ARTIFICIAL INTELLIGENCE

CONTRIBUTORS

Max Bramer — The Open University
Alan Bundy — Edinburgh University
Jadzia Cendrowska — The Open University
William F. Clocksin — Cambridge University
Lesley Daniel — Immediate Business Systems

Peter G. Davey — Oxford University
Ben du Boulay — Sussex University
Marc Eisenstadt — The Open University
John Frisby — Sheffield University
Steven Hardy — Sussex University
Tony Hasemer — The Open University
Jim Howe — Edinburgh University
Joachim Laubsch — University of Stuttgart
Paul Lefrere — The Open University
John Mayhew — Sheffield University
Tim O'Shea — The Open University
Gordon Plotkin — Edinburgh University
Graeme Ritchie — Heriot-Watt University
Joe Rooney — The Open University
Jon M. Slack — The Open University
Henry Thompson — Edinburgh University

ARTIFICIAL INTELLIGENCE

Tools, Techniques, and Applications

TIM O'SHEA
MARC EISENSTADT

Editors

The Open University

HARPER & ROW, PUBLISHERS, New York
Cambridge, Philadelphia, San Francisco,
London, Mexico City, São Paulo, Sydney

Sponsoring Editor: John Willig
Project Editor: David Nickol
Designer: T. R. Funderburk
Production: Delia Tedoff
Compositor: Science Press
Printer and Binder: R. R. Donnelley & Sons Company
Art Studio: Vantage Art, Inc.
Cover Art: Anne Youkeles

ARTIFICIAL INTELLIGENCE: Tools, Techniques, and Applications

Copyright © 1984 by Harper & Row, Publishers, Inc.

Library of Congress Cataloging in Publication Data

Main entry under title:

Artificial intelligence.

    1. Artificial intelligence. I. O'Shea, Tim,
1949-   . II. Eisenstadt, Marc, 1947-   .
Q335.A788 1984   001.53'5   84-502
ISBN 0-06-041894-X

To our children
Catherine Elisabeth O'Shea
and
Nathan Eisenstadt

CONTENTS

Preface   ix

PREFACE

This book is designed for the newcomer to artificial intelligence (AI). The original impetus for this volume was an AISB (Society for the Study of Artificial Intelligence and Simulation of Behaviour) school that was organised for advanced undergraduate and beginning graduate students in computer science and psychology, as well as for professionals engaged in their first industrial AI endeavour. Our intention has been to provide both academic and industrial readers with clear tutorial accounts of a representative sample of mainstream AI topics. Toward this end, we have provided detailed implementation notes and/or annotated bibliographies as appropriate.

The book covers three main topics: tools, techniques, and applications of AI. Part I, "Tools," is concerned with special-purpose programming languages that are used by AI workers and the advanced software environments that support these languages. The part begins with a chapter on PROLOG, a language rapidly gaining in popularity as a vehicle for the design and implementation of expert systems. LISP, the *lingua franca* of AI, is introduced in the next chapter, aimed at the complete novice, followed by a chapter delving into some of the advanced capabilities of LISP as used by modern AI researchers. The last chapter in Part I describes a software environment that offers the features of both LISP and PROLOG, along with the facilities to assist the user in editing, running, and debugging AI programs.

"Techniques," Part II, provides insight into the practice of AI. Of particular interest are the critical and creative techniques that are involved in obtaining a Ph.D. in AI, the scientific techniques that are used in the construction of psychological models, the mathematical techniques that are needed in robot design, and the parsing techniques that lie at the root of modern computational linguistics.

Part III, "Applications," deals with a selection of areas in which AI has proved successful: language processing, computer vision, robotics, text processing, planning, and expert systems. Each chapter includes a discussion of the history, fundamental results, and important research problems relevant to that particular area.

At the Open University we are committed to an educational ideology based on making knowledge and intellectual skills accessible to the widest possible audience. We hope that in reading these chapters you will find, as we have, that our authors have made a number of important aspects of the practice of AI both intelligible and exciting.

We have received a great deal of administrative and secretarial assistance in running the AISB school and in editing this book. For this help, we would particularly like to thank Pat Cross, Claire Jones, Diane Mason, Doreen Warwick, and Olwyn Wilson.

Tim O'Shea
Marc Eisenstadt

PART I

TOOLS

CHAPTER 1

AN INTRODUCTION TO PROLOG

WILLIAM F. CLOCKSIN

INTRODUCTION

PROLOG is a practical and efficient computer programming language that was invented around 1970 by Alain Colmerauer and his associates at the University of Marseille (Roussel, 1975). With the advent of very efficient implementations of PROLOG (Warren, 1979), it has since become a natural choice for solving problems that involve symbolic representations of objects and relationships between objects. The fundamental basis of PROLOG is the notion of logic programming, in which computation can be viewed as controlled logical inferences (Kowalski, 1979). This, in turn, grew out of work in computer-aided theorem proving (Robinson, 1965).

PROLOG is now being used for many applications of symbolic computing, including

- relational data bases and expert systems
- mathematical logic, theorem proving, semantics
- abstract problem solving and plan formation
- understanding natural language
- architectural design, site planning, logistics
- symbolic equation solving, compiler writing
- biochemical analysis and drug design

PROLOG is an unusual but exceptionally simple language. Newcomers to PROLOG find that the task of writing a PROLOG program is not similar to specifying an algorithm in the

1

same way as in a conventional programming language. Instead, PROLOG programmers ask these questions of their problem:

- What formal facts and relationships occur in the problem?
- What relationships are true about the answer?

The PROLOG approach is to specify known facts and relationships about a problem. It is not always necessary to see the solution to a problem as a step-by-step sequence of "instructions." When the computer is programmed in PROLOG, how the computer actually carries out the computation depends partly on the logical relations inherent in PROLOG statements, partly on what new facts PROLOG can "infer" from the given ones, and only partly on explicit control information that is supplied by the user.

PROLOG provides an implementation of many aspects of program execution that are useful for programs of interest to researchers in artificial intelligence, such as nondeterminism, parallelism, and pattern-directed procedure call. However, these sophisticated techniques are used in the internal operations of the PROLOG system and thus are hidden from the programmer. The PROLOG programmer sees a rule-based language that is reminiscent of, but not to be confused with, first-order predicate calculus. PROLOG provides a uniform data structure, called the *term,* out of which all data, as well as PROLOG programs, are constructed. A PROLOG program consists of a set of clauses, where each clause is either a fact about the given information or a rule about how the solution may relate to or be "inferred" from the given facts. Thus, PROLOG can be seen as a first step towards an ultimate goal of programming in logic (Kowalski, 1979).

It is perhaps a tribute to PROLOG that so many people in the world have been motivated to learn it by referring to concise reference manuals and a few published research papers, and by word of mouth. More recently, a collection of papers on logic programming research has been edited by Clark and Tärnlund (1982), and a textbook of practical PROLOG programming has been published (Clocksin & Mellish, 1981). The textbook goes into much more detail and explanation than is possible in this chapter. The purpose here is to give you an idea of what it is like to program in PROLOG and to show how this relates to programming techniques that are of interest to researchers in the area of artificial intelligence.

A PROLOG PRIMER

The act of programming in PROLOG consists of

- specifying some facts about objects and relationships
- specifying rules about objects and relationships
- asking questions about objects and their relationships

The program that is presented to a PROLOG system consists of a data base that contains the facts and rules that are relevant to the problem. To solve the problem, the user asks questions about whether certain relationships are true. PROLOG is a conversational system: A computer terminal is used to enter facts, rules, and queries; the answers are printed on the terminal's display.

PROLOG distinguishes between different modes of entry. *Consult* mode is used to enter facts and rules, and *query* mode is used to enter queries. In the examples below, the special prompt characters **?–** indicate *query* mode, while the absence of these characters indicates *consult* mode.

Let us consider facts. When we say "John owns the book," we are declaring that a relationship, ownership, exists between one individual object "John" and another individual object denoted by "the book." This relationship has a particular order: John owns the book, but the book does not own John. When we ask the question "Does John own the book?" we are attempting to find out about a relationship. The statement "John owns the book" translates into a PROLOG fact as follows:

    owns(john, book).

The following points about this notation are important. First, the names of all relationships and objects must begin with a lowercase letter. Second, the relationship is written first, the objects involved are written separated by commas, and the whole group of objects is enclosed in a matching pair of round brackets. Third, a full stop comes at the end of the fact. Fourth, the objects listed within the brackets must appear in a consistent order. The particular order is not important provided that the programmer is consistent. In the above example, we have put the owner first, and the object owned second. So, the fact likes(john, mary) is not the same fact as likes(mary, john). If we wish to represent the fact that John likes Mary, and that Mary likes John, we must say so in two separate facts.

The name of the relationship is called a *predicate,* and the objects inside the brackets are called the *arguments*. So, the above example is a fact about the predicate likes, which has two arguments, john and mary.

It does not matter to PROLOG if we declare facts that are not true in the real world. We could write king(john, france) to assert that "John is the King of France" (being king relates a monarch with a country). In the real world this is obviously false, not least because the monarchy was abolished in France sometime around 1792. But PROLOG neither knows nor cares. PROLOG simply allows you to express arbitrary relationships among objects.

Next, questions. Once we have collected some facts together, we can ask questions about them. Such a collection is called a *data base.* Here is a sample data base of friends, consisting of a collection of likes predicates:

    likes(john, mary).
    likes(john, fred).
    likes(mary, fred).
    likes(fred, john).

Assuming the above facts had been suitably entered in *consult* mode, we could now ask "Does John like Mary?" by typing:

    ?– likes(john, mary).

To answer this question, the PROLOG system examines each entry in the data base looking for facts that match the question. A question and a fact match if their predicates are spelled the same, and if they have the same arguments. In this case, there is indeed a matching fact, so the PROLOG system answers **yes**. Given the above data base, if you ask the question

> **?–likes(mary, jane).**

then the PROLOG system will answer **no**. This response actually means "cannot be proved by what is in the data base."

It is also possible to use variables. In PROLOG, a variable takes the place of an object that we may be unable or unwilling to name at the time we write the program. For example, we could ask the question "Is there some thing X that John likes?" by typing:

> **?– likes(john, X).**

Any name that begins with an uppercase letter is a variable. In the preceding data base two facts would match this question. The first matching fact is likes(john, mary), so PROLOG would print out

> **X = mary**

and wait for a reply from you. If you type the RETURN key on the keyboard, the system will abandon the search for more matching facts. If you type a semicolon, then the system will continue the search. A complete interaction might look like this:

> **?– likes(john, X).**
> **X = mary;**
> **X = fred;**
> **no**

The last reply is **no**, meaning that there are no more facts that can satisfy the question.

Another way to ask more complicated questions is to use conjunctions. If we want to know whether John and Mary like each other, we can state the question in the form of two goals, separated by a comma. The comma is pronounced "and":

> **?– likes(john, mary), likes(mary, john).**
> **no**

Using variables, we can ask if John likes anyone who likes John:

> **?– likes(john, X), likes(X, john).**
> **X = fred**

In the first goal of this question X is initially unknown. We say that X is not instantiated (meaning that it does not have an instance). However, when searching the data base, PROLOG finds a fact that matches if X is mary. The variable X is now instantiated to mary. As a result, any occurrence of X in the question is replaced by mary. Next, the second goal is considered: likes(mary, john). This goal fails, as there is nothing to match it in the data base. But there might be some other fact that matches the first goal (remember we had not exhausted the data base on the first goal). Indeed there is, when X is fred. So now, X is instantiated to fred, and the second goal is tried again: likes(fred, john). This time the goal succeeds because a matching fact is found in the data base. Both goals thus succeed, and PROLOG prints out the first answer as already shown.

It is important to understand the idea that PROLOG alternates successively between two neighbouring goals in a conjunction to find an answer that satisfies them both. An arbitrary number of goals that are separated by conjunctions may participate in this way. This is the basis of a very powerful technique known as *backtracking*. The PROLOG textbook goes into much detail about how backtracking works and how to take advantage of it to solve your problems. We have more to say about backtracking later.

Rules

Often it is helpful to express a fact in the form of a rule. For example, if we wanted to express the fact that John likes everyone who likes wine, it would be tedious to add additional facts to the data base to express this. It would be far simpler to store a *rule* about what John likes, instead of listing all the people whom John likes. Suppose we wished to represent the rule that John likes some thing X provided that X likes wine. We write this as a rule, made up of a head and a body. The head and body are separated by a :- symbol like this:

likes(john, X) :- likes(X, wine).

This rule is pronounced "John likes X provided that X likes wine." You could also say, "John likes X if X likes wine." Rules may be entered in the data base the same way as facts. When programming you will generally put a mixture of facts and rules in the data base. An entry in the data base, whether a fact or a rule, is called a *clause*. When PROLOG encounters a rule when searching the data base for a clause matching a question, it attempts to match the head of the rule with the goal in the question (using the definition of "match" previously given). If the two match, then the body of the rule contains subgoals which must be satisfied in order to satisfy the original goal. The preceding rule contains only one subgoal in its body.

Consider a very simple rule that tells us about sisters. Suppose we are given two people called X and Y. Person X is a sister of person Y provided that X is female and X and Y have the same parents. This definition translates directly into a PROLOG rule as follows:

sister(X, Y) :- female(X), parents(X, Ma, Pa), parents(Y, Ma, Pa).

This rule is read "it is a fact that X is a sister of Y provided that: X is female, and the parents of

X are some objects Ma and Pa, and the parents of Y are the same Ma and Pa." Let us supply some facts that will help the preceding rule to succeed:

```
female(alice).
female(victoria).
male(albert).
male(edward).
parents(edward, victoria, albert).
parents(alice, victoria, albert).
```

We have said "it is true that Alice is female," "it is true that Edward is male," "it is true that the parents of Alice are Victoria and Albert," and so forth. The single foregoing rule, together with these six facts, permit us to ask questions about certain relationships about a certain family.

```
?– sister(alice, edward).
yes
```

It is a fact that Alice is a sister of Edward. Let us try a few more questions, shown with the answer that PROLOG gives. Notice the use of variables in some questions:

```
?– sister(alice, victoria).
no
?– sister(alice, alice).
yes
?– sister(alice, X).
X = edward
?– sister(X, Y).
X = alice, Y = edward;
X = alice, Y = alice
?– sister(X, X).
X = alice
?– sister(X, Y), parents(Z, _, Y).
no
```

(Using an underline character when a variable is allowed means the anonymous, or "don't care" variable.) The last question asked if X is the sister of someone (Y) who is the father of a child (Z). The answer PROLOG gives is **no**. This means that there is nothing in the data base that can satisfy such a question. Notice that the **male** facts in the data base are never used by this rule. In this sense they are redundant, but we listed them here to give a sense of completeness. Notice that the **sister** rule makes explicit the notion that a female is her own sister. It is possible to modify the rule to add an extra condition that the two candidate objects for sisterhood must be different objects.

BACKTRACKING

How is a PROLOG question (or goal) evaluated by the system? Consider the last question concerning sisters and parents. Since these two goals are connected by a conjunction, PROLOG needs to find some instances in the data base that satisfy both goals. Think of a conjunction of goals connected by ',' as a sequence of neighbours. To satisfy a conjunction of goals, we make an attempt to satisfy each goal in the conjunction, from left to right. First, sister(X, Y). Are there any facts or rules in the data base to satisfy this? The data base is searched from top to bottom. Immediately it finds our rule for sister as previously shown. Since there is a new set of goals to process (the definition of sister), the left-to-right evaluation will proceed for female, parents, and parents again. If they all succeed, then we are back to the question at hand, and attempt to satisfy parents(Z, _, Y).

Given a particular goal, the goal may either succeed or fail when an attempt is made to satisfy it. If it succeeds, then PROLOG attempts to satisfy its neighbour on the right. If there are no more neighbours on the right, then the entire conjunction succeeds. If, however, a goal fails, then an attempt is made to resatisfy its neighbour on the left. Since there can be more than one possible answer to a goal, resatisfying a goal allows the goal to succeed with an alternative answer. If a goal fails, and it does not have a left-hand neighbour to resatisfy, then the entire conjunction fails.

What about variables during backtracking? Any variables that happen to be in a goal may become instantiated to some data structure when the goal succeeds. As soon as a variable becomes instantiated to some data structure, every occurrence of the variable (having the same name) in the goal will be "instantly" instantiated to the same data structure. If a goal fails, then any variables that may have been instantiated by the goal's previous success (if any) are forgotten. This is the essence of backtracking. Attempting to satisfy a conjunction of goals essentially does a depth-first left-to-right search of a proof tree. The process of instantiation is called *binding* in the pattern-matching example discussed in Chapter 3.

Here is a collection of simple one-rule examples, together with some explanation of new parts. Each rule uses backtracking to find a set of objects that satisfy each goal in the body of the rule.

Example 1

"John likes anyone who likes wine and food."

    likes(john, X) :- likes(X, wine), likes(X, food).

It can be established that john likes X provided that X likes wine and X also likes food.

Example 2

"X was on the throne during year Y if: X reigned between years A and B, and year Y falls between years A and B." In this example we assume that clauses defining years_of_reign exist in the data base. Notice that the underline character '_' can be included within a name (as in

years_of_reign) to improve legibility. In this context it cannot be confused with the "anonymous variable," which is just the underline character '_' on its own. The infix operators '>=' and '=<' have the usual meanings of "greater than or equal to," and "less than or equal to," respectively:

```
on_throne(X, Y) :-
        years_of_reign(X, A, B), Y >= A, Y =< B.
```

Relevant clauses for the data base pertaining to the fifteenth-century House of Avis (Portugal) are

```
years_of_reign(duarte, 1433, 1438).
years_of_reign(alfonso_V, 1438, 1481).
years_of_reign(john_II, 1481, 1495).
```

Example 3

"The population density of X is Y." Here we assume that clauses for relating a country with its population, and a country with its area, are provided in the data base. The infix operator **is** evaluates the arithmetic expression on its right-hand side and matches it with the object on its left-hand side. Remember this because we shall use **is** later.

```
density(X, Y) :- population(X, P), area(X, A), Y is P / A.
```

Relevant clauses for population and area (in millions of people and millions of square miles) for 1976 might look like

```
population(usa, 203).      area(usa, 3).
population(india, 548).    area(india, 1).
population(brazil, 108).   area(brazil, 3).
```

GENERAL DATA STRUCTURES

More interesting examples involve data structures other than numbers and atoms. Arbitrary data structures are represented as terms that can have any number of components. For example, we could define a structure called book, with three components: title, author, and serial number. Then, a particular copy of *Wuthering Heights* (the passionate and savage novel by Emily Bronte, the nineteenth century Yorkshire author) is an individual and may be denoted as

```
book(wuthering_heights, bronte, 1756820)
```

and could take part in questions just as any other individual:

```
?- owns(john, book(wuthering_heights, bronte, 1756820)).
?- owns(john, book(X, bronte, _)).
```

In these examples we are asking whether John owns a particular book that we may be able to describe with more or less detail. Given a structure such as book(X, Y, Z), the atom book is called the *functor,* and the arguments enclosed in the brackets are called the *components.* When used as an individual, as in the preceding example, the structure can never be mistaken for a goal or clause. However, notice that clauses (facts and rules) are represented as structures. This is no accident. The notion that programs should be written by using the same data structures that are manipulated by programs is a feature that PROLOG shares with LISP, as described in Chapters 2 and 3.

For another use of structures, the Portuguese monarchs from the previous section can be represented more flexibly as a structure. We choose monarch as the functor, and the name, "serial number," and country ruled as components. For example, we could represent

```
monarch(john, 2, portugal).
monarch(john, 2, sweden).
```

because both Portugal and Sweden were reigned by different John II's.

```
years_of_reign(monarch(duarte, 0, portugal), 1433, 1438).
years_of_reign(monarch(john, 2, portugal), 1481, 1495).
years_of_reign(monarch(john, 3, sweden), 1568, 1592).
on_throne(Country, Monarch, Serial, Year) :-
        years_of_reign(monarch(Monarch, Serial, Country), A, B),
        Year >= A,
        Year =< B.
```

Notice that the variable Monarch is distinct from the functor monarch. This example will work even if we leave out the serial number of a monarch by replacing its component in the query by an uninstantiated variable. For example, to ask which John ruled an unknown country in 1588 (the year of the Spanish Armada), we would ask

```
?- on_throne(C, john, S, 1588).
C = sweden, S = 3
```

As with other languages used by researchers in artificial intelligence, a data structure known as the *list* plays an important role in PROLOG programming. The list cell, which is represented as a predicate (named '.'), has two arguments called the *head* and the *tail.* Lists are binary trees that are constructed from list cells. As with LISP, denoting binary trees by using the dot notation can be cumbersome. So, there is a simpler notation for lists. Terminal nodes of the tree are written, separated by commas, and all are enclosed in a pair of square brackets. The empty list is denoted [ ]. Examples of lists are

```
[john, wants, to, stroke, the, cat]
[the, cardinal, drew, off, each, plum, coloured, shoe]
[[This], list(is, made + of), [Several, [types]], of, structure]
[ ]
```

The notation [X | Y] denotes the list whose head is X and tail is Y. This is used in pattern matching. For example, suppose we wish to define a predicate that succeeds if its first argument is a member of the list given as its second argument. The first clause about this problem is that "it is a fact that X is a member of a list if X is the head of the list." The second clause is "X is a member of the list if X is a member of the tail of the list." Putting these together in a procedure yields

```
member(X, [X | _]).
member(X, [_ | L]) :- member(X, L).
```

We can ask the following questions:

```
?- member(darwin, [marx, darwin, freud]).
yes
?- member(X, [marx, darwin, freud]).
X = marx;
X = darwin;
X = freud
```

There are three possible solutions to the second question, so the **member** goal succeeds once for each of the three queries shown.

Here is an interesting way to use **member** to find out if two lists differ—that is, if one list has an element that is not in the other. This is an example of what some people call "nondeterministic programming," which relies on the preceding definition of **member** that allows backtracking:

```
differ(X, Y) :- member(Z, X), not(member(Z, Y)).
```

To evaluate this, PROLOG bashes back and forth between the two neighbouring **member** goals until both are satisfied or both fail. The goal not(X) succeeds if its argument fails when considered as a goal. Likewise, it fails if its argument succeeds.

As another example of backtracking, here is a program to search a maze. The goal go(X, Y) succeeds if it is possible to go from room X to room Y:

```
go(X, X).
go(X, Y) :- door(X, Z), go(Z, Y).
```

To supply a maze, we simply add to the data base facts about where the doors are:

```
door(a, b).     door(b, e).
door(b, c).     door(d, e).
door(c, d).     door(e, f).
door(g, e).
```

The previous go procedure might get into loops by researching rooms it has searched before. To avoid this, we can keep a list of room numbers that we have visited and ensure that we enter only rooms we have not been to before. In this modified version of the program, T is our "trail" of room numbers, represented as a list:

```
go(X, X, _).
go(X, Y, T) :- door(X, Z), not(member(Z, T)), go(Z, Y, [Z | T]).
```

The rightmost go goal collects the current room number (Z) for its list (by making a list that has Z as its head, and the "list so far" (T) as its tail. The whole thing is passed to the recursive call of go. The question you would ask to search a maze would initialise the list to the empty list for normal use (as in the query **?-** go(a, z, [ ]).). Initialising the list to contain some room numbers would permit the program to search the maze, avoiding those rooms.

CONTROL OF BACKTRACKING

There is a special goal called the "cut," which is used to make backtracking programs more efficient where necessary. The cut is written as an exclamation mark, '!'. The cut goal always succeeds, but if an attempt is made to resatisfy it, all its left-hand neighbours fail immediately. Furthermore, the *parent goal* fails. That is to say, the goal that invoked the rule in which the cut is encountered fails. To put this another way, the success of the cut commits the system to the first successful satisfaction of its left-hand neighbours. Consider the following example:

```
a :- b, c, d, e.
b.
c.
d :- f, g, !, h, j.
f.
g.
?- a.
```

We attempt to satisfy the a rule, and goals b and c succeed. Next, the d goal in the body of the a rule becomes the parent goal, and then the f and g goals succeed. Then the cut goal succeeds. At this point, the system becomes committed to the solution that satisfied f and g. The h goal will be considered next. If it fails, causing the cut to be resatisfied (entered from the right), then the parent goal d (in the a rule) fails.

One special way to use this is to commit the system to only one answer from a goal that may have more than one answer, as in our question

```
?- member(X, [marx, darwin, freud]).
```

If member were to be defined as:

```
member(X, [X | _]) :- !.
member(X, [_ | T]) :- member(X, T).
```

then the system would be committed to the first answer and would fail on backtracking:

```
?- member(X, [marx, darwin, freud]).
X = marx;
no
```

If the member question is to be interpreted as a predicate, then this is a more efficient definition. If, however, it is desired that member acts as a generator of members, then the definition without the cut is needed. This is analogous to the use of generators described in Chapter 3.

It is important to recognize that the cut provides "shortcuts" to the normal backtracking process. This is unappealing to logic programming purists, because the effect of the cut cannot be conveniently represented within the semantics of logic. However, the cut is needed to write practical programs. It is not difficult to learn to use the cut properly. Provided that we need to use the cut, we may as well make the best of it and not consider it as an unsightly blemish.

PATTERN MATCHING

Advantages of pattern matching can be shown by writing a program to convert one arithmetic expression into another. Compilers are an especially attractive example. The Edinburgh PROLOG compiler (Warren, 1979), which generates very efficient code for the DECsystem-10, is written in PROLOG.

Let us develop an example that converts an expression into its symbolic derivative. This is often presented as a list of rules in mathematics books, and it is nice to find that the rules translate easily into PROLOG. We use the functors $+$, $-$, and so forth to represent nonterminal nodes of expression trees. These functors have a built-in syntax declaration as right-associative infix operators with the usual precedence relationship. We define the predicate d(X, Y, Z) as meaning "the derivative of X with respect to Y is Z." Here are a few derivative rules in PROLOG. Note the similarity to tables of derivatives as found in mathematics texts:

```
d(X, X, 1).
d(C, X, 0) :- atomic(C).
d(U + V, X, A + B) :- d(U, X, A), d(V, X, B).
d(U − V, X, A − B) :- d(U, X, A), d(V, X, B).
d(C * U, X, C * A) :- atomic(C), C \= X, d(U, X, A).
d(U * V, X, B * U + A * V) :- d(U, X, A), d(V, X, B).
```

And that is a working program. Here is a question and the answer:

```
?- d(x * x − 2, x, A).
A = x * 1 + 1 * x − 0
```

The goal atomic(X), whose definition is built into the PROLOG system, succeeds if its argument is an atom or an integer, and fails otherwise. We use it here to check whether we are finding the derivative of a constant. The infix "not the same as" operator '\=' fails if its two arguments match, and succeeds otherwise.

The preceding answer is not in an algebraically simplified form. However, we can provide a straightforward simplifier, which consists of two clauses plus some facts about algebra. The simp predicate is defined such that the goal simp(X, Y) simplifies the expression X, obtaining the expression Y. The first clause given below simply states that an atom simplifies to itself, and there are then no more solutions. The second clause unpacks an expression tree into its node and two branches by using the comp predicate (defined below), then simplifies each branch recursively, then uses comp again to recompose the expression with simplified branches (called S), and then finally checks to see if S is a simplified form by using the s predicate (defined below). Any simplified form found (F) is instantiated as the second argument to simp.

```
simp(E, E) :- atomic(E), !.
simp(E, F) :-
      comp(E, Op, L, R),
      simp(L, X),
      simp(R, Y),
      comp(S, Op, X, Y),
      s(S, F).

comp(X + Y, +, X, Y).
comp(X − Y, −, X, Y).
comp(X * Y, *, X, Y).

s(X * 1, X).        s(1 * X, X).
s(X * 0, 0).        s(0 * X, 0).
s(X + 0, X).        s(0 + X, X).
s(X − 0, X).
```

Notice that there are pairs of **s** facts for addition and multiplication to account for commutativity. This works as follows: To simplify an expression E by using the **s** table, we need first to simplify the left-hand argument, then simplify the right-hand argument, and then see if the resulting pieces are in our table. Since we recursively simplify the subcomponents of E, it will be in a simplified state when it is time to see if it is in the table. At the "leaves" of the expression tree there are either integers or atoms. These are simplified into themselves by the first **simp** clause.

A "pretty printer" is used to display the tree structure of expressions by using carriage returns and spaces appropriately. Every programmer has a favourite way to print out tree structures. The pretty printer that follows is very simple. It takes two arguments: a term to print and an indentation level. The procedure is recursive in nature, and the indentation level is incremented and passed on to the next recurrence if there is a term "deeper" in the tree. The **comp** predicate from above is used to obtain the node and branches of a subtree:

```
pp(X, I) :- atomic(X), writeln(I, X), !.
pp(X, I) :-
        comp(X, Op, A, B),
        writeln(I, Op),
        I1 is I + 4,
        pp(A, I1),
        pp(B, I1).


writeln(S, T) :- tab(S), write(T), nl.
```

The auxiliary predicate **writeln** contains some goals for writing characters to the user's terminal. The goal **writeln(S, T)** indents by S spaces, writes the term T, and returns to a new line. The initial call of **pp** must set the indentation count to some initial value (say, 0):

```
?- pp(x * 1 + 1 * x − 0, 0).
```

The output is shown in Figure 1.1 opposite. To the practised eye this looks reasonably natural, but we have drawn in branches to connect the nodes of the tree. More sophisticated pretty printers will do this automatically.

By providing a simplifier and an equation pretty printer, we could define a predicate to do all the work:

```
diff :-
        write('Type the Expression:'),
        read(Exp),
        d(Exp, x, Deriv),
        simp(Deriv, Simplified),
        write('The derivative w.r.t. x is:'),
        pp(Simplified, 0).
```

The preceding differentiator, simplifier, and pretty printer handle only the binary operators, addition and multiplication. Handling other operators does not present a problem, because one

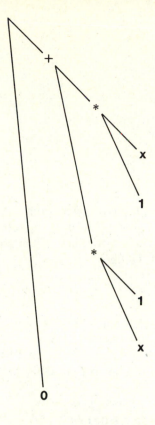

yes

Figure 1.1   The output of **?- pp** (x ∗ 1 + 1 ∗ x − 0, 0).

simply adds more rules to cope with the new expected input. For example, adding the following rule would make the simplifier cope with unary operators:

    simp(X, Y) :- comp(X, Op, Sarg), simp(Arg, Sarg), s(Op, Sarg, Y).

To simplify multiple unary minus, we must add a **comp** rule such as comp(minus(X), minus, X) and an **s** rule such as s(minus(minus(X)), X).

A practical simplifier would not use the **comp** predicate, because the number of facts defining it would be as large as the number of different kinds of nodes in the expression tree. For such applications, PROLOG has a built-in predicate that converts a structure into a list of its functor and components (and vice versa). The predicate, denoted as an infix operator '=..', succeeds if its left-hand argument can be decomposed into a list of functor and components given on the right-hand side. Normally we would write the second **pp** clause from above without using comp as follows:

```
pp(X, I) :-
      X =.. [Op, A, B],
      writeln(Op, I),
      I1 is I + 4,
      pp(A, I1),
      pp(B, I1).
```

GRAMMAR RULES

Because the basic computational mechanism of PROLOG is a top-down search through a tree of goals, representing parsing problems is especially suited to the PROLOG approach. A grammar rule notation can be used for conveniently expressing the grammar of the problem. Consider the following sentence that is represented as a PROLOG list:

[the, cardinal, drew, off, each, plum, coloured, shoe]

Among the constituents of this sentence there can be included the noun phrase, verb phrase, determiner, adjectives, and so forth. We can represent these constituents as structures, and the grammar to recognise and generate them can be defined as PROLOG predicates. A PROLOG program to parse (as well as generate) a family of sentences including the preceding one is

```
sentence(np(X), vp(Y))          --> noun_phrase(X), verb_phrase(Y).
noun_phrase(det(X), Y)          --> determiner(X), mod_noun(Y).
verb_phrase(v(X), np(Y))        --> verb(X), noun_phrase(Y).
verb_phrase(cv(X, Y), np(Z))    --> verb(X), adverb(Y), noun_phrase(Z).
verb_phrase(cv(X, Y), np(Z))    --> verb(X), noun_phrase(Z), adverb(Y).
mod_noun(n(Y))                  --> noun(Y).
mod_noun(cn(X, Y))              --> mod_adjective(X), mod_noun(Y).
mod_adjective(X)                --> adjective(X).
mod_adjective(ca(X, Y))         --> adverb(X), mod_adjective(Y).
determiner(the)                 --> [the].
determiner(each)                --> [each].
determiner(an)                  --> [an].
noun(cardinal)                  --> [cardinal].
noun(shoe)                      --> [shoe].
noun(plum)                      --> [plum].
verb(drew)                      --> [drew].
adjective(coloured)             --> [coloured].
adjective(cardinal)             --> [cardinal].
adjective(plum)                 --> [plum].
adverb(plum)                    --> [plum].
adverb(off)                     --> [off].
```

In this notation, nonterminal constituents are represented as structures, of which their components are descendants in the parse tree. Components of the structures on the left-hand side of the ––> arrow are assembled into the parse tree as a result of PROLOG's pattern-matching (unification) mechanism. Terminals in the lexicon appear on the right-hand side as atoms enclosed in square brackets. PROLOG systems provide facilities, either built-in or as library programs, to accept the preceding notation and translate it rule by rule into equivalent clause notation. This program generates a parse tree of the previous sentence that looks like this when printed by using the pretty printer (as redefined above):

```
s
 \
  np
   \ \
    \ det
    \    \
    \    the
    \
     n
      \
       cardinal
  vp
   \ \
    \ cv
    \   \
    \   drew
    \
    off
     np
      \ \
       \ det
       \    \
       \    each
       \
        cn
         \ \
          \ ca
          \   \
          \   plum
          \
          coloured
           n
            \
             shoe
```

This grammar should also be able to parse sentences such as "the cardinal drew an off coloured plum," which might be appropriate when describing someone of high clerical office who is sketching a fruit of unappetising appearance. It is easy to extend such grammars to account for number agreement, ensuring that articles match their subjects (preventing "an cardinal"), dealing properly with objects of transitive verbs, representing semantic information about the sentence, and so forth.

Another example shows a way to extract a "meaning" of the sentence without using an intermediate parse tree. The following rules translate a sentence (in a restricted grammar) into a representation of its meaning in predicate calculus notation:

s(P)	——> np(X, P1, P), vp(X, P1).
np(X, P1, P)	——> det(X, P2, P1, P), n(X, P3), rel(X, P3, P2).
vp(X, P)	——> transv(X, Y, P1), np(Y, P1, P).
vp(X, P)	——> intrans(X, P).
rel(X, P1, and(P1, P2))	——> [that], vp(X, P2).
rel(_, P, P)	——> [ ].
det(X, P1, P2, forall(X,(implies(P1, P2))))	——> [every].
det(X, P1, P2, exists(X, and(P1, P2)))	——> [a].
n(X, man(X))	——> [man].
n(X, woman(X))	——> [woman].
transv(X, Y, loves(X, Y))	——> [loves].
intrans(X, lives(X))	——> [lives].

For example, if the (ambiguous) sentence "every man loves a woman" is parsed by the preceding grammar rules, the following structure is obtained:

   forall(X, implies(man(X), exists(Y, and(woman(Y), loves(X, Y))))).

This parse corresponds to the interpretation "every man has (his own particular) woman whom he loves." Another parse, corresponding to the meaning "there exists precisely one woman whom every man loves," is available, if required, by backtracking. The second parse results in the following structure:

   exists(Y, and(woman(Y), forall(X, implies(man(X), loves(X, Y))))).

In this program, components of structures are used to represent the meanings of phrases. The last component actually specifies the meaning representation, however, the meaning of a phrase may depend on several other factors given as the other arguments. For example, the verb "lives" gives rise to a representation of the form lives(X), where X is something standing for the person who lives. In the case of "every," the meaning has to be applied to a variable and two propositions containing that variable. The result is a representation that denotes "if substituting an object for the variable in the first proposition yields something true, then substituting the same object for the variable in the second proposition will also yield something true."

Finding symbolic derivatives, simplification, and grammar rules are only a few examples of problems that are conveniently handled by PROLOG. When a problem is cast into the form of rules, at any given point there is a program that works. It may not compute answers for all the questions you ask, but it is a matter of adding more rules to cover these cases. Furthermore, if the program has been made modular, and PROLOG makes this easy to do, then there is usually no need to rewrite existing parts of the program when modifications are required. For many people, including most artificial intelligence programmers, this is an attractive methodology for programming. At any given point there is something that works. It is easier to build on a *working* program no matter what size it is. Program construction then involves the task of adding more rules while maintaining a working structure. This seems to be exactly the opposite methodology that is promoted by languages such as Pascal, for which the Pascal programmer is not always able to have a working program until every last detail of the problem specification is known.

APPLICATIONS

The aforementioned examples are toy examples, in both content and style of interaction. However, there exist large artificial intelligence programs that are written in PROLOG. One example is the Mecho program, which solves mechanics problems that are stated in English (Bundy et al, 1979). The Mecho program contains three modules: a module that translates the English input into a symbolic representation of the meaning of the input, a module that uses knowledge of mechanics to set up the equations of the problem, and a sophisticated module that forms analytic solutions of equations and inequalities. Each module of the program is written in PROLOG. Another good example is the ORBI expert system for environmental resource evaluation, which will be discussed subsequently.

Program transformation is another important application. The PROLOG compiler itself is an example, because PROLOG procedures that are tail recursive are automatically translated into a form that executes iteratively (Warren, 1979). Compilation by recursive descent is a natural by-product of the standard flow of control in PROLOG programs; the properties of the logical variable, data structures as programs, and lack of side effects make it easy to maintain symbol tables, resolve effective addresses, and operate on programs. These features will become increasingly important when interactive programming environments are more widely appreciated outside the laboratory. Just as production engineering (the design of tools and manufacturing methods) plays an important part in the manufacturing industry, the design and use of interactive programming environments should be a more important part of commercial software engineering in the future.

PROLOG programs are being used in industrial applications, especially in Hungary (Santane-Toth & Szeredi, 1982), where the industrial use of PROLOG has been encouraged by the government. Applications include: using knowledge about chemical interactions to design drugs, and about building codes and architectural practise to design buildings, and for software engineering. At present in Britain and Japan there is some investigation into the possibilities of employing PROLOG in production planning, industrial process control, and strategy control for flexible automation systems.

PROLOG is suitable as an implementation language for expert systems (Michie, 1980). One can consider an expert system as consisting of three parts: a data base of knowledge about a particular domain, an "inference engine," and an interface for communicating with the user. PROLOG itself provides the data base and one kind of inference engine. Other types of inference engines as well as interfaces to the user and to remote data bases can be implemented in PROLOG. Two systems in particular are impressive: the Chat system (Warren & Pereira,

1981), which answers questions that are stated in English about a geographical data base, and the ORBI system (Pereira, Sabatier, & d'Oliveira, 1982), an expert system that is concerned with environmental resource evaluation. The Chat system can answer questions (stated in English) such as, "Which are the continents in which no country contains more than two cities whose population exceeds 1 million?" Chat first parses the query, translating it into a logical expression that can be evaluated as a PROLOG program (this step takes 160 milliseconds for the previous query). Next, Chat rewrites the logical expression to obtain an expression that probes the data base more efficiently (58 milliseconds for the above). Finally, the optimised expression is evaluated as a PROLOG goal to probe the data base (754 milliseconds).

Answering a query is only part of the problem. The ORBI system can answer questions (stated in Portuguese) such as whether a particular map reference is suitable for an industrial site. Furthermore, ORBI can "explain" its reasoning in a way that makes sense to the user (who is trained but who is not an expert). The authors of ORBI found PROLOG to be "an excellent language for expert system implementation," and gave these reasons:

1. The various components of an expert system are integrated into the same simple formalism: natural language processing, knowledge base, explanation facility, relational data base, metaknowledge (information about how to use knowledge), and interpreters for specialised control.
2. Compactness of expression, together with an efficient implementation, permits programs as complex as expert systems to be used practically.
3. The dual semantics, declarative and procedural, facilitates the development of metaknowledge features.

In summary, we have learned that PROLOG has been applied in a number of areas outside pure research. As has been said by Warren (1979), many of the applications are large and complex programs that probably would never have been written at all, were it not for the relative ease of writing them in PROLOG.

References

Bundy, A., Byrd, L., Luger, G., Mellish, C., and Palmer, M. 1979. Solving mechanics problems using meta-level inference. In *Expert Systems in the Micro-Electronic Age,* ed. D. Michie. Edinburgh, Scotland: Edinburgh University Press.

Clark, K. L., and Tärnlund, S.-A., eds. 1982. *Logic Programming.* New York: Academic Press.

Clocksin, W., and Mellish, C. 1981. *Programming in Prolog.* New York: Springer-Verlag.

Kowalski, R. 1979. *Logic for Problem Solving.* Amsterdam: North Holland.

Michie, D. 1980. Expert systems. *Computer Journal* 23: 369–376.

Pereira, L. M., Sabatier, P., and d'Oliveira, E. 1982. ORBI—An expert system for environmental resource evaluation through natural language, Report FCT/DI-3/82, Departamento de Informatica, Universidade Nova de Lisboa, Lisbon, Portugal.

Robinson, J. A. 1965. A machine-oriented logic based on the resolution principle. *Journal of the Association for Computing Machinery* 12: 23–41.

Roussel, P. 1975. *Prolog: Manuel de Reference et d'Utilisation.* Marseille-Luminy: Groupe d'Intelligence Artificielle.

Santane-Toth, E., and Szeredi, P. 1982. Prolog applications in Hungary. In *Logic Programming,* eds. K. L. Clark and S.-A. Tärnlund. New York: Academic Press.

Warren, D. 1979. Prolog on the DECsystem-10. In *Expert Systems in the Micro-Electronic Age,* ed. D. Michie. Edinburgh, Scotland: Edinburgh University Press.

Warren, D. H. D., and Pereira, F. C. N. 1981. An efficient easily adaptable system for interpreting natural language queries, Research Paper 155, Department of Artificial Intelligence, University of Edinburgh, Edinburgh, Scotland.

Winston, P., and Horn, B. K. P. 1981. *LISP*. Reading, Mass: Addison-Wesley.

CHAPTER 2

AN INTRODUCTION TO LISP

TONY HASEMER

INTRODUCTION

LISP is an artificial intelligence programming language. That is to say, programs written in LISP tend to be, in some way, models or mimics of some kind of human cognitive ability, as distinct from the number-crunching packages, stock control routines, and so on for which languages of the FORTRAN or COBOL type are more suitable. In fact, LISP knows very little about numbers—a quirk that some students of the language find utterly endearing. Instead, LISP deals with symbols: mainly alphanumeric symbols such as English words, but in principle a symbol can be composed of any combination of the characters on a terminal keyboard. According to its own rules of syntax, LISP combines these symbols into characteristic "shapes," like sentences, and then manipulates the sentences to produce the equivalent of paragraphs and even of whole chapters. To call LISP a programming *language* is not merely a bit of wishful thinking, because—in the same way that some things that can be said in French do not translate directly into English and vice versa—LISP expressions can be sufficiently rich or complex in content that a description of their purposes in English becomes a very long-winded affair indeed. As with foreign-language speakers, experts in LISP tend to think in LISP.

LISP is a highly interactive language—it talks back to you. What it actually does is to *read* what you type in, *evaluate* it, and then *print* the result on your terminal. That's easy to understand if you imagine wanting to know the answer to some simple sum, such as 3 plus 4: If you used the proper LISP format, which is (+ 3 4), LISP would read your question, evaluate it (i.e., work out the answer) and print 7. But a precisely analogous thing happens when you type in symbols that are *not* numeric. In this case the evaluation process (finding the answer, or finding out what your input means) is rather like looking up an unknown word in a dictionary, and similarly, the "meaning" of your input may well be a very much more complex object than the input itself. For example, the word *democracy* might represent a very large amount of interconnected information. LISP provides you with a relatively small initial dictionary and then allows you to add to, delete from, or alter the contents of the dictionary as you think fit. That is, LISP has a dictionary in which to look things up, but you the user will have control over what it finds there.

LISP Terminology

I will now clarify a few terms that LISP speakers use to describe what they are doing. Strictly speaking, any set of symbols that is legal in LISP is a LISP *s-expression,* and as Winston tells you in his excellent books (Winston 1980; Winston & Horn, 1981), the *s* stands for symbolic. But it has become commonplace to distinguish between an *atom*—a single "word" with no brackets (i.e., no LISP punctuation)—and an *expression,* which is any legal set of symbols including two or more brackets. And in order for a set of symbols to form a legal LISP expression, the numbers of opening and closing brackets *must* balance. Here are four legal LISP s-expressions:

```
tony
(run)
(+ 3 4)
(foo (bar glort))
```

and here are three examples that are not legal s-expressions:

```
tony)
(ru)n
(foo (bar glort)
```

An opening bracket tells LISP that you have begun to say something to it. Within what you say—the expression—you are allowed arbitrarily to nest smaller expressions; so that the only way LISP has of knowing that you have finished all of what you wanted to say is when you type the final balancing bracket. Here's a very simple LISP expression (I only want you to get used to how such things look for the moment—don't try to understand them):

```
(setq x 'cat)
```

and here's a more complex one:

```
(arbitrate-between (policies-of government) (needs-of unemployed))
```

Notice the shapes of these. Each pair of brackets encloses its own expression, and expressions can occur within other expressions: In the second case an expression whose first symbol is arbitrate-between contains two other expressions, one beginning with policies-of and the other with needs-of. LISP understands such a structure, as I am about to explain.

The cycle of reading, evaluating, and printing repeats over and over for as long as you continue a session with LISP. Not surprisingly, it is referred to as the read-eval-print loop. But it's not only at the top level—from typed input, around the loop, and back to the terminal—that LISP always returns a value. *Everything* in LISP gets evaluated at some point, and its value is the result of that evaluation. The inner expressions in the second of the preceding examples return values (when evaluated) that are then used as elements in the evaluation of the outer expression. To put that another way, you couldn't arbitrate-between (whatever that may mean) two things until you knew what those two things were. Provided that you stick to acceptable LISP syntax when typing in your inputs, the LISP evaluator is very clever, and *always* evaluates expressions, subexpressions, sub-subexpressions, and so on in the correct order—that is, the innermost first.

As for values, atoms have the value that you give them. You'll see how to do so in a minute. A LISP expression (sentence) has a value that is the overall result of evaluating that expression, as *monetarism* might be the overall meaning of the first subexpression in our example. And the value of a program, when executed, is the value of the last expression in that program as the evaluator works on it. Do you see the pattern? If you type in a simple thing, LISP merely evaluates it and gives you back the result. If you type in a thing within a thing, LISP evaluates the inner thing in order to evaluate the outer thing and gives you back the final result. In this respect the analogy between a LISP expression and an English sentence falls down: English sentences have their own internal structures that are extraordinarily rich and varied; and people have spent and still do spend many years of their lives in trying to express that richness in the relatively restricted structures that are afforded by programming languages.

USING LISP

When you summon LISP on your computer, what you get each time is a new, unused LISP with a small basic dictionary as I've already mentioned. Its contents remain under your control as previously seen (i.e., you can change the meanings therein), but it holds around 200 words whose meanings were originally supplied by the designers of the language. These words are the names of inbuilt system programs and are what makes your computer behave like a LISP machine, rather than a FORTRAN machine or a PROLOG machine. Three of them are read, eval, and print. You'll come across more in the course of this chapter. Your unused LISP, or the computer on which it runs, will also have an editor of some sort, so that you can write and modify your own programs. In effect the programs you write will, when finished, be used in exactly the same way as the programs supplied by the designers—will be so exactly like them, in fact, that you could if you liked write new versions of read, eval, and print, and your new versions would replace the old ones. Many long-term LISP users eventually write their own read-eval-print loops, in order to do clever things that satisfy their own personal needs or tastes. It is even possible in this way to make LISP behave as though it were a different language altogether. People say that one of the major advantages of LISP is that it is "indefinitely extensible," which means simply that if you don't like what it does, or how LISP does it, you're perfectly free to rewrite it so that it behaves the way you want it to. More than any other programming language, your LISP can be your own personal affair. Of course, there are dangers in that as well as advantages.

Lists

LISP's basic "shape," the equivalent of a sentence, is a *list*. Hence the language's name: *LIS*t *P*rocessing language. LISP is adept at building lists, accessing or changing various elements of them, or joining bits of them onto other lists. At first sight this may not appear to be a very useful ability, but in fact a great deal of what we refer to as "cognitive" activity involves, or can be reduced to, following an ordered list of tasks. Following a recipe in order to cook a meal is a good example; playing bridge is another. So the simplest type of LISP program is a routine that tells the computer to carry out a set of instructions in a given order: it is a *list* of things for the machine to do. Inside LISP, each of the individual instructions will probably itself be a list, and so on down to arbitrary levels of complexity. The magic bit of LISP is that it automatically knows how to sort out such nests of lists—which bits to process first and what to do with the results of that processing—so that what you, the user, get at the end of it all is what your program asked for.

LISP represents a list quite simply:

(write a letter)

is a list of three elements. And

(write a (thankyou letter))

is also a list of three elements, the first two of which are write and a, and the third of which is a sublist consisting of the two elements thankyou and letter. The complexity of these lists is arbitrary (i.e., it is up to you).

Which is all very interesting, but what does it *mean?* The answer is that as far as the computer is concerned it means nothing at all. To the computer the word *write* and the word *zxcvb* are equally meaningful (or meaningless); they are *symbols* to be manipulated according to your instructions and to the syntactic rules of LISP.

Variables

In LISP there are three main ways of giving meaning to a symbol. There are others, but the two I'm about to describe are by far the most common, and it would be difficult to write a LISP program without them. The third is less commonly used, but actually is the key to understanding how LISP really works. Taking the first two first, and continuing the language analogy for a moment, you can either make the symbol represent a fact, a piece of data, as the word letter symbolises an object, or you can make it represent on *action* whose *result* is a piece of data. The correct terminology here is to say that the action *returns* the piece of data: policies-of computes the policies from whatever its input data is; write would produce something written. It would also be better if from now on I referred to symbols as *atoms,* which is the proper LISP name for them. In most dialects of LISP, an atom can consist of almost any combination of keyboard characters, but in general it should not begin with a numeral (unless, of course, the whole atom is a number—such as 3572), and naturally there are a few reserved characters—you'll meet one of them, the single quote, shortly.

The concept of a variable (noun) having a value (meaning) is sometimes a sticky one for newcomers to programming. Some people find it easier to think in terms of the *x*s and *y*s of algebra or graphs, where the *unknown* is given a name (*x* or *y*) and the value has to be found by some mathematical process. But the essential point is that the variable itself means nothing, it is merely a symbol via which one can "get at" the value. As with the algebraic example, the same variable (the same symbol or name) can have different values at different times. The variable itself is no more than the *name* of the atom that holds the current value. When you type that name into LISP, LISP responds by telling you what the current value of that atom is.

The link between the name and whatever value it has at present is known as the *binding*. You can, for example, bind x to 3, after which every time you refer in your program to x, LISP understands 3; and later you can rebind x to cat. This destroys the original link between x and 3 and substitutes a link from x to cat, so that from then on if you say x, LISP understands cat.

The value of x is not necessarily just another symbol such as 3 or cat. It may be some hugely complex piece of data such as we humans would understand from the name-symbol "democracy." In LISP you are free to bind more or less any piece of data to any arbitrarily chosen symbol, and obviously it makes life easier to be able to refer to x when writing a program, rather than typing out the entire meaning of the word *democracy*. In the simplest case, the variable is the name of some object and its value is the object itself. But hopefully there are no real "cats" inside your computer, and so that particular object can only be represented by another symbol. LISP doesn't mind: It is happiest with pure symbols and leaves the thorny problem of their meaning up to you.

So, we can invent nouns that we intend to write into our programs, and we can assign meanings to those nouns. Besides that we have the unusual facility of changing the meanings as we go along, if we want to. (Don't panic, the ways of doing that are very easy, as you'll see shortly.) The other thing we want to be able to do is to create *functions,* which will operate on those nouns to produce different nouns. The same principle applies, in that we bind a value to a symbol, but in this case the value is not a fact but is a thing to do. Once this has been done, and when we subsequently type the symbol correctly into LISP, LISP understands not an object as before but that it must *do* something—something that we specified ourselves when we bound the symbol concerned to the "meaning." Apparently, the process of creating the binding in this case is different from before, and indeed, it is referred to differently: We *bind* a variable to a value, but we *define* a function—even though deep inside LISP itself the two operations are more or less identical.

Binding Variables to Values

Now it is time for a few practical examples of what I've been discussing. First, binding a variable to a value—here's one way to do that in LISP:

```
(setq x 'cat)
```

The setq is a LISP reserved word—also known as a system function—which any unused LISP knows about already. It is in fact a function whose effect is to create the binding between the following symbol x and the third item in that list. The third item, as you can see, is the word oat. *You* know what it means, and it is irrelevant that the machine does not. If you typed the aforementioned line (exactly!) into LISP, the machine would respond with the new value of x; that is to say, it would respond

cat

And if you now typed simply

x

you would get the same result. What LISP habitually does, as I have already said, is to *read* your typed input, *evaluate* it, and then *print* the result back at you.

One thing needs explaining—that little quote mark before the word that was to become the value of x. What that does, as your typed input chunters faithfully around the read-eval-print loop is to *prevent* the evaluation from happening. The effect is that whatever follows the quote (in this case another symbol) is handled verbatim, exactly as you typed it. If you were to omit the quote, LISP would try to evaluate cat. But it can't: As far as the machine is concerned, cat is just a symbol to which you the user have as yet attached no meaning. You may already have discovered that if you type the preceding example in without the quote you get an error message, such as **cat unbound variable**, which is LISP's way of saying "What? I don't understand you."

For consistency, you might expect that the x ought to have a quote, too, since it is the *symbol* (shape) x, and not the value of x, to which you wish to bind a value. And you'd be quite right:

    (set 'x 'cat)

would do exactly the same thing. But all dialects of LISP provide setq, which is short for *set quote* and which is reputed to save time in typing. Whatever you may think of that justification, notice that the single quote in LISP behaves very much as inverted commas do in English: It translates into some such phrase as "I mean precisely this."

Creating Functions

The preceding is a thumbnail sketch of how values are bound in LISP. Now I want similarly to give you a quick taste of how functions are created. So, here's a silly schematic LISP program to give you the idea:

```
(defun make-pancake (x y z)
       (weigh out 3 ounces of x)
       (mix in 1 z)
       (add 5 ounces of y)
       . . . .)
```

Notice a number of things. First, the word defun, which means *define a function*. (The dialect of LISP that I'm showing you is MacLISP. Many other dialects use de, or define.) The name of the function follows the defun, and then a list of variables (x y z), whose values will be the materials, or data, on which the function will be expected to work. In the previous example you might expect to get a pancake if you made x, y, and z, respectively, flour, milk, and an egg. But if you tried to use your function on tar, feathers, and a cross cat, you'd end up with something else entirely. The point here is that LISP functions are processes: You give the process name a meaning by defining it with defun, but that meaning only makes sense within a given context, or environment. To try to do the backstroke while negotiating a complicated roundabout in your car is another example of a process applied in the wrong environment. So don't expect your LISP functions to work as you wanted them to unless you use them with the right variables around. I'll have more to say about variables later.

Second, notice that however long or complicated a function may become, the left-hand and right-hand brackets always balance. Remember, LISP uses brackets, and patterns of brackets, much as English uses various punctuation marks—to disambiguate or separate parts of sentences or whole sentences from one another. Thus, each separate instruction within a function has its own pair of brackets to separate it from the preceding and following instructions, and the function as a whole (the sentence) similarly has an outer pair of its own. Other high-level programming languages use keywords such as begin and end for the same purpose; one of the minor joys of LISP is that all that extra typing is quite unnecessary.

Third, what I have sketched is how you would write a function—how you would tell LISP what this new word make-pancake is supposed to mean. Actually using ("calling") a function once you have written it is achieved simply by typing its name into the computer, together with a suitable set of values for the variables (egg, flour, milk). You can define a function with any number of variables, including none, but thereafter you must supply a value for each of them every time the function is called ("used").

What does all this add up to? Well, when you sit down at the computer it knows nothing at all except how to "do" LISP. And LISP, as I've already said, operates with lists. So, to teach it a new word (make-pancake), we supply it with a list whose first element is the word defun. (By the way, defun is an inbuilt LISP function that remembers your new word-definition as you write it):

```
(defun make-pancake (x y z)
      (weigh out 3 ounces of x)
      (mix in 1 z)
      (add 5 ounces of y)
      . . . .)
```

The second element of the list is the new word itself, and the third element is another list—that of the variables on whose values the function will work—in the context of which the new word will have its expected meaning or effect. These variables are known as the *arguments* of the function: In this case the arguments of the function make-pancake are x, y, and z. The remaining elements are the actual instructions—and when you later call your new function the computer will execute these instructions in turn until it reaches the end, which it will recognise when it sees the final balancing bracket.

A REAL LISP FUNCTION

OK, now let's write a function that will really do something, although something pretty pointless, but which I hope will tie all of the preceding discussion together for you. We're going to create a list as the value of a variable, and to define a function to manipulate that list for us.

First, the list itself. As previously mentioned, we don't want to have to type the whole list out every time we refer to it inside our function. And in any case, since the function is intended to change the list, it might be hard to know exactly what to type at any given point. So what we do is bind the list to some variable—some name—so that whenever we refer to the variable, LISP will understand that we mean the current list. Here we go:

    (setq animals '(lion grouper rat whale butterfly cat))

Now we have a variable whose value is that list. Notice that the brackets around the list of animals make it into a *unit,* the *whole* of which is handled verbatim by LISP's evaluator. If you now type

    animals

into LISP, it will reply with the list

(lion grouper rat whale butterfly cat)

If you don't know what a grouper is, look it up. Groupers are fun.

Returning for a moment to the analogy between a program and an ordered list of things to do, imagine that you might want to deal with the first element of the list and then cross it out—remove it from the list to show that it was done—whereupon you would proceed to the next item, and so on. Or alternatively, you might decide that butterfly doesn't really belong in there because it's not a *real* animal (there's no meat on it), and so you might want simply to remove butterfly but to leave the rest of the list unchanged. Or you might think that the list isn't nearly long enough and want to add some more members to it. All these things are astonishingly easy in LISP, because LISP is designed to process lists and so naturally has system functions at hand for just that purpose.

Some Examples to Try

Try typing the following:

    (setq animals (cdr animals))

Sorry about the cdr. Most LISP system functions are highly mnemonic. But some of the very simplest are hangovers from the days before LISP itself was even considered. This one stands for contents of decrement register, but don't worry about that. Just remember that cdr returns a list minus its first element.

Notice carefully what we're doing here. Overall, we are changing the value of the symbol animals from the original long list to one that is one element shorter. In detail, LISP starts as usual with the innermost nested part of our instruction, that is, with

(cdr animals)

There are no quotes anywhere here, so the whole of that little piece can be evaluated as it stands. The value of animals is what we set it to be previously.

(lion grouper rat whale butterfly cat)

and the value of cdr is the command to LISP to find out what that list would look like with its head (first element) removed. So the innermost part of our instruction returns a truncated version of the original animals list, which LISP then uses as data with which to carry out the remainder of our instruction. You can imagine, if you like, that somewhere inside LISP that original instruction now looks like

(setq animals "to the result of what you just did")

Of course, you don't see any of this going on—it happens too fast to see anyway. Only the final result will be returned to the terminal for you to read. Intermediate results such as that of the cdr are returned to some place within the computer's memory that LISP knows about but which doesn't matter to us.

So all that remains for LISP to do now is to *set* (*quote,* i.e., the symbol) animals to the new version of the list, and after that LISP dutifully returns the new value of animals to your terminal:

(grouper rat whale butterfly cat)

Notice in passing that cdr, in common with almost all LISP functions, does *not* alter the value of the data it works on. That's why we needed to use a setq. To prove this, type

(cdr animals)

to which LISP will reply

(rat whale butterfly cat)

that is, the "tail" of the latest value of the symbol animals. But if you now type

animals

you'll see that the value of the symbol itself is unchanged:

(grouper rat whale butterfly cat)

A companion function to cdr is car. Whereas odr gives you the tail of the list, the list minus its first element, car gives you only the first element—but again and as usual, the list itself is unchanged by the operation of car by itself:

>	(car animals)

returns

>	**grouper**

and

>	animals

returns

>	**(grouper rat whale butterfly cat)**

Now let's get rid of the scrawny **butterfly**. Type

>	(setq animals (remove 'butterfly animals))

and LISP will return

>	**(grouper rat whale cat)**

This time, we've told LISP to remove the quoted, and therefore verbatim, word **butterfly** from the list which is the value of **animals**, and then to give the symbol **animals** this new value. As you can see from what LISP returns, that's exactly what it does. In case your dialect of LISP doesn't have the function **remove**, I'll show you later how to define it yourself.

Adding New Elements

There are two possible things that we might want to do in adding new animals to the list: We might want to add just one animal, or a whole new list. LISP allows for either, via judicious use of the functions cons and append. Cons adds a new single element on to the front of an existing list:

>	(setq animals (cons 'dog animals))

returns

>	**(dog grouper rat whale cat)**

Append joins a new list on to the end of an existing list:

    (setq animals (append animals '(ostrich python)))

    returns

(dog grouper rat whale cat ostrich python)

Adding a new single element on to the end of an existing list is achieved by using append with the single new element that is formed into a list just as ostrich and python were

    (setq animals (append animals '(flea)))

Adding a new list on the front of an existing one is also done with append, but with its *arguments* reversed:

    (setq animals (append '(mouse tweetie-pie) animals)

And after all those setqs, our list of animals is now quite long:

(mouse tweetie-pie dog grouper rat whale cat ostrich python flea).

   One more thing, and then we really will write that long promised LISP function. That thing is an essential to almost any program—the ability to write a *conditional* clause so that the machine will do either one thing or another, depending on various conditions. In LISP, the conditional form looks like this:

    (cond (⟨test-1⟩ ⟨action-1a⟩ ⟨action-1b⟩ . . .)
          (⟨test-2⟩ ⟨action-2a⟩ ⟨action-2b⟩ . . .)
          (. . .   . .)
          (⟨test-N⟩ ⟨action-Na⟩ ⟨action-Nb⟩ . . .))

The tests and actions can each be any legal LISP s-expression, from simple atoms to the most complicated series of function calls that you care to dream up. That is why I have enclosed them in angle brackets: to indicate that they represent arbitrary pieces of LISP code.
   What LISP does on encountering such a sentence is to evaluate the first of the tests, to see if it comes out as true or false. It doesn't matter how complicated the test may be—only the result it finally returns is counted. If it comes out as true, LISP performs the corresponding action-1a, then action-1b, and so on, and completely ignores the rest of the cond. If it comes out as false, LISP goes on to evaluate the second test to see if that comes out as true, and if so to carry out action-2a, action-2b, and so on, and then to ignore the rest of the cond as before. Again, any action performed can be as complex as you like, and the result of the whole cond is the value that is returned by the very last action performed. There can be as many test-action lines as you

like, and on each of them there is one test followed by any number (including none) of actions. Very often an experienced programmer will make the final line an "if all else fails" case by writing simply t as the test. In LISP, t signifies *true* and nil signifies *false,* so that a t clause (test-action line) ensures that the last test, if no other, always succeeds and that the corresponding actions, if any, are always carried out.

To be precise, I should tell you that in most dialects of LISP the empty list, that is, ( ) or nil, signifies false but anything that is *not* nil signifies true. Thus, the test in a cond clause could return anything at all that was not nil, and the corresponding action(s) would be executed. OK—if that isn't very clear, the easiest way to clarify it is to show you an example. We're not going to forget about our list of animals, having gone to such trouble to create it, but just for the sake of this quick example, let's have a new list, called creatures, which so far has only one element:

```
(setq creatures '(pussy))
```

And here's the cond I want to show you:

```
(cond ((null creatures) (print 'nothing))
      ((cdr creatures) creatures)
      (t (print 'creatures)))
```

Can you see what the cond would do? Well, the ⟨test⟩ in the first clause is

```
(null creatures)
```

and null, as you may have guessed, is a system function that returns t if a list is empty and nil otherwise. Since the list creatures is not empty (it has a pussy in it), this first clause returns nil and the cond moves on to the next clause. Here it finds

```
(cdr creatures)
```

And what's the value of creatures minus its first element? nil again, I'm afraid. So the cond is left with nothing but its t clause to look at, and there the ⟨action⟩ is

```
(print 'creatures)
```

that is, print the (quoted) symbol creatures. And that is what the cond does.

So, here at last is the real LISP function:

```
(defun shorten (l)
    (cond ((null l) nil)
          (t (print l)
             (shorten (cdr l)))))
```

What this function does is print out successive cdrs of its argument, that is, of the input list l. Applying it to our list of animals, which you would do by typing in

(shorten animals)

the print instruction would produce on your terminal

mouse tweetie-pie dog grouper rat whale cat ostrich python flea
tweetie-pie dog grouper rat whale cat ostrich python flea
dog grouper rat whale cat ostrich python flea
grouper rat whale cat ostrich python flea
rat whale cat ostrich python flea
whale cat ostrich python flea
cat ostrich python flea
ostrich python flea
python flea
flea
nil

Let's go through the preceding definition line by line and see how it works. defun, as we saw before, says to LISP "give the following meaning to the word shorten, and the name shorten itself is followed by a list of the data on which shorten will work—in this case a list that is symbolised by l. When we call (use) shorten we'll type

(shorten animals)

whereupon l is bound to the then value of animals. Notice, in passing, that animals itself is not actually referred to within shorten—only l is. That means that when shorten has done all its stuff and comes to an end, animals will still have its same old value, despite the fact that shorten uses progressively smaller lists as the value of l. If you like, l's value is initially a *copy* of the value of animals. That's how it comes about that most system functions, such as cdr—which are essentially no different from the functions you write yourself—don't alter the values of what you feed into them.

The first clause of the cond says, "If the list is empty, do nothing." The first time around, of course, the list is by no means empty, so this clause fails and LISP goes on to the second clause. This is a t clause, as previously described, and must operate if all else fails. So LISP proceeds to execute the corresponding action, which in this case is a series of two actions. The first action here says "print the list," and LISP does so, onto your terminal of course, because that is the effect of print. And the second action calls shorten all over again, with a different argument—a different initial value for l—that is the cdr of the original value. So during the second run of shorten the list that gets printed is the cdr of the original; during the third run it is the cdr of that, and so on until the list is exhausted. During the final run of shorten the list is empty, thus, the first clause of the cond fires so that LISP then *does* nothing as instructed by the nil action. This trick, that of making a function call itself, is known as recursion, which I'll return to later on. First, I want to tell you about the all-important third way of giving *meaning* to a LISP symbol.

THE LISP DATA BASE

Try typing in

> (putprop 'cat 'whiskers 'features)

and LISP will return

> **whiskers**

But if you type

> cat

you'll get an error message. There is no sense in which whiskers has been made the value of anything. Putprop is different from setq. Nonetheless, something has been achieved, for if we type

> (get 'cat 'features)

LISP will faithfully return

> **whiskers**

Via putprop, LISP associates a *value* (whiskers) with an *atom* (cat), but only as a certain kind of *property* (features). You could also type

> (putprop 'cat 'tiddles 'name)

And now LISP would still return **whiskers** if you typed

> (get 'cat 'features)

but would return **tiddles** if you asked it to (get 'cat 'name). Try it. What's more, putprop doesn't restrict you to single entries:

> (putprop 'cat '(tail miaow whiskers) 'features)

will return

> **(tail miaow whiskers)**

To see what has happened, use another system function, plist, which is the mnemonic for *property list:*

> (plist 'cat)

LISP returns

(name tiddles features (tail miaow whiskers))

(*Note:* In many dialects of LISP the cdr of a *quoted* atom, for example, (cdr 'cat), returns its property list, in which case the plist function doesn't exist.)

Every symbol in LISP may be visualised as carrying a list of properties around with it. As usual, the contents of that list are (almost) entirely under your control; but LISP reserves certain entries on it for its own use. Otherwise, it would be possible for a ham-fisted user to destroy his/her LISP completely by doing the wrong things to the property list. The property list is the means by which LISP does what it does, such as keeping track of the meanings you assign to various symbols. Some dialects of LISP will let you inspect the whole list with plist (or cdr); others keep certain parts hidden so you won't be tempted.

The way to alter these entries once they're made is to use a combination of putprop and get:

(putprop 'cat (remove 'miaow (get 'cat 'features)) 'features)

What happens here is that the evaluator starts, as usual, with the most deeply nested part of the instruction, in this case

(get 'cat 'features)

and that returns, internally to LISP, of course:

(tail miaow whiskers)

That three-element list is then used as the data used to evaluate the next most deeply nested part of the instruction. As before, you can imagine that somewhere inside LISP the whole thing now looks like:

(putprop 'cat
          (remove 'miaow "from the result of what you just did")
          'features)

(I've had to use three lines because the instruction has grown too long for one line. LISP doesn't care about extraneous spaces, and I'll explain later why the lines are indented.) OK, so removing miaow from (tail miaow whiskers) leaves **(tail whiskers)**. Now the original instruction could look like

(putprop 'cat "the latest result" 'features)

in other words,

(putprop 'cat '(tail whiskers) 'features)

The effect of this new **putprop** is to overwrite (obliterate) any existing values of the property **features**, so that

(get 'cat 'features)

now returns

(tail whiskers)

The property list is a very neat and tidy way of associating with LISP atoms any values that you want to be permanent, without affecting the ability of the same atoms to be bound or defined in the usual way. LISP itself keeps all of what it knows about any given symbol on the symbol's property list. If you try

(plist 'shorten)

you'll see that in among various arcane words there is also recognisably the function we wrote.

And—this is the exciting fact—when you type into LISP an expression consisting of symbols to which you have assigned various meanings—some of them values and some of them functions—the evaluator only has to look at the property list of each to know exactly what you intended. Every unquoted symbol you type into LISP must have a property list of some kind if LISP is to understand it (whether or not the particular dialect you're using will let you see it), and the so far apparently magic system functions, **defun** and **setq**, achieve their effects simply by **putpropping** values onto the list under standard property headings. When we told LISP to **shorten** our list of **animals** the evaluator knew, just by looking to see which of these standard headings had values associated with them, that **shorten** was a call to a function, and **animals** was a list of data.

(Unfortunately, the MacLISP dialect doesn't show **setq**'d values on its property lists. It associates values with symbols in a slightly different way. But the preceding example remains a good *model* of what happens, and in many other dialects it is literally true.)

LEVELS, RECURSION AND ITERATION

When you are typing directly into LISP from your terminal, programmers say that you are working at "top level." They have this image of the computer according to which whatever you type has to dive deep inside the machine in order to get itself executed, so that execution occurs at "one level down." And if what you type is a function call, so that when it is executed it produces a further set of instructions for the machine to execute, those new instructions have to dive even deeper to be worked on by the machine at "two levels down," and so on. This image of how the machine handles nested instructions is intuitively helpful rather than physically accurate, but I recommend it as an aid to understanding and I use it in what follows.

Let's return now to the question of recursion. It is often handy, as it was in our **shorten** function, to have the machine do the same thing over and over as it executes a program. And the first thing to note here is that obviously a stop signal or stop condition must become effective at some point; otherwise the machine goes on and on doing the same thing forever. I'll come back to how to stop it in a minute.

In programming there are two ways in which you can do the same thing repeatedly. One is called *recursion,* and the other is called *iteration.* Beginners often find the distinction quite hard to grasp, so I'll do my best to explain it clearly. Recursion is what shorten did: It actually contained a line of LISP code that made shorten happen again inside itself—a part of the execution of shorten involved executing shorten again. A visual analogy is the effect you get when standing between two parallel mirrors: endless copies of your reflection stretching away to infinity. Or a drawing such as

That is recursion, and what distinguishes it from anything else is that executing, say, shorten, involves also executing an inner *copy* of the function, within which there occurs another copy, and so on. Recursion *does not* involve executing the *same* copy of the function more than once.

Here is shorten again:

```
(defun shorten (l)
      (cond ((null l) nil)
            (t (print l)          <--
               (shorten (cdr l)))))
```

As it runs, and as the LISP evaluator reaches the end of the line I've arrowed, a whole new version of the function is set up, with a different argument (different input data to work with). When the evaluator reaches the same point in the new **shorten**, the same thing happens again. This repeats until at some point the last line sets up a new version of **shorten** with an empty list as its argument. On that cycle the arrowed point is never reached, because the **cond** directs the evaluator elsewhere, namely, to a **nil** or "do-nothing" instruction. Once again (so that the diagram I want to draw doesn't fill the rest of this book), let's start with a fairly short input list for our function to work on

   (setq animals '(dog cat mouse))

Here is a representation of what happens when we type in

(shorten animals)

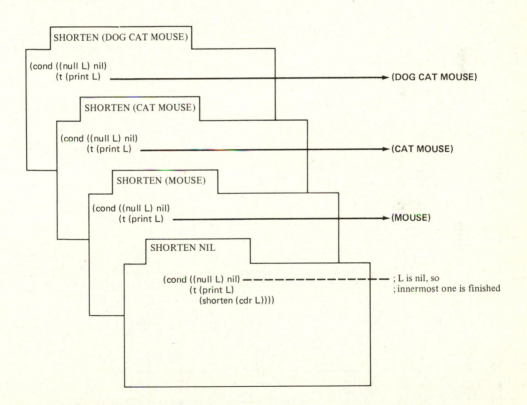

OK, having dutifully done nothing on the cycle where the data have been reduced to nil, what does the machine do next? Well, it has to finish off all those partially completed serial versions of **shorten**, and then it can return to top level and to you. To make this a bit clearer, let's rewrite the last line of the function

```
(defun shorten (l)
      (cond ((null l) nil)
            (t (print l)
               (shorten (cdr l))   )))
```

The bit after the space on the last line is what remains to be executed, in each of the series of **shortens**. Fortunately, in this particular case, there is nothing there, just the official (according to the bracketing conventions) end of each. But we could rewrite **shorten** in yet another way

```
(defun shorten (l)
      (cond ((null l) nil)
            (t (shorten (cdr l))
               (print l))))
```

This time, the list l isn't printed on each *forward* cycle of the recursion as before, but is left over until the cond has finally brought the recursion to an end. Whereupon each of the **print** commands is executed in turn, one at each level of the recursion as it "unwinds."

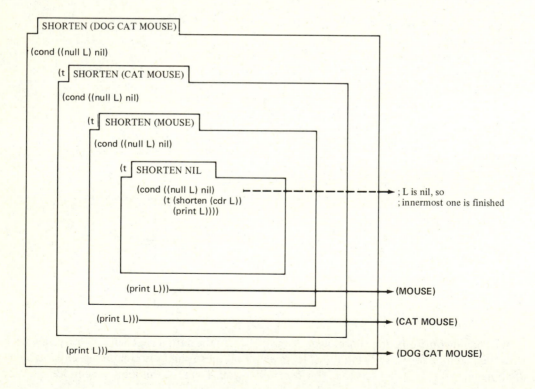

So what happens is that the version of I with only one element left—that is, (mouse) in the preceding example—is printed first. In practice, this is the version of I that existed when the cdr of I was an empty list, or nil. Then, the next shortest version, with two elements, is printed, and so on, right up to the full list. Try it.

ITERATION

The other way to do the same thing repeatedly is very much simpler, and is called *iteration*. You've heard of the word "re-iteration," to do with repeating words or phrases? Well, iteration is the same thing applied to a program. An iterative function contains a loop. Unlike recursion, only one copy of the function is ever executed, and so there is no unwinding involved. It's only a straightforward loop, just as you would expect from the name. One way of expressing the difference between recursion and iteration is that the former takes place at progressively deeper levels, whereas the latter occurs all on one level. An iterative loop involves the following steps:

1. Bind some variables.
2. Test the variables to see if the exit (stop) condition applies. If so, exit. If not, go on to (3).
3. Change the values of the variables in some way.
4. Go back to (2).

This format is invariable whatever the programming language, since it is merely an English-language description of what *must* happen if a loop is to work. Advanced dialects of most modern programming languages take advantage of this commonality, making themselves easier to read by expert programmers who don't have expertise in that particular language by using what have become known as structured programming concepts. Basically, this means that the vast majority of the programs that are written can be broken down into English-language describable chunks like the loop description I've just given you. The programming language can also provide comparable chunks of code whose syntax is fixed, so that you the user only have to fill in the slots with the names of your own local variables, and so on, to be guaranteed a working segment of your overall program. Unfortunately, exactly what structures you have available depends entirely on what dialect of LISP you're using, so for the purposes of this chapter I'll stick with the very basic (and, in some programmers' eyes, disreputably old-fashioned) prog loop. All LISPs have it; and you may find it an interesting exercise to find out what structures your own LISP offers that could improve the style or readability of the programs I write.

This is how a basic prog loop looks:

```
(prog ⟨vars⟩
      tag
      ⟨stop-test⟩
      ⟨. . body . .⟩
      (go tag))
```

As you can see, the loop corresponds very closely to the verbal steps I've already given. The body can be any sequence of LISP instructions you like, the assumption being that at least one of them will change the value of some variable and that that variable's value will be tested in the stop-test. Here's an example:

```
(defun shorten (l)
     (prog ( )
           tag
           (cond ((null l) (return nil))
                 (t (print l)
                    (setq l (cdr l))
                    (go tag)))))
```

Notice how the first clause of the cond is the stop-test, and how its t clause is the body of the prog construct. Notice also that after printing the current value of the list l, instead of recalling shorten with a truncated argument, we stay within the *same* call to it, explicitly resetting l to its own cdr and then repeating the section of code between the tag and the instruction to (go tag). This cycling continues until the stop-test succeeds (until l is null), whereupon the return instruction halts it. You aren't obliged to return nil. You can return anything—as complicated a series of LISP expressions as you like—the final value of which becomes the final value of the prog. In the preceding verbal description of a loop, point (1) says "Bind some local variables." *Binding* means giving them some values, and in the prog construct any variables whose names (symbols) are placed within the pair of brackets immediately following the atom prog itself are automatically bound (setq'd) to nil. But shorten doesn't need any such variables, so the brackets above form an empty list. I return to the subject of these local variables in the next section.

We could make shorten correspond even more closely to the verbal description of a loop by using the system function and instead of cond. And takes any number of arguments and evaluates them in order until one of them returns **nil**, or until there are no arguments left. For example,

```
(and 'cat 'dog nil 'mouse)
```

will return **nil**, but

```
(and 'cat 'dog 'mouse)
```

will return **mouse**. So here's another version of the iterative shorten:

```
(defun shorten (l)
     (prog ( )
           tag
           (and (null l) (return 'done))
           (print l)
           (setq l (cdr l))
           (go tag)))
```

Since (null I) returns **nil** unless the list I is empty, the return never gets executed until that point. This version of **shorten** will do exactly what the others did, but it will also print **done** when it has finished.

SCOPE OF VARIABLES

As mentioned earlier, once a value has been bound to a variable, that binding remains in force until you the user change it. This is always true when the binding is done from top level—that is, from the keyboard. Bindings created from within your functions (like the sequential bindings of I in the last section) *can* be permanent, but more often than not they will go away, and when they are finished with, the variable name will become unbound. Variables (the names of variables) whose bindings remain true throughout the execution of an entire program—which may contain literally scores of small functions about the size of **shorten**—are known as "global" variables; those whose bindings are set up within a single function and are lost when the function ends are said to be "local" to that function. And, of course, there are various states in between: It is perfectly reasonable that you might want a variable to be assigned at one point in your program, to retain its value during the execution of several subroutines, and only then to lose it. This area over which the variable keeps its binding is referred to as its *scope*.

Consider now something I said in the preceding section: The value of the list I used by **shorten** was a *copy* of the actual list of **animals**. What LISP functions habitually do with their arguments is to make a copy of each, on which the function will operate, and then when execution of the function is complete the old value is restored. In other words, within **shorten** itself I was bound to various successive values—none of which could possibly affect the value of **animals**—and at the end of **shorten** the list I became unbound: It had no value at all. Exactly the same thing would happen were we to rewrite **shorten** by using the symbol **animals** in place of I. Despite the fact that during execution of **shorten** the list of **animals** had several different values, once **shorten** was over, **animals** would be restored to what it was originally. This is an example of a variable, I or **animals**, being purely local to **shorten**; and an important part of the point of specifying such variables when the function is originally defined is that from then on LISP knows that their scope is local. The symbols that you put where the arrow is in the following example acquire values that are strictly local to **shorten**: Using them outside the body of the definition of that function will cause an error: As mentioned earlier, these variables are known as the *arguments* to the function:

```
(defun shorten (    ) . . .)
                 ↑
```

Suppose that at the same time we had another variable lying around, say, an n which we had previously bound to 30 by doing a **setq** from top level. We could insert into **shorten** a line saying

```
(setq n (difference n 1))
```

so that every time **shorten** was executed the value of n was reduced by one. But because n itself was not specified as a local variable when shorten was defined, its old value is *not* restored when the execution of shorten is complete. In this case n is a global variable and its value will be permanently changed every time you call shorten. Try it:

```
(setq n 30)
```

then

```
(defun shorten (l)
      (prog ( )
            tag
            (and (null l) (return 'done))
            (print l)
            (setq n (difference n 1))
            (setq l (cdr l))
            (go tag)))
```

The preceding notation for arithmetic-type operations, where the "operating" function is specified first, is used throughout LISP and is known as prefix functional notation. In arithmetic terms, (difference n 1) is equivalent to $(- n\ 1)$ instead of the more usual $(n - 1)$, but it means the same thing. Later on I mention other LISP functions that work similarly, for example, (equal n 3) returns t only if $n = 3$.

The point here is that it is very sloppy programming practice, not to mention needlessly wasteful of your computer's memory space, to create global variables when local ones will do. And later, when you try to understand your older programs, you'll find it much easier if you have kept all your variables tidy, with obvious and clearly defined scopes. Prog allows you to have local variables that are not included in the function definition, and which as already mentioned are automatically preset to nil for you. The advantage of this facility may not be too obvious when the only real function you've seen is shorten in various guises. But suppose, for example, that you wanted to count how many times your program cycled through its loop. You could use n, despite the fact that n already has a value outside the boundaries of shorten, like this:

```
(defun shorten (l)
      (prog (n)
            (setq n 0)
            tag
            (and (null l) (return n))
            (print l)
            (setq n (plus 1 n))
            (setq l (cdr l))
            (go tag)))
```

You have to setq n to zero initially, because in almost all LISPs nil and 0 are not the same thing. Thereafter n is augmented by one each time around the loop, and its final value is returned when l becomes empty.

FROM ALGORITHMS TO CODE

Earlier you saw the comment that some aspects of human cognitive ability can be reduced to the process of going through an ordered list of actions, crossing them off one by one, until the end of the list is reached and some overall effect is achieved. Now we can extend that analogy a little, because any one item on the list may itself be quite a complex sublist of instructions: In the final program it may be represented as a prog loop, for example. But each step, each item on the list, can be viewed as a coherent "chunk" of activity, or as a subgoal on the way to the final goal. Ideally, steps do not interact, so that step 3 does not have to be done in some idiosyncratic way because step 7 will change things later. In a well-written computer program there will be a "master" function, which is analogous to you following a recipe or whatever; and the master function will call a sequence of lesser functions, each of which will perform just one of the steps that are required to produce the end result. This technique—dividing the overall problem or task into discrete subtasks and of carrying them out in an ordered way—is known as structured programming, and is very much in vogue just now. The structured programming constructs which I mentioned before, and which MacLISP as well as other high-level languages have, are intended to make programs easier both to write and to read.

Writing out (in English) the list of steps that your program must follow is known as "writing the algorithm," but obviously not just any old list will do: The algorithm is not finished until every step in it can be directly translated into things of which the computer is capable. To close this chapter I'll run through the writing of an algorithm and its translation into workable code to give you the flavour of how such things are accomplished.

The Towers of Hanoi

There is a famous AI problem that is variously referred to as the Tower of Brahma or the Towers of Hanoi. It is rumoured that somewhere in the mysterious East a succession of Buddhist monks devote their lives to solving the problem by hand, and that when they have done so the world will end. The problem has also been produced as a child's toy. It has a wooden base up from which poke three pegs. On one peg is a set of discs or rings, like miniature gramophone records, decreasing in size from the bottom up. The number of rings need not be specified: The minimum is obviously three if the problem is not to be trivially simple; it is said that the poor monks have to deal with sixty-four of them.

The rules of the game are: (1) move only one ring at a time and (2) never place a larger ring on top of a smaller one. The objective is to transfer the entire pile of rings from its starting peg to either of the other pegs—the target peg:

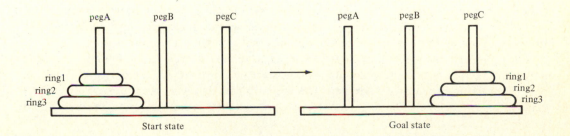

Start state   Goal state

Our purpose now is to write a program to solve this problem, that is, to print out the moves that are necessary to go from the starting state to the goal state. In order to do this, we need two things: a way of representing any "current" state of the problem—how it looks after *n* moves—and a program that can operate on that representation until the goal state is reached. Notice that for AI purposes this is *all* that the computer does: It manipulates its data (its symbols) until they fall into some desired pattern. As ever, the significance of that pattern is up to us, and the question of giving the computer arms and hands with which to solve a physical representation of the problem is beyond the scope of our present concerns. We will solve the Towers of Hanoi problem by using a formalism known as the production system, which can itself be handled very easily in LISP.

Production Systems

The *production system* (PS) is an AI technique that is often used for modelling the kinds of processes that I've been talking about: those that can be reduced to a set of rules or instructions. The advantage of the PS is that it makes the rules explicit and therefore easy to change. Its disadvantage is that it is relatively difficult to see at a glance exactly what happens as the program containing the PS is executed.

The principle is easy enough. The moment-by-moment progress of the running program towards its objective is represented in a special temporary store called the *working memory* (see below), and according to the contents of this memory, at any time one or more of the rules will be applicable—will "fire"—and in so doing will change the contents of the memory so that a different rule or rules become applicable. And so on, until a special rule fires which says in effect "That's it, objective achieved," and the whole thing stops. The example I'm going to show you is, to be honest, very much in the class of production systems made easy, and purists would certainly want to say that it isn't a "proper" production system at all. But it will give you a good insight into how such a program is designed.

In this particular example, representation of any problem state is fairly simple, but you can probably imagine that to represent some intermediate stage in a game of chess or in parsing a paragraph might be a much more complex affair. For convenience we give the pegs alphabetic names and the rings numeric names. Our working memory contains only four elements: the names of the three pegs, each associated with the numbers of the rings that are currently held on it, plus a statement of the program's current goal—that is, which of the rings it is currently trying to move.

The program's method of tackling the problem is fairly analogous to the way in which you or I might handle it. It knows from game rule (2) that its first need is to move the largest ring onto the target peg; but it can't do that directly because there are other rings on top of it, and so moving it would contravene game rule (1). So, it needs to clear those smaller rings away. It considers the second largest ring first, but, of course, the same objections apply. Thus, it still needs to clear away the smaller rings from on top of the second largest ring. Eventually it comes to one it can move: the very smallest. And it moves that smartly to the target peg.

Then it repeats the preceding process, trying to move the largest ring and finding that it can only move the top one on the same pile. And because of game rule (2) the only place that top ring can go is on the middle, spare peg. The program now tries yet again to move the largest ring. If there were only three rings to start with, this can now be done under game rule (1), but unfortunately its intended destination—the target peg—is now obstructed by the smallest ring, so that moving anything onto it would break game rule (2). Thus, the target peg must now be cleared, according to the same game rules and therefore by the same programmatic method. Once it is clear, the largest ring can be moved onto it. Repetition of this entire process eventually produces the desired result, and fairly obviously this is the case no matter how many rings are involved.

The Rules in English

The steps behind the previous section can be encapsulated as follows:

1. If the target peg holds all the rings 1 to n, stop because according to game rule (2) they must be in their original order and so the problem is solved.
2. If there is no current goal—that is, if a ring has just been successfully moved, or if no rings have yet been moved—generate a goal. In this case the goal is to be that of moving to the target peg the largest ring that is not yet on the target peg.
3. If there is a current goal, it can be achieved at once if there are no smaller rings on top of the ring to be moved (i.e., if the latter is at the top of its pile), and if there are no smaller rings on the peg to which it is to be moved (i.e., the ring to be moved is smaller than the top ring on the peg we intend to move it to). If this is the case, carry out the move and then delete the current goal so that rule 2 will apply next time.
4. If there is a current goal but its disc cannot be moved as in rule 3, set up a new goal: that of moving the largest of the *obstructing* rings to the peg that is neither of those specified in the current goal (i.e., well out of the way of the current goal). Delete the current goal, so that rule 3 will apply to the new goal next time.

The production system takes a set of rules such as 1 to 4 and a working memory (WM) such as that previously described. It applies each rule in turn to the WM; sometimes the rule will fire and alter the WM, sometimes not. When it reaches the end of the set of rules, it starts again from the top, and so on, until the "win" rule (rule 1) fires to stop the process. In principle the rules are completely independent of one another, and any of them may fire during each cycle. In more complicated production systems several rules will fire during the same cycle, and in such cases a subsidiary set of rules, known as conflict resolution rules, have to be employed. Luckily, we won't need them.

More sophisticated production systems can look for matches between *patterns* of data comprising the rules and *patterns* of data that are held in working memory. For our purposes, and to avoid the complexities of sophisticated pattern-matching strategies, it will be simpler to write LISP functions that are capable of diving right into working memory to find out what is actually there.

The Working Memory

As already mentioned, this will contain four elements. In LISP terms, it will be a *list* of four elements. The first one will contain the current goal if any, but at the start of the problem there is no current goal (rule 2 hasn't fired yet to create one). So the initial condition of the goal slot in WM is nil:

```
((goal nil). . . .)
```

Each of the remaining three elements of WM concerns one of the three pegs:

```
((goal nil)
 (pegA . . .)
 (pegB . . .)
 (pegC . . .))
```

and at the start of the problem only pegA has any rings (all of them) on it:

```
((goal nil)
 (pegA (1 2 3))
 (pegB nil)
 (pegC nil))
```

Notice that I've faithfully written in the nils to represent empty segments of memory, even though LISP will do nothing with them. This is a good habit to acquire, because not only does it make the initial state of WM easier for us humans to read but it also ensures that later on, when you come to do more advanced programming in which LISP *does* need to be told specifically about the existence of nothings, you won't forget to put them in!

Another thing to notice here is that the numeric names of the rings also express their sizes: ring2 is bigger than ring1, and so on. Furthermore, the order of the numbers in the pegA list expresses the order in which those rings would appear on a real, physical pegA. That is to say, the smallest ring, which under game rule (2) must be at the top of the pile, is the first in the list.

Now that we've decided on the form our initial WM is to take, it's a trivial matter to make this into a function that will reestablish the start of the problem each time we run our program:

```
(defun reset ( )
       (setq wm '((goal nil)
                  (pegA (1 2 3))
                  (pegB nil)
                  (pegC nil))))
```

Reset needs no arguments, no local variables, because all it does is a setq to bind the atom wm to a quoted (verbatim) pattern of symbols. If you define reset by typing it into the machine, then run it by typing (reset), and then type wm, you'll see that that binding has been successfully accomplished.

At this point, if you are going to try out the following examples, you should ask someone who knows, or consult the necessary manuals, in order to determine how to operate whichever of the many available editing systems your computer has. You need to be able both to keep your routines, such as reset, on a "file" and to "load" the contents of the file into your LISP at any time. The procedure probably isn't complicated, but there certainly isn't room here to cover all the possible variations. If for some reason you aren't able to use an editor, you could (very carefully!) type the functions into LISP as I describe them to you. The whole set of functions will form a "suite" which will correctly operate together without you having to do anything special to ensure that they do. But, once you have logged off, you'll have to type the whole lot in again the next time you want to use them. So use an editor if you can.

Accessing Working Memory

Notice that each element of working memory is of the same form:

    (⟨item-name⟩   ⟨data⟩)

This was deliberate on my part, because we can now write a single "accessing function" which will retrieve from working memory any piece of data we may need. Like this (read on to see what assoc does):

```
(defun fetch (item)
    (second (assoc item wm)))
```

When you have a data structure such as our working memory, something that consists of a list of sublists, any specific sublist can be retrieved by using the system function assoc. Assoc takes two arguments: an atom and a list. The atom is a "key" and the list is the list of sublists, known as an *alist* (association list). Assoc looks down the alist until it finds a sublist whose first element is the same as the key, and then it returns the whole sublist. Thus,

    (assoc 'pegA wm)

would return

    (pegA (1 2 3))

   However, what we usually want to get at is the data rather than a list of the data and its item name. In other words, we want the second element of what assoc returns. LISP doesn't give you the function second for free: It expects you to use combinations of cars and cdrs to achieve the same effect. But this is a case where I don't like the way LISP does things: second is far easier to understand when one is reading code. And, as I mentioned near the beginning of this discussion, if you don't like the way LISP does things, you're quite free to change it. So let's create the function second; it only takes a minute.

```
(defun second (l)
    (cadr l))
```

And that's it. Notice the cadr. That's a combination of a cdr, which the LISP evaluator will execute first, embedded in a car, which the evaluator executes subsequently:

(cadr l)   is equivalent to   (car (cdr l)).

Since

(cdr '(pegA (1 2 3))   is   **((1 2 3))**

and

(car '((1 2 3))   is   **(1 2 3)**,

(second '(pegA (1 2 3)))   returns   **(1 2 3)**.

In most dialects of LISP, you're allowed to concatenate cars and cdrs. Thus

(caddr x)   is equivalent to   (car (cdr (cdr x))).

We will use fetch, which in turn of course will use (call) second, whenever we want to get at a specific piece of data held in working memory.

The Rules in LISP

The four rules now need to be reexpressed in (translated into) LISP. This isn't difficult, except that in the process I have to tell you about a number of LISP system functions that you haven't as yet come across. And as mentioned earlier, the property list is a handy place to keep this kind of "permanent" data.

Rule 1

We'll call our first rule p1, and here's what it looks like:

If (equal (fetch 'pegC) '(1 2 3)) then (setq halt t)
         ⟨condition⟩   ⟨action⟩

This could represent the first of the four rules, which said, If the target peg holds all the rings 1 to n, stop because according to game rule (2), they must be in their original order and so the problem is solved. Here's how we can translate this rule even further into LISP, by using the property list of the atom p1 to hold the ⟨condition⟩ and ⟨action⟩ halves:

(putprop 'p1 '(equal (fetch 'pegC) '(1 2 3)) 'condition)
(putprop 'p1 '(setq halt t) 'action)

As in an ordinary cond, the rule is split into two parts, a condition and an action, and only if the condition is satisfied will the program go on to execute the action. The two halves are associated with the atom p1 under different properties (headings) on its property list, and if via your editor you type the previous two lines into your file, the whole rule will automatically be put onto p1's property list every time you load the file into LISP. All that the preceding rule, the win rule, says is: "If pegC holds all the rings, set a flag (halt) which will stop the cycling of the production system." You'll see exactly how that happens in a minute.

Rule 2

Rule 2 needs to say as its condition part "If there is no current goal . . ." for which

    (null (fetch 'goal))

will do admirably. So here's the condition part of rule p2:

    (putprop 'p2 '(null (fetch goal)) 'condition)

And the rest of rule 2, the action part, says first, ". . . find the biggest ring that is not yet on the target peg . . ." which in LISP could look like this:

    (setq ringX (apply 'max (append (fetch 'pegA) (fetch 'pegB))))

In other words, make a list (append) of the rings on both pegA and pegB, and find the *biggest* of those. And, remember, the two lists of rings on the two pegs are lists of numbers. There is a LISP function max, which finds the largest of a set of numbers, but unusually among LISP functions it doesn't like being given a list to deal with: (max 1 2 3) returns **3**. But as you now know, append would return, '(1 2 3), and (max '(1 2 3)) will not work. The way around this minor problem is to interface max to append's list via the system function apply, which handily takes as its arguments the name of some other function—in this case max—and a list (see Chapter 3 for a formal definition of apply).

And the remainder of rule 2 says ". . . and set up the goal of moving that ring to the target peg." So here's the whole of the condition part of rule 2. It looks pretty hairy, but please read on. You'll find that it's not really hairy at all:

    (putprop 'p2 '(and (setq ringX
                    (apply 'max
                        (append (fetch 'pegA)
                            (fetch 'pegB))))
                (deposit 'goal (list 'move
                        ringX
                        'from
                        (pegof ringX)
                        'to
                        'pegC)))
        'action)

The actual format of the goal created by rule 2 (what it looks like) may seem unnecessarily complex, full of quoted atoms that can only be of use to us as human observers. But if you get "bugs" (errors) when you have typed all these pieces of code into LISP, such human-oriented additions will help. They also have another rather neat purpose, as you'll see later.

The function deposit replaces an existing working memory element with a new one; and pegof, as its name implies, returns the name of the peg that holds the ring that is given as pegof's single argument. We'll write both of these shortly. List is a system function and simply creates a list out of as many arguments as you care to give it.

In passing, observe but don't be confused by the indentations of the preceding lines of code. Generally speaking, LISP code is written so that each unbalanced opening bracket on a line causes the succeeding line to be indented by a small fixed number of characters (look at one of the preceding function definitions to see how this works). In addition, where multiple arguments such as those to list in the previous section won't all fit on the line, the conventions allow you to place the arguments vertically beneath one another as I have. During execution, LISP ignores all spaces, and so it sees the atoms that follow list as being continuous until the opening bracket just before list itself is balanced by the closing bracket just after pegC—which is exactly what we want it to do. The only point of the indentation is to make the intentions of the programmer clearer to anyone reading the code.

Rule 3

Rule 3 says "If there *is* a goal . . ." which we can translate into LISP very simply by telling the computer to fetch whatever is in the wm's goal slot. If fetch returns anything, there must be a goal there. But rule 3 goes on to say "achieve the goal if certain conditions apply," and whether or not these conditions do apply has to be found out from the contents of the goal itself. The goal might be "move ring3 (the largest) from pegA to pegC," and under the terms of rule 3 we'll need to know, before trying to achieve the goal, whether or not ring3 is obstructed by smaller rings on either its own or its target peg. Now, we don't want to waste time by fetching the goal every time we need to look at this or that bit of it. So we fetch it once and bind the result of the fetch to some variable—for convenience, a variable called *goal*. And remember that the binding function, setq, returns the value it binds. So if

```
(setq goal (fetch 'goal))
```

returns anything other than **nil**, we know that there must have been a goal there and at the same time have achieved the desired time-saving binding.

So here's the condition part of rule 3:

```
(putprop 'p3 '(and (setq goal (fetch 'goal))
                   (smallerp (second goal)
                             (car (fetch (sixth goal))))
                   (equal (second goal)
                          (car (fetch (fourth goal)))))
        'condition)
```

The actual format of the goal we know from rule 2, which is the only goal-creating rule so far. The format is

```
(move ringX from pegX to pegY)
```

and having set (bound) our variable goal to this, the next thing rule 3 asks us to do is to see if the ring concerned—a number, remember—is smaller than the top ring on the destination peg, in this example, pegY.

(In LISP, functions that only return either **t** or **nil** and which are used as tests are known as "predicates"; hence, the **p** on smallerp: It's not a misprint.)

Now, if we fetch the last member of **goal**, we'll get a list of numbers, or **nil**, depending on what rings if any are currently on that peg. The first of that list is the top one and is necessarily the smallest (game rule 2). And if goal's ring is smaller than that—has a lower number as its name—we're in good shape.

The last test required by rule 3 is to see if goal's ring has any smaller rings on top of it. And of course it won't have if it is itself the top ring on its own peg. The preceding **equal** clause ascertains that.

Notice that each of the three tests ultimately will return either **nil** or non-**nil**, so that if any of them fails the whole **and** will return **nil**, as I said before. We'll write smallerp and sixth shortly.

Assuming that it returns non-**nil** or **t**, we now need to write the action part of rule 3, which is quite simple:

```
(putprop 'p3 '(and (move (second goal) (fourth goal) (sixth goal))
                   (deposit 'goal nil))
         'action)
```

The function move, which we will write later on, alters wm so that goal's ring disappears from the peg where it is and reappears on its intended new peg. Deposit, as I said before, replaces the existing goal with its own second argument—in this case with nil. So that deposit effectively deletes the current goal for us.

Rule 4

Being the most complicated of the four rules, rule 4 naturally has the hairiest-looking code. But if you're still with me so far, I don't think you'll have much trouble with it. Here's the condition part:

```
(putprop 'p4 '(and (setq goal (fetch 'goal))
                   (setq pegX (otherpeg (fourth goal) (sixth goal)))
                   (setq ringY (apply 'max
                                 (smallerthan (second goal)
                                    (append (fetch (fourth goal))
                                       (fetch (sixth goal)))))))
         'condition)
```

OK—the **and** has three arguments, as we can see from the vertical line of setqs, and each of these will as before return either **nil** or non-**nil**. The first clause of the **and** is the same as that of rule 3, so we needn't go through that again. PegX is another variable that is allowed to be global, as was ringX in a previous section, and is set by another of our not as yet written functions, otherpeg, to have as its value the only peg that is *not* mentioned in the current goal.

RingY is another such variable, and according to the words of rule 4 must be bound to the largest of the rings that obstruct movement of the ring mentioned in the goal. Since all these rings must, according to game rule (2), be smaller than goal's ring, we can write a function smallerthan which takes two arguments: goal's ring and a list of all the rings on both that ring's own peg and the peg to which the goal wishes to move it. Both these pegs are, of course, mentioned in goal itself. There may be more than one obstructing ring, so smallerthan will have to return a list—even if it is a list of only one ring—so once again we need the ugly dodge of max and apply to find which is the biggest one.

And that's more or less it for the rules. The remaining action part of rule 4 is simple by comparison:

```
(putprop 'p4 '(deposit 'goal (list 'move
                             ringY
                             'from
                             (pegof ringY)
                             'to
                             pegX))

            'action)
```

Auxiliary Functions

Now let's get some of these "dogsbody" functions out of the way, and then only the really interesting stuff that actually makes the production system work remains to be done.

Now that you've seen how to write second, fourth and sixth are almost trivial:

```
(defun fourth (l)              (defun sixth (l)
    (cadddr l))                    (cadr (cddddr l)))
```

Pegof takes the name of a ring as its single argument, and calls fetch to look into the current wm to see which peg's list of rings includes that argument. It uses the system function member, which takes two arguments and returns something other than nil if the first argument is a member of the second:

```
(member 'a '(a b c)) returns non-nil
(member '(b c) '((a b) (b c) (c d))) returns non-nil
(member 'b '((a b) (b c) (c d))) returns nil
```

I've carefully told you non-nil rather than t, because many dialects of LISP, including MacLISP, return either nil or that subpart of the second argument that *begins* with the first argument:

```
(member 'b '(a b c)) returns (b c)
(member 'f '(a b c)) returns nil.
```

You can probably imagine that sometimes this is very useful. But for our purposes here you can if you like think of member as simply returning **t** or **nil**.

```
(defun pegof (ring)
      (cond ((member ring (fetch 'pegA)) 'pegA)
            ((member ring (fetch 'pegB)) 'pegB)
            ((member ring (fetch 'pegC)) 'pegC)))
```

Smallerp does almost the same thing as the system function called lessp. But lessp will only handle numbers, and unfortunately, we need our **smallerp** function to cope with possible **nil**s as well—when there are *no* rings on the current target peg. So let's just put the ordinary lessp inside a cond after trapping any **nil**s:

```
(defun smallerp (a b)
      (cond ((null b) a)
            ((null a) b)
            (t (lessp a b))))
```

Smallerthan is a slightly different kettle of fish. In this case we need a function that takes a list of rings and returns all those members of the list that are smaller than some model ring. We use a small loop to get the effect we want:

```
(defun smallerthan (model l)
      (prog (result)
            loop
            (cond ((null l) (return result))
                  ((lessp (car l) model)
                    (setq result (cons (car l) result))))
            (setq l (cdr l))
            (go loop)))
```

The loop syntax sets us up a local variable, called result, into which we put all the successful candidates as a later cond test is applied to each member of the list in turn. When we've exhausted the list l, we get the loop to return the result—the order of the rings in it doesn't matter because eventually we're going to apply max to it.

The test, each time around the loop, inspects the first member of l. Only if it is *less* than the model (numerically) does it cons it onto result. Whether or not it does, l is then setq'd to its own cdr, ready for the next cycle of the loop. Otherpeg is simple:

```
(defun otherpeg (peg1 peg2)
      (car (remove peg1 (remove peg2 '(pegA pegB pegC)))))
```

In English, this says "whatever two peg names I feed in as arguments, delete them both in turn from a list of all three pegs and return the remainder to me—or, rather, the car of the remainder since the remainder will still be a list." Deposit, remember, overwrites an existing element of working memory:

```
(defun deposit (heading item)
     (setq wm (remove (assoc heading wm) wm))
     (setq wm (cons (list heading item) wm)))
```

The first line assocs a heading—say, 'goal—with wm, returning perhaps **(goal nil)**. That gets removed from wm by the remainder of the first line. The second line merely conses a list of the same heading and the new item, perhaps '(goal (move ring3 from pegA to pegC)) onto the truncated wm, restoring it to its normal four-element length.

Now, notice what such a procedure—that is, removeing one element and then consing on another—would do to a simpler list:

```
(setq animals '(grouper leviathan phoenix))
```

returns, of course,

(grouper leviathan phoenix).

Then,

```
(setq animals (remove 'leviathan animals))
```

returns

(grouper phoenix),

and

```
(setq animals (cons 'pussy animals))
```

returns

(pussy grouper leviathan).

That is, the procedure can, unless the item removed happens to be the very first item, change the order of the remaining items in the sense that what was originally the second element no longer is, and so on. Exactly that happens to our wm as various bits are removed from it and various other bits are added. But because we're finding the bits we want to remove via assoc rather than via functions such as car, second, third, and so on, the order of wm's elements doesn't matter.

Some dialects of LISP, including MacLISP, do not have the function remove. The point here is that remove, in common with all the other system functions you've seen, does not alter the values of its arguments. The nearest thing that MacLISP has to an equivalent function is called **delete**, and it *does* affect the value of its second argument. When **delete** is applied to a list, that list is permanently changed, and its original value is nowhere to be found. **Delete** is known as a "destructive" function. There are one or two other LISP functions that behave in this unusual way—and indeed, their destructiveness can in some circumstances be very useful. However, to save you from any problems along these lines, here is the definition of a nondestructive **remove**:

```
(defun remove (e l)
      (cond ((null l) nil)
            ((equal e (car l)) (cdr l))
            (t (cons (car l) (remove e (cdr l))))))
```

This is, incidentally, a nice example of how recursion can be used to achieve quite complicated effects. Notice the recursive call to itself on the last line. Here's a quick description of how it works:

If the list l is empty, the function returns **nil**, which is reasonable enough. If l's first element is the one we want removed, the function returns the **cdr** of l, which is also reasonable. It's the last line that is clever. Do you remember how the evaluator always starts with the most deeply nested s-expression? Well, on the last line of **remove**, the most deeply nested expression is (cdr l), which the evaluator works out so as to use it as the second argument of a new call to **remove** itself. Suppose that the *original* call to **remove** had been:

```
(remove 'leviathan (grouper leviathan pussy)).
```

You can probably see that the *new* call to **remove** on the last line will then have these arguments:

```
(remove 'leviathan '(leviathan pussy))
```

and of course during this new call to **remove** the second line of the **cond** will be activated because the element we want to remove is now at the head of l. So the **cond**'s second line returns

(pussy).

All this, remember, is happening during activation of the last line of the *original* call to **remove**. And that line hasn't been finished with yet. It has done something with the **cdr** of its l, the *original* l, and now it has to do something with the **car**. That is, it has to **cons** that **car** onto the front of whatever result it has achieved so far. And that result, as I've just explained, is

(pussy).

So the total effect of the last line of the **cond** is

```
(grouper pussy)
```

which is exactly what we wanted. It tends to be a bit of a brain-twisting exercise to follow the recursion step by step as shown with a longer original version of l. But the logic does hold, and the definition of remove that I've given you will work with any length of l you like.

As already explained, move changes the innards of wm so that it represents some new problem state, perhaps after moving ring3 from pegA to pegC as previously shown

```
(defun move (ring frompeg topeg)
      (deposit frompeg (remove ring (fetch frompeg)))
      (deposit topeg (cons ring (fetch topeg)))
      (print (fetch 'goal))
      t)
```

The first line fetches from the wm-heading which is the value of frompeg ('pegA, maybe) the list of whatever rings are currently on that peg. It then deposits into wm the result of removeing from that list the value of ring ('ring3). The second line does the same set of operations but this time conses in ring so that it becomes part of the list of rings associated in wm with topeg ('pegC). Finally, move performs the all-important operation of printing a note on the terminal each time a ring is moved from one peg to another. Move is called only by rule 3, which is the only rule that does any ring moving.

Now we come to the last and most exciting part of our definition writing. After this one, the program will actually *work*! The remaining function is what is known as the "interpreter" of our production system. In a full-blown ps, this would handle all the complicated pattern-matching and conflict resolution strategies (i.e., what to do if two or more rules are activated simultaneously). Ours will be a somewhat skeletal affair but serviceable nonetheless. It consists of two nested prog loops, which I write out as two separate functions:

```
(defun psi ( )
     (prog (rules halt ringX ringY pegX goal)
          (reset)
          (setq rules '(p1 p2 p3 p4))
          loop
          (and halt (return nil))
          (process rules)
          (go loop)))

(defun process (rules)
     (prog ( )
          loop
          (cond ((null rules) (return nil))
               (halt (return nil))
               ((eval (get (car rules) 'condition))
               (eval (get (car rules) 'action))))
          (setq rules (cdr rules))
          (go loop)))
```

Actually, that's not all of it—there are some refinements to come. But it's enough to start with, and provided that you had typed all the rest of the code in correctly, it would work. And the way to get it to work is simply to type

(psi)

which will call all that you have already seen into operation as and when required.

The outer function—psi—runs reset, and then sets up the value of the variable rules. This latter operation is just to save you the bother of typing the list of rules as an argument to psi every time you call it. Then it goes into a loop. Within the loop, it first checks to see that halt is not t (which it won't be the first time around because, remember, prog initialises all its variables to nil, and halt is one of those in the list following the atom prog), and then calls the inner function, process, to work on the list of rules. When process has finished, psi's loop re-iterates so that unless rule 1 has meanwhile set halt to t, process will be called again with the same argument. (The same argument because no matter what process may have done to the value of the variable rules in the course of its own operations, it restored that value when it had finished.)

Process consists of another loop that evaluates each rule in turn by taking the car of successive cdrs of the value of rules. In each case, if the condition part of the rule evaluates to t, the action part of the rule is carried out—by the simple expedient of making the condition part the test and the action part the action in an ordinary cond clause. Process stops iterating, and finishes altogether, either when there are no more rules to work on (i.e., when the value of rules has been cdred down to nil) or when and if rule 1 setq halt to t.

The overall effect is that each rule is taken in turn, and if it fires its action part is executed. When the list of rules runs out, the system starts again with the list restored to its original value. And when the objective is achieved, rule 1 ensures that the whole program comes to a halt.

The only thing left to do now is to put in some nice print statements, so that you can see your production system working.

```
(defun process (rules)
    (prog ( )
        loop
        (cond ((null rules) (return nil))
              (halt (return nil))
              ((eval (get (car rules) 'condition))
               (eval (get (car rules) 'action))
               (princ (car rules)) (princ "fired.")
               (princ "new goal:") (princ (fetch 'goal))))
        (setq rules (cdr rules))
        (go loop)))
```

I've added only two lines, inside the cond of process.

Princ is a system function. LISP has two main printing functions; the other is print, as used in our routine move. Print prints its argument and then does a carriage return. Princ does the same without the carriage return but has another advantage: If its argument is enclosed within double quotes, whatever is inside the quotes is printed verbatim, whereas the quotes themselves are not printed at all. This allows you to have lowercase printouts as before; but you must be careful to include within the quotes any interword spaces that may be necessary to make the final printout look right.

Debugging

It's quite unlikely that even if you type in the whole of the above very carefully, your production system will work the first time. Don't be discouraged: Even the best programmers think it a triumph if they write a totally bug-free program at the first go. So to conclude here are a couple of hints about how to debug what you have on your file.

Your LISP will certainly have some kind of tracer, which at the very least will show you which of your routines calls which other(s), and will print the arguments to each as the routines are entered or exited. So if you type, for example,

 (trace deposit)

and then run your production system as usual, trace will be activated every time the function deposit is called during that run, and will show you what data it received each time and what it returned. You'll probably be quite interested to watch a run of your program with *every* function traced, if you can be bothered to type them all in:

 (trace psi second fourth sixth pegof . . . ⟨etc⟩)

Incidentally, the simple command

 (untrace)

switches off the tracer altogether.

If you're lucky your LISP may have a stepper, which is a kind of slow-motion tracer that allows you to watch every single thing that happens as your entire program is executed. And there will probably be some kind of "break package"—a special set of functions or keyboard commands that can halt a running program while you investigate what is going on at that point. Ask someone who knows to show you what your LISP can do in this respect.

If all else fails, the answer is to insert temporary print statements into your routines so that the machine prints information on your terminal as the program runs. Note that since they are to be temporary, bare calls to print (with one argument) will do. All those ands and ors won't be necessary. There are two handy ways of using print:

 (print variable-name) or (print (list . . . variable-names . . .))

In one of those ways you can have the machine tell you, say, what is the value of wm (what is in working memory) at any point where you choose to insert

 (print wm)

into your code; and so on.

Finally, assuming that all is well with your **ps**, this is the printout you should get when you run it. It solves the Towers of Hanoi problem with three rings on the starting peg. Of course, you'll get different, and longer, printouts if you change the definition of **reset** so that **pegA** initially has four or five (or more) rings on it. But be careful—the number of moves that are required to solve the problem can soon get very large indeed!

```
p2 fired. new goal: (move 3 from pegA to pegC)
p4 fired. new goal: (move 2 from pegA to pegB)
p4 fired. new goal: (move 1 from pegA to pegC)
(move 1 from pegA to pegC)
p3 fired. new goal: nil
p2 fired. new goal: (move 3 from pegA to pegC)
p4 fired. new goal: (move 2 from pegA to pegB)
(move 2 from pegA to pegB)
p3 fired. new goal: nil
p2 fired. new goal: (move 3 from pegA to pegC)
p4 fired. new goal: (move 1 from pegC to pegB)
(move 1 from pegC to pegB)
p3 fired. new goal: nil
p2 fired. new goal: (move 3 from pegA to pegC)
(move 3 from pegA to pegC)
p3 fired. new goal: nil
p2 fired. new goal: (move 2 from pegB to pegC)
p4 fired. new goal: (move 1 from pegB to pegA)
(move 1 from pegB to pegA)
p3 fired. new goal: nil
p2 fired. new goal: (move 2 from pegB to pegC)
(move 2 from pegB to pegC)
p3 fired. new goal: nil
p2 fired. new goal: (move 1 from pegA to pegC)
(move 1 from pegA to pegC)
p3 fired. new goal: nil
p1 fired. new goal: nil
nil
```

Notice that this printout contains two sorts of things: the print statements we put in so that you can see your **ps** working; and the printing done by **move**. You can suppress the former by what is known as "commenting out" the two printing lines in **process**. All you have to do is preface each of them with a semicolon, for example,

```
;(princ (car rules)) (princ " fired. ")
```

When LISP sees a semicolon, it completely ignores anything that follows it on the same line. The idea is that you can put in among the actual lines of your definitions lines of "comments" that—later on when you've forgotten all that you have read here—will remind you how the functions themselves work. So, if you comment out both the printing lines in **process** and run **psi** again, your program will now print out only the moves that are necessary to solve the problem:

```
(move 1 from pegA to pegC)
(move 2 from pegA to pegB)
(move 1 from pegC to pegB)
(move 3 from pegA to pegC)
(move 1 from pegB to pegA)
(move 2 from pegB to pegC)
(move 1 from pegA to pegC)
nil
```

The LISP Experience

If you have worked your way carefully through the examples in this chapter, and have come to terms with the intricacies of your own local LISP system and editing facilities, then you have overcome the first important hurdle on the road to AI programming. It takes thousands of hours of hands-on use to become an expert. Persevere! Chapter 3 describes some of the more powerful capabilities of LISP as used by modern AI practitioners.

ADVANCED LISP PROGRAMMING

JOACHIM LAUBSCH

INTRODUCTION

Programming in artificial intelligence and cognitive simulation is concerned with modelling the behavior of complex systems. A fundamental technique for modelling a complex system is to decompose it into modules that interact via *special purpose languages*. A good example is Winograd's (1972) SHRDLU, where the parsing module was written in a special purpose language to express syntactic rules, and the inference and planning module was written in Micro-Planner, a special purpose language that is designed to represent inference rules and the control of their use.

The advantage of a special purpose language is that it allows a higher level of abstraction, thus making it easier to write and understand a program. LISP's main virtue is that it provides a large tool box with which one may construct an application-specific language. What makes LISP extensible?

- Procedures and data are uniformly represented as list structures. You can write procedures that analyse or construct other procedures.
- The writing of an interpreter for an embedded language is easy. The debugging facilities of LISP can be adapted to the embedded language.
- LISP's parser (the function *read*) is programmable. If you prefer Algol-like syntax you can modify the reader. An example of this is the CLISP front end for InterLISP (Teitelman, 1978). The same holds for the printing functions.
- Macros allow you to extend the language by specifying transformations.

- A rich set of primitive procedures can be combined to build larger building blocks.
- Representation-independent programming is supported by letting you separate the use of a data structure from its concrete implementation.

Although the history of artificial intelligence programming languages has resulted in a number of "higher level languages" (see Bobrow and Raphael, 1974), LISP has remained the main workhorse of AI programming. In part, the reason for the failure of these higher level languages is that the constructs provided by them—such as chronological backtracking, data bases with multiple contexts, or pattern-directed invocation—were often found to be too general for particular applications. This chapter will examine some techniques of general utility in building a system that is tailored to your own needs.

Since the invention of LISP 1.5 (McCarthy et al., 1965), several dialects of LISP have emerged. The most commonly used are:

- *MacLISP* has an efficient compiler and many packages of useful functions (Pitman, 1983). Its descendant, LISP Machine LISP (Weinreb & Moon, 1981), provides extensions for multiple processes, object-oriented programming, and manipulation of bitmap graphics.
- *Franz LISP* is essentially an implementation of (most of) MacLISP on the VAX under Unix.
- *Rutgers/UCI LISP* is an extension of Stanford LISP 1.6, incorporating some of the program editing and debugging ("break") packages that were originally developed for InterLISP. UCI LISP is described in detail in Meehan (1979).
- *InterLISP* offers an integrated program development environment. It introduced data-type definition facilities and primitives to implement advanced control structures, like coroutines or backtracking. The language and environment are described in Teitelman (1978).
- *Common LISP* represents a joint effort of the LISP community to propose a language standard for LISP implementations on new hardware (Steele, 1982). All these dialects extend the *expressiveness* and *power* of LISP 1.5 by a large number of primitives and library packages, data-types, control structures, and abstraction facilities. The result is a *general systems programming language* (Weinreb & Moon, 1981) for production of high-quality compiled code and is augmented by extensive *user-aids* to form a total *programming environment* (Teitelman & Masinter, 1981). The LISP programming environment is just as extensible as the language, because *everything* is written in LISP. For example, if you need to extend the editor you do not have to know another language and its interface conventions. You simply add LISP code. The Multics *Emacs* implementation is a good example of how a powerful extensible editor can be written in LISP (Greenberg, 1980).

Since language definition is such an important issue in the design of complex systems, and LISP itself provides a good model of how a language can be defined by an *interpreter,* we will first describe the basic LISP interpreter. Its core is the interpreter function **eval**. If you have understood **eval**, you will have understood the essentials of LISP.

The next section outlines the definition of a simple LISP interpreter that is close to the original definition of LISP 1.5 (McCarthy et al, 1965). Similar descriptions can be found in Allen (1978), McCarthy and Talcott (1978), Steele and Sussman (1978a), or Winston and Horn (1981). This description of the interpreter will use *production*-like rules to capture the essence of LISP's semantics but will not deal with sequential programs, fancy control structures, side effects, error treatment, special forms, and macro definitions. Later we will see how these rules can be translated into LISP procedures. Key terms are introduced *in italics*, whereas abstract ("nonterminal") symbols are enclosed in angle brackets, for example, ⟨tail⟩. Lowercase symbols will stand for variables and uppercase symbols for constants. The dot (".") separates the left and right elements of a pair. Three dots ("...") are used to indicate ellipsis, meaning "more of the same can (optionally) go here."

THE LISP INTERPRETER

Main routine: eval
Purpose: eval computes the value of a symbolic expression exp in an environment env.

Data Structures

· exp is a *symbolic expression*

Syntactically, a *symbolic expression* is either an atom or a pair, whose left and right parts are symbolic expressions. Nil and T as well as other symbols and numbers are atoms. Pairs are represented as (⟨left⟩.⟨right⟩).

For example, the following are symbolic expressions:

```
a   X   Foo   G007   +    plus
0   −1   3.14   0.001
(a . b)   (x . 3)
(a . (b . 1))   ((a . T) . c) . Nil)
```

But (a . b . c) is not.

Lists are a special kind of symbolic expression. A *list* is either the empty list or a pair whose left is a symbolic expression and whose right is again a list. The *empty list* is represented as ( ). A nonempty list is represented as (⟨head⟩ . ⟨tail⟩).

For example, the following are lists:

```
( )   (1 . ( ))   (a . (1 . ( )))   (+ . (a . (1 . ( ))))
```

Since this is cumbersome to read, we write

```
( )   (1)        (a 1)            (+ a 1)
```

instead, that is,

```
(1)          is a list with head 1 and tail ( ).
(a 1)        is a list with head a and tail (1).
(+ a 1)      is a list with head + and tail (a 1).
```

In LISP, the symbol Nil and the empty list ( ) denote the same object.

- env is a *list* of *bindings*.

A *binding* is a pair whose left is a *name* (a symbol), and whose right is a *value* (a symbolic expression).

For example,

(a . 1)   is a binding with name a and value 1
(x . (a b c))   is a binding with name x and value (a b c).

An environment is represented as a list of bindings:

(((⟨name1⟩ . ⟨value1⟩)   (⟨name2⟩ . ⟨value2⟩) . . .)

Such a structure is also called an *association list*. The empty environment is ( ), which will also be used to signify "don't care" environments, that is, environments whose bindings are of no consequence to the example being presented. Thus,

((a . 1) (x . (a b c)))

is an environment with the same bindings as those in the preceding example.

Rules

To describe a rule, we use the notation:

eval [⟨exp-pattern⟩, ⟨env-pattern⟩] => ⟨result-pattern⟩

which can be read as "To evaluate some expression of the form ⟨exp-pattern⟩ in an environment of the form ⟨env-pattern⟩, transform it into ⟨result-pattern⟩."

Square brackets are used to indicate the arguments to a function, with the individual arguments separated by commas. The arrow => indicates that the result of a particular function is shown on the right. Thus, in this notation we would say

plus [3, 4] => 7

although in LISP the actual code would look like this:

(plus 3 4)

The values returned by actual LISP functions will also be shown on the right of an arrow but printed in **THIS TYPE FACE** to indicate that this is the value that a running LISP interpreter would print out on your terminal, for example:

(plus 3 4) => **7**

1. *Constants* evaluate to themselves in any environment:

> eval [x, env] => x, where x is a constant.

Nil, T, and numbers are constants.

EXAMPLES:

> eval [1, ( )] => 1
> eval [T, ( )] => T

2. *Variables* are evaluated by looking up their value in the environment:

(a)
> eval [v, ((v . x) . e)] => x

Here, env is ((v . x) . e), an environment whose first binding is (v . x) and whose rest is e. The value of v is the value of the first binding.

EXAMPLE:

> eval [a, ((a . 3) (b . 4))] => 3

(b)
> eval [v, ((w . x) . e)] => eval [v, e]

where the name of the first binding w is unequal to v.

The value of v is looked up in the remaining environment e. The value of v in an empty environment is undefined.

EXAMPLES

> eval [b, ((a . 3) (b . 4))] => eval [b, ((b . 4))] => 4
> eval [c, ((a . 3) (b . 4))] => eval [c, ((b . 4))] => eval [c, ( )] is undefined.

3. *Quoted expressions* (written as (**quote** x) or 'x) evaluate to whatever is being quoted:

> eval [(QUOTE x), e] => x

EXAMPLES:

> eval [(quote a), ((a . 3) (b . 4))] => a
> eval [(quote (quote a)), ( )] => (quote a)

4. A *combination* is evaluated by applying its first element (the operator) to the list of evaluated arguments:

---

eval [(f a1 a2 . . .), env]
=> apply [f, (eval [a1, env]   eval [a2, env]   . . .), env]

(f a1 a2 . . .) is a combination with operator f and arguments a1, a2, . . . The LISP convention is to write the operator *before* the arguments (*prefix* notation). Certain special forms (quote, cond, and function) are *not* operators.

EXAMPLES

(a) eval [(+ 1 2), ( )] => apply [+, (1 2), ( )] => 3

We see later how apply works. In this case the operator + is a primitive function. + is applied to the argument list (1 2) and returns 3.

(b) eval [(+ a b), ((a . 1) (b . 2))]

First, the arguments are evaluated:

> eval [a, ((a . 1) (b . 2))] => 1
> eval [b, ((a . 1) (b . 2))] => eval [b, ((b . 2))] => 2

Then the list of evaluated arguments is produced: (1 2), and + is applied to it exactly as in (a)

(c) eval [((lambda (x) (+ x x)) a), ((a . 3))]
   => apply [(lambda (x) (+ x x)), (3), ((a . 3))]

Here, the operator of the combination is

> (lambda (x) (+ x x))

a so-called *lambda-form*. A lambda-form is like a function but does not have a name. It has the syntax

> (lambda (⟨v1⟩ ⟨v2⟩ . . .) ⟨body⟩)

The list (⟨v1⟩ ⟨v2⟩ . . .) is called the *bound variable list*. The ⟨body⟩ is a single expression.

In (lambda (x) (| x x)) the bound variable list contains only x, and the body is (+ x x). This lambda-form is a function that doubles its argument. We see later how apply deals with lambda-forms.

5. *Conditional expressions* have the syntax

(cond ⟨clause1⟩ ⟨clause2⟩ . . .),

where a clause has the form (⟨test⟩ ⟨consequent⟩).

Conditional expressions are evaluated by finding the first clause whose test is not Nil and then evaluating its consequent:

> eval [(COND (test1 consequent1)
>   (test2 consequent2) . . .), env]
> => eval [consequent$_i$, env]
> where test$_i$ is the first test such that
> eval [test$_i$, env] does not evaluate to Nil.

EXAMPLE

eval [(COND ((> x 0) x) (T (minus x))), ((x . −3))]

The first clause is ((> x 0) x). Evaluating its test gives

eval [(> x 0), ((x . −3))] => apply [>, (−3 0), ((x . −3))]

The operator > applied to (−3 0) returns Nil, and the next clause (T (minus x)) is considered. Since the test T is not Nil, the consequent is evaluated:

eval [(minus x), ((x . −3))]
=> apply [minus, (−3), ((x . −3))] => 3

6. An *expression* of the form (FUNCTION ⟨function⟩) evaluates to what is called a *functional object*. ⟨function⟩ is a lambda-form or a symbol naming a lambda-form:

> eval [(FUNCTION f), e] => (FUNARG f e)

The functional object produced by eval is represented as the list

(FUNARG f e)

Such an object is like a function but has its own environment associated with it. We see later that functional objects can occur as operators in combinations and be applied to arguments.

EXAMPLES

(a) eval [(function (lambda (x) (+ x dx))), ((dx . 0.001))]
   => (funarg (lambda (x) (+ x dx)) ((dx . 0.001)))

This is a functional object that, if applied to an argument, will increment it by 0.001. Note that if the expression had been evaluated in an environment with some other binding of dx, then a different functional object would have been produced.

(b) eval [(function (lambda (x y) (cond ((f x y) x) (T y)))),
          ((f . <))]
   => (funarg (lambda (x y) (cond ((f x y) x) (T y)))
              ((f . <)))

This functional object will return the minimum of two numbers, since f is bound to < (the "less than" symbol). If the expression had been evaluated when f was bound to >, then the resulting functional object would compute the maximum instead.

Subroutine: **apply**
Purpose: To apply a function **fun** to a list of already evaluated arguments **args** in an environment **env**.
Rules:

1. If **fun** is a *primitive operation* (such as cons, car, cdr, atom, eq, +, >, etc.), that primitive is called with the appropriate arguments:

> apply [fun, (a1 a2 . . .), env]
> => call fun with (a1 a2 . . .)

EXAMPLES

apply [+, (1 2), ( )] => 3
apply [>, (1 2), ( )] => Nil
apply [cons, (1 2), ( )] => (1 . 2)

2. If fun is a *symbol that the user has defined* to stand for a lambda-form, that lambda-form is retrieved and applied:

> apply [fun, (a1 a2 . . .), env]
> =>apply [lambda-fun, (a1 a2 . . .), env]
> where lambda-fun is the lambda-form associated with
> fun by definition.

EXAMPLE

Supposing **double** had been defined by the user as

> (lambda (x) (+ x x))

then

> apply [double, (2), ( )]
> => apply [(lambda (x) (+ x x)), (2), ( )]

The rule for evaluating the last form is shown next.

3. A *lambda-form* is applied by evaluating its **body** in an environment where its bound variables are bound to **args**:

> apply [(LAMBDA (v1 v2 . . .) body), (arg1 arg2 . . .), env]
> => eval [body, ((v1 . argl) (v2 . arg2) . . . . env)]

EXAMPLE

> apply [(lambda (x) (+ x x)), (2), ( )]
> => eval [(+ x x), ((x . 2))]
> => apply [+, (2 2), ((x . 2))] => 4

4. A *functional object* is applied by applying its function to the arguments in its *own* environment:

> apply [(FUNARG ⟨function⟩ ⟨environment⟩), args, env]
> => apply [⟨function⟩, args, ⟨environment⟩]

EXAMPLE

```
apply [(funarg (lambda (x) (+ x dx)) ((dx . 0.001))), (1), ( )]
=> apply [(lambda (x) (+ x dx)), (1), ((dx . 0.001))]
=> eval [(+ x dx), ((x . 1) (dx . 0.001))]
=> 1.001
```

5. If **fun** is any other expression, this is evaluated and its value is applied instead:

```
apply [fun, args, env]
=> apply [eval [fun, env], args, env]
```

EXAMPLES

```
apply [delta, (2), ((delta . (funarg (lambda (x) (+ x dx)) ((dx . 0.001))))))]
=> apply [(funarg (lambda (x) (+ x dx)) ((dx . 0.001))), (2),   . . .]
=> apply [(lambda (x) (+ x dx)), (2), ((dx . 0.001))]
=> eval [(+ x dx), ((x . 2) (dx . 0.001))] => 2.001
```

With this rule we can evaluate expressions that produce functional objects. Suppose the user had defined **twice** as the lambda-form

```
(lambda (f) (function (lambda (x) (f (f x))))).
```

Twice is a function that returns a function that will apply its argument twice. Thus, the combination

```
((twice 'double) 3)
```

should apply **double** twice and compute (double (double 3)).

```
eval [((twice 'double) 3), ( )]
=> apply [(twice 'double), (3), ( )]
```

Evaluating the first of the inner terms gives us

```
eval [(twice 'double), ( )] => apply [twice, (double), ( )]
=> apply [(lambda (f) (function (lambda (x) (f (f x))))), (double), ( )]
=> eval [(function (lambda (x) (f (f x)))), ((f . double))]
=> (funarg (lambda (x) (f (f x))) ((f . double)))
```

Substituting this in the outer form yields

=> apply [(funarg (lambda (x) (f (f x))) ((f . double))), (3), ( )]
=> apply [(lambda (x) (f (f x))), (3), ((f . double))]
=> eval [(f (f x)), ((x . 3) (f . double))] => . . . => 12

Since f is bound in the environment to double, this rule will cause double to be applied twice.

IMPLEMENTING THE LISP INTERPRETER IN LISP

As an exercise, we program the rules of eval and apply in LISP itself. Of course, this is circular, but it may actually be a practical way to implement an interpreter, if we used a simpler subset of LISP instead and compiled into another language, possibly using an existing LISP system (Sussman et al, 1981). Our implementation will give us a concrete model of defining a language through its interpreter.

Summary of Primitive Language Constructs

Before starting, let us summarize the primitive language constructs of LISP, as introduced in Chapter 2.

1. Defining a Function

■ (defun ⟨name⟩ ⟨vars⟩ ⟨body⟩)

defines a function with name ⟨name⟩. The arguments to defun are not evaluated. ⟨vars⟩ is a list of names to give to the arguments of the function, and ⟨body⟩ will be evaluated if the function is applied. Another way to see this is that the lambda-form

(lambda ⟨vars⟩ ⟨body⟩)

becomes associated with ⟨name⟩.

EXAMPLE

(defun square (n) (times n n))

associates (lambda (n) (times n n)) with square. Thus to evaluate (square 3) in environment env will cause rules 2 and 3 of apply to evaluate (times n n) in the environment: ((n . 3) . env).

2. Constructing a Pair

■ (cons ⟨arg1⟩ ⟨arg2⟩)

Cons constructs and returns a pair whose left part is the value of ⟨arg1⟩ and whose right part is the value of ⟨arg2⟩.

EXAMPLES

    (cons 'a 'b) => **(a . b)**
    (cons 'b Nil) => **(b)**
    (cons 'a (cons 'b Nil)) => **(a b)**

3. Constructing a List

■ (list ⟨arg1⟩ ⟨arg2⟩ . . .)

The function list is a primitive list-constructor that may take n ($n \geq 0$) arguments. Any nonempty list can equally be constructed by cons instead, since such a list is a subset of pairs whose right is either a list or ( ).

EXAMPLES

    (list) => **( )**
    (list 'a) => **(a)**   This is the same as (cons 'a Nil)
    (list 'a (cons 'b 1) '(c d)) => **(a (b . 1) (c d))**

4. Recognizing Objects

■ (consp ⟨arg⟩)

Consp returns T if its argument is a pair and Nil otherwise.

EXAMPLES

    (consp (cons Nil Nil)) => **T**
    (consp Nil) => **Nil**
    (consp (list 1 2 3)) => **T**

■ (listp ⟨arg⟩)

Listp returns T if its argument is Nil or a pair and Nil otherwise.

EXAMPLES

    (listp (cons Nil Nil)) => **T**
    (listp Nil) => **T**
    (listp (list 1 2 3)) => **T**

■ (atom ⟨arg⟩)

An atom is recognized by the predicate **atom**. Atom returns **T** if its argument is an atom, and **Nil** otherwise.

    EXAMPLES

        (atom 'foo) => **T**
        (atom Nil) => **T**
        (atom 3) => **T**
        (atom (cons 1 2)) => **Nil**

■ (symbolp ⟨arg⟩)

A symbol is recognized as a nonnumerical atom.

    EXAMPLES

        (symbolp 'foo) => **T**
        (symbolp Nil) => **T**
        (symbolp '(a)) => **Nil**

■ (numberp ⟨arg⟩)

A number is recognized by **numberp**.

    EXAMPLES

        (numberp 3) => **T**
        (numberp Nil) => **Nil**
        (numberp '(2 4)) => **Nil**

5. Selecting Parts of Pairs or Lists

■ (car ⟨arg⟩)

A pair's left part (or a nonempty list's first element) is selected by **car**.

    EXAMPLES

        (car (cons 'a 'b)) => **a**
        (car (list 'a 'b)) => **a**

■ (cdr ⟨arg⟩)

A pair's right part (or a nonempty list's tail) is selected by cdr.

EXAMPLES

    (cdr (list 'a 'b 'c)) => **(b c)**
    (cdr '(a)) => **Nil**
    (cdr '((a b c) . d)) => **d**

■ (c{a|d}...r ⟨arg⟩)

Compositions of car and cdr can be abbreviated.

EXAMPLES
    (car (cdr l))   can be written as   (cadr l)
    (cdr (car (cdr l))) can be written as   (cdadr l)

6. Equality of Objects

■ (eq ⟨arg1⟩ ⟨arg2⟩)

Eq returns T if its arguments are the same objects and Nil otherwise. Symbols that print the same are eq. Numbers should be compared with equal. Lists that print the same are equal but not necessarily eq. The empty list ( ) is eq to Nil, that is, (null x) is the same as (eq x Nil).

7. Conditional Expressions

■ (cond (test1 consequent1)
        (test2 consequent2)
        . . .)

This has a value that is found by examining its clauses in sequence as described in rule 5 of eval. If all tests are Nil, cond returns Nil. In the example that follows, a semicolon (;) is used to indicate comments. Items to the right of the semicolon are ignored by LISP.

EXAMPLE

The function merge inserts a number into a list such that all numbers before it are smaller or equal.

```
(defun merge (element list)
    (cond  ((null list) (list element))      ;if list is empty, return (element)
           ((< element (car list))            ;if element smaller than list's head,
            (cons element list))              ;return (element . list)
           (T (cons (car list)                ;else cons the head of list onto
                (merge element (cdr list))))))  ;the result of merging element with
                                              ;the tail of list
```

Let us try out merge. LISP prints out the result (indicated here as following =>).

```
(merge 2 (  )) => (2)
(merge 2 '(3)) => (2 3)
(merge 2 '(1 3)) => (1 2 3)
```

Note that in the last example merge calls itself. Let us trace merge:

```
(trace merge)
(merge 2 '(1 3))
>> merge    element = 2    list = (1 3)
    >> merge    element = 2    list = (3)
    << merge    value = (2 3)
<< merge    value = (1 2 3)
```

Merge is an example of a recursive function. We see more of these later.

Now we are well equipped to program the LISP interpreter according to the *rules of evaluation.* We call it eval* in order not to confuse it with the already defined eval of the running system.

```
1       (defun eval* (exp env)
2           (cond ((atom exp)                    ;exp is an atom
3               (cond ((eq exp 'Nil) 'Nil)       ;rule 1 of eval
4                   ((eq exp 'T) 'T)
5                   ((numberp exp) exp)
6                   (t (lookup exp env))))        ;rule 2 of eval
7           ((eq (car exp) 'QUOTE)               ;exp is a list
8               (cadr exp))                       ;rule 3 of eval
9           ((eq (car exp) 'COND)
10              (evcond (cdr exp) env))           ;rule 5 of eval
11          ((eq (car exp) 'FUNCTION)
12              (make-funarg (cadr exp) env))     ;rule 6 of eval
13          (t (apply* (car exp)
14                  (evlist (cdr exp) env)
15                  env))))                       ;rule 4 of eval
```

The first cond clause considers expressions that are atoms. Constants are handled in lines 3 to 5. Variables are evaluated by using the function lookup (line 6):

```
16      (defun lookup (name env)
17          (cond ((null env) (error))
18              ((eq (caar env) name) (cdar env))        ;rule 2a of eval
19              (t (lookup name (cdr env)))))))           ;rule 2b of eval
```

Lookup finds the binding of name in the association list env, and returns its value, for example:

```
(lookup 'b '((a . 3) (b . 4))) => 4
```

Lookup may have to scan the association list for a while (calling itself recursively) if the binding is near the end of a long list. Thus, looking up a variable's value is inefficient, since it requires search. Some LISP systems adopt a technique called *shallow binding,* which allows direct access to the value but requires more work if environments change (which is infrequent).

The next three clauses treat the special forms: QUOTE, COND, and FUNCTION. Quoted expressions (lines 7 to 8) are trivial. Conditional expressions (lines 9 to 10) are handled by evcond:

```
20      (defun evcond (clauses) env)
21          (cond ((null clauses) (error))
22              ((eval* (caar clauses) env)        ;test of clause1 succeeds
23               (eval* (cadar clauses) env))      ;evaluate its consequent
24              (t (evcond (cdr clauses) env))))
```

Evcond gets a list of clauses and evaluates the test of the first one. If the test succeeds it evaluates the consequent, otherwise it calls itself with the remaining clauses until there are none left. This we consider to be an error, because rule 5 of eval left it undefined. Many LISP systems would actually return Nil in that case.

Expressions of the form (FUNCTION ⟨function⟩) are treated next (lines 11 to 12). We delegate this task to make-funarg which constructs a funarg as a list:

```
25    (defun make-funarg (fun env) (list 'funarg fun env))
```

Combinations fall into the remaining class of expression and are treated in the last clause (lines 13 to 15). First evlist is called to make a list of evaluated arguments

```
26    (defun evlist (forms env)
27        (cond ((null forms) Nil)
28            (t (cons (eval* (car forms) env)
29                (evlist (cdr forms) env)))))
```

Then the operator of the combination, list of evaluated arguments, and environment are handed over to apply*:

```
30    (defun apply* (fun args env)
31         (cond ((isprimitive fun)                    ;rule 1 of apply
32              (primitive-call fun args))
33             ((isuser-defined fun)                   ;rule 2 of apply
34              (apply* (get-definition fun) args env))
35             ((islambda fun)                         ;rule 3 of apply
36              (eval* (lambda-body fun)
37                    (bind (lambda-vars fun) args env)))
38             ((isfunarg fun)                         ;rule 4 of apply
39              (apply* (funarg-function fun)
40                     args
41                     (funarg-env fun)))
42             (t (apply* (eval* fun env) args env))))) ;rule 5 of apply
```

To decide which of the five rules of apply should be used, we have defined the following *recognizers* for functions:

Isprimitive does not return Nil for primitive functions.

```
43    (defun isprimitive (fun)
44         (cond ((symbolp fun)
45              (member fun '(cons list car cdr eq + . . .)))
46             (T Nil)))
```

Isuser-defined does not return Nil for functions defined with defun.

```
47    (defun isuser-defined (fun)
48         (cond ((symbolp fun) (get-definition fun))
49             (T Nil)))
```

Get-definition is a function that retrieves the lambda-form associated with fun, for example:

   (get-definition 'square) => **(lambda (x) (* x x))**.

In many LISP systems the property list associated with a symbol is used for storing the definition. The property list of a function's name would have under some attribute a representation of its lambda-form, which get-definition would retrieve.

Islambda returns T, if fun is a lambda-form.

```
50    (defun islambda (fun)
51         (cond ((atom fun) Nil)
52             (T (eq (car fun) 'lambda))))
```

Isfunarg returns **T** if **fun** is a functional object:

```
53    (defun isfunarg (fun)
54        (cond ((atom fun) Nil)
55            (T (eq (car fun) 'funarg))))
```

The following are selectors for lambda-forms and funargs:

```
56    (defun lambda-vars (l) (cadr l))
57    (defun lambda-body (l) (caddr l))
58    (defun funarg-function (l) (cadr l))
59    (defun funarg-env (l) (caddr l))
```

Rule 1 of **apply** (lines 31 to 32) and rule 2 (lines 33 to 34) are trivial. Rule 3 (lines 35 to 37) treats lambda-forms. Here we have to bind the bound-variable list to **args** and add these bindings to the front of **env**:

```
60    (defun bind (vars args env)        ;given an environment return a new one
61        (cond ((null vars) (cond ((null args) env) (T (error))))
62            ((null args) (error))
63                                        ;if both args and vars are nonempty lists then 'pair off'
64                                        ;the first var with the first arg, i.e. (var1 . arg1),
65                                        ;cons that onto the environment, i.e. ((var1 . arg1) . env),
66                                        ;and recursively bind the remaining args to the new
67                                        ;environment
68            (t (bind (cdr vars) (cdr args)
69                (cons (cons (car vars) (car args)) env)))))
```

EXAMPLE

```
(bind '(x y) '(2 3) '((x . 1) (y . foo)))
=> ((y . 3) (x . 2) (x . 1) (y . foo))
```

Note that **lookup** will find the binding of x to 2 if called with this environment. Rule 4 (lines 38 to 41) simply extracts the function and the environment and calls **apply∗** recursively. The last case (line 42) evaluates the function in the given environment and calls **apply∗** with the result.

LIMITATIONS OF THE INTERPRETER

We have omitted the definition of primitive functions and left out the details of what goes on if the user defines a symbol as a function (i.e., uses **defun**). Another limitation of our **eval** is that it does not allow a side effect on the binding environment. In real LISP systems this is accomplished through the *assignment* construct setq:

    (setq var form)

evaluates form, causes the variable var to be bound to form's value, and returns it. If the variable had been bound, its old value is forgotten. If it was unbound, it becomes bound at the *global* level (also called "top level").

To interchange the values of x and y, one could write

    . . .

    (setq y ((lambda (tem) (setq x y) tem) x))

    . . .

The lambda-form saves the old value of x as tem before setting x to y. It then returns tem. We have now allowed for the body of a lambda-form to contain more than one form. All forms will be evaluated but the last value is the value of the lambda-form. This is called progn in many LISP dialects and is only necessary if you must use side effects.

We also omitted the prog-*feature* (McCarthy et al, 1965) which allows you to write sequential programs with goto and return. Many modern LISP systems still have this feature for historical reasons but have introduced abstract constructs for iteration (do, for, loop, repeat etc.) and nonlocal exits (catch and throw in MacLISP or UCI-LISP). Some dialects (e.g., TLC-LISP [Allen, 1980]) have eliminated prog altogether. It is not necessary to learn how prog works, and if you translate an algorithm that uses goto into functional style, it will usually become clearer.

PROGRAMMING SCHEMATA

For the beginner it is useful to "internalize" a few often repeated patterns of program writing (schemata). Those familiar with FORTRAN or BASIC will have difficulties understanding *recursion*. The *rules of eval* as well as the definition of the preceding data structures were often recursive.

To define a concept recursively, split up the problem into *base* cases and *recursion* cases. A recursion case expresses the problem in terms of a "reduced" problem. For example, look at the definition of "symbolic expression" already given.

base:　　An atom is a symbolic expression.

recursion: If x and y are symbolic expressions, then the pair whose left is x and right is y is a symbolic expression.

Similarly, the recursive function lookup (given above) can be viewed this way:

base:　　If env is empty, no value is found. If the first binding's name is name, return its value.

recursion: Lookup name in the rest of the environment.

The best way to learn the use of recursive programming schemata is to try to understand examples, possibly by tracing them out on the computer. For example, to trace lookup (defined above), we say

```
(trace lookup)
(lookup 'b '((a . 3) (b . foo)))
>> lookup   name = b   env = ((a . 3) (b . foo)))
   >> lookup   name = b   env = ((b . foo)))
   << lookup   value = foo
<< lookup   value = foo
```

It is a myth that recursion is inefficient. A smart compiler often transforms recursive calls into iterative code (Risch, 1973). *Tail recursion*—where the last form to be evaluated in the body of the function is a call to itself (as in lookup or bind)—can also be interpreted iteratively. The *VLISP* interpreter (Greussay, 1976), for example, converts tail recursion to iteration. We will now study one particular recursive schema, which has many variations. A thorough treatment of recursive programming techniques is given by Burge (1975).

A Schema for Tree Recursion

input: A tree that is either an atom (terminal node) or a pair whose left and right parts are trees.

algorithm: If the tree is an atom, apply the function term-val to it, returning its value. If the tree is a pair, apply the function compose to the tree recursion of its left part and the tree recursion of its right part and return whatever compose returns.

subroutines: (1) Term-val gives the value at terminal nodes of the tree. (2) Compose is a function of two arguments that accumulates them into a single expression.

In our notation we will surround the slots of the schema by "<" and ">." A template for a tree recursion function definition is

```
(defun <tree-recurse> (tree)
    (if (atom tree) (<term-val> tree)
       (<compose> (<tree-recurse> (left tree))
                  (<tree-recurse> (right tree)))))
```

Note that (if <test> <then-form> <else-form>) is just a shorter way of writing

```
(cond (<test> <then-form>) (t <else-form>))
```

A typical example would be the fringe function which computes a list of all terminal nodes of a tree from left to right. We can define fringe if we realize that it is an instance of the tree-recursion schema with the slots filled as follows:

```
<tree-recurse>   = fringe
<term-val>       = (lambda (x) (cons x nil)) = ncons
<compose>        = append
```

Append could be defined as

```
(defun append (a b)
    (if (null a) b
        (cons (car a) (append (cdr a) b))))
```

For example, if we had the tree

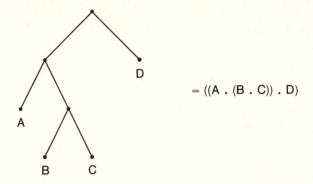

= ((A . (B . C)) . D)

the result of (fringe tree) would be (A B C D). For this representation of a tree, the accessor **left** is car, and the accessor **right** is cdr. Filling the slots of the schema, we can write fringe:

```
(defun fringe (tree)
    (if (atom tree) (ncons tree)
        (append (fringe (left tree))
                (fringe (right tree)))))
```

Let us trace fringe:

```
(setq a-tree '((A . (B . C)) . D)) => ((A . (B . C)) . D)
(fringe a-tree)
>> fringe    tree = ((A . (B . C)) . D)
    >> fringe    tree = (A . (B . C))
        >> fringe    tree = A
        << fringe    value = (A)
        >> fringe    tree = (B . C)
            >> fringe    tree = B
            << fringe    value = (B)
            >> fringe    tree = C
            << fringe    value = (C)
        << fringe    value = (B C)
    << fringe    value = (A B C)
    >> fringe    tree = D
    << fringe    value = (D)
<< fringe    value = (A B C D)
```

Everytime we want to define a tree-recursion function we could take <tree-recurse> as a schema for doing this. Alternatively, we may have defined a function tree-recurse which takes as arguments the tree and the term-val and compose functions:

```
(defun tree-recurse (tree term-val compose)
    (if (atom tree) (term-val tree)
        (compose (tree-recurse (left tree) term-val compose)
                 (tree-recurse (right tree) term-val compose))))
```

Then, an alternate definition of fringe would be

```
(defun fringe (tree)
    (tree-recurse tree (function ncons) (function append)))
```

Yet another possibility is to define a "function-producing" function def-tree-recurse that could generate a function according to this schema, for example:

```
(def-tree-recurse 'fringe 'ncons 'append)
```

would produce the preceding definition of fringe. We see later how to define a function such as def-tree-recurse by using *macros*. Tree recursion, as defined here, assumes a binary tree with terminal nodes being atoms. We could extend the schema to *n*-ary trees and arbitrarily defined terminal nodes. Further, in general, we may not want to accumulate the results of the lower nodes but search through or modify the tree. Also, we might invent more mnemonic versions of def-tree-recurse or define an editing template, which the user fills in like a form.

Iteration over Lists

A very useful schema is to apply a function repeatedly to all elements or tails of a list and accumulate the results. Although this can be done recursively, it is more convenient to use a *mapping* function. A mapping function applies some function to the successive elements or tails of one (or more) lists and returns a result list containing the respective results of these applications.

One mapping function is mapcar, a LISP primitive that could be defined as

```
(defun mapcar (fun list)
    (cond ((null list) Nil)
          (t (cons (fun (car list))
                   (mapcar fun (cdr list))))))
```

Mapcar applies fun to each element of list and composes the results as elements into the resulting list. For example, to produce a list of squares from a list of numbers, we could write

```
(defun squarelist (l)
    (mapcar (function square) l))
```

Thus,

      (squarelist '(1 2 3)) => **(1 4 9)**

Several extensions and variations on mapping are usually predefined in LISP:

1. It is possible to map a function with n ($n > 1$) arguments over n lists.

    EXAMPLE

```
(defun pairlis (names values)
      (mapcar 'cons names values))
```

    (pairlis '(a b c) '(1 2 3)) => **((a . 1) (b . 2) (c . 3))**

2. The function can be applied to each *element* or *tail*.

    EXAMPLE

    map maps over successive tails:
    (map 'print '(a b c)) prints
    (a b c), **(b c)**, **(c)**

3. The results can be appended instead of consed together.

    EXAMPLES

    (a) mapcan is like mapcar, except that it composes the results of the function as segments into a list.

```
(mapcan (function (lambda (x) x))
        '(Nil (foo) ( ) (bar baz))) => (foo bar baz).
```

    (b) mapcon is like mapcan in that it composes segments but is like map in that it applies the function to successive tails. With it, we could define a function that eliminates duplicates from a list:

```
(defun nodups (list)
      (mapcon (function (lambda (tail)
                            (if (member (car tail) (cdr tail)) nil
                               (ncons (car tail)))))
            list))
(nodups '(a b a c b)) => (a c b)
```

EXTENDING THE LANGUAGE BY DEFINING MACROS

A simple way to extend LISP is through *macro expansion*. Our simple LISP interpreter did not treat macros. What we want is to have <form1> *transformed* into <form2> so that **eval** can evaluate <form2> instead. For example, we might like to say

> (second x) which is transformed to **(car (cdr x))**

which is then evaluated. Below we will write <form1> ==> **<form2>** to express <form1> being transformed by macro expansion to **<form2>**.

To accomplish the transformation before evaluation, we define **second** as a macro that produces the transformation. For defining a macro, **defmacro** is used. It is like **defun** except that the body of the definition specifies the transformation to perform.

> (defmacro second (arg) (list 'car (list 'cdr arg)))

When **eval** sees (**second** x), it notices that **second** is defined as a macro. The body of the definition is evaluated while **arg** is bound to x, giving the list (**car** (**cdr** x)). Then **eval** tries this new form in the original environment.

A macro definition using **defmacro** looks as follows (in MacLISP):

> (defmacro <name> <pattern>
>   <body-form1> <body-form2> . . .)

The <pattern> is any symbolic expression that is made out of symbols and conses. When the macro call is expanded, the symbols in <pattern> are bound to corresponding parts of (the tail of) the call, for example:

macro call:	(second '(a b c))
tail of call:	('(a b c))
pattern:	(arg)
binding:	arg = '(a b c)
==>	**(car (cdr '(a b c))**

In many other dialects of LISP, **arg** in the preceding example would be bound to the entire macro call; that is,

> arg = "(second '(a b c))".

In such dialects, the body of the macro needs to be modified accordingly.

A very important use of macros is to define a function that does not evaluate all its arguments (see Pitman [1980]). Such functions are called "special forms" in LISP 1.5 because the evaluation of the arguments are carried out specially by this function (e.g., **quote** and **cond**). An example is the form (**if** test then-form else-form). Defining **if** as a normal function would regrettably cause **else-form** to be evaluated even if the value of **test** were non-Nil!

Clearly, this would cause append (see above) not to terminate. Instead, we define if as a macro, so that

```
(if test then-form else-form) ==>
(cond (test then-form) (T else-form))
```

The definition is as follows:

```
(defmacro if (test then-form else-form)
        (list 'cond (list test then-form) (list T else-form))
```

Writing macros is simplified by using the "inverse quoting" notation that is found in MacLISP (indicated by the back-quote character " ` "). Instead of the symbolic expression constructors: cons, list, and append, we write down the "image" of the list and "unquote" those subexpressions that are to be evaluated by prefixing them with the character ",". Thus,

```
(list 'cond (list test then-form) (list T else-form))
```

can be written as

```
`(cond (,test ,then-form) (T ,else-form))
```

Now we can define the schema to generate a tree-recursion function, as described in the earlier section on programming schemata.

```
(defmacro def-tree-recurse (name term-val compose)
        `(defun ,name (tree)
                (if (atom tree) (,term-val tree)
                    (,compose  (,name (left tree))
                               (,name (right tree))))))
```

An important macro is let:

```
(let ((var1 form1) (var2 form2) . . .)
    body-form1 body-form2 . . .)
==>
((lambda (var1 var2 . . .)
        body-form1 body-form2 . . .)
    form1 form2 . . .)
```

Note that form1, form2 . . . are evaluated *before* their values are bound to var1, var2, and so on. Thus, a later form cannot use the binding of a variable that is computed by an earlier form. If the sequential binding is intended, a very similar construct (called let*) can be defined. This is left as an exercise for the reader. Let us define let:

```
(defmacro let (varlist . body)          ; pattern is a pair!
        '((lambda ,(mapcar 'car varlist)
                ,@body)
         ,@(mapcar 'cadr varlist)))
```

At expansion time, varlist is bound to ((var1 form1) (var2 form2) . . .) and body is bound to (body-form1 body-form2 . . .). Note that we have used another trick of inverse-quoting: The ,@ prefix within inverse-quote means that the following term should evaluate to a list whose elements are to be *spliced* in as a segment into the surrounding list. For example, if x = (c d), then: '(a b ,@x e) => **(a b c d e)**.

USING CLOSURES TO DEFINE GENERATORS

The form (closure <variables> <function>) produces a functional object that contains an environment in which <variables> are bound according to the values they have at evaluation at the time of closure. A *closure* is like a **FUNARG** (see above), except that it contains only an explicitly mentioned environment (<variables>). Closures are a convenient tool for an *object-oriented* programming style: Objects are active entities that react to messages, a style used very effectively in SMALLTALK (Xerox Learning Research Group, 1981). In the following example we define a *stack* as a *procedure* that obeys the usual stack operations:

```
(defun make-stack ()
    (let ((stack nil))
        (closure '(stack)
                (lambda (op)
                    (cond ((eq (car op) 'push)
                            (setq stack (cons (cadr op) stack)))
                        ((eq (car op) 'pop)
                         (cond ((null stack) (error "stack empty"))
                                (t (let ((top (car stack)))
                                        (setq stack (cdr stack))
                                        top))))
                        ((eq (car op) 'empty)) (null stack))
                        (t (error "unrecognized stack-operation"))))))))
```

The behaviour of the stack is abstractly described in terms of the possible operations on it. Closures support a programming style that separates the behavioural description from the actual implementation.

Let us see now how we can create a stack! We call make-stack, which then returns a functional object.

```
(setq S1 (make-stack))
```

S1 is a functional object like a funarg, but its environment contains only the variable **stack** with value Nil. Since S1 behaves like a function, we can use it as the operator of a combination. For example, if we want to push the element "a" onto the **stack**, we would call S1 with (push a):

(S1 '(push a)) => **(a)**

Intuitively, what we're doing is sending an object called S1 the following message: "push a onto yourself." The first cond clause is evaluated, and in S1's environment **stack** is now bound to (a). We now apply S1 to other operations:

(S1 '(push b)) => **(b a)**
(S1 '(pop))   => **b**
(S1 '(empty)) => **Nil**

S1 is a functional object (and not a data structure) that maintains its own environment for binding the variable **stack**. Other stacks could be created similarly and would not be affected by operations on S1, since each possesses its own variable **stack**.

What have we done? We organised the behaviour of a stack into *one* module. Depending on the operation **op**, the stack will behave in the described way. Push and **pop** operations alter the variable **stack** by using **setq** only locally. Bindings of **stack** outside the closure are not affected. (As an exercise the treatment of closures in our simple LISP interpreter is left to the reader. *Hint:* It is very similar to funarg, but you have to implement setq also.)

Now that we have learned how to make functions behave as ordinary objects we will see how to use closures to write a function that produces a list of possibilities. Such a possibility list is called a *generator*. A generator contains the first possibility explicitly and a *continuation* to compute another generator. The continuation is a functional object with enough of the environment saved to produce the next possibility and the next continuation. The following example shows how closures help define generators.

Suppose we want to create a generator for natural numbers starting at n:

```
(defun gen-numbers (n)
       (list n (closure '(n)
                    (lambda ( ) (gen-numbers (+ n 1))))))
```

For convenience and increased readability, let's assume that closures are printed out in the form

{**closure with**
env = <**an association list of bindings**>
function: <**the function of the closure**>}

Here, then, is the generator at work:

```
(setq N1 (gen-numbers 3))=>
   (3 {closure with
       env = ((n . 3))
       function: (lambda ( ) (gen-numbers (+ n 1)))})
```

Our generator has the form

```
(<first possibility> <continuation>)
```

The continuation is a function that yields another generator.

To see what we can do with such generators, let us define some operations on them:

1. The empty generator is represented as the empty list:

```
(defun empty (gen) (null gen))
```

2. We get the first possibility from the generator by first:

```
(defun first (gen)
       (if (empty gen) (error "generator is exhausted")
          (car gen)))
```

3. We get the next possibility by next:

```
(defun next (gen)
       (if (empty gen) (error "generator is exhausted")
          (apply (cadr gen) Nil)))
```

Notice that the lambda-function shown in the closure earlier has no arguments, hence the Nil on the last line. The lambda-function does not need any arguments because the binding of n will be correctly retrieved from the closure's environment.

```
(first N1)=>3
(setq N1 (next N1))=>
      (4 {closure with
            env = ((n . 4))
            function: (lambda ( ) (gen-numbers (+ n 1)))})
(first N1) => 4
```

Now let us become more ambitious: We define a pattern matcher that returns the possibility list of all the ways in which a pattern could match a target datum. This matcher compares a single-level list structure pattern against a datum. Pattern-elements may be constants (atoms), *element-variables* (?x) or *segment-variables* (!x). Segment-variables (in contrast to element-variables) match any segment of zero or more elements of a list and make it necessary to backtrack, since in general there will be several alternatives of partitioning the data into segments. The following code is a slight variation of the matcher presented in the SCHEME manual (Steele & Sussman, 1978b). It shows how a backtracking control structure can be implemented with closures.

We define the function **match** that matches a pattern (**pat**) against a datum (**dat**):

```
(defun match (pat dat)
      (match1 pat dat '( ) (function (lambda ( ) nil))))
```

The workhorse is the function

```
(match1 pat dat bdgs fail)
```

which keeps a list of bindings (**bdgs**) and a functional argument (**fail**). Initially **bdgs** are empty and the continuation is a function that returns the empty generator. **Match1** always returns a generator, that is,

```
( )          ;the empty generator
```

or

```
(<first possibility> <continuation>)
```

As with our number generator we can keep on calling the continuation until it eventually runs out the alternatives and returns ( ) — the empty generator.

To prepare, let us first describe some auxiliary functions:

Recognizers:

(isconstant x)	is satisfied if x is an atom.
(iselement-var x)	is satisfied if x is an element-variable.
(issegment-var x)	is satisfied if x is a segment-variable.
(isbound var alist)	is satisfied if var is bound on alist.

Selectors:

(lookup var alist)	finds the value var is bound to on alist.
(nfirst list n)	returns a list of the n first elements of list.
(nrest list n)	returns list with its n first elements removed.

Constructor:

(bind var val alist)	returns a list whose first element is the binding of var to val and whose rest is alist.

Here, then, is the definition of **match1**. The real workhorse function, **match-segment-var** (line 34) will be described momentarily.

```
1 (defun match1 (pat dat bdgs fail)
2                                        ;bdgs: a list of bindings of variables in pat
3                                        ;fail: a continuation function to be called for backtracking
4                                        ;to the next alternative if pat does not match dat
5   (if (null pat)        ;hopefully, many recursive invocations leave both
6     (if (null dat)      ;pat and dat empty, resulting in . . .
7                         ;a list of bdgs and continuation, i.e.
8       (list bdgs fail)    ;normal successful outcome.
9       (fail))           ;only pat is null . . . better backtrack
10    (let ((p1 (car pat)))    ;pat is not null . . . focus on (car pat)
11      (cond
12        ((isconstant p1)    ;pat begins with a constant
13         (cond ((null dat) (fail))    ;empty dat? backtrack
14               ((eq p1 (car dat))    ;1st parts match, so . . .
15                (match1 (cdr pat) (cdr dat) bdgs fail)    ;match rest
16               (t (fail))))    ;constant doesn't match . . . backtrack
17        ((iselement-var p1)    ;pat begins with element variable, e.g. ?x
18         (cond ((null dat (fail))    ;empty dat? backtrack
19               ((isbound p1 bdgs)    ;p1's got a value already
20                (if (equal (lookup p1 bdgs) (car dat))    ;p1's value matches (car dat)
21                    (match1 (cdr pat) (cdr dat) bdgs fail)    ;so match rest
22                    (fail)))    ;p1's value didn't match (car dat), so backtrack
23               (t (match1 (cdr pat) (cdr dat)    ;p1 has no value, so match rest . . .
24                          (bind p1 (car dat) bdgs)    ;forcing p1 to match (car dat)
25                          fail))))    ;and passing along continuation
26        ((issegment-var p1)    ;pat begins with segment variable, e.g. !y
27         (if (isbound p1 bdgs)    ;got value already?
28             (let* ((seg (lookup p1 bdgs)) (seglen (length seg)))    ;look it up
29               (cond ((< (length dat) seglen) (fail))    ;too short . . . adios
30                     ((equal (nfirst dat seglen) seg)    ;early items match, so . . .
31                      (match1 (cdr pat) (nrest dat seglen)    ;match rest
32                              bdgs fail))
33                     (t (fail))))    ;same length but mismatch . . . backtrack
34             (match-segment-var pat dat bdgs fail 0)))    ;invoke workhorse!
35        (t (error "illegal pattern" pat)))))))    ;give up
```

The following is a summary of how match1 works:

1. If both pat and dat are Nil, we terminate with a generator whose first possibility is bdgs and whose continuation is fail (line 8). This is the normal successful termination.
2. If pat is exhausted, but something is still left in dat, our current bdgs fail to match. We try the next alternative by calling the continuation fail (line 9).
3. If the head of pat is a constant or an element variable, but dat is empty, we also try the next alternative (lines 13 and 18).
4. If the head of pat is a constant that is the same as the head of dat, we recursively invoke

match1 with the remaining **pat** and **dat**, the same **bdgs** and continuation (lines 14 to 15). If they are not the same, we try a new alternative (line 16).

5. If the head of **pat** is an element variable that is already bound, we look whether its binding is the same as the head of **dat** and proceed as in case 4 (lines 19 to 22). If the element variable was not yet bound, we add the binding and recurse as before (lines 23 to 25).

6. If the head of **pat** is a bound segment variable (line 27), then there are three subcases:
   (a) If the remaining **dat** is shorter than the segment, the match must fail and we try another alternative (line 29).
   (b) If **dat** begins with **seg**, we succeed and match the rest of **pat** against a **dat** from which **seg** is removed (lines 30 to 32).
   (c) If **dat** does not begin with **seg**, we try the next alternative (line 33).

7. If the head of **pat** is a segment variable that was not yet bound (line 34), we have to try all segments of **dat** that start with length 0 up to the length of **dat**. This is what **match-segment-var** does.

The function **match-segment-var** will try segments of increasing length and construct the appropriate continuation function. Its definition follows:

```
1 (defun match-segment-var (pat dat bdgs fail length-so-far)
2     (if (> length-so-far (length dat))   ;not enough left in dat to match ...
3        (fail) ;so backtrack
4        (match1 (cdr pat) ;do main match routine ...
5               (nrest dat length-so-far) ;on what's left after ...
6                    ;forcing match against first length-so-far elements:
7               (bind (car pat) (nfirst dat length-so-far) bdgs)
8               (closure '(pat dat bdgs fail length-so-far)
9                       (lambda ( )
10                              (match-segment-var pat dat bdgs fail
11                                      (+ length-so-far 1)))))))
```

If the length of the segment exceeds the length of the datum, it fails. Otherwise it will match the remaining datum and pattern after binding (**car pat**) to the segment with a length equal to **length-so-far** (line 7). But its continuation will try segments that are one element longer (line 11). This continuation must be callable anywhere and must still have the current **pat**, **dat**, **bdgs**, **fail**, and **length-so-far** available. Thus, we construct a closure where all these belong to the environment. The function of the closure will call **match-segment-var** with an incremented **length-so-far**.

EXAMPLE

The possibilities for

    match '(!x ?y !x !z) '(a b a a b))

are shown overleaf:

```
((x . ( ))    (y . a)    (z . (b a a b)))
((x . (a))    (y . b)    (z . (a b)))
((x . (a b)) (y . a)    (z . ( )))
```

Instead of returning all possibilities at once, match will return a generator:
($\langle$first-possibility$\rangle$ $\langle$continuation$\rangle$).

```
(setq G1 (match '(!x ?y !x !z) '(a b a a b)))
=> (((x . ( )) (y . a) (z . (b a a b))) ⟨cont1⟩)
```

where $\langle$cont1$\rangle$ is the continuation that is represented as a closure. (We avoid writing it out in full, since it would be rather lengthy.) By repeated application of the continuation, we obtain the remaining possibilities. To get the next one, a segment of length 5 would be tried for z. But that fails, and a segment of length 1 for x is tried, which succeeds. Here is how the continuation would be invoked, assuming the function next is defined precisely as it was in the gen-numbers example presented earlier:

```
(setq G1 (next G1))
=> (((x . (a)) (y . b) (z . (a b))) ⟨cont2⟩)
```

Now a segment of length 2 for x is tried and succeeds:

```
(setq G1 (next G1))
=> (((x . (a b)) (y . a) (z . ( )) ⟨cont3⟩)
```

until

```
(setq G1 (next G1)) => Nil
```

As an exercise for the reader, try tracing the possibilities generated by

```
(setq G2 (match '(!x !y) '(a b)))
(setq G2 (next G2))
```

and so on.

Generators are useful in situations where it is unnecessary (or impossible) to compute all alternatives at once. The computation of the other alternatives is delayed until needed. For example, a syntactic parser could return a generator for the alternative parse trees which a semantic module could examine one by one. The important point is that the semantic computation is conceptually separate from the syntactic one; that is, both processes act like coroutines.

DATA-DRIVEN PROGRAMMING

Data-driven programming consists of associating a function with the data and embedding the knowledge of how to deal with the specific datum in that function. Consider the matching example above. The basic structure of match1 is to check for the type of pattern-element and dispatch to code that deals with that case. Suppose we would also allow restricted variables and evaluated forms in the pattern. Then match1 would have the structure:

```
(cond ((isconstant 〈pattern-element〉) . . .)
       ((iselement-var 〈pattern-element〉) . . .)
       ((issegment-var 〈pattern-element〉) . . .)
       ((isrestricted-var 〈pattern-element〉) . . .)
       ((isevaluated 〈pattern-element〉) . . .)
       . . .)
```

Instead we could write

```
(cond ((isconstant 〈pattern-element〉) . . .)
       ((ismatch-var 〈pattern-element〉)
        (apply (get-match-function 〈pattern-element〉)
               (list pat dat bdgs fail)))
       . . .)
```

Each type of pattern-variable is represented as a list with a distinguished symbol as its first element. E.g. ?x is represented as (*evar* x), and *evar* is the distinguished symbol indicating the type element-variable. ismatch-var would return T for any match variable:

```
(ismatch-var '?x) => T
(ismatch-var '!x) => T
```

get-match-function retrieves the code for the type of pattern variable and apply runs it with the appropriate arguments. How can we associate the code with the type of variable? Usually the *property list* of the distinguished symbol is used to store the associated function. In LISP every symbol may have a property list (given by the function plist):

```
(plist 〈symbol〉) =>     (〈attribute1〉 〈value1〉
                         〈attribute2〉 〈value2〉
                         . . .
                         〈attributen〉 〈valuen〉)
```

The function (get symbol attribute) accesses the value of symbol's attribute. The function

```
(putprop symbol value attribute)
```

assigns value as the new value for symbol's attribute. For example, if the element-variable ?x were represented as (*evar* x), the match-function for element-variables could be defined as

```
(putprop '*evar*
         '(lambda (pat dat bdgs fail)
              (let ((p1 (car pat)))
                 (cond ((null dat (fail))
                        ((isbound p1 bdgs)
                         (if (equal (lookup p1 bdgs) (car dat))
                             (match1 (cdr pat) (cdr dat) bdgs fail)
                             (fail)))
                        (t (match1 (cdr pat) (cdr dat)
                                   (bind p1 (car dat) bdgs)
                                   fail)))))
         'match-function)
```

and get-match-function would retrieve that definition. We can do the same for all other types and define the recognizer for match variables as

```
(defun ismatch-var (object)
    (cond ((atom object) Nil)
          ((get (car object) 'match-function) T)))
```

This is the basic mechanism, and we can make this more transparent by defining a match-function definer that accomplishes this and also ensures that the function is compiled.

The important point about data-driven programming is that it allows incremental additions without changing the general algorithm. For example, we could extend match to deal with *restricted* variables. A restricted variable is like an element-variable, but it matches only if some predicate is satisfied.

Let $(name).(predicate) be our external notation for a restricted variable (where ⟨predicate⟩ is a one-argument function returning T or Nil). For example, $x.numberp would only match numbers. We can program LISP's reader to transform the external notation into an internal one such as

```
(*rvar* ⟨name⟩ ⟨predicate⟩)
```

by using *read-macros*. Then $x.numberp reads in as (*rvar* x numberp).

We can now extend match by putting a function on its property list that first checks the predicate on the datum and then does the same as for element-variables:

```
(putprop '*rvar*
         '(lambda (pat dat bdgs fail)
              (if (null dat) (fail)
                  (if ((restriction (car pat)) (car dat))
                      . . . proceed as for element variable . . .
                      (fail))))
         'match-function),
```

where restriction extracts the predicate from a restricted variable. As an exercise, the reader may wish to extend the matcher to accept alternatives

(*any* {⟨constant⟩ | ⟨variable⟩} . . .)

by defining the appropriate match-function for *any*.

REPRESENTATION-INDEPENDENT PROGRAMMING

LISP allows writing programs in a very obscure way, by encoding the data representation in the algorithm. Typically such programs use the *general* constructors, recognizers, modifiers, and selectors (cons, list, atom, rplaca, car, cdr, etc.) for *specific* data structures. If the programmer chooses a new representation for that data structure (i.e., because of a modification of the problem), the program has to be altered in a nonlocal way, and it becomes necessary to understand which specific operation was intended by the general operation. Particularly in assignment there are many alternate forms that depend on the chosen representation. Through the language extension facility of LISP, a generic assignment (called **setf** in MacLISP) and a structure definition function (called **defstruct** in MacLISP) have been provided. Charniak, Riesbeck and McDermott (1980) show how a similar extension can be implemented and use the representation-independent style throughout their book. Illustrations of **defstruct** and **setf** follow.

The Structure Definition Function defstruct

With **defstruct** we can define a structured object. The effect of **defstruct** is the definition of a set of macros for *creating* a structure, *recognizing* it, and *accessing* parts of it. We will only describe the most elementary features of **defstruct**. You can find out more in Weinreb and Moon (1981) or Steele (1982).

Consider the example of writing a program that deals with ships, and you are interested in their position, velocity, and mass:

```
(defstruct (ship)
      x-pos y-pos x-vel y-vel (mass 500))
```

This declares that every ship has the components x-pos, y-pos, x-vel, y-vel, and mass. The mass is defaulted to 500. This declaration automatically defines

1. The *constructor:* make-ship

EXAMPLES

```
(setq titanic (make-ship))
(setq qe2 (make-ship mass 300 x-pos 50 y-pos 10))
```

These expressions build structures of type ship. Notice that make-ship can take a variable number of arguments and that the order of arguments is flexible as well. If a component is not specified, its value defaults to Nil unless a different default has been previously specified in the defstruct declaration.

2. The *accessor-functions:* ship-x-pos ship-y-pos ship-x-vel ship-y-vel ship-mass. The convention is that the name of the structure will be prefixed to the component.

EXAMPLES

    (ship-x-pos qe2) => **50**
    (ship-mass titanic) => **500**
    (ship-x-pos titanic) => **Nil**

3. The *recognizer:* ship-p

    (ship-p qe2) => **T**

4. The function setf is extended to work on structures of type ship.

    (setf ⟨structure-access⟩ ⟨value⟩)

means that the accessed structure is altered such that a subsequent ⟨structure-access⟩ operation would result in ⟨value⟩.

EXAMPLE

    (setf (ship-x-vel qe2) 10)

sets the x-vel component of qe2 to 10. Setf is like setq but it works on structures as well as on variables.

The function defstruct allows a concise way of defining the basic operations to be used with a structure. There is also a standard way of printing a structure:

    (print qe2)

prints

    #S(ship x-pos 50
            y-pos 10
            x-vel 10
            y-vel ( )
            mass 300)

The # sign is a read macro that allows anything followed by #S to be read in again to produce the same structure. We now program a data-base facility in the representation-independent programming style, using **defstruct** (see Charniak, Riesbeck, and McDermott, 1980, Chaps. 11, 14).

Discrimination Nets

A simple way of building a data base of assertions like

(loves mary fred) (loves mary tom)

is to represent it as a list. Unfortunately, as the data base grows it becomes more time consuming to find an entry (since we have to examine the entire list in the worst case).

To retrieve all love relationships, we could search for the pattern (loves ?x ?y) and obtain a list of bindings. In this case, instead of searching the entire data base, we need only examine those assertions whose first element is loves. In a discrimination net, entries are stored in groups that can be discriminated by having different elements in some *position,* for example, the first element (or CAR) position. We only consider a discrimination *tree* for lists of atoms as entries. (Other cases with arbitrary lists, variables, and multiple indexing are also treated in Charniak, Riesbeck, and McDermott, 1980.)

By discriminating successfully on the CAR of the assertion, we would obtain a tree like the following:

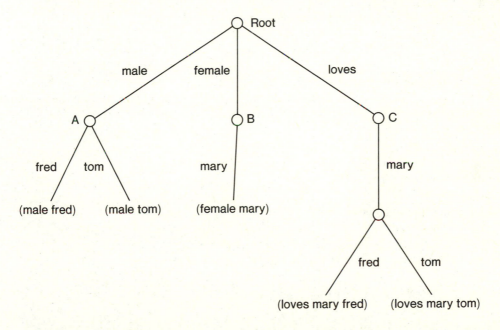

We define the representation of such trees by defining *node* and *link* structures (using defstruct):

(defstruct (node) entry links)

A node has the components entry and links. Defstruct defines the selector functions node-entry and node-links and the constructor for nodes make-node which will use the default Nil for entry and links. The component links is a list of structures of type link:

```
(defstruct (link) key node)
```

A link has as components a key that is the name of the branch and a node that it points to. For example, to build the preceding discrimination tree by hand, we could first build the node labeled A:

```
(setq A (make-node
                links (list (make-link
                                key 'fred
                                node (make-node entry '(male fred)))
                        (make-link
                                key 'tom
                                node (make-node entry '(male tom))))))
```

Similarly, we can build nodes B and C. Then Root is defined by

```
(setq Root (make-node
                links (list (make-link key 'male node A)
                        (make-link key 'female node B)
                        (make-link key 'loves node C))))
```

Obviously this is a tedious way to build a discrimination net, and we will examine soon how to add entries more elegantly. Let us see first how we can fetch an entry from the net. The idea is to scan the successive keys of the entry and simultaneously proceed down the tree along the links with these keys. A useful function is one that finds the link from a node along a key:

```
(defun successor-link (key node)
        (find-node key (node-links node)))

(defun find-node (key links)
        (cond ((null links) Nil)
                ((equal key (link-key (car links))) (car links))
                (T (find-node key (cdr links)))))
```

For example, in the previous data base

```
(successor-link Root 'loves)
```

would return the link with key = **loves** and node = **C**.

If a node has no successor along a key, successor-link will return Nil. We define *fetching an entry from a node* as tracing down a path from the node along those links that are the successive elements of the entry.

```
(defun fetch-entry (entry node)
    (cond ((null node) Nil)
          ((null entry) (node-entry node))
          (T (fetch-entry (cdr entry)
                          (next-node (car entry) node)))))

(defun next-node (key node)
    (let ((link (successor-link key node)))
        (if (link-p link) (link-node link) Nil)))
```

If a node has no successor-link on a particular key, next-node returns Nil and so will fetch-entry.

How can we build a discrimination tree? The function add-entry will examine the tree as fetch-entry did, but if it comes to a node with no proper successor link, it will insert one:

```
(defun add-entry (entry node)
    (let ((final (fetch-final-node entry node)))
            ;final will be the terminal node of the tree at which the
            ;entry is inserted.
        (cond ((node-entry final) entry) ;entry is already there
              (t (setf (node-entry final) entry)))))
            ;assign entry as the entry of final
```

To fetch the final node, we proceed almost as with fetching, except when we come to a node with no link for the next element of the entry (the key), we insert a link with this key and a new empty node:

```
(defun fetch-final-node (entry node)
    (if (null entry) node
        (fetch-final-node (cdr entry)
                          (next-node-insert (car entry) node))))
```

The function next-node-insert is like next-node, except that if no link is found under node, a link will be created and inserted:

```
(defun next-node-insert (key node)
    (let ((link (successor-link key node)))
        (if (link-p link) (link-node link)
                ;link is already there: return its node
            (let ((new-node (make-node)))
            ;no link for key: create new link with node = a new node
                (setf (node-links node)
                      (cons (make-link key key node new-node)
                            (node-links node)))
            new-node))))
            ;add a link with key to new-node under the links of the given node
```

Let us try out add-entry by building the preceding data base:

```
(setq Root (make-node)) => #S (node entry Nil links Nil)
(add-entry '(male fred) Root) => (male fred)
Root =>
#S (node
      entry Nil
      links (#S (link
                   key male
                   node #S (node
                                entry Nil
                                links (#S (link
                                            key fred
                                            node #S (node
                                                         entry (male fred)
                                                         links Nil)))))))

(add-entry '(male tim)) => (male tom)
```

and so on will build up the discrimination tree.

Retrieving Patterns from a Discrimination Net

The function fetch-entry works for entries that are lists of constants. If aside from constants, we also allowed variables, an entry like (loves ?x ?y) could give us all candidates in the data base. The idea is to use a function fetch-candidates to provide us with a list of all candidates and then match each of these to filter out the good ones. (*Note:* As an exercise write fetch-candidates to return a possibility list, using the idea of a generator discussed earlier.) How can we modify fetch-entry to take care of variables in the entry?

```
1     (defun fetch-candidates (pat node)
2          ;returns a list of assertions that possibly match
3          (cond ((null node) Nil)
4                ((null pat) (list (node-entry node)))
5                ((isvariable (car pat))
6                 (mapcan (function (lambda (link)
7                                      (fetch-candidates (cdr pat)
8                                                        (link-node link))))
9                          (node-links node)))
10               (T (fetch-candidates (cdr pat)
11                                    (next-node (car pat) node)))))
```

Two modifications were necessary to obtain fetch-candidates from fetch-entry:

1. The function fetch-candidates returns a list of assertions. Line 4 achieves this for the basic case, lines 6 to 9 for the variable case, and lines 10 to 11 for the recursive one.

2. Variables in entries have to be treated specially (line 7), so we insert a clause to catch this case. It ignores the variable position: For each node in the node's links, fetch the candidates for the remaining pattern.

Both changes were local and did not involve interaction with the other code. Even if a programmer had not known the details of representation for the discrimination tree, he or she could have made this change. But had we used the primitive operations (like (cons (cadr x) (caddadr x))), there would have been severe problems for anyone attempting to modify the code.

As an exercise, you may like to write a **retrieve** function that accepts a pattern and produces all binding lists. The idea is first to fetch all the candidate entries for the pattern and then use a pattern-matcher (like our **match** function) to find the bindings of the variables. For example:

(retrieve (loves ?x ?x) Root)

would return **Nil** in our data base.

What has the representation-independent style of programming bought us? First, the mnemonic names aid our understanding. Second, the logical dependency between functions manifests itself, and the implementation-dependent representation is concealed. For example, if we were to use a different representation of the data base such as property lists for nodes, we would only have to change the structure definition. Third, if we were to modify the program (e.g., by allowing multiple discrimination instead of only under the car of an entry), it would be possible to find automatically all places where the links of a node are accessed or modified. InterLISP's Masterscope (Masinter, 1980) provides us with such a facility.

THE INTERACTIVE ENVIRONMENT

When you run LISP on your computer you will be interacting with the *top level* of LISP. As described in Chapter 2, this is a loop where the user is asked to type in a form, which is then evaluated. The result is printed out on the terminal and the top level asks for another form to evaluate. The function **toplevel** implements this read-eval-print loop (and also allows you to augment it to treat particular error conditions, enter another language, etc.). You can now incrementally add definitions (using **defun** or **defmacro**), assign values, load files, edit, and so on. Aside from this basic interaction a "real" LISP system will offer you many interactive aids to develop programs and monitor their behavior. In practice, the paper and pencil phase of programming can be eliminated. This is the purpose for designing a *programming environment* (Sandewall [1978] provides a survey of programming environments).

The purpose of a programming environment is to facilitate the intellectual step from conception of an idea to the running and correct implementation of a program. It supports various aspects of programming: the design and production of programs and their understanding and use. "The main activity of programming is not in the origination of new independent programs, but in the integration, modification and explanation of existing ones" (Winograd, 1979). Thus, to have an expressive language is only one aspect of a productive programming environment. The major contribution to productivity is an integrated and knowledgeable support system of *programming tools*.

The traditional approach of separate editing, compilation, loading, and test phases (which was invented during the time of batch-processing) is inadequate, since in an interactive environment this cycle

1. is too long for minor changes
2. requires that the user focuses his attention on bookkeeping tasks that are unrelated to his conceptual task
3. is inadequate because it does not support explorative programming where tentative modifications are made to enhance the user's understanding of the problem by experimentation

InterLISP's programming environment is designed to support an incremental style of program writing without intermediate compile and load phases. As soon as you have typed in a function definition, you may run it. If it produces an error, the system may repair it (e.g., spelling or syntactic errors) or put you into a *break* loop in which you can investigate the cause of the error (by examining the current environment) and then edit the function tentatively and continue the computation. If the change was undesirable, you can *undo* it. The benefit of being able to correct "on the fly" may be large if you had a high investment in getting to the point that produced the error.

Unfortunately, such tools are complex, and novices will not be able to use them adequately. The purpose of advanced programming environments (as found in InterLISP or LISP Machine LISP) is to support expert programmers who work on large programs. It will take novices much more time to learn how to use the tools effectively than it takes them to learn the language. There are various on-line aids (like **HelpSys** in InterLISP) to give you instruction on issues you specify. As your programs grow, you will gradually acquire the skills to maintain them.

Tools are programs that operate on user programs. An important aspect of tools is their *integration:* The environment should give the user the illusion of working with a "knowledgeable assistant." What are the tools in a program development system?

1. Aids to design and modify programs (*editor*).
2. Aids to present visually (multiple views of) programs such that their logical structure is reflected in the layout (*prettyprint*).
3. Aids to file (alternate versions of) programs automatically when modifications are made (*librarian*).
4. Aids to annotate programs by comments, specifications, or test examples. Some of this documentation may be generated automatically; all of it has to be selectively accessible.
5. Aids to support program understanding: *Masterscope* (Masinter, 1980) is a tool for global program analysis. It can present an overview of the calling structure of a program or its parts; it shows how a piece of program is used and answers questions (in a subset of natural language) about control or data flow. More complex aids (which are still relatively experimental or confined to a subset of LISP) include tools to infer types, detect bugs, prove some property of a program, or verify with respect to specifications.

6. Aids to monitor program execution. A *trace* facility allows you selectively to show function invocation and argument passing. A *break* facility lets you interrupt the computation under prespecified conditions. A *stepper* combines the options of tracing and breaking, but lets you dynamically specify break conditions and subexpressions whose evaluation is to be monitored. With *baktrace* you can find out how the program got to the breakpoint. A *meter* facility gives you statistics on program execution which may be valuable to decide on optimizations.

It is crucial to have all these aids potentially at your disposal in any state. A few examples of highly desirable (and currently available) integrated tools may illustrate this:

· The editor should recognize syntax errors while you type and should support a visual representation by: (1) automatic indentation (as **prettyprint** would) and (2) blinking balanced parentheses (to support visualization of logical blocks).
· You should be able to request documentation about a function call to find out how to supply its arguments while editing.
· The editor should know if you change a function definition and be able to guide you to all places in the program where other functions called it. (This is not trivial if data-driven programming is used.)
· If a computation is suspended at a breakpoint because it was undefined, you should be able to call the editor to define the function, do some computation to try it out, and then continue execution from the breakpoint, possibly with additional trace specifications.

Currently used LISP systems vary only little in the supported language, but largely in the available program development tools. One difference between the editors of InterLISP and MacLISP is that in InterLISP the editor manipulates the internal representation of the program (a "residential" editor [Sandewall, 1978]). MacLISP uses a separate editor (Emacs [Stallman, 1980]) that operates on the source code. Both offer structure-oriented commands as opposed to character- or line-oriented commands. InterLISP's editor is more fully integrated with the rest of the tools, whereas Emacs makes more use of screen-oriented operations (e.g., pointing). Developments of both dialects on powerful personal computers (Bawden et al, 1979; Burton et al, 1980) are combining the advantages of both approaches into systems that support multiple windows on high resolution displays (Teitelman, 1977). Such systems can enhance programmer productivity considerably because much typing is substituted by selecting from menus, and the display of multiple windows (a simulated "desktop") supports alternate views of your program and helps to organize your agenda of tasks.

It becomes important to *extend and adapt tools to an embedded application language*. For example, a production rule system for modelling expert behaviour will have its own interpreter, and it is desirable to have, say, a tracing facility that allows monitoring the backward-chaining of rules. It is not necessary to start from scratch if application specific tools are needed. The extensibility of InterLISP's program development tools is based on the following design principle:

Anything that can be done from the terminal should also be do-able by a program.

This is accomplished through

1. separation of the command language from the programs that implement the code manipulation
2. use of primitive operations out of which the standard aids are built
3. sublanguages that drive standard tools
4. "hooks" that allow the user to supply his or her own function to handle a special case.

The InterLISP manual describes in detail all the environment facilities that are necessary to extend user aids. Most other LISP systems either offer only rudimentary extension facilities for the environment or require the user to study the code that implements the various existing tools.

References

Allen, J. R. 1978. *The Anatomy of Lisp*. New York: McGraw-Hill.

Allen, J. R. 1980. TLC-Lisp documentation. Redwood Estates, Calif.: The Lisp Company.

Bawden, D., Greenblatt, R., Holloway, J., Knight, T., Moon, D., and Weinreb, D. 1979. The Lisp machine. In *Artificial Intelligence: An MIT Perspective,* vol. 2, eds. P. Winston and R. Brown. Cambridge, Mass: MIT Press.

Bobrow, D. G., and Raphael, D. 1974. New Programming Languages for A.I. Research. *Computing Surveys* 3(6): 154–174.

Boyer, R. S., and Moore, J. S. 1979. *A Computational Logic*. ACM Monograph Series. New York: Academic Press.

Burge, W. H. 1975. *Recursive Programming Techniques*. Reading, Mass.: Addison-Wesley.

Burton, R. R., Kaplan, R. M., Masinter, L., Sheil, B. A., Bobrow, D. G., Deutsch, L. P., Bell, A., and Haugeland, W. S. 1980. Papers on Interlisp-D. Xerox Cognitive & Instruct. Sc. Tech. Rep. CIS-5. Palo Alto, Calif.: Xerox PARC.

Charniak, E., Riesbeck, C., and McDermott, D. V. 1980. *Artificial Intelligence Programming*. Hillsdale, NJ: Erlbaum.

Greenberg, B. S. 1980. Prose and CONS—Multics EMACS: A Commercial Text Processing System in Lisp. *Conference Record of the 1980 Lisp Conference,* Stanford, Calif., pp. 6–12.

Greussay, P. 1976. Iterative interpretations of tail-recursive LISP procedures. Dep. d'Informatique, TR 20-76, Université de Paris VIII—Vincennes.

Masinter, L. 1980. *Global Program Analysis in an Interactive Environment,* SSL-80-1. Palo Alto, Calif.: Xerox PARC.

McCarthy, J. 1978. A Micro Manual for Lisp—Not the whole Truth, *ACM SIGPLAN Notices, History of Programming Languages Conf.* 13: 215–216.

McCarthy, J., Abrahams, P., Edwards, D., Hart, T., and Levin, M. 1965. *LISP 1.5 Programmer's Manual*. Cambridge, Mass.: MIT Press.

McCarthy, J., and Talcott, C. 1978. *LISP Programming and Proving*. Stanford, Calif.: Stanford University. (unpublished).

Meehan, J. 1979. *The New UCI LISP Manual*. Hillsdale, NJ: Erlbaum.

Pitman, K. 1980. Special Forms in Lisp. *Conference Record of the 1980 Lisp Conference*. Stanford, Calif., pp. 179–187.

Pitman, K. 1983. *The Revised MacLISP Manual*. Technical Report TR-295. Cambridge, Mass.: MIT Laboratory for Computer Science.

Risch, T. 1973. RemRec—A Program for Automatic Recursion Removal in Lisp. Datalogilab., DLV 73/24. Uppsala, Sweden: Univ. Uppsala Institute for Informatics

Sandewall, E. 1978. Programming in the interactive environment: The Lisp experience. *Computing Surveys* 10(1):

Stallman, R. M. 1980. EMACS Manual for TWENEX Users. AI Memo 555. Cambridge, Mass.: MIT Artificial Intelligence Laboratory.

Steele, G. L., ed. 1982. Common Lisp Manual. Pittsburgh, Pa.: Carnegie-Mellon University Computer Science Department.

Steele, G. L., and Sussmann, G. J. 1978a. The Art of the Interpreter or The Modularity Complex (Parts Zero, One, and Two). AI Memo 453. Cambridge, Mass.: MIT Artificial Intelligence Laboratory.

Steele, G. L., and Sussman, G. 1978b. The revised report on SCHEME, a dialect of LISP. AI Memo 452. Cambridge, Mass.: MIT Artificial Intelligence Laboratory.

Sussman, G. J., Holloway, J., Steele, G. L., and Bell, A. 1981. Scheme-79: Lisp on a Chip. *Computer Magazine.* IEEE July 1981: 1–21.

Teitelman, W. 1977. A Display Oriented Programmer's Assistant. Proc. IJCAI-5. Cambridge, Mass.

Teitelman, W. et al. 1978. *INTERLISP Reference Manual.* Palo Alto, Calif.: Xerox PARC.

Teitelman, W., and Masinter, L. 1981. The InterLisp Programming Environment. *Computer Magazine,* IEEE April 1981: 25–33.

Touretzky, D. S. 1983. *A Summary of MacLisp Functions and Flags,* 5th ed. Pittsburgh, Pa.: Carnegie-Mellon University Computer Science Department.

Weinreb, D., and Moon, D. 1981. *Lisp Machine Manual,* 3rd ed. Cambridge, Mass.: MIT Artificial Intelligence Laboratory.

Winograd, T. 1972. *Understanding Natural Language.* New York: Academic Press.

Winograd, T. 1979. Beyond programming languages. *Comm. ACM* 22(7): 391–401.

Winston, P. H., and Horn, B. K. 1981. *Lisp.* Reading, Mass.: Addison Wesley.

Xerox Learning Research Group. 1981. The Smalltalk-80 System. *Byte* (August 1981): 36–48.

Annotated Bibliography

Allen, J. R. *The Anatomy of Lisp.* New York: McGraw-Hill, 1978.

Allen gives you an in-depth understanding of a major portion of computer science by focusing on LISP. The working of a LISP system is made transparent enough so that you could design your own. Representation-independent programming is explained and used throughout. The best time to read it is after you have had some hands-on experience. John Allen also has implemented the TLC-LISP system that runs on many micros (see *Byte,* August 1979 issue).

Burge, W. H. *Recursive Programming Techniques.* Reading, Mass.: Addison-Wesley, 1975.

This is not a text on LISP but is on recursion and the theory of computation that requires some mathematical inclination. After studying it you will think LISP without knowing that you learned it.

Charniak, E., Riesbeck, C., and McDermott, D. V. *Artificial Intelligence Programming.* Hillsdale, NJ: Erlbaum, 1980.

Not an introductory text on LISP but is for the reader who has had a basic LISP course and is interested in AI. This is the best available workbook. Because it gives many problems and solutions for nontrivial problems in the field, you learn to program by understanding how experts would do it. Rather than only commenting code, the authors abstract the underlying methodology. The representation-independent style is used. It is tailored to UCI-Lisp but that should not put you off, because code is given to implement the specific constructs in your dialect. This can be used as a workbook to keep you busy for a year, and then you will be a "competent AI programmer." Most problems can be solved with a small system, such as VLISP for the PDP-11 or TLC-LISP on various micros.

Friedman, D. *The Little Lisper*. Science Research Associates.

A very concise and entertaining short introduction for the novice.

Henderson, P. *Functional Programming, Application and Implementation,* London: Prentice-Hall, 1980.

Henderson describes in an introductory way techniques that are used in writing functional programs. It uses LISP in many of the examples and shows how to implement a "LISPkit." It treats many advanced topics such as backtrack programs, delayed evaluation, and higher order functions. Although not an introductory text on LISP programming, it provides a deep understanding of the semantics of functional languages. This text could be integrated well into a computing science curriculum, because it interrelates the theory of programming, compilers, programming languages, and data structures concisely. The examples are well chosen, illustrate the concepts, and motivate programming exercises.

McCarthy, J., Abrahams, P., Edwards, D., Hart, T., and Levin, M. *LISP 1.5 Programmer's Manual*. Cambridge, Mass.: MIT Press, 1965.

Describes the original language that nobody uses anymore. It is interesting if you want to understand the metacircular definition of an interpreter. For that purpose you might also want to read a pedagogical introduction (see Steele & Sussman, 1978a).

McCarthy, J., and Talcott, C. *LISP Programming and Proving*. Stanford, Calif.: Stanford University, 1978 (unpublished draft).

Aside from a concise and formal introduction to LISP, this yet unpublished textbook introduces techniques for proving properties of LISP programs. It presupposes that you have an elementary understanding of first-order logic. In conjunction with the Boyer-Moore theorem prover for recursive functions (available in InterLISP or MacLISP) and their book (Boyer & Moore, 1979), it would provide a thorough understanding of (automatic) program verification techniques.

Meehan, J. *The New UCI LISP Manual*. Hillsdale, NJ: Erlbaum, 1979.

This is the printed version of the on-line manual that comes with Rutgers UCI-LISP for the DEC System-10 or -20.

Pitman, K. *The Revised MacLISP Manual*. Technical Report TR-295. Cambridge, Mass.: MIT Laboratory For Computer Science, 1983.

Part of the MacLISP reference manual for the DEC System-10 or -20 comes on-line with the system, but you will have to use other on-line documentation to make use of many clever features that were later added at MIT or CMU. It is advisable also to get the much shorter manual of Touretzky (1983) to use in conjunction with Pitman's welcome revised edition.

If you are running MacLISP under TOPS-20 (sometimes called "TWENEX"), you should also get Emacs (Stallman, 1980) for a general purpose editor that is tailored to LISP.

Schank, R. C., and Riesbeck, C. K. eds *Inside Computer Understanding: Five Programs Plus Miniatures*. Hillsdale, NJ: Erlbaum, 1981.

A workbook for those with interest in natural language processing, especially the Yale approach. It shows and explains microversions of many large programs that were developed at Yale. The microversions capture the main idea and give you a good starting point to understand the fully grown system or design your own extension. All microversions can be solved with a small system, such as VLISP for the PDP-11 or TLC-LISP on various micros.

Shapiro, S. C. *Techniques of Artificial Intelligence*. New York: Van Nostrand, 1978.

If you have studied an introductory AI textbook, and are introduced to LISP, say, by Winston and Horn, using this book will be a substitute for an AI programming "apprenticeship." It is an enjoyable educational experience to work through this collection of solutions to several nontrivial AI problems. Most problems can be solved with a small system, such as VLISP for the PDP-11 or TLC-LISP on various micros.

Siklossy, L. *Let's Talk Lisp*. Englewood Cliffs, NJ: Prentice-Hall, 1976.

A useful textbook for the beginner with no mathematical or computer science background. It gives many elementary examples and exercises.

Teitelman, W. et al. *InterLISP Reference Manual*. Palo Alto, Calif.: Xerox PARC, 1978.

This very detailed documentation of the InterLISP programming environment requires familiarity with LISP. It is also available on-line (with a nice front end query language).

Weinreb, D., and Moon, D. *LISP Machine Manual*. 3rd ed. Cambridge, Mass.: MIT Artificial Intelligence Laboratory, 1981.

A good LISP background is necessary to understand it. Some newer language constructs (closures, stack groups, flavors, multiple values, and structures) are explained in a tutorial manner. Good reading if you want to know what you are missing in your current dialect of LISP.

Winston, P. H., and Horn, B. K. *LISP*. Reading, Mass.: Addison-Wesley, 1981.

This is my favourite text for a beginner. No programming and little mathematics background are required. The MacLISP dialect is used. It gives many introductory examples from all fields of AI, simplified enough to be digestible by a novice.

CHAPTER 4

A NEW SOFTWARE ENVIRONMENT FOR LIST-PROCESSING AND LOGIC PROGRAMMING

STEVEN HARDY

INTRODUCTION

Artificial intelligence research involves, among other things, making computers do tasks that are easy for people but hard for computers—such as understanding English or interpreting pictures. Since this is difficult, AI researchers use programming systems that facilitate the development of programs and are prepared to sacrifice some runtime efficiency to pay for this. Programs that are written using AI programming systems usually need more memory and run more slowly than equivalent programs that are written with conventional programming systems. However, with the decreasing cost of computer hardware, AI programming systems are now within the economic reach of many computer users and there is now no justification for non-AI programmers to use poor program development tools simply because of their cost.

This chapter describes the POPLOG programming system that was developed at Sussex University. It is currently implemented on the VAX range of computers, manufactured by Digital Equipment Corporation (DEC). These computers are classified as large minicomputers. They have a 32-bit word size which means that programs can become very large—many hundreds of times larger than is possible with a 16-bit machine such as the IBM personal computer. A medium-sized VAX computer at Sussex easily supports around twenty simulta-

ACKNOWLEDGMENT: The POPLOG system is the result of work by many members of the Cognitive Studies Programme at Sussex University. John Gibson, Chris Mellish, and Aaron Sloman made especially large contributions.

neous users of the POPLOG programming system. To ensure portability, POPLOG is based on VMS, the standard operating system that is provided by DEC.

In some respects, the decision to base POPLOG on standard hardware and software is a little old-fashioned. The current vogue in AI-programming system design is to use specialized hardware such as the LISP machine (see Weinreb, 1979). LISP is the AI programming system that is most used in the United States. The LISP machine is a special type of computer that is designed to run LISP with the same efficiency with which a conventional system runs on a conventional computer. It is a single user system—each programmer has his or her own computer, each broadly comparable in power to a VAX. We simply could not afford to buy twenty LISP machines and neither, we think, will many potential users of the POPLOG system.

The phrase "programming system" is used when referring to POPLOG in place of the more usual "programming language" because POPLOG, like BASIC, provides a complete "environment" for the programmer to work within. Moreover, there are *two* programming languages that are available in POPLOG, POP-11, and PROLOG. Typically, a POPLOG user will invoke the POPLOG system immediately after logging in and remain there until returning to the monitor to log out. Within the POPLOG system, the programmer can perform all the activities that are associated with programming. Programs can be edited, compiled, debugged, and documented all without once leaving POPLOG. Full access to system utilities, such as MAIL, is available. The POPLOG programming system includes the following:

- VED, an extendable screen editor, which can display up to two windows simultaneously.
- A POP-11 compiler, which translates POP-11 programs into VAX machine code. The compiler can be invoked as a subroutine by user programs.
- Debugging tools, which enable the programmer to locate program faults. These work at the same source code level; the programmer need not be aware that POP-11 is compiled into machine code. For example, during breakpoints the user can give arbitrary POP-11 commands.
- An on-line documentation system that allows the user to access *Help* and *Teach* files to obtain aid and instruction respectively on how to use the POPLOG system.
- A PROLOG compiler that translates PROLOG programs into VAX machine code. PROLOG provides a relational data base with limited theorem-providing capability (see Chapter 1).

There are numerous advantages to combining these components into a single system. For example, while the editor is being used the state of the user's computation (such as constructed data structures) is retained. The editor and compilers share memory and so can easily communicate. When, for example, a POP-11 procedure is edited, only that one procedure need be recompiled and not the entire program. Programs can be written partly in POP-11, a sequential procedural language, and partly in PROLOG, a backtracking declarative language. This provides a significant advantage over stand-alone PROLOG systems where *everything* must be written in "logic," even those parts that are more naturally or efficiently expressed procedurally.

Procedures that are written in other programming languages (such as FORTRAN or C) may be incorporated into programs that are written to use POPLOG. Although these "external procedures" may not be altered during a single session with POPLOG, this nevertheless provides a very powerful facility. A vision program, for example, may do low level array manipulation in FORTRAN, intermediate level processing in POP-11, and high level scene analysis in PROLOG.

Since PROLOG is described elsewhere in this volume, in this chapter we concentrate on the POP-11 programming language and how it interacts with the VED screen editor (similar interactions are possible between PROLOG and VED).

THE POP-11 PROGRAMMING LANGUAGE

In this section a number of examples of programs that are written in POP-11 are presented. They get increasingly complicated. Although POP-11 has many characteristics in common with languages like Pascal, it also has a number of advanced features that facilitate the writing of programs to solve complex problems. POP-11 is a dialect of POP-2 that has been extensively developed at Sussex University. Other dialects of POP-2 exist, notably GLUE and WonderPOP but all share the important features of the original which is described in Burstall (1971). The majority of POP-11 users have no conception of its full power; many are content to treat it as little more than an interactive Pascal. Indeed, POP-11 has been used to teach AI and programming to hundreds of psychology and philosophy undergraduates at Sussex University.

The final part of this section is a discussion of the way POP-11 is implemented. POP-11 is written almost entirely in POP-11 and so can easily be extended.

An Old Favourite: Factorial

Bowing to an old tradition, we present as our first example of a POP-11 procedure the definition of *factorial*. The simplest way of writing this procedure is recursively, thus

```
define factorial(number) -> result;
    if number = 1 then
        1 -> result
    else
        number * factorial(number - 1) -> result
    endif
enddefine;
```

We can invoke this procedure, thus:

```
factorial(5) =>
** 120
```

The symbol "=>" is called the print arrow and instructs POP-11 to print out the value of the expression to its left. The output is preceded by two asterisks, for example:

```
factorial(5) + factorial(5) =>
** 240
```

The fact that the formal parameter to factorial is called number has no significance to the POP-11 compiler. It might just as well have been called, say, x. Any type of object (e.g., number or string) can be assigned to any variable. This is not to say that POP-11 is a typeless language. Every object has a type and it is not possible, for example, to subtract a number from a string. The subtraction procedure checks at runtime that the arguments it has been given are numbers and if not it reports an error to the user. This would happen if we applied factorial to, say, a string:

```
factorial('seven') =>
MISHAP: NON NUMBERS FOR ARITHMETIC OPERATION
INVOLVING: 'seven' − 1
DOING: factorial
```

The definition of factorial uses what is termed an "output variable"; in this case it is called result. Whatever is "assigned" to this variable is the result of the procedure call. Assignment statements in POP-11 look like this:

```
expression −> variable
```

For example:

```
1 −> result
```

This assigns the number 1 to the variable result. The final value of this variable is the result of the procedure call. As with the formal parameter number, there is no significance to the word result. The procedure could have been equivalently written as

```
define factorial(x) −> y;
    if x = 1 then 1 −> y else x * factorial(x − 1) −> y endif
enddefine;
```

Notice, too, that new lines have no significance in POP-11.
    Factorial can also be defined iteratively, thus

```
define factorial(number) −> result;
    vars index;
    1 −> result;
    for index from 1 to number do
            index * result −> result
    endfor
enddefine;
```

The second line of this definition uses the keyword vars to tell the POP-11 compiler that the variable index is "local" to this procedure. The semicolon after the declaration is a "separator." If a procedure definition has several steps, then they must be separated by semicolons. This procedure has two main steps—assigning 1 to result and a "for loop." Notice that the value of the variable result is changed several times when this procedure is applied; it is the final value of result that is the result of the procedure.

The meaning of for loops in POP-11 is very similar to their meaning in other programming languages. In this case the controlled statement

    index * result –> result

is executed with index being first 1, then 2, then 3, and so on, up to the value of number.

Notice that in POP-11 most syntactic constructions have an opening keyword (e.g., for) and a closing keyword that is formed by prefixing end onto the opening keyword (e.g., endfor). Although this is verbose, it is easy to read and remember and means that when the POP-11 compiler detects syntax errors, it can give more useful information than would be possible if the same closing keyword were used for many constructions.

A number of control statements can be used in loops. The statement quitloop, for example, can occur anywhere in the body of a loop and immediately stops the loop. Quitloop is syntactic sugar for a simple goto to an implicit label that is placed after the end of the loop. Other "jumpout" constructions in POP-11 are more powerful; catch and throw, for example, provide a structured form of nonlocal gotos.

Variables

POP-11 is a "dynamically scoped" language. This refers to the way "free variables" are treated. Had the variable index not been declared as local to factorial, then the POP-11 compiler would have looked in the environment of the procedure that invoked factorial to see if index were a local variable of that. If not, the POP-11 compiler would look in the environment of that procedure's invoker and so on, until it either found an active procedure with index as a local variable or else reached the end of the procedure-calling chain and found the global variable index. This is to be contrasted with the mechanism that is used in "lexically scoped" languages such as ALGOL where free variables are looked for in lexically enclosing procedures. A technique called "shallow binding" is used to ensure that POP-11 variables can be accessed extremely rapidly (with only one memory reference). In a later section we describe how POPLOG is implemented in more detail.

Surprisingly, procedure definitions in POP-11 are simply syntactic sugar for assignment statements. When a definition of, say, factorial is encountered, the POP-11 compiler simply assigns a "procedure record" to the variable factorial. Thus, the following is permissible:

    factorial –> temp;
    temp(5) =>
    ** 120

More surprisingly, we can do

```
5 -> x;
factorial(x) =>
** 120
factorial -> temp; x -> factorial; temp -> x;
x(factorial) =>
** 120
```

Treating procedures as objects like any other, for example, numbers, which can be moved around from variable to variable, has many advantages. For instance, it is easy to redefine procedures in POP-11—one simply assigns a new procedure to an existing variable. Also, procedures may be passed as arguments, returned as results, stored in data structures, and, as we see later, dynamically constructed like any other data structure!

DATA STRUCTURES

POPLOG includes a rich set of *predefined* types of data structure, including:

integers	in the range −536870911 to 536870911
decimals	"real" numbers (both single and double precision)
strings	one-dimensional arrays of "bytes"
vectors	one-dimensional arrays of any object
arrays	any number of dimensions
properties	hash-coded "arrays," any object can be a subscript
pairs	as in LISP
procedures	structures containing machine code
externals	procedures written in some language other than POP-11 such as FORTRAN or assembly language
closures	a combination of a procedure and an environment
processes	see below
devices	descriptions of external objects like disc files

One additional vitally important data structure is the "word" which is modelled on the LISP atom. In essence, a *word* is a string with additional properties that has been entered in the POPLOG dictionary. There is only one copy of any word (unlike strings where there may be several strings containing the same letters). Words in POP-11 are also variables; among the properties that a word has are its value and its syntactic type.

User Defined Structures

The user may define new types of data structure if the predefined types of data structure are inappropriate. One way of declaring a new type of data structure is to use a "recordclass" statement which is analogous to the MacLISP **defstruct** function described in Chapter 3. For example,

```
recordclass person name age sex;
```

This tells POP-11 that **person** is a new type of data structure that has three components: a **name**, an **age** and a **sex**. *Instances* of data structures are not *declared* in POP-11 but are *created* by using a "constructor" procedure. The constructor procedure is defined automatically by POP-11 when the **recordclass** statement is used. The convention is that this constructor procedure is named by concatenating the string **cons** with the label identifying the **recordclass** structure (**person** in the preceding example) to yield a unique name (e.g., **consperson**). Here is an example of how such a constructor procedure is used:

```
consperson("steve", 33, "male") -> p;
```

This creates a new **person** structure whose **name** is **steve**, whose **age** is 33, and whose **sex** is **male**. The new structure is stored in an area of memory called the *heap* and a pointer to (i.e., the address of) the new structure is assigned to the variable **p**. We can use the new structure, thus:

```
age(p) =>
** 33
age(p) + 1 -> age (p);
age(p) =>
** 34
```

Notice that structures are accessed by using procedures; the procedure assigned to the variable **age** accesses the second component of a **person** structure. This convention makes it particularly easy to make a program independent of the form in which data are stored since there is no syntactic distinction between accessing a field of a structure and applying any other procedure to the structure. We might, for example, decide to alter our representation of a **person**, thus

```
recordclass person name yearofbirth sex;
```

If we have a global variable containing the current year, we can now write an ordinary procedure called **age**, thus

```
define age(x) -> result;
     currentyear - yearofbirth(x) -> result
enddefine;
```

If the value of **currentyear** changes, then this will be reflected in the result of future calls of **age**. For example:

```
consperson("steve", 1949, "male") -> p;
1984 -> currentyear;
age(p) =>
** 35
currentyear + 1 -> currentyear;
age(p) =>
** 36
```

We may even define an updater for age that will allow us to *assign* to the age of a person, even though there is no age field as such. With this new representation, an assignment to age should be translated to an assignment to the yearofbirth. The appropriate definition is

```
define updaterof age(newage, x);
     currentyear − newage −> yearofbirth(x);
enddefine;
```

We can use this new procedure as follows:

```
currentyear =>
** 1985
age(p) =>
** 36
38 −> age(p);
yearofbirth(p) =>
** 1947
```

Memory Management

POPLOG includes a "garbage collector." This manages the heap where all structures that are created by the user are stored. When a temporary data structure is no longer accessible by the user (e.g., no user variables "point" to it), the garbage collector reclaims the space that is occupied by the inaccessible structure. It is not possible for the user to find the actual address of a structure and, in fact, the garbage collector will rearrange the heap periodically to coalesce reclaimed memory.

Using Lists

The most commonly used data structures in POP-11 are lists and words. These are modelled on the data structures that are provided in LISP. A list is a linked collection of primitive data structures, called pairs. Pairs have two components, a hd and a tl. A three-element list of the words steve, is, and happy could be created by the following command:

```
conspair("steve", conspair("is", conspair("happy", nil))) −> x;
```

The hd of the first pair is a pointer to the first element of the list; the tl of the first pair is a pointer to a second pair. The hd of the second pair is a pointer to the second element and its tl is a pointer to a third pair. The hd of the third pair is a pointer to the third element of the list, and its tl is a distinguished object nil, thus

```
hd(x) =>
** steve
hd(tl(x)) =>
** is
hd(tl(tl(x))) =>
** happy
```

Although there is a default way of printing data structures, the user is allowed to override this default and to specify precisely how structures of any given type are to be printed. POP-11 already has a special way of printing pairs, thus

```
x =>
** [steve is happy]
```

Additionally, square brackets [and] have been defined as syntax words in POP-11 so that users may create lists without explicit use of conspair. (How new syntax words are created is discussed later.) The preceding list could have been created more simply with the statement

```
[steve is happy] —> x;
```

Such expressions are termed *structure expressions*. They are evaluated into data structures. In the previous example, the structure could be created at "compile time" since all its constituents are known then. This is not usually the case; usually data structures are created out of components that are being held in variables and are not known at compile time. For example, if the variable adj contains some word, then the user can create a three-element list of the words steve, is, and the value of adj. Thus

```
[steve is ^adj]
```

The up-arrow, ^, tells POP-11 that it is the *value* of adj that is wanted and not the word *adj* itself. If the value of a variable is a list, the double up-arrow, ^^, tells POP-11 to insert *all* the elements of that list as elements of the new list, for example,

```
[red orange yellow] —> x;
[blue ^^x] =>
** [blue red orange yellow]
[^^x blue] =>
** [red orange yellow blue]
[^^x are all colours] =>
** [red orange yellow are all colours]
```

The up-arrow is thus equivalent to the MacLISP comma (,), and the double up-arrow is equivalent to the MacLISP ,@.

Thus, the preceding example in MacLISP would look like this:

```
(setq x `(red orange yellow))
(red orange yellow)
`(blue,@x)
(blue red orange yellow)
`(,@x blue)
(red orange yellow blue)
`(,@x are all colours)
(red orange yellow are all colours)
```

Since most POP-11 users use structure expressions, there is no need for them to know about conspair. This eliminates many minor programming errors. Structure expressions can be used to create all types of data structure, not just lists.

Pattern Assignments

To complement structure expressions, POP-11 provides a *pattern assignment* statement for decomposing lists without the explicit use of hd and tl. A typical pattern assignment is

```
x --> [?a ?b ?c];
```

This statement takes the list that is the value of the variable x and assigns the first element of the list to a, the second to b, and the third to c. Unless the list has exactly three elements, an error message is generated. A more complicated example of a pattern assignment is

```
x --> [?a ??b ?c];
```

The double question mark indicates that b is to be given a list as value. The first element of x is assigned to a, the last to c, and a list of the intervening elements to b. If x was initially [steve is very happy], then a will be set to steve, b to [is very], and c to happy. Using structure expressions and pattern assignments, one can easily write a procedure to produce a copy of a list with some given item deleted; thus

```
define delete(item, list) -> result;
     vars x, y;
     list --> [??x ^item ??y];
     [^^x ^^y] -> result
enddefine;

delete ("very", [steve is very happy]) =>
** [steve is happy]
```

A Simple Data Base Package

Structure expressions and pattern assignments are used to provide a simple data-base facility in POP-11. The variable database is a list of structures. The procedure add inserts a structure in this list, remove removes a structure and lookup locates a structure; thus

```
define add(item);
     [^item ^^database] -> database
enddefine;

define remove(item);
     vars x, y;
     database --> [??x ^item ??y];
     [^^x ^^y] -> database
enddefine;

define lookup (item);
     vars x, y;
     database --> [??x ^item ??y]
enddefine;
```

Lookup will usually be given a pattern as argument; the effect of using lookup is to assign to the variable in that pattern, thus

```
[ ] —> database;
add([steve is happy]);
add([frank is busy]);
database =>
** [[frank is busy] [steve is happy]]
lookup([?p is happy]);
p =>
** steve
```

Lookup generates a runtime error if nothing in the data base matches the required item.

Finally, forevery constructions allow programs to iterate over all instances of a set of patterns in a given list, for example:

```
forevery  [[?x is a bachelor] [?x is rich]]  in database do
      add([mary wants [^x loves mary]])
endforevery;
```

A Simple Parser

Pattern assignments may contain restrictions; these are elements in the pattern that restrict the values that can be assigned to a variable. For example, the statement

```
[i saw 3 ships] ——> [??x ?y:isinteger ??z]
```

is an example of a restricted pattern assignment. The variable y is constrained to accept as value only an integer. Thus the result of the preceding assignment would be to give x the value [i saw], y the value 3, and z the value [ships].

If we have written procedures called nounphrase and verbphrase which, respectively, return **true** if given a noun phrase and a verb phrase, then the following statement will succeed (i.e., not cause an error) only if the value of list is a "sentence":

```
list ——> [??x:nounphrase ??y:verbphrase]
```

The variables x and y will be set, respectively, to the portion of list that is the noun phrase and the portion that is the verb phrase. Should the subprocedures nounphrase and verbphrase return anything other than **true** or **false** (say, parse trees), then x and y will be set to the results of those procedures.

So that we can tell *whether* list is a sentence (it may not be), we use the procedure matches. If matches can perform a pattern assignment without error, it returns **true**, otherwise it returns **false**. The following is a procedure that recognizes a 'sentence' and returns a parse tree for it (or else returns **false** if its argument is not a 'sentence'):

```
define sentence(list) —> result;
    vars X, Y;
    if list matches [??X:nounphrase ??Y:verbphrase] then
        [sentence ^X ^Y] —> result
    else
        false —> result
    endif
enddefine;
```

The definition of **nounphrase** is equally straightforward:

```
define nounphrase(list) —> result;
    vars X, Y;
    if list matches [?X:determiner ??Y:adjnoun] then
        [nounphrase ^X ^Y] —> result
    else
        false —> result
    endif
enddefine;
```

This says that a noun phrase is a **determiner**, followed by an **adjnoun**. An **adjnoun** is either simply a **noun** or else an **adjective**, followed by an **adjnoun**:

```
define adjnoun(list) —> result;
    vars X, Y;
    if list matches [?X:noun] then
        X —> result
    elseif list matches [?X:adjective ??Y:adjnoun] then
        [adjnoun ^X ^Y] —> result
    else
        false —> result
    endif
enddefine;
```

A verb phrase is defined as a verb, followed by a nounphrase, thus:

```
define verbphrase(list) —> result;
    vars X, Y;
    if list matches [?X:verb ??Y:nounphrase] then
        [verbphrase ^X ^Y] —> result
    else
        false —> result
    endif
enddefine;
```

To complete our parser we need procedures to recognize the syntactic class. A simple way to do it is to use the member function to see if the word in question is a member of the known list of correct words in a particular syntactic class. For this example, we assume that the only known words, and their syntactic classes, are as follows:

Words	Syntactic Class
the	determiner
each	determiner
cardinal	noun
purple	adjective
discarded	verb

Thus, our syntactic class recognizers are trivially defined:

```
define determiner(word) —> result;
     if member(word, [the each]) then
          [determiner ^word] —> result
     else
          false —> result
     endif
enddefine;

define noun(word) —> result;
     if member(word, [cardinal shoe]) then
          [noun ^word] —> result
     else
          false —> result
     endif
enddefine;

define adjective(word) —> result;
     if member(word, [purple]) then
          [adjective ^word] —> result
     else
          false —> result
     endif
enddefine;

define verb(word) —> result;
     if member(word, [discarded]) then
          [verb ^word] —> result
     else
          false —> result
     endif
enddefine;
```

We can now test our parser, thus:

```
sentence ([the cardinal discarded each purple shoe]) =>
** [sentence
      [nounphrase [determiner the] [noun cardinal]]
      [verbphrase  [verb discarded]
                   [nounphrase [determiner each]
                               [adjnoun [adjective purple]
                                        [noun shoe]]]]]
```

The form of this parser is so straightforward that it is easy to write a program that will *generate* the preceding program, given a description of the grammar. POP-11 contains such a program in the library (see below). The programs generated by the library package are less simplistic than that previously shown which is *not* recommended as a way of writing parsers; the example is shown only to illustrate structure expressions and pattern assignments.

The grammar and example described here are similar to those in Chapter 1 on PROLOG. This will enable the reader to compare a POP-11 program with a similar PROLOG program. Bear in mind that the PROLOG example showed only the input to the corresponding PROLOG library program and not the output of the program, as shown here.

PROCEDURE CLOSURES

POP-11 provides a number of mechanisms for dynamically creating new procedures as a program is running. In this section, which can be skipped on first reading, we illustrate the way one such technique, called *partial application* or *closures,* is used for input and output in POP-11 and also how it could be used to implement PROLOG.

Closures in Input and Output

Partial application is a technique whereby a procedure and some arguments for that procedure can be "frozen" together to create a new procedure (or *closure* as it is sometimes called). A closure needs fewer arguments than the original procedure; if *all* the arguments were frozen in at the time the closure was created, then it will need no additional arguments at all. Partial application is used to provide elegant input/output mechanisms in POP-11, and this application is a good introduction to closures. POP-11 provides a number of primitive procedures for accessing disc files. With some simplifications, two of these are:

- Sysopen which takes as argument the name of a disc file and returns a "device descriptor" for reading from that file.
- Sysread which takes as argument a device descriptor, created by **sysopen**, and returns the *next* character from the disc file.

Thus

```
sysopen('foobaz') -> d
```

The variable **d** will now hold a device descriptor for the file called **foobaz**. To read the first character from this file, we would do

```
sysread(d) =>
```

A subsequent call to **sysread** with the same descriptor will get the second character, and so on. We can "partially apply" **sysread** to the device descriptor **d**, and assign the result of this application to a variable. Thus, if we type in

```
sysread(% d %) —> p;
```

then the variable **p** will hold a closure. Notice that partial application is denoted by *decorated* parentheses, (% and %). We can now simply apply **p** to read successive characters from the file, thus:

```
p( ) =>
```

Sysread and sysopen are packaged up into a procedure called **discin** which takes as argument a file name and returns a procedure that reads from that file, thus:

```
define discin(filename) —> result;
    sysread(% sysopen(filename) %) —> result
enddefine;
```

```
discin('foobaz') —> p;
p( ) =>
```

As in MacLISP closures, the new function **p** needs no arguments, precisely because the binding of the file name to 'foobaz' is now internally stored as part of **p**'s own personal environment.

Closures and PROLOG

In this section a highly simplified account of the way PROLOG is implemented in POPLOG is given; Mellish and Hardy (1983) provide a fuller account. PROLOG is implemented by using a technique called *continuation passing*. In this technique, procedures are given an additional argument, called a *continuation*. This continuation (which is a procedure closure) describes whatever computation remains to be performed once the called procedure has finished *its* computation. This is precisely the same technique as that used in Chapter 3 for implementing generators. In conventional programming the continuation is represented implicitly by the return address and code in the calling procedure. Suppose, for example, that we have a procedure, called **prog**, that has just two steps: (1) calling the subprocedure **foo** and then when that has finished execution, (2) calling the subprocedure **baz**, thus:

```
define prog( );
    foo( );
    baz( );
enddefine;
```

Were this procedure to be rewritten by using explicit continuations, then baz would be passed as an extra argument to foo since baz is the continuation for foo. Actually, it is not quite that simple, since prog itself would also have a continuation and this must be passed to baz as *its* continuation, thus:

```
define prog(continuation);
     foo(baz(% continuation %))
enddefine;
```

So, if we invoke prog we must give it explicit instructions, continuation, as to what is to be done when it has finished. Prog invokes foo, giving foo as its continuation the procedure baz, which has been partially applied to the original continuation since that is what is to be done when baz (now invoked by foo as its continuation) has finished its task.

This apparently roundabout way of programming has an enormous advantage—since procedures have explicit continuations, there is no need for them to "return" to their invoker. Conventionally, subprocedures returning to their invokers means: "I have finished—continue with the computation." With explicit continuations, we can assign a different meaning to a subprocedure returning to its invoker, say "Sorry—I wasn't able to do what you wanted me to do."

Prog accomplishes its task by first doing foo and then doing baz. The power of continuation programming is made clear if we define a new procedure newprog, thus:

Try doing FOO but if that doesn't work then try doing BAZ

This is represented as follows:

```
define newprog(continuation);
     foo(continuation);
     baz(continuation);
enddefine;
```

If we now invoke newprog (with a continuation), then it first calls foo (giving it the same continuation as itself). If foo is successful, then it will invoke the continuation. If not, then it will return to newprog which then tries baz. If baz too fails (by returning), then newprog itself fails by returning to *its* invoker.

PROLOG Predicates and Continuations

Consider the following PROLOG procedure:

```
happy(X) :- healthy(X), wise(X).
```

This says that x is happy if x is healthy and wise. If this is the only definition of happy, then we may translate this to the following POP-11 procedure:

```
define happy(x, continuation);
      healthy(x, wise(% x, continuation %))
enddefine;
```

A call of this procedure can be interpreted as meaning: Check that x is **happy** and if so do the continuation.

This is accomplished by passing x to **healthy** but giving **healthy** a continuation which then passes x across to **wise**. Let us suppose that someone is **healthy** if he or she either **jogs** or else **eats cabbage**. In PROLOG, we would say

```
healthy(X) :- jogs (X).
healthy(X) :- eats (X, cabbage).
```

This can be translated as

```
define healthy(x, continuation);
      jogs(x, continuation);
      eats(x, "cabbage", continuation);
enddefine;
```

Finally, let us assume that we know that **chris** and **jon** both jog. In PROLOG, this would be

```
jogs(chris).
jogs(jon).
```

We can represent this as a POP-11 procedure, thus:

```
define jogs(x, continuation);
      if x = "chris" then continuation( ) endif;
      if x = "jon" then continuation( ) endif;
enddefine;
```

The translation of **jogs** is too simplistic. It does not cater for the case where x is unknown, and we wish to *find* someone who **jogs**. This is dealt with in the actual PROLOG subsystem of POPLOG by representing unknowns by data structures whose contents are initially **undef**, a unique word. Instead of simply comparing x with the word **chris**, **jogs** instead tries to "unify" the data structure with the word **chris**. PROLOG procedures are translated directly into virtual machine code and not into POP-11 procedures.

Coroutines and Generators

POPLOG allows programs to be written as a number of cooperating processes. Only one process may be active at any given moment and it must explicitly relinquish control of the processor before any other process may run. This restricted multiprocessing facility is called *coroutining*. To illustrate the use of coroutines, we present a program to solve the "same fringe" problem.

The same fringe problem consists of writing some program to take two arbitrarily shaped trees and determine if the *fringe* (the list of all terminal nodes) of the two trees is identical. This is true for the following two trees, which both have fringes [A B C]:

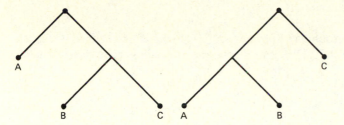

What makes this problem difficult is that although one can write a recursive program to traverse one tree, it is very hard to write a program to traverse two differently shaped trees. The solution is to have one *process* per tree. These processes perform a simple recursive traversal of their single tree, pausing after finding each element of the fringe.

We can easily represent trees like those in the figure with lists, thus:

    [A [B C]]   [[A B] C]

We represent a node of the tree as either a word (meaning we are at a tip of the tree and the word is on the fringe) or else as a list of subtrees. For simplicity, we say that nodes are either tips or else have exactly two subtrees. A procedure to traverse such a tree is

```
define traverse(tree);
     if islist(tree) then
            traverse(tree(1));
            traverse(tree(2));
     else
            suspend(tree, 1)
     endif
enddefine;
```

The notation **tree(1)** denotes the first subtree. POP-11 allows lists (and many other structures) to be accessed as if they were one-dimensional arrays. Thus, if the **tree** given to **traverse** is a list, then **traverse** calls itself recursively—first on the first subtree and then on the second subtree. If the **tree** given to **traverse** is *not* a list, then it must be a tip, that is, a word on the fringe. In this case **traverse** calls the procedure **suspend**, telling it to return one result, namely, the tip word. **Suspend** halts the current process and restarts the process that invoked it. To create a process, we use the procedure **consproc**. Basically, **consproc** takes as argument a procedure and returns a process that when invoked with **runproc** will call the given procedure. **Consproc** must also be given the arguments that will be needed by the procedure and a count of the number of arguments. The following procedure, **fringeprocess**, takes as argument a tree and returns as results a process that will traverse the given tree:

```
define fringeprocess(tree);
      consproc(tree, 1, procedure x; traverse(x); termin endprocedure)
enddefine;
```

(The notation **procedure . . . endprocedure** specifies an "anonymous" procedure; these are called "lambda expressions" in LISP.) We can apply the preceding procedure to some particular tree, thus:

```
fringeprocess([[a b] [c [d e]]]) -> x;
```

The value of x is now a process that can be run with **runproc**. **Runproc** also needs to know whether any data items are to be passed to the process; in this case there are none. **Runproc** will start the process which will enter **traverse** and continue execution until it reaches a call of **suspend**. The parameter to **suspend** will then be passed back to the calling process as the result of **runproc**, thus

```
runproc(0, x) =>
** a
```

We now have the first element of the fringe of the tree that is given to **fringeprocess**. The process held in the variable x is now suspended halfway through the execution of **traverse**. If we invoke **runproc** repeatedly, we will get the subsequent elements of the fringe; thus

```
runproc(0, x) =>
** b
runproc(0, x) =>
** c
```

Eventually, the process in x will terminate and produce **termin** as its result, indicating that we have reached the end of the fringe. (Termin is a unique object used by POP-11 programs to signify that a "stream" has terminated.)

It is a simple matter to write a procedure that takes two trees, creates processes for each of them, and then compares the results given by the two processes, thus:

```
define samefringe(t1, t2);
      vars x1, x2, p1, p2;
      fringeprocess(t1) -> p1;
      fringeprocess(t2) -> p2;
      repeat forever
            runproc(0, p1) -> x1;
            runproc(0, p2) -> x2;
            if x1 = termin and x2 = termin then return(true) endif;
            unless x1 = x2 then return(false) endunless;
      endrepeat;
enddefine;
```

Return is a keyword to force immediate termination of a procedure call. This is used as soon as two fringe elements are different. If the trees have identical fringes, then the two subprocesses will eventually return **termin** simultaneously and the **repeat** loop will be broken. If the fringes are different, then the PROLOG garbage collector will recover the space that is occupied by the now unwanted processes.

The reader will note the similarity between testing the "outputs" of two processes and testing two lists for equality. POP-11 provides a mechanism by which a process can be made to *appear* to be a list of its outputs. The following expression

```
pdtolist(runproc(% 0, fringeprocess(tree) %))
```

evaluates to a *dynamic list*. Dynamic lists are data structures that *appear* to be simple lists. The normal list processing procedures, like **hd** and **tl** will work on them. *Actually,* the elements of a dynamic list are evaluated only when they are required. If we were to access the third element of the dynamic list that is created by the preceding expression, then POP-11 would arrange for the process to be run three times without us being aware of it.

HOW POPLOG IS IMPLEMENTED

The POPLOG system is implemented almost entirely in POPLOG. There are three reasons for this:

- It gives the user almost unlimited power to tailor the system to his or her own requirements.
- It is the easiest way of implementing the system—POPLOG is a powerful programming tool and using it in its own construction is very convenient.
- It makes the POPLOG system inherently portable. At a time when there are so many exciting developments in hardware design we wanted the POPLOG system to be relatively independent of any actual computer. About three man-months of work should be sufficient to move the system to any 32-bit computer. Since the essential programming tools, such as a screen editor, are already in POPLOG, the user of POPLOG is also relatively independent of the operating system.

The Overall Structure

The POPLOG system can be visualized as an inverted pyramid resting upon the POPLOG virtual machine. The POP-11 and PROLOG compilers translate programs into instructions for this machine. Nearly all the POPLOG system, including the screen editor and the compilers themselves, is written in POP-11 and so can be translated into POPLOG virtual machine code.

POPLOG virtual machine code is itself the apex of a pyramid and can be translated into the machine code of the actual machine on which POPLOG is running. For user programs, POPLOG contains an in-core assembler which translates POPLOG virtual machine code directly into running programs in memory.

To produce the running code for the POPLOG system itself, a different mechanism must, of course, be used. This is accomplished by having a "bootstrap" version of the POPLOG system which simply makes a list of POPLOG virtual machine code instead of translating it into running programs in memory. A stand-alone program (written in POP-11, naturally) translates this list into the assembly language that is provided by the host operating system. Once in this form, it is easy to "link in" programs that are written in languages other than POPLOG and then use the standard assembler to produce a running program. This arrangement is illustrated here:

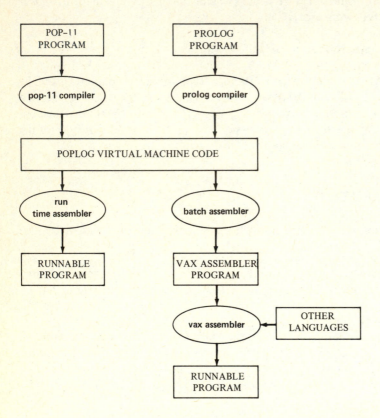

To transport the POPLOG system to a new computer we need to rewrite only the two assemblers for the new computer. The batch assembler (used for compiling the POPLOG system itself) makes many machine-dependent "optimizations." Most importantly, it replaces calls of certain key procedures (such as addition) by suitable inline code. As the batch assembler is table driven, it is easy to modify it for a new type of computer.

The Virtual Machine

An understanding of the POPLOG virtual machine is of great help in understanding POP-11. This machine is conceptually very simple and the mapping between POP-11 instructions and virtual machine instructions is also simple. POPLOG is based on a stack-oriented machine. Expressions in POP-11 are translated into instructions for this machine. For example, the assignment statement

    x + y —> z;

translates into the virtual machine instructions

```
push    x       —Put the value of variable X on the stack
push    y       —Put the value of variable Y on the stack
call    +       —Call the addition procedure, which removes
                    two elements from the stack and replaces them by their sum
pop     z       —Remove one element from the stack and store in the variable Z
```

A second stack is used to save the values of local variables during procedure calls. For example, the procedure

    define double(x); x * 2 enddefine;

translates to

```
save     x      —Save the value of variable X on the system stack
pop      x      —Set variable X from the user stack
push     x      —Put the value of X onto the user stack
pushq    2      —Put the integer 2 onto the user stack
call     *      —Call the multiplication procedure
restore  x      —Restore the value of X from the system stack
```

These instructions are translated to true machine code and then packaged up into a "procedure record" which is then assigned to the variable **double.**

Understanding this simple two-stack mechanism makes it easy to understand many features of POP-11. For example, it is clear that procedures can have more than one result (i.e., procedures can leave more than one thing on the stack); it is even possible for procedures to have a variable number of results (although this can lead to obscure programs).

Notice, too, that POP-11 has a simple way of assigning scope to variables. All occurrences of the same variable name (say x) refer to the same location; on entry to a procedure the current value of its local variables are saved and then on procedure exit they are restored. That is, POP-11 is "dynamically bound" with "shallow binding." This has the advantage that procedures are not associated with any particular environment; a procedure is simply a collection of instructions that can be executed any time and in any environment.

Also, it can be seen that it is necessary for the addition procedure, say, to check that it has been given two numbers, since the addition procedure can be invoked at any time whatever the state of the stack.

In POPLOG it is not variables that are typed, it is objects. A POP-11 procedure cannot *insist* that it be given only, say, integers; if this is crucial to the procedure's operation, then it must perform this type-checking itself. It is not generally recognized that typed variables greatly restrict the type of procedure that can be written. For example, the sort procedure in the

POP-11 library takes two arguments: a list of any type of object and a boolean procedure that embodies the ordering criteria. Such a procedure could not be written in a strongly typed language, such as Pascal, because the precise type of the procedure is not known at compile time (it is known that it must return a truth value, but it is not known what type of argument it requires; in fact, it might be given *any* type of argument).

The simple representation for procedures, combined with the ability to call the compiler recursively, gives the user great flexibility. Crucially, the user can write programs that *construct* procedures by assembling the text for the procedure and then compiling that text. The ability to do this is often of great importance in AI programs, where a program may wish to extend itself on the basis of the data it is given.

Defining Syntax Words

The POPLOG virtual machine is available to the user as a set of procedures for "planting" virtual machine code instructions. This means that the POP-11 compiler itself can be written as a set of POP-11 procedures. Indeed, some infrequently used syntactic constructions are defined by quite ordinary POP-11 procedures that are stored in the "auto loadable" library.

Suppose, for example, that POP-11 did not already have an until loop. The form of such a loop is

```
until condition do actions enduntil
```

The POPLOG virtual machine instructions for such a loop are

```
label L 1
⟨code for the condition⟩
ifso L2
⟨code for the actions⟩
goto L 1
label L2
```

The **ifso** virtual instruction is a conditional **goto**. It removes one element from the top of the user stack, and if it is not **false**, transfers control to the given label.

The user could add **until** loops to POP-11 by defining the following procedure:

```
define syntax until;
     vars L 1, L 2;
     gensym( ) –> L 1;
     gensym( ) –> L 2;
     plantlabel(L 1);
     compileto("do");
     plantifso(L2);
     compileto("enduntil");
     plantgoto(L 1);
     plantlabel(L2);
enddefine;
```

The procedure **compileto** reads in and compiles text up to the given closing keyword, in this case, **enduntil**. The various plant procedures create POPLOG virtual machine code. The procedure **gensym** creates unique words for use as labels.

Should one **until** loop be nested inside another, then the preceding definition of **until** will be invoked recursively by **compileto**.

THE ENVIRONMENT

As already shown, POP-11 is a powerful and flexible programming language. Programming languages, however, are only one of the tools that the programmer needs. Programmers typically spend much of their time interacting with ancillary programs like editors and debugging packages. Perhaps the most crucial advantage POPLOG offers the programmer is that all the necessary tools are integrated into a single "programming environment." Most significantly, a powerful screen editor, called *VED*, is intimately linked to the compilers and the runtime system. This means that the familiar edit-compile-test-debug cycle in which so much programmer time is spent can be appreciably speeded up.

The Text Editor

Since programmers spend more time modifying programs than running them, it is important that they have good editing facilities. POPLOG accomplishes this by building the editor into the runtime system, thus allowing the user to edit and recompile portions of his or her program as it is being developed and tested.

POP-11 is primarily intended for interactive use from a terminal. In earlier implementations of POP-11 the compiler read a stream of definitions and imperatives from the user's terminal and wrote back any output. In this new implementation for the VAX a text editor, called VED, is interposed between the user and the POP-11 compiler, as shown here:

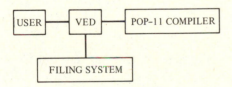

Notice that the user is always communicating with VED, the text editor. The PROLOG compiler occupies a similar place to the POP-11 compiler in this scheme.

The user's VDU screen continuously displays a portion of some selected file or files. These files may either belong to the user or be files "belonging" to POPLOG (such as documentation or tutorial files). When the user presses the DOIT button, part of the "current" file is sent to the POP-11 compiler. The compiler compiles the fragment of text that is sent to it and sends back any output to VED which splices the output into the current file and hence displays the output on the user's VDU screen. Because the output is stored in an edit file, it is easy to review any output that has scrolled off the top of the VDU screen.

This may sound very complicated, but in practice it is very simple since the scope of the DOIT button will default to any fresh text that is typed in since the DOIT button was last pressed. A simple interaction with POPLOG will consist of the user typing in a command, pressing the DOIT button, and observing the output; this cycle is then repeated. If a definition needs to be modified, two or three keystrokes after editing suffice to have the procedure recompiled and incorporated into the existing compiled program.

Debugging Tools

The POP-11 compiler can be invoked during breakpoints. This allows the user to give any POP-11 command—for example, to examine or change variables, or even to edit and recompile procedures. Breakpoints occur when (1) there is an error, (2) code execution reaches a declared breakpoint (set, perhaps, by editing a procedure definition to include a call of the compiler), or (3) the user interrupts a running program.

Since POP-11 procedures can be manipulated by POP-11 programs, debugging tools can be written in POP-11 itself. (This feature of POP-11 is shared by LISP and other AI languages.) For example, in the POPLOG library there is a short program (about fifty lines) that will add "trace" printing instructions to specified procedures.

The Documentation System

One big advantage of having a screen editor built into the POPLOG system is that it greatly simplifies providing documentation for the on-line user. A simple editor command, such as

> help for

tells the editor that the user wants to look at the *help file* for for (one of the iterative constructions in POP-11). The editor assigns a "window" on the user's VDU screen and within that window displays the wanted documentation. The documentation is visible as the user ponders over the file he or she is editing which is also visible. If the information given is insufficient, the user can give the command:

> teach for

This selects the *teach file* for for. Teach files are generally much longer and are tutorial introductions to the use of POPLOG.

A third level of documentation, reference files, are provided for those who want more precise details of how the system works. These are primarily intended for experienced programmers.

The Library

An essential component of POPLOG is the associated program library. POPLOG has an "auto-loading" mechanism that causes library files to be automatically compiled and included into any user program that references them. As part of the undergraduate teaching programme, a number of simplified AI programs have been written and these are available for incorporation into user programs. They include a suite of programs for operating on line drawings, an

ELIZA-like program, a structure data base, and a parser generator program that writes parsers in POP-11, given a context free grammar. All library programs may be perused with the editor and the **showlib** command.

CONCLUSIONS

The POPLOG system for the VAX computer, although originally developed for AI research, has features that make it useful in more general applications. The system provides an excellent environment for the programmer. He or she need not ever leave this environment since it includes needed utilities such as text editors, documentation, and debugging tools. The compiler itself is not intrusive, generally doing the right thing by default (e.g., recompiling edited text). The system is efficient enough to be used for its own development (i.e., the compiler, screen editor, etc. are all written in POP-11). The system runs on an unmodified VMS operating system and will be made available on other machines and operating systems.

Bibliography

Burstall, R., Collins, D., and Popplestone, R. *Programming in POP-2*. Edinburgh, Scotland: Edinburgh University Press, 1971.

This book describes the earliest version of POP-2. In addition to a primer, it also has many demonstration programs that, unfortunately, are badly written with excessive use of GOTOs, and so on.

Clocksin, W., and Mellish, C. *Programming in PROLOG*. New York: Springer-Verlag, 1981.

This book is a reference manual for, and introduction to, PROLOG.

Green, T., and Guest, D. An Easily-implemented Language for Computer Control of Complex Experiments. *International Journal of Man-Machine Studies* 6 (1974):335–359.

This paper describes GLUE, a dialect of POP-2, used for controlling psychology experiments.

Hewitt, C. *Viewing Control Structures as Patterns of Passing Messages*. Artificial Intelligence memo 410. Cambridge, Mass.: Massachusetts Institute of Technology, 1976.

Reading this paper, which introduces the ACTOR model of computation, will help the reader understand more about the continuation passing style of programming.

Holloway, J., Lewis, G., Sussman, G., and Bell A. *The SCHEME-79 Chip*. Artificial Intelligence memo 559. Cambridge, Mass.: Massachusetts Institute of Technology, 1980.

This describes a hardware implementation of the SCHEME interpreter. See Sussman and Steele, (1975) for an account of this language.

Lieberman, H., and Hewitt, C. *A Real Time Garbage Collector That Can Recover Temporary Storage Quickly*. Artificial Intelligence memo 569. Cambridge, Mass.: Massachusetts Institute of Technology, April 1980.

One of the serious disadvantages of the POPLOG programming environment is that periodically it takes time out to reorganize its memory—a process called *garbage collection*. This paper describes one method of overcoming this problem. As POPLOG is not used for real-time work we have not attempted to use any of the ideas in this paper. With the decreasing cost of computer memory, the problem may go away as we might expect computers to have such massive amounts of memory that either garbage collection will be unnecessary or else can be postponed until a noncritical time (like overnight).

Mead, C., and Conway, L. *Introduction to VLSI Systems.* Reading, Mass.: Addison-Wesley, 1979.

It is becoming increasingly important for programming system designers to consider whether their design could exploit special purpose hardware. This was not an issue in the design of POPLOG since we wished to use standard, commercially available hardware; the interested reader, however, may wish to consult this introduction to VLSI design.

Mellish, C., and Hardy, S. Implementing PROLOG in POP-11. In *Issues in PROLOG Implementation,* ed. J. A. Campbell. New York: Wiley, 1983.

This paper describes the way in which PROLOG has been implemented in the POPLOG system and outlines the advantages of putting a PROLOG compiler into a good programming environment.

Sussman, G. J., and Steele, G. L. *SCHEME: An Interpreter for Extended Lambda Calculus.* Artificial Intelligence memo 549. Cambridge, Mass.: Massachusetts Institute of Technology, 1975.

A very worthwhile paper that describes a collection of issues about implementing interpreters for the lambda calculus. In particular, there is a useful discussion of the relative merits of "dynamic" and "static" binding.

Weinreb, D., and Moon, D. *LISP Machine Manual.* Cambridge, Mass.: Massachusetts Institute of Technology, 1979.

The reference manual for the MIT LISP machine. This is only for the very dedicated, as it explains very little of the philosophy behind using single user computers.

PART II

TECHNIQUES

CHAPTER 5

HOW TO GET A PH.D. IN AI

ALAN BUNDY
BEN DU BOULAY,
JIM HOWE
and
GORDON PLOTKIN

Getting a Ph.D. is hard work. This chapter gives advice about various aspects of the task. The examples presented here are based on existing practices in the Department of Artificial Intelligence at the University of Edinburgh. Nevertheless, the main issues will be of direct relevance to students who are pursuing Ph.D.'s (and, in fact, masters degrees) in artificial intelligence or AI-related research at other institutions.

At most academic institutions that are offering postgraduate training in AI research, getting a Ph.D. involves writing a thesis and sitting an oral examination. The oral is generally used to ask for clarification of the thesis, so that the main burden of assessment falls on the thesis.

WHAT IS A THESIS?

The definition of an adequate thesis differs according to the type of research degree, Ph.D., M.Phil, or M.Sc, and from institution to institution. The requirements for the Edinburgh University Ph.D. are typical and are reproduced below.

The thesis, to be judged adequate, must be an original work that displays knowledge of the field, combined with the exercise of critical judgement, and contain material that is worthy of presentation as a definite contribution to knowledge. The main text, which normally should not exceed 100,000 words, must also be satisfactory in respect to its literary presentation.

This definition may not be very helpful. How original and significant must Ph.D. research be? The phrase "contain material that is worthy of presentation" suggests a simple rule of thumb. It should be possible to distill from the thesis a paper that is worthy of publication in a journal. This is not an infallible guide—refereeing standards are not always what they should be; the final decision rests with the examiners. The Edinburgh University's definition of a Master's thesis is similar and refers to a record of research or a critical survey of knowledge in an approved area of study. In this case publication in a journal would not be expected and a departmental technical report would suffice. Most departments doing AI research publish and circulate a series of technical reports or memos.

If you are unfamiliar with the standards that are expected in a journal paper or research report, read some of them! Read some theses, too. Do not be intimidated by lengthy theses: Some Ph.D. students spend five or six years writing them!

A TYPICAL PROGRAMME OF POSTGRADUATE STUDY

Producing a thesis in the three- or four-year time span that is normally allotted by sponsors is hard. Very few students can manage it. However, achieving some milestones along the way is a useful discipline, which is mainly up to you to accomplish.

A very helpful milestone is preparing a thesis proposal sometime during your first year. This should be widely circulated inside (and perhaps outside) your department and approved by your supervisor.

The proposal should contain (not necessarily in this order)

1. a description of the proposed project (the problem, motivation, and proposed approach)
2. an account of any work you have done in the area to date (with reference to any papers or programs you have written)
3. a bibliography and short survey of the area
4. an approximate timetable

Although the length of the proposal is determined by your own judgment of need, 3000 words would be a good target length.

By the end of the third year of a three-year programme, the minimum achievement is that all experimental and programming work should have been completed. In addition, your thesis writing plan should have been constructed and approved by your supervisor. Ideally, the first draft of the thesis should also be ready for scrutiny by your supervisor before the end of the third year of study, otherwise the writing may be delayed by you taking employment elsewhere upon completion of your three-year postgraduate study. Also, notice that the organisation and presentation of the material in the dissertation must be completely satisfactory or the examiners may ask that the thesis be rewritten. Thus, getting your supervisor's advice about presentation is a critical part of the writing that should be done before leaving your department. Experience shows that most students have difficulty in organizing their material satisfactorily. Show drafts of your thesis to as many people as possible who are willing to read and comment on it, including your internal examiner.

STANDARD PITFALLS FOR POSTGRADUATE STUDENTS

There are a series of standard traps that are lurking to catch postgraduate students, or anyone who is doing research for the first time. It is best to be aware of these, so that you have an outside chance to avoid them. Some pitfalls are described now.

Solving the World

Most students pick research goals that are far too ambitious. This is particularly easy to do in AI. So many tasks that humans find simple turn out to be really difficult to model. Obviously, the main burden of helping you to choose a suitable topic will rest with your supervisor. In addition, you should read the literature and talk to fellow workers to find out about the state of the art. One good source of ideas is the "further work" sections of papers. Read these works critically. Another good source is redoing poor work properly.

Manna from Heaven

Having chosen a topic, what do you do next? It is no good sitting in your room with a blank piece of paper and a pencil, waiting for divine inspiration for good ideas. What you can do is the following:

1. Read the literature. Read with a question in mind; for example, What is wrong with this? How can I use this? and so on.
2. Talk to people. Do not go in hiding. Do not be ashamed of your ideas. Other people's will often be sillier.
3. Tackle a simplified version of your problem. Ask your supervisor for exercises, miniprojects, and so on.
4. Write down your ideas in a working paper. Imagine that you are explaining your ideas to someone. You will be amazed at how half-baked ideas take shape and bugs are exposed through these simple practices.
5. Give a talk to a small group. This has the same effect as (4).

Computer Bum

Computers are very seductive. You can spend years at a terminal debugging your programs and tuning up the input/output routines. You get a satisfying sense of achievement when a bug is exposed or a nice output is generated. This is illusory! Your program must be explainable at a higher level than code for it to help you make a real contribution to knowledge.

Try to plan your program theoretically before going to the terminal. If you must work some of it out at the terminal, do so only briefly and then work out the theory. If you find this difficult, try to describe how it works to a friend, in a paper, or at a seminar. If people do not understand, it is your fault—try harder.

Yet Another Language

A terminal case of "computer bum" is to get involved in writing yet another programming language. Of course, the existing languages do not offer *exactly* what you need for your project, but that is no excuse for writing another one. You can usually find a reasonable candidate and add what you need to it. Writing a useful, new language requires an encyclopaedic knowledge of AI needs and experience of systems programming. No one will use the language you write—not even you! You will have spent all your time on the language and none on the project with which you started. If you really believe that existing languages are inadequate, then write a paper on them, carefully describing the deficiencies. If you do a good enough demolition job, enhanced languages will spring up overnight.

Micawberism

Gathering experimental data can be fun and gives all the appearances of productive work. Make sure that you know what class of result you are attempting to establish with your experiments.

1. Talk to people, explain what you think your experiment might show.
2. Imagine the experiment is finished and you have "the data"; what exactly would you do with it?
3. Try out the experiment on one or two people first, and in addition, try out the analysis. Don't keep running experiments in the hope that something will turn up.

Ivory Tower

Single-minded dedication to your topic is good, but do not shut out the rest of the world completely. Keep in touch with the state of the art in related fields. Talk to others about their research. Attend selected seminars and lectures. Set aside a part of the week for reading reviews and abstracts and skimming subject-related papers.

Misunderstood Genius

It is all too easy to believe that no one understands your ideas because you are a genius and the others are all "looneys" and charlatans. Try to keep your equilibrium.

Love of Jargon

AI is full of jargon: Try to rephrase your ideas by using ordinary English; try to rephrase your ideas in someone else's jargon. Do your ideas come out differently?

Love of Complexity

It is *not* a virtue to make a complicated program—it is just a nuisance to others. Do it as simply as possible. Occam was perfectly right.

Lost in Abstraction

To be worthwhile your research should be aimed at understanding some major property of intelligence, for example, controlling search, representing knowledge, learning. However, to achieve anything, you must tackle the abstract property in a concrete situation; that is, you must build a program to do some task that requires the search to be controlled, and knowledge to be represented, and learned. Tackling the problem in the abstract will only lead to paralysis and frustration.

Ambitious Paralysis

Having high standards for your finished product is good, but you should not apply the same standards to your initial attempts or you may never get started. Do something simple, then apply your standards to refine it into a worthy thesis.

PSYCHOLOGICAL HURDLES

Research itself shares the same psychological difficulties as other creative endeavours, such as writing novels and plays or painting pictures. Some of these problems and their antidotes are set out now.

Mental Attitude

Part of a researcher's skill includes an appropriate mental set to his or her work. This can be learned, if you know your goals and have enough determination. One of the main ingredients of this mental attitude is a belief in what you are doing. Do not be afraid of a little egotism! You must believe that the problem you are tackling is important and that your contribution to the solution is significant. Otherwise, how are you to generate the energy or ambition to struggle through the long hours of hard work that are required? (Edison said that genius was 1% inspiration and 99% perspiration, and he should have known.) To obtain this self-assurance, first select a research topic in which you can believe. Of course, do not become so arrogant that you no longer can listen to criticism. You must be prepared to modify your ideas if they are wrong.

Research Impotence

For many people, research prowess is yet another virility symbol. Lack of success at research can be accompanied by the same feelings of inadequacy and impotence as postmature virginity. Like sexual impotence, research impotence is a self-fulfilling prophecy. Doubts about your own ability can affect your frame of mind, causing the dedication and enthusiasm that are necessary to produce results to diminish or even evaporate. To avoid this vicious circle, you should realise that research ability does not depend on some magic essence; it is a skill that can be learned, like any other skill. You, too, can do original research by following the instructions in this chapter.

Dealing with Criticism

All of us find criticism hard to take, but some hide it better than others. To make progress in your research, you will have to learn both to seek out and take criticism into account and to differentiate between valid and invalid criticism. If you feel too close to the subject to decide, ask a friend for a second opinion. If the criticism is invalid, maybe the critic has misunderstood. Can you improve your explanation?

You have to learn to take some knocks—rejections from journals, rough rides in question time—in order to achieve your goal. Take it with a smile. Learn what you can. Don't be tempted to give up—you are in good company. In studying the lives of famous scientists, you will find that many of them had to endure very heavy criticism. In fact, some of the best work is the product of personal feuds—each scientist pushing him- or herself to outdo the other. This is where faith in yourself will be fully tested.

Early Morning, Cold Start

Almost everyone finds it difficult to start work at the beginning of the working day, but once he or she has begun, it is relatively easy to keep going. The remedy is twofold:

1. Make yourself a regular working schedule—and stick to it. It doesn't have to be 9:00 AM to 5:00 PM, but there should be a definite time of day when you start to work. Otherwise you will be postponing the evil moment with endless, routine, domestic chores.
2. Make sure you leave some nonthreatening, attractive task to do first. For instance, do not stop writing the day before at the beginning of a new hard section. Leave something easy to start writing: a paragraph that is routine for you or a diagram to draw.

Theorem Envy

You have chosen a new field where the research methodology has not yet been developed. You may get a hankering for the methodology you were raised on. For mathematicians, for example, this might be the longing to prove clean clear theorems—theorem envy. For engineers, this might be screwdriver envy, and so on. Be wary! Only try to prove a theorem if it is clearly relevant to your overall purpose. For instance, proving the termination of a procedure you have found to be useful may well be relevant. Finding a procedure whose termination you can prove, but which is not otherwise interesting, is not relevant.

Fear of Exposure

You have a great idea and all you have to do is test it by proving a theorem, writing a program, explaining it to a friend and so on. But something is holding you back. You find it difficult to start work. Could it be that you are secretly afraid that your idea is not so great after all? Hard experience has taught you that ideas that appear to be solutions to your problems in the middle of the night, evaporate in the cold dawn. Courage! Research is always like this. Ten steps forward and nine steps back. The sooner you subject your idea to the acid test, the sooner you will discover its limitations and be ready for the next problem.

If I Can Do It, It's Trivial

Once you have seen the solution to a problem, it appears trivial. Then it is tempting to say, "That's too easy, I'll try something else." This is a nonterminating loop! Your solution won't be trivial to other people (probably it will be wrong or overcomplex) and should be used anyway as a basis for further work. Motto: Do the easiest thing first, then stand on shoulders and do the next easiest thing, and so on—a better infinite loop.

CHOOSING A RESEARCH PROJECT

Your research project must fulfill the following criteria:

- You must be enthusiastic about it.
- Solving the problems it entails must be worthy of a Ph.D.
- It must be within sight of the state of the art, i.e. it must be "do-able" in three or four years.
- There must be someone in your department willing to supervise it.

The importance of enthusiasm cannot be overestimated. You are going to need all that you can raise to give you the perseverance and motivation to see you through what will be a hard, lonely, and unstructured period. Choosing both a problem you consider of central importance (although you cannot expect to bite off more than a small chunk of it) and an area that utilizes your already proven abilities (e.g., mathematical reasoning for mathematicians; natural language for linguists), can be very helpful. Beware of selecting an area that is new to you because of its superficial appeal. The gloss will soon wear off when you are faced with the hard grind that is necessary to get a basic foundation in it.

Having chosen the general area or problem you want to work on, you must try to define a specific project. This is where your supervisor comes in. Find a member of academic or research staff whose interests lie in this area and who is prepared to advise you. He or she may have some projects to suggest and will also be able to pass an opinion on the worthiness and do-ability of anything you suggest. On the whole, beginning students tend to underestimate the worthiness and overestimate the do-ability of projects—sometimes modest-sounding projects prove harder than they appear at first. So *do* listen to your supervisor's advice and don't fall into the "solving the world" pitfall.

Get your supervisor to suggest some reading material. You will find suitable projects in the further work and suggested readings sections of papers and theses. It is good research methodology to continue working on a problem at the point where someone else stopped. You may find some work that you consider has been done badly and contemplate redoing it properly. Perhaps you can simpify the program, relate it to other work, or build a more powerful program.

Projects that you should avoid because they lead to bad research are programs that do a task without addressing any important issues and programs that are not based on previous work (also see the section on standard pitfalls).

RESEARCH METHODOLOGY

Stage 1

Think of a scenario—that is, a sample output that would show that your computer program was exhibiting the ability you want it to model. In mathematical reasoning this scenario might be a proof; in natural language, a sample dialogue; in vision, the recognition of a scene, and so on.

Stage 2

Hypothesise what processes might achieve such a scenario. Outline the procedures and data structures that might be involved. Try to make these as general as possible. See the problems you encounter as examples of general problems. Do not use ad hoc mechanisms except to overcome problems that are not central to the issue you are addressing. Use existing AI mechanisms wherever appropriate. Showing that a problem can be solved with an existing mechanism is also a research achievement!

Stage 3

Think of further scenarios. See whether your proposed program could cope with them. Use them to refine, generalize, extend, and debug it.

Stage 4

When you are statisfied that your proposed program is stable, choose the programming language that fits your needs the closest and implement your program. Debug it on the scenarios in stages 1 and 3.

Stage 5

Find some scenarios that you have not previously considered and run your program on them. Modify your program until it is robust—that is, runs on a wide range of scenarios and does not collapse ignominiously every time you input a new one.

Stage 6

Describe your program by using language that is independent of your particular implementation.

N.B. Stages 4 and 5 will take longer than you think—years not months—so leave plenty of time!

SOME CRITERIA FOR ASSESSING AI RESEARCH

Two criteria that are often advanced for assessing AI research are psychological validity and technological applicability. Unfortunately, neither of these apply to the bulk of AI research. AI can be regarded as analogous to applied mathematics, with the role of pure mathematics being played by computer science and the role of physics being played by the cognitive sciences: psychology, linguistics, and so on. Under this analogy the purpose of AI is to provide and explore *computational techniques* for cognitive modelling. (The word *technique* is meant to be interpreted in a very broad sense.) However, AI is in such a very early stage of development that, for most cognitive tasks, we are hard pressed to find *one* suitable technique. Mainstream AI is concerned with extending the range of techniques that are available.

How are these techniques to be assessed? There is an unwritten set of criteria in wide usage, as can be seen from the ready agreement among critics on the *faults* in a piece of research, but not on its virtues. This is not a coincidence. These criteria can be concretized by generalizing from particular faults and negating the result. Here are the resulting criteria.

Clarity

The technique should be explained in a clear way. In particular, the explanation should be free of program code. Often the explanations provided by authors, although code free, are so vague as to be meaningless, for instance, the use of terms like "knowledge based," "frames," and so on. The explanation should be sufficiently clear so that an experienced AI practitioner would be able to implement the technique from it. This ideal is seldom attained.

The explanation should account for the performance, successful or otherwise, of the program. This seems obvious, but detailed study often reveals discrepancies between the explanation and the program. Retrospective analysis of a program will often show the original explanation to be almost irrelevant to the program's success.

A program with impressive performance, which is claimed to be in a finished state, but which has no clear explanation of the techniques it is based on, is worse than useless. No one can build on the work nor can anyone redo it properly without having the originality questioned.

Power

The more powerful the technique the better. Programs get credit for range and efficiency; techniques get credit for generality. As McDermott observes, AI programs often only work on the worked example in the paper. On other examples, in the words of Bobrow, "they turn to simulating gross aphasia or death." A famous natural language program is reputed to require four versions to produce all its published dialogue and to fail ignominiously on other dialogues. Can such a program be said to have proved the value of the techniques it embodies?

Parsimony

The simpler the technique the better. Occam's razor surely has a place in AI. On the other hand, many influential AI workers have argued that AI programs must *necessarily* use redundant (multiple) representations of knowledge, be highly complex, and so on. These apparently contradictory views can be reconciled by accepting that, although totally irredundant and very simple programs may be unattainable, irredundancy and simplicity are still important goals for which to strive. Some researchers have misunderstood this and have made a *virtue out of necessity* by presenting redundancy and complexity as features.

Originality

The technique or its application should be novel. The novelty of a technique is potentially hard to judge when the technique has been explained by using new terminology for old ideas. For instance, the following have all been used to describe forwards reasoning: antecedent theorems, demons, event driven, bottom up.

Most theoretical work should take the form of extending or clarifying old techniques, that is, it should generalize empirically established success. Workers in resolution theorem-proving used to be criticised for pursuing theoretical results independently of their practical utility. The activity of applying old techniques to new domains is sadly undervalued. If we are to account for a wide range of intelligent behaviour, we should surely be looking for a few simple techniques with wide applicability. It is not desirable for new techniques to be invented for each new domain.

Completion

The work should be in a finished state. This depends on where it is published: half-baked ideas, progress reports, and partially implemented programs are suitable for technical reports and conference proceedings, but not for theses or journal articles, except in a clearly marked "further work" section. It should *always* be made clear what has not been finished.

Hand simulations are not to be trusted. A large part of AI philosophy rests on the observation that unpredicted problems are uncovered during the process of implementation of any but the simplest techniques. If a technique is simple enough to be hand simulated, then it should be trivial to implement.

Despite the claim that these criteria are in wide usage, they are nevertheless poorly understood. With poorly understood criteria it is always easier to identify a blatant violation than to judge the extent of fulfillment, hence the ready agreement about faults but the lack of agreement on the virtues of a piece of AI research. It is to be hoped that this explicit formulation of the criteria will make such agreement easier to obtain.

WRITING PAPERS

Research papers are the major product of AI research. They are the yardstick by which individual and group progress and success are measured. Therefore they are very important and you should devote a large part of your research career to writing them. Besides being the primary means of communicating with the rest of the AI world, writing papers is also a good vehicle for clarifying and debugging your ideas.

As well as the dizzy heights of books, theses, and journal articles, there are various lesser forms of writing. You should understand what these are so that you can make full use of them. Writing should be a regular part of your life. Keep records of everything you do—notes of your ideas, documentation of programs, lecture notes, notes on papers you read, and so on. These serve several purposes—an aid to your memory (you will be amazed at how quickly you forget), a vehicle for clarification (often you will find that problems appear and are solved as you try to explain things to yourself), and as a starting point for a paper. Make sure you write them legibly enough to read later and that you file them somewhere you can recover them. Some people find it very useful to type them into the computer (learn about your local editor and text formatter).

Technical Reports

Most departments run series of research memoranda or technical reports. These are for descriptions of research work, either finished or in progress. You should not be afraid of presenting ideas that are not fully developed. Make writing your ideas in technical reports a regular habit. If your ideas are mere rubbish, then the sooner other people can see and appraise them, the better it is for you.

Journal Articles

When you and your supervisor think that you have something worth publishing in an outside publication, you should submit a paper to a journal. Choose one from the list provided in the "Useful Sources" section. In preparing the paper for publication, make sure that credit is given to everyone who has helped with its preparation, for example, your supervisors and anyone who has contributed ideas, others who have commented on the draft, and so on. Where a contribution is significant, consider joint authorship. Remember to acknowledge sources of support such as the source of your research studentship and related support for facilities that are used for the research, and so on. If uncertain, consult your research supervisor about these points. You will submit several copies of the paper to the journal. These will be vetted by several referees who are chosen by the journal editor. Do not be too downhearted if it is rejected—you will be in good company. Read the referees' comments carefully. Are they right or have they misjudged your work? Was your choice of journal appropriate? Consider submitting your paper elsewhere, but first take into account those criticisms you consider valid.

Conference Proceedings

A lesser form of publication is the proceedings of a conference. Conferences will often consider descriptions of work in progress. They will usually be refereed just like journal articles. Both papers and verbal presentations usually have strict length limits (from five to fifteen pages and 10 to 30 minutes respectively), so be prepared to be concise. Presenting a paper at a conference will be very valuable for you: You will get feedback from a wider audience than usual; you are more likely to meet people—more so than a nonparticipant would—and will find it easier to get funding to attend.

GUIDE TO WRITING

During the course of your research project you will need to write many documents: a thesis proposal and outline; research notes; conference and journal articles; and finally, the thesis itself. The standard of writing for journals, conferences, and theses is not high and has been a major cause of rejection in all three cases. A badly written thesis is not usually a cause for total failure but can cause soul-destroying delays while it is rewritten and reexamined. Poor writing will also make it difficult for others to understand your work. It is, therefore, quite important that you learn to write well. This section contains some tips and rules for improving your writing. Nobody knows enough about good writing to do more than that.

There are no hard and fast rules for good writing, but if you are going to break one of the following rules, you should have a good reason and do it deliberately, for instance, you want to overwhelm the funding agency with jargon rather than have them understand how little you actually achieved.

- Tell a story. Your paper should present an argument that you are advancing, for which your research provides evidence. Make sure you know this story. Summarise it in a few words on paper or to a friend. Be certain the story is reflected in the title, abstract, introduction, conclusion, and structure of the paper.

- Present your case so that it *cannot* be *misunderstood*. Think of your audience as intelligent but ignorant of your topic and given to willful misunderstanding. Make sure that the key ideas are stated transparently, prominently, and often. Do not tuck several important ideas into one sentence with a subtle use of adjectives. Do not assume that any key ideas are too obvious to say. Say what you are going to say, say it, and then say what you just said.

- Do not try to say too much in one paper. Stick to the main story and only include what is essential to it. Reserve the rest for another paper. A reader should get the main idea of the paper from the first page. Long-rambling introductions should be pruned ruthlessly.

- Follow the basic framework for a scientific paper: What is the problem? What did you use to tackle it? What results followed?

- Have a particular reader in mind as you write, to keep the technical standard of the paper uniform.

- Do not feel that you must start writing at the beginning. In particular, the introductory remarks are best written when you know what will follow. Start by describing the central idea, for example, your main technique, procedure, or proof. Now decide what your hypothetical reader *has to know* in order to understand this central idea and put this information into the introductory sections/chapters.

- Use worked examples to illustrate the description of a procedure. Do not use them as a substitute for that description.

- State clearly what is new or better about what you have done. Make explicit comparisons with closely related work.

- Define a new term, if you find yourself using a long noun phrase to refer to the same entity or idea several times. Do not define a new term unless you really need it.

- Learn to use a typewriter (all nine fingers), a screen editor, a text formatter, and a spelling corrector. Type your paper into a computer, either directly or from notes or from a hand-written manuscript. This will save time when it comes to alterations, corrections, and so on. Run the finished product through a spelling corrector.

- Ask several people to read the draft versions. Expect to spend time incorporating their suggestions into the text. If they did not understand, it is your fault, not theirs. It is discourteous to ask someone to reread a paper if you have not yet considered his or her previous comments.

STAYING IN TOUCH

Staying in touch with related research is one of the main subgoals of obtaining a research degree. Some of the difficulties were raised at a "research difficulties" meeting, held in the Edinburgh AI department, in the context of reading habits. Here is a relevant quote from the minutes of that meeting:

> Reading is difficult: The difficulty seems to depend on the stage of academic development. Initially it is hard to know what to read (AI abstracting is poor, and many documents are unpublished), later reading becomes seductive and is used as an excuse to avoid research. Finally one lacks the time and patience to keep up with reading (and fears to find evidence that one's own work is second rate or that one is slipping behind).

Clearly there are ways of staying in touch other than reading, but similar difficulties apply. One still has to maintain a proper balance between learning about other people's work and getting on with one's own.

It may be helpful to think of the work of others as arranged in concentric circles around your own, where the relevance of the work decreases as you get farther from the centre. For instance, if you were studying anaphoric reference, then the inner circles would consist of other work on anaphora; the middle circle would consist of work in natural language understanding and computational linguistics and the outer circle would contain other work in AI and linguistics. You can add extra circles to taste. Obviously, you can afford to spend less time keeping in touch with the work in the outer circle than with that in the inner circle, so different study techniques are appropriate for the different circles.

Outer Circle

You can achieve an appropriate level of familiarity with the work in this circle by skimming papers or reading the abstracts. An incomplete list of abstracts can be found in *SIGART* and in the *ACM Computing Reviews,* but generally AI abstracting is poor. It is a good idea to set aside an hour each week for visiting the library to skim the latest arrivals. An alternative to skimming is attending conferences to listen to both the short presentations and the longer tutorial addresses. It is also very valuable to approach people in the coffee room or corridor and engage them in a short conversation about their latest ideas.

Middle Circle

Here you need to spend some more time. The methods described for outer circle are still applicable but are not sufficient—you will also need to read some papers right through and engage in some longer conversations. You will want to read some more specialized textbooks, attend seminars, and so on. It is worthwhile to keep a record of papers you have reviewed and some comments about them, otherwise the benefits derived from reading them will evaporate as your memory fades. Some people find a card indexing scheme valuable here.

Inner Circle

For a really deep understanding, reading a paper once is not sufficient. You should read it several times and get involved in it. Work through the examples. Set yourself some exercises. Get in touch with the author about it. Talk or write to him or her with a list of queries and/or criticisms. Trying to teach some work to others is one invaluable way to get a deep understanding of it. Offer a seminar, either formal or informal, or give a lecture to your fellow postgraduate students. You will need your own personal copy of papers that you are using heavily. If you don't have one, photocopy someone else's.

When reading a paper you will find that you understand it better if you have a question in mind which you hope the paper will answer. The precise question will depend on the circumstances, but it might be one of the following: "Can I use this technique in my program?" "How does this paper tackle the x problem?" "Is this acceptable as a journal article?" "How can I present this idea to my class?"

Finally, don't be afraid to admit your ignorance by asking questions. Everybody feels sensitive about his or her areas of ignorance, and in a field as multidisciplinary as AI, we all necessarily have wide areas of ignorance. People enjoy answering questions—it makes them feel important. You can usually get a far better feel for a piece of work by discussing it with someone who understands it than by only reading the paper.

THE EXAMINATION OF THESES

After you have written and rewritten your thesis to your supervisor's satisfaction, then you are ready to submit it. Make sure that your thesis is in accord with the guidelines that are given in your institution's regulations.

Sitting an oral examination is a little like debugging a program. The thesis is the program, you are the programmer, the degree standards are the language syntax, and the examiners are the interpreter. During the examination you will get various error messages. These messages do not need to be taken at face value—they may be based on a misunderstanding—but they cannot be ignored. Assume that each error message will lead to some alteration in your thesis. Of course, you hope that this will only be a minor alteration, but do not let this hope blind you to the possibility that the problem is more fundamental. Do not get aggressive or defensive with your examiners. You cannot bludgeon or sweet-talk them into passing you, any more than you can force or persuade the computer to accept your "buggy" program. What you have to do is clarify your own thinking, clear up any misunderstandings between you and your examiners, make sure you understand how to correct your thesis, and then correct it. The oral examination is a cooperative process. Your examiners want to pass you. Give them all the help they need.

USEFUL SOURCES

The following list includes journals that are known to publish AI papers. The information on each journal is arranged in the order of title of journal, name and address of most appropriate editor for sending AI material to, and the type of AI material that the journal accepts.

General AI Journals

Artificial Intelligence
Bobrow, D., Xerox PARC, 3333 Coyote Hill Rd, Palo Alto, CA, U.S.A.
General artificial intelligence.

Cognitive Science
Charniak, E., Brown University Dept. of Computer Science, Providence, RI, 02912, U.S.A.
General AI, psychology, and language.

Other Journals Accepting AI Material

Journal of the Association for Computing Machinery
Nilsson, N., SRI International, 333 Ravenswood Rd., Menlo Park, CA, U.S.A.
Theory of computation and mathematical type, AI papers (e.g., theorem proving).

International Journal of Man-Machine Studies
Gaines, B., Centre for Man-Computer Studies, 24–28 Oval Road, London NW1 7DX.
Computer assisted instruction, natural language understanding, speech, bionics.

Cognitive Psychology
Hunt, E., Department of Psychology, University of Washington, Seattle, WA 98195, U.S.A.
AI of direct interest to cognitive psychologists.

Newsletters

AISB Quarterly (Society for the Study of Artificial Intelligence and Simulation of Behaviour)
Scanlon, E., Institute of Educational Technology, The Open University, Walton Hall, Milton Keynes, England.
Short general interest articles, conference reports, titles of recent papers, and so on; not technical articles.

AAAI Magazine (American Association for Artificial Intelligence)
Engelmore, B., Teknowledge Inc., 525 University Ave., Palo Alto, CA 94301, U.S.A.
Similar to *AISB Quarterly* but includes technical articles. Up-market presentation.

SIGART Newsletter (Association for Computing Machinery Special Interest Group in Artificial Intelligence)
Price, K., Image Processing Institute, University of Southern California, Los Angeles, CA 90007, U.S.A.
Similar to but less amusing than *AISB Quarterly*, includes abstracts of papers as well as titles.

Regular Conferences

IJCAI (International Joint Conference on Artificial Intelligence)
Biennial on odd years.
The major AI conference.

ECAI (European Conference on Artificial Intelligence)
Biennial on even years. Major European event. Replaces British-based AISB conferences.

AAAI (American Association for Artificial Intelligence)
Annual except when IJCAI is in U.S. Major U.S. event.

IFIP (International Federation for Information Processing)
Major computer conference. Has AI section.

Writing Technique

There is a good guide to style and presentation of scientific papers in Vernon Booth, "Writing a Scientific Paper," *Biochemical Society Transactions* (1975) 3:1–26. Helpful information about writing theses is given by C. J. Parsons in *Theses and Project Work*. London: Allen & Unwin, 1973.

Resource Handbook

The Handbook of Artificial Intelligence, vols. I, II, eds. A. Barr and E. A. Feigenbaum; vol. III, ed. P. Cohen and E. A. Feigenbaum. Los Angeles: William Kaufman, 1981/2. It contains over two hundred short articles that summarize most of the important AI programs and methodologies. It is a valuable reference source and contains extensive pointers to the existing literature.

CHAPTER 6

COGNITIVE SCIENCE RESEARCH

JON M. SLACK

THE BIRTH OF A NEW DISCIPLINE

Language, thought, and intelligent behaviour are areas of study that by their very nature embrace a range of established academic disciplines. Linguists, psychologists, computer scientists, neuroscientists, educationalists, and epistemologists all have an interest in explaining or modelling some aspect of the behaviour that we assume is a product of cognitive functions. Although the disciplines have very different origins and traditions, they share a common interest in a set of overlapping problems and issues. In the last decade the awareness of these common issues has grown, leading to the emergence of a new interdisciplinary research domain, known as *cognitive science*. Being a cognitive scientist means that you are interested in a certain class of problems relating to natural and artificial intelligence. These problem areas include knowledge representation, inference, language comprehension and production, question answering, image understanding and perception, learning, problem solving, and planning. Even though these overlapping issues provide a sound basis for the creation of a new scientific discipline, they are not sufficient; a common language is also required. Being a cognitive scientist also means that you take a specific approach to these problems, using constructs such as semantic nets, scripts and frames, production systems, ATN grammars, prototypes, heuristic search, and goal-oriented languages, to list just a few. Because cognitive science began as an interdisciplinary subject, cognitive scientists tend to come from a wide variety of academic backgrounds, bringing with them a range of skills and techniques. Cognitive science tries to embrace this wide range of tools and marry the results of quite disparate analyses. The new discipline would be of little value if it merely represented a collection of independent studies that happened to relate to the same problem. For cognitive science to establish itself, one of its main objectives must be to integrate different analyses of the same problem through its common theoretical approach. Thoroughbred cognitive scientists need to take account of the range of possible analyses that are applicable to their areas of interest. To achieve this they are forced to extend their expertise and learn a range of new skills. As the discipline matures, it will be the range of skills at their disposal that will be the hallmark of good cognitive scientists. At the same time, the emerging discipline does not want to fall victim to the old saying "Jack of all trades—Master of none."

The ultimate goal of cognitive science is to explain every aspect of cognition, preferably in terms of a single theory that is built around a few fundamental principles.

The theoretical foundations of cognitive science are rooted in logic and computation theory (Brainerd & Landweber, 1974; Minsky, 1967) from which Newell and Simon (1976) have derived their notion of "physical symbol systems." This notion defines a general class of systems that have the capacity to hold and transform symbols, or more generally, symbolic structures, but exist as physical entities. Human beings and computers are the prime examples of such systems. The idea formalizes, to a certain extent, the philosophy that binds cognitive science as a discipline. Within this metatheory, human cognition is the product of a system that has the characteristics of a physical symbol system, and the main endeavour of cognitive science is the investigation of such systems. Cognitive scientists believe that the notion of a physical symbol system is as fundamental to cognitive science as the theory of evolution is to all biology. This metatheory totally constrains the form of the expression of theories within cognitive science.

Norman (1980) outlines a set of twelve issues that he believes provide a comprehensive definition of the field. But these issues cannot be studied as isolated domains; knowledge of a wide range of behaviour and the underlying interactions is the key to understanding cognition.

> We need to study a wide range of behaviour before we can hope to understand a single class. Cognitive scientists as a whole ought to make more use of evidence from the neurosciences, from brain damage and mental illness, from cognitive sociology and anthropology, and from clinical studies of the human. These must be accompanied, of course, with the study of language, of the psychological aspects of human processing structures, and of artificially intelligent mechanisms. The study of Cognitive Science requires a complex interaction among different issues of concern, an interaction that will not be properly understood until all parts are understood, with no part independent of the others, the whole requiring the parts, and the parts the whole. (Norman, 1980, p. 1)

This view of the cognitive scientist puts the emphasis on the skills of being able to build theories through the integration of evidence from a diversity of sources and the ability to "communicate" within a variety of disparate disciplines.

Once the essence of a theory has emerged, it develops through the interplay of empirical work and theory building. The original ideas are transformed into hypotheses that have to be potentially falsifiable. The researcher then constructs controlled situations within which these hypotheses can be tested. The results of the research mould the theory into shape. As the body of empirical findings grows, the original theory is required to account for more and more behavioural data. To do this the original theory invariably needs to be extended or modified. Changes to the theory stimulate further empirical work that may lead to further changes in the theory. In this way the theory is "bootstrapped up" from its original core propositions to produce a complex set of interrelated hypotheses.

At this stage in theory development the main purpose of empirical research is to analyse and delineate the individual components of cognition and their interrelations. The range of analytic tools that are available to the cognitive scientist is quite diverse, including discourse analysis, protocol analysis, and a multitude of experimental techniques. Some of these tools require the ability to create rigorously controlled tasks, whereas others are dependent on the selection and analysis of some appropriate sequence of behaviour. Experimental work embraces both aspects, putting the emphasis on good design. This entails minimizing the effects of uncontrolled factors and eradicating the influence of possible confounding variables. Although experimentation has tended to be the dominant form of empirical research within the discipline, cognitive scientists do not restrict the types of empirical evidence they are willing to incorporate into a project. Building working models is the approach that is contributed by the discipline of artificial intelligence which, being a synthetic science, strives to combine the elements of cognition that are isolated by the analytic sciences into a functioning whole. In this sense, creating a working model can be viewed as a form of experiment in that the resulting program tests whether the theory being modelled is cohesive and whether its dynamic features are viable. In fact, many researchers within artificial intelligence regard writing programs as equivalent to running experiments (Simon, 1969).

Only when a theory has been relatively well specified through empirical research is it possible for the researcher to begin to build a working model. But why bother building a working model when the theory is already worked out? There are a variety of benefits for the researcher that accrue from building working models. First, although the theory is well specified already, certain concepts and ideas may remain imprecise. Model building forces the researcher to be explicit; every structure needs to be defined, each stage of a process specified.

Second, as Norman stressed in the preceding quote, cognition is the product of a complex system of interacting components and to understand it requires a research tool that allows one to come to grips with the complexity of these interactions. A computer simulation provides just such a tool, as the researcher can observe directly how the various processes, programmed as subroutines, interact. In addition, the program functions as a memory pad, allowing the researcher to keep track of numerous components and their interactions.

Third, the simulation can be used to generate new hypotheses that necessitate further empirical work which in turn results in an elaboration of the theory. Being explicit about the nature of a particular process may force the model builder to consider alternative forms which can be transformed into specific hypotheses and compared empirically.

Fourth, with complex theories it is often difficult to work out all the possible predictions that can be made; these predictions become more evident in running a simulation model. Also, the simulation can often produce unexpected results that have implications for the form of the theory. The relationship that should exist between a theory and a program that simulates it has yet to be established within cognitive science. Although working models are always generated from theories, no guidelines have been worked out that specify how the principles that constitute the theory should correspond to the components of the program. Some researchers claim that the simulation program *is* the theory (Newell & Simon, 1961; Kosslyn, 1980). Others claim that the program does not embody the theory as such; rather, they use computer simulations to test out the predictions of their theories (Anderson & Bower, 1973). For them, a working model in cognitive science has the same standing as computer simulations of theories in physics and in other sciences.

The issue is further complicated by the distinction that is drawn by Marr (1977) within artificial intelligence between two types of theory, Type 1 and Type 2. A Type 1 theory embodies a computational theory for the problem being answered, as well as a description of a program that implements it. A Type 2 theory, on the other hand, corresponds to a program that provides the solution to a problem through the complex interaction of numerous processes. This latter type of solution cannot be decomposed into a set of clear principles, which constitute the computational theory at the core of a Type 1 solution. In cognitive science, the researcher needs to establish a Type 1 theory in explaining human cognition. However, the distinction cannot be applied so easily, since most Type 1 theories in cognitive science also involve Type 2 theories.

The program simulating a theory often goes beyond the principles that are specified in the theory, and in significant ways. The model builder is often forced to specify the solutions to particular problems in the form of ill-defined interactions between processes, even though the working model, as a whole, is derivable from a single underlying theory. Moreover, it is not always possible to derive a Type 1 theory for a particular aspect of cognition; certain cognitive functions may well be the product of the continued interaction of a large collection of processes operating on a diverse range of knowledge. Given the complexity of the issue, it remains to be seen whether cognitive scientists will converge in their approach to the use of working models in theory development. Chapter 10 discusses the significance of Marr's distinctions in the context of research on computer vision.

A cognitive science project weaves together three strands of research activity: theory development, empirical research, and model building. Each of these activities has far less impact in isolation from the other two. *Theory development* elaborates the set of constructs from which empirical research and model building take their impetus; the theory guides the experiment and forms the basis for the model. *Empirical research* validates and constrains the theory and determines the parameters of the working model. *Model building,* which in cognitive science usually involves designing and building computer simulations, instantiates and extends the theory and generates new hypotheses that need to be tested empirically. Models and theories are not identical. A working model embodies a theory and as such is constrained by it, but not all the components of the model relate to the theory. Models are made up of three types of components: (1) those that relate directly to the theory—components that either model some element of the theory or have implications for it; (2) those that are completely irrelevant to the theory—such as aspects of the model that are determined by hardware factors; and (3) those that are not easily classified into the previous two categories. When building a model of a theory, the researcher must use these categories to classify the different elements of his or her model in order to counter any criticism of it as being ad hoc.

AN EXAMPLE OF COGNITIVE SCIENCE RESEARCH

It is easier to illustrate the range of tools and techniques that are used by cognitive scientists in the context of a specific research program. I have chosen to describe the exploration of the cognitive processes underlying the use of visual mental imagery. There are a number of reasons for this choice.

1. The concept of imagery has a long and controversial history within psychology, dating back to the philosophical origins of the discipline.
2. Research on visual mental imagery, due to the nature of the concept, explores questions that are fundamental within cognitive science, relating to the form and processing of internal representations of knowledge.
3. Research in this area spans the wide range of techniques, tools, and approaches that are encompassed by the new discipline.
4. Kosslyn (1980) has proposed a general theory of visual mental imagery that attempts to draw together evidence from a range of sources in true cognitive science style. This is the theory that forms the focus for the rest of the chapter.

To get a feel for the phenomenon of visual mental imagery, try to answer the following question: Do tigers have striped tails? In trying to answer this question, most people report first "looking" at a mental image of a tiger, then "scanning" the image and "zooming in" on the rear in order to have a "close look" before answering the question on the basis of what they "see." This type of "mental picturing" is a common psychological phenomenon and is associated with a variety of cognitive tasks; experimental subjects have reported using imagery when trying to make sense of complex sentences (Jorgensen & Kintsch, 1973) and as an aid to memory recall (Bower, 1970; Paivio, 1971). Research on visual mental imagery explores what images are, how they are produced, how and when they are used, and what it means to "look at" and "transform" them. In terms of the language that unifies cognitive science, this means *building a model of visual mental imagery that specifies the underlying knowledge structures and processes that operate on them.*

The form of the knowledge structures underlying mental images is the issue of contention on which the controversy surrounding the topic centres. Although most people agree that imagery is a vivid and undeniable phenomenon, its basis and functional role in cognition are strongly debated issues within cognitive science. A number of cognitive scientists have proposed general models of cognition based on the belief that all knowledge of the world is best represented by some form of propositional knowledge structure or code (Anderson, 1976; Norman, Rumelhart, & the LNR Research Group, 1975; Schank, 1972). These models try to account for all aspects of cognition, including mental imagery, in terms of the interactions of a relatively small set of processes and higher-order process models, all of which operate on proposition-based knowledge structures. Propositions are abstract languagelike structures that represent facts about the world, and their discrete form makes them particularly suitable as data structures for processing by digital computers.

On the other side of the debate are those who believe that image codes are utilized in cognition, in addition to proposition codes (Paivio, 1971; Kosslyn, 1980). These structures are no longer conceived of as "pictures in the head"; rather, they have quasi-pictorial characteristics and are mapped into a "medium" that has the properties of a coordinate space. In this sense, image codes are not languagelike and their correspondence to the things they represent is "nonarbitrary." Having the properties of a coordinate space means that the medium within which images are instantiated has built into it a system of interrelated constraints that determine the way images operate and behave. Images have been classified as "analogue representations" because their functional properties are the product of the constraints intrinsic to their representational medium. This debate, usually referred to as the "propositional versus analogue (spatial)" issue, has filled the pages of many journals and conference proceedings, and theoretical arguments as well as empirical evidence have been used as ammunition on both sides. But what sort of criteria can be used for deciding the issue in favour of one side or the other?

Working from First Principles

In cognitive psychology competing theories tend to be compared experimentally: The psychologist searches for an experimental task or situation for which the alternative theories make different predictions about the subjects' responses. These behavioural predictions are compared with the results of the experiment to determine which theory produces the "best-matching" predictions, and thus has the greater validity. It would be nice if it were possible to apply the same approach to the propositional versus analogue issue. Unfortunately, it is not possible to discriminate between alternative theories of representation in terms of behavioural predictions.

This point was demonstrated by Anderson (1978) by using some of the principles of computation theory (Minsky, 1967). Anderson argued that it is impossible to test theories of representation without making certain assumptions about the processes that operate on them. Behavioural data are always the product of a set of processes that act upon a specific form of representation. Thus, although behavioural predictions can be used to discriminate among theories, such theories must make statements about both the type of representation and the nature of the processes that act on them. This means that experiments in cognitive science should always test representation-process pairs. Anderson supported his argument by showing that, given any model consisting of a representation-process pair, it is possible to generate alternative models consisting of different representation-process pairs that are indistinguishable in terms of their behavioural predictions. The different models make up for differences in representation by proposing compensating differences in the processes. However, it is not possible for two arbitrary models to mimic each other; the theories of representation underlying the models must satisfy a condition that is referred to as "preservation of internal distinctions." Two theories of representation satisfy this condition if there is a one-to-one mapping, f, between them that has a computable inverse, denoted f^{-1}; that is, the inverse mapping is capable of specification (the concept of a computable function is central to computation theory but is beyond the scope of the present chapter; the interested reader is referred to Minsky, 1967). If there is such a mapping, then the distinctions among knowledge structures in one representation are preserved by the distinctions among knowledge structures in the other representation. Further, if the inverse mapping, f^{-1}, is also one to one, then the two models are capable of mutual mimicry. Anderson argues that image-based models and proposition-based models can mimic each other as it is possible to define a one-to-one function between an image code representation and a propositionalization of it, and vice versa.

Anderson's proof of behavioural mimicry went even further and showed that not only can one model mimic the observable behaviour of another model, but the two sets of procedures that produce that behaviour could, theoretically, be isomorphic. For example, consider a task in which a subject is shown a picture depicting the spatial relations between various objects and is at some later time asked questions about the picture and the response times are measured. A proposition-based model of the task might posit that the information in the picture is stored in long-term memory in the form of a set of propositions that represent the spatial relations between the objects. When the subject is asked a question such as "Is the ball on top of the table?" the set of propositions is searched by activating all the propositions linking "ball" and "table," and each proposition activated is compared with the propositional structure representing the question. Based on the outcome of the comparison process the appropriate response is executed. This model could be mimicked by an image-based model as follows: The propositions representing the picture in long-term memory are transformed into a composite image that represents the identical information. This image is then searched for spatial relations that link the ball and table. Each relation found is then compared with an image that represents the spatial relation being questioned. The outcome of the image comparison process is transformed back into the corresponding propositional structure that is then executed as the response. The two sets of processes are isomorphic in that they perform the same operations but on different types of data structure.

Denoting the set of processes that operate on the propositional representations as T_p, the set of processes that operate on the image-based representations as T_i, and the function that maps image representations onto propositional representations as $f: I \rightarrow P$, then T_p is equivalent to $f \cdot T_\mathrm{i} \cdot f^{-1}$, where $f^{-1}: P \rightarrow I$ maps propositions onto images, and T_p operating on propositions is isomorphic to T_i operating on images. That is, the set of proposition-based processes, T_p, can be mimicked by the application of f^{-1}, transforming the propositional representation into an equivalent image representation, followed by the application of T_i which performs manipulations on the images that are equivalent to the operations T_p carries out on the propositions. The resulting image representation is then transformed back into propositions through the application of f. On the basis of this equivalence, you could argue that the two models could be distinguished in terms of response times, as f and f^{-1} are bound to take some finite time to compute. But the proposer of the image-based model might argue that the set of processes $f \cdot T_\mathrm{i} \cdot f^{-1}$ can be executed in the same time period as the set of processes T_p. For this to be the case, f and f^{-1} have to be computed at high speed and T_i has to be computed faster than T_p. That is, the image search and comparison processes have to be faster than the corresponding proposition-based processes.

This argument is plausible if you assume that an image medium is far better suited to processing spatial relations than the equivalent propositional representation. Thus, the two models not only mimic each other but also reproduce the same time relationships. What this shows is that, theoretically, it is impossible to decide the propositional versus analogue issue on the basis of the behavioural predictions of models arising from different forms of representation. This does not mean that the issue is totally indeterminate; other criteria can be applied that might produce a decisive result. For example, it may be possible to distinguish one form of representation from another at the biological level. It's plausible that physiological data, such as that relating to hemispheric differences in processing spatial as opposed to linguistic material (see Bub & Whitaker, 1980), may provide a clue to the types of representation that are used in visual and verbal tasks.

In addition, the criteria of parsimony and efficiency may be useful in determining whether different types of representation are used in different tasks, or whether a single abstract form of representation underlies all cognition. For example, some recent research has shown that in matching either two pictures or a picture and a verbal description, subjects' response times are differentially affected by complexity; stimulus complexity affects the picture-description matching task, but not the picture-picture task (Nielson & Smith, 1973). These results seem to imply that different codes are used in the different tasks.

However, as Anderson's "proof of mimicry" showed, it is possible to create a model employing a single propositional representation that can adequately account for the data. Such a model would need to invoke the notion of processing propositions in parallel in order to explain the lack of effect due to complexity in the picture-picture matching task. Unfortunately, it is also necessary to assume that this form of high-speed processing is not used when matching verbal information. This assumption makes the model seem grossly inefficient, compared to the "dual-code" (two-code) model that proposes specialized representations for the efficient processing of different types of stimulus information. All these possibilities are considered in detail by Anderson (1978).

Kosslyn's Theory of Mental Imagery

The distinction between a theory and a model in cognitive science was discussed earlier and is particularly pertinent to Kosslyn's work on visual mental imagery. His research program was a prototypical cognitive science project containing the three important strands of theory development, empirical research, and model building. Starting with a basic conception, or metaphor, for mental imagery, he explored its implications through a comprehensive program of empirical research. As his experimental work uncovered more and more information about the nature of mental imagery, the original metaphor gradually developed into a complex theory. His original conception, referred to as the *cathode ray tube (CRT)* metaphor (Kosslyn, 1975), depicted mental images as displays on a CRT-like spatial display medium. This metaphor was quickly refined as it became possible to provide more precise definitions for visual mental images. The accumulation of experimentally validated hypotheses allowed Kosslyn to construct a general theory of mental imagery that, in his own words, consisted of the specification of "law-like relations among 'functional capacities' of the brain" (Kosslyn, 1980, p. 116).

Once the theory was sufficiently well specified, Kosslyn and his associates began the task of transforming it into a working model so they could investigate the way in which its different components interacted. As a cognitive scientist, Kosslyn's goal was to provide an explanation of mental imagery by using the language of "structure and process." His theory took the form of a collection of interrelated, lawlike statements about the knowledge structures that represent images and the processes that manipulate those structures. The working model, which took the form of a computer simulation, mapped the components of the theory into a specific modelling environment that embodies the constraints resulting from the particular programming language used, the choice of system architecture, and the limits of the processing capacity. The model was seen as a particular instantiation of the theory within the general "computer-brain" analogy. As such, Kosslyn was forced to "fill in" certain details that were not specified within the theory but which were necessary for the model to work. Some of these details proved theoretically important and led to further experimental work which in turn resulted in the theory being extended or modified.

In describing Kosslyn's theory, one must remember that although it is possible to describe the knowledge structures as independent entities separate from the processes that act on them, the two can never really be divorced. As Anderson (1978) pointed out, models within cognitive science by necessity have to be expressed in terms of structure-process pairs. The knowledge structures that are described later are relatively meaningless if considered independently of the particular processing system within which they function. Equally, the nature of a particular process is constrained by the form of the knowledge structures it operates on. Thus, although the structures and processes are described separately, they comprise a whole that represents a particular theory of mental imagery.

Images, according to Kosslyn, have two components, a "surface representation" and a "deep representation." The *surface representation* corresponds to one's experience of the image and has quasi-pictorial features. The image is manifest within an "image space" that has similar properties to a CRT-like display but does not imply a physical existence. The image space might exist as the activation of a particular network of neurons in the brain or as the contents of a display file or image array within a computer. Surface representations are generated from *deep representations* which are abstract knowledge structures that are stored in long-term memory.

The major properties of the image space were determined empirically and are as follows: (1) The space is finite, having a definite shape and size (Finke & Kosslyn, 1980; Kosslyn, 1978). This means that the "mind's eye" subtends a particular visual angle. (2) The image space functions as a coordinate space and has metric properties (Kosslyn, 1975). (3) When images are generated within the space they have limited resolution (Kosslyn, 1976). That is, parts of subjectively smaller images are more difficult to "see" because the detail is obscured. (4) In addition, the image space has a resolution gradient, the resolution being highest at the centre and decreasing towards the periphery (Kosslyn, 1978). (5) Images are transient; once a portion of the image space has been activated, thereby forming an image, it begins to decay. Kosslyn (1975) proposed this property as an explanation for his finding that images of objects in complex contexts were more degraded than images of the same objects in simple contexts, the reason being that the image of the object had more time to decay while generating the complex scene as compared with the simple scene.

The contents of the image space are images of objects or scenes. The correspondence between an image and the object it represents is "nonarbitrary" in the sense that each part of an image corresponds to some part of the object. Further, an image representation is a structure-preserving mapping in that the positions of different parts of an object relative to each other are preserved in the image of the object. Kosslyn believes that image to object mappings are products of the human visual system and as such are genetically determined. The knowledge structures from which the surface images are generated are of two forms, which Kosslyn refers to as "literal" and "propositional." Both types of knowledge structure are stored in long-term memory which is organized in the form of a network.

The relations between the structural components of Kosslyn's model are depicted in Figure 6.1. Each object concept that is stored in long-term memory has associated with it an ordered list of propositional knowledge structures, denoted in Figure 6.1 by the identifier prp. For the purposes of Kosslyn's project the lists contain specified categories of information as follows: (1) the parts that make up an object, for example, the proposition hasa reartire from the car.prp list in Figure 6.1; (2) the location of those parts on the object, location under-rearwheelbase in list reartire.prp; (3) the size class of a part or object, size: medium in car.prp; (4) an abstract

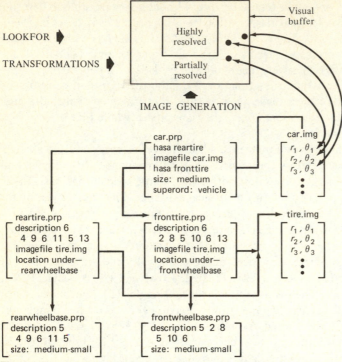

Figure 6.1   A schematic representation of the structures posited by
Kosslyn's theory. The words in large type indicate the
major processes and the locus of their action.

description of a part or object's appearance, **description 6 4 9 6 11 5 13** in the list **reartire.prp**;
(5) the name of the object's superordinate concept, **superord:vehicle** in car.prp; and (6) the
name of the literal knowledge structures that are used to generate an image of the object,
imagefile car.img also in the list **car.prp**. A list is accessed through its concept name and is
searched serially, starting at the top.

   The propositional structures that are posited by Kosslyn have the same format and serve the
same function, as those used in other proposition-based theories of cognition (Anderson, 1976;
Norman, Rumelhart, & the LNR Research Group, 1975). In fact, Kosslyn's restricted
knowledge network can be considered as part of a larger knowledge base that underlies all
aspects of cognition. This has to be the case for imagery to be involved in other cognitive tasks,
such as language understanding, fact retrieval, and problem solving.

   The literal knowledge structures encode information about how objects and scenes look—
they are not descriptions; rather, they are a product of the visual system and represent
"primitive" images. A surface image is generated by activating its underlying literal knowledge
structure, denoted in Figure 6.1 by the file identifier img.

   As yet, Kosslyn's theory does not specify the precise format of these structures. However, it
does specify their organization. The literal knowledge structure that is linked to each object
concept in memory embodies a "skeletal encoding" of the object that defines its overall shape or
structure within the surface image. The detail of the image is built up by activating the literal

encodings that are associated with each of the object's parts. The parts of an object are named in its list of propositions that link to equivalent proposition lists for each of the parts, and one of the propositions in each of these lists names the literal encoding for that part; for example, one of the propositions stored in the reartire.prp list is imagefile tire.img. Thus, the complete literal encoding for an object is distributed over the part-of, or hasa in Figure 6.1, hierarchy that describes the object's structure and components. The properties of the deep representations are, like the properties of the surface images, based on an impressive corpus of empirical research (Kosslyn, 1980).

Kosslyn has so far specified four basic types of imagery processing that can be combined to build specific models of experimental tasks. The different types of processes are those used in generating, inspecting, and transforming images, as well as those that are necessary for information retrieval from long-term memory. These processes will be discussed in more detail in the next section. In addition to these processes, Kosslyn's research project is presently looking at the way in which images are used in reasoning and how they function as mnemonic devices.

Establishing the Facts and Resolving the Issues

The experience and use of mental imagery cannot be conceived of as an independent, unitary facet of human cognition. Rather, it is associated with an array of related psychological phenomena, and before giving an account of how it works, one must delimit the boundaries of the problem. This is one of the key functions of empirical research: to determine exactly what it is that needs to be explained. Only through empirical investigation of the phenomena is it possible to isolate and refine the important information-processing problems that should be resolved through the development of the theory.

One of the key questions that Kosslyn had to answer before creating a working model of image formation and processing was whether images are stored as single memory units that are simply retrieved and activated or whether some form of constructive process is involved. That is, are images stored as wholes and transferred as such to the image space when needed or are they actively built up in the image space from component primitive images? To answer this question, Kosslyn and his associates designed the following experiment: Subjects were asked to study a collection of drawings of animals. Two versions of each drawing were produced, in one version the animal was drawn in outline, in the second version the same outline sketch was filled in with detail, providing an internal texture to the drawing. Each subject studied only one version of each drawing and equal numbers of "detailed" and "undetailed" versions. The subjects were told that their memory for the drawings would be tested. The drawings were removed after being studied for a set duration, and the subjects were asked to form an image of each drawing at the onset of the appropriate cue. They were requested to press a response key as soon as they could see each image as sharply and clearly as possible. The time that was taken by a subject to generate each image was recorded. After making a response, the subject was shown both versions of the drawing of the animal he or she had just imaged, and asked to indicate which version he or she had previously studied. This part of the procedure was included to ensure that the subjects paid close attention to the detail of the drawing, and also to obscure the main purpose of the experiment which was to analyse the differences in the image-generation times.

The design of the experiment also required the use of a control group of subjects who performed a similar sequence of tasks but who received instructions that did not mention the use of imagery. After studying the pictures, the control subjects were asked to "quickly review the properties of the pictured animals, as if in preparation for a test" (Kosslyn, 1980, p. 95) and to press the response key when they felt they had reviewed all the properties that were contained in each previously studied picture.

The underlying rationale of the experiment is that if images are formed by integrating component images rather than retrieved from memory as single units, then the detailed versions of the drawings should take longer to image than the outline versions. This is because the more detailed version of a drawing should produce more memory units or encodings at the time of study which will require more time to be recomposed when forming an image of the drawing. On the other hand, if the images of the drawings are stored in memory as single units, the image-formation times should not differ for the two versions because the task involves the activation of a single unit regardless of whether it encodes a detailed or outline version. The results of the experiment showed that there was a significant difference in the image formation times for the two conditions; on average, detailed drawings took approximately 200 milliseconds longer to image than outline drawings.

According to the rationale of the experiment, this finding implies that images are not simply retrieved and played back as single units, but are actively constructed from component image elements. However, it is possible to account for this finding in terms of a proposition-based model. According to such a model, both versions of a drawing are represented in memory by a list of propositions that encode the various properties of the drawings—detailed versions producing longer lists of properties than outline versions. The longer response times are the result of having to scan through longer property lists that are associated with the detailed drawings, rather than being the product of the image-formation processes. Fortunately, Kosslyn was able to counter this alternative explanation by analysing the response times of the control subjects. Because these subjects were asked to "review the properties of the pictured animals," their response times are presumably a measure of the time it takes to scan through the lists of properties. However, Kosslyn found that there was no reliable difference between the average response times for the two versions of a drawing, indicating that the length of a property list did not affect a subject's response time. This rather counterintuitive result is not that surprising when you consider that the scanning rates for such property lists have been estimated at only a few milliseconds per item. Thus, the proposition-based explanation of the large difference in image-formation times can be ruled out on the basis of the performance of the control group.

This example highlights the essential skills of the empirical researcher. First, it is to isolate the particular issue of interest. This entails determining the important questions about imagery that need to be answered. Second, a theoretical language must be chosen within which answers can be generated. The researcher constructs a theory that describes the functional operations underlying the cognitive domain of concern. Third, the issue being investigated needs to be formulated as one or more specific hypotheses that take the form of precise relationships between variables that can be manipulated by the researcher and observable behaviour that he or she can in some way measure. This usually involves searching for a suitable experimental task or observational setting for which the theory makes specific predictions. Fourth, the researcher has to design a tightly controlled experiment that manipulates the variables of interest, while at the same time reducing the possible effects of other variables that might influence the subjects' behaviour. The aim of the experimenter is to rule out any alternative explanations for the predicted results.

Building a Working Model

Through the interplay of theory development and empirical research, Kosslyn and his research team developed a general theory of image processing in terms of the interactions of a number of basic components. The theory specifies the nature and properties of these components, which have been validated experimentally. However, it does not provide a good description of their interactions, even though the theory specifies them indirectly. One of the main advantages of building working models of complex cognitive theories, as discussed earlier, is that they allow the researcher to gain a better understanding of how the theory functions as a whole. Interacting processes and knowledge structures are easier to conceptualize as a working computer program consisting of a set of subroutines, a control structure, and specified data structures. Kosslyn and Schwartz (1977) built such a program as a working model of Kosslyn's theory. The rest of this section is based on their work.

The task of building a working model can be broken down into a number of different stages, each stage involving slightly different skills. Starting with a description of the theory in terms of the empirically derived properties of the basic components and their interactions, this needs to be translated into the language of "structure and process." The basic components must be specified as data structures and the dynamic elements of the theory as processes. The model builder then has to decide on the programming environment within which to build the simulation; this decision usually comes down to choosing the most appropriate programming language, given the specification of the model. The next stage involves transforming the rather abstract structure-process description into equivalent elements within the chosen programming language. This entails modelling the data structures by using the data types and structures that are available within the language and writing efficient subprograms to model the individual processes that are put together according to the specification of the control structure to create a "runnable" program. The final stage usually requires the model builder to "debug" his or her program to get it to run.

As part of his experimental work, Kosslyn (1976) showed that when subjects use imagery to verify properties of named animals, their response times are faster, the larger the size of the property relative to the size of the imaged animal. However, if subjects imaged only the local region where the property ought to be found, and did not consult an image of the whole animal, the size of a property no longer influenced verification time. For example, subjects were quicker at deciding that a lion has a tail than deciding that a lion has whiskers. But there was no difference in their response times for these two decisions when they were asked to image the back end of a lion prior to deciding about the first property and to image the head of a lion prior to deciding on the latter property. Let us consider how to simulate the cognitive processing that is involved in this sort of "verification task." The working model resulting from this endeavour should, theoretically, be capable of mimicking, in terms of overall processing time, the behavioural data that are generated by the subjects. The goal is to build a working model of Kosslyn's theory that simulates the cognitive processes underlying a subject's responses in a specific experimental task. That is, we want to build a specific model—one that embodies a general theory.

From the outset, it is important for the model builder to be aware of (1) those elements of his or her model that are relevant to the theory, (2) those that are irrelevant to the theory, and (3) those that are neutral. For example, one of the first decisions to be made in modelling image processing is how to represent the image space. The theory states that the image space functions as a finite, coordinate space, but this description does not specify how it is best represented as a data structure within the computer. As model builder, you have to decide on the best data structure. As long as the chosen structure has the functional properties of a finite, coordinate space, its exact format is irrelevant to the theory. However, the choice of structure may then be guided by other constraints, such as certain data structures being more suitable than others for processing as coordinate spaces.

The most appropriate form of data structures is usually the first decision to be made; the decision being guided by the form of the processes that are specified by the theory. The precise form of the processes is detailed next, outlining the form of the input data structures, the form of the output, and the algorithm that performs the transformation. The control structure, specifying the order in which the processes operate, is the last component to be designed. The range of specific models embraced by a general model makes use of a common set of so-called "primitive" processes, but each has a unique control structure. These processes are used as building blocks to contruct specific models that correspond to the alternative control structures that can be imposed on them. However, not all possible control structures correspond to meaningful specific models.

Starting with a collection of interrelated empirical findings from which you can infer the functional properties of the image-processing system, you then need to create a description of the model, specifying the precise form of the knowledge (data) structures and the processes that act on them. The core decision on which the project hinges, in building a working model of mental imagery, is what type of data structure should be used to model the image space. The major features of the image space, derived from Kosslyn's research, were described in a previous section, and can be summarised as (1) the image space is of fixed shape and size, (2) it functions as a coordinate space, (3) it has limited resolution, (4) it has an inherent resolution gradient, and (5) images within the space decay over time. This list of properties can be modelled in a variety of ways, but each model must specify some type of data structure that, combined with a set of elementary processes, such as a decay process, exhibits these properties.

In his theory, Kosslyn refers to the image space as the "visual buffer" which he implemented as a two-dimensional array, called the *surface matrix*. Continuing the CRT-display metaphor, each element of the array functions as an individual pixel, and a surface image corresponds to a configuration of activated elements in the array that depicts an object or objects. Representing the visual buffer as a matrix of dots has the built-in property of limited resolution. The clarity of a surface image is limited by the number of dots that are activated in forming it; a subjectively small, complex image maps a large amount of detail onto a small number of dots, thereby losing resolution. The fall-off in resolution from the centre of the visual buffer was modelled by using a high-resolution window; outside this window information—that is, dots—was lost at an increasing rate towards the periphery. The decay property can be simulated by using dots of different density, with a decay process transforming the density values of the activated regions on a regular cycle. Each element of the matrix is referenced through a set of polar coordinates that allow the literal encodings underlying the image of an object to be represented as files of coordinates specifying the elements that need to be activated in the surface matrix to depict the imaged object. The propositional knowledge structures that are stored in long-term memory are represented by list structures. These structures are linked to form a network of interconnected higher-order lists and files that constitutes the data base of the model. These relations between the structural components of Kosslyn's model are depicted in Figure 6.1.

Having translated the description of the functional properties of the basic components into a specification of structures and processes, you now have to decide on the most appropriate programming language in which to construct your working model. Different languages have been designed for processing different types of data structures, as discussed in other chapters in this volume. For example, LISP was originally designed for manipulating symbolic list structures, whereas a language like FORTRAN was designed for numerical computation and is particularly suitable for writing programs that operate on matrix structures. Other languages, like APL and modern dialects of LISP, are convenient for handling both these types of data structure. Of course, the choice of programming language is actually irrelevant to the theory and may have to be decided on totally practical grounds, such as choosing from the limited range of languages that are available to you on the machine that you are using. But if a real choice does exist, then the decision ought to be determined by the relative efficiency of each language for processing the types of data structures that are defined by the model. In the context of the present example, you would obviously want to choose a language that was suitable for manipulating matrices (arrays) but which also possessed the capacity for efficient list structure processing.

At this point you have a description of the data structures, processes, and control structure that together constitute a specific model of image processing. In addition, you have decided on the most appropriate language, or possibly languages, for building the working model. Now let's consider some of the problems that have to be overcome in creating the implementation.

The first problem relates to the manifest form of the image. The surface matrix is best represented by a two-dimensional array of finite size, the elements of which need to function as independently activated pixels with a range of intensity values. A matrix structure containing integer values ranging over the scale 0 to 7, for example, where 0 represents zero pixel activation and 7 corresponds to fully activated, would be a suitable implementation of the surface matrix. The contents of the matrix—that is, the image—could easily be displayed on the appropriate graphics peripheral.

A less sophisticated implementation, not incorporating the decay property of images, can be used to output to an ordinary visual display unit. Using a matrix structure of size 24 (VDU lines) by 80 (characters per line), one could set the elements at either "1", activated, or " ", nonactivated. Simulating the resolution gradient requires the surface matrix to be partitioned into a number of concentric frames or windows, the central window corresponding to the high-resolution region. Information is lost (activation levels set to 0) at an increasing rate, moving from the centre to the outer frames. For example, in the VDU implementation, setting the central window to an area of 12 (lines) by 32 (characters) allows the rest of the matrix to be partitioned into three workable resolution regions, each frame increasing the size of the window by 4 (lines) and 16 (characters). Within the four regions the information fall-off rates could be set at; (1) high-resolution window—no loss of information; (2) inner resolution region—information lost at a rate of one-in-four; (3) middle resolution region—a one-in-two rate; and (4) outer resolution region—a three-in-four rate. The resolution gradient is presumably a "firmware" feature of the image space, but in the working model it must be simulated in software. The process that is required to implement this property operates on the surface matrix, setting "1"s to " "s at random according to the specified resolution loss partitions. All the processes that operate on the surface matrix will use a set of standard matrix manipulation routines, and it is worthwhile creating a library of such routines that can be called by the different high-level processes.

The literal encodings, or image files, are easily represented by files or records consisting of the matrix coordinates (array subscripts) of those elements of the surface matrix that need to be activated (set to 1) when the image is generated. Each object, or subpart, which can be referenced by the system, has an image file linked to it.

The propositional structures are best implemented in the form of linked list data structures, the linking embodying the network organization of the propositions. The processes operating on these structures need to make use of recursive list processing if they are to work efficiently. Thus, a language like FORTRAN, although highly suitable for coding the matrix operations, would be cumbersome in coding the procedures that operate on the proposition data base because it is a nonrecursive language. PASCAL, on the other hand, is a recursive language, and is compatible with processing the data base structures but is slightly less efficient in processing array structures. A possible compromise, alluded to earlier, is to build a library of matrix transformation subroutines that are coded in FORTRAN which can be addressed by the top-level simulation program which is coded in PASCAL. This type of external referencing is allowable within the PASCAL language.

Let's now look more closely at the processes that act on the surface matrix and data base. To simulate the cognition underlying the type of property verification task previously outlined, one needs to decompose the task into a sequence of more elementary processes. For example, if the simulation program knows about vehicles, a typical property question might be "Does a van have a rear bumper?" To answer this question the program needs to generate an image of a van at the correct level of resolution so that an answer can be produced as the result of inspecting the image. To achieve this the program could utilise the following subroutines, or processes, in the order listed:

1. **Generate** an image of the vehicle; regenerate the image to take account of the decay feature of the image space.
2. **Look up** the location of the queried part in the propositional list for the imaged object.
3. **Assess** the resolution level of the image to verify that the queried part is detectable; if this subroutine returns a negative value, additional subroutines are called which adjust the size of the image appropriately.
4. **Scan** the surface image in the direction of the location of the queried part; the direction is inferred from the location information that is retrieved from the proposition list.
5. **Inspect** the appropriate section of the high-resolution window to detect the queried part; this subroutine exhibits a restricted form of pattern recognition.
6. **Iterate** over the last two steps until the high-resolution window in centred on the region where the queried part should be located.
7. **Respond Yes** as soon as the **Inspect** subroutine returns a positive value, otherwise a **No** response should be made on completing the search.

Most, if not all, of these processes would call lower-level processes that operate directly on the surface matrix and data base structures. Hard-copy examples of possible surface images are shown in Figure 6.2—Figure 6.2*a* shows the initial image at the correct level of resolution, and Figure 6.2*b* shows the final image that can be inspected for the queried part.

The working model previously described differs only slightly from the program developed by Kosslyn (1980) for inspecting images that is shown in flow-diagram form in Figure 6.3. The

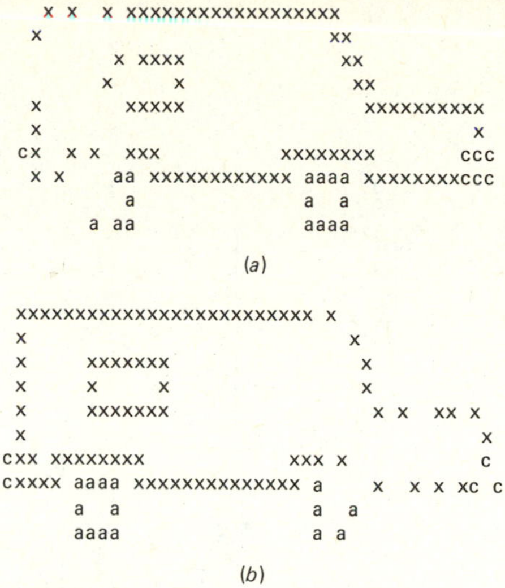

```
  x  x    x  xxxxxxxxxxxxxxxxxxx
  x                           xx
        x  xxxx              xx
      x      x              xx
  x        xxxxx                  xxxxxxxxxx
  x                                        x
 cx  x  x   xxx            xxxxxxxx       ccc
   x  x     aa  xxxxxxxxxxxx aaaa  xxxxxxxxccc
           a                    a  a
         a  aa                 aaaa
```

(a)

```
xxxxxxxxxxxxxxxxxxxxxxxxxxx  x
x                            x
x      xxxxxxx               x
x      x     x               x
x      xxxxxxx             x  x    xx  x
x                                      x
cxx  xxxxxxxx             xxx  x        c
cxxxx  aaaa  xxxxxxxxxxxxxxx  a    x  x  x  xc  c
      a   a                  a   a
      aaaa                   a   a
```

(b)

Figure 6.2

theory only specifies the high-level processes as listed, but to create a working model, one needs to define each of these processes in coded form, which means working out their precise nature. However, the details of the corresponding subroutines are often largely irrelevant to the theory. For instance, to write the **assess** subroutine you have to devise some measure of the resolution level of a surface image and a subprocess that will determine this measure as well as check it against the resolution level value that is stored in the description of the queried part. But, given the present level of detail of the theory, the quantification method chosen for the resolution level measure will not have major consequences for theory development. This means that, depending on the state of the theory, a lot of the effort that goes into building working models is not guided by the theory, leaving the model builder to rely on his or her knowledge of efficient program construction to decide many of the modelling issues that emerge.

The obvious question that arises from having designed and built a working simulation of a cognitive process, such as image inspection, is what do you gain from the exercise? Before you can even begin to create a working program you need to have a clear and unambiguous description of the model in terms of the structures and processes involved, so why not leave it at that? The problem is that models developed on paper are, by their very nature, poor at representing their inherent dynamic properties. As most models within cognitive science usually comprise a complex system of interacting components, only through building working models is it possible to fully appreciate the nature of these interactions. For example, consider the model of image inspection, previously developed. As a model worked out on paper, it is not obvious that step (3) is really necessary, and the model builder may not appreciate the importance of the resolution level of the image as a factor that influences the detectability of its different parts. Only when a running program is built may the importance of the resolution level be realised. A simulation of the model without step (3) would work when inspecting images of certain subjective sizes for certain properties, but it would not work in all cases. The program would sometimes return a negative response because the **inspect** subroutine cannot detect the queried

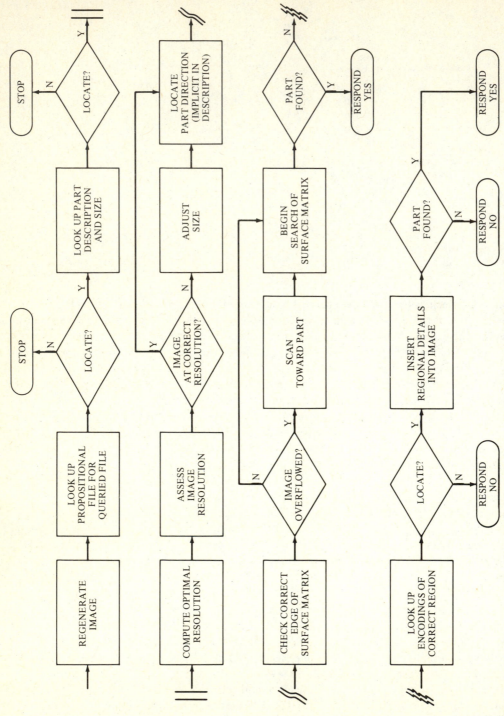

Figure 6.3   A flowchart outlining how images are searched to determine whether the object has a named part.

part, since the subjective size of the image is too small, resulting in the part being partially obscured. To circumvent this problem, one must introduce step (3) into the working model to check that the image is at the correct level of resolution for the queried part to be recognized by the **inspect** subroutine. The model builder is forced to augment his or her model in order for it to function as a working program. Having produced a solution to the problem that works within the program, he or she then needs to consider its implications for the original theory. Is the resolution level check a valid procedure to introduce into the theory? How can the existence of such a procedure be tested empirically? In a cognitive science project, the researchers would try to devise an experimental situation that could falsify the new extension to the theory. In fact, Kosslyn (1975) provided convincing evidence for the resolution check procedure in his experiments in which subjects answered property questions after producing appropriate images of varying subjective size.

In putting together a working model of their theory, Kosslyn and Schwartz (1977) came across numerous unexpected results, an example of which is quoted here:

> In an earler version of the program . . . expansion did not clarify parts of the image in this model . . . and thus the model seemed in need of revision. Upon altering the implementation . . . we were surprised to discover that resolution was no longer indexed by simple dot density: more dots were now filled in as the image expanded. Thus, the previous technique of using decreased dot density as a direct index of increased resolution failed to work; the program faltered in assessing whether to zoom in or pan out. We solved this problem by indicating where cells of the activated partition buffer were overprinted (by using capital letters). Thus, as more dots, including those overprinted, appear in a given area, resolution tends to decrease (because contours are obscured). Overprinting is taken to correspond to increased density and brightness, a claim which seems potentially testable. (Kosslyn & Schwartz, 1977, p. 294)

It has already been emphasized that not every facet of a working model's design has implications for the theory. The model builder has to develop a clear conception of which design decisions are relevant to the theory and which are not. As part of the preceding working model, it was necessary to design a pattern-recognition subroutine (**inspect**), a crucial component that is needed for recognizing and classifying the different parts of an imaged object. However, the precise form of the subroutine is irrelevant to the theory of mental imagery being simulated. Although pattern recognition is an extremely important topic within cognitive science, it should be realised that modelling a cognitive function as complex as mental imagery is bound to raise a host of issues that are beyond the scope of a particular project. The model builder cannot hope to solve all the problems of cognition, however bold and grand the original undertaking. Those aspects of the model that are specified by the theory obviously place constraints on the form of the pattern-recognition subroutine. For example, the theory specifies the type of data structures on which the subroutine operates. But because of the modular structure of the model, a subroutine that satisfies the specified constraints can be "imported" into the program. At this stage of development of the theory, the form of the subroutine is not important, only the result it returns is crucial for the model.

Kosslyn's (1980) theory does not specify the exact form of the pattern-recognition subroutine. In his working model, pattern recognition is embodied in a process called *find* which is a fundamental component of both the image-generation and image-inspection processes. This subroutine searches the surface matrix for a particular part or region of an image by accessing the description of the part that is stored in the list of propositions that are linked to the part's name. The subroutine then executes, in an ordered sequence, the tests that constitute the description. For example, referring to Figure 6.1, in looking for the reartire of the imaged car in the surface matrix, the find subroutine accesses the proposition file of the target part, reartire.prp and retrieves the description proposition, description 6 4 9 6 11 5 13. The numbers listed in the description refer to "mysterious" test subroutines that, when run in sequence, enable find to locate the target part in the surface matrix. These subroutines are mysterious in the sense that Kosslyn and Schwartz do not explain how they work, but it is clear that Kosslyn does not consider the form of the find subroutine as crucial to his theory, as evidenced in the following quote:

> I make no claims that the specific procedures used by FIND actually reflect those used by people; to solve this problem would be to solve much of the problem of how people recognize patterns. Instead, I simply make the very weak claim (which can hardly be wrong) that some kinds of procedures are used in order to classify spatial patterns; the particulars of our procedures were constructed simply for convenience, and none of the explanatory power of the model rides on the details of these procedures. (Kosslyn, 1980, p. 149)

This does not mean that, as research on mental imagery progresses, the form of the pattern-recognition subroutine will never be delineated within the theory. Rather, it is realised that there are more pressing issues concerning the relation between visual mental imagery and visual perception that need to be tackled first. Kosslyn's theory is by no means considered definitive, even by Kosslyn (1980) himself. The extent to which image processing and perceptual processing overlap is a key issue and has stimulated some important empirical research (Finke & Schmidt, 1978; Pinker, 1980). The advances made in this area could well have implications for any theory of mental imagery. In particular, this research may bring to light more details concerning the form of the pattern matcher used for classifying images that, in turn, could place further constraints on the image-generation and image-inspection processes that Kosslyn posited.

THE EMERGING DISCIPLINE

This chapter has illustrated the broad range of skills embraced by cognitive science research. The cognitive scientist has to knit together the different theoretical constructs, methodologies, and approaches that are established within the subdisciplines. This task forces him or her to develop the requisite skills to a high level. In fact, in order to communicate within the interdisciplinary field he or she needs to adopt the role of Jack-of-all-trades. However, the cognitive scientist can never afford to fall victim to the second half of the saying, Master-of-none, because cognitive science will always derive its content from its subdisciplines. The constituent research fields will never lose their identity within cognitive science, rather, the new research field will always draw on the many relevant advances made within psychology, artificial intelligence, and so on. If cognitive science ever became divorced from its origins, it would quickly stagnate due to the lack of fresh ideas and concepts.

Even as the subject evolves its own metatheory, the fundamental principles on which the theory is based will necessarily be derived from other fields. This is not a criticism of the new subject, it is just a restatement of the fact that as a research area, cognitive science is defined mainly in terms of the issues it tackles rather than its approach. Many of these arguments, however, could have been applied equally well to subjects such as psychology and sociology in their infancy. It is not the case that the interdisciplinary area will ever subsume the constituent disciplines. On the contrary, the new field will most probably be absorbed into the existing disciplines as a major interdisplinary topic. This prognosis has implications for the training of cognitive scientists, the main one being that cognitive science programmes are better suited to the postgraduate rather than to the undergraduate level.

References

Anderson, J. R. 1976. *Language, Memory and Thought*. Hillsdale, N.J.: Erlbaum.

Anderson, J. R. 1978. Arguments concerning representations for mental imagery. *Psychological Review* 85: 249–277.

Anderson, J. R., and Bower, G. H. 1973. *Human Associative Memory*. New York: Winston.

Bower, G. H. 1970. Imagery as a relational organizer in associative memory. *Journal of Verbal Learning and Verbal Behavior* 9: 529–533.

Brainerd, W. S., and Landweber, L. H. 1974. *Theory of Computation*. New York: Wiley.

Bub, D. N., and Whitaker, H. A. 1980. Lexical access and imagery: Would the right hemisphere please stand up? *Cognition and Brain Theory* 4(1): 61–68.

Finke, R. A., and Kosslyn, S. M. 1980. Mental imagery acuity in the peripheral visual field. *Journal of Experimental Psychology: Human Perception and Performance* 6: 126–139.

Finke, R. A., and Schmidt, M. J. 1978. The quantitative measure of pattern representation in images using orientation-specific color aftereffects. *Perception and Psychophysics* 23: 515–520.

Jorgensen, C. C., and Kintsch, W. 1973. The role of imagery in the evaluation of sentences. *Cognitive Psychology* 4: 110–116.

Kosslyn, S. M. 1975. Information representation in visual images. *Cognitive Psychology* 7: 341–370.

Kosslyn, S. M. 1976. Can imagery be distinguished from other forms of internal representation? Evidence from studies of information retrieval time. *Memory and Cognition* 4: 291–297.

Kosslyn, S. M. 1978. Measuring the visual angle of the mind's eye. *Cognitive Psychology* 10: 356–389.

Kosslyn, S. M. 1980. *Image and Mind*. Cambridge, Mass.: Harvard University Press.

Kosslyn, S. M., and Schwartz, S. P. 1977. A simulation of visual imagery. *Cognitive Science* 1: 265–295.

Marr, D. 1977. Artificial intelligence—A personal view. *Artificial Intelligence* 9: 37–48.

Minsky, M. 1967. *Computation—Finite and Infinite Machines*. Englewood Cliffs, N.J.: Prentice-Hall.

Newell, A., and Simon, H. A. 1961. GPS, a program that simulates human thought. In Billing, H. (Ed.), *Lernende Automaten*. Munich: Oldenbourg KG.

Newell, A., and Simon, H. A. 1976. Computer science as empirical inquiry: Symbols and search. *Communications of the ACM* 19(3): 113–126.

Nielson, G. D., and Smith, E. E. 1973. Imaginal and verbal representations in short-term recognition of visual forms. *Journal of Experimental Psychology* 101: 375–378.

Norman, D. A. 1980. Twelve issues for cognitive science. *Cognitive Science* 4: 1–32.

Norman, D. A., Rumelhart, D. E., and the LNR Research Group. 1975. *Explorations in Cognition*. San Francisco: Freeman.

Paivio, A. 1971. *Imagery and Verbal Processes*. New York: Holt, Rinehart and Winston.

Pinker, S. 1980. Mental imagery and the third dimension. *Journal of Experimental Psychology: General* 109: 354–371.

Schank, R. C. 1972. Conceptual Dependency: A theory of natural language understanding. *Cognitive Psychology* 3: 552–631.

Simon, H. A. 1969. *The Sciences of the Artificial*. Cambridge, Mass.: MIT Press.

Annotated Bibliography

Anderson, J. R. *Language, Memory and Thought*. Hillsdale, N.J.: Erlbaum, 1976.

A perfect example of the cognitive science approach. Anderson gives a general explanation of a large domain of cognition, including language understanding, memory retrieval, and learning. The text illustrates perfectly the amalgamation of experimental psychology and model building. Some of the early chapters also provide a good introduction to the major issues and concepts that form the basis for the new discipline.

Gentner, D., and Stevens, A. L. (Eds.). *Mental Models*. Hillsdale, N.J.: Erlbaum, 1983.

A new collection of articles on the use of the concept of mental models to explain how humans reason about the way the world works. The book typifies the growing literature within cognitive science, with articles written by psychologists, AI researchers, anthropologists, and education technologists. As with most edited collections, the level and quality is variable. But it is a nice example of the way the different disciplines have converged on the same concept, and ultimately, the same approach—the emergence of cognitive science.

Kosslyn, S. M. *Image and Mind*. Cambridge, Mass.: Harvard University Press, 1980.

Another good example of cognitive science research—the illustrative research discussed in this chapter is based on this work. The book gives an initial, but relatively comprehensive, account of the phenomena associated with the experience and use of mental imagery. In addition to discussing the philosophical issues concerning imagery, it describes a computer simulation that embodies Kosslyn's theory. The theoretical development is well supported by a range of ingenious experiments. At the meta-level, the book affords the ideal skeletal structure for a cognitive science project.

Norman, D. A. (Ed). *Perspectives on Cognitive Science*. Hillsdale, N.J.: Erlbaum, 1981.

The founding fathers give their views on the major issues that unite cognitive science researchers. The book includes Norman's article, outlining the twelve issues that in his opinion map out the content of the discipline. In addition, it contains articles by Simon and Newell that delineate the theoretical foundations of the subject. An inclusive range of in-depth analyses of key topics makes up the complement of the chapters. As an introduction to the new discipline, it's a must. But don't expect to be taught how to do cognitive science—the aim of the text is to delimit what it is.

Norman, D. A., Rumelhart, D. E., and the LNR Research Group. *Explorations in Cognition*. San Francisco: Freeman, 1975.

Arguably, the first cognitive science text. The book describes a set of interrelated research projects that were carried out by the LNR group, covering almost every aspect of cognition—problem solving, language comprehension, perception, reasoning, and cognitive development. All the projects use a common form of representation, called an active semantic network, which is a form of schemata representation developed by Norman and Rumelhart. The book gives a cogent demonstration of the unitary nature of cognition and the importance of the issue of representation in explaining it. A very readable and well-illustrated text.

Schank, R., and Abelson, R. *Scripts, Plans, Goals and Understanding: An Inquiry into Human Knowledge Structures.* Hillsdale, N.J.: Erlbaum, 1977.

Representing our knowledge of the world is probably the most crucial problem that cognitive science needs to tackle and solve. Schank and Abelson's book is currently the most precise and successful attempt. It does not solve the issue, but the questions it raises strike at the heart of the problem and are going to require answers before cognitive science can progress much further. In addition to all the theory, the authors touch on the specifics of knowledge representation and organization—What do we need to know about the world, or rather, some subdomain of it, in order to understand it? The book also shows that an understanding of human motivation, the "Achilles' heel" of cognitive science and all its related subdisciplines, is essential to our ability to make sense of the world. A useful text for the researcher who is interested in modelling higher-order knowledge structures—their representation, organization, and processing.

Schank, R., and Reisbeck, C. K. *Inside Computer Understanding: Five Programs Plus Miniatures.* Hillsdale, N.J.: Erlbaum, 1981.

This book scrutinizes some examples of the model-building side of cognitive science research as carried out at Yale. The models are based on Schank's theoretical work which is briefly outlined in the introductory chapters. Rather than just describe how the programs work, the authors present a complete description of how the models were built, including actual code, flow diagrams, and even "hands-on" exercises that allow the reader to build his or her own miniature version of each program. Moreover, part of the book is devoted to a scaled-down version of LISP which can be used to build the miniature versions. A very worthwhile text for the novice model builder.

CHAPTER 7

ROBOT CONTROL SYSTEMS

STEVEN HARDY

INTRODUCTION

This chapter outlines some of the problems that are associated with controlling robots. It is assumed that the reader has no knowledge of robot control systems beyond that of the informed person. The issues discussed are:

- arm geometry
- choice of coordinate system
- calculation of forces required to maintain, or change, the robot's position
- calculation of a good path between a starting position and a desired position
- compliant motion
- choice of language in which to instruct the robot

These issues are discussed in a manner that is appropriate to the general reader. A more complete treatment of some issues can be found in Waters (1979); a useful compendium of some research papers is found in Brady (1982) and Winston (1979).

ARM GEOMETRY

The most obvious feature of any robot is its physical construction. To the reader it may well be the *only* significant feature! The way the various components of a robot (or arm, since that is all

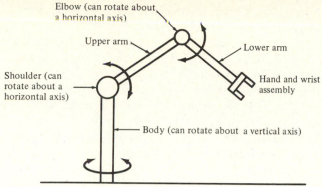

Figure 7.1   A typical robot arm.

most current robots consist of) are connected together is sometimes referred to as the "arm's geometry." Figure 7.1 is a depiction of a typical robot arm.

The arrangement is like a desk lamp; the lamp (or hand) can be positioned at any place within a sphere bounded by the lengths of the upper and lower arms. The lamp itself can then be pointed in any desired direction.

This geometry is similar to that of the PUMA arm (see Chapter 8). An alternative geometry is to do away with the elbow and lower arm and instead make the upper arm telescopic, like the Unimate arms.

In general, one will try to design an arm so as to minimize the task of controlling it. Typically, the axes of rotation of the various joints will be made to intersect; this simplifies calculating the position of the hand, given the position of the joints (see the section on coordinate systems). Other constraints on arm geometry come from the desire for power and accuracy. If, for example, the motors driving a joint are mounted on the joint itself, then the weight of the motor must be subtracted from the amount of useful load that the arm can carry. If the motors are positioned in the base, with a gear chain transmitting power to the joint, then some positional inaccuracy will almost certainly be introduced by the gear chain, thus reducing accuracy. Safety issues are also important; what, for example, will happen to the arm if the power fails? It might be disastrous for an industrial robot to drop its load in the event of a fault.

Many novel arm geometries have been tried. For example, the MIT robotics group has constructed a more obviously anthropomorphic arm with a ball and socket joint at the shoulder and four "tendons," spirally wrapped around a telescopic arm. The wrist can be positioned anywhere on the surface of a sphere by pulling on the four tendons; it can also be rotated about an axis, passing along the arm. Unfortunately, calculating the precise tensions with which to pull upon the four tendons to produce some motion has proved very difficult and so the arm is not yet practically useful.

CHOICE OF COORDINATE SYSTEM

Suppose you were blindfolded and you allowed someone to reposition your hand. You would have a good sense of where your hand was—whether close to your nose, say, or close to your heart. This is due to a sixth sense, known as kinesthesis, of which we are largely unaware. A robot control system must have this sense, too. It must be able to work out where its hand is.

The joints of the arm will be instrumented so that the control system can tell the angle made at each joint; the control system can "read off" the position of the hand in "joint coordinates," but will have to compute its position in "world coordinates" if that is needed. It may not be needed; the system could work entirely in joint coordinates. This would imply that the robot would think of its nose as being at the point its hand is at when its joints are bent in a particular way, rather than thinking of its nose as being in the middle of its face.

The calculation of cartesian world coordinates is not unduly complex for an arm designed so that the various axes of rotation intersect. We shall consider a simple two-dimensional example, as depicted in Figure 7.2. The position of the wrist is

$$x = A * \cos(a) + B * \cos(a + b)$$
$$y = A * \sin(a) + B * \sin(a + b)$$

(An asterisk denotes multiplication, as in FORTRAN.) The formulae become more complicated if the number of joints is increased (the wrist must also be considered since it will usually alter the position of the hand slightly as it alters the orientation).

Now consider the inverse problem—How can the control system compute the joint coordinates that are needed to position the hand at a particular world position? Unfortunately, there isn't always a single solution and finding the solutions is hard. It is not appropriate to give the complete solution in a chapter of this type—see Waters (1979) for the details. If the two components of the arm of Figure 7.2 are both unit length (i.e., $A = B = 1$) then the formulae are comparatively simple:

$$b = \arccos((x * x + y * y - 2)/2)$$
$$a = \arctan(y/x - b/2)$$

Computing joint coordinates is time consuming and robot control systems must work in real

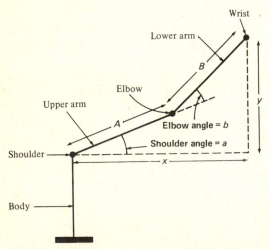

Figure 7.2   Position of wrist assembly (two dimensions only).

time. Anyone who can come up with a cheap way of doing it really fast (perhaps with special-purpose chips) will be doing robot control system designers a big favour!

One way around the problem is to make the arm large. That way, small changes in a and b will cause large changes in x and y. If the upper arm is kept almost vertical and the lower arm is kept almost horizontal, then the sine and cosine terms can be replaced by approximations; there is then almost a direct mapping between joint coordinates and world coordinates. See Figure 7.3 for an illustration.

The choice between whether to use joint coordinates or world coordinates is not a simple one. In joint coordinates a position is specified by the angles that are made at the robot joints; in world coordinates a position is specified independently of the particular arm that is being used. World coordinates are usually preferable since these will be more readily understandable to a human programmer. Moreover, the shape of object, such as a cube, will be distorted in joint space (i.e., there will be no simple relationship between the coordinates of the vertices of the cube as there is with cartesian coordinates). Furthermore, the joint space "shape" of a real-world object changes in different regions of joint space. For example, the difference between the coordinates of the ends of a rod will vary with the position of the rod, relative to the base of the arm. Altering a program that is written in terms of joint coordinates to cater for, say, a slightly different work space layout, can be almost impossible; altering a program that is written in cartesian coordinates will usually be much simpler.

Even if one has made the decision to use cartesian coordinates, it will be necessary to decide on an origin for that coordinate system. The obvious choice is to take coordinates that are relative to a "frame of reference," centred on the shoulder of the robot with its axes aligned with the horizontal and vertical. However, such a decision may well prove very inconvenient. For example, if one were describing how to insert a peg into a hole, one would probably prefer to use

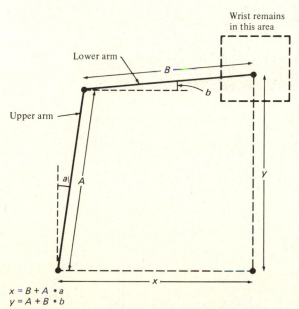

$x = B + A * a$
$y = A + B * b$

Figure 7.3   The effect of making the arm large.

a coordinate system that is aligned with the axis of the hole. If one were using the robot to remove objects from a conveyor belt, one might want a frame of reference that was moving with the belt. One might even want the frame of reference to be realigned for each object if the objects on the belt were in random orientation. For some tasks, such as polishing a convex mirror, one might prefer to use spherical coordinates in place of cartesian ones. If the mirrors were on a moving belt, one might want to superimpose the spherical coordinate system onto a moving cartesian frame in which the motion of the belt is described. Ideally, therefore, a robot control system will provide powerful tools for shifting between coordinate systems. As we have seen, this is difficult to provide. The topic of coordinate systems is raised again in the section "Gently Does It," which concerns compliant motion.

CALCULATION OF FORCES

Let us suppose that the motor at each joint of our arm can be instructed to exert a particular torque on that joint. Further, suppose that the arm is completely frictionless so that if no torque is exerted, then the arm will fall to the ground in an untidy heap. Now let us consider the task of keeping the arm fixed in some position.

If the control system knows exactly how heavy each component of the robot is and the position of its centre of gravity, then the control system can calculate the torque that is required at each joint. The torque that is required at the elbow, for example, will be related to the weight of the lower arm and hand assembly and the angle that the lower arm is making with the vertical. If the lower is upright, then no torque should be required. The torque at the shoulder is related to the torque at the elbow, the weight of the upper arm, and the position of the upper arm. If both the upper arm and lower arm are vertical (i.e., the robot is stretching up as far as it can), then again, no torque should be needed at the shoulder. Let us suppose that the simple arm of Figure 7.2 is holding an object of mass M in the hand and that the masses of the two arm components are MA for the upper arm and MB for the lower arm. Further, assume that the two arm components are uniform so that their centres of gravity are at their midpoints. This is illustrated in Figure 7.4.

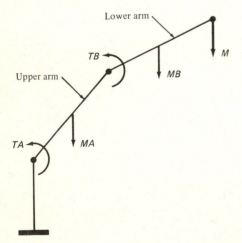

Figure 7.4   Torque needed to remain stationary.

TA is the torque that is required at the shoulder and *TB* is the torque that is required at the elbow. If the arm is stationary, then these two torques are given by the formulae

$$TB = MB * B * (\cos (a + b)/2) + M * B * \cos (a + b)$$
$$TA = (MA/2) * A * \cos (a)$$
$$+ MB * (A * \cos (a) + B * \cos (a + b)/2)$$
$$+ M * (A* \cos (a) + B * \cos (a + b))$$

If the arm is very light in comparison to its load, these formulae simplify to

$$TB = M * B * \cos (a + b)$$
$$TA = M * (A * \cos (a) + B * \cos (a + b))$$

Calculating the torques that are required for a more realistic robot can be very difficult, as can be imagined by trying to compute the torques that are required to keep a stick man in some fixed position.

Unfortunately, even if the calculations can be made, they will still be inaccurate. Maybe the weight of the hand isn't quite known exactly, maybe the position sensors are not exactly right, maybe the motors cannot generate exactly the requested torque. Since this "open-loop" control strategy won't work, the robot system must take account of the difference between the actual position and the desired position. This can be used to calculate an error term to add to the torques that are already computed. The simplest "closed-loop" strategy is to compute feedback for each joint separately; if the shoulder joint, say, is slightly off, then the torque at that joint is slightly altered, independent of the state of the other joints. This is a dubious strategy since the joints aren't independent—rotating the body will move the hand and a centripedal force will be needed to prevent the hand from flying outwards. This difficulty can be overcome to some extent by moving the arm only slowly.

We can illustrate the general problem by considering a simple arm with only one limb that we wish to keep horizontal but which is sagging *a* degrees. This is illustrated in Figure 7.5

Since the arm is sagging, the torque at the joint is obviously too small. We should increase it by some amount that is dependent on *a*—say, *G* * *a*, where *G* is described as the "gain factor." This will cause the arm to rise towards the desired position. Unfortunately, as it rises, the arm acquires momentum. Thus, when it reaches the desired position, its momentum will carry it farther than desired. By then, the error angle *a* will have become negative and the error

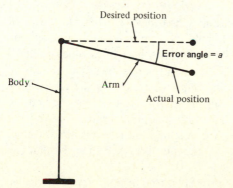

Figure 7.5   A sagging arm.

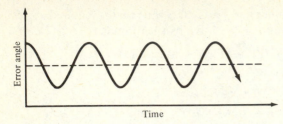

Figure 7.6   Oscillation in error angle.

feedback (i.e., $G * a$) will be pulling the arm downwards against the direction of its motion. Thus, the arm will oscillate as shown in Figure 7.6

Making the gain factor larger is no help. This will simply make the magnitude of the oscillations larger (indeed, if we make the gain factor sufficiently large, then the oscillations get larger and larger as time goes on). A partial solution is to introduce a "damping" term proportional to how fast the arm is moving. If the arm is already moving towards the desired position, the damping term reduces the amount of extra torque that is applied. Unfortunately, the robot arm (as described earlier) is not instrumented to tell the control system how fast it is moving, but only where it is; thus, the control system must test the position of the arm periodically (say, a hundred times a second) and subtract positions to get an idea of the arm's velocity. Worse still, the optimal values for the gain and damping factors depend on the configuration of the arm and what load it is carrying.

Unsurprisingly, many arm manufacturers dodge this issue. They may adopt the simplest solution of having unnecessarily massive motors that are capable of quick response and having a simple closed loop around each joint. If the motors are powerful enough, and the joints appropriately damped, this strategy will be enough to maintain the arm in a stationary position without any calculations at all. As computer power becomes cheaper relative to the cost of electric motors, we can expect more computationally expensive strategies to come into use. Let us hope this is soon—were I to be close to a robot carrying a bucket full of molten metal I would want to be sure that, if necessary, it could stand absolutely still whilst I got out of the way. If the calculation required for it to do this took several seconds, then in that time it might have already fallen over.

GETTING FROM *A* TO *B*

Our next problem is moving the hand from one position to another. The simplest way of accomplishing this is to use the mechanism that is used to hold the arm steady, but giving it the new desired position. The error term will be huge, so the motors will be told to generate large torques. The arm will wildly swing across to its new position and probably overshoot. The path taken by the arm and the time taken will be hard to predict. Suppose, for example, that the only difference (in joint space) between the initial position and the final position is that the body of the robot arm is swung around; all other joints maintain their position. Simply rotating the body, however, will cause the hand to traverse a *circular* arc. A similar situation is illustrated in Figure 7.7. A person would simultaneously bend and then unbend his or her elbow so that the hand would travel on a straight path.

Ideally, we should like to *choose* what trajectory the arm takes and at what speed it travels. Typically, we'd prefer the hand to move in a straight line in world coordinates, as opposed to a

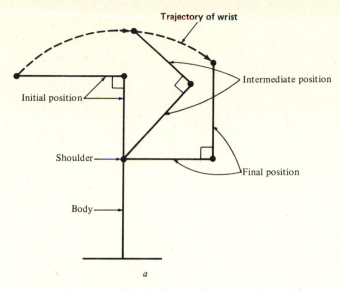

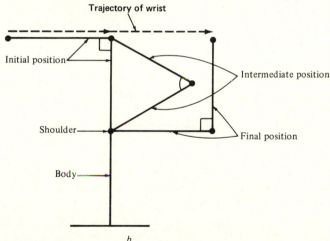

Figure 7.7   (*a*) In joint space: Only shoulder joint rotates; elbow
stays at 90°. (*b*) In world space: As shoulder rotates,
elbow closes and reopens.

straight line in joint coordinates. A straight line can be described with a simple formula; we may
describe a wanted trajectory with some simple formulae relating the cartesian positions of the
wrist (i.e., *x* and *y*) to the time (say, *t*), thus:

$$x(t) = x0 + xv * t$$
$$y(t) = y0 + yv * t$$

(*x*0 and *y*0 are the initial position of the wrist; *xv* and *yv* describe the desired velocity of the
wrist.) Unfortunately, the control system would prefer a trajectory in terms of *a* and *b* (the joint
angles) which are the only variables it can directly control. Transforming the formulae for *x*(*t*)

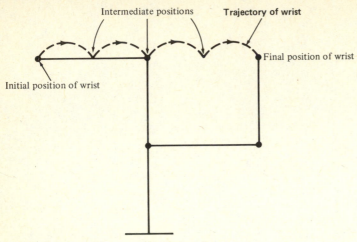

Figure 7.8   Breaking a trajectory into fragments.

and $y(t)$ into expressions for $a(t)$ and $b(t)$ is, in general, extremely difficult. One solution (described in Paul [1975]) is to break up the trajectory into many small sections (each, say, lasting a hundredth of a second); the x and y coordinates are computed for each instant and these are translated (using the static "world to joint" coordinate transformation described earlier) into joint coordinates. Between these positions, the arm is allowed to travel in a straight line in joint space. Since the positions are very close together, the overall effect is that we get a final trajectory that is close to the desired straight line in world coordinates. Figure 7.8 illustrates this for one example.

There are many constraints on trajectories; unless the motors are hugely overpowerful we will occasionally find that a desired trajectory requires more strength than our arm has. To achieve better control over the arm, we need to understand its dynamic behaviour. We should be able to compute the torques that are required, not just for maintaining a given position, but also for maintaining a given trajectory. The calculation is difficult and time consuming. Centrifugal forces and Coriolis forces can make the arm behave in strange ways. (Coriolis forces come from a moving body's "desire" to maintain its angular momentum; if the body of the robot is rotating and the arm is pulled in, then Coriolis forces will tend to make the body rotate faster to compensate for the smaller moment of inertia—an effect spectacularly exploited by ice-skaters.)

In the absence of a way of calculating the behaviour expeditiously, we must be extremely cautious. By making the motors powerful, and by moving the arm slowly, we will get by in most situations.

WHICH WAY TO GO

Working out a trajectory from one place to another is no simple matter. We need to avoid trying to pass the hand through the object being manipulated, for example. If two robots are working in close proximity, they must not collide. Someday we'll have robot control systems that can take a description of the arm itself (i.e., its shape) and of the objects in the environment and work out on their own how to get from one place to another.

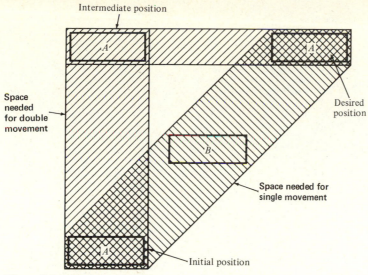

Figure 7.9   Space needed for movement as polygons.

One approach to solving this problem is based on viewing the world as a collection of polyhedra that move in straight lines. Although not all objects are polyhedral (e.g., spheres and cylinders) this simplification has several advantages:

- It is compact. A polyhedron can be described as being the volume that is contained by a number of planes (e.g., six planes for a cube, five for a pyramid) and a plane can be described in just four numbers.
- It is easy to determine whether two polyhedra overlap by using this representation.
- If a polyhedron moves in a straight line, then the volume it sweeps out is also a polyhedron. Thus, the control system need deal with only one type of shape (the polyhedron).

This is illustrated, in two dimensions, in Figure 7.9. The task is to move polygon *A* to the indicated desired position without hitting polygon *B*. By examining the polygonal area that is swept out by *A*, if it is moved straight to the goal position, we can see that it intersects with polygon *B*. Thus, we must make the move in two stages, as indicated. One problem with this account is that when a polyhedron is *rotated,* it does not sweep out a polyhedral volume. For an account of how to solve this and other problems see Lozano-Perez (1980).

GENTLY DOES IT

At present, almost all robot systems use position control. That is, the desired behaviour of the arm is described in terms of the positions it must pass through. However, many tasks cannot be described solely in terms of desired positions. Consider the task of opening a door; the robot hand could be directed to the door handle, told to grasp it, and then told to move along a circular arc in the horizontal plane. Suppose that the door hinges aren't perfectly vertical. The door handle will "want" to travel along a trajectory very close to a horizontal arc—but maybe not

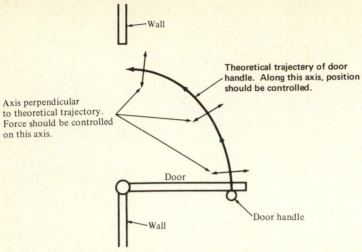

Figure 7.10 Theoretical trajectory of a door handle.

close enough to prevent the robot from pulling the door handle off the door. This is illustrated in Figure 7.10. Or again, consider the task of drawing a circle on a blackboard that is screwed to a supposedly vertical wall. There is a strong possibility that the robot might merely wave the chalk around in the air and miss the wall completely; it might try to drive the chalk into the wall if the blackboard is farther forward than expected. (If the robot's motors are powerful enough, it might even demolish the wall!)

Finding ways of describing such simple tasks is surprisingly hard. One recent line of research (Mason, 1979) suggests that for all tasks there is a "natural" coordinate system where the directions of the axes are defined by physical constraints and by the task itself. The robot hand must be controlled by a combination of position control (along the "task axes") and by force control (along the "physical constraint axes"). For the "door-opening" task, depicted in Figure 7.10, the natural coordinate system is one in which one axis is the circular arc upon which the door handle should travel; the second axis is vertical; and the third axis is horizontal and

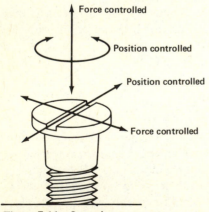

Figure 7.11 Inserting a screw.

perpendicular to the first two axes. The control system will be told to control the *position* along the circular arc (since this is a task axis) but minimize the *force* along the other two axes (since these are physical constraint axes). Figure 7.11 illustrates the axes for the task of using a screwdriver. One axis (a task axis and so position controlled) is a rotational axis about the length of the screwdriver; a second axis is perpendicular to the slot in the head of the screw (this is a physical constraint axis and force should be minimized); a third axis is parallel to the slot (this is a task constraint, the screwdriver is free to move along this axis so its position must be controlled); the fourth axis is along the length of the screwdriver (this is a physical constraint and the control system must maintain a slight positive pressure along this axis).

THE USER INTERFACE

How should the system appear to the user? A robot that can only be programmed by someone with a Ph.D. in computer science isn't a lot of use. One technique is to have a "teach" mode. The robot is manually controlled by use of a button box that directly drives the joints. The arm is manoeuvred through a series of positions, each of which is stored by the control system. The arm can then be told to replay the stored sequence of moves over and over again. Practically none of the problems previously described arise. The system need know about only joint coordinates. It need have only one way of moving from one position to another (say, joint interpolation). It's obvious as to why this approach is often employed in simple applications such as spray painting.

A better approach, embodied in the VAL language (Unimation, 1979), is to write programs to control the arm in an easy to use language. Perhaps because BASIC is so popular, VAL programs look a bit like BASIC. VAL allows the user to express positions in a variety of ways—in terms of joint coordinates, world coordinates, tool coordinates, or even in terms of user-defined coordinate systems. Conditional behaviour is much easier to express in a written language than with a teach mode. VAL also has a REACT statement, allowing the user to specify actions to be performed when some external event happens.

The ideal user interface to a robot system would be one with which we supply only a description of the objects to be manipulated and how they are to be assembled. Such descriptions are often already available in machine-readable form as the output of CAD systems. Systems such as RAPT (Popplestone, 1977) are the first steps towards programs that take declarative descriptions of some task and synthesize robot control programs by using techniques that are drawn from artificial intelligence research into automatic problem solving and automatic programming.

CONCLUSIONS

Usually, we associate automation in the factory with mass production. Conventional automatic machines are usually specific to one (generally repetitive) task. Thus, they are suitable only for long production runs where the high initial cost of the machinery can be recouped over a considerable period of time. The inherent flexibility of *programmable* robots offers the promise of production lines that are not tied to any particular product but which can be converted to producing new products very rapidly. However, this has not happened; robot systems are *not* used for very short production runs. Typical of most industrial applications of robotics are tasks in the motor industry where robots are programmed to perform some simple repetitive task (like spot welding or spray painting) and then continue to perform that task day in and day out.

Those familiar with the history of research into artificial intelligence will recognize this pattern. Many branches of AI have started with hopes that very rapidly a high degree of competence would be achieved. These hopes have been dashed as researchers realised that there were many different theoretical problems needing solution. Once the initial euphoria has died down, sustained research will slowly come to grips with the problem. Machine translation (MT) is the paradigmatic example of this. Only now, more than twenty years after the first MT projects are we seeing the first practical applications of natural language understanding programs.

In this chapter, I have outlined some of the theoretical problems that must be solved before we will have truly flexible automation systems. Current research, however, is more at the stage of identifying problems than solving them. Inadequate solutions to deep theoretical problems are deeply embedded in the crude control systems for most commercial robot systems; this makes them unsuitable for research use and suitable only for simple repetitive tasks in industry. With sustained research, gradual improvements can be expected, but it will be a long time before robots make human labour unnecessary.

Annotated Bibliography

Brady, M., and Hollerbach, J. *Robot Motion: Planning and Control*. MIT Press Series in AI. Cambridge, Mass.: MIT Press, 1982.

This book contains a valuable collection of articles describing current research problems in robot control systems. Some basic issues are also covered. This book is the recommended next reading after this chapter. Short versions of some of the articles cited in this bibliography are in this collection.

Feldman, J. AL: A Programming System for Automation. Technical Report No. AIM-243. Stanford, Calif.: AI Lab, Stanford University, 1973.

AL is a high-level programming language for describing robot assembly tasks. It includes unusual facilities such as the ability to *simulate* the operation of a control program and check for problems such as collisions between the robot and the work place. Not only is simulation much safer than using the actual robot, it is also much faster, allowing control programs to be developed "off line."

Lozano-Perez, T. Spatial planning with polyhedral models. Ph.D. thesis. Cambridge, Mass.: MIT AI Lab., 1980.

This Ph.D. thesis describes the advantages of considering all objects as polyhedral for the purposes of trajectory planning. The necessary algorithms are given in detail in LISP.

Lozano-Perez, T. Robotics. *Artificial Intelligence* 19(2): 1982.

A short (six-page) summary of key issues with a useful annotated bibliography of readily accessible papers on the issues discussed in this chapter.

Mason, M. T. Compliance and Force Control for Computer Controlled Manipulators. Technical Report No. TR-515. Cambridge, Mass.: MIT AI Lab., 1979.

This Ph.D. thesis is concerned with the theory underlying compliant motion and describes the concept of "task defined" and "physically defined" axes that are, respectively, position and force controlled.

Nevins, J. L., and Whitney, D. E. Research on Advanced Assembly Automation. Charles Stark Draper Laboratory, 1977.

This paper is mostly concerned with the problem of compliant motion. It includes a description of the "remote centre compliance" wrist assembly. This device makes it much easier to insert a peg into a hole—a classic robot assembly problem. It is an example of a "passive" compliance device. The wrist is attached to the robot arm with a collection of springs; only the *position* of the arm is controlled directly—the springs "control" the compliance of the object being manipulated.

Paul, R. B. Manipulator path control. In *Proceedings, 1975 International Conference on Cybernetics and Society*. New York: IEEE.

This paper describes how, by breaking a trajectory into fragments, we can eliminate the need for transforming the description of some trajectory from some world-oriented coordinate system to a joint-coordinate system.

Paul, R. B. *Robot Manipulators: Mathematics, Programming and Control*. Cambridge, Mass.: MIT Press, 1981.

An introduction to the theoretical issues underlying robot control systems.

Popplestone, R. A Language for Specifying Robot Assembly. Research Report 29. Edinburgh: Department of AI, University of Edinburgh, 1977.

This is an early paper describing the RAPT project at Edinburgh. Robot assembly tasks are described in a declarative language, based on predicate logic. RAPT, part compiler and part problem solver, translates this description into low-level instructions for controlling the robot arm.

Unimation, Inc. *User's Guide to VAL*. Danbury, Conn., 1979.

This document describes how to use the VAL robot control langauge. VAL allows the user to write programs in terms of either joint coordinates or a user-defined cartesian frame of reference. VAL also has a "teach" mode for creating programs by manually moving the arm through a sequence of moves. Thus, VAL is a good working compromise between practicality and theoretical power.

Waters, R. Mechanical Arm Control. Technical Report No. AIM-549. Cambridge, Mass.: MIT AI Lab., 1979.

This paper provides an enormously valuable summary of solutions of three classic robot control problems: (1) How to map between coordinate systems, (2) calculation of detailed trajectories, and (3) calculation of forces. Emphasis is given to ways of speeding up these calculations. Readers should be competent programmers and applied mathematicians.

Winston, P., and Brown, R. (Eds.). *Artificial Intelligence: An MIT Perspective, Vol. II*. MIT Press Series in AI. Cambridge, Mass.: MIT Press, 1979.

The second section of this volume contains four papers on robotics. Of special interest is a paper by T. Lozano-Perez describing the LAMA language for giving high-level descriptions of robot assembly tasks.

CHAPTER 8

KINEMATIC AND GEOMETRIC STRUCTURE IN ROBOT SYSTEMS

JOE ROONEY

ROBOTICS AND MANIPULATION

The word *robot* was introduced originally by Capek (1923) in his play *R.U.R.* (Rossum's Universal Robots)—a satire on mechanised civilisation. This described humanoid machines, manufactured to provide humankind with a "race" of worker slaves, capable of performing a wide variety of tedious tasks without complaint, in manual, clerical, or domestic environments. In the play, the word is used in the sense of "worker" (indeed, it is derived from the Czech word *robotit* meaning *to drudge*), which is very close to the sense in which we would use it today.

Historically, the concept of an autonomous machine arose repeatedly as a theme, although it was usually associated with toys, magic, fantasy, or entertainment, rather than with a practical purpose (Reichardt, 1978). Furthermore, the idea has often been used as a symbol or metaphor. Thus, many works of fiction deal with the state and/or progress of a society (or the lack of it) in terms of such machines. Capek's *R.U.R.* (1923) and Butler's *Erewhon* (1872) are clearly in this category. More recently, the possible capabilities and shortcomings of the machines themselves have been explored. Most notably in this area has been the work of the science fiction writer, Asimov, who first coined the word *robotics* and who devised three (albeit rather primitively expressed) rules of robot conduct—*the three laws of robotics*. These can be found in his collection of robot short stories, *I, Robot* (Asimov, 1950).

The exploitation of an autonomous or semiautonomous machine in an industrial environment is a relatively recent phenomenon. In particular, the development of the modern industrial robot was based initially on two postwar technologies—namely, the NC machine tool, used in manufacturing industry, and the master-slave manipulator, used for handling radioactive materials. Since then, there have been rapid advances and today the industrial robot is able to perform a wide range of tasks in various types of environments as outlined in Chapter 12 (see also, Engelberger [1980]). As a result, the field of robotics is now beginning to attract considerable support, both within and outside the manufacturing context.

Ostensibly, a true robot system would be the archetypal intelligent machine, interacting with its environment in a purposive, adaptive, and "intelligent" manner. As yet, no such system exists. Instead, the traditional approach to robotics in artificial intelligence work usually centres on an investigation of the capabilities of "abstract" robot systems, without much regard to their physical implementation. Essentially, the problem of designing or operating this type of "paper" robot then reduces to one or more particular examples of problem solving, pattern recognition, strategic planning, and so on, where we seek to determine what type of behaviour is *logically* possible. Thus, it has been proved that paper robots can (in theory) be self-organising, self-repairing, and self-reproducing. But again, progress has been slow in the physical implementation of such ideas.

In contrast to the AI and cybernetic approaches, the approach to robotics in industry has generally been much more pragmatic and mundane, so that, as yet, only very primitive systems have evolved. Nevertheless, these have now reached a level of operational sophistication and reliability, high enough to allow them to be used routinely on the shop floor. In the near future it is expected that "relevant" AI techniques and ideas will be introduced into industrial robot systems to enhance their basic capabilities and improve their adaptability to changing environmental circumstances.

Let us now take a closer look at the subject of robotics. First of all, it should be noted that the application areas for robot systems are wide ranging, both inside and outside the industrial context. They can be (and are) used to replace men in hazardous, remote, or monotonous environments. In manufacturing industries typical applications include: welding, component assembly, and paint spraying. Outside industry, recent application areas are: underwater exploration and welding; bomb disposal; mining; handling of radioactive, chemical, or biological material; planetary surface investigation; artificial-limb replacement; and so on. At present, these systems do not exhibit a high degree of autonomy (with the exception of the planetary probes) and, in fact, are often controlled remotely by human operators. Nevertheless, it is valid to refer to them as robot systems because they possess many of the attributes (albeit in a primitive form) that are associated with robots. What are these attributes?

One of the chief distinguishing features of a robot system is that it be capable of physically processing the external real world in addition to its information-processing abilities. It is, therefore, more than just a realisation of a Turing Machine, because we must take account of the range of *physical* possibilities as well as the range of logical possibilities in its design and operation. In a robot system we are more interested in what it is possible to *do,* and in what it is possible to *make,* rather than just in what it is possible to *compute.* (We might refer to such a system as a Manufac—Turing Machine!)

At the very least a robot design should incorporate the following subsystems:

- *receptors* (sensors, etc.) for abstracting information from the environment (or from itself)
- *effectors* (actuators, etc.) for implementing a course of action

- *controllers* and *processors* for interpreting input information and generating output strategies
- *memories* and *registers* for storing data and information structures, procedures, and plans of action

Furthermore, the operation of a robot system should involve at least the following functional areas:

- manipulation/locomotion
- sensing/perception
- command/control
- representation/modelling

This chapter examines the structure of some of these subsystems and functional areas. In particular, it concentrates mainly on manipulation and its associated manipulator systems, since this is perhaps the least developed area in artificial intelligence work.

If you find it surprising that manipulation should be a topic in AI, then just consider the two most often quoted attributes that distinguish humans as intelligent beings—namely, their "linguistic ability" and their "manual dexterity." Without the former, their reasoning powers and communication skills would be greatly impaired, if not eliminated; without the latter, their technology would have been a nonstarter, and painting, sculpture, instrumental music, and dance would not exist.

The subject of manipulation has three main aspects. (1) It is concerned with the shape, symmetry, location, orientation, and motion of individual physical objects, together with their spatial and temporal interrelationships. (2) It is concerned with the procedures that are required to construct or change these properties. (3) It is concerned with the physical design of the manipulator systems that are necessary to implement the procedures. Therefore, it involves many different ideas and techniques from various types of geometry and from kinematics. In this chapter we will restrict ourselves to a discussion of some of these aspects, with particular emphasis on the design of robot manipulator systems.

STRUCTURE IN ROBOTICS

The design of a robot system naturally involves many different factors. These include the nature of the physical objects, properties or attributes to be processed; the required degree of interaction (or experimentation) of the system with the objects and the environment; and the level of sophistication of the system and its techniques for evaluating input information and implementing output strategies. However, one of the more important factors determining the design is the *structure* of the system. This is primarily concerned with the shapes, positions, orientations, interconnections and juxtapositions of the subsystems and components. It is sensible to base the design on a proper understanding of the range of theoretically possible structures. This chapter examines some of these, particularly kinematic and geometric structures.

Kinematics is concerned primarily with the *motion* of the manipulator systems. Since motion is perceived as a continuous change of position in space within a certain interval of time, it is not surprising that all physical objects and systems exhibit some kinematic behaviour as they move, change shape, or evolve. (Of course, the kinematic aspects may be irrelevant in a particular situation, or their effects may be relatively insignificant.) For the purposes of robot manipulation, the aim is to investigate how to arrange and interconnect various types of kinematic components so as to produce manipulator systems that can transmit, control, or constrain relative motions. This is what is meant by *kinematic structure*. In particular, we often seek to determine those mechanical arrangements that allow the system to have a certain type of motion (say, parallel to a given plane) and to exhibit a definite amount of freedom of motion (referred to as *degrees of freedom*).

As an illustration, suppose a kinematic system is to be designed as a component subsystem in a manipulator configuration so that it has just *one* degree of freedom of motion. (The complete manipulator requires at least *six* degrees of freedom in order to operate in three-dimensional space.) This means that its motion is to be completely determined by a single input variable (such as the angular displacement of one motor shaft). How many "distinct" systems are possible and what structure do they have?

Clearly, the number of possible kinematic arrangements is unlimited, but if we impose some restrictions on the type and size of the system, we can reduce the possibilities to a small finite set. For example, with the following six physical conditions imposed, there are only nineteen essentially distinct systems (see Fig. 8.1):

- The system should be a *planar kinematic system* so that all components move in parallel planes.
- The joints should all be of the same type (say, pin-joints) and should each connect only two components together.
- The system, at most, should have eight components (links).
- The system should be kinematically *closed loop* so that disconnecting any one joint will not separate the system into two parts.
- The system should not have a *separating* component whose removal would separate the system into two parts.
- No connected subsystem consisting of two or more components should have zero degrees of freedom (i.e., is immobile).

In general, these conditions would be too restrictive for manipulator components and subsystems. Thus, for example, one usually requires that the system have more than one degree of freedom, that it be *spatial* (rather than planar), and that the joints be of more than one type (say, rotational pin-joints and translational hydraulic rams). Furthermore, many existing systems are kinematically *open-loop* systems, in that they consist of a serial arrangement of links and joints that are similar to a human arm (e.g., the PUMA robot is of this type). Alternatively, they may have subsystems of this type, and in general, they will contain a total of more than eight component links. Nevertheless, the preceding conditions do provide a relatively simple introduction to the relevant concepts at this stage. The resulting nineteen systems satisfying these constraints are illustrated schematically in Figure 8.1. Notice that some of the conditions are conditions on the organisation and interconnection of component parts, which are

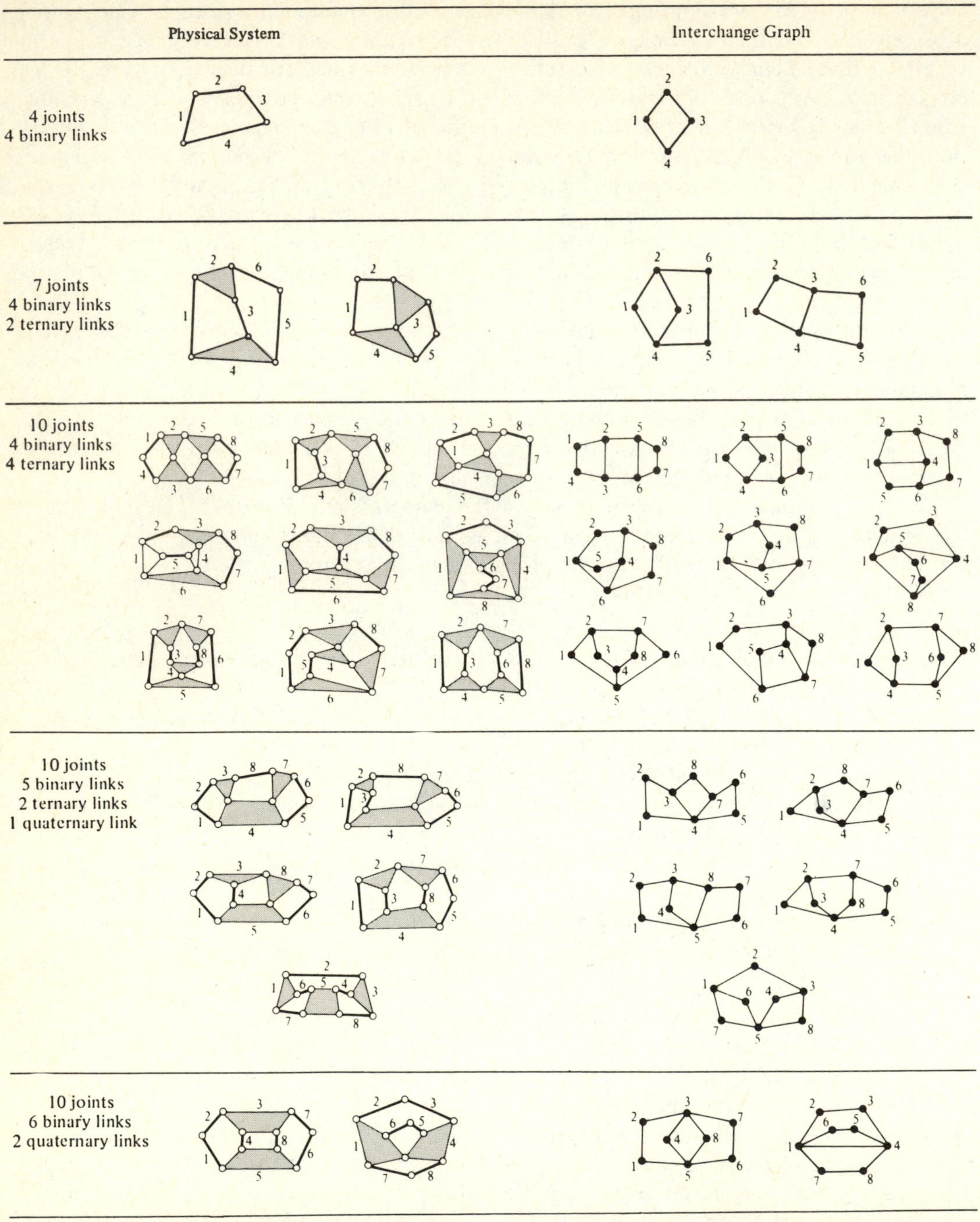

Figure 8.1 The nineteen possible one-degree-of-freedom planar kinematic systems imposed restrictions on connectedness, and so on. (*Source:* Open University course TM361: Graphs Networks and Design—Unit 10, p. 58.)

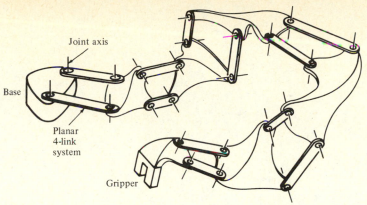

Figure 8.2 A six-degree-of freedom spatial kinematic system, constructed from six one-degree-of-freedom planar kinematic systems.

best expressed using a *graph* representation. In Figure 8.1 each system is shown with its corresponding *interchange graph* (in which the vertices represent the component links and the edges represent the joints). This is useful in the description and construction of possible kinematic systems and in their classification.

Despite the fact that these kinematic systems are of a very special type (i.e., one degree of freedom, planar systems, etc.) they do offer certain potential advantages, to the designer, over more complicated arrangements. Thus, for example, we may consider constructing a six-degree-of-freedom spatial system by connecting six one-degree-of-freedom planar systems in series (Fig. 8.2). In fact, several so-called "parallelogram" manipulators are of this type since they consist mainly of a serial arrangement of four-link planar parallelogram kinematic systems (e.g., the articulated "set-square" mechanism found on a draughtsman's drawing board and shown in Fig. 8.3). These are sometimes easier to design and have the advantage of allowing each degree of freedom to operate independently without disturbing the orientation of the

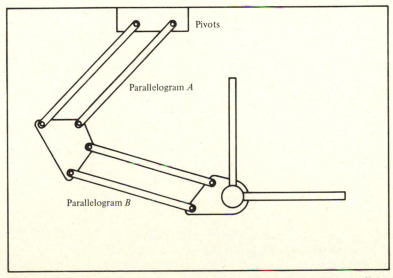

Figure 8.3 Draughtsman's articulated set-square mechanism—a parallelogram manipulator.

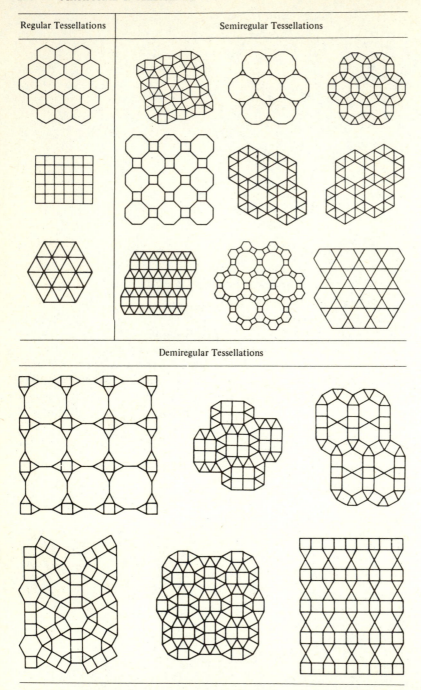

Regular Tessellations

Semiregular Tessellations

Demiregular Tessellations

Figure 8.4 Regular, semiregular, and demiregular planar tessellations. (*Source:* Pearce, *Structure in Nature Is a Strategy for Design.* Cambridge, Mass., MIT Press.)

gripper (or set-square in the case of the draughting instrument). However, they do not usually allow sufficient design flexibility in that such arrangements restrict the dexterity of the system because they are inherently planar, so we must consider more general, truly spatial, systems.

We now briefly discuss *geometric structure*. In the present context this is concerned primarily with the precise shapes, sizes, positions and orientations of objects in space. The latter may be the component links of a manipulator, or the workpieces themselves, but we choose a different example, taken from a sensing system rather than from a manipulation system. Thus, suppose we seek to design a vision sensor or a tactile sensor. At present, such systems contain arrays or grids of similar components that are sensitive to light or to physical contact. The precise shapes and arrangements of these *pixels* (or "tactiles") are clearly important parameters in the design and operation of the sensor.

As an illustration, suppose we seek arrangements that possess a high degree of "regularity" or symmetry and which consist of arrays of a single type, or a small number of types, of component. These are reasonable conditions to impose in that they should facilitate the design and operation (i.e., scanning patterns, etc.) of the device. How many "distinct" arrangements are possible?

As in the case of the kinematic systems, the number of possible geometric arrangements for such a sensor is unlimited, but we illustrate a small set of possibilities in Figure 8.4. These are essentially the three *regular* plane tessellations (consisting of congruent regular polygons of a single type in edge-to-edge contact); the nine *semiregular* plane tessellations (consisting of congruent regular polygons of more than one type in edge-to-edge contact, with the same arrangement of polygons meeting at each vertex); and a selection from the infinite number of possible *demiregular* tessellations (consisting of congruent regular polygons of more than one type in edge-to-edge contact, but in which there are two or more types of arrangements of polygons meeting at a vertex). Obviously, we have severely restricted the possibilities by constraining the pixels to have regular convex polygonal shapes and the arrangements to those in which polygons share only complete edges without overlapping, and so on. Nevertheless, many of these arrangements offer potential advantages to the designer.

For instance, the regular hexagonal array has every pair of adjacent pixels sharing a common edge, whereas in a more conventional square (or rectangular) array, diagonally juxtaposed pixels share only a common vertex (Fig. 8.5). This can be useful in interconnecting pixels and in reducing extraneous effects on the discretised image that are caused by rotation of the pixel plane about the line of sight. Additional advantages are offered by the semiregular arrange-

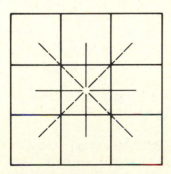

Edge adjacency = 4

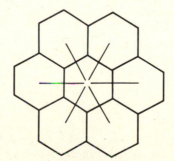

Edge adjacency = 6

Figure 8.5 Comparison of adjacency for square array and hexagonal array of pixels.

ments since these provide two or more different pixel types that may be useful for configurations in which each pixel has one or more adjacent local memory stores or in which each pixel has an associated detector of motion/contrast/a particular colour, and so on. However, in general, we must consider more complicated systems such as rectangular dissections, nonregular tessellations, and nonconvex pixels in order to obtain sufficient design flexibility.

So far we have looked briefly at two areas in which structure plays an important role (namely, the kinematic structure of manipulator systems and the geometric structure of sensor systems) and we considered relatively simple examples. In any real system the structure can be considerably more complicated than in these examples, but they illustrate the main features. In particular, notice that any complexity in the system arises in two main forms: (1) *The individual component parts may have a complex shape and/or structure* and (2) *The components may be organised or interconnected in a complex arrangement.* Both aspects concern us here and we now examine kinematic structure from this viewpoint.

KINEMATIC ELEMENTS AND ARRANGEMENTS

In a robot system the task of the manipulator is usually either to locate an external object in position (such as a component in a subassembly, or a welding gun, etc.) or to move that object from position A to position B in a definite sequence of motions (perhaps along a specified path at a specified rate, etc.). Ideally, the manipulator system should satisfy two basic requirements:

- the ability to *grasp* arbitrarily shaped objects and temporarily hold them stationary without disturbing their initial positions and orientations
- the ability to *displace* objects in 3D space from one arbitrary position and orientation to another

These requirements are difficult (if not impossible) to satisfy in practice. The first demands the existence of a *general-purpose* gripper or hand, which can grasp an object regardless of its shape, size, mass, flexibility, or surface texture. The second demands the existence of a *general-purpose* manipulator arm, which can reach every position with every possible orientation (including those inside itself), regardless of how near or far it is, or of what obstructions may be present.

Most existing systems do not attempt to achieve such generality, and so they usually avoid these problems. For example, many current designs incorporate special-purpose grippers for handling particular sizes and shapes of objects, such as cuboids, cylinders, and so on (Fig. 8.6). These are often restricted in their degrees of freedom and ranges of motion, as are many manipulator arms. Furthermore, all these systems are designed to operate within a finite workspace and have a limited amount of dexterity in avoiding obstacles, reaching into confined spaces, or maintaining their full quota of degrees of freedom throughout all parts of that workspace.

At present there are four main kinematic types of robot manipulators that are classified according to relatively crude criteria. The four classes are designated as *cartesian, cylindrical, spherical polar,* and *articulated,* depending on the gross characteristics of the associated workspaces (Fig. 8.7). The articulated type is the more general arrangement, but in fact, all

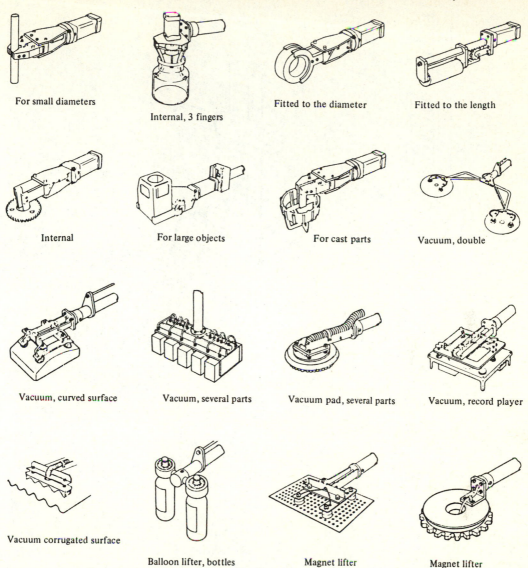

For small diameters

Internal, 3 fingers

Fitted to the diameter

Fitted to the length

Internal

For large objects

For cast parts

Vacuum, double

Vacuum, curved surface

Vacuum, several parts

Vacuum pad, several parts

Vacuum, record player

Vacuum corrugated surface

Balloon lifter, bottles

Magnet lifter

Magnet lifter

Figure 8.6   Examples of special-purpose robot grippers. (*Source:* G. Lundström, L. Lundström, and A. Arnström, *Industrial Robots—A Survey*. Bedford, England, International Fluidics Services, 1972, p. 10.)

four types are essentially anthropomorphic arrangements, with their actuated joints arranged in series. They also usually have very special geometry, with adjacent joint axes that are parallel or intersecting in groups (at a "wrist" joint, e.g.) and where there are few, if any, offsets between adjacent links in the systems. Thus, most existing manipulator designs tend to be variations on a few well-tried kinematic themes rather than radically new types of systems.

However, recently several novel types of kinematic designs have been investigated in detail. Thus, Hunt (1982) has examined various geometric arrangements for in-parallel-actuated

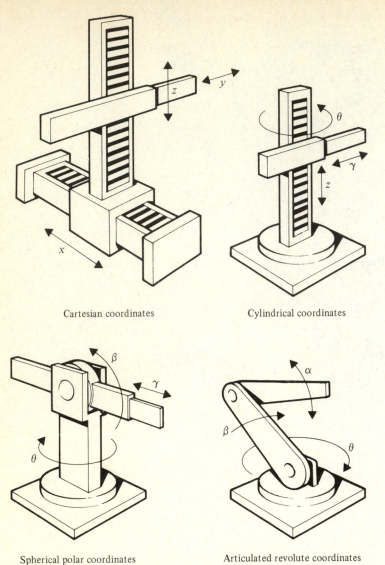

Cartesian coordinates

Cylindrical coordinates

Spherical polar coordinates

Articulated revolute coordinates

Figure 8.7 Four "kinematic types" of robot manipulators. (*Source:*
J. F. Engelberger, *Robotics in Practice*. London, Kogan
Page, 1980, p. 31.)

manipulators and has outlined the principles involved in their kinematic design. Many of these
are based on the flight-simulator system (Fig. 8.8) and are decidedly nonanthropomorphic.
Such systems have multiloop kinematic structures and these latter have been analysed in
general by Earl and Rooney (1982) for the purpose of generating new manipulator designs (Fig.
8.9).

The kinematic structure of a robot manipulator has two main aspects—namely, the
kinematic elements and their *kinematic arrangement*. The former refers to the types of
components that are present in the system, whereas the latter refers to how these are organised.
We restrict our attention to the rigid components of a manipulator system and ignore the

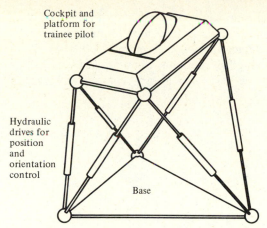

Cockpit and
platform for
trainee pilot

Hydraulic
drives for
position
and
orientation
control

Base

Figure 8.8   The Stewart platform flight-simulator system.

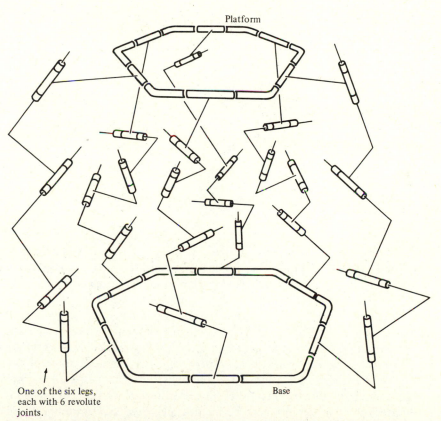

Platform

One of the six legs,
each with 6 revolute
joints.

Base

Figure 8.9   Multiloop kinematic system with more general nonanthropomorphic type and arrangement of joints than in the Stewart platform.

flexible, fluid, or electrical subsystems. The basic, rigid component elements are then referred to as *kinematic links* or simply, *links* (think of the links of a chain). Similarly the basic interconnections between links are referred to as *kinematic joints* or, simply, *joints*. Thus, the pedestal, "upper arm," "forearm," and gripper "fingers" represent examples of the links in a typical robot-manipulator system, whereas the "waist," "shoulder," "elbow," and "wrist" represent obvious examples of the joints (Fig. 8.10).

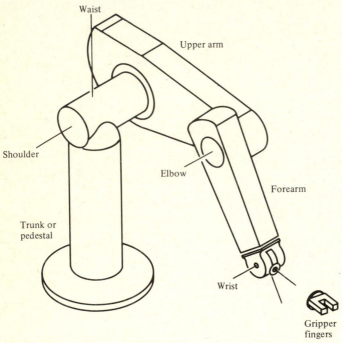

Figure 8.10 The links and joints of a typical industrial robot manipulator.

What types of links are possible in more general designs? If we ignore the detailed geometry of a link, then we may classify a link simply by the number of joints associated with it. Thus, a terminal link (in an open-loop manipulator), such as the pedestal or the gripper (treated as a single link), is a *unary link*, since it is connected to only one other link via a single joint. The intermediate links (in an open-loop manipulator), such as the "upper arm" and "lower arm," however, are *binary* links, since they have two joints associated with them (one on each end). Continuing in this way, we may define *ternary, quaternary,* and, in general *r-ary links* which have three, four, and *r* joints associated with them, respectively. For example, some of the "polar-coordinate" types of robot (Fig. 8.7) contain ternary links, whereas the parallelogram types (Fig. 8.2) usually contain quaternary links. We illustrate the various types of link in a simple sequence in Figure 8.11. For completeness we include a *nullary link* (one having no joints associated with it). We depict the links schematically by using open circles to denote potential joints and also illustrate some of the alternative geometric forms (unlimited in number) that each link can take.

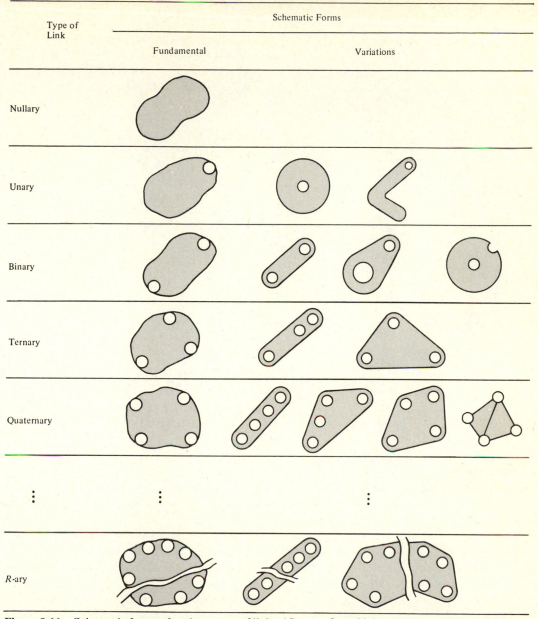

Figure 8.11   Schematic forms of various types of links. (*Source:* Open University course TM361: Graphs Networks and Design—Unit 10, p. 10.)

Notice that the fundamental schematic form for each particular type of link represents an irregularly shaped body, with the potential sites for joint connections conveniently located around the perimeter. In particular cases the joints can be of different types, have different sizes and shapes, and be distributed in a more organised way, such as along a straight strip. In this respect, it is not entirely accidental that the variations of form resemble "Meccano-like"

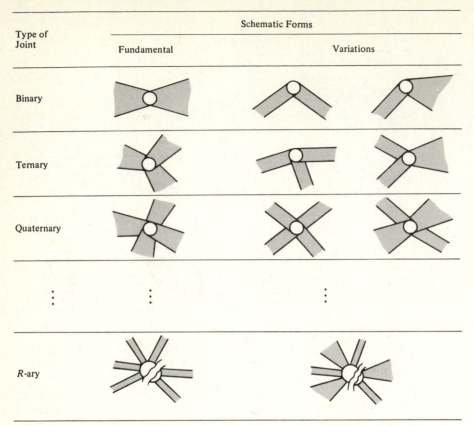

Figure 8.12   Schematic forms of various types of joints. (*Source:* Open University course TM361: Graphs, Networks and Design—Unit 10, p. 11.)

components, although for links with four or more joints we can obtain solid polyhedral arrangements in addition to the familiar "strip" and "plate" types. In all cases the detailed shape is of secondary importance at this stage, since we are interested only in the *number, type,* and *arrangement* of joints on each link.

We now look in more detail at the concept of a *joint*. So far we have defined a joint as a connection between links but have said little about the nature of this connection. Of course, we have implicitly assumed that the joint allows relative motion to take place between the links, so that we exclude from the outset such things as welds, glued joints, or rigidly bolted connections. The mobile types of joints may be classified in a scheme that is analogous to that for links. We again ignore, for the moment, the nature and detailed geometry of a joint and classify it simply by the number of links associated with it. Thus, a *binary joint* connects two links together, a *ternary joint* connects three links, and, in general an *r-ary joint* connects *r* links. We illustrate these types schematically in Figure 8.12. Notice that nullary joints and unary joints do not occur, because, in practice, these are meaningless: A joint must connect at least two links together.

The fundamental schematic form of each particular type of joint represents a site where the appropriate number of links are connected together. In general, each of the links meeting at the joint can be of any type (unary, binary, ternary, ..., r-ary), which has been indicated by not specifying the shape of the shaded areas. In particular cases all sorts of different types and shapes of links can meet at the joint, such as binary (or r-ary) strips, ternary (or r-ary) plates, or polyhedral solids, joined at their vertices or edges. We indicate this in Figure 8.12 by giving the variations of schematic form.

Now we have previously defined an r-ary link as one having r joints associated with it, but this can lead to difficulties if these joints are themselves multiple joints (i.e., not binary joints). It is often more convenient to define the r-ary link as one that is connected to r other links. However, if all the joints are binary joints, then these two definitions of r-ary links are equivalent. Henceforth we will restrict our attention primarily to binary joints. This can be justified by the fact that, in practice, an r-ary joint can be regarded (in several different ways) as consisting of $r - 1$ binary joints.

A kinematic system consists of various kinematic links that are interconnected by various types of kinematic joint. So far we have examined the basic elements (r-ary links and r-ary joints) but have not as yet discussed the possible kinematic arrangements that are constructed from these elements. For example, how many systems is it possible to construct by using just four links and allowing only binary joints? If we ignore the geometrical aspects and consider just the "topological" arrangements, then it is possible to form six different connected systems. These are illustrated in Figure 8.13 and they contain several types of links (ranging from unary to ternary) and various numbers of joints (ranging from 3 to 6).

Notice that two arrangements are *open-loop,* two are *single-loop,* and the remaining two are *multiloop* kinematic systems. Furthermore, one of the open-loop arrangements has three branches and one of the single-loop systems has a loop and a branch, so the six systems are quite distinct topologically. Therefore, each of them has a different *kinematic structure.* This can be represented by using graph theoretic concepts (Berge, 1977) and techniques, where an r-ary link is modelled by a vertex of degree r and a binary joint is modelled by an edge joining the two appropriate vertices. We will return to this representation in the final section of the chapter.

Physically, there are many possible types of binary joints, of all shapes, sizes, and designs, but so far we have ignored these aspects. How many fundamentally different designs are possible? In the nineteenth century the German kinematician Franz Reuleaux (1876) investigated binary joints in his attempts to derive a classification scheme for machines. He distinguished two basic types of binary joints, which he referred to as *higher kinematic pairs* and *lower kinematic pairs.* (He used the term pair for a binary joint to indicate that only *two* bodies or links are involved in the joint.)

His classification depends on how the two links make contact. Thus, if they are in *point contact* or *line contact* the binary joint would be a higher pair, whereas a *surface contact* gives rise to a lower pair. Examples of point contact are: a pencil point, in the act of drawing on a sheet of paper, or a compass point, placed at the centre of a circle to be drawn.

Line contact occurs when a cylinder rolls on a plane, for example, and is commonly found in many machines—a cam and tappet (a single straight line of contact), two simple gear wheels meshing (a single straight line), a railway locomotive wheel in contact with the track (a single straight line), or a piston ring in contact with its cylinder wall (a circle of contact). These examples are illustrated in Figure 8.14.

Surface contact naturally occurs when the two links share part or all of one or more common surfaces. Typical examples are provided by many everyday "machines" such as a wheel and its axle, or the three kinds of door-hinge systems shown in Figure 8.15. Notice that the surfaces

Interchange Graph	Corresponding System

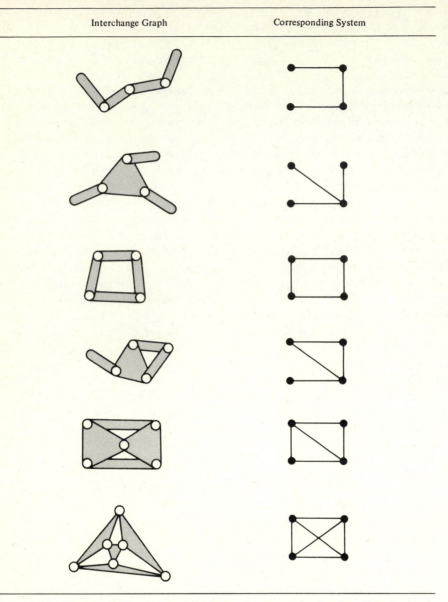

Figure 8.13   The six distinct connected kinematic systems having four links and only binary joints. Their interchange graphs are also shown. (*Source:* Open University course TM361: Graphs, Networks and Design—Unit 10, p. 26.)

remain in contact throughout the relative motion, although the particular segment of surface that is common to both bodies (links) may change. Also, notice that since no object is perfectly rigid, *exact* point or line contact can never occur in practice, so that all binary joints have surface contact on a small enough scale. (i.e., there will always be a small "contact patch").

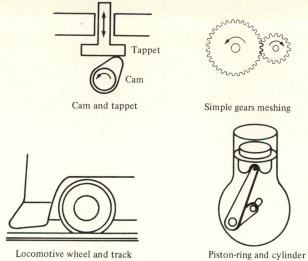

Cam and tappet   Simple gears meshing

Locomotive wheel and track   Piston-ring and cylinder

Figure 8.14   Examples of line contact between pairs of components.

We may summarise Reuleaux's classification as follows:

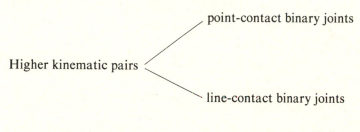

Of the two types of pairs, the lower pairs are the more interesting in the present context. Indeed, much of the history and evolution of machines has been devoted to the development of lower

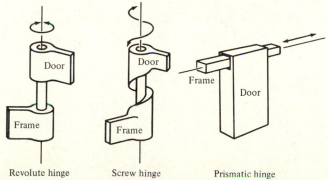

Revolute hinge   Screw hinge   Prismatic hinge

Figure 8.15   The three types of door-hinges having surface contact between the two links.

pairs, whereas more primitive machines tend to involve many simple higher pairs. We concentrate mainly on lower pairs.

Reuleaux defined just six different lower pairs (Fig. 8.16) having surface contact and these are:

1. the *revolute* pair
2. the *screw* pair
3. the *prismatic* pair
4. the *cylindric* pair
5. the *spherical* pair
6. the *planar* pair

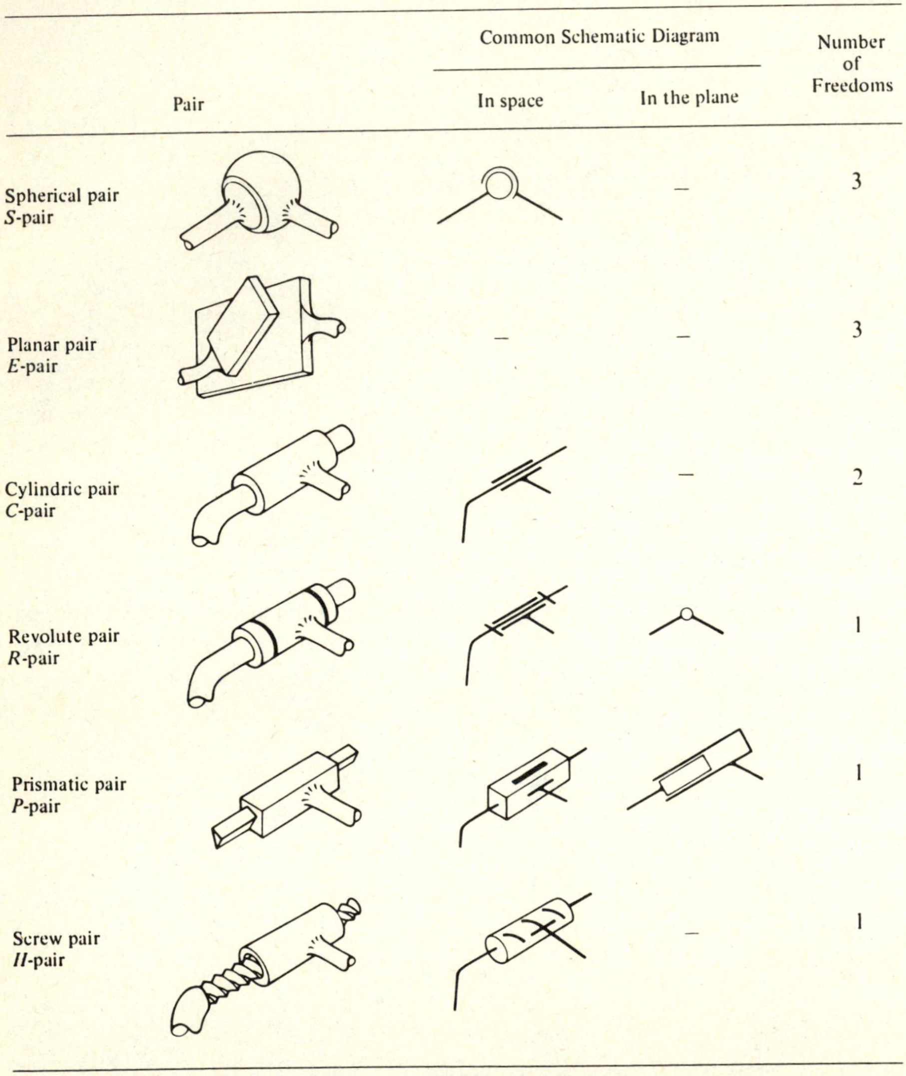

Pair	Common Schematic Diagram		Number of Freedoms
	In space	In the plane	
Spherical pair S-pair		—	3
Planar pair E-pair	—	—	3
Cylindric pair C-pair		—	2
Revolute pair R-pair			1
Prismatic pair P-pair			1
Screw pair II-pair		—	1

Figure 8.16 Reuleaux's six lower kinematic pairs. (*Source:* K. H. Hunt, *Kinematic Geometry of Mechanisms.* Oxford, Clarendon Press, 1978, p. 8.)

We have already seen examples of the first three in the guise of the three types of door hinges. The remaining three are also commonly found in most machinery. A simple example of a cylindric pair is provided by a bolt mechanism that is used to lock a door, where the bolt can both *slide* and *rotate* so that the contact surfaces are portions of circular cylinders. Similarly, the ball joint found on car-suspension systems or on rearview mirrors is a common example of a spherical pair. Here the ball and socket are in contact over a portion of the surface of a sphere. Finally, an example of a planar pair is provided by, say, an orbital sander and a work surface, where the surface of contact is a plane.

Reuleaux's six lower pairs are the most important surface-contact binary joints and all other types can be derived from them. In fact, it is even possible to derive all six pairs from just one fundamental one—the screw pair. To see how this is done, we must consider the relative motions involved in a kinematic pair, since this is essentially what distinguishes the six types from one another.

In Figure 8.16 we have illustrated the six lower pairs in schematic form. The revolute, prismatic, and screw pairs each have one degree of freedom associated with them, which means that the relative displacement of the two links involved in the pair is specified in terms of a single parameter. The revolute allows only rotation through an *angle,* the prismatic allows only translation through a *distance,* and the screw allows only a screw displacement involving a coupled rotation and translation through an angle and distance (related via the *pitch* of the screw). Each of these three pairs has a definite axis associated with it, which is the key to their interrelationship.

The screw pair reduces to both the revolute and the prismatic pairs, as special cases, in the following way (Fig. 8.17). If the pitch of the screw is infinite such that the screw threads become parallel to the axis of the screw, the joint allows only translation without rotation. It then operates as a prismatic pair. Similarly, if the pitch of the screw is zero such that the screw threads become perpendicular to the screw axis, the joint allows only rotation without translation. It then operates as a revolute pair.

For the remaining three pairs the situation is slightly more complicated, since each has more than one degree of freedom. Thus, the cylindric pair allows independent rotation and translation so that two parameters (an angle and a distance) are involved in specifying the relative displacement. This joint can be simulated by a combination of a revolute pair and a prismatic pair, in series, with parallel or collinear axes as shown in Figure 8.18. Alternatively, two different coaxial screw pairs in series can replace the cylindric joint, and so on.

The planar pair permits relative translation in two independent directions on the surface of contact, as well as relative rotation about a normal to this surface so that it has three degrees of freedom in all. It can be simulated in several ways such as by two prismatic pairs and a revolute pair in series (with the revolute axis perpendicular to both prismatic axes), for example, as shown in Figure 8.18.

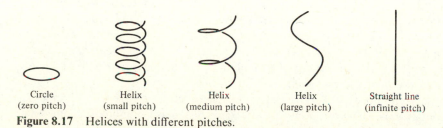

| Circle | Helix | Helix | Helix | Straight line |
| (zero pitch) | (small pitch) | (medium pitch) | (large pitch) | (infinite pitch) |

Figure 8.17   Helices with different pitches.

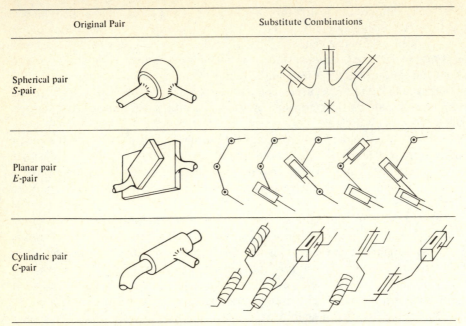

| Original Pair | Substitute Combinations |

Figure 8.18   Substitute combinations of lower pairs. (*Source:* K. H. Hunt, *Kinematic Geometry of Mechanisms.* Oxford, Clarendon Press, 1978, pp. 8–9.)

Finally, the spherical pair permits relative rotations about three independent axes and therefore can be considered to be a combination of three revolute pairs in series, such that their three axes are concurrent with the centre of the original sphere. Again, this is illustrated by Figure 8.18.

We have now shown how all six Reuleaux pairs can be derived from just one type (the screw pair) and its special cases (the revolute and the prismatic). Indeed, the whole subject of kinematic structure could be based on this one type of joint. It is no accident that this is the case, because screw motion and screw systems are fundamental concepts in theoretical mechanics. In fact, Ball (1900) in his *Theory of Screws* constructed an elegant mathematical description of 3D kinematics and dynamics which has recently been rediscovered, extended, and applied to spatial mechanisms and manipulators by several researchers, including Hunt (1978), Bottema and Roth (1979), Phillips and Hunt (1964), Rooney (1975; 1978), and so on. The importance of screw theory can be gleaned from the following observations:

- Any system of forces acting on a rigid body in 3D space cannot be reduced, in general, to either a single force or a single couple (i.e., a combination of two equal and opposite forces). However, it can always be reduced to a *combination* of a single force and single couple, where the force has an associated line of action and the couple lies in a plane perpendicular to this line of action. The resulting force-couple combination, together with the line of action, is known as a *wrench* on a screw (axis).
- The displacement of a rigid body in 3D space is not in general either a pure translation or a pure rotation about an axis. However, it can always be expressed as a combination of a rota-

tion about and a translation along a definite line; and it is then referred to as a *screw displacement* about a screw axis.

The most general motion of a rigid body in 3D space is a screw motion consisting of a *twist* about a screw axis. At any instant there exists a line (not necessarily within the body) about which the body is instantaneously rotating and along which it is instantaneously translating. This *instantaneous screw axis* moves continuously in space as the motion progresses.

We will return to discuss briefly some of these ideas in the following sections where we concentrate on the screw joint and, in particular, on systems utilizing its special cases—the revolute and prismatic joints. Notice that we are not concerned with the detailed construction of any of these joints so that we ignore aspects concerned with bearings, drives, and lubrication. Instead, we concentrate on their geometry.

KINEMATIC GEOMETRY

So far we have discussed the various types of links and joints (Figures 8.11 and 8.12) that may occur in a kinematic system; the Reuleaux classification scheme for binary joints (Figure 8.16 shows the lower pairs); and some of the possible types of interconnection for systems with a certain number of links (Fig. 8.13). In each case we have been concerned primarily with the "topological" design and arrangement of the components. This enables us to deduce certain global characteristics for a given kinematic system by using various combinatorial techniques. For instance, the *gross mobility* (an integer indicating the degree of overall freedom of movement of the system) can be determined, using a counting argument, as follows.

Thus, suppose we consider two unconnected links, one of which is free to move in any way in 3D space. Then the free link possesses *six* degrees of freedom with respect to the other (fixed) link. This is because six independent parameters are required to specify their relative position and orientation (Fig. 8.19). These might be the three x, y, and z coordinates of the centre of mass of the link, together with the yaw, pitch, and roll angles defining its attitude or orientation (as in the case of an airplane). We say that this two-link system has a mobility of six.

For each new free link added to the system we introduce a further six degrees of freedom. So, for a system of n unconnected links, with one link fixed as a reference link, we have $6(n - 1)$ degrees of freedom, and hence the mobility is $6(n - 1)$ in this case. However, if any of the links

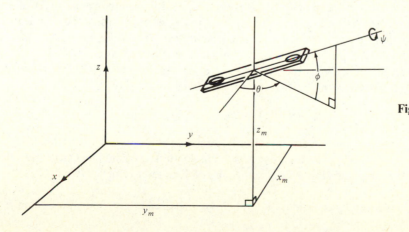

Figure 8.19   The six parameters specifying the position and orientation of one link with respect to another in 3D space.

are interconnected by joints, then these remove freedoms and reduce the mobility. A single revolute pair, for instance, reduces the relative freedom, or mobility, of the two links in the pair from six to one, because the relative position and orientation is now specified by a single parameter—the angular displacement at the joint (see Figure 8.16). Introducing a revolute pair between two links, therefore, removes five degrees of freedom from the system. In general, if we interconnect the system with j_R revolute pairs we remove $5j_R$ degrees of freedom and hence reduce the mobility by $5j_R$.

Similar arguments apply to the prismatic pair and the screw pair since each of these also removes five freedoms. The cylindric pair, however, only removes four freedoms, since it allows two relative degrees of freedom (between the two links involved), specified by an independent rotational displacement and a translational displacement. Finally, both the planar pair and the spherical pair each remove only three degrees of freedom since they each require three parameters to specify their configuration (two translational and one rotational displacement for the planar pair; three rotational displacements for the spherical pair).

We can now write down the following expression for the mobility of any system of links that are interconnected by Reuleaux lower pairs;

$$M = 6(n - 1) - 5j_R - 5j_P - 5j_H - 4j_C - 3j_E - 3j_S \qquad (1)$$

where M is the mobility of the system
  j_R is the number of *revolute* pairs
  j_P is the number of *prismatic* pairs
  j_H is the number of *screw* pairs
  j_C is the number of *cylindric* pairs
  j_E is the number of *planar* pairs
  j_S is the number of *spherical* pairs

This expression (known as a *mobility criterion*) is based entirely on a simple counting argument, and in general, if the value of M given by equation (1) is greater than zero, then the system should be *mobile* (i.e., relative motion can take place between the component links). If $M \leq 0$, then the system should be *immobile* and acts as a structural framework. If $M < 0$ (i.e., strictly less than zero), then the system is also said to be *overconstrained*. In this case one or more freedoms can usually be added to the system to increase M from its negative value up to zero without altering its immobile state.

Expressions that are similar to equation (1) can be written down for various special types of systems. The most common example occurs when all the links in a system are restricted to move always parallel to a given plane. Such systems are termed *planar* kinematic systems and usually involve just revolute joints and prismatic joints. In this case the revolute axes are all perpendicular to the given plane, whereas the prismatic axes are parallel to this plane. If we exclude all joints except revolutes, the mobility criterion for planar systems of this type is

$$M = 3(n - 1) - 2j_R \qquad (2)$$

Here each link has only three degrees of freedom initially, such as the x and y coordinates, say, to locate its centre of mass over the plane, together with a single angle to define its orientation with respect to a normal to the plane (Fig. 8.20), and each revolute joint removes two of these (leaving one).

The two mobility criteria given by equations (1) and (2) can be used to give some indication

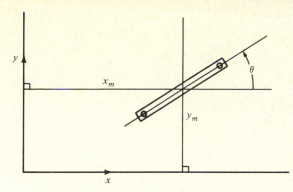

Figure 8.20 The three parameters specifying the position and orientaton of one link with respect to another in 2D space.

of how a kinematic system will behave, based only on a knowledge of the number and type of links and joints that are present. Unfortunately, there are so many exceptions to the rule that neither equation (1) nor equation (2) is very useful without some further information on the detailed structure and geometry of the systems. At least three different "problems" can arise. For example, the interconnections may be such that one part of the kinematic system (considered as a subsystem) is overconstrained, whereas another part is underconstrained, so that the two effects cancel (algebraically) and the total mobility lies somewhere in between the two extreme values.

This situation is illustrated by Figure 8.21 which compares two planar systems (with the same number of links and joints), both having mobility zero according to equation (2), but whose true mobilities differ. The mobility criterion is unsatisfactory here since in real systems the overconstrained and underconstrained parts do not neutralize each other in general, because of the way the two subsystems are joined together. What happens is that the underconstrained part usually dominates and gives the whole system its mobility. This phenomenon provides a good argument for constructing a system in stages (or as a modular design), so that at each stage, or level, the mobility is the value that is ultimately required for the whole system.

The second type of problem that arises is concerned with *passive* degrees of freedom. This occurs chiefly when a system contains binary links that are interconnected by spherical pairs. Now in equation (1) we see that each spherical pair imposes three constraints and removes

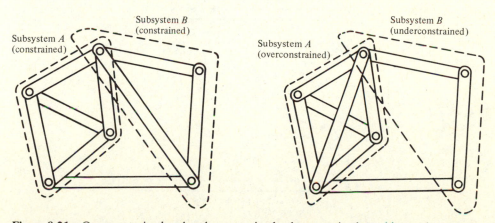

Figure 8.21 Overconstrained and underconstrained subsystems in planar kinematic systems.

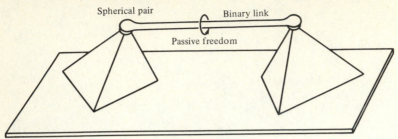

Figure 8.22   The passive degree of freedom of a binary link connected at two spherical pairs to any system.

three degrees of freedom from a given system, so that j_S spherical pairs remove $3j_S$ freedoms. This is usually true, but in the case of a binary link with a spherical pair at each end, we can see from Figure 8.22 that the two pairs do not remove all six degrees of freedom from the binary link, as one would expect. This is because the link always retains a single *passive* freedom of rotation about its own longitudinal axis. Any passive degree of freedom of this sort does not affect the real mobility of the system as a whole, since each binary link can happily rotate independently. It does, however, affect the mobility criterion (equation (1)) since each binary link associated with two spherical pairs will essentially conceal a degree of freedom.

The third main type of problem that arises with mobility criteria is caused by particular geometrical configurations that affect the mobility of the system. A simple example is afforded by a single-loop planar system with four links and only revolute pairs (Fig. 8.23). Normally, this would have a mobility of one according to equation (2), but if the lengths of three of the links add up to the length of the fourth link, then the system will not move (i.e., it will have an effective mobility of zero), despite the fact that the link interconnections have not changed in any way. Furthermore, it is a simple matter to choose link lengths so that it is not even possible to connect the system together as a closed-loop configuration, because some links are too short (or too long).

A more interesting example of the preceding type of geometrical problem is provided by the planar five-link system in Figure 8.24. If we construct such a system by using two ternary links,

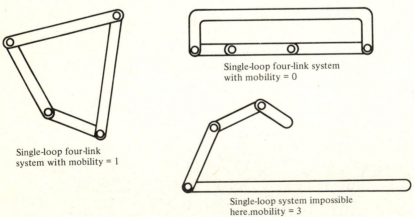

Single-loop four-link
system with mobility = 1

Single-loop four-link system
with mobility = 0

Single-loop system impossible
here. mobility = 3

Figure 8.23   Particular geometrical configurations that affect mobility.

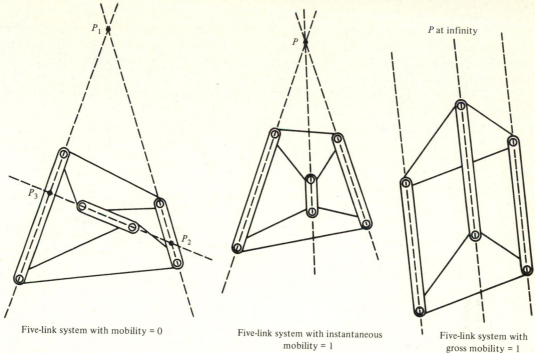

Five-link system with mobility = 0

Five-link system with instantaneous
mobility = 1

Five-link system with
gross mobility = 1

Figure 8.24   Instantaneous mobility and gross mobility in planar systems.

three binary links, and only revolute pairs, we obtain a "two-loop" arrangement as shown. For a random choice of link lengths or link shapes, this system will be an immobile structure (i.e., $M = 0$ according to equation (2), since the number of links, $n = 5$, and the number of revolute pairs, $j_R = 6$). However, it is possible to choose the dimensions of the links in such a way that the three imaginary straight lines, joining the two revolute pairs on each binary link, all intersect in a single point, P, instead of in three separate points. If this occurs then the components of the system can move relative to one another, through a small range on either side of their "equilibrium" position (shown in Fig. 8.24), and we refer to this as an *instantaneous mobility*. In practice, we usually obtain quite a reasonable range of motion about the equilibrium position because of a certain amount of "stretch" and "give" in the physical components. (No material is completely rigid and so it deforms slightly to accommodate small stresses.)

With this choice of dimensions the condition for the instantaneous mobility is destroyed as soon as the system moves slightly, because the three lines cease to intersect in a single point. However, the instantaneous mobility can become a *gross mobility* if the point of intersection, P, is chosen to be at infinity. The dimensions must then be such that the three lines are always parallel, in which case the three binary links have the same length and the two ternary links must be congruent triangles.

These problems highlight the difficulties that are encountered in the design of kinematic systems and emphasise the importance of the geometric structure. What, therefore, determines the geometry of a kinematic system? The answer is again the type and arrangement of joints. But this time we must consider the geometrical arrangement rather than just the topological arrangement. In the previous section we discussed six types of binary joint (the Reuleaux lower pairs) and indicated how these are interrelated, all based essentially on the screw pair. This provides the key to an understanding of the geometry. In fact, the whole subject of kinematics can be based on the "theory of screws" as originally expounded by Robert Ball (1900), but for our purposes we concentrate on just one aspect; namely, that a screw pair has a particular line (the axis of the joint) associated with it.

In a kinematic system, such as a manipulator, the joints interconnecting the links define a

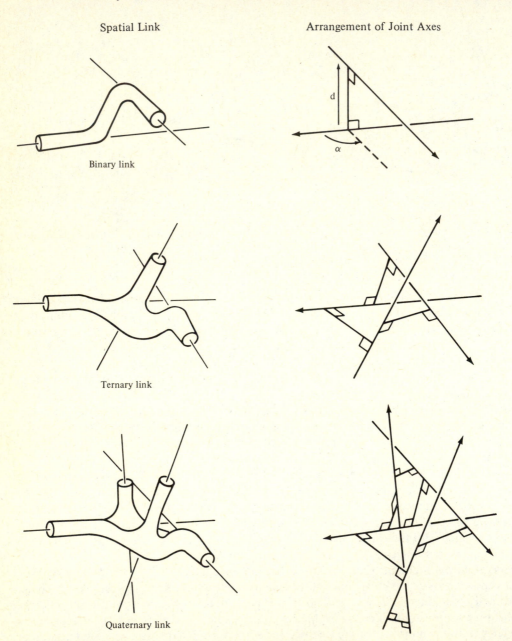

Spatial Link   Arrangement of Joint Axes

Binary link

Ternary link

Quaternary link

Figure 8.25   The skew joint axes of spatial links with revolute joints.

system of lines in 3D space. It is then the position, orientation, and juxtaposition of these lines (rather than the detailed shapes and sizes of the links and joints) that determine the basic geometry of the manipulator. This emphasis on *line geometry,* rather than on the usual point geometry, has important implications for the mathematical representation and modelling of robot manipulators, and we will consider this aspect in the final section.

For a binary link having two revolute joints, the axes of these joints would, in general, be two *skew* lines (i.e., nonintersecting and nonparallel). For a ternary link the three revolute joint axes would form a configuration of three skew lines. For a quaternary link one would have four skew lines, and so on, and so for an *r*-ary link, the essential geometry is defined by a configuration of *r* skew lines. These arrangements are illustrated by Figure 8.25. Now any two skew lines define a unique *common perpendicular line* that intersects both of the lines orthogonally (Fig. 8.26). The configuration can then be specified with respect to this line in terms of two parameters— the *twist angle, α,* between the two joint axes, and the *common perpendicular distance, d,* separating the axes along the common perpendicular line. Three skew lines define three common perpendicular lines, and hence define three twist angles and three common perpendicular distances. Four skew lines define six common perpendicular lines (i.e., one for each pair of joint axes), and so on, and so for *r* skew lines there are $_rC_2 = r!/2! \, (r-2)!$ common perpendicular lines, distances, and twist angles. The geometry of a general spatial system, constructed from *r*-ary links that are interconnected with, say, revolute pairs, is therefore, described by a complicated configuration of skew lines that are specified by many twist angles and distances.

Various important special cases can be derived by choosing particular values for the link parameters. Thus, for example, if all the twist angles are zero, then the joint axes become parallel and all links are constrained to move only in parallel planes. The members of this class are referred to as *planar* systems and Figures 8.23 and 8.24 illustrate two examples. (Figure 8.1 shows an additional nineteen planar systems satisfying various conditions on mobility and interconnection, etc.)

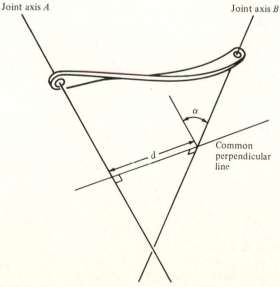

Joint axis *A*   Joint axis *B*

α

Common
perpendicular
line

d

Figure 8.26   A binary link with two skew joint axes.

Alternatively, if all the common perpendicular distances are zero, then the joint axes all intersect in a single point. These systems are referred to as *spherical* systems because all the links are constrained to move only on the surfaces of concentric spheres. Figure 8.27 compares the line geometry of three four-link systems—namely, a spatial, a planar, and a spherical configuration. Each is shown as a closed-loop and as an open-loop arrangement (such as in an articulated manipulator). Notice that the physical shape, size, and position of the links are not especially relevant to the kinematic geometry. This is particularly true in the case of the spherical systems, where the common perpendicular lines cannot be used sensibly as links because they have zero length. Here the links are usually taken to be defined by arcs of great circles, although straight chords (not perpendicular to the joint axes, of course) would also suffice. Clearly, appropriate link shapes are chosen in practice to satisfy other criteria, such as minimum restriction on ranges of motion, avoidance of mutual interference between links, and so on.

We now examine the geometry of a particular type of manipulator—the articulated design. This consists of a sequence of links that are connected in series to form an open-loop spatial kinematic system. For example, the PUMA robot, shown in Figure 8.10, is of this type and consists of seven links (two unary and five binary), connected serially by six revolute pairs, which produce the six degrees of freedom that are required at the gripper. In Figure 8.28 we illustrate the arrangement of joint axes for the PUMA. It can be seen that axes 1 and 2 intersect at right angles, as do axes 3 and 4, axes 4 and 5, and axes 5 and 6. Furthermore, axes 2 and 3 are parallel, and axes 4, 5 and 6 all intersect in the same point at the "wrist." The geometry is, therefore, far from the most general arrangement possible, since most common perpendicular distances are zero and twist angles are either zero or right angles.

The most general configuration of joint axes for a seven-link, six-revolute serial manipulator

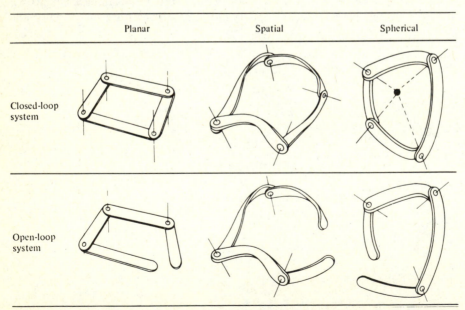

Figure 8.27   A comparison of the line geometry of planar, spatial, and spherical four-link kinematic systems. (*Source:* Open University course TM361: Graphs, Networks and Design—Unit 10, p. 20.)

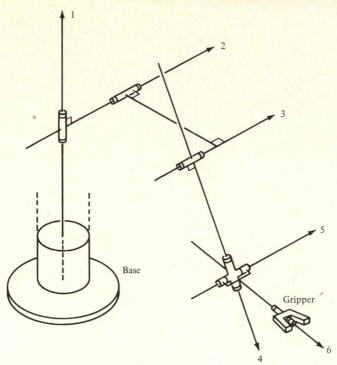

Figure 8.28 The arrangement of revolute joint axes for the PUMA industrial robot.

is shown in Figure 8.29. Here all common perpendicular distances are nonzero and twist angles are neither zero nor $\pi/2$. In addition, there is an *offset* distance at each joint, which defines the relative separation of the two adjacent common perpendicular lines meeting the joint axis. This arrangement provides a high degree of dexterity and flexibility in the workspace. However, it is much more difficult to design, analyse, and control such a system because the extra complication introduced by having all joint axes skew, with an offset distance at each, leads to highly nonlinear coupled equations describing the geometry. These are usually very difficult to solve (particularly in real time) and often prove to be intractable.

As an indication of the type of difficult problem encountered with such a manipulator, consider the question of what values to assign to the joint angles in order to locate the gripper at a specified position in space with a specified orientation. We refer to a particular set of joint angles as a manipulator *posture*. If we examine a simple case such as a four-link planar manipulator with just three parallel revolute joint axes (Fig. 8.30), then we can see immediately that there is generally more than one set of joint angles (i.e., posture) for a fixed gripper position and orientation. For this planar system there are clearly just *two* postures. However, in general, it is extremely difficult to determine the *number* of postures and even more difficult to derive the appropriate values for the joint variables. Thus, it has only recently been shown, after intensive efforts, that the general spatial serial arrangement of six revolutes (all skew with offsets), illustrated in Figure 8.29, has *thirty-two* postures, and even this result is not yet widely accepted (Rooney & Duffy, 1972; Duffy & Rooney, 1974; Duffy & Derby, 1979; Duffy & Crane, 1980). Note that the special geometry of the PUMA (zero common perpendicular distances and offsets; zero or $\pi/2$ twist angles) reduces the number of postures drastically from thirty-two to *eight*. For the PUMA these consist of combinations of "elbow up" or "elbow

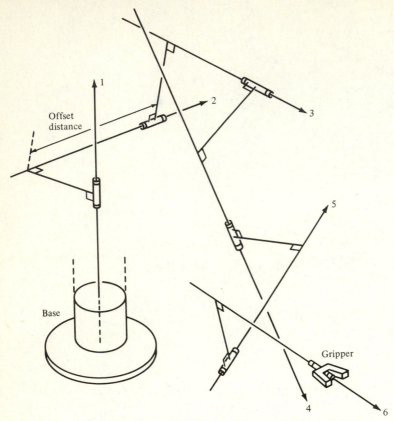

Figure 8.29   The most general arrangement of revolute joint axes incorporating offsets at each joint.

down," right-arm," or "left-arm," and "flipped-wrist" or "nonflipped-wrist" modes (thus, giving $2^3 = 8$ possible postures).

A practical design that is based on the general geometry would be difficult to implement at present. Nevertheless, it is sensible to consider theoretically the most general type of system, despite the difficulties, because this will reduce to most of the other types as special cases. Furthermore, the kinematic design of spatial manipulators is still at such a primitive stage that

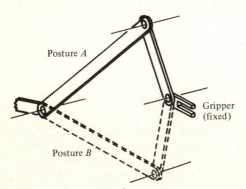

Figure 8.30   The two postures of the three-revolute planar manipulator.

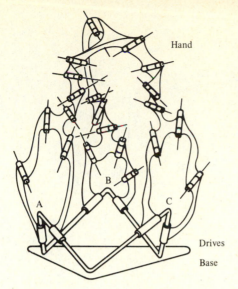

Hand

Drives

Base

Figure 8.31 Multiloop spatial manipulator, constructed from spherical subsystems *A*, *B*, and *C*.

the range of possible systems and their behaviour modes have not been explored, even superficially. This is particularly true of multiloop systems where the links and joints are arranged in parallel rather than serially as in an open loop. We illustrate an example of this type in Figure 8.31, where the system is constructed in a modular fashion from spherical subsystems.

One advantage of this type of parallel arrangement is that some or all the driven joints (i.e., the drives) can be located on the base, instead of having to be distributed serially along the manipulator. This may reduce the masses and inertias that have to be moved and so improve the performance. But obviously, the structure and geometry are more complicated, and certainly the determination of numbers and types of postures becomes a serious problem. However, these problems may prove to be relatively unimportant for some applications, such as those where the range of motion, or size of workspace, is to be restricted, or where high precision takes priority.

Before ending this section, we consider briefly the difficult subject of *screw systems*. We have already seen how the lower pair joints can all be based on just one—the screw pair. Moreover, as stated in the previous section, the most general displacement of any body in 3D space is a screw displacement and its motion at any instant is a screw motion. How does this relate to manipulator geometry?

Suppose we consider just two links joined at a revolute pair. The relative motion is then always a pure rotation about the axis of the joint. This represents a special case of a screw motion without sliding along the screw axis. If we now add a third link and join it in series at another revolute pair to the second link, the relative motion of the third with respect to the second is again a pure rotation about the new joint axis. But if we now ask about the motion of the third with respect to the first link, this is not so obviously determined because there is no direct connection between these two links at a joint.

To see what happens, consider a special case, namely, that in which the two revolute axes are parallel so that we have a planar system (Fig. 8.32). There is then a theorem in kinematics

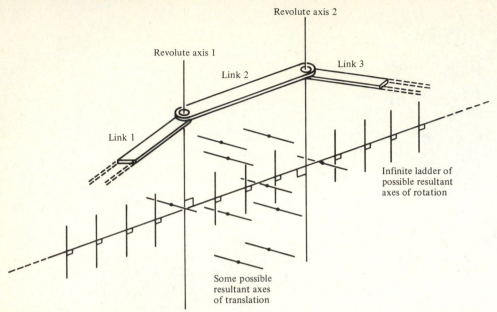

Figure 8.32   The instantaneous relative motions of three planar links connected in series at revolute pairs.

(Hunt, 1978) that states that the instantaneous motion of link 3 with respect to link 1 must always be either

- a pure rotation about an axis chosen from an infinite collection of possible axes forming the "rungs" of a "ladder" defined by the two given joint axes

  or

- a pure translation along an axis chosen from another infinite collection of possible axes that are perpendicular to the plane of the preceding ladder

Reference to Figure 8.32 should make the situation clear. Which particular axis is the appropriate one is only determined when the angular velocities about the given joint axes are known. These also define the magnitude of the resultant rotation or translation.

Returning now to the spatial case where the axes of the two revolute joints are skew (Fig. 8.33), we find that a similar situation arises, but now the instantaneous motion of link 3 with respect to link 1 is always a *screw motion* (not just a pure rotation or a pure translation this time) about an axis chosen from an infinite collection of possible axes. However, these axes no longer form the rungs of an infinite ladder, but instead, they form the generators of a twisted self-intersecting, finite ruled surface known as a *cylindroid* (Fig. 8.34). In effect, the ladder becomes twisted and finite in extent as soon as the two given revolute axes defining it are no longer parallel. Which particular screw axis is the appropriate one is only determined when the angular velocities about the given joint axes are known. These also define the *pitch* and the *magnitude* of the resultant screw motion.

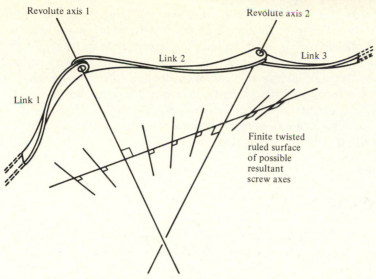

Figure 8.33   The instantaneous relative motions of three spatial links connected in series at revolute pairs.

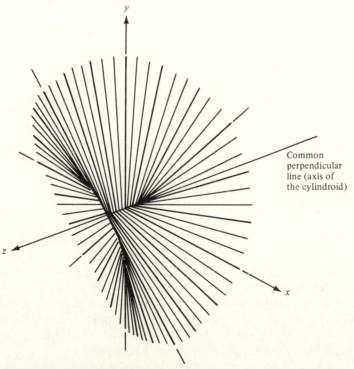

Figure 8.34   The cylindroid ruled surface.

If we have a manipulator system consisting of a serial arrangement of more than two revolute joints, then similar considerations apply to the range of possible resultant screw motions. However, we now have a collection of possible resultant screw axes that form a more complicated screw system than the cylindroid. In fact, it is generally a higher-order arrangement that is not a ruled surface (a single infinity of lines), but instead, is either a *congruence* (a double infinity of lines) or a *complex* (a triple infinity of lines). These geometrical screw systems will not be discussed further here. An excellent treatment is given in Hunt (1978), where these ideas are also used to investigate analogous constructs arising in dynamics, from a consideration of general systems of forces acting on rigid bodies.

MATHEMATICAL REPRESENTATIONS

As stated in the first section of this chapter, there are at least four main functional areas involved in the design and operation of a robot system, namely,

· manipulation/locomotion
· sensing/perception
· command/control
· representation/modelling

The fourth area is of a rather different character from the first three in that it is essentially nonspecific. Generally, it is concerned with the representation and modelling of the external environment, the internal states of the system, the required tasks to be executed, and the available operational strategies that the system has access to, or has the capability to perform. These usually involve the construction of data structures, information structures, algorithms and heuristics, either at the initial programming stage or interactively during system operation. In the present context, however, we are more interested in the types of representations that are useful in modelling aspects of the kinematic design of manipulator systems. Such representations are important for generating, constructing, enumerating, and classifying those systems that are physically and logically possible. Here we consider some representations for describing the topological and geometric structures that are suitable for robot manipulator designs.

Consider first the topological structure of a manipulator. We seek to represent the links, the joints, and their interrelationships. This can obviously be achieved in many ways but one of the more useful approaches utilizes the *interchange graph* concept. Each link is represented by a *vertex* (i.e., a point) and each binary joint is represented by an *edge* (i.e., a finite line segment—not necessarily straight). Two links connected at a joint then become two vertices sharing a common edge, and an *r*-ary link is modelled by a vertex of degree *r* (i.e., a vertex shared by *r* edges). This type of representation is useful when there are only binary joints present, illustrated by Figure 8.35. If more than one type of binary joint is present, for example, several of the six Reuleaux pairs of Figure 8.16, this can be dealt with by labelling or colouring the appropriate edges to distinguish the different types on the interchange graph.

The interchange graph representation is so called because one appears to interchange the role of links and joints in transferring from the system to the graph, so that links become points

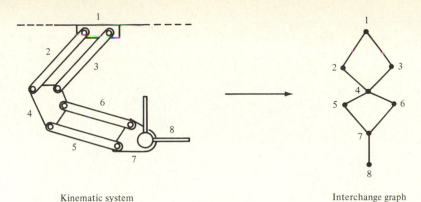

Kinematic system   Interchange graph

Figure 8.35 The interchange graph representation for the set-square mechanism of Figure 8.3.

(resembling joints) and joints become edges (resembling binary links). This is possible when there are only binary joints present. If there are r-ary joints, then these cannot be modelled effectively by a single edge (which associates only two vertices), because more than two links are involved in the joint (and hence more than two vertices must be associated). Such systems require a *hypergraph* representation (Berge, 1977) if the 'interchange' idea is to be used. We, therefore, restrict ourselves to systems containing only binary joints (for simplicity) since r-ary joints ($r > 2$) can always be decomposed into ($r - 1$) binary joints.

As an example of the use of the interchange graph, consider the problem of enumerating (or logically constructing) all possible systems of a given type. Thus, if we require all possible connected four-link systems with only (unspecified) binary joints, we can begin by representing these with four vertices (the links), and then connect the vertices in all possible ways with single edges (the binary joints). There are just six possible configurations and the resulting systems have already been shown in Figure 8.13, together with their interchange graphs. Similarly, Figure 8.1 illustrates the nineteen possible mobility one planar systems with only revolute binary joints and with the various other restrictions on connectedness that were mentioned earlier.

The interchange graph representation can be used in a more positive way than in the previous examples, as a means of constructing manipulator systems from particular types of components. Thus, in Earl and Rooney (1982) it is shown how to construct large classes of multiloop manipulator arrangements by using modular components whose interchange graphs are trees. Two types of components are considered—namely, *drive* components and *distribution* components. The former contain all the driven joints and the latter serve to distribute the motion throughout the system to the required output sites (Figure 8.36). Any particular system can be constructed in terms of the interchange graphs of the components. The rules of construction (expressed in graph terminology) then ensure the appropriate distribution of mobility throughout the system and also determine the allowable sites for the location of the drives (i.e., driven joints). The situation is illustrated by Figure 8.37, which shows the graph of the multiloop system that is presented in Figure 8.31.

We turn now to the representation of geometric structure. In the previous section we emphasised the fact that line geometry is more important than point geometry in determining the geometric structure of manipulators because it better describes joint axes, screw displacement axes, and so on.

227

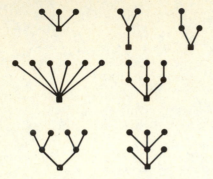

Some rooted trees for drive components

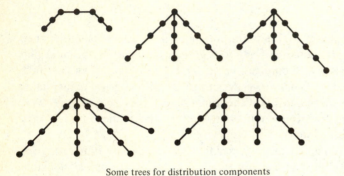

Some trees for distribution components

Figure 8.36 Interchange graph for drive and distribution components.

But how do we represent line geometry mathematically? Well, if the positions of the lines are ignored and we take account only of their directions, then the usual technique is to represent each line by a *unit vector*. This is sometimes also referred to as a unit *free vector* (Brand, 1947), because it can be located anywhere in space, at whichever point is convenient (as long as it maintains its direction), without affecting the analysis. The unit vector, **V**, representing any one

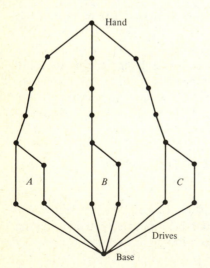

Figure 8.37 The interchange graph for the multiloop system in Figure 8.31.

line, can be written in terms of its three real number *components* as (L, M, N). Given any two such unit vectors, say, $\mathbf{V}_1 = (L_1, M_1, N_1)$ and $\mathbf{V}_2 = (L_2, M_2, N_2)$, it is usual to define a *dot product;* $\mathbf{V}_1 \cdot \mathbf{V}_2 = L_1 L_2 + M_1 M_2 + N_1 N_2$, and a *cross product;* $\mathbf{V}_1 \times \mathbf{V}_2 = (M_1 N_2 - M_2 N_1, N_1 L_2 - N_2 L_1, L_1 M_2 - L_2 M_1)$. The dot product is a real number and can be shown (Brand, 1947) to be equal to $\cos \alpha$, where α is the real angle between the lines (Fig. 8.38). The cross product is a vector and its magnitude can be shown (Brand, 1947) to be equal to $\sin \alpha$. Moreover, the line associated with this cross-product vector is perpendicular to both of the original lines.

If these lines are themselves perpendicular, then the dot product of their vectors is zero. Similarly, if the lines are parallel, then the cross product of their vectors has zero magnitude. In this way the algebra introduced by using vectors, real number components, dot products, cross products, and so on, can be used to describe and/or determine the directional relationships between two or more lines. Furthermore, as we will see later, by introducing matrix or quaternion techniques, the effect of a rotation through an angle θ about a line through the origin (Fig. 8.41) can be analysed in terms of this vector algebra.

Now in the case of a manipulator the significant lines, such as joint axes, have definite (although not necessarily fixed) locations in space. We must, therefore, represent the *position* of each line, in addition to its direction. The usual vector algebra is not sufficiently powerful (at least in its simple form) to achieve this. However, it is possible to represent the direction and position of a line with an *ordered pair* of vectors. The first vector defines the direction of the

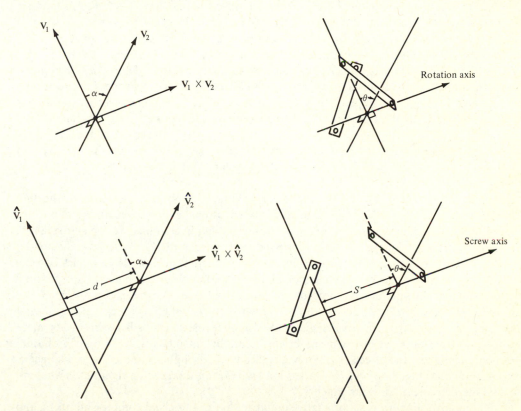

Figure 8.38   The real angle between intersecting lines and the dual angle between skew lines.

line, whereas the second specifies its *moment* about the origin so that in combination with the first it defines the position of the line (see Fig. 8.40).

A novel type of vector algebra can be constructed for these ordered pairs of vectors, which are then referred to as *dual vectors* (Brand, 1947). It is directly analogous to the usual vector algebra, but with a new kind of dot product and cross product. These are used as before to specify relationships between lines (now skew), and we will discuss them shortly. The dual vectors differ from the familiar (real) vectors in that their components are no longer just single real numbers but are instead ordered pairs of real numbers. Similarly, the dot product of two dual vectors is an ordered pair of real numbers, and the cross product has a "magnitude" that is an ordered pair of real numbers.

The occurrence of ordered pairs of real numbers is quite natural in the context of the geometry of skew lines. Thus, consider how to describe their juxtapositions. Each pair of skew lines defines *two* (unique) real parameters—namely, the *twist angle, α,* between the lines, measured about the common perpendicular line, and the *common perpendicular distance, d,* separating the lines, and measured along the common perpendicular line (Fig. 8.38). The configuration can, therefore, be described by the ordered pair of real numbers, (α, d). This should be contrasted with the case of two intersecting lines, which are conveniently described by a single real number, α, the angle between them.

Now in this latter situation the dot product of their corresponding (real) vectors is equal to $\cos \alpha$, a real number. Is there an analogous expression when the lines are skew? It turns out that such an expression does exist, and it is very simple and elegant. It is based on an algebra that is similar to the complex number algebra. This is derived by combining the real parameters, α and d (for two skew lines) into a single algebraic entity known as a *dual number* (Yaglom, 1968; Brand, 1947). This is a type of "generalised complex number" having the form, $\alpha + \epsilon d$ (where $\epsilon^2 = 0$) : the more usual complex number, $\alpha + id$ (where $i^2 = -1$) being less useful in this context. A dual number used in this way is referred to as the *dual angle* between the skew lines (Brand, 1947; Study, 1901), and it can be shown (Rooney, 1975b) that the dot product of the two dual vectors representing the lines is then equal to $\cos(\alpha + \epsilon d)$, the cosine of the dual angle between the lines. Furthermore, the dual vectors themselves have components that are ordered pairs of real numbers, and these can also be written as dual numbers, so that a dual vector then has dual number components.

The preceding discussion illustrates some of the advantages obtained by introducing the dual numbers and their algebra. They enable us to derive equations, expressions, and relationships for skew lines directly from known expressions for intersecting lines. Thus, we replace each real angle with a corresponding dual angle and expand the resulting dual equations, and so on by using the algebraic rules defining the dual numbers and their functions. Real angles become dual angles, real vectors become dual vectors, and their real number components become dual number components. The overall procedure uses a principle known as the *principle of transference* (Rooney, 1975b) and the resulting dual vector algebra provides a powerful and concise tool for representing the directional and positional relationships between two or more skew lines. Furthermore, as we will see briefly later, by introducing dual matrix or dual quaternion techniques, the effect of a screw displacement through an angle θ and distance S about a general line (Fig. 8.43) can be analysed in terms of this dual vector algebra. So what are these dual number and dual vector algebras?

The dual number algebra is superficially similar to that of the usual complex numbers, and two dual numbers can be added, subtracted, multiplied, or divided, in general. The difference arises because we have $\epsilon^2 = 0$ rather than $i^2 = -1$. Thus, for example, two dual numbers $a_1 + \epsilon b_1$, and $a_2 + \epsilon b_2$ are multiplied as follows:

$$
\begin{aligned}
(a_1 + \epsilon b_1)(a_2 + \epsilon b_2) &= a_1 a_2 + \epsilon^2 b_1 b_2 + \epsilon(a_1 b_2 + a_2 b_1) \\
&= a_1 a_2 + \epsilon(a_1 b_2 + a_2 b_1)
\end{aligned}
\tag{3}
$$

It is possible to define functions of a dual variable (analogously to functions of a complex variable) by using a formal Taylor series expansion, together with the property $\epsilon^2 = \epsilon^3 = \epsilon^4 = \cdots = 0$ (Brand, 1947). Thus, given a dual number, $a + \epsilon b$, we define any function, f, as follows:

$$
\begin{aligned}
f(a + \epsilon b) &= f(a) + \epsilon b f'(a) + \epsilon^2 \frac{b^2}{2!} f''(a) + \cdots \\
&= f(a) + \epsilon b f'(a)
\end{aligned}
\tag{4}
$$

In particular, the sine and cosine functions with dual-number arguments become

$$
\sin(a + \epsilon b) = \sin a + \epsilon b \cos a
\tag{5}
$$

$$
\cos(a + \epsilon b) = \cos a - \epsilon b \sin a
\tag{6}
$$

and these are important for manipulator kinematics.

To see how one takes advantage of the dual-number algebra, consider the representation of the spatial relationships between lines. For example, a general line in space can be described by three dual angles, since it is skew to the three x, y, and z coordinate lines (Fig. 8.39). These might be $\alpha_x + \epsilon d_x$, $\alpha_y + \epsilon d_y$, and $\alpha_z + \epsilon d_z$. Now if the given line passes through the origin, then

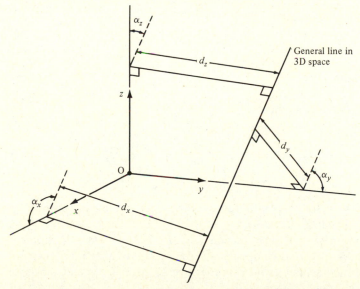

Figure 8.39   The three dual direction cosines, $\cos(\alpha_x + \epsilon d_x)$, $\cos(\alpha_y + \epsilon d_y)$, and $\cos(\alpha_z + \epsilon d_z)$, of a directed line in space.

only the three "twist" angles, α_x, α_y, and α_z, are nonzero. The line can now be represented by a free vector (L, M, N), whose three real-number components are the direction cosines of the line, so that we have

$$L = \cos \alpha_x$$
$$M = \cos \alpha_y \tag{7}$$
$$N = \cos \alpha_z$$

By analogy we can similarly represent the general line (i.e., not through the origin) by a *dual vector* $(\hat{L}, \hat{M}, \hat{N})$, whose three dual-number components are the *dual direction cosines* of the line, so that now we have

$$\hat{L} = \cos (\alpha_x + \epsilon d_x)$$
$$\hat{M} = \cos (\alpha_y + \epsilon d_y) \tag{8}$$
$$\hat{N} = \cos (\alpha_z + \epsilon d_z)$$

Expanding the right-hand sides of equations (8), using equation (6), we obtain

$$\hat{L} = \cos \alpha_x - \epsilon d_x \sin \alpha_x$$
$$\hat{M} = \cos \alpha_y - \epsilon d_y \sin \alpha_y \tag{9}$$
$$\hat{N} = \cos \alpha_z - \epsilon d_z \sin \alpha_z$$

and if we define

$$L_0 = -d_x \sin \alpha_x$$
$$M_0 = -d_y \sin \alpha_y \tag{10}$$
$$N_0 = -d_z \sin \alpha_z$$

we obtain from equations (7), (9), and (10)

$$\hat{L} = L + \epsilon L_0$$
$$\hat{M} = M + \epsilon M_0 \tag{11}$$
$$\hat{N} = N + \epsilon N_0$$

Equation (11) can be written as a vector equation:

$$\hat{\mathbf{V}} = \begin{bmatrix} \hat{L} \\ \hat{M} \\ \hat{N} \end{bmatrix} = \begin{bmatrix} L \\ M \\ N \end{bmatrix} + \epsilon \begin{bmatrix} L_0 \\ M_0 \\ N_0 \end{bmatrix} \tag{12}$$

from which it is clear that the dual vector $(\hat{L}, \hat{M}, \hat{N})$, representing a general line in 3D space, is essentially a pair of real vectors. The first, (L, M, N), gives the direction and magnitude of the line, whereas it is shown in Rooney (1975b) that the second, (L_0, M_0, N_0) represents the *moment* of the line about the origin (Fig. 8.40). The six components L, M, N, L_0, M_0, and N_0 are referred to as the *Plücker coordinates* of the line, but notice that they are not all independent, since we usually represent the line with a *unit* dual vector, so that

$$L^2 + M^2 + N^2 = 1 \tag{13}$$

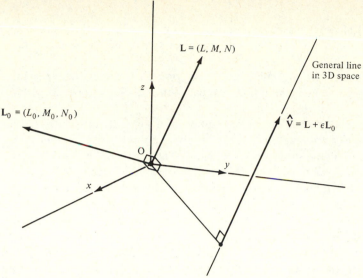

Figure 8.40 The six Plücker coordinates (L, M, N, L_0, M_0, N_0) of an arbitrary line in space.

and moreover, the direction vector and the moment vector are orthogonal, so that

$$LL_0 + MM_0 + NN_0 = 0 \tag{14}$$

The two conditions (13) and (14) imply that there are only four independent Plücker coordinates for a given line.

The representation of a line in 3D space, by a unit dual vector is a very useful description, for we can define dot and cross products for pairs of dual vectors, which lead to very simple criteria for parallelism, intersection, orthogonality, and so on.

The dot product for dual vectors $\hat{\mathbf{A}}$ and $\hat{\mathbf{B}}$ is simply

$$
\begin{aligned}
\hat{\mathbf{A}} \cdot \hat{\mathbf{B}} &= (\mathbf{A} + \epsilon\mathbf{A_0}) \cdot (\mathbf{B} + \epsilon\mathbf{B_0}) \\
&= \mathbf{A} \cdot \mathbf{B} + \epsilon (\mathbf{A} \cdot \mathbf{B_0} + \mathbf{A_0} \cdot \mathbf{B})
\end{aligned} \tag{15}
$$

which is a dual number. The cross product for $\hat{\mathbf{A}}$ and $\hat{\mathbf{B}}$ is similarly given by

$$
\begin{aligned}
\hat{\mathbf{A}} \times \hat{\mathbf{B}} &= (\mathbf{A} + \epsilon\mathbf{A_0}) \times (\mathbf{B} + \epsilon\mathbf{B_0}) \\
&= \mathbf{A} \times \mathbf{B} + \epsilon (\mathbf{A} \times \mathbf{B_0} + \mathbf{A_0} \times \mathbf{B})
\end{aligned} \tag{16}
$$

which is a general dual vector.

If $\hat{\alpha} = \alpha + \epsilon d$ is the dual angle between the lines defined by $\hat{\mathbf{A}}$ and $\hat{\mathbf{B}}$, then it can be shown (Brand, 1947) that

$$\hat{\mathbf{A}} \cdot \hat{\mathbf{B}} = \cos \hat{\alpha} = \cos \alpha - \epsilon d \sin \alpha \tag{17}$$

and

$$\hat{\mathbf{A}} \times \hat{\mathbf{B}} = \sin \hat{\alpha} \, \hat{\mathbf{E}} = (\sin \alpha + \epsilon d \cos \alpha) \, \hat{\mathbf{E}} \tag{18}$$

where $\hat{\mathbf{E}} = \mathbf{E} + \epsilon\mathbf{E_0}$ is a unit line vector representing the common perpendicular line to the $\hat{\mathbf{A}}$ and $\hat{\mathbf{B}}$ lines.

If the dot product (eq. (17)) of two nonparallel unit dual vectors is real (i.e., the ϵ component is zero), then the two associated lines intersect. If the dot product is zero, then the lines intersect at right angles.

If the cross product (eq. (18)) of two-unit dual vectors is a *pure* dual vector (i.e., only the ϵ component is nonzero), then the two associated lines are parallel. If the cross product is zero, then the lines are collinear.

Dual-number representations also arise in the description of a general rigid body *spatial screw displacement*. This involves a real angle of rotation, θ, about a screw axis, together with a real distance of translation, S, along the screw axis (Fig. 8.38). The dual number $\theta + \epsilon S$ is then referred to as the *dual angular displacement* about the screw axis. However, a screw displacement requires more information for its specification than just the dual angular displacement. We also need to know the screw axis itself. As we saw previously, this can be represented by a dual vector, involving three additional dual numbers, so it seems that, in all, four dual numbers are required (three to define the three dual angles that the screw axis makes with the x, y, and z coordinate lines and the fourth to specify the magnitudes involved in the actual screw displacement about the screw axis). Of course, these four dual angles are not all independent because of the two conditions (eqs. (13) and (14)) imposed on the Plücker coordinates of the line. So, of the eight real parameters involved in the four dual angles, only six are independent.

It is possible to represent a screw displacement algebraically in terms of a hypercomplex number known as a *dual quaternion* (Rooney, 1978). This was originally invented by Clifford (1873) as an extension of Hamilton's real *quaternion* (Hamilton, 1899). A *real* quaternion q is essentially an algebraic construct that is similar to a complex number but consisting of four real components instead of two. It has the form

$$q = a + ib + jc + kd \tag{19}$$

where

$$i^2 = j^2 = k^2 = ijk = -1 \tag{20}$$

and a, b, c, and d are real.

Two such quaternions may be added, subtracted, multiplied, or "divided" within a definite system of rules (the normal rules of algebra together with those given in eq. (20)), forming a (noncommutative) algebra. However, because of the noncommutativity, division requires pre- or postmultiplication by an inverse. Thus, the inverse of q in equation (19) is defined as

$$q^{-1} = \frac{a - ib - jc - kd}{a^2 + b^2 + c^2 + d^2} \tag{21}$$

that $qq^{-1} = q^{-1}q = 1$. To divide p by q, we then have a choice of two different quotients, namely, $q^{-1}p$ and pq^{-1}.

A real quaternion is useful in representing spatial rotations about a fixed point (Rooney, 1977). For example, the quaternion representing a rotation through angle θ, about a line through the origin with direction cosines, l, m, and n, (Fig. 8.41), has the form

$$q = \cos\frac{\theta}{2} + il\sin\frac{\theta}{2} + jm\sin\frac{\theta}{2} + kn\sin\frac{\theta}{2} \tag{22}$$

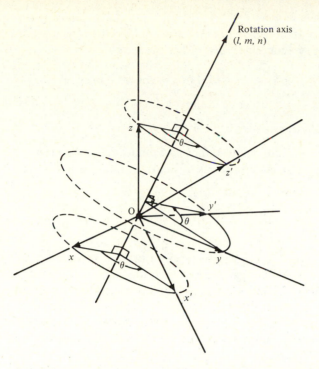

Figure 8.41 A rotation of the coordinate system through angle θ about an axis through the origin with direction cosines (l, m, n).

A point r in space is also represented by a quaternion with zero the first component and with its x, y, and z coordinates forming the remaining three components; thus,

$$r = ix + jy + kz \tag{23}$$

The result of the rotation represented by q (given by eq. (22)), acting on any point r (given by eq. (23)) is then expressed, in terms of quaternion multiplication, by the transformation

$$r' = q^{-1}rq \tag{24}$$

where r' is the new position of the point. The effects of performing particular rotations about the x, y, and z axes, respectively (with the origin as fixed point), are illustrated by Figure 8.42.

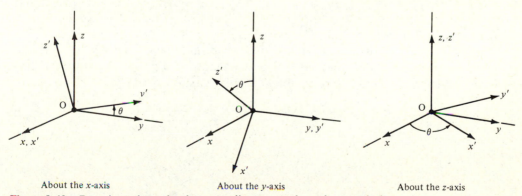

About the x-axis   About the y-axis   About the z-axis

Figure 8.42   Rotations about the three coordinate axes through an angle θ.

The preceding quaternion representation, with four real components, may be contrasted with the more usual 3×3 real matrix representation, which has nine real components. The matrix, $\mathbf{M}$, representing the same rotation through θ about line (l, m, n) has the form

$$\mathbf{M} = \begin{pmatrix} l^2 (1 - \cos\theta) + \cos\theta & ml (1 - \cos\theta) + n\sin\theta & nl (1 - \cos\theta) - m\sin\theta \\ lm (1 - \cos\theta) - n\sin\theta & m^2 (1 - \cos\theta) + \cos\theta & nm (1 - \cos\theta) + l\sin\theta \\ ln (1 - \cos\theta) + m\sin\theta & mn (1 - \cos\theta) - l\sin\theta & n^2 (1 - \cos\theta) + \cos\theta \end{pmatrix} \quad (25)$$

A point $\mathbf{r}$ in space is represented by a 3×1 column matrix, formed from its x, y, z coordinates and the result of the rotation on $\mathbf{r}$ is then expressed in terms of matrix multiplication by the transformation

$$\mathbf{r}' = \mathbf{M}\mathbf{r} \quad (26)$$

where $\mathbf{r}'$ is the new position of the point.

Clearly, the quaternion representation (eq. (22)) is concise, elegant, and less redundant than the equivalent matrix representation (eq. (25)). But there is a certain trade-off involved in using the former, because of the slightly greater complexity of the transformation required to operate on a point (compare eqs. (24) and (26)). However, if several successive transformations are to be performed (as is usual for manipulator kinematics), the quaternion representation is the more efficient approach. Furthermore, one of its main advantages is that it represents the rotation explicitly in terms of the axis of rotation.

We conclude this chapter by briefly returning to the general spatial screw displacement and dual quaternions. The formalism for this representation is very similar to that for the real quaternions that were previously considered, except that now there is no fixed point in the body to be screw displaced and we describe the geometry in terms of lines. A dual quaternion $\hat{q}$ is again an algebraic construct but it consists of four *dual* components, which therefore involve eight real components in all. It has the form

$$\hat{q} = (a + \epsilon a_0) + i(b + \epsilon b_0) + j(c + \epsilon c_0) + k(d + \epsilon d_0) \quad (27)$$

where

$$i^2 = j^2 = k^2 = ijk = -1, \quad \epsilon^2 = 0 \quad (28)$$

and a, a_0, b, b_0, c, c_0, d, and d_0 are real.

Two such dual quaternions may be added, subtracted, multiplied, and divided within a definite system of rules, again, forming a (noncommutative) algebra. As with the real quaternions, division requires pre- or postmultiplication by an inverse defined as

$$\hat{q}^{-1} = \frac{(a + \epsilon a_0) - i(b + \epsilon b_0) - j(c + \epsilon c_0) - k(d + \epsilon d_0)}{(a^2 + b^2 + c^2 + d^2) + 2\epsilon(aa_0 + bb_0 + cc_0 + dd_0)} \quad (29)$$

so that

$$\hat{q}\hat{q}^{-1} = \hat{q}^{-1}\hat{q} = 1$$

The dual quaternion representing a screw displacement through angle θ and distance S,

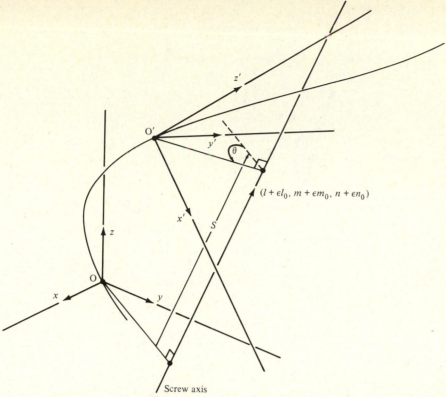

Figure 8.43 A general spatial screw displacement of the coordinate system through angle θ and distance S about an axis with dual direction cosines $(l + \epsilon l_0, m + \epsilon m_0, n + \epsilon n_0)$.

about a general line with dual direction cosines $(l + \epsilon l_0)$, $(m + \epsilon m_0)$, and $(n + \epsilon n_0)$ (Fig. 8.43), then has the form

$$
\begin{aligned}
\hat{q} = {} & \left(\cos \frac{\theta}{2} - \epsilon \frac{S}{2} \sin \frac{\theta}{2} \right) \\
& + i \left[l \sin \frac{\theta}{2} + \epsilon \left(l \frac{S}{2} \cos \frac{\theta}{2} + l_0 \sin \frac{\theta}{2} \right) \right] \\
& + j \left[m \sin \frac{\theta}{2} + \epsilon \left(m \frac{S}{2} \cos \frac{\theta}{2} + m_0 \sin \frac{\theta}{2} \right) \right] \\
& + k \left[n \sin \frac{\theta}{2} + \epsilon \left(n \frac{S}{2} \cos \frac{\theta}{2} + n_0 \sin \frac{\theta}{2} \right) \right]
\end{aligned}
\tag{30}
$$

A general line $\hat{r}$ in space is also represented by a dual quaternion with zero first component and with its three dual direction cosines forming the remaining three components; thus,

$$
\hat{r} = i(L + \epsilon L_0) + j(M + \epsilon M_0) + k(N + \epsilon N_0)
\tag{31}
$$

Finally, the result of the screw displacement represented by $\hat{q}$ (given by eq. (30)), acting on any

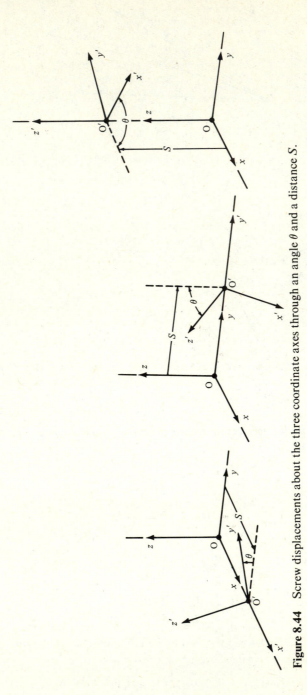

Figure 8.44 Screw displacements about the three coordinate axes through an angle θ and a distance S.

line $\hat{r}$ (given by eq. (31)) is then expressed, in terms of dual quaternion multiplication, by the transformation

$$\hat{r}' = \hat{q}^{-1}\hat{r}\hat{q} \tag{32}$$

where $r^{\wedge\prime}$ is the new position of the screw displaced line. The effects of performing particular screw displacements about the x, y, and z axes, respectively (no fixed point), are illustrated by Figure 8.44.

This dual quaternion representation with four dual components (and hence eight real components) may be contrasted with the more usual 4×4 real matrix representation that is commonly used for general spatial displacements. This has 16 real components, although four of these are always either zero or unity (Rooney, 1978) and is similar in form to the 3×3 real matrix of equation (25). As with the real quaternion, the dual quaternion is concise and elegant, and for several successive transformations it is more efficient than the matrix. However, one of its chief advantages is that it represents the screw displacement explicitly in terms of the screw axis.

In this chapter we have examined some of the concepts and ideas involved in robot manipulator kinematics and in this section we reviewed some of the mathematical techniques and representations that are used to describe kinematic geometry. These areas are usually neglected, despite their central role, for two main reasons: first, there is a general lack of awareness and understanding of the nature and extent of the principles involved in manipulation, and second, 3D kinematics is conceptually difficult, requiring advanced mathematical techniques and representations. It is hoped that this chapter has gone some way towards altering the situation.

References

Asimov, I. 1950. *I, Robot*. London: Panther Science Fiction/Granada Publishing.

Ball, R. S. 1900. *The Theory of Screws*. Cambridge, England: Cambridge University Press.

Berge, C. 1977. *Graphs and Hypergraphs*. Amsterdam: North-Holland.

Bottema, O., and Roth, B. 1979. *Theoretical Kinematics*. Amsterdam: North-Holland.

Brand, L. 1947. *Vector and Tensor Analysis*. New York: Wiley.

Butler, S. 1872. *Erewhon, or, Over the Range*. Harmondsworth: Penguin English Library.

Čapek, K. 1923. *R.U.R. (Rossum's Universal Robots)*. Oxford: Oxford University Press.

Clifford, W. K. 1873. Preliminary sketch of biquaternions. In *Proceedings of the London Mathematical Society* 4(64,65): 381–395.

Duffy, J., and Crane, C. 1980. A displacement analysis of the general spatial 7-link, 7R mechanism. *Mechanism and Machine Theory* 15: 153–169.

Duffy, J., and Derby, S. 1979. Displacement analysis of a spatial 7R mechanism—A generalised lobster's arm. *Trans. ASME Journal of Mechanical Design* 101: 224–231.

Duffy, J., and Rooney, J. 1974. Displacement analysis of spatial six-link, 5R-C mechanisms. *Trans. ASME Journal of Applied Mechanics* 41(series E,3): 759–766.

Earl, C. F., and Rooney, J. 1982. Some kinematic structures for robot manipulator designs. ASME paper 82-DET-89 in 17th Biennial Mechanisms Conference, Washington, D.C. September. (In press)

Engelberger, J. F. 1980. *Robotics in Practice*. London: Kogan Page.

Hamilton, W. R. 1899. *Elements of Quaternions*, Cambridge, England: Cambridge University Press.

Hunt, K. H. 1978. *Kinematic Geometry of Mechanisms*. Oxford: Clarendon Press.

Hunt, K. H. 1982. Structural kinematics of in-parallel-actuated robot-arms. ASME paper in 17th Biennial Mechanisms Conference, Washington, D.C., September.

Phillips, J. R., and Hunt, K. H. 1964. On the theorem of three axes in the spatial motion of three bodies. *Australian Journal of Applied Science* 15: 267–287.

Reichardt, J. 1978. *Robots: Fact, Fiction and Prediction*. London: Thames & Hudson.

Reuleaux, F. 1876. *The Kinematics of Machinery*. New York: Dover (Reprint 1963—Original, Macmillan).

Rooney, J. 1975a. On obtaining the velocity motor of any link in a general *n*-link spatial manipulator. In *Inst. Mechanical Engineering Proceedings of the Fourth World Congress of IFToMM* 5: 1083–1087, Newcastle-upon-Tyne, September.

Rooney, J. 1975b. On the principle of transference. In *Inst. Mechanical Engineering Proceedings of the Fourth World Congress of IFToMM* 5: 1089–1094, Newcastle-upon-Tyne, September.

Rooney, J. 1977. A survey of representations of spatial rotation about a fixed point. *Environment and Planning B* 4: 185–210.

Rooney, J. 1978. A comparison of representations of general spatial screw displacement. *Environment and Planning B* 5: 45–88.

Rooney, J., and Duffy, J. 1972. On the closures of spatial mechanisms. ASME paper 72-Mech-77 in 12th ASME Mechanisms Conference, San Francisco, October.

Study, E. 1901. *Geometrie der Dynamen*. Leipzig: Teubner.

Yaglom, I. M. 1968. Complex Numbers in Geometry. New York: Academic Press.

Annotated Bibliography

Asimov, I. *I, Robot*. London: Panther Science Fiction, Granada Publishing, 1950.

This is a collection of short science fiction stories, each about a particular aspect of possible robot behaviour. The robots are considered to be machines, designed and engineered to perform specific tasks and services, and are not presented primarily as menacing threats to humanity. These stories are memorable in that they explore robot "psychology" and introduce both the term *robotics* and the famous *three laws of robotics*, namely,

1. A robot may not injure a human being, nor, through inaction, allow a human being to come to harm.
2. A robot must obey the orders given it by human beings, except where such orders would conflict with the first law.
3. A robot must protect its own existence as long as such protection does not conflict with the first or second law.

Many subsequent science fiction stories have been based on the implementation and/or logical consistency of these three laws.

Ball, R. S. *The Theory of Screws*. Cambridge: Cambridge University Press, 1900.

This little known classic (with classic author and title) has only recently been rediscovered and its central importance is now recognised in the kinematic geometry of mechanisms and manipulators. It is a mathematical treatise that derives and develops an elegant theory for representing the general motion (under a general system of forces) of systems of rigid bodies in three-dimensional space. A stimulating read, although heavy going for those without a mathematical background or some knowledge of theoretical mechanics.

Berge, C. *Graphs and Hypergraphs*. Amsterdam: North-Holland, 1977.

An advanced textbook and comprehensive reference on graph theory. It is also one of the few books on graphs that also discusses hypergraphs in the same context.

Bottema, O., and Roth, B. *Theoretical Kinematics*. Amsterdam: North-Holland, 1979.

This book presents a predominantly algebraic approach to the subject, by an eminent mathematician (Bottema) who has long been an active force in algebraic geometry and kinematics, and an equally well-respected leader in the kinematics community (Roth). The treatment is largely analytical and mathematically demanding of the reader. However, the presentation is very good, being clear and concise on most topics. The authors mainly treat the idealized linear elements (points, lines, and planes) embedded in kinematic spaces and investigate the geometric properties that arise under those transformations referred to as *motions*. An excellent advanced text, appealing to the theoretically minded and mathematically oriented reader—not for the beginner.

Brand, L. *Vector and Tensor Analysis*. New York: Wiley, 1947.

This highly recommended text is one of the best that is available on the subject. It is clearly written and provides a unified comprehensive coverage of most types of vector, tensor, and related concepts, encountered in applied mathematics. This includes much interesting discussion of their interrelationships. It is also one of the few modern texts that discusses *dual vectors, motors, quaternions, dyadics,* and so on, and it does this consistently within the same framework.

Butler, S. *Erewhon, or, Over the Range*. Harmondsworth: Penguin English Library, 1872.

In this unconventional novel, Butler uses the device of an imaginary journey to a bizarre place (Erewhon) to satirize society. It was inspired by Darwin's *Origin of Species* and has many interesting passages on the evolution of form and of consciousness in plants, animals, humans, and machines. His treatment of machines is particularly interesting and he deals with several aspects of their possible future development which are uncannily close to the reality of subsequent events. Some of the topics discussed include, the trend towards miniaturization, the effects of autonomous (intelligent) behaviour, and ultimately machine (intellectual) superiority over humans. Of course, eventually the Erewhonians forbid all machines.

Čapek, K. *R.U.R. (Rossum's Universal Robots)*. Oxford: Oxford University Press, 1923.

This classic play by the Czech novelist Karel Čapek is the source of the word *robot* (from *robotit: to drudge*), used in its modern sense to signify an autonomous machine that is manufactured to provide a general-purpose workhorse for humankind. The play provides an entertaining read, although it presents a rather sinister and gloomy viewpoint on the future of human–robot interaction, since the robots eventually destroy humankind and then replace them.

Clifford, W. K. "Preliminary sketch of Biquaternions." In *Proceedings of the London Mathematical Society* 4(64,65): 381–395, 1873.

This technical paper is the original source of the *dual quaternion* concept, which Clifford refers to as *biquaternions*. However, Hamilton had used the latter word for quaternions with complex number components, whereas Clifford uses it to refer to quaternions with *dual number* components (his own invention). An interesting read, although the notation needs updating.

Duffy, J., and Crane, C. "A Displacement Analysis of the General Spatial 7-Link, 7R Mechanism." *Mechanism and Machine Theory* 15: 153–169, 1980.

This technical paper represents a major advance in the field of mechanism analysis. The determination of the input–output equation (and, in particular, its degree) for the 7-revolute mechanism is central to the task of specifying joint angles for a 6-revolute manipulator, given its gripper position and orientation. After many years work by several researchers (including the author of this chapter), this intractable problem appears now to have been solved. The authors finally derived a degree 32 equation, indicating thirty-two postures for the associated 6-revolute manipulator with general geometry. However, they failed to obtain any choice of parameters (twist angles, etc.) that would give thirty-two real solutions.

Duffy, J., and Derby, S. "Displacement Analysis of a Spatial 7R Mechanism—A Generalised Lobster's Arm." In *Trans. ASME, Journal of Mechanical Design* 101: 224–231, April 1979.

In this technical paper, an input–output equation of degree 24 is derived for a 7-revolute single-loop spatial linkage, with consecutive joint axes intersecting. The kinematic geometry of the associated open-loop manipulator, obtained from the linkage, resembles that of a lobster's arm.

Duffy, J., and Rooney, J. "Displacement Analysis of Spatial Six-link, 5R-C Mechanisms." In *Trans. ASME, Journal of Applied Mechanics,* 41 (Series E,3): 759–766, September 1974.

In this technical paper the input–output equations (relating two angular variables) for two 6-link single-loop spatial linkages, with five revolutes and one cylindric joint, are derived. The difficult derivation shows (for the first time) that these equations are of degree 16, and hence the linkages have sixteen distinct closures in general. A manipulator based on either linkage could therefore adopt sixteen different postures.

Earl, C. F., and Rooney, J. "Some Kinematic Structures for Robot Manipulator Designs." ASME paper 82-DET-89 in 17th Biennial Mechanisms Conference Washington D.C., September 1982. (To be published in ASME Journal Mechanical Design.)

This is a technical paper dealing mainly with nonanthropomorphic manipulator designs in terms of their kinematic structure. Modular designs are derived by using two types of components (actuation and distribution). Some knowledge of kinematics and familiarity with graph theory are assumed.

Engelberger, J. F. *Robotics in Practice.* London: Kogan Page, 1980.

This recent text by the so-called "father of industrial robots," and the founder and president of Unimation, Inc., the world's first and (currently) largest industrial robot company, is an excellent introduction to the subject of robotics in the manufacturing context. The main emphasis is placed on applications and application areas rather than on robot designs and associated software structure, but this is appropriate for the intended audience. The treatment is comprehensive, although it is aimed more at managers than at engineers. The book is recommended reading for anyone who is interested in the industrial robot field.

Hamilton, W. R. *Elements of Quaternions.* Cambridge, England: Cambridge University Press, 1899.

This classic text by the famous Irish mathematician, Hamilton, was the culmination of many years of work, aimed at deriving a logically consistent algebra for ordered triples of real numbers that would be as useful as the real number algebra, and the complex number algebra (for ordered pairs of real numbers). In fact, Hamilton showed the task to be impossible for triples but derived a suitable algebra for ordered quadruples of real numbers—hence the name *quaternion.* Subsequent work by Gibbs led to the separation of the multiplication rule for quaternions into two parts—the dot product and the cross product—in common use today for ordered triples (i.e., vectors in 3D space). A very interesting book, although heavy going for the nonmathematician.

Hunt, K. H. *Kinematic Geometry of Mechanisms.* Oxford: Clarendon Press, 1978.

This excellent recent text on kinematic geometry by a world leader in the subject (and the originator of much of it) presents, in an eminently readable form, a concise and lucid exposition of the principles. It is greatly complemented by the many clear figures illustrating (often conceptually difficult) ideas and by the liberal use of several alphabets to distinguish different mathematical constructs. The book provides a more geometrical approach to the *theory of screws* than is found in Ball (1900) and so is more accessible. It also advances the subject considerably in its application to spatial linkage systems and robot manipulators. It is not aimed specifically at any one particular audience, although it probably falls between final year undergraduate and postgraduate levels. The book will appeal to those of a theoretical disposition, and will be attractive to anyone with a well-developed geometric appreciation and/or intuition.

Hunt, K. H. "Structural Kinematics of In-Parallel-Actuated Robot-Arms." ASME paper in 17th Biennial Mechanisms Conference, Washington, D.C., September 1982.

This is a technical paper dealing with some nonanthropomorphic manipulator designs based on the Stewart platform (which is used as a flight simulator). A knowledge of kinematics is assumed, although the presentation is excellent with good clear diagrams.

Phillips, J. R., and Hunt, K. H. "On the Theorem of Three Axes in the Spatial Motion of Three Bodies." *Australian Journal of Applied Science* 15:267–287, 1964.

This technical paper is one of the first in recent times to discuss the theory of screws and its modern application to systems of interconnected rigid bodies in space. In particular, it reintroduces the *cylindroid,* a ruled surface (of central importance in kinematic geometry) whose generators are possible screw axes. As is usual from these two pioneering authors, the presentation is good, with excellent clear diagrams illustrating the conceptually difficult geometry.

Reichardt, J. *Robots: Fact, Fiction and Prediction.* London: Thames & Hudson, 1978.

This nontechnical book presents a useful overview of the past, present, and possible future of robots and related devices or systems. In particular, it has a brief illustrated chronology of the field, covering most of the significant events in mythology, literature, art, and technology. The approach is entertaining and provides interesting background material in an accessible form.

Reuleaux, F. *The Kinematics of Machinery.* New York: Dover (Reprint, 1963—Original, Macmillan, 1876).

This classic nineteenth-century text by the German kinematician Franz Reuleaux was the first systematic attempt to derive a classification scheme for machines. It was a major pioneering work which has only been bettered recently. Definitely recommended—it provides a very interesting and well-written development of the subject, and discusses general issues of design, innovation, and so on in wider contexts.

Rooney, J. "On Obtaining the Velocity Motor of any Link in a General *n*-Link Spatial Manipulator." In *Inst. Mechanical Engineering Proceedings of the Fourth World Congress of IFToMM* 5:1083–1087, Newcastle-upon-Tyne, September 1975.

This technical paper investigates the use of *motors* (another name for dual vectors) to derive the instantaneous screw motion of any component in a manipulator system. The resulting complicated algebraic expressions are greatly simplified by utilizing a recursive notation, previously developed by the author.

Rooney, J. "On the Principle of Transference." In *Inst. Mechanical Engineering Proceedings of the Fourth World Congress of IFToMM* 5:1089–1094, Newcastle-upon-Tyne, September 1975.

This technical paper derives and proves the direct relationship between systems of intersecting straight lines (involving *spherical geometry*) and general systems of skew lines (involving *spatial geometry*), in terms of dual numbers and dual vectors. The original proof by Kotelnikov was lost during the Russian Revolution.

Rooney, J. "A Survey of Representations of Spatial Rotation About a Fixed Point." *Environment and Planning B* 4: 185–210, 1977.

This technical paper presents a comparison of five methods of representing a general rigid-body rotation about a fixed point. Unlike the screw-displacement case in Rooney (1978), there is now no distinction between point transformations and line transformations. The "best" representation is shown to be the *unit real quaternion*.

Rooney, J. "A Comparison of Representations of General Spatial Screw Displacement." *Environment and Planning B* 5: 45–88, 1978.

This technical paper presents a comparison of eight methods of representing a general spatial rigid-body screw displacement. A distinction is made between the screw displacement of points and that of lines. The *4 × 4 real matrix* operating on a column vector of homogeneous coordinates is shown to be the "best" representation for point transformations. The *unit dual quaternion* is similarly found to be the "best" representation for line transformations.

Rooney, J., and Duffy, J. "On the Closures of Spatial Mechanisms." ASME paper 72-Mech-77 in 12th ASME Mechanisms Conference, San Francisco, October 1972.

A technical paper that derives the number of *closures* for a range of 3-, 4-, 5-, 6- and 7-link single-loop spatial linkages and structures. These closures can be directly related to the *postures* of spatial manipulators.

Study, E. *Geometrie der Dynamen*. Leipzig: Teubner, 1901.

Study was the first to introduce the notion of a *dual angle* in this pioneering work. However, it is now difficult to obtain in translated form.

Yaglom, I. M. *Complex Numbers in Geometry*. New York: Academic Press, 1968.

An essential book for anyone who is interested in geometric algebras. It discusses many different "generalised" complex and hypercomplex numbers with an emphasis on geometrical application. In particular, it introduces the familiar *complex number* $a + ib$ (where $i^2 = -1$), and two related numbers:—the *dual number*, $a + \epsilon b$ (where $\epsilon^2 = 0$), and the *double number*, $a + \iota b$ (where $\iota^2 = +1$). The book goes on to discuss *quaternions, dual quaternions, octonions,* and so on. Many of these are useful in geometry and kinematics.

CHAPTER 9

IMPLEMENTING NATURAL LANGUAGE PARSERS

HENRY THOMPSON
and
GRAEME RITCHIE

This chapter provides a detailed discussion of two techniques for implementing natural language parsers. We assume that the reader had some familiarity with both LISP (see Chapters 2 and 3) and the fundamentals of syntax and syntax diagrams. The role of parsers in natural language processing, and some of the difficult representational and design issues involved, are discussed in Chapter 11.

The first type of parser we will discuss is known as a *nondeterministic* parser. Such a parser is so called not because it behaves in a random fashion, but rather, because the action to be performed at any moment (i.e., the syntactic structure to be built) is *not* uniquely determined by the current state of the parser and the current input symbol. In other words, the parser makes its "best guess" at any moment but may have to back up if its best guess turns out later to be wrong. To see why this may be useful, try parsing the following sentence:

THE OLD MAN THE BOATS.

This sentence is difficult for most people to parse, because we tend to assume that MAN is a noun and OLD is an adjective. In fact, this sentence only makes sense if it is reparsed, taking OLD as a noun (as in THE OLD RECEIVE PENSIONS) and MAN as a verb (as in MAN THE

SAILS). A nondeterministic parser would be capable of backing up and trying this second alternative once it realized that its first parse was unsuccessful. Nondeterminism requires special machinery for storing alternative interpretations and for maintaining alternative pending hypotheses. One way of providing this machinery involves a formalism known as the *chart,* which is described in detail in the first part of this chapter.

The second kind of parser we will deal with, called a *deterministic* parser, would stick with its first interpretation of the above sentence, even though it might be wrong. Deterministic parsing is computationally less demanding than nondeterministic parsing, since it has no automatic mechanism for finding multiple interpretations of a sentence. This means that it is likely to be more error-prone than nondeterministic parsing, but this can be a blessing in disguise if the designer of a parser intends it to be stumped by sentences that people find very difficult to parse. The secret of deterministic parsing lies in making choices intelligently, thus minimizing the number of erroneous parses. Intelligent choices usually depend on some mechanism for sneaking a look at upcoming parts of the input sentence, and it is here that special *lookahead* machinery is required. This machinery is the heart of the deterministic parser described in detail in the second half of this chapter.

For both types of parsers that are presented subsequently, a general introduction to the relevant technique is given, followed by a step-by-step specification of the LISP functions that are necessary to implement it. The functions are shown in the InterLISP dialect (Teitelman, 1978) in order to improve readability and are reworked into a minimal dialect of LISP in the appendices.

NONDETERMINISTIC PARSING: THE CHART

The original conception of the *chart* as a representation for syntactic structure is based on work by Earley (1970), Kay (1973), and Colmerauer (1970). The easiest way to think about a chart is to regard it as a variant of a syntax tree, with the added virtues of being able to represent alternative parses and also to represent pending hypotheses. To illustrate this, let's look at a traditional syntax diagram for the sentence that was presented earlier, THE OLD MAN THE BOATS:

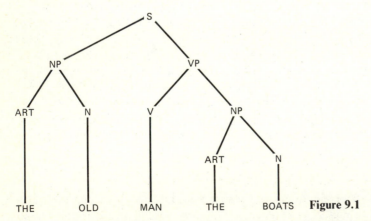

Figure 9.1

The preceding syntax diagram uses *nodes* in a *tree* to depict both terminal symbols (such as OLD) and nonterminal symbols (such as NP). The chart alters this perspective slightly by using *edges* in a *graph* to depict terminal and nonterminal symbols. Figure 9.2*a* shows the chart representation for the same sentence as that shown in Figure 9.1.

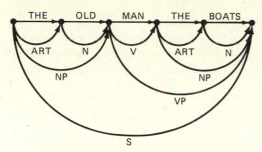

Figure 9.2*a*

A sentence is parsed by constructing edges that span (i.e., "account for") increasingly large sections of the original graph of terminal symbols, which is simply

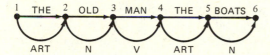   **Figure 9.2*b***

In actual practice, the first level of nonterminal symbol (i.e., a word's syntactic class) can be obtained quickly from a prestored lexicon, so that the initial chart on which the parser does its hard work looks more like that shown in Figure 9.2*c*. We number the nodes for ease of reference, as discussed here. This example has so far been biased in order to show only the

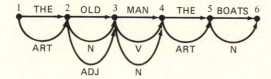   **Figure 9.2*c***

correct outcome. The chart representation begins to come into its own when we allow it to contain syntactic alternatives. Thus, **OLD** might be either an adjective or a noun, and **MAN** might be either a noun or a verb. This is represented in a straightforward way in the chart by allowing multiple edges, as shown in Figure 9.2*d*. When a "spanning edge" is constructed

Figure 9.2*d*

during the parse, its internal representation contains information about which nodes it connects and which particular edges it subsumes. Thus, the edge labelled **NP** contains internal details to the effect that it connects nodes 1 and 3 and that it subsumes the first two, **ART** and **N** edges (Fig. 9.2*e*). We will use square brackets in the diagrams to indicate subsumed edges: that is,

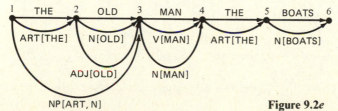

Figure 9.2*e*

NP [ART,N] means that the edge labelled **NP** subsumes, or spans, the edges labelled **ART** and **N**. The precise details of which edges are involved requires a more complicated internal format, which we will describe later.

During the course of parsing, pending hypotheses can also be represented in the chart, using *active edges* (Kay, 1980). To illustrate briefly, if our parser expects to encounter a noun phrase that in turn is expected to consist of an article followed by a noun, we can depict that expectation in the chart as shown in Figure 9.2*f*. Other hypotheses can be represented similarly.

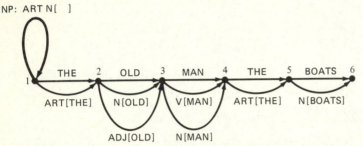

Figure 9.2*f*

The active edge shown at the top will in effect slowly leapfrog across the chart, with ever more spanning edges being constructed along the way.

Where the inactive edges of the chart represent complete constituents, the active edges represent incomplete constituents. Where inactive edges indicate the presence of such and such a constituent, with such and such a substructure, extending from here to there, active edges indicate a stage in the search for a constituent. As such, they must record the category of the constituent under construction, its substructure as found so far, and some specification of how it may be extended and/or completed. The next section describes how this is done.

The Fundamental Rule

The basic event in chart parsing is the encounter between active and inactive edges. If an active edge and an inactive edge meet, and the inactive one satisfies the needs of the active one, then a new, more complete edge can be built. This is the *fundamental rule* of active chart parsing, and can be expressed more explicitly as follows:

The Fundamental Rule

Whenever the far end of an active edge *A* and the near end of an inactive edge *I* meet for the first time, if *I* satisfies *A*'s conditions for extension, then build a new edge as follows:

· Its near end is the near end of *A*.
· Its far end is the far end of *I*.
· Its category is the category of *A*.
· Its contents are a function (dependent on the grammatical formalism employed) of the contents of *A* and the category and contents of *I*.
· It is inactive or active depending on whether or not this extension completes *A*.

Note that neither *A* nor *I* is modified by the preceding process—a completely new edge is constructed. In the case of *A*, this may seem surprising and wasteful of space, but in fact, it is crucial to the proper handling of ambiguity. It guarantees that all parses will be found, independent of the order in which operations are performed. Whenever further inactive edges are added at this point the continued presence of *A*, together with the fundamental rule, ensures that alternative extensions of *A* will be pursued as appropriate.

A short example in terms of a trivial context-free phrase-structure rule should make the workings of the fundamental rule clear. Figures 9.3*a* to 9.3*d* show the parsing of **THE MAN** by the rule **NP** —> **Art N**. In these figures, inactive edges are light lines below the row of vertices. Active edges are heavy lines above the row. Figure 9.3*a* simply shows the two inactive edges for the string with form-class information.

Figure 9.3*a*

Figure 9.3*b* shows the addition of an empty active edge at the left-hand end of the chart. We will discuss where it comes from in the next section. Its addition to the chart invokes the fundamental rule, with this edge being *A* and the edge for **THE** being *I*.

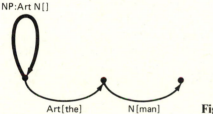

Figure 9.3*b*

The notation here for the active edges is the category being sought, in this case **NP**, followed by a colon, followed by a list of the categories that are needed for extension/completion, in this case, **Art** followed by **N**, followed by a bracketed list of subconstituents, in this case, empty. Since the first symbol of the extension specification of *A* matches the category of *I*, a new edge is created by the fundamental rule, as shown in Figure 9.3*c*.

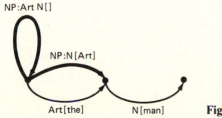

Figure 9.3*c*

This edge represents a partially completed **NP**, still needing an **N** to complete, with a partial structure. Its addition to the chart invokes the fundamental rule again, this time with it as *A* and the MAN edge as *I*. Once again, the extension condition is met, and a new edge is constructed. This one is inactive, however, as nothing more is required to complete it.

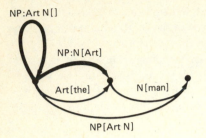

Figure 9.3*d*

The fundamental rule is invoked for the last time, back at the left-hand end of the chart, because the empty NP edge (active) now meets the complete NP edge (inactive) for the first time, but nothing comes of this as Art does not match NP, and so the process comes to a halt with the chart as shown in Figure 9.3*d*.

Implementation: The Chart and the Fundamental Rule

In this section we will provide detailed specifications for an implementation of the data structures of the chart and the workings of the fundamental rule, relative to one particular grammatical formalism. As will be discussed subsequently, other formalisms can easily be substituted without major changes.

Before plunging in, a note on the presentation of the implementation. In the body of the text we will use InterLISP, for its naturalness and readability. Marginal comments are given in italics, and preceded by a semicolon. In the appendix to this chapter there is a complete implementation in a minimal LISP—we believe it should run on virtually any LISP, provided the arguments to the mapping functions are correct(ed). Function names that follow are presented as the first element of a square-bracketed list, followed by the lambda-form which defines the function. Thus, the notation

```
[GetVertex
    (LAMBDA (n)
        (OR (CAR (NTH Vertices n))
            (HELP "not a vertex number" n)))]
```

is identical to the following format as used in Chapters 2 and 3:

```
(defun GetVertex (n)
        (or (car (nth vertices n))
            (help "not a vertex number" n)))
```

The following examples use "assignment arrows" rather than SETQ, so that

```
N <— 3
```

is equivalent to

> (SETQ N 3)

First, the chart itself. It consists of vertices and edges. From a vertex we need to access incoming and outgoing edges. We will keep active and inactive edges separate, and identify each vertex with a number, giving the following record structure:

> (Record Vertex
>   ((activeIn . activeOut)
>   vNumber inactiveIn . inactiveOut))

In InterLISP, records provide a perspicuous way for creating and accessing structured data objects. The preceding declaration names the record **vertex** and lays out its component parts. It is analogous to the **defstruct** facility of MacLISP, described in Chapter 3. The special function **create** builds instances of named records:

> (create ⟨recordname⟩ ⟨fieldname1⟩ <− ⟨value1⟩ . . .)

Suffixed field names of the form ⟨record⟩:⟨fieldname⟩ extract and set fields. For example, the first vertex from Figure 9.3*d* would look like this:

> (((({*empty NP edge*}) . ({*partial NP edge*} {*empty NP edge*}))
>   1 NIL . ({*complete NP edge*} {*Art edge*}))

(Here and subsequently we use forms like {*Art edge*}, {*edge 3*}, {*vertex 2*} to indicate the presence of the complete structure for the indicated edge or vertex.) If V1 were bound to this structure, then the value of V1:inactiveOut (read as the inactiveOut field of record V1) would be

> ({*complete NP edge*} {*Art edge*})

and

> V1:inactiveOut <− NIL

would change the structure to

> (((({*empty NP edge*}) . ({*partial NP edge*} {*empty NP edge*})) 1 NIL . NIL)

For edges we must have the category they represent, their left and right ends, their contents, and, if active, what they need to be extended. An identifying number is added as well, giving the following record structure:

> (Record Edge ((cat eNumber left . right) contents . needed))

We could put the edges themselves into the vertices, and vice versa, but the resulting circular structures, although perfectly useable, would be hard to debug. For the purposes of this implementation, then, we will put edges in vertices, but only vertex *numbers* in edges. For example, the partial NP edge from Figures 9.3c and 9.3d would be

((NP 4 1 . 2) ({*Art edge*}) . (N)).

Using vertex numbers in edges will necessitate a lookup when we need to find the left or right end of an edge. Opting for simplicity over efficiency, we will keep a numerically ordered list of vertices, and use the function NTH to find them (here and in subsequent function definitions, sample calls and return values are illustrated):

```
[CreateVertex
    (LAMBDA NIL
        (PROG (vertex)
            (vertex <- (create Vertex
                            vNumber <- (VertexCount <- (ADD1 VertexCount))))
            (Vertices <- (NCONC1 Vertices vertex))
            (RETURN vertex)))]
```

Call: (CreateVertex)   Return: **(NIL 1 NIL)**

```
[GetVertex
    (LAMBDA (n)
        (OR (CAR (NTH Vertices n))
            (HELP "not a vertex number" n)))]
```

Call: (GetVertex 1)   Return: **(NIL 1 NIL)**

As edges also need a counter installed, we have as well:

```
[CreateEdge
    (LAMBDA (cat needed contents left right)
        (create Edge cat <- cat
                    needed <- needed
                    contents <- contents
                    left <- left:vNumber
                    right <- right:vNumber
                    eNumber <- (EdgeCount <- (ADD1 EdgeCount))))]
```

Call: (CreateEdge 'NP '(Art N) NIL {*vertex 3*} {*vertex 3*})
Return: **((NP 5 3 . 3) NIL . (Art N))**

Note that as what we will mostly pass around are actual vertices, we now extract the vertex numbers for inclusion in the edge. The same record will be used for both active and inactive edges—we can always tell what we've got by what field of a vertex we got it from. Also, the **needed** field will be **NIL** for inactive edges, non-**NIL** for active ones.

We need not only create edges but also actually need to install them in the chart. For this we use a pair of functions, one for each sort of edge:

```
[AddActiveEdge
    (LAMBDA (left right cat contents needed)
        (PROG (edge)
            (edge <- (CreateEdge cat              ; make the edge
                                  needed
                                  contents
                                  left
                                  right))
            (left:activeOut <- (CONS edge left:activeOut))    ; add it to
            (right:activeIn <- (CONS edge right:activeIn))    ; the vertices
            (for inactive in right:inactiveOut       ; the fundamental rule
                do (push Agenda
                        (create Config active <- edge
                                       inactive <- inactive)))))]
```

Call: (AddActiveEdge {*vertex 3*} {*vertex 3*} 'NP NIL '(Art N))
Return: **NIL**

```
[AddInactiveEdge
    (LAMBDA (left right cat contents)
        (PROG (edge)
            (edge <- (CreateEdge cat              ; make the edge
                                  NIL             ; inactive, so nothing needed
                                  contents
                                  left
                                  right))
            (left:inactiveOut <- (CONS edge left:inactiveOut))    ; add it to
            (right:inactiveIn <- (CONS edge right:inactiveIn))    ; the vertices
            (for active in left:activeIn       ; the fundamental rule
                do (push Agenda
                        (create Config inactive <- edge
                                       active <- active)))))]
```

Call: (AddInactiveEdge {*vertex 3*} {*vertex 5*} 'NP '({*Art edge*} {*NP edge*}))
Return: **NIL**

These functions make use of another InterLISP facility, the iterative statement. Such constructs as

```
(for VAR in LIST do FORM1 . . .)
```

and

```
(while CONDITION collect FORM2)
```

allow the perspicuous expression of mapping operations. The first will evaluate FORM1 repeatedly, with VAR bound to each element of LIST in turn. The second will assemble a list of the result of the repeated evaluation of FORM2, as long as CONDITION remains true. Other keywords such as on, for iteration over tails instead of elements, and thereis, for iterative search for a non-NIL value, will be used later in what we hope is a straightforward interpretable fashion.

In these functions the fundamental rule has appeared. There are two ways that two edges can meet for the first time—when a new active edge is added, at its far (right) end, and when a new inactive edge is added, at its near (left) end. Thus, the two loops at the end of the previous functions go through the appropriate edge set at the relevant vertex and create instances of a record called a Config, which are then added to a list called Agenda. A Config is just a pair of edges:

```
(Record Config (active . inactive))
```

It records a possible occasion for the fundamental rule to operate. We could, of course, have simply called a function to implement the fundamental rule inside each of the loops, but using an agenda gives us a simpler organisation and allows us flexibility with respect to the choice of *depth-first* versus *breadth-first* search. If we use the agenda as a last-in-first-out queue of tasks, processing will be depth-first, backtracking style. If on the other hand, we run first-in-first-out, processing will be breadth-first, pseudo-parallel style. This will be clearer subsequently.

If the agenda is a queue of configurations for submission to the fundamental rule, then the basic operation of the chart parser is to remove Configs from the agenda and check them against the fundamental rule:

```
[Run
   (LAMBDA NIL
      (bind current                        ; declares current as a local variable
         while (current <- (pop Agenda))
         do (TryToExtend current:active
                          current:inactive)))]
```

It is the function **TryToExtend** that actually implements the fundamental rule:

```
[TryToExtend
   (LAMBDA (active inactive)
      (PROG (needed newContents)
            (needed <- active:needed)
            (if (Match (CAR needed)          ; see if we can extend
                       inactive:cat
                       inactive:contents)
                then                                      ; success -
                    newContents <- (CONS inactive         ; add the sub-tree
                                         active:contents)  ; to the contents
                    (if (CDR needed)          ; do we still need more?
                        then (AddActiveEdge        ; yes—active
                                (GetVertex active:left)
                                (GetVertex inactive:right)
                                active:cat
                                newContents
                                (CDR needed))   ; remaining needs
                        else (AddInactiveEdge   ; no — inactive
                                (GetVertex active:left)
                                (GetVertex inactive:right)
                                active:cat
                                (REVERSE newContents))))))))]
```

```
Call: (TryToExtend '((NP 17 3 . 3) NIL . (Art N))
                   '((Art 3 3 . 4) ((lex the)) . NIL))
Return: NIL
```

If one compares this definition with the specification of the preceding fundamental rule, one can see how each clause in the specification is realised in the code. A number of incidental decisions have also been made, which must be explained before the code is completely clear.

First of all, a very simple format for the grammar has been chosen: context-free phrase-structure rules represented as

```
(Record Rule (lhs . rhs))
```

where **lhs** is the left-hand side, an atomic category, and **rhs** is a list of atomic categories making up the right-hand side. Thus, a trivial grammar for a small bit of English would be

```
(S NP VP)
(VP V NP)
(NP Art N)
(NP PropN)
```

It should be clear from this how to construct an active edge, given a rule—the lhs goes into the cat field, and the rhs is the needed field. (CAR edge:needed) will always be the next category needed, (CDR edge:needed) the rest, if any.

What about inactive edges? Before looking at complex constituents, a detour to consider the dictionary is needed. In order to avoid issues that are not central to our concerns, we will assume that a function called Defns exists that will provide for any atom corresponding to a (possibly inflected) word, a list of definitions, each consisting of a category and a (possibly empty) list of feature markings:

    (Record Definition (category . features))

The category will go in the cat field, whereas the features will go in the contents field—one inactive edge per definition. Code to implement a version of Defns in a simple, straightforward way can be found in the appendix.

As for the contents field of inactive edges representing nonterminal nodes, we will simply have there a list of the subsidiary inactive edges representing the subordinate nodes, thus giving a simple tree structure. In the preceding definition of TryToExtend, the reader will note that in order to save storage, the subtree is in fact accumulated *backwards*, by CONSing on the front, and only put in its proper order once the whole has been found.

A more complex use of the contents field could, of course, be made in a more sophisticated system, together with more complex rules. It is as a hint in this direction that the function Match is called to determine whether or not to proceed:

```
[Match
      (LAMBDA (rulepart cat contents)
            (EQ rulepart cat))]
```

    Call: (Match 'NP 'NP '({*Art edge*} {*N edge*}))   Return: **T**

If rules and contents were more complex, that complexity would have to be discharged here (and in the construction of new contents from old).

Now that all the subsidiary bits have been laid out, the reader is encouraged to look back at the definition of TryToExtend and see that all of it is now clear and that it does faithfully implement the fundamental rule.

We can now recapitulate the preceding example (Fig. 9.3*a* to 9.3*d*), showing this time the actual edges:

Edge[cat: Art	contents: ((lex the))	left: 1
eNumber: 1	needed: NIL	right: 2]
Edge[cat: N	contents: ((lex man))	left: 2
eNumber: 2	needed: NIL	right: 3]

Figure 9.4*a*

Here we suppose that the actual word (or root) is found as the value of the lex feature in the preterminal edge.

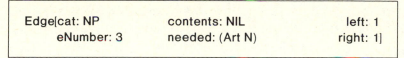

Edge[cat: NP   contents: NIL   left: 1
        eNumber: 3   needed: (Art N)   right: 1]

Figure 9.4*b*

Note that the first empty, active edge begins and ends at the same vertex. When **edge 3** is added to the chart, a Config consisting of it and **edge 1** will be put on the agenda, taken off, given to TryToExtend; Match will confirm that (CAR {edge 3}:needed) = {edge 1}:cat; and the next edge will be built:

Edge[cat: NP   contents: ({edge 1})   left: 1
        eNumber: 4   needed: (N)   right: 2]

Figure 9.4*c*

The insertion of this edge yields another new Config, consisting of it and **edge 2**, and once again, Match will succeed when TryToExtend processes it:

Edge[cat: NP   contents: ({edge 1}{edge 2})   left: 1
        eNumber: 5   needed: NIL   right: 3]

Figure 9.4*d*

As the constituent is now complete, this edge will be added as inactive. Note that the subconstituents are in the correct order, as the result of the final REVERSE.

One more Config gets built, consisting of **edges 3** and **5**, but when Match comes to compare Art and NP, it fails, and with the agenda empty, processing will cease.

We require only two more things before our parser is essentially complete—a source for preterminal **edges** such as 1 and 2, and a source for empty active **edges** such as 3. The former come from the dictionary, the latter from the grammar—in the next section we will see how.

Implementation: Lexical Edges and Seek

We already have all the information we need with respect to lexical (preterminal) edges. We can build an initial chart out of edges constructed from lexical entries:

```
[Chart
   (LAMBDA (words)
      (PROG (start left right)
            (EdgeCount <− 0)
            (VertexCount <− 0)
            (Vertices <− NIL)
            (Agenda <− NIL)
            (start <− left <− (CreateVertex))
            (for w in words
                 do (right <− (CreateVertex))
                    (for def in (Defns w)
                         do (AddInactiveEdge
                                 left
                                 right
                                 def:category
                                 def:features))
                    (left <− right))))]
```

Call: (Chart '(the man))   Return: **NIL**

Well, now we have a chart, but with no active edges it won't *do* anything. To get active edges we must first decide whether to parse *top-down* or *bottom-up* (see Chapter 11). We will choose top-down for explicit exemplification here, but later we suggest how to do bottom-up as well.

To go top-down, we must begin with a hypothesis that we are seeking to confirm. We start from the initial symbol and try to find a way to expand it into the preterminal string. In the chart what this means is that we need empty active edges at the left-hand end of the chart, one for each rule that expands the initial symbol. If we suppose that the variable TopCat contains that symbol, then what we would like is a function Seek, such that if we added

. . . (Seek TopCat start)

to the end of the definition of the preceding Chart, the right thing would happen. And in fact, if we assume that all the rules are gathered together in a list called Grammar, the definition of

Seek is straightforward:

```
[Seek
    (LAMBDA (cat vertex)
        (for rule in Grammar
            do (if (EQ rule:lhs cat)
                then (AddActiveEdge
                        vertex
                        vertex
                        cat
                        NIL
                        rule:rhs))))]
```

Call: (Seek 'S {*vertex 1*})   Return: **NIL**

We can now get started, but we still won't ever get an edge like edge 3 in Figure 9.4*b*. If we think carefully about what top-down parsing means, it is clear what we have missed. Whenever we make a hypothesis (i.e., build an active edge), we must see if that engenders any further hypotheses (i.e., subsidiary active edges). That is, when we build an active edge, we must add more active edges, looking for that which the original edge needs next. Now that we have Seek, this can easily be done by adding:

```
. . . (Seek (CAR needed) right) . . .
```

to the definition of AddActiveEdge. The worked example that follows should make clear why this is the right thing to do. Note that when (CAR needed) is a preterminal, no new edges will be built, since by definition there are no (nonlexical) rules in the grammar expanding a preterminal.

We only need one more small piece, and our parser is complete. The function Chart will build an initial chart and insert the first crucial active edge(s). Behind the scenes the fundamental rule (as expressed in AddActiveEdge and AddInactiveEdge) will put Configs on the agenda. But no one will take them off—we need to add a call to Run to our definition of Chart. And once it comes back, indicating that everything that can be done has been done, we also need to communicate the results, if any. So our final addition, at the end of the definition of Chart, is

```
(Run)
(for edge in start:inactiveOut
    do (if (AND (EQ edge:right
                    right:vNumber)
                (EQ edge:cat TopCat))
        then (ShowEdge edge)))
```

The final loop will call a function ShowEdge to display those inactive edges of the correct category that span the chart.

Implementation: A Complete Example Run

Let us now work through a simple example, showing each edge as it is built and the state of the agenda as we go. The agenda entries are shown as pairs of edge numbers, rather than of actual edges, for the sake of concision. The reader may find it helpful to construct a diagram such as those in Figures 9.3a to 9.3d as she or he reads through the example. We will use the simple grammar that has previously been given.

```
(SETQ Grammar '((S NP VP)
                (VP V NP)
                (NP Art N)
                (NP PropN)))
```

```
(Chart '(Kim likes the apple))
```

[cat: PropN eNumber: 1	left: 1 right: 2	needed: NIL contents: ((lex Kim))]	
[cat: V eNumber: 2	left: 2 right: 3	needed: NIL contents: ((lex likes))]	These four all come from the loop in Chart.
[cat: Art eNumber: 3	left: 3 right: 4	needed: NIL contents: ((lex the))]	
[cat: N eNumber: 4	left: 4 right: 5	needed: NIL contents: ((lex apple))]	
[cat: S eNumber: 5	left: 1 right: 1	needed: (NP VP) contents: NIL]	This one is from the Seek in Chart.

Agenda: ((5 . 1))

[cat: NP eNumber: 6	left: 1 right: 1	needed: (Art N) contents: NIL]	These two are from the Seek in AddActiveEdge and were provoked by edge 5.
[cat: NP eNumber: 7	left: 1 right: 1	needed: (PropN) contents: NIL]	

Agenda: ((7 . 1)(6 . 1)(5 . 1))

Note that as Art and N are preterminals, not expanded by any rule in Grammar, no further edges come from the Seek in AddActiveEdge at this point. Rather, at this point Run is called, and Configs start coming off the agenda.

(7 . 1) succeeds, giving

| [cat: NP | left: 1 | needed: NIL |
| eNumber: 8 | right: 2 | contents: ({edge 1}] |

        Agenda: ((7 . 8)(6 . 8)(5 . 8)(6 . 1)(5 . 1))

(7 . 8) and (6 . 8) fail
(5 . 8) succeeds, giving

| [cat: S | left: 1 | needed: (VP) |
| eNumber: 9 | right: 2 | contents: ({edge 8}] |

        Agenda: ((9 . 2)(6 . 1)(5 . 1))

| [cat: VP | left: 2 | needed: (V NP) |
| eNumber: 10 | right: 2 | contents: NIL] |

From the Seek in AddActiveEdge provoked by edge 9.

        Agenda: ((10 . 2)(9 . 2)(6 . 1)(5 . 1))

(10 . 2) succeeds, giving

| [cat: VP | left: 2 | needed: (NP) |
| eNumber: 11 | right: 3 | contents: ({edge 2})] |

        Agenda: ((11 . 3)(9 . 2)(6 . 1)(5 . 1))

| [cat: NP | left: 3 | needed: (Art N) |
| eNumber: 12 | right: 3 | contents: NIL] |

| [cat: NP | left: 3 | needed: (PropN) |
| eNumber: 13 | right: 3 | contents: NIL] |

From the Seek in AddActiveEdge provoked by edge 11.

        Agenda: ((13 . 3)(12 . 3)(11 . 3)(9 . 2)(6 . 1)(5 . 1))

(13 . 3) fails
(12 . 3) succeeds, giving

| [cat: NP | left: 3 | needed: (N) |
| eNumber: 14 | right: 4 | contents: ({edge 3})] |

        Agenda ((14 . 4)(11 . 3)(9 . 2)(6 . 1)(5 . 1))

Note that at this point we have a partial S, a partial VP, and a partial NP, each waiting on the next to provide what it needs.

(14 . 4) succeeds, giving

| [cat: NP | left: 3 | needed: NIL |
| eNumber: 15 | right: 5 | contents: ({edge 3}{edge 4})] |

        Agenda: ((11 . 15)(12 . 15)(13 . 15)(11 . 3)(9 . 2)(6 . 1)(5 . 1))

(11 . 15) succeeds, giving

[cat: VP   left: 2   needed: NIL
 eNumber: 16   right: 5   contents: ({edge 2}{edge 15})]

    Agenda: ((9 . 16)(10 . 16)(12 . 15)(13 . 15)(11 . 3) (9 . 2)(6 . 1)(5 . 1))

(9 . 16) succeeds, giving

[cat: S   left: 1   needed: NIL
 eNumber: 17   right: 5   contents: ({edge 8}{edge 16})]

    Agenda: ((5 . 17)(6 . 17)(7 . 17)(10 . 16)(12 . 15)
      (13 . 15)(11 . 3)(9 . 2)(6 . 1)(5 . 1))

All the remaining Configs on the agenda fail, and edge 17, which spans the chart and is of the right category, is then the one correct analysis.

Left Recursion and Redundancy Checking

The previous example does no more than illustrate the basic workings of the chart-parsing process. Important aspects of the chart-parsing approach are not illustrated, in particular, the way in which duplication of effort is avoided in ambiguous situations. That must be left to the interested reader to investigate, but there is one other thing we must do before we leave the chart. As presented, our implementation cannot deal properly with many collections of rules. For instance, if we added the following three rules to our grammar, to introduce prepositional phrases, several problems would arise:

  (PP Prep NP)
  (VP V NP PP)
  (NP NP PP)

First of all, our preceding example sentence would now receive two identical analyses, as the final NP would be sought (and found) twice, once by the original VP rule and once by the new one. Worse yet, the new NP rule is *left-recursive*, and would cause the parser to go into an infinite loop. Seeking an NP would cause an active edge embodying the new rule to be built, which would in turn cause an NP to be sought, and so on.

Fortunately, the chart makes it easy to correct both these problems. They both arise because Seek is called more than once with the same arguments—category sought and vertex. We need to ensure that only the first such call actually causes any edges to be built. By checking at the beginning of Seek to see whether the right sort of empty active edge is already present, we can easily bring this about. We wrap the old body of Seek in the following conditional:

```
[Seek
  (LAMBDA (cat vertex)
    (if (NOT (for e in vertex:activeOut
               thereis (AND (EQ e:right vertex:vNumber)
                            (EQ e:cat cat))))
      then as before]
```

The loop in the preceding conditional checks to ensure that no empty (i.e., starting and finishing at this vertex) active edges are already present, looking for the same category. Since such edges can only have come from a previous, identical call to Seek, their presence means the current call need do nothing.

With this addition our parser is complete. A full listing of a "dialect-neutral" version, including a driver and output routines, together with a simple dictionary package, can be found in the appendix. It should be emphasized that this is a stripped out, minimal set of code, and that the first thing anyone who proposes to use it should do is add tracing and debugging tools. Nothing is more frustrating than to be simply told "No parses"—a usable system must provide some means of finding out *why*.

Extensions and Modifications

There are a number of different directions in which one might extend the system as it stands. Features were mentioned previously, as a way of increasing the power of the grammatical formalism. Other extensions to an essentially context-free phrase-structure formalism are possible: Thompson (1981, 1982) describes a chart-based parser for Generalised Phrase Structure Grammar (Gazdar, 1981) which incorporates a number of such extensions. One can also move in another direction, away from phrase structure rules altogether. For instance, both recursive transition nets and augmented transition nets can be comfortably handled with a chart parser. In these cases it would be a state in the net that would fill the needed field in an active edge, recording the status of a partial analysis. This approach is described in Kaplan (1973).

It is also easy to change the decisions we made about various issues. Breadth-first processing can be obtained by taking Configs off the agenda from the other end. Bottom-up analysis will result if Seek is invoked not on the addition of active edges, but rather, on the addition of inactive ones. The interested reader is encouraged to take the code from the appendix and start experimenting. Hands-on experience is the best teacher—enjoy!

DETERMINISTIC PARSING: LOOKAHEAD

Some computational linguists try to overcome the problem of partial (local) structural ambiguity by allowing the parser to use information about several constituents (not just one word) when making structure-building decisions. Recent interest in this approach was sparked by the proposals put forward by Marcus (1980).

In Marcus's model of parsing, constituents (i.e., fragments of the syntax tree) can be held in two temporary stores (the stack and the buffer). The parser consists of a set of rules that define what action is to be taken on the basis of the contents of the two stores.

What follows is not so much a simplified Marcus parser as a "rational reconstruction" of the essential character of a stack and buffer parser, drawing on his ideas, as well as others from those who have followed him, including Church (1980), Milne (1982), and Berwick (1982).

The Stack and the Buffer

The *stack* is a conventional, last-in-first-out store, onto which items can be *pushed* (i.e., inserted at the top) and from which they can be *popped* (i.e., removed from the top). Items on the stack are usually partially built syntactic subtrees that have yet to acquire some of their child nodes. The initial node in the syntax tree (usually an S node for a sentence) is pushed onto the stack at the start of the parse, and the whole parse tree is gradually built onto it (upside-down, as it were), with intermediate structures being taken on and off the stack as necessary. Most of the activity is with respect to the top node of the stack, which is called the *current node*.

The buffer is (roughly) a first-in-first-out queue of items waiting to be processed, although various operations can be performed on the buffer that alter the steady right-to-left flow of items through the buffer. Items in the buffer are generally single lexical entries or complete syntactic subtrees (e.g., a structure representing an NP) that have been completed but not yet attached to any of the nodes waiting on the stack.

Lexical entries usually come into the buffer at the *right* end, as needed (discussed later). They are formed by removing words from the *left* end of the input string and looking them up in the lexicon. Lexical entries may also be inserted directly into the buffer at specified points as a result of explicit action in a grammar rule.

Nodes (i.e., syntactic subtrees) are built on the stack. They may be *dropped* from the top of the stack into the buffer. Dropped items are inserted at the left end of the buffer (i.e., they go to the front of the queue).

Figure 9.5 shows how these structures might look at the start of a parse (Fig. 9.5*a*), during the parse (Fig. 9.5*b*), and after the parse has finished (Fig. 9.5*c*). Square brackets ([ ]) here and below denote syntactic nodes, braces ({ }) are for lexical entries.

a   Stack: −1 [S]
       Buffer: ⟨empty⟩
       Input String: John likes the park

b   Stack: −1 [VP {V (lex likes)}]
             −2 [S [NP {PropN (lex John)}]]
       Buffer: 1 [NP {Art (lex the)}
                     {N (lex park)}]
             2 {Punct (lex /.)}
       Input string: ⟨empty⟩

c   Stack: −1 [S [NP {PropN (lex John)}]
                 [VP {V (lex likes)}
                     [NP {Art (lex the)}
                         {N (lex park)}]]]
       Buffer: 1 {Punct (lex /.)}
       Input string: ⟨empty⟩

Figure 9.5

In Figure 9.5*b* the stack has two entries: an incomplete VP and an incomplete S. The buffer contains an NP and the lexical entry for a period. In Figure 9.5*c* the NP has been incorporated into the VP, which has been attached to the S to complete the parse.

Grammar Rules

A rule consists of a set of *conditions* (i.e., tests, or prerequisites) and a list of *actions*. The conditions specify tests that nodes on the stack and/or nodes or lexical entries in the buffer must satisfy for the rule to be applicable. Tests will typically be in terms of syntactic categories and features.

Also, each rule has a *priority*, which is a positive whole number indicating the order in which rules are to be tried; rules with lower priority numbers are tried first.

Figure 9.6 shows a sample rule.

Name:	NP+PP
Packet:	VPGram
Priority:	10
Conditions:	(−1 VP) (1 NP) (2 PP) (3 Punct)
Actions:	(Attach 1 −1) (Attach 1 −1)

Figure 9.6

We have adopted the following convention for referring to items in the stack and buffer, both in conditions and in actions:

- Positive integers refer to items in the buffer, left to right.
- Negative integers refer to items on the stack, top to bottom.

Hence, the meaning of this rule, which is named NP+PP and has priority 10, is roughly as follows: "If the current node is a VP, and the buffer begins with an NP node, followed by a PP node and then a punctuation mark, then attach the NP node and then the PP node to the VP node."

If a buffer position is ever addressed that does not contain an entry, sufficient words are removed from the input string, looked up in the lexicon, and inserted in the buffer to fill the addressed position. If the input string is exhausted, periods (.) are filled in instead. Limitations elsewhere ensure against infinite regress (discussed later).

Notice that both the Attach commands refer to position 1 in the buffer—this is because once the NP node has been attached to the VP node, it is automatically lifted out of the buffer, thus leaving the PP node in position 1. The current node is still the VP node, since attachment merely adds a child node to the current node, without pushing the child node onto the stack. The execution of this rule would transform a position like Figure 9.7*a* into Figure 9.7*b*:

```
a    Stack: −1 [VP {V (lex gives)}]
             . . .
     Buffer: 1 [NP {Art (lex the)}
                   {N (lex book)}]
             2 [PP {Prep (lex to)}
                   [NP {Art (lex the)}
                       {N (lex man)}]]]
             3 {Punct (lex /.)}


b    Stack: −1 [VP {V (lex gives)}
                   [NP {Art (lex the)}
                       {N (lex book)}]]
                   [PP {Prep (lex to)}
                       {NP {Art (lex the)}
                           {N (lex man)}]]]]
             . . .
     Buffer: 1 {Punct (lex /.)}
```

Figure 9.7

The other piece of information given in the preceding rule is VPGram, the name of the *packet* to which this rule belongs. A grammar for a stack and buffer parser consists of a set of packets, where a packet is a named collection of rules. As the parser processes the sentence, it maintains a short list of *active* packets, and only rules that are in the currently active packets can be used. Packets are added to, or removed from, the active list by the actions of rules. There are also some links between the active list and the nodes on the stack.

Thus the basic operation of the parser is to choose from the rules in the active packets the highest priority rule whose conditions are all satisfied and execute all its actions. This continues until no active rule is satisfied, at which point the parsing effort is complete. It has been successful provided that

1. the stack is fully connected—that is, each node is a subnode of the next, all the way to the initial S node;
2. the input string is empty;
3. the buffer is empty (except for final punctuation).

Unanchored Matching

Marcus proposed a special mechanism, called the *attention shift*, to allow phrases (typically NPs) to be built in a relatively autonomous way, so that rules for building clauses (e.g., the one previously given) can treat both words and whole phrases uniformly, once this special mechanism has prebuilt the phrases and placed them in the buffer.

Marcus's mechanism was special purpose and perhaps more complex than necessary. After observing that the conditions that test buffer entries amount to an "anchored" pattern, we provide "unanchored" patterns as well, achieving the same effect. An *anchored* pattern is one whose elements must be matched by the elements of the target starting at a specific position, typically, as in our case, the left end of the target. An *unanchored* pattern, on the other hand, can match starting at *any* position in the target. We adopt the convention that sets of conditions beginning with an exclamation point (!) are unanchored. Not only may they match starting at any point in the buffer, but also if they do match successfully, subsequent references into the buffer are effectively displaced rightwards, so that references to buffer positions in actions will be interpreted correctly. This displacement continues in effect until explicitly undone and may, of course, happen recursively. An example should clarify what all this means.

Suppose we go back to the example in Figure 9.5, at a different stage (Fig. 9.8):

Buffer: 1 [NP {PropN (lex John)}]
         2 {V (lex likes)}
         3 {Art (lex the)}
         4 {N (lex park)}

Figure 9.8

The following rule, for initiating NPs, would not match if the conditions were interpreted as anchored (Fig. 9.9):

Name: StartNP
Packet: Pool
Priority: 0
Conditions: ! (1 Art)
Actions: (NewNode 'NP) (Attach 1 −1)
               (Activate NPParse)

Figure 9.9

But as it contains the signal for unanchored matching, it does match, with the following effect, where the arrow −> indicates where the address 1 used to point in the buffer (Fig. 9.10):

Stack: −1 [NP {Art (lex the)}]
            . . .
Buffer: −> [NP {PropN (lex John)}]
            {V (lex likes)}
         1 {N (lex park)}

Figure 9.10

Note, in particular, that the effective beginning of the buffer has been displaced to the right, so that 1 refers to what is actually the third item in the buffer. Thus, the result of the Attach action was what was wanted, and the following rule can now complete the story (Fig. 9.11):

```
Name:           SimpleNP
Packet:         NPParse
Priority:       10
Conditions:     (1 N)
Actions:        (Attach 1  −1) (Drop) (Restore)
```

Figure 9.11

The two new actions here are Drop and Restore. The Drop pops the top item (in this case the newly constructed NP) off the stack and inserts it at the front of the (effective) buffer. Thus, after the Drop but before the Restore the situation is as follows (Fig. 9.12):

```
Stack: ...
Buffer: −> [NP {PropN (lex John)}]
           {V (lex likes)}
        1  [NP {Art (lex the)}
           {N (lex park)}]
```

Figure 9.12

The Restore action moves the effective beginning of the buffer back to its previous position, indicated in the preceding diagrams by the arrow −>. Since it is possible for an unanchored match to occur at any time, multiple displacements may occur, so there is actually a stack of previous positions. Successful unanchored matches push the current position onto this stack before displacing, and Restore takes the most recent entry off this stack and restores the current position there. Note that a rule with an unanchored pattern must take *some* action to ensure that it does not immediately match again, or an infinite loop will occur. Thus, the rule in Figure 9.9 Attaches the Art, thereby removing it from the buffer and preventing the rule from matching again at the same place.

Maintaining the Set of Active Packets

Certain packets of rules (the StartPackets) are made active initially (i.e., at the start of each parse) to initiate the process. Subsequently, packets are activated or deactivated as explicitly requested by the actions of rules. However, packets are considered to be active *with respect to* the top node on the stack, and when it changes, the set of active packets may change as well.

When a new current node is created (on the top of the stack), this in a sense signals the start of a new subtask—the building of this subtree. When a node is completed, and popped off the stack, that subtask has been completed and the parser can then resume what it was doing before. To reflect this flow of work between different subtasks, there are explicit connections between the nodes on the stack and sets of packets. When a new node is pushed onto the stack, the current set of active packets is temporarily hidden and a new set is established (associated with this new node); when that node is eventually popped off the stack, its associated set of packets vanishes and the previous set is reinstated. So although at any given moment there is exactly one set of packets active, there may be others that have been temporarily shelved and which are associated with nodes farther down the stack.

Hence, the packets that are activated at the start of the parse are associated with the initial node that is on the stack. The question arises—Are there any packets that should always be active? That is, are there any rules that are so general or so global in their applicability that we would want them always to be available? If so, there is a need, within the grammar, for a list of **AlwaysActivePackets** that will automatically be activated whenever the creation of a new node creates a new context. It is an open question whether such a facility is really necessary, but we have included it in our implementation and use it in the worked example.

Actions Available

In this section we give a brief description of each of the actions that are available for use in rules. Each of them is in fact a LISP function, and so the actions of a rule are simply **EVAL**uated when the rule is invoked. Examples of use can be found in the worked example presented later.

(Attach subPlace supPlace cFlg)
Attaches the node or lexical entry addressed by **subPlace** to the node addressed by **supPlace** as its next descendant. If **subPlace** addresses an entry in the buffer, it removes the entry from the buffer. If **subPlace** addresses a node and **cFlg** is **non-NIL** then the newly attached node is pushed onto the stack, becoming the current node, and the packets named in **AlwaysActive-Packets** become the active packets. Negative integers address nodes on the stack, from the top down. Positive integers address entries in the buffer, from the left. Category names address the first node of the given category on the stack. For example, (Attach 2 'S) would attach the second entry in the buffer to the first S node on the stack, working down from the top (current) node.

(NewNode cat)
Makes a new node of category **cat**, and pushes it onto the stack, making it the current node. The packets named in **AlwaysActivePackets** become the active packets.

(Drop)
Pops the current node off the top of the stack and places it at the front (left end) of the buffer, moving items to the right as necessary to accommodate it. The set of active packets is reset from the new current node.

(Close)
Pops the current node off the top of the stack. It is so called because it typically signals the completion or closure of a constituent. Not allowed unless the node is attached to some other node (see discussion in next section). The set of active packets is reset from the new current node.

(Restore)
Returns the effective beginning of the buffer (the point addressed by 1) back to where it was before the most recent displacement.

(InsertAt word place)

Places the lexical entry for word into the buffer at the position addressed by place, moving items to the right to make room as necessary.

(Activate packetName1 . . . packetNameN)

Activates the named packets. Note that as the active packets are a set, multiple activation of the same packet has no noticeable effect.

(Deactivate packetName1 . . . packetNameN)

Deactivates the named packets.

Determinism and Ambiguity

What is it about this stack and buffer approach that merits the appellation *deterministic*? How does it deal with structural and form class ambiguity? We now summarise the limitations on the mechanism.

First of all, there is no explicit mechanism that is provided for multiple analyses. At each point in an analysis the highest priority active rule whose conditions are satisfied will be invoked. Even if the grammar actually contains two rules of the same priority, both active and both satisfied, there is only an indeterminacy, not nondeterminism. Depending on particular implementations, one or the other will be invoked and the other irretrievably lost.

Second, certain constraints are built into the mechanism to defeat any attempt at covert pseudo-parallelism. Taken together, these constraints ensure that any structure that is built must be incorporated in the final analysis, thus making it impossible to carry along two or more partial analyses for a time, subsequently discarding all but one, which would be a sort of pseudo-parallelism. This is the origin of the constraint on Close, previously mentioned: Without this restriction it would be possible to do exactly that.

The other mechanism on which some limitation must be imposed is that of lookahead. If no limit were imposed, then what amounts to a backtracking parser could be implemented, first determining the correct analysis path by examining all possible alternatives, without building any structure; then having made the choice, building the one result.

Thus, for both practical and theoretical reasons, most systems of this sort limit the amount of lookahead. There are three places where limits can be imposed. First of all, one may limit how far into the buffer any rule may look. For instance Marcus's (1980) system only allows addresses in the buffer up to 3, whereas Milne's (1982) is restricted to 2. Second, one may limit the position at which the beginning of unanchored patterns may match. Again, in Marcus's system this limit is (position) 3, whereas Milne's system does not allow unanchored matching at all, effectively making this limit 1. Finally, there is the question of limiting the recursion of unanchored matches. One can either do this directly or indirectly by limiting the total amount of displacement the buffer is allowed to undergo. Marcus takes the latter approach, setting this limit at 3 as well.

Taken together, these various limits combine to place an upper bound on the total number of entries in the buffer—in Marcus's system this is 5, in Milne's 2. In the interests of simplicity, the implementation described subsequently incorporates only the second limitation—that on the origin of unanchored matches. Some limit here is necessary to prevent infinite search; otherwise, the mechanism that fills unaddressed buffer positions would cause the buffer to grow indefinitely.

But we still have not fully addressed the question of structural ambiguity. Indeed, by adding some limit on the lookahead allowed the parser, we have added to the set of (by definition) intractable global ambiguities those cases of local ambiguity that cannot be diagnosed within the given limit. Various approaches to this problem are possible, but they are all (necessarily) extrasyntactic in character. They typically combine some appeal to semantic and/or contextual information to make the choice, with some possibility for backtracking with respect to such choices. This higher-order nondeterminism is usually defended as being justifiable on psychological grounds, but the status of the psychological evidence that is advanced in favour of these claims is unclear at best. The reader who is interested in more details on either the extrasyntactic mechanisms themselves or the justifications provided for them is referred to the published descriptions of the various systems, for example Marcus (1980) and Milne (1982).

The other problem that we have not dealt with is form class ambiguity. Marcus, in fact, did not deal with it in his system, and neither do we in the implementation that we give here. Milne presents an elegant method for dealing with the problem in many cases. It amounts to allowing multiple lexical entries to be entered in the buffer, but once one part of such an entry matches a pattern element, it is as if the other parts were not there. Thus, if we change the example discussed in Figures 9.4 to 9.8 to John likes the saw, and assume that the word *saw* has a two-part lexical entry, one part for each of its readings as noun and as verb, then the analysis would proceed as before, with the verbal reading disappearing after the matching of this entry with N in the invocation of the NPParse rule. The interested reader is encouraged to experiment with the inclusion of such a mechanism in the implementation that follows.

Implementation: The Stack and the Buffer

The stack is a list of instances of the following record:

    (TypeRecord Node
        (cat super packets . subnodes)).

The cat field contains the atomic category name; super contains the parent in the tree structure being built, if any; packets contains the names of the packets that are active in association with this node, and subnodes contains the children in the tree structure, if any.

The buffer is a list of instances of the Node record and the Lex record:

    (TypeRecord Lex body),

where the body field is just a standard lexical entry as for the nondeterministic parser (but see the discussion on ambiguous words). Type records differ from ordinary records in that they contain a hidden key that allows the predicate type? to identify instances. Thus, for example:

    (type? Node ⟨expr⟩)

will be T iff ⟨expr⟩ evaluates to an instance of the Node record.

Both the stack, stored in the global variable Stack, and the buffer, stored in the global variable Buffer, are initialised to NIL; that is, they start empty.

One function serves to mediate all access to the stack and the buffer as far as references to it from conditions and actions are concerned:

```
[Item
    (LAMBDA (address)
        (PROG (ref)
            (if (NUMBERP address)
                then (if (ILESSP address 0)                    ; on stack
                    then (RETURN (OR [CAR (NTH Stack (IMINUS address))]
                                     [HELP "address not valid"]))
                elseif (IGREATERP address 0)                   ; in buffer
                    then ref<—(IPLUS address Offset)
                        (FillBuffer ref)
                        (RETURN (CAR (NTH Buffer ref))))
            elseif (LITATOM address)           ; scan up stack for category
                then (RETURN (OR (bind node
                                    first (node <— (CAR Stack))
                                    while (type? Node node)
                                    do (if (EQ address
                                              node:cat)
                                          then (RETURN node)
                                          else node <— node:super))
                                 (HELP "not found on stack" address))))
            (HELP "can't interpret address" address)))]
```

Call: (Item +n)	Return: Buffer item n
Call: (Item −n)	Return: Stack node n
Call: (Item ⟨cat⟩)	Return: First stack node with category ⟨cat⟩

This function interprets three different kinds of address. The first term of the conditional deals with negative integers, which refer to nodes on the stack, by negating the argument and selecting that element from the list in Stack. The stack is also accessed by the third term of the conditional, which deals with nonnumeric arguments. These are assumed to be category names, and the stack is scanned via the *super* link for a node of the given category.

The second term of the conditional deals with positive integers, which refer to items in the buffer. Here we immediately confront two aspects of the implementation of the buffer mechanism. As the preceding discussion makes clear, addresses in the buffer are not absolute, but relative to the currently effective displacement. In this implementation, this displacement is stored as an absolute numerical offset in the global variable Offset, initially 0. Thus, to determine the referent of any buffer address, we add it to the current value of Offset, as shown. We also see here the mechanism that automatically fills in the buffer as needed. This is implemented by the following functions:

```
[FillBuffer
    (LAMBDA (i) (while (IGREATERP i BufferEnd)
                    do (Input)))]
```

Call: (FillBuffer 3)

```
[Input
  (LAMBDA NIL
      Buffer <- (NCONC1 Buffer (MakeWord (OR (pop InputString) '.)))
      BufferEnd <- (ADD1 BufferEnd))]
```

Call: (Input)

The global variable **BufferEnd**, initially 0, holds the length of the buffer, indicating the maximum permissible absolute buffer address at any time. Thus, it can be seen that together **FillBuffer** and **Input** operate to add items to the end of the buffer until the argument to **FillBuffer** is a valid address. If the input string (in the variable **InputString**) is at any time exhausted, periods are used.

The function **MakeWord** simply looks up words in the lexicon, using the same basic routine and record as the chart parser, and after checking that no polysemy is involved, returns an instance of the **Lex** record:

```
(Record Definition (category . features))
```

```
[MakeWord
   (LAMBDA (word)
      (PROG (lv)
            (lv <- (Defns word))
            (if (CDR lv)
                then (HELP "can't handle multiple defn's for word"
                           (CONS word lv))
                else (RETURN (create Lex body<-(CAR lv))))))]
```

Call: (MakeWord 'John)   Return: **(Lex PropN**
                                       (PN 3sg)
                                       (lex John))

Packets, Rules, and Tests

We turn now to packets and rules, which are instances of the following records:

```
(Record Packet (name . rules))
(Record Rule (name packet priority tests . actions))
(Record Test (address . conditions))
```

A *packet* is a name and a list of rules. For reasons that will become clear when we look at the parsing process itself, this list must be in priority order, with the highest priority rule given first.

Rules themselves consist of a name, the name of the packet they belong to, a priority, and lists of tests and actions. Tests have the form shown, although since the only condition implemented is category identity, multiple conditions will not make sense. Thus, all tests in the examples discussed here will be of the form (address ⟨cat⟩).

Tests are evaluated by the following function:

```
[DoTest
  (LAMBDA (address conditions)
    (PROG (item)
          (item <- (Item address))
          (if (for c in conditions
                   always (EQ c
                              (if (type? Node item)
                                  then item:cat
                                  elseif (type? Lex item)
                                  then item:body:category
                                  else (SHOULDNT))))
              then (RETURN address)))))]
```

Call: (DoTest 2 'NP)   Return: if 2 --> (Lex PropN . . .) then **NIL**
                                      if 2 --> (Node NP . . .) then **2**

Given that only one condition is present, the loop is unnecessary, but it is there to support subsequent expansion to more complex conditions. Note that the function Item, previously defined, is used to access items in the buffer, so the address will be interpreted relative to any displacement in force.

DoTest is called by the following function, which implements both anchored and unanchored matching:

```
[DoTests
  (LAMBDA (tests)
    (if (NEQ (CAR tests) '!)               ; anchored
        then (for test in tests
                  always (DoTest test:address
                                 test:conditions))
        else (for i from 0 to (SUB1 WindowSize)      ; unanchored
                  do (if (for test in (CDR tests)
                             always (DoTest (if (AND            ; in the buffer
                                                 (NUMBERP test:address)
                                                 (IGREATERP test:address 0))
                                             then (IPLUS i test:address)
                                             else test:address)
                                            test:conditions))
                         then (Offset i)             ; displace
                              (RETURN T)))))]
```

Call: (DoTests '((1 V)(2 NP)(-1 S)))   Return: **T** or **NIL**

The first term of the conditional is for the anchored tests, which lack the initial !, and is a simple conjunction of calls to DoTest. The second term implements the unanchored option. Each position in the current buffer is considered as the possible start for a matching of the tests, within a window determined by the variable WindowSize, set to 3 in this implementation. This is done by trying *relative* displacements of 0 through WindowSize − 1, added to the address of each test that refers to the buffer. If a position is found where all the tests succeed, then the function **Offset** is called to effect the displacement:

```
[Offset
    (LAMBDA (j) (push OffsetStack Offset)
                Offset <- (IPLUS Offset j)))]
```

Call: (Offset 1)

The current displacement is pushed onto a stack of saved offsets, and the new absolute displacement is formed by adding the argument to the old value. The fact that all references into the buffer are relative to the current value of **Offset**, as in the preceding definition of **Item**, means that this change in value effects the desired displacement.

Displacements are undone by popping the stack:

```
[PopOffset
    (LAMBDA NIL Offset <- (pop OffsetStack))]
```

Call: (PopOffset)

The next question of concern is how the rules are invoked—How is it arranged that the highest priority rule from an active packet whose tests are satisfied is run? The answer is in the following function, whose repeated running is the heart of the parsing process:

```
[DParse
    (LAMBDA NIL
        (PROG (ruleset best top this rule)
                (ruleset <- (for p in ActivePackets
                                collect (p:rules)))
        LP1 (for rs on ruleset
                when (CAR rs)
                do (this <- (OR (CAAR rs):priority
                                DefaultPriority))
                    (if (OR [NULL top] [LESSP this top])
                        then top <- this
                            best <- rs))
            (if top
                then                        ; top priority rule is head of
                    rule <-(CAAR best)      ; first queue in best
                    (RPLACA best (CDAR best))  ; this changes ruleset,
                    (if (DoTests rule:tests)   ; but not ActivePackets
                        then (for action in (rule:actions)
                                    do (EVAL action))
                            (RETURN T))
                else                        ; no rules left
                    (RETURN))
            (top <- NIL)                    ; that rule failed, try again
            (GO LP1)))]
```

Call: (DParse)

The structure of this admittedly complex function is not as bad as it looks at first sight. It consists of an initial loop, which gathers the rules from the active packets (which are maintained in a list as the value of the global variable ActivePackets) into a list of lists called ruleset, and then a main loop, which has two parts. The first part selects the list of rules in ruleset whose first rule has the highest priority. Provided the lists themselves are in priority order, this will be the highest priority active rule. Note that if the priority field of a rule is NIL, the value of the global variable DefaultPriority, which is initialised to 10, is used. In the second part, this rule is then removed from ruleset (although not, of course, from the packet itself), and its tests are evaluated. If they succeed, the actions of the rule are performed, and the function returns T. If they fail, we loop back, and try again with the next highest priority rule. If no rule is found whose tests are satisfied, then the parse is finished, for good or ill, and the function returns NIL.

Actions

The part of the function DParse that performs the actions of a rule simply uses EVAL to do this. As previously discussed, this is because actions are simply in the form of s-expressions. This section presents the code for each of the actions.

```
[Attach
    (LAMBDA (subPlace supPlace cFlg)
        (PROG (sub sup)
                (sub <- (Item subPlace))
                (sup <- (Item supPlace))
                (sup:subnodes <- (CONS sub sup:subnodes))
                (if (AND [NUMBERP subPlace] [IGREATERP subPlace 0])
                    then (RemBuf subPlace))    ; from buffer—take it out
                (if (type? Node sub)
                    then sub:super <- sup        ; back pointer
                        (if cFlg        ; put it on bottom of stack as well
                            then (PushStack sub))
                    elseif cFlg
                        then (HELP "Can't make non-node current" sub))))]
```

Call: (Attach 1 −1)

The basic operation here is the addition of the subordinate item to the list of subnodes in the parent. If the new subordinate is a node, its backpointer is set appropriately, and if cFlg is set, it is pushed on the stack as well. The effects of this on the active packets will be discussed subsequently. If the new subordinate comes from the buffer, it is removed therefrom, using the following function:

```
[RemBuf
  (LAMBDA (position)
    (PROG (afterPos tail)
          (afterPos <- (IPLUS position Offset -1))
          (if (ZEROP afterPos)
            then (pop Buffer)
            else tail <- (NTH Buffer afterPos)
                 (RPLACD tail (CDDR tail)))
          (BufferEnd <- (SUB1 BufferEnd))))]
```

Call: (RemBuf 2)

This is just straightforward list manipulation. Note that the argument is interpreted relative to the value of Offset and that the value of BufferEnd is updated.

Back to actions:

```
[NewNode
    (LAMBDA (cat) (PushStack (create Node cat <- cat)))]
```

Call: (NewNode 'NP)

Again, see the following discussion on the effect of this on the active packets.

```
[Drop
    (LAMBDA NIL (Insert (PopStack) 1))]
```

Call: (Drop)   Return: **(Node NP . . .)**

Drop uses another buffer manipulation utility:

```
[Insert
  (LAMBDA (item position)
    (PROG (afterPos tail)
          (afterPos <- (IPLUS position Offset -1))
          (FillBuffer afterPos)
          (if (EQ afterPos 0)
            then (push Buffer item)
            else tail <- (NTH Buffer afterPos)
                 (RPLACD tail (CONS item (CDR tail))))
          (BufferEnd <- (ADD1 BufferEnd))))]
```

Call: (Insert '(Node NP . . .) 1)

More straightforward list manipulation, again relative to the current displacement in Offset. FillBuffer is also used, to ensure enough list to manipulate.

Before returning to actions, it is important to note that Insert and RemBuf are *not* actions as such. They are utility routines and should not appear in grammars. The assertions made about the nature of this parser depend on the actions that appear in rules being drawn from the list in the earlier Actions Available section and nowhere else. The use of EVAL to perform them is an implementation detail only and should not be interpreted as license to include arbitrary s-expressions in rules.

```
[Close
    (LAMBDA NIL
        (if (CAR Stack):super
            then (PopStack)
            else (HELP "can't close unattached node"
                        (CAR Stack):cat)))]
```

Call: (Close)

Note that we canot use this to throw a node away—it must be attached somewhere.

```
[Restore
        (LAMBDA NIL (PopOffset))]
```

Call: (Restore)

Restore is simply the public name for PopOffset, previously defined.

```
[InsertAt
        (LAMBDA (word place) (Insert (MakeWord word) place))]
```

Call: (InsertAt 'for 2)

InsertAt uses the utility already defined in this section.

```
[Activate
    (NLAMBDA packets
        (for p in packets
            unless (ASSOC p ActivePackets)
            do (push ActivePackets
                    (OR [ASSOC p PacketLibrary] [HELP "not a packet" p]))))]
```

Call: (Activate packet1 packet4)

The arguments to this function, which is a no-spread **NLAMBDA**, are an arbitrary number of packet names, which are implicitly quoted. The variable **p** will thus, in the example call, range over the names **packet1** and **packet4**. For each name, if no packet of that name is already active, one is found in the value of the global variable **PacketLibrary** and added to the active list in **ActivePackets**. Thus, **PacketLibrary** is the permanent home of **packets**, that is, the grammar.

```
[Deactivate
    (NLAMBDA packets
        (for p in packets
            do (ActivePackets <− (DREMOVE (ASSOC p ActivePackets)
                                          ActivePackets))))]
```

Call: (Deactivate packet2 packet5)

These last two actions are for the *explicit* manipulation of the set of active packets. The section that follows describes the implementation of the *implicit* effects of operations on the stack.

Implicit Activation and Deactivation of Packets

The set of active packets is associated with the current node in the stack and changes as the stack changes. The following functions, which are used to push and pop nodes from the stack, implement this behaviour:

```
[PushStack
    (LAMBDA (node)
        (if Stack
            then (CAR Stack):packets <− (ActivePacketNames))
        (push Stack node)
        ActivePackets <− NIL
        (APPLY (FUNCTION Activate) AlwaysActivePackets))]
```

Call: (PushStack '(Node NP . . .))

Aside from the actual pushing of the node onto the stack, three things happen here. *Before* the stack is changed, the names of the currently active packets are stored into the **packets** field of the current node. The function that collects them is straightforward:

```
[ActivePacketNames
    (LAMBDA NIL
        (for p in ActivePackets
            collect (p:name)))]
```

Call: (ActivePacketNames)   Return: **(packet1 packet4)**

Second, the set of active packets is cleared. Finally, the function/action **Activate** is applied to the value of the global variable **AlwaysActivePackets**. The grammar writer should therefore set this to a list of the names of those packets that she or he wishes always to have active.

The other half of the process is as follows:

```
[PopStack
   (LAMBDA NIL
      (PROG1 (pop Stack)
             (ActivePackets <- NIL)
             (APPLY (FUNCTION Activate) (CAR Stack):packets)))]
```

Call: (PopStack)

As well as popping the top node off the stack, this sets the set of active packets to be those named in the **packets** field of the new top (current) node, thus restoring the situation properly.

Starting, Finishing, and in Between

What remains is just the beginning, middle, and end. That is, what stitches all this together? Most of the answer is in the following function:

```
[Det
   (LAMBDA (InputString)
      Buffer <- Stack <- ActivePackets <- OffsetStack <- NIL
      Offset <- 0
      BufferEnd <- 0
      (NewNode TopCat)
      (APPLY (FUNCTION Activate) StartPackets)
      (while (DParse))
      (ShowResults Stack Buffer))]
```

Call: (Det '(Robin likes the child))

After a number of variables are initialised, we first create the first node on the stack, using the value of the variable **TopCat** as the category thereof. This will normally be S. Then we activate those packets that are named in the list **StartPackets**, which the grammar writer should set appropriately. Then as long as **DParse**, previously described, continues to find some rule to invoke, it will be recalled, but once it fails to do so, the loop will terminate. Then the function **ShowResults** is called to display the results, if any:

```
[ShowResults
   (LAMBDA (stack buffer)
     (if (OR (for n in buffer
                   thereis (NOT (AND [type? Lex n]
                                      (EQ n:body:category 'Punct])))
             InputString)
       then (PRINT "No Parse"))
     (if (NOT (for s on stack
                   while (CDR s)
                   always (EQ (CAR s):super (CADR s))))
       then (PRINT "Stack not fully connected"))
     (PrintNode (CAR (LAST stack))))]
```

Call: (ShowResults)

We know, because **Det** set it up that way, that the last node on the stack is the top of the tree. But before we print it out, we must check to see that a number of conditions are satisfied, or we have not actually successfully parsed the input. First of all, the input must have been completely exhausted. Second, the buffer must be empty as well, except for possible residual extraneous punctuation. Finally, even if these conditions are met, but the stack is not knit together into one tree, there is still a problem—the analysis is not complete.

The system is now complete. Some additional material, for printing results, interfacing to the user, and building the **PacketLibrary**, are not discussed here but do appear in the appendix.

A Sample Run

To help explicate the workings of the system as implemented, as well as the underlying concepts, we close with a trace of a complete analysis of a simple sentence. The grammar we use here is necessarily trivial but is designed to illustrate the operation of the various mechanisms and includes a simple realisation of the rule of Dative Shift, producing the same analyses for both **Kim gave the book to Robin** and **Kim gave Robin the book**. The run that is shown here is given the latter sentence for input and uses the following grammar, arranged in packets:

```
Packet: S-Start
     Name: Subj
     Priority: 10
     Conditions: (1 NP)
     Actions: (Attach 1 −1) (Deactivate S-Start) (NewNode 'VP) (Activate Parse-VP)

Packet: Parse-VP
     Name: Obj
     Priority: 10
     Conditions: (1 NP)
     Actions: (Attach 1 −1) (Attach −1 −2)
```

Name: Vb
Priority: 10
Conditions: (1 V) (2 NP)
Actions: (Attach 1 −1)

Name: IObj
Priority: 5
Conditions: (1 NP) (2 NP)
Actions: (Attach 2 −1) (Attach −1 −2) (InsertAt 'to 1)

Name: PMod
Priority: 10
Conditions: (1 PP)
Actions: (Attach 1 −1)

Packet: CPool
Name: PNP
Priority: 0
Conditions: ! (1 PropN)
Actions: (NewNode 'NP) (Attach 1 −1) (Drop) (Restore)

Name: SNP
Priority: 0
Conditions: ! (1 Art)
Actions: (NewNode 'NP) (Attach 1 −1) (Activate NPack)

Name: PP
Priority: 1
Conditions: ! (1 Prep) (2 NP)
Actions: (NewNode 'PP) (Attach 1 −1) (Attach 1 −1) (Drop) (Restore)

Packet: NPack
Name: NPN
Priority: 10
Conditions: (1 N)
Actions: (Attach 1 −1) (Drop) (Restore)

The SStart packet is in StartPackets and the CPool packet is in AlwaysActivePackets.

Using this grammar, and with the limit on unanchored matching set to 3 (buffer positions 1, 2, and 3), we get the following behaviour during parsing, where at each step we show on the first line the rule that is selected, the absolute displacement relative to which it has matched and will take effect, and the names of the active packets. On the second line we show the buffer and the top (current) node on the stack as they are at the instant the indicated rule matches, but *before* its actions take effect. The effect of the actions may be understood by comparing the state of the packet set, buffer, and stack on the given lines (the *before* state) and the next lines (the *after* state). In cases where the displacement in the buffer is nonzero, the effective start of the buffer is indicated by underlining. Comments are given in italics.

(Det '(Kim gave Robin the book))

CPool is always active, and the rules in it have high priority, in order to get NPs and PPs built quickly.

Rule: PNP	Offset: 0	Packets: S-Start CPool
Buffer: Kim		Top of Stack: [S]

Here we see unanchored matching take effect.

Rule: PNP	Offset: 2	Packets: CPool S-Start
Buffer: NP gave Robin		Top of Stack: [S]

Rule: Subj	Offset: 0	Packets: S-Start CPool
Buffer: NP gave NP		Top of Stack: [S]

The subject has been attached, but we don't see it since the VP node has been pushed on top. Note the change in active packets. But before we can parse the VP, the high priority rules in CPool are tried, and we get another NP.

Rule: SNP	Offset: 2	Packets: Parse-VP CPool
Buffer: gave NP the		Top of Stack: [VP]

Here we have a change of packets within a displacement. Note that as we finish this and drop it off the stack, Parse-VP *automatically comes back.*

Rule: NPN	Offset: 2	Packets: NPack CPool
Buffer: gave NP book		Top of Stack: [NP (Art (lex the))]

Rule: Vb	Offset: 0	Packets: CPool Parse-VP
Buffer: gave NP[Robin] NP[the book]		Top of Stack: [VP]

Look carefully at the definition of this rule, to see how it "undoes" the Dative Shift.

Rule: IObj	Offset: 0	Packets: CPool Parse-VP
Buffer: NP[Robin] NP[the book]		Top of Stack: [VP (V (lex gave))]

Rule: PP	Offset: 0	Packets: CPool Parse-VP
Buffer: to NP[Robin]		Top of Stack: [VP (V (lex gave))
		[NP (Art (lex the))
		(N (lex book))]]

Rule: PMod	Offset: 0	Packets: Parse-VP CPool
Buffer: PP		Top of Stack: [VP (V (lex gave))
		[NP (Art (lex the))
		(N (lex book))]]

And so the final result is

```
[S [NP (PropN (lex Kim))]
   [VP (V (lex gave))
       [NP (Art (lex the))
           (N (lex book))]
       [PP (Prep (lex to))
           [NP (PropN (lex Robin))]]]]]
```

That's all there is—the interested reader is referred to the appendix to this chapter, where she or he can find a complete set of "neutral LISP" definitions with which to experiment.

APPENDIX: CODE LISTINGS

This appendix presents complete listings of all the code that is necessary to implement both parsers that are described in this chapter. The language is close to a minimal, neutral dialect of LISP. With the exception of possibly changing the order of the arguments to push and to the mapping functions, one should be able to run it as is on most LISP systems. Note also that (NTH x n), as used in InterLISP, is equivalent to (NTHCDR x (SUB1 n)) in MacLISP. Some marginal comments on functions that were not previously discussed are provided.

Simple Dictionary

```
[Defns
  (LAMBDA (word)
    (OR (Lookup word)
        [PROGN (PRINTC "Please enter definition for ")
               (PRINC word)
               (PRINTC "Format is either single—(cat (f v) . . .) − or
                          list of same")
               (TERPRI)
               (Enter word (READ))
               (Defns word)])))]

[Lookup
  (LAMBDA (word)
    (MAPCAR (FUNCTION LexAug) (CDR (ASSOC word Dict))))]

[Enter
  (LAMBDA (word defs)
    (SETQ Dict
          (CONS (CONS word
                      (COND ((OR (LITATOM defs)
                                 (EQ (U-CASE (CAR defs)) 'E))
                             (ERR 'ABORT))
                            ((ATOM (CAR defs)) (LIST defs))
                            (T defs)))
                Dict)))]
```

```
[CheckRed
   (LAMBDA (fp)
      (COND ((NULL (ASSOC (CAR fp) feats)) (SETQ feats (CONS fp feats)))))]

[LexAug
   (LAMBDA (def)
      (PROG (cat feats)
            (SETQ feats (CDR def))
            (MAPC (FUNCTION CheckRed)
                  (CDR (ASSOC (SETQ cat (CAR def)) Redun)))
            (COND ((NULL (ASSOC 'lex feats))
                  (SETQ feats (APPEND feats (LIST (LIST 'lex word))))))
            (RETURN (CONS cat feats))))]
```

The following is a very small sample dictionary and feature redundancy table.

```
(SETQ Dict (QUOTE ((to (Prep))
                  (book (N))
                  (gives (V (#objs 2) (PN s3)))
                  (runs (V (PN s3) (#objs 0) (lex run)))
                  (like (V (#objs 1)))
                  (and (Conj))
                  (that (Comp))
                  (with (Prep))
                  (Mary (PropN))
                  (scope (N))
                  (a (Art (PN s3)))
                  (park (N))
                  (in (Prep))
                  (/'s (Pos))               ; / is the literal insert char
                  (duck (N))
                  (saw (V)
                       (V (Tns pst) (lex see)))
                  (likes (V (PN s3) (#objs 1) (lex like)))
                  (men (N (PN pl) (lex man)))
                  (man (N))
                  (the (Art (PN s3 pl)))
                  (/. (Punct (type final)))
                  (John (PropN)))))

[SETQ Redun (QUOTE ((N (PN s3))
                   (PropN (PN s3))
                   (V (Tns pres) (#objs 0 1) (PN sg pl))]
```

Nondeterministic Parser

The principal difference between this implementation and the one presented in the text is the absence of the InterLISP record constructions. Creation, access, and modification functions are thus needed for **Vertices** and **Edges**. First for vertices:

```
[CreateVertex
    (LAMBDA NIL
        (SETQ Vertices
            (NCONC1 Vertices
                    (LIST (CONS NIL NIL)
                          (SETQ VertexCount (ADD1 VertexCount))
                          NIL)))
        VertexCount)]

[GetVertex
    (LAMBDA (n)
        (OR (CAR (NTH Vertices n)) (HELP "not a vertex number" n)))]

[GetEdgeList                         ; the args type and direction are
    (LAMBDA (vertex type direction)  ; used here and below
        (SELECTQ type                ; to select the field
                [inactive (SELECTQ direction
                          (in (CADDR (GetVertex vertex)))
                          (out (CDDDR (GetVertex vertex)))
                          (SHOULDNT))]
                [active (SELECTQ direction
                        (in (CAAR (GetVertex vertex)))
                        (out (CDAR (GetVertex vertex)))
                        (SHOULDNT))]
                (SHOULDNT)))]        ; general error message

[GetVertexNumber
        (LAMBDA (vertex) (CADR vertex))]

[AddToEdgeList
    (LAMBDA (vertex type direction edge)
        (SETQ vertex (GetVertex vertex))
        (SELECTQ type
                [inactive (SELECTQ direction
                          (in (RPLACA (CDDR vertex)
                                      (CONS edge (CADDR vertex))))
                          (out (RPLACD (CDDR vertex)
                                       (CONS edge (CDDDR vertex))))
                          (SHOULDNT))]
                [active (SELECTQ direction
                        (in (RPLACA (CAR vertex)
                                    (CONS edge (CAAR vertex))))
                        (out (RPLACD (CAR vertex)
                                     (CONS edge (CDAR vertex))))
                        (SHOULDNT))]
                (SHOULDNT)))]
```

The next section is for **edges**:

```
[CreateEdge
    (LAMBDA (cat needed contents left right)
        (CONS (CONS cat
                    (CONS (SETQ EdgeCount (ADD1 EdgeCount))
                            (CONS left right)))
            (CONS contents needed))))]

[GetCat
        (LAMBDA (edge) (CAAR edge))]

[GetEdgeNumber
        (LAMBDA (edge) (CADAR edge))]

[GetContents
        (LAMBDA (edge) (CADR edge))]

[GetNeeded
        (LAMBDA (edge) (CDDR edge))]

[SetNeeded
        (LAMBDA (edge needed) (RPLACD (CDR edge) needed))]

[GetLeft
        (LAMBDA (edge) (CADDAR edge))]

[GetRight
        (LAMBDA (edge) (CDDDAR edge))]
```

The next section of code reproduces the functions that are presented in the text. The careful reader will note that the exact pattern of actual vertices versus vertex numbers is not exactly reproduced, but otherwise the functionality is identical:

```
[AddActiveEdge
    (LAMBDA (left right cat contents rhs)
        (PROG (edge)
                (SETQ edge (CreateEdge cat rhs contents left right))
                (AddToEdgeList left 'active 'out edge)
                (AddToEdgeList right 'active 'in edge)
                (Seek (CAR rhs) right)
                (MAPC (FUNCTION
                        (LAMBDA (inactive)
                            (SETQ Agenda (CONS (CONS edge inactive) Agenda))))
                    (GetEdgeList right 'inactive 'out))))]
```

```
[AddInactiveEdge
   (LAMBDA (left right cat contents)
      (PROG (edge)
            (SETQ edge (CreateEdge cat NIL contents left right))
            (AddToEdgeList left 'inactive 'out edge)
            (AddToEdgeList right 'inactive 'in edge)
            (MAPC (FUNCTION
                     (LAMBDA (active)
                        (SETQ Agenda (CONS (CONS active edge) Agenda))))
                  (GetEdgeList left 'active 'in))))]


[Run
   (LAMBDA NIL
      (PROG (current)
         LP (COND (agenda (SETQ current (CAR Agenda))
                          (SETQ Agenda (CDR Agenda))
                          (TryToExtend (CAR current) (CDR current))
                          (GO LP)))))]


[TryToExtend
   (LAMBDA (active inactive)
      (PROG (needed newContents)
            (SETQ needed (GetNeeded active))
            (COND ((Match (CAR needed)
                          (GetCat inactive)
                          (GetContents inactive))
                   (SETQ newContents (CONS inactive (GetContents active)))
                   (COND ((CDR needed)
                          (AddActiveEdge
                             (GetLeft active)
                             (GetRight inactive)
                             (GetCat active)
                             newContents
                             (CDR needed)))
                         (T (AddInactiveEdge
                             (GetLeft active)
                             (GetRight inactive)
                             (GetCat active)
                             (REVERSE newContents)))))))))]


[Match
      (LAMBDA (rulepart cat contents) (EQ rulepart cat))]
```

```
[Chart
   (LAMBDA (words)
      (PROG (start left right)
            (SETQ EdgeCount 0)
            (SETQ VertexCount 0)
            (SETQ Vertices NIL)
            (SETQ Agenda NIL)
            (SETQ start (SETQ left (CreateVertex)))
       LP (COND (words (SETQ right (CreateVertex))
                       (MAPC (FUNCTION
                                (LAMBDA (def)
                                   (AddInactiveEdge
                                      left
                                      right
                                      (CAR def)
                                      (CDR def))))
                             (Defns (CAR words)))
                       (SETQ words (CDR words))
                       (SETQ left right)
                       (GO LP)))
            (Seek TopCat start)
            (Run)
            (MAPC (FUNCTION
                     (LAMBDA (edge)
                        (COND ((AND (EQ (GetRight edge) right)
                                    (EQ (GetCat edge) TopCat))
                               (ShowEdge edge)
                               (TERPRI)))))
                  (GetEdgeList start 'inactive 'out))))]


[Seek
   (LAMBDA (cat vertex)
      [PROG (edges)
            (SETQ edges (GetEdgeList vertex 'active 'out))
       LP (COND ((AND (EQ (GetRight (CAR edges)) vertex)
                      (EQ (GetCat (CAR edges)) cat))
                 (RETURN))
                ((SETQ edges (CDR edges))
                 (GO LP)))
            (MAPC (FUNCTION
                     (LAMBDA (rule)
                        (COND ((EQ (CAR rule) cat)
                               (AddActiveEdge vertex vertex cat
                                              NIL (CDR rule))))))
                  Grammar)])]
```

Finally, here are a number of ancillary functions that are not actually described in the text: One for driving the parser repeatedly, and providing a simple way of reparsing the previous string, and two for printing results.

```
[RunChart
  (LAMBDA NIL
    (PROG (inp)
      LP (TERPRI)
         (PRINC "Parse as")
         (PRIN TopCat)
         (PRINC ":")
         (Chart (COND ((EQ (SETQ inp (READ)) 'P)          ; 'p' gives the
                        (PRIN PreviousString)             ; previous string
                        (TERPRI)
                        PreviousString)
                       ((LISTP inp) (SETQ PreviousString inp))  ; a list is saved
                       (T (RETURN))))                     ; and parsed,
         (GO LP)))]                                       ; anything else exits

[ShowEdge
  (LAMBDA (edge)
    (ShowContents (GetCat edge) (GetContents edge) (POSITION)))]

[ShowContents
  (LAMBDA (cat contents col)
    (TAB col)
    (PRINC "(")
    (PRINC cat)                     ; Show the category and then
    (SPACES 1)                      ; the contents in
    (SETQ col (POSITION))           ; horizontal tree style
    (MAPC (FUNCTION
            (LAMBDA (p)             ; check to see if we've hit bottom
              (COND ((PreTerminal cat) (PRINC p))          ; Bottoming out
                     (T                                    ; Recurse to next level in tree
                       (ShowContents (GetCat p) (GetContents p) col)))))
          contents)
    (PRINC ")"))]

[PreTerminal
  (LAMBDA (cat) (NOT (ASSOC cat Grammar)))]
```

Deterministic Parser

Again, the principal difference between this implementation and the one presented in the text is the absence of the InterLISP record constructions. Creation, access, and modification functions are thus needed for nodes:

```
[CreateNode
    (LAMBDA (cat) (LIST 'Node cat NIL NIL))]

[GetSubNodes
    (LAMBDA (node) (CDDDDR node))]

[AddToSubNodes
  (LAMBDA (node newSub)
    (RPLACD (CDDDR node) (CONS newSub (CDDDDR node))))]

[SetSuper
    (LAMBDA (node newSup) (RPLACA (CDDR node) newSup))]

[GetSuper
    (LAMBDA (node) (CADDR node))]

[GetCat
    (LAMBDA (node) (CADR node))]

[NodeP
    (LAMBDA (ptr) (EQ (CAR ptr) 'Node))]

[GetPackets
    (LAMBDA (node) (CADDDR node))]

[SetPackets
    (LAMBDA (node packets) (RPLACA (CDDDR node) packets))]
```

Access functions for rules:

```
[GetPriority
    (LAMBDA (rule) (CADDR rule))]

[GetTests
    (LAMBDA (rule) (CADDDR rule))]

[GetActions
    (LAMBDA (rule) (CDDDDR rule))]

[GetPacket
    (LAMBDA (rule) (CADR rule))]
```

And a type predicate for lexical entries:

```
[LexP
     (LAMBDA (ptr) (EQ (CAR ptr) 'Lex))]
```

The next section reproduces the functions presented in the text. First the actions:

```
[Drop
     (LAMBDA NIL (Insert (PopStack) 1))]

[InsertAt
     (LAMBDA (word place) (Insert (MakeWord word) place))]

[Activate
   (NLAMBDA packets          ; takes an arbitrary number of unevaluated args
      (MAPC (FUNCTION
                 (LAMBDA (p)
                    (COND ((NOT (ASSOC p ActivePackets))
                           (SETQ ActivePackets
                                   (CONS (OR [ASSOC p PacketLibrary]
                                             [HELP "not a packet" p])
                                         ActivePackets))))))
            packets))]

[Deactivate
   (NLAMBDA packets           ; takes an arbitrary number of unevaluated args
      (MAPC (FUNCTION
                 (LAMBDA (p)
                    (SETQ ActivePackets
                            (DREMOVE (ASSOC p ActivePackets) ActivePackets))))
            packets))]

[NewNode
     (LAMBDA (cat) (PushStack (CreateNode cat)))]

[Attach
   (LAMBDA (subPlace supPlace cFlg)
      (PROG (sub sup)
            (SETQ sub (Item subPlace))
            (SETQ sup (Item supPlace))
            (AddToSubNodes sup sub)
            (COND ((AND [NUMBERP subPlace] [GREATERP subPlace 0])
                   (RemBuf subPlace)))     ; from buffer—take it out
            (COND ((NodeP sub)
                   (SetSuper sub sup)
                   (COND (cFlg           ; put it on bottom of stack as well
                          (PushStack sub))))
                  (cFlg (HELP "Can't make non-node current" sub))))))]
```

```
[Close
   (LAMBDA NIL
      (COND ((GetSuper (CAR Stack)) (PopStack))
            (T (HELP ''can't close unattached node''
                  (GetCat (CAR Stack))))))]

[Restore
      (LAMBDA NIL (PopOffset))]
```

Next, the buffer and stack utilities:

```
[Item
   (LAMBDA (address)
      (PROG (ref)
            (COND
               ((NUMBERP address)
                (COND ((LESSP address 0)          ; on stack
                       (RETURN (OR [CAR (NTH Stack (Difference 0 address))]
                                   [HELP ''address not valid''])))
                      ((GREATERP address 0)       ; in buffer
                       (SETQ ref (PLUS address Offset))
                       (FillBuffer ref)
                       (RETURN (CAR (NTH Buffer ref))))))
               ((LITATOM address)                 ; scan up tree for category
                (RETURN (OR [PROG (node)
                                  (SETQ node (CAR Stack))
                             LP  (COND ((AND node [NodeP node])
                                        (COND ((EQ address (GetCat node))
                                               (RETURN node))
                                              (T (SETQ node (GetSuper node))
                                                 (GO LP)))))]
                            [HELP ''not found on stack'' address]))))
            (HELP ''can't interpret address'' address)))]

[Offset
   (LAMBDA (j)
      (SETQ OffsetStack (CONS Offset OffsetStack))
      (SETQ Offset (PLUS Offset j)))]

[PopOffset
      (LAMBDA NIL (SETQ Offset (pop OffsetStack)))]

[Input
   (LAMBDA NIL
      (SETQ Buffer (NCONC1 Buffer (MakeWord (OR   [pop InputString]   '/.))))
      (SETQ BufferEnd (PLUS BufferEnd 1)))]
```

```
[Insert
   (LAMBDA (item position)
      (PROG (afterPos tail)
            (SETQ afterPos (PLUS position Offset −1))
            (FillBuffer afterPos)
            (COND ((EQ afterPos 0) (SETQ Buffer (CONS item buffer)))
                  (T (SETQ tail (NTH Buffer afterPos))
                     (RPLACD tail (CONS item (CDR tail)))))
            (SETQ BufferEnd (PLUS BufferEnd 1))))]


[FillBuffer
   (LAMBDA (i)
      (PROG NIL LP (COND ((GREATERP i BufferEnd) (Input) (GO LP)))))]


[PopStack
   (LAMBDA NIL
      (PROG1 (CAR STACK)
             (SETQ Stack (CDR Stack))
             (SETQ ActivePackets NIL)
             (APPLY (FUNCTION Activate) (GetPackets (CAR Stack)))))]


[RemBuf
   (LAMBDA (position)
      (PROG (afterPos tail)
            (SETQ afterPos (PLUS position Offset  −1))
            (COND ((GE afterPos BufferEnd) (SHOULDNT)))
            (COND ((ZEROP afterPos) (SETQ Buffer (CDR Buffer)))
                  (T (SETQ tail (NTH Buffer afterPos))
                     (RPLACD tail (CDDR tail))))
            (SETQ BufferEnd (DIFFERENCE BufferEnd 1))))]


[ActivePacketNames
      (LAMBDA NIL (MAPCAR (FUNCTION CAR) ActivePackets))]


[PushStack
   (LAMBDA (node)
      (COND (Stack (SetPackets (CAR Stack) (ActivePacketNames))))
      (SETQ Stack (CONS node Stack))
      (SETQ ActivePackets NIL)
      (APPLY (FUNCTION Activate) AlwaysActivePackets))]
```

```
[MakeWord
   (LAMBDA (word)
      (PROG (lv)
            (SETQ lv (Defns word))
            (COND ((CDR lv)
                   (HELP ''can't handle multiple defn's for word''
                         (CONS word lv)))
                  (T (RETURN (CONS 'Lex (CAR lv)))))))]
```

Now, the essential parsing functions:

```
[Det
   (LAMBDA (InputString)
      (SETQ Buffer
            (SETQ Stack (SETQ ActivePackets (SETQ OffsetStack NIL))))
      (SETQ Offset 0)
      (SETQ BufferEnd 0)
      (NewNode TopCat)
      (APPLY (FUNCTION Activate) StartPackets)
      (PROG NIL LP (COND ((DParse) (GO LP))))
      (ShowResults Stack Buffer))]


[DParse
   (LAMBDA NIL
      (PROG (ruleset best top this rule)
            (SETQ ruleset (MAPCAR (FUNCTION CDR) ActivePackets))
        LP (SETQ rs ruleset)
        LP1 (COND (rs (COND ((CAR rs)
                             (SETQ this
                                   (OR [GetPriority (CAAR rs)]
                                       DefaultPriority))
                             (COND ((OR [NULL top] [LESSP this top])
                                    (SETQ top this)
                                    (SETQ best rs)))))
                      (SETQ rs (CDR rs))
                      (GO LP1)))
            (COND (top    ; top priority rule is head of best queue
                   (SETQ rule (CAAR best))
                   (RPLACA best (CDAR best))
                   (COND ((DoTests (GetTests rule))
                          (MAPC (FUNCTION EVAL) (GetActions rule))
                          (RETURN T))))
                  (T (RETURN)))        ; no joy at all
            (SETQ top NIL)
            (GO LP)))]
```

```
[DoTests
 (LAMBDA (tests)
  (COND
   ((NEQ (CAR tests) '!)
    (PROG (test)
       LP (COND (tests (SETQ test (CAR tests))
                      (COND ((DoTest (CAR test) (CDR test))
                             (SETQ tests (CDR tests))
                             (GO LP))
                            (T (RETURN))))
               (T (RETURN T)))))
   (T (PROG (i test tp)        ; unanchored
          (SETQ i 0)
        LP (COND ((GREATERP i (DIFFERENCE WindowSize 1)) (RETURN)))
          (SETQ tp (CDR tests))
       LP1 (COND
            (tp (SETQ test (CAR tp))
               (COND ((DoTest (COND ((AND [NUMBERP (CAR test)]
                                          [GREATERP (CAR test) 0]
                                     (PLUS i (CAR test)))
                                    (T (CAR test)))
                              (CDR test))
                     (SETQ tp (CDR tp))
                     (GO LP1))
                    (T (SETQ i (PLUS i 1)) (GO LP))))
            (T (Offset i) (RETURN T))))))))]
```

```
[DoTest
  (LAMBDA (address conditions)
     (PROG (item)
          (SETQ item (Item address))
         LP (COND (conditions
                   (COND ((EQ (CAR conditions)
                           (COND ((NodeP item) (GetCat item))
                                 ((LexP item) (CAR (CDR item)))
                                 (T (SHOULDNT))))
                          (SETQ conditions (CDR conditions))
                          (GO LP))
                         (T (RETURN))))
                 (T (RETURN address)))))]
```

```
[ShowResults
   (LAMBDA (stack buffer)
      (COND
         ((OR [PROG (n)
                LP (COND (buffer (SETQ n (CAR buffer))
                              (COND ((AND [LexP n]
                                             [EQ (CAR (CDR n)) 'Punct])
                                        (SETQ buffer (CDR buffer))
                                        (GO LP))
                                    (T (RETURN T))))
                         (T (RETURN)))]
                InputString)
             (TERPRI)
             (PRINC ''No Parse'')
             (TERPRI)))
         (COND ((PROG (s)
                   (SETQ s stack)
                LP (COND ((CDR s)
                           (COND ((EQ (GetSuper (CAR s)) (CADR s))
                                    (SETQ s (CDR s))
                                    (GO LP))
                                 (T (RETURN T))))
                         (T (RETURN))))
             (TERPRI)
             (PRINC ''Stack not fully connected'')
             (TERPRI)))
         (PrintNode (CAR (LAST stack)))))]
```

Some printing routines that give slightly different pictures from those in the text:

```
[PrintNode
   (LAMBDA (node)
      (COND ((LexP node) (PrintLex (CDR node)))
            ((NodeP node)
             (PROG (pos)
                (PRIN (GetCat node))
                (SPACES 1)
                (SETQ pos (POSITION))
                (MAP (FUNCTION
                        (LAMBDA (np)
                           (PrintNode (CAR np))
                           (COND ((CDR np) (TAB pos)))))
                     (REVERSE (GetSubNodes node)))))))]
```

```
[PrintLex
   (LAMBDA (lab)
      (PRIN (CAR lab))
      (SPACES 1)
      (PROG1 (POSITION)
             (MAP (FUNCTION
                     (LAMBDA (f)
                        (PrintFP (CAR f))
                        (COND ((CDR f) (SPACES 1)))))
                  (CDR lab))))]
```

```
[PrintFP
   (LAMBDA (fp)
      (PRINC "[")
      (PRIN (CAR fp))
      (MAPC (FUNCTION (LAMBDA (v) (SPACES 1) (prin v))) (CDR fp))
      (PRINC "]"))]
```

A top level to read repeatedly input and call **Det**, and remember the previous input for possible reuse by typing P :

```
[RunDet
   (LAMBDA NIL
      (PROG (inp)
         LP (TERPRI)
            (PRINC "Parse as ")
            (PRIN TopCat)
            (PRINC ": ")
            (Det (COND ((EQ (SETQ inp (READ)) 'P)
                        (PRIN PreviousString)
                        (TERPRI)
                        PreviousString)
                       ((LISTP inp) (SETQ PreviousString inp))
                       (T (RETURN))))
            (GO LP)))]
```

And finally, a utility to take a list of rules and put them into packets, in priority order, all in the PacketLibrary:

```
[PackPacks
   (LAMBDA (rules)
      (SETQ PacketLibrary NIL)
      (MAPC (FUNCTION StuffRule) rules))]
```

```
[StuffRule
  (LAMBDA (r)
    (PROG (p)
          (COND ((NOT (SETQ p (ASSOC (GetPacket r) PacketLibrary)))
                 (SETQ PacketLibrary
                       (CONS (SETQ p (CONS (GetPacket r)))
                             PacketLibrary))))
          (RPLACD p
                  (INSERT r              ; sorted insertion
                    (CDR p)
                    (FUNCTION
                      (LAMBDA (X Y)
                        (LE (OR [GetPriority X] DefaultPriority)
                            (OR [GetPriority Y] DefaultPriority)))))))))]
```

To illustrate the use of the rule-packing facility, there follows a subset of what might appear on a grammar file to be loaded in—key variables are set, the rules are read in, and then packed into the library.

```
(SETQ TopCat 'S)

(SETQ StartPackets '(S-Start CPool))

(SETQ AlwaysActivePackets '(CPool))

(SETQ WindowSize 3)

(SETQ DefaultPriority 10)

(SETQ Rules (QUOTE ((SNP CPool
                      0
                      (! (1 Art))
                      (NewNode 'NP)
                      (Attach 1 −1)
                      (Activate NPack))
                    . . .
                    (IObj Parse-VP
                      5
                      ((1 NP) (2 NP))
                      (Attach 2 −1)
                      (Attach −1 −2)
                      (InsertAt 'to 1)))))

(PackPacks Rules)
```

References

Berwick, R. 1982. Locality principles and the acquisition of syntactic knowledge. Ph.D. thesis. Cambridge, Mass.: MIT AI Lab.

Church, K. M. 1980. On memory limitations in natural language processing. Master's thesis. Cambridge, Mass.: MIT Laboratory for Computer Science.

Colmerauer, A. 1970. Les Systèmes-Q ou un Formalisme pour Analyser et Synthetiser des Phrases sur Ordinateur. Montreal: Internal Publication 43, Departement d'Informatique, Université de Montreal.

Earley, J. 1970. An efficient context-free parsing algorithm. *Communications of the Association for Computing Machinery.* 13(2): 94–102.

Gazdar, G. 1981. Phrase Structure Grammar. In Jacobson and Pullman (Eds.), *The Nature of Syntactic Representation.* Dordrecht: Reidel.

Kaplan, R. 1973. A general syntactic processor. In Rustin, R. (Ed.), *Natural Language Processing.* Englewood Cliffs, N.J.: Prentice-Hall.

Kay, M. 1973. The MIND system. In Rustin, R. (Ed.), *Natural Language Processing.* Englewood Cliffs, N.J.: Prentice-Hall.

Kay, M. 1980. Algorithm schemata and data structures in syntactic processing. In *Proceedings of the Symposium on Text Processing.* Nobel Academy. (In press). (Also, Technical Report No. CSL-80-12. Palo Alto, Calif.: Xerox Palo Alto Research Center.)

Marcus, M. P. 1980. *A Theory of Syntactic Recognition for Natural Language.* Cambridge, Mass.: MIT Press.

Milne, R. W. 1982. Predicting garden path sentences. *Cognitive Science* 6: 349–373.

Teitelman, W. 1978. *The InterLISP Reference Manual.* Palo Alto, Calif.: Xerox Palo Alto Research Center.

Thompson, H. S. 1981. Chart parsing and rule schemata in GPSG. In *Proceedings of the 19th Annual Meeting of the Association for Computational Linguistics.* Alexandria, Va: Association for Computational Linguistics. (Also, DAI Research Paper 165. Edinburgh: Department of Artificial Intelligence, University of Edinburgh.

Thompson, H. S. 1982. Handling metarules in a parser for GPSG. In Barlow, M., Flickinger, D., and Sag, I. (Eds.), *Developments in Generalized Phrase Structure Grammars: Standard Working Papers in Grammatical Theory,* Vol. 2. Bloomington, Ind.: Indiana University Linguistics Club.

CHAPTER 10

COMPUTER VISION

JOHN MAYHEW
and
JOHN FRISBY

INTRODUCTION

In this chapter, vision is considered as a sequence of processes that are successively extracting visual information from one representation, organising it, and making it explicit in another representation to be used by other processes. Viewed in this way, it is conceptually convenient to treat vision as computationally modular and sequential. This is not to deny that future implementations of competent visual systems will find it advantageous to utilise modules that are operating in parallel and that complex control structures managing their interactions might be necessary, both within and between levels in a processing hierarchy. It is, however, to suggest that at present it seems best to direct attention to understanding the principles that can underlie the design of modules that are capable of extracting useful information from a particular type of visual information.

That approach is different in character from the fashionable artificial intelligence approach to vision of a decade or so ago. The guiding theme then was the design of control processes that could deploy "the right knowledge at the right time" to solve the task in hand. With the realisation that the failings of poor representations cannot be indefinitely relieved by ever more elaborate and ad hoc control structures, that era has given way to the current period which is characterised by much more careful examination of what were often regarded hitherto as relatively uninteresting "low level" visual processes. Undoubtedly one of the central figures bringing about that change was David Marr, and a good deal of what is said in this chapter bears the stamp of his considerable influence.

Marr has argued that an information-processing problem can and should be understood at

301

three separate levels and that failure to distinguish the different kinds of issues involved at each one has hindered progress not only in AI but also in psychology and neurophysiology (his recent book, Marr [1982] gives the best overview of his thinking). The topmost level, Level 1, Marr believed should be concerned with devising a computational theory or method that is capable of dealing in principle with the problems of the task in question; Level 2 should develop algorithms implementing the theory; and Level 3 should deal with hardware. According to Marr, the task for the researcher in AI is to work mainly at Level 1, that is, isolate an information-processing problem (identify a tractable goal) and find (prove) a method for its solution. The questions at this level are of the sort: "How is it possible in principle to extract the shape of an object from the shading information in the image?" "What use can be made of the optics of the situation? If the optics is not enough, what assumptions can be made about the nature of the world that can serve as constraints upon which to base secure computational strategies?" and so on. The answer of Horn and his colleagues to this set of questions is a detailed analysis of the intricate relationship between image intensities and the nature of the surfaces in the scene from whence they arise. This analysis considers such things as the position of the light source and the position and orientation of surfaces in relation both to the source and to the observer's viewing position. Thus, Ikeuchi and Horn (1981) proved that 3D-shape recovery from image intensity data is possible if (1) the surface is assumed to give perfectly uniform diffuse reflection; (2) the surface is assumed to be locally smooth; and (3) surface orientation is known for certain places in the image. This proof amounts to a theorem and it stands whether or not any particular visual system uses the method proved. Also, the validity of the theorem is independent of questions arising in connection with the choice of algorithms based on the theorem (of which there may in principle be many, some more convenient than others for a given application). Finally, the truth of the theorem is quite separate from questions to do with hardware. In short, Level 1 is logically prior to Levels 2 and 3, although in practice the difficulties involved in securing principled methods at Level 1 are such that any insights obtained from computational experiments, visual illusions, and so on (Level 2), or even neurophysiology (Level 3), are of course, to be seized upon. Indeed, one of the most stimulating aspects of Marr's work is his integration of work at all three levels, while keeping clearly distinct the relevant issues for each one.

There are strong implications from this both for AI and for psychology and neurophysiology. As far as AI is concerned, it provides a framework for evaluating the worth of putative AI research results, fads, and fashions. Also, if AI's global aim is to devise principled solutions to well-formed information-processing problems, it is sensible to begin with the easy ones and thereby build upon a strong base. Accordingly, the problems of early vision are, Marr suggests, ideal starting points for trying to understand the complexities of the information-processing capacities of the human mind. He argues that, given our obvious competence in this domain, it seems likely that the effect of evolutionary pressure has been to hardwire solutions to some tractable computational problems. If so, it should be possible to discover the principles underlying these solutions as a sound first step on the way to larger questions.

Of course, Marr realised that although certain information-processing problems may be amenable to principled computational theories (termed by him 'Type 1' theories; Marr [1977]), others may not have that inherent structure. Problems of the latter kind are those that can be solved only by the simultaneous action of a considerable number of processes whose interaction is its own simplest description (a 'Type 2' theory). Marr claimed that most early AI programs amounted to Type 2 theories. The danger with such theories is that

> they can bury crucial decisions, that in the end provide the key to the correct Type 1 decomposition of a problem, beneath the mound of small administrative decisions that are inevitable whenever a concrete program is designed . . . with any candidate for a Type 2 theory, much greater importance is attached to the performance of the program [and] since its only possible virtue might be that it works, it is interesting only if it does. Often, a piece of AI research has resulted in a large program without much of a theory, which commits it to a Type 2 result, but that program either performs too poorly to be impressive or (worse still) has not even been implemented. Such pieces of research have to be judged very harshly, because their lasting contribution is negligible. (Marr, 1977, p. 39)

This danger is to be avoided, the argument runs, by seeking Type 1 theories first, a goal obviously implying the need to choose a tractable yet nontrivial problem domain. When armed with a collection of successful Type 1 solutions, and that prospect is within sight for low-level vision, then it may be easier to think more clearly about genuine Type 2 problems. That will perhaps mean a return to problems of control but from a much stronger vantage point than hitherto.

As for psychology, the levels framework offered by Marr provides a much needed clarity about objectives. The psychophysics of vision can now be given the valuable task of asking whether or not a particular computational theory is implemented in the human visual system: Experiments can be designed to test whether human vision has certain predictable attributes if such and such a theory were implemented within it. Less theoretically driven studies can be valuable if done by way of seeking clues about computational theories, but otherwise such studies seem increasingly misplaced. In particular, the postulation of "mechanisms" to explain phenomena, outside any attempt to ask what functional role such mechanisms might have as implementing a computational theory, is a misguided activity. Almost the whole of the vast and still expanding literature on spatial frequency channels (see later) might turn out to be an example of such misplaced endeavour. Naturally enough, Marr's criticism of such an entrenched orthodoxy has made his approach rather unpalatable to some psychophysicists who hold defiantly to their traditional position that "phenomena/mechanisms" are worth studying per se, regardless of questions about their functional significance. In our opinion, that view will gradually wither as achievements mount in theorising at Level 1. In passing, we might note here that we strongly suspect that Helmholtz would have felt instantly at home in Marr's writings.

As for the scope of this chapter, it must necessarily be severely restricted by considerations of length. Rosenfeld's annual bibliography in the *Journal of Computer Graphics and Digital Image Processing* lists some 900 papers that were published during 1980 on various facets of image processing, and clearly no summary of that literature can be contemplated in an introductory chapter of the present kind. Instead, we choose to illustrate the themes that have already been introduced, with a review of the computational structure of the task of extracting the shape of objects from edge information contained in static monochromatic images. The annotated bibliography provides references to other important areas of achievement within the overall conceptual framework we espouse (e.g., structure from motion, shading, and texture), as well as giving starting points for entering the vast pattern recognition literature.

CARTOONS

The fact that a cartoon or line drawing can be perceived at all is of interest. It implies that the information it makes explicit is sufficient for the successful operation of processes that extract shape and pattern. A cartoonlike representation making explicit image intensity changes is called the *primal sketch* by Marr (1976). In Marr's view the computation of the primal sketch is one of the first important functions of early visual processing. It is important because it provides a data base about the image that is utilized by subsequent visual processes.

The Grey Level Image (GLI)

The grey level image (GLI) is a point-by-point representation of image intensities from which the primal sketch is computed. The GLI is formed by the optical image triggering various photochemical and/or photoelectric processes and its important property is that it is pointilliste. That is, it makes explicit only local (receptor or pixel) intensity values: all other information is left implicit. The GLI can be thought of as an array of numbers defining the altitudes of points on a hilly terrain (height = intensity), in which case the primal sketch computation is the business of describing the ridges, slopes, valleys, and so on comprising that terrain.

Measuring Gradients and Gradient Changes with Spatial Operators

If the primal sketch is a description of a hilly landscape, then it is sensible to begin its computation with the measurement of gradients and changes in gradients. This section describes some ways for measuring gradients that have proved useful in image processing, and its presumes very little familiarity with the field. More knowledgeable readers are invited to skip ahead to the next section.

The gradient of a slope, as anyone who ever climbed a hill will know, is simply the ratio of how far you go up (down is a negative slope), divided by how far you went along. Those readers who can remember their elementary calculus will recall that the gradient at a point on a curve is given by the first differential (=first derivative). Fortunately for those whose memory of the calculus is hazy, almost no knowledge of mathematics is required for grasping the key ideas about how gradients can be measured in images. This is because there is a remarkably simple and direct way of computing a quantity that serves as a close approximation to the first derivative.

Consider Figure 10.1*a*, which shows the profile of a hilly terrain. The gradient at Q is steeper than at S: walking up the hill at P takes you considerably higher than at S for the same lateral distance. A measure of the gradient at each point can be found by subtracting a measure of the height of the terrain on one side from a similar measure of the height on the other side. Obviously, the larger the number obtained, the greater the slope will be.

A simple way to effect this subtraction is to multiply the chosen height value on one side by -1 and the height value on the other side by $+1$, and then add the two quantities so obtained (Fig. 10.1*b*). In the image-processing literature this is called applying a *spatial operator,* in this case a $-1/+1$ operator. Closely allied terms to *operator* are: *weighting function, mask* (a term much used by Marr), *template* (often used when the operator defines a pattern or feature that is being searched for, rather than when a gradient is being measured), and *receptive field* (used in the neurophysiological literature).

Of course, as the gradient of the profile being measured in Figure 10.1*a* varies from place to

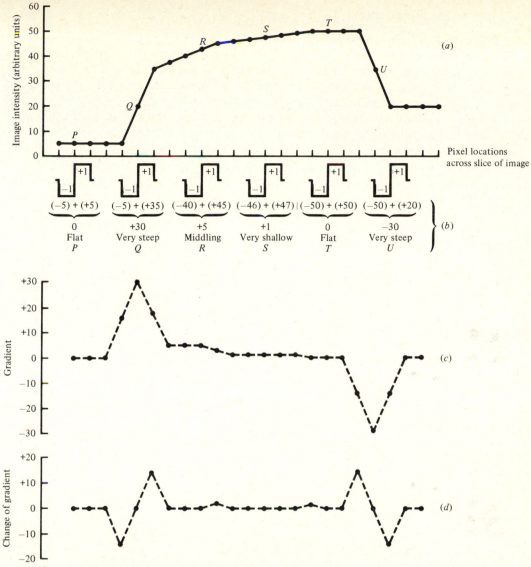

Figure 10.1 Measuring gradients and changes of gradients in image intensities. (*a*) Image intensity profile; (*b*) using the $-1/+1$ operator; (*c*) convolution profile showing first derivative of (*a*), as obtained using $-1/+1$ operator; (*d*) convolution profile showing second derivative of (*a*) as obtained using $-1/+2/-1$ operator. See text.

place, it is necessary to apply the $-1/+1$ operator all along it, rather than just at the points P, Q, R, S, T, and U, chosen for illustration. The application of an operator all over an image is called *convolution;* the operator is said to have been "convolved with" the image. Figure 10.1*c* presents a "convolution profile," derived from Figure 10.1*a*, using the $-1/+1$ operator. It shows that when the intensity profile is flat, the output given by this operator is 0 (as required), on the steepest parts the output is $+30$ or -30 (arbitrary units, with the sign indicating up or down gradients), and on the shallowest slope it is $+1$.

It should be clear from this example that applying an operator is a purely local affair, the -1 and $+1$ multiplications (weightings) and the summing of the results being done for each point separately. But how local is local? Should the -1 and $+1$ weightings be applied only to points immediately adjacent to the point whose gradient is being measured, or should some average of nearby points be used, for example, by weighting a number of points on one side -1, and a similar number on the other side $+1$, and then adding the whole lot up? In other words, how wide should the gradient measuring device be? The answer is that there is no one answer. That is, a range of different sizes is needed to cope with the fact that intensity gradients of differing steepness occur in most natural images. This point can be appreciated by inspecting Figure 10.2*a*, which illustrates the problem that would be faced in trying to measure shallow slopes with a very small operator: The difference in heights measured by a small operator would not differ much in size and might well be missed altogether despite the presence of an appreciable nonzero slope, particularly if the point whose gradient was being measured happened to be sitting on a small local plateau whose flatness was uncharacteristic of the overall slope. On the other hand, a larger $-1/+1$ operator that summed heights over a greater spatial range would be much more sensitive to shallow slopes but the bind then would be that such a wide operator would blur out any small dips or bumps on the slope that might be significant (Fig. 10.2*b*). These considerations force the use of a range of spatial operators to cover the range of gradients that need to be extracted, a state of affairs that is mirrored in the building industry: A bricklayer's level is longer than a carpenter's, and surveyors stand at opposite ends of fields and shout to one another. The problem of detecting gradients of differing *scale,* as it is termed, will be discussed further in the next section.

Measuring gradients is a useful thing to do but it is also desirable to extract information about changes in intensity gradients. Changes in intensity gradients are significant because they are usually caused by things in the world that the visual system wants to know about, such as illumination changes, surface orientation changes, and changes in surface reflectance (e.g., the edges of objects or surface markings).

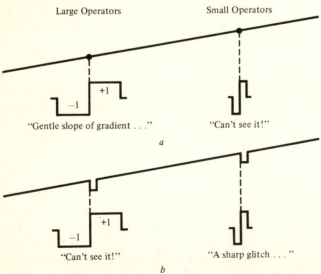

Figure 10.2 Measuring gradients at different scales using operators of different sizes.

One way in which a gradient change can be located is to search for a peak in the first derivative profile. Figure 10.3 illustrates the fact that a sharp slope (Fig. 10.3*a*) produces a sharp peak in its first derivative (Fig. 10.3*b*). This peak would occur in the convolution profile of a $-1/+1$ operator which, as previously explained, delivers an approximation to the first derivative.

The first derivative measures gradients, the second derivative measures changes of gradients. Consequently, an alternative approach to finding the location of a change in gradient is to obtain a second derivative profile and then to locate within it points of significant gradient change. The second derivative of a sharp edge is shown in Figure 10.3*d*, where it can be seen that a sudden intensity change is located at the point where the second derivative passes from

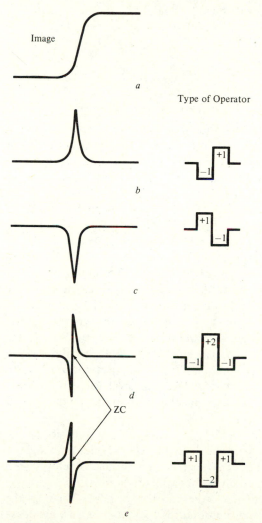

Figure 10.3   The intensity change in (*a*) gives rise to a peak (*b* and *c*) in its first derivative and to a zero crossing (ZC) in its second derivative (*d* and *e*) (*Source:* After Marr, 1982).

positive to negative, a point called naturally enough a "zero crossing" (ZC). Hence, locating a ZC in the second derivative is an alternative way of finding a change in intensity gradient. (Technically, a ZC is defined as the intersection of the zero plane ($z = 0$) with a surface $z = f(x, y)$; if you are on a beach and you have got one wet foot and one dry, then you have found one.)

The spatial operator that delivers a measure of the second derivative has the form $-1/+2/-1$ (or equivalently but with opposing sign, $+1/-2/+1$; Figs. 10.3d, 10.3e). The basic idea underlying this operator is that at a point where gradient changes (e.g., V in Fig. 10.4), the gradient to the right is bound to be different from the gradient to the left. So if we measure the gradient to the right and subtract it from the gradient to the left, we obtain a measure of their difference and hence a measure of the second derivative. An easy way to do this in a single convolution is to use an operator built up in the following way:

V		V = point in image being measured
-1	$+1$	Gradient rightwards of V
	$-(-1+1)$	Subtraction of gradient leftwards of V

-1	$+2-1$	Resulting operator

Figure 10.1d shows the result of convolving this operator with the intensity profile used in Figure 10.1a and, as required, it can be seen that deviations from zero mark points of gradient change. The size of the operator's output reflects the sharpness of the change and its sign ($+$ or $-$) gives the direction of the change. Also, it will be seen that a ZC occurs at the point of steepest gradient.

Mention has already been made of the fact that a $+1/-2/+1$ operator would have given an exactly equivalent result, except for sign (Fig. 10.3). Biological visual systems are usually equipped with both types of operator, the $-1/+2/-1$ type being called an "on center unit" (Fig. 10.4) because light falling on its center "excites" it, and the $+1/-2/+1$ type being termed an "off-center unit" because light shone on its center "inhibits" it. The reason biological systems bother with both types of device (computers need only one or the other) is generally believed to be because nerve cells cannot signal negative numbers directly (unlike computers, of course). According to this view, neural units of the on-center and off-center types signal the negative and positive parts, respectively, of the required convolution profile. If this interpretation is correct, then the need for the two types of units arises solely from a biological hardware limitation, and has nothing to do with the underlying computation being performed. This is a fine example of the need to keep considerations of a hardware kind, Level 3, clearly distinct from the quite different business of trying to understand the computational task being undertaken, Level 1, as discussed in the introduction.

For purposes of exposition, only one-dimensional (1D) slices of an image intensity profile have been considered so far. However, a visual image is usually a 2D array of intensities and the question arises as to how the operators just described can be extended to cope satisfactorily with real images. One simple way this can be done is to keep the operators functional 1D devices by making masks sensitive to gradients in one particular orientation only. This is done by the simple expedient of elongating each operator, as shown in Figures 10.5a and 5b, in which case the operators are said to provide "directional derivatives" because the derivative is tied to a particular orientation.

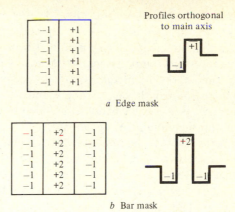

a Edge mask

b Bar mask

Figure 10.5   Operators giving directional derivatives.

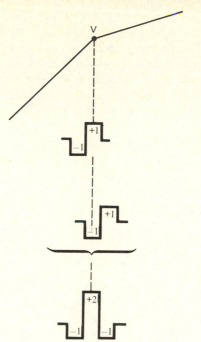

Figure 10.4   Detecting the gradient change at *V* can be done using a $-1/+2/-1$ operator. See text.

It is of considerable interest to note how these directional masks bear a strong resemblance to the receptive fields of so-called "simple cells" that were found in the striate cortex of cats by Hubel and Wiesel (for a review of their work, see Hubel [1982]). This similarity tempted Marr (1976) into believing that simple cells really are devices for delivering directional derivatives, and he based his first conception of how the primal sketch might be computed upon that idea. If this approach is adopted, obviously measurements will need to be taken in a fairly large number of different orientations at each point in the image, and so a very large population of similar devices will be necessary. This may help explain the crystal-like replicating architecture of the striate cortex. However, alternative interpretations of this hardware are available, not least of which is Marr's own changed account when he later reworked the problem of computing the primal sketch (Marr & Hildreth, 1980).

Marr (1976) called the extended $-1/+1$ operator shown in Figure 10.5 an "edge mask" and the device with a central "excitatory" region bounded by two "inhibitor" flanks a "bar mask." It is important to remember that these names reflect the superficial structure of the masks, and nothing more. Viewed from the theoretical vantage point of the primal sketch, such masks are properly interpreted as gradient-measuring devices, not as edge or bar feature detectors. Indeed, the masks shown would be quite hopeless feature detectors because their outputs would be grossly ambiguous: Is a given level of response due to a high contrast edge/bar of nonoptimal orientation, or to a low contrast edge/bar of optimal orientation? The same point can be appreciated by reconsidering the output convolution profiles in Figures 10.1*c* and 10.1*d*.

Edge and bar detectors? No. These devices measure gradients and changes in gradients. (Of course, whether that is a proper interpretation of simple cells is quite another matter.)

The approach to measuring gradients by using directional derivatives imposes certain severe and unnecessary computational overheads. Apart from the sheer number of operators that have to be applied, the oriented masks tend to deliver measurements that are smeared over parts of the image to which they do not apply, and cleaning these up can be a difficult task. The question thus arises: Is it possible to do the gradient measuring job in 2D images by using isotropic (i.e., nonorientationally tuned) operators?

It turns out that the first derivative cannot be measured with an isotropic operator, but the second derivative can be obtained by using the "Laplacian," which is an operator with a circularly symmetric field (Fig. 10.6; Think of it as an operator of the $-1/+2/-1$ or $+1/-2/+1$ type spun around its center). However, in order to consider how the Laplacian might best be used, it is desirable to explore in more depth the structure of the primal sketch computational task.

Marr and Hildreth's Theory of the Primal Sketch

The primal sketch computation requires accurate measurements of intensity gradients of differing scale (steep to shallow), and at the same time it is necessary to locate gradient changes from these measurements with precision. Relating this problem to the issues raised in the introduction, the question arises: Is it possible to devise a Type 1 computational theory about the design of a measuring device that is suitable for these twin purposes? Marr and Hildreth (1980) believe that it is, arguing as follows:

1. No single measuring device can be optimal simultaneously at all scales (see the previous section). It follows that one must find a way of dealing separately with changes occurring at different scales. This consideration leads to the specification of several gradient measurement devices, each suited to a limited range of slopes (or changes of slope). Using the concepts of spatial frequency (SF), one can express this requirement as the need for gradient measures that are well localised on the SF domain (high and low SFs being equivalent to steep and shallow intensity changes respectively).

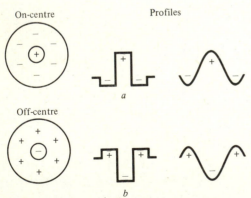

Figure 10.6   Operators of the Laplacian type. + means excitatory, − means inhibitory (i.e., + and − weightings, respectively).

2. Things in the world that give rise to intensity changes in the image are typically lines, edges, blobs, shadows, and so on. An important property of such "primitives," and one that must be preserved by a device well suited to measuring their gradients, is that they are spatially localised. It follows that each device must, at its own scale, utilise a smooth average of nearby points, rather than any kind of average of widely scattered points, as the latter would distort positional information.

3. The problem is that the requirements for good localisation in the SF and positional domains are in opposition. For example, if one uses as a measuring device a receptive field that is designed to serve as an ideal spatial frequency (SF) filter (i.e., a filter with sharp SF cutoffs: Fig. 10.7b), then the side lobes of such a field produce echoes from strong intensity changes. The echoes appear as gradient changes in the convolution profile that have no direct physical correlate in the visual world. A narrow-band filter thus produces noise, when viewed from the perspective of solving the computational task of locating intensity changes in the image that correspond to physical attributes of the scene (the central requirement of the primal sketch computation). Equally, if one uses a receptive field that is designed to maximise localisation in the spatial domain, then side lobes are acquired in the SF domain (Fig. 10.8b). The result then is that the receptive field misses some significant intensity changes because it averages out changes occurring over a wide range of scales.

4. Marr and Hildreth's answer to this conflict of interests is to use smoothing filters to select information from the GLI at different scales, but to choose a type of smoothing that optimises the opposing demands of SF and positional localisation. A well-known theorem (see Marr and Hildreth [1980]) shows that the only smoothing distribution that is appropriate is the normal or Gaussian distribution. This theorem thus provides a principled (Type 1) justification for Gaussian smoothing. For Marr and Hildreth, therefore, the first step in the primal sketch computation is to convolve the image (I) with a range of Gaussians (G) of differing size (i.e., differing standard deviation, σ). In symbols, this step is expressed as $G*I$.

5. Intensity changes in $G*I$ can be characterised by the zero crossings in the second directional derivative, D2($G*I$). (D2 is read as "delta squared" and means the second derivative). Due to the derivative rule for convolutions, this can be written as D2$G*I$. D2G is thus an operator that can be convolved with I to give exactly the same result as using a D2 operator to "look at" the results of the $G*I$ convolution. That is, a single convolution with the D2G operator will suffice. The profile of this operator at right angles to its main axis (remember, the argument so far is still concerned with the computation of a directional derivative, so the operator would look roughly like Figure 10.5b in shape) is of the Mexican hat type (Fig. 10.9). This operator would examine only a portion of the image's SF spectrum, determined by the size of the Gaussian smoothing. Figures 10.7 and 10.8 show the performance of the D2G operator in comparison with two SF filters.

6. It is desirable if possible to use an isotropic operator for measuring gradients, as described earlier. There is no such operator for delivering the first derivative, but the Laplacian is suitable for measuring the second derivative, given some weak assumptions (see Marr and Hildreth [1980]). The end result of this analysis of the design of a suitable operator thus becomes a "Laplacian convolved with a Gaussian."

The preceding analysis concludes Marr and Hildreth's Type 1 design for a good gradient-measuring device. However, they have a lot more to say about how it might be implemented in terms of algorithms (Level 2) and hardware (Level 3). In particular, it turns out that a good approximation to D2G can be obtained by using an operator termed a *DOG* ("difference of

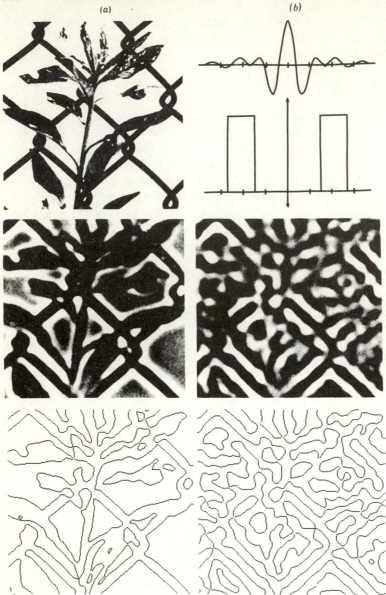

Figure 10.7 Comparison of the performance of Marr and Hildreth's D2G with a filter with sharp SF cutoffs. Column (*a*) shows an image, its convolution with D2G, and the ZCs extracted from that convolution. Column (*b*) shows the receptive field for a pure octave bandpass filter, its frequency selectivity, and then the convolution and ZCs obtained using this filter. Note that the ZC array contains echoes of the strong edges in the image caused by the side lobes of the receptive field. These ZCs have no correlates in the original image and hence constitute unwanted noise as far as Marr and Hildreth's theory is concerned. The width of the central excitatory region of both filters is the same. (*Source:* From *Proceedings of the Royal Society of London, Series B,* vol. 207, pp. 187–217, 1980. Copyright 1980 by the Royal Society, London, England. Used with permission of the Royal Society.)

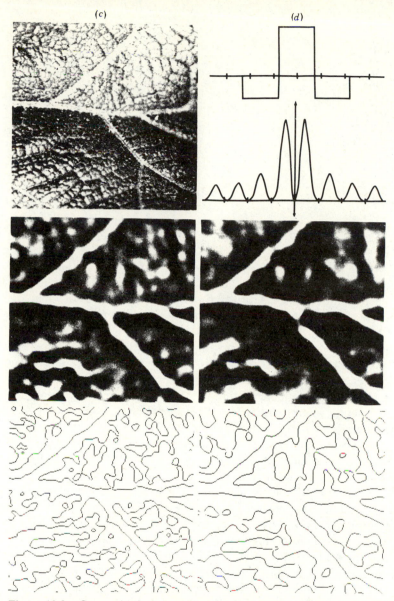

Figure 10.8 Comparison of the performance of D2G (column *c*) with a filter providing a square-wave approximation to the second derivative (column *d*; layout as in Fig. 10.7). The latter operator sees relatively few ZCs compared with D2G due to the way its broad SF selectivity blurs out desirable information. The central excitatory region of both filters is the same (but larger than for Fig. 10.7). (*Source:* From *Proceedings of the Royal Society of London, Series B,* vol. 207, pp. 187–217, 1980. Copyright 1980 by the Royal Society, London, England. Used with permission of the Royal Society.)

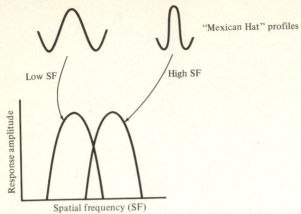

Figure 10.9   "Mexican Hat" operators of the D2G type with their associated spatial frequency selectivities (not drawn to scale).

Gaussians"). This is an operator that is created by the addition of one positive and one negative Gaussian-weighting function, with the variance of the two Gaussians having a ratio of about 1.6 (Fig. 10.10). A number of operators of this type can be used to span the different scales of image gradients that need to be extracted.

Interestingly, it has been known for more than 15 years that the receptive fields of many cells in the first stages of the mammalian visual pathway can be well described as DOGs (see Marr and Hildreth [1980] for references). It can therefore now be appreciated that mammalian biological visual hardware (Level 3) is implementing a pretty good Level 1 theory of measurement devices for extracting intensity changes. Psychophysical experiments on "SF channels" suggest that the human visual system does likewise (Wilson & Giese, 1977; an SF channel is simply a population of cells that are tuned to be selective for a limited range of SFs). The earlier estimate of four channels sampling at different scales (Wilson & Bergen, 1979) has now been revised to six (Wilson, 1983), each with a bandwidth of about 1.5 octaves.

The reason that this issue has been developed here at some length is because it neatly illustrates the general approach that was adopted by Marr. Great emphasis is placed on task analysis and that involves clear thinking about what is being computed and why. It was because one was trying to build a primal sketch optimising the SF and positional localisation trade-off that one arrived at the specification of the DOG operator. A different computational goal might have led to quite a different result. For example, if one had been concerned with developing a model of object recognition based on Fourier filtering, then sharply tuned filters might have been preferred rather than the relatively broad-band filters that are the end result of Marr's analysis.

Having analysed clearly the task requirements, the search is then on for a principled solution to the problems encountered. That is quite different from what has happened in a great deal of the pattern recognition literature that is concerned with edge detection, a literature often interested in trying out one operator after another with little thought given to fundamental design questions (but see Haralick [1980] for a review of that literature, plus an account of his own edge operator which is far from ad hoc; he has taken the approach of trying to specify the best-fit polynomial that describes the image intensities). Finally, the approach blends nicely with neurophysiological and psychophysical studies, leaving one with a deeply satisfying

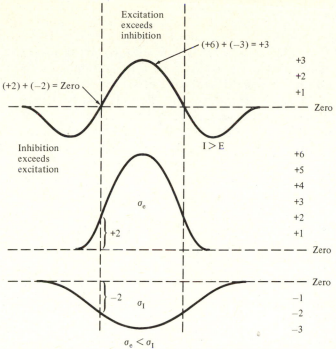

Figure 10.10   The "Mexican Hat" receptive field as a "difference of Gaussians" (DOG).

explanation of some well-known but hitherto poorly understood characteristics of biological hardware and human vision. One can go so far as to say that even if the account turns out to be wrong, it serves as a fine model of what type of answer would count as a proper understanding of a problem in vision.

Nevertheless, it remains true that the elegant analysis of Marr and Hildreth is still highly controversial as a general theory of edge detection and that other candidates exist (e.g., Haralick [1980]; see also Binford [1981], for a critique of the Marr/Hildreth theory). Moreover, the Marr/Hildreth account was based upon some earlier attempts that were barely Type 1 in character. Thus, Marr's (1976) seminal paper on the primal sketch used orientationally tuned filters with no clear Type 1 reasons for doing so, his choice being largely driven, it seems, by neurophysiological results, suggesting that such filters might exist in the mammalian visual cortex. Nor did the 1976 paper provide a theoretical justification for DOGs. That came later, as did the idea of a Laplacian convolved with a Gaussian and the use of ZCs (Marr [1976], used peaks from oriented operator outputs to deliver the same type of information that Marr and Hildreth obtained by using ZCs from circularly symmetric masks). These developments arose when Marr returned to the question of how to compute the primal sketch, aware of the compromises he had made in his original paper and the need to probe deeper into the computational nature of the task. That subsequent probing no doubt benefitted a great deal from the kind of difficulties that were evident in the computational experiments reported in the 1976 paper. The point here, of course, is not to say that computational experiments are a bad thing but to insist that they must be seen for what they are—trial runs helping to suggest a clarification of the task being solved and what might constitute a Type 1 solution.

Locating Intensity Changes

As already mentioned, the candidate proposed by Marr and Hildreth to serve as a suitable primitive for this purpose is the ZC (Fig. 10.3d). ZCs have the advantage of being readily accessible (i.e., easily located in convolutions) but they also have the advantage of being "complete." That is, if the filter used has a bandwidth of about 1 octave, or if a broader band filter is used but with slopes around the ZC taken into account, then it might be possible to reconstitute the image from the convolution profile (Logan's Theorem: see Marr et al., [1979]; Poggio et al. [1982] extend Logan's theorem to 2D). This is important, not because it is desirable to reconstitute the image, of course, but because it means that ZCs plus their slopes contain all the important information, albeit some of it implicitly.

Although the ZC has considerable practical and theoretical attractions, it is nevertheless the case that the human visual system seems also to use peaks, at least for stereoscopic vision in cases where luminance changes are confounded with disparity changes. In that circumstance, ZCs are in principle unsuitable (this is a Type 1 justification for peaks: see Mayhew and Frisby [1981] whose use of peaks from the second-derivative convolution profile is, of course, not to be confused with taking peaks from the first derivative; Fig. 10.3).

Grouping of Primitives Within Channels

Marr's (1976) version of the primal sketch computation proposed two "grouping operations" for delivering assertions about image intensity changes: within channel and cross channel. This approach was continued in Marr and Hildreth (1980) but with ZCs replacing peaks as the elementary primitives to be grouped.

Within the SF channel, the grouping process joins locally adjacent ZCs into small "edge segments" and assigns them an orientation. ZCs are by their nature continuous as are the edges of "objects," giving a simple Type 1 justification for the grouping process. The locations of sudden changes of ZC orientation (corners), closures (blobs), and line ends or terminations are also made explicit at this stage.

Marr's neurophysiological candidate for carrying information about ZC edge segments is the well-known "simple cell" of Hubel and Wiesel (1959), with the orientational tuning of this cell reflecting the way it groups ZCs collinearly (see Fig. 10.11 which is based on Marr and Hildreth [1980]; Marr and Ullman [1981], develop this account to take note of directional selectivity; see also Zucker [1982]). This interpretation of simple cells marks a sharp change from the original 1976 primal sketch paper that treated simple cells as oriented SF filters, following suggestions to that effect from Campbell and Robson (1968). In the current account, simple cells carry the first "raw" symbolic assertions about "what is there," whereas in the former theory they still served as gradient measurement devices.

Testing these different views (which may, of course, turn out not to be exclusive in that simple cells are a broad class of unit) is presently a neurophysiological issue of considerable interest and a good example of how a computational theory can open up neurophysiological questions, which it is difficult to conceive arising, at least in a precise form, in any other way. (For completeness, one should perhaps emphasise that other interpretations of the functional role of Hubel and Wiesel units and/or SF channels abound, although not all have the precision of those just mentioned.)

The other grouping process organises ZC segments across SF channels. The principle here is

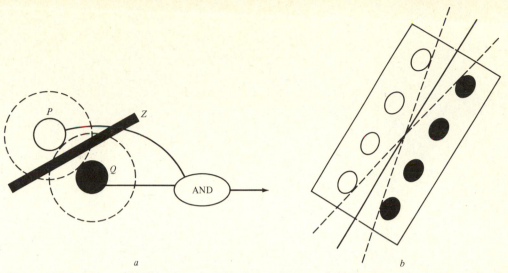

a   *b*

Figure 10.11   Marr and Hildreth say of this figure: "Proposed mechanism whereby some simple cells detect zero-crossing segments. In (*a*), if *P* represents an on-centre geniculate *X*-cell receptive field, and *Q*, an off-centre, then if both are active, a zero-crossing *Z* in the Laplacian passes between them. If they are connected to a logical **AND** gate, as shown, then the gate will "**detect**" the presence of the zero-crossing. If several are arranged in tandem, as in (*b*), and also connected by logical **AND**'s, the resulting operation detects an oriented zero-crossing segment within the orientation bounds, given roughly by the dotted lines. This gives our most primitive model for simple cells. Ideally, one would like gates such that there is a response only if all *P*, *Q* inputs are active, and the magnitude of the responses then varies with their sum." (*Source:* Reproduced from Marr and Hildreth, 1980, with permission as described in legend for Fig. 10.7.)

that of "spectral continuity." An isolated event in the spatial domain (position) produces a continuous event in the frequency domain (size), that is, an isolated edge in the luminance profile will produce broad spectrum activity that will appear in the convolution surfaces of all the differently scaled DOGs (Fig. 10.12). One can, therefore, argue that spatially coincident ZCs in the different channels *must* be derived from the same object in the image. The reason one needs to consider the cross-channel spectrum is that the output from a channel considered in isolation is ambiguous ('edge blind,' cf. the colour blindness of a monochromat; also see earlier remarks on the ambiguity of operators regarding feature detection). In contrast, the spectrum of ZC amplitudes that are obtained from two or more channels provides a "signature tune" that can be interpreted and from which a description of the luminance edge can be computed, which is the next stage of the process.

Interpretation of Local ZC Groupings: The Raw Primal Sketch

The mapping of grouped ZC "microsegments" into a descriptive vocabulary of edges, bars, lines, blobs, and so on is not yet satisfactorily understood (Hildreth, 1981), either in terms of the processes or of the particular items in the vocabulary, but something like it must happen to produce an explicit description of local image intensity changes—what Marr calls the "raw primal sketch." It has, of course, been implemented in Marr's program but problems have been

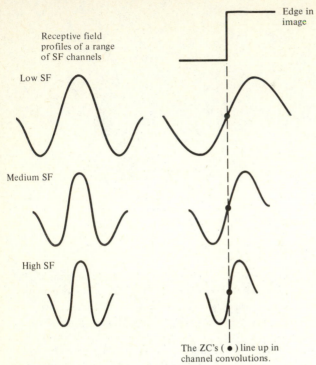

Receptive field
profiles of a range
of SF channels

Edge in
image

Low SF

Medium SF

High SF

The ZC's (●) line up in
channel convolutions.

Figure 10.12   An isolated edge produces spatially coincident ZCs in different SF channels (all profiles diagrammatic only).

found to arise from the processing of dense textures that disrupt the spatial coincidence of the ZCs.

The Full Primal Sketch

The information made explicit in the raw primal sketch is still local. It may be regarded as being at the same level as a child's "join-the-dots" puzzle, that is, large-scale contours and regions have yet to be made explicit from local information about them. Of course, for the visual system the game involves a lot more than joining up successively numbered dots. First, there are an awful lot of dots, and second, they do not just carry a number but instead, carry a description. For example, what the grouping operations have to decide at this stage is whether to join together under a single assertion two local descriptions such as:

'edge' (contrast: 4)   and   'edge' (contrast: 3)
      (orientation: 15)   (orientation: 16)
      (fuzziness: 5)   (fuzziness: 6)

or whether some alternative grouping with some other description is to be preferred.

It is at this level of the computation that a functional role arises for the Gestalt "figural grouping principles" of continuity, proximity, similarity, and so on. There are two major guiding principles for the development of these grouping operations.

Dots ——— become ———→ Clusters ——— become ———→ Lines —— become —→ Arrow shape

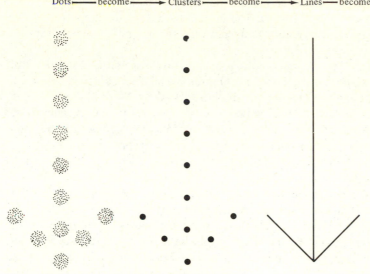

Figure 10.13   The principle of explicit naming.

The first is strategic and is the principle of "explicit naming": If you want to treat a group of things as a single entity, give it a name. The power of explicit naming is illustrated in Fig. 10.13. The patches of dots are grouped together, using the principles of similarity and proximity, and each one is given the name *cluster* (with parameters of size and location but with those details not shown). The clusters are then grouped, using the principle of continuity (sometimes called *curvilinear aggregation*) to yield a new set of elements called *lines*. The lines are then ready for shape classification as an arrow by later postprimal sketch processes. The result of the repeated application of figural grouping processes is thus to generate increasingly abstract entities: The lines shown in Figure 10.13 are, of course, only "virtual lines," having no existence as such in the image. The creation of virtual entities is possible because once a "thing" has been given a name (Marr calls the names "place tokens"), then the entity can be manipulated, acquire properties, be grouped, or be input to any of the processes that have access to the particular level of processing under consideration. This is the essence of symbolic computation.

The second major principle affecting grouping operations is tactical, called the principle of *least commitment:* errors are costly so do not do anything you might have to undo. Thus, in Marr's primal sketch, as in many other low-level labelling programs in computer vision, grouping does not occur in a single pass but instead involves several stages that are characterised by the progressive relaxation of the requirements for joining elementary descriptions. At first, only those entities whose descriptions agree very closely are grouped to form a single unit, and then only if no plausible alternative is available. If there is a plausible alternative, or if there is only a partial match in the description, then the decison is held in abeyance until further comparison and interpolation between descriptions of other elements have been completed, in the hope that disambiguating information will arrive from elsewhere (e.g., a plausible but not very good alternative being excluded by virtue of its capture by another group into which it fits perfectly; note the principle of least commitment at work here). The use of so-called "relaxation processes" for achieving mutually consistent groupings of raw primal sketch entities is described in the next section.

The assertions of the raw primal sketch can also be grouped by using processes of texture discrimination (for a review, see Julesz [1981]). The basic idea here is to compare adjacent regions for the density and type of elements that comprise them, and thereby assert the existence of entities when differences are found.

For Marr, the final outcome of grouping operations and texture discrimination is the "full primal sketch." This is a representation making explicit region boundaries, object contours, and primitive shapes or configurations (an example of the latter used by Marr is the eyes–nose triangle of Fig. 10.14). The full primal sketch embodies some aspects of what is called *scene segmentation* in the pattern recognition literature. This is a process of grouping together those parts of an image description that come from an object in the scene prior to their recognition. We discuss some of the very considerable difficulties that have been experienced with segmentation later in the chapter.

It is an important aspect of Marr's theory that the computation of the full primal sketch is knowledge free, in the sense that no knowledge of particular objects that might or might not be present is used. In short, Marr's approach at this level is to try to describe attributes of the image without forming any hypotheses of what things might be in the associated scene. Thus, the contours in Figure 10.14 were made explicit without any help from knowledge that the image was that of a teddy bear.

Of course, the computation of the full primal sketch does rely on knowledge of the visual world but that knowledge is of a very general kind. Thus, the Type 1 justification for the grouping principles employed is that they capitalise on the usual properties of object contours, regions, and so on, and not on the properties of specific objects that might be present. When Marr first forwarded his theory, that kind of knowledge-free approach was directly against the current AI fashion which argued that smart visual systems knew a great deal about what there was to be scene. For example, Shirai's (1973) edge finder attempted to use downward flowing high-level knowledge of what *should be there,* given the current object hypothesis, to influence the low-level processing of what *actually is there.* But this tactic spawns a really difficult problem, namely, how can high-level semantic knowledge be interfaced with low-level grouping processes (later we give an account of some "model-driven" attempts to do so). The success of Marr's primal sketch program underlined the principle that good representations simplify problems of control (the corollary of which might be—if you have a bad representation, who cares if you patched around it with control).

Relaxation Processes: Understanding Grouping at Level 2

The grouping operations, previously described, typically have to deal with an enormous amount of image data. If grouping is attempted by using sequential labelling operations utilising contextual information about 'sensible' neighbouring grouping possibilities, then the process is intrinsically very slow. One approach to overcome this limitation is to begin by assessing the

---

Figure 10.14   The primal sketch. (*a*) Grey levels in image; (*b*) intensity map of image; (*c*) segments of the raw primal sketch before much grouping has taken place; (*d* to *f*) groups found during extraction of the full primal sketch. (*Source:* From "Early Processing of Visual Information" by D. Marr, *Philosophical Transactions of the Royal Society of London,* vol. 275, no. 942. October 19, 1976, copyright 1976 by the Royal Society, London, England. Used with permission of the Royal Society.)

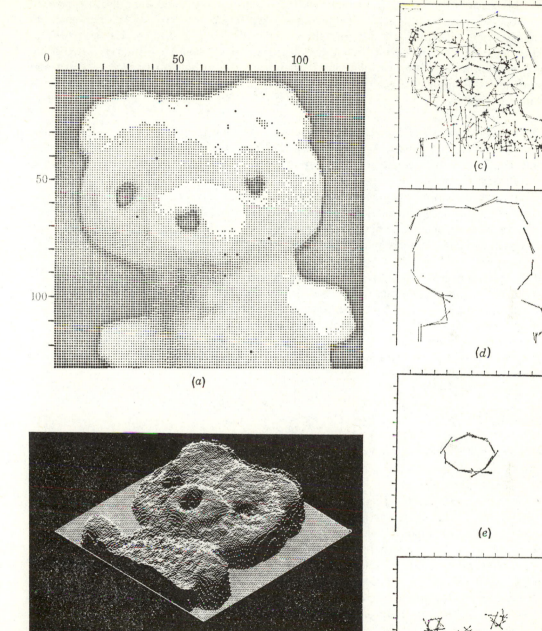

(a)

(b)

(c)

(d)

(e)

(f)

grouping possibilities for every part independently and in parallel and then to compare each part's assessment with those of local neighbouring parts in order to detect and correct potential inconsistencies, repeating this process with as many cycles as necessary. Using iteratively cycling local neighbourhood interactions to obtain a globally consistent interpretation of an image is often termed a *relaxation process,* or alternatively a *cooperative process.* Davis and Rosenfeld (1981) provide a good review and state that, very generally, a relaxation process is organised as follows:

1. A list of possible labels is independently selected for each picture part, based on the intrinsic characteristics of the part. A measure of confidence can be associated with each possible label and it is tacitly assumed that the correct label for each part is on the initial list of labels for that part.
2. The possibilities (and confidences) for each part are compared with those for related parts, based on a model for the relationships among the possible labels of picture parts. Labels are deleted or confidences are adjusted to reduce inconsistencies.
3. Step (2) can be iterated as many times as required

Obviously, any particular application of a relaxation process will need to consider carefully how to specify label relationship models, estimate confidences, and so on. It is in completing that specification that Level 1 considerations dealing with the computational structure of the task in hand are crucially important. The relaxation process itself is simply a useful general-purpose algorithmic tool, and hence is clearly to be categorized as Level 2 in nature. A further instance of its use is described later for the (quite different) task of line labelling in blocks world research.

SILHOUETTES

Silhouettes tell us more than they should. This point is admirably illustrated by the party game of configuring one's hands to produce shadows that are seen as funny faces, animals, and so on. The shadows could in principle be generated by an infinity of different objects, hands being just one possibility, and yet the visual system arrives at a particular interpretation—in this case, amusingly *not* the hands that actually create the shadows. Why and how does it do so?

One of the most important themes in current work on computer vision is to develop the research strategy that if a visual information-processing task is clearly impossible, and yet we do it, then we must be making some assumptions (see Ullman [1979] for an application of this strategy to the problem of extracting structure from motion). Marr (1977b) makes the point that because shadowgraphs are a 'successful yet impossible' trick, implicit in the way we represent a silhouette (or more generally, an occluding contour—the visible boundary between an object and its background; Fig. 10.15) there must be some a priori assumptions. The question is: What are they? Marr (1977b) proposes the following:

1. Each point on the contour generator projects to a different point on the occluding contour in the image. (The contour generator is the set of points on the generating surface that projects to the occluding contour; Fig. 10.15).

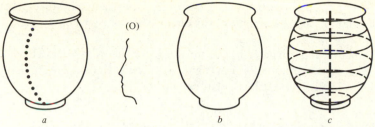

Figure 10.15   Analysis of occluding contour. A three-dimensional surface (*a*) that from the viewpoint of the observer (O) generates the occluding contour shown in (*b*). The dots on the surface of (*a*) are termed the 'contour generator' of the occluding contour by Marr. Given assumptions described in the text, it can be proved (Marr 1977b) that the generating surface of an occluding contour is a 'generalised cylinder', i.e. a surface created by moving a cross section, whose size and shape can vary, along an axis, as illustrated in (*c*).

2. Nearby points on the occluding contour arise from nearby points on the generating surface.

3. The contour generator lies wholly in a single plane.

Assumptions (1) and (2) say that where the occluding contour looks continuous it really is, and (3) says that convex/concave segments of the contour reflect similar properties of the generating surface.

Marr has proved that if all these assumptions hold, then the generating surface is a *generalised cylinder* (sometimes also called a *generalised cone*). This is a surface created by moving a cross section along an axis (Fig. 10.15c). The cross section may vary smoothly in size and shape, and the axis need not remain straight along the length of the cylinder. (Imagine the craft of "throwing a pot." The potter's thumbs, moving up and changing their distance from the center of rotation of the wheel, sweep out a generalised cylinder of circular cross section, with size variations introduced by the potter as he throws a bowl, vase, etc.)

The important strong psychological assumption being advanced here is that human beings have generalised cylinders as a major component of their representation for shape.

Marr has also shown that the parameters for a generalized cone can be recovered not only from a silhouette but also from the contours in more usual images. That is, they can be derived from contour groupings appearing in the full primal sketch and interpreted as the boundary where an object occludes its background. This amounts to the claim that generalised cylinders are an accessible representation for shape. The importance of this will become clear in the following section.

STICK FIGURES

Continuing the theme, stick figures, like cartoons and silhouettes, are greatly impoverished sources of information and yet they work. Possibly one reason that pipe cleaners can be used to construct the inhabitants of the child's farmyard is that they make explicit the disposition and relative sizes of the axes of generalized cones. Following the example of cartoon figures, the implication is that the axes of generalised cylinders may provide the basis for representation of a 3D shape that is sufficient for recognition.

To understand the significance of this suggestion, one must ask the question as to what in principle would constitute a *good* representation for a 3D shape (a Type 1/Level 1 question, of course). Marr and Nishihara (1978) list three criteria that can be applied:

· *Accessibility*. This is the computational cost of extracting the representation from the image.
· *Scope and Uniqueness*. For what class of shapes is the representation suitable and do the shapes in that class have canonical descriptions in the representation? A canonical representation is one in which a particular shape has a unique description in the representation: Obviously recognition is facilitated if different views of the same object produce the same shape description. A noncanonical representational scheme would have to face the difficult problem of deciding whether two (or more) descriptions describe the same object, or whether they arise from different objects.
· *Stability and Sensitivity*. Can the representation be used to capture both the similarities and the differences between objects? These opposing requirements can be met only if the representation allows a decoupling between stable information capturing the more general and less varying properties of a shape, from information sensitive to the finer distinctions between shapes.

Marr and Nishihara then list three design considerations for a representation that need to be met, bearing the foregoing criteria in mind:

· *Coordinate System*. Should the coordinate system be viewer or object centered? The major considerations here are the criteria of *accessibility* and *scope/uniqueness* as just described. A viewer-centered description may be more accessible, but when used for recognition it will obviously be noncanonical and thus costly in storage (perhaps leading to the need to store a lengthy list of different descriptions, one for each possible or at least frequent view of a given object). On the other hand, an object-centered coordinate system is probably more expensive to extract from the image in the first place but it will have lower recognition and storage costs. Marr and Nishihara argue that the advantages of an object-centered coordinate system greatly outweigh the cost of its extraction from the image.
· *Choice of Primitives*. Should the elementary units of the representation be volumetric or surface based, and what size should they be? An example of the former is a stick figure representation, based on generalised cones, with each stick representing a particular volume of space filled by a part of the 3D shape (a suggestion originally made by Binford [1980]). A surface-based representation might describe an object in primitives such as surface patches or regions (e.g., Ullman [1983]), and that might be feasible for simple geometric figures (see the following discussion below on the blocks world) but not so easy for a shape such as a giraffe. Origami might provide a surface-based challenge to a volumetric representation, but it could be that some of the "art" of Origami derives from its use of a very unsuitable

medium to represent complex shapes. In any event, the most important consideration seems to be that volumetric primitives explicitly carry information about the spatial disposition of the parts of an object that are only implicit in a surface-based representation. In both cases, the size of the primitives will determine what information cannot be carried, what information can be made explicit, and what information is implicit (and possibly costly to extract later if required).

Organisation. Should all the primitives be at the same level, or should there be a modular structure to the representation? The latter is the obvious choice because: (1) it exploits the principle of explicit naming (the description 'sheet of stamps' says something that is only implicit in *several hundred small patches*) and (2) a hierarchical modular design enables one to solve the stability/sensitivity conflict, for higher-in-the-hierachy descriptions are intrinsically stable, whereas lower-order descriptions will capture fine detail.

Accordingly, Marr and Nishihara (1978) chose an object-centered, volumetric, modular, and hierarchical representation (Table 10.1 and Fig. 10.16). This is a representation particularly well suited to the description of shapes made from the conjunction of generalised cylinders (the sort of objects that grow naturally and hence have well-defined axes) and particularly ill-suited to the description of the shape of crumpled newspapers and many other objects.

TABLE 10.1

DESIGN CHOICE	CRITERIA
1. Coordinate System: Viewer-centered or object-centered?	Accessibility, and scope and uniqueness
2. Primitives: Volumetric or surface-based?	Scope and uniqueness
3. Organisation: Modular/hierarchical or single level?	Stability and sensitivity

To summarize the argument so far: stick figures work because they make explicit the disposition and relative sizes of generalised cylinders; silhouettes work because we assume their contours are generated by generalised cylinders. The stick figure representation is obviously a kind of "structural description," that is, a list of "parts" and the relationships among them, but goes well beyond any previous scheme of that type in the refined analysis of the problems and the use of the axes of generalised cylinders as the parts.

Marr and Nishihara (1978) call the relationships describing the conjunction of the axes of component cylinders the *adjunct relations* (Fig. 10.16). Thus a person and a tailless horse might be regarded as having the same number of parts (a trunk, four limbs, a neck, and a head), but they can be distinguished, among other things, of course, by differences in the relative sizes of the components and the "admissable" range of angles at which component axes connect to the principal axis.

To summarise Marr and Nishihara (1978)—to recognize a visual object is to extract from the image a (hierarchically organised) description of the orientation of its principal and component axes, their adjunct relationships, and relative lengths. Then, with the principal axis as the basis of the object-centered coordinate system, the description is matched to a canonical model that is held in a memory.

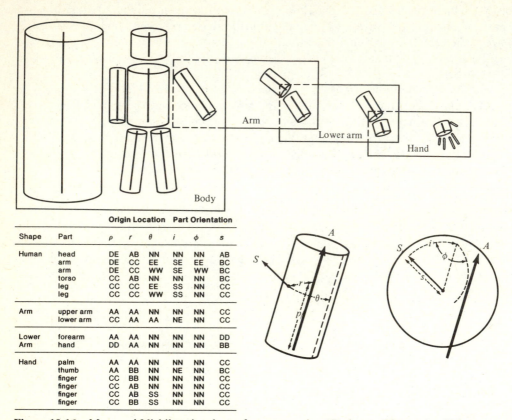

Shape	Part	Origin Location			Part Orientation		
		ρ	r	θ	i	φ	s
Human	head	DE	AB	NN	NN	NN	AB
	arm	DE	CC	EE	SE	EE	BC
	arm	DE	CC	WW	SE	WW	BC
	torso	CC	AB	NN	NN	NN	BC
	leg	CC	CC	EE	SS	NN	CC
	leg	CC	CC	WW	SS	NN	CC
Arm	upper arm	AA	AA	NN	NN	NN	CC
	lower arm	CC	AA	AA	NE	NN	CC
Lower Arm	forearm	AA	AA	NN	NN	NN	DD
	hand	DD	AA	NN	NN	NN	BB
Hand	palm	AA	AA	NN	NN	NN	CC
	thumb	AA	BB	NN	NE	NN	BC
	finger	CC	BB	NN	NN	NN	CC
	finger	CC	AB	NN	NN	NN	CC
	finger	CC	AB	SS	NN	NN	CC
	finger	CC	BB	SS	NN	NN	CC

Figure 10.16   Marr and Nishihara's scheme for representing 3D shapes. They write: "The arrangement of 3-D models into the representation of a human shape. First the overall form—the "body"—is given an axis. This yields an object-centered coordinate system which can then be used to specify the arrangement of the 'arms', 'legs', 'torso', and 'head'. The position of each of these is specified by an axis of its own, which in turn serves to define a coordinate system for specifying the arrangement of further subsidiary parts. This gives us a hierarchy of 3-D models: we show it extending downward as far as the fingers. The shapes in the figure are drawn as if they were cylindrical, but that is purely for illustrative convenience: It is the axes alone that stand for the volumetric qualities of the shape, much as pipecleaner models can serve to describe various animals. The illustration also includes a printout of the 3-D model representation as it is stored for use in a computer. The essence of the coding is to express how the various subsidiary axes relate to the shape as whole: where are they, which way are they, which way are they pointing, and how long are they? For each of the modules, the first three quantities shown in the computer code specify the location of the proximal end of the axis: p gives its position along the length of the axis of the overall shape, r gives its distance outward therefrom, and θ gives the angle at which it is found. The last three quantities specify the orientation of the subsidiary axis. Two angles, i and ϕ, serve to give its direction and a number, s, gives its length. In all cases, angles are specified by a set of compass directions and lengths by a system of line-segment names; the details need not concern us." (*Source:* From "Visual Information Processing: Artificial Intelligence and the Sensorium of Sight" by D. Marr and H. K. Nishihara, 1978, *Technology Review,* vol. 81, October. Alumni Assoc. of MIT, Cambridge, Mass. Figures from "Representation and recognition of the spatial organization of three dimensional shapes" by D. Marr and H. K. Nishihara, *Proceedings of the Royal Society of London,* Series B, vol. 200, pp. 269–294, Copyright 1978 by the Royal Society, London, England. Used with permission of the Royal Society.)

The catalogue of stored models can be accessed in three different ways:

- *The Specificity Index*. This is the most general method exploiting the hierarchical structure of the representation. It is essentially to search in a coarse-to-fine manner through a hierarchical network of increasingly finer structural details until the limit of the resolution of the description is reached and/or recognition is achieved. If this search is conducted by using only the information contained in a 2D description of the image, such as that delivered by the primal sketch, then the orientation information in the adjunct relationships in the object-centered description can only be loosely specified. However, once the data-driven access to the stored model is successful, the top-down constraints provided by the stored adjunct relationships may be used to recover the 3D disposition of the object with reference to the viewer.
- *The Adjunct Index*. This utilises details of adjunct relationships to access the hierarchy of 3D models in the catalogue at a finer level of detail than the specificity index. Thus, if the to-be-matched description has specific details relating the orientation of the principal axis to some of its components, then one can access the catalogue appropriately, that is, it is the adjunct relationships (among others) that allow one to distinguish between bipeds and quadrapeds.
- *The Parent Index*. This is the access for top-down processing from the highest level. If a bit of the image is identified as a horse's head, then that information can be used to access the 3D-model catalogue directly, and the 3D model selected enables one to exploit a considerable number of constraints, for example, where in the image to expect to find the rest of it, the dip angle of an ambiguous axis, and so on.

The research question that Marr and Nishihara did not answer, although they clearly saw it as having considerable importance, and Marr gave it great prominence in his book, was how to recover their object-centered 3D-shape representation from a viewer-centered 3D-shape representation of the surfaces in the scene. Their preliminary studies investigated recovery only from 2D in the full primal sketch. The next section considers that question in some detail.

THE MISSING LINK: THE NEED FOR INTERMEDIATE REPRESENTATIONS

Marr and Nishihara (1978) explored the recovery of their object-centered 3D-shape representation from 2D data in the full primal sketch. Attempting to leap in a single bound from 2D or "pictorial" representations to 3D models has been characteristic of (all?) early computer vision systems and helps explain their uniformly poor performance. It is now generally recognized in the image-understanding community (although perhaps not in the pattern recognition one), that what is required is one or more intermediate representations that capture the 3D characteristics of surfaces in the scene and that 3D models should be fitted to the data in those representations, not to earlier ones.

The Problems of Image Segmentation

The problems to be faced in moving directly from pictorial data to 3D models are various and severe. They are best illustrated by considering the problem of "segmenting" pictorial data. Segmentation is a central concept in the pattern recognition and image processing (PRIP) literature and roughly corresponds to the separation of "figure from ground" in the psychological literature (see Marr [1982, p. 270]). The basic idea is that the first step to be taken in dealing with a pictorial representation is to break up its parts into regions that are meaningful for the task in hand. In the case of object recognition, this amounts to the claim that it is necessary to begin by clustering together picture parts that comprise an object and then to attempt to recognise what object produced that cluster.

The typical difficulty experienced with this approach is that it is often impossible to segment out a desired region by using grouping mechanisms based on bringing together similar picture parts. Regions that are important for object recognition do not necessarily have any distinctive visual characteristics, or else object boundaries are obscured by, say, shadows or occlusions from other objects that combine to produce segmentations of a picture into regions that have no semantic unity. And obviously, it is hardly surprising if recognition proves difficult by using segmented-out regions that do not correspond to genuine scene entities.

The PRIP literature continues to regard segmentation as a major image-processing goal, probably because in limited and well-defined industrial domains various region-growing procedures have proved of commercial value. In sharp contrast, the image-understanding (IU) community, whose approach is exemplified by Marr, is concerned with building general-purpose vision systems and in understanding the best known systems of that type (natural ones). They now generally accept the need to avoid altogether the classic segmentation problem, and instead, begin by building much richer representations of scene surfaces than the simple boundaries of the primal sketch before attempting to fit 3D-object models. This distinction between PRIP and IU probably now constitutes *the* salient difference between their endeavours. Even in the case of ACRONYM, probably the most successful 3D-object recognition system to emerge from IU that goes straight from a 2D image to a 3D model (doing so with a highly sophisticated and powerful inference engine; Brooks [1981]), it is now recognised that a volumetric intermediate-level data-base, rather than the present pictorial one, will prove essential for future progress (Binford, 1982).

Intrinsic Images

Barrow and Tenenbaum (1978, 1981) have coined the term *intrinsic images* for intermediate representations that make explicit various aspects of visible surfaces. Intrinsic images are maps that lay out in image (and hence viewer-centered) coordinates the local properties of surfaces such as their illumination, reflectance, orientation, and distance. One possible implementation of such a scheme offered by Barrow and Tenenbaum is illustrated in Figure 10.17 and we cannot improve on their description of it as

> a stack of registered arrays representing the original image (top) and the primary intrinsic image arrays. Processing is initialised by detecting intensity edges in the original image, interpreting them . . . and then creating the appropriate edges in the intrinsic images (as implied by the descending arrows). Parallel local operations (shown as circles) modify the val-

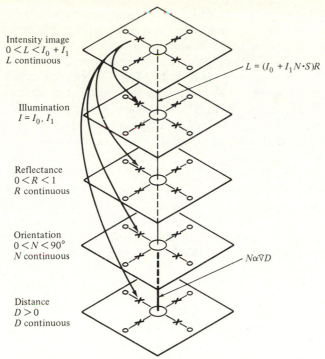

Intensity image
$0 < L < I_0 + I_1$
L continuous

$L = (I_0 + I_1 N \cdot S)R$

Illumination
$I = I_0, I_1$

Reflectance
$0 < R < 1$
R continuous

Orientation
$0 < N < 90°$
N continuous

$N \alpha \nabla D$

Distance
$D > 0$
D continuous

Figure 10.17   Barrow and Tenebaum's parallel computa-
tional model for recovering intrinsic images.
See text for details. (*Source:* Reproduced with
permission from A. R. Hanson and E. M.
Riseman (Eds). *Computer Vision Systems.*
Academic Press, NY, 1978.)

ues in each intrinsic image to make them consistent with intra-image continuity and limit
constraints (e.g., reflectance must be between 0 and 1). Simultaneously, a second set of
processes (shown as vertical lines) operates to make the values at each point consistent with
the corresponding intensity value, as required by the inter-image photometric constraint. A
third set of processes (shown as X's) operates to insert and delete edge elements, which in-
hibit continuity constraints locally. The constraint and edge modification processes operate
continuously and interact to recover accurate intrinsic scene characteristics and to perfect
the initial edge interpretation. The system functions like an analog computer: as a value in
one image increases, say to improve continuity, corresponding values in other images must
increase or decrease to maintain consistency with the observed intensity at that point.
Within each image, values tend to propagate in from boundary conditions established along
edges. This resembles relaxation processes . . . (Barrow & Tenenbaum, 1978).

The 2½D Sketch

Barrow and Tenenbaum's (1978) concept of an interacting stack of intrinsic images is similar in
some respects to Marr's notion of the 2½D sketch. Marr uses the latter term for a viewer-

centered (hence the term *sketch*) representation, making explicit the depths, local orientations, and discontinuities of visible surfaces, created and maintained from a number of cues (e.g., stereopsis, structure from motion, optical flow, occluding contours, surface contours, texture, texture contours, shading; Marr [1982]). The computation of the $2\frac{1}{2}$D sketch is for Marr the final objective of early visual processing. It is at the limit of what Marr felt tempted to call "pure perception—the recovery of surface information by purely data-driven processes without need for particular hypotheses about the nature, use, or function of the objects being viewed . . . (the $2\frac{1}{2}$D sketch) provides a representation of objective physical reality that precedes the decomposition of the scene into objects and all the concomitant difficulties associated with object recognition" (Marr, 1982, p. 269).

To summarize this section: The emerging consensus view in the IU community is that representations that are intermediate between 3D models and the inherently 2D pictorial data of the primal sketch are essential for general-purpose vision systems. This is obligatory because the main factors that determine the intensity values in an image are illumination, surface geometry, surface reflectance, and vantage point, and the effects of these various factors in forming natural images need to be disentangled before higher level processes concerned with object recognition can have much chance of success.

OUTLINE FOR A GENERAL-PURPOSE VISION SYSTEM

In this section we integrate what has gone before by providing an abbreviated specification for the architecture of a general-purpose vision system up to the level of object recognition. Although configured as a serial process of transformation between layered representations, it must be emphasised that outputs of intermediate levels may (and in the human almost certainly do) support various and different tasks (navigation, orientation, manipulation, etc.), so that it is not envisaged that information must pass right through the system before being used. The control structure should not be regarded as rigid either; that is, it should be possible for (at least adjacent) layers to communicate, thus providing a sensible mix of bottom-up/top-down processing.

In this specification, each section first states the information that is carried explicitly at a given level and then gives the transformations that are carried out to achieve the next level of representation.

Grey Level Image(s)

Assuming a sensor/image aquisition process, we have as the first level in the processing hierarchy—pointilliste 2D array(s) of intensity measurements. Like an array of numbers, all the explicit information is local and all the structural information is implicit.

Transformations from this level are mainly local operations of spatiotemporal differentiation at different scales and resolutions, augmented by first-order statistical grouping processes. The assumptions here are that reflectance changes over space/time correspond to important physical events in the world, that is, illumination and object discontinuities and boundaries. These changes project into the image as intensity changes over different scales.

Raw Primal Sketch (Static) and Optical Flow field (Motion)

These are iconic (imagelike) representations describing the location, scale, magnitude of the intensity changes in the images, edge features, and local first-order statistics (texture). The optic flow field is a local representation describing the velocity vector at every image location. Its computation has not been discussed earlier for reasons of space but it can be thought of as a "movement analogue" of the raw primal sketch.

The key aspect of representations at this level is that they are descriptions of the image; hence, they are often called *pictorial*.

Transformations from this level to the next level up, which is concerned with representing attributes of scene surfaces, assume surface continuity, the geometry of projection, photometry, models of surface junctions, tangency, and occlusion. The processes include stereopsis, shape from . . . shading, texture, contour, motion parallax, and so on. The theoretical understanding and discovery of principled solutions to these "classical" visual phenomena/problems is one of the jewels in the crown of recent IU research.

Intrinsic Images

This is the first level at which descriptions of the scene become explicit. The intrinsic images describe, in viewer-centered coordinates, information about intrinsic surface properties, for example, surface distance, orientation, reflectance, illumination, texture/material properties, and so on.

Transformations from this level exploit analogues of iconic grouping processes to recover surface boundaries. Assumptions of surface homogeneity to interpret surface boundaries produce a segmentation of the scene in terms of surfaces and volumes. This is the present research frontier for much IU work and successful systems can be expected fairly soon.

$2\frac{1}{2}$D Sketch

A $2\frac{1}{2}$D sketch is an explicit 3D representation of the scene in a viewer-centered coordinate system that integrates all the information contained in the intrinsic images. It is this and the previous level of representations that have been weak or missing from most earlier vision/ object-recognition systems. (A possible and limited exception is Kanade's system, described subsequently, which recovers the quantitative shape of planar, or nearly planar, surfaced objects.)

Transformations from this level map the viewer-centered shape representation to object-centered shape representations. The models here will be modular and exploit both volumetric and surface primitives in a hierarchical geometry of 3D structure. Attainment of useful vision systems at this level can be expected reasonably soon if only because a large number of researchers are now working on them. Almost certainly, the control structure will involve some goal-directed top-down seepage into this level.

Complex 3D-Object Models for Recognition

The representations at this level are a rich mixture of symbolic relational and geometric structures. They will be object-centered (viewpoint-independent), hierarchical, and canonical.

Everybody seems to agree on that. However, we doubt whether the representation should be generic over tasks. For example, we would not expect the same representation to be equally suitable for an object-recognition task and a manipulator to help guide the blind.

TOY BLOCKS

Earlier sections have omitted all reference to what has until recently generally been considered as *the* AI-vision-domain—"blocks world scene analysis." It has been natural to exclude this research until now because we have wanted to cast our introduction within the conceptual framework offered by Marr. His work, with its emphasis on natural images from complex scenes and its concern to learn from biological visual systems, was developed at least partly as a reaction against the relatively narrow and deliberately simplified confines of blocks world work. Even so, blocks world research has contributed several important developments and any tutorial review of the present kind would be negligent if it omitted to introduce them. Readers who become impatient with the rather in-grown feel of this section can simply skip it. However, they should note that the gradient-space representation (see subsequent discussion below), which grew out of blocks world work, has found application in many other fields. Readers should also be aware that this section is more of a commentary and contains less elementary introductory material than previous sections.

The major goal of blocks world vision research has been to arrive at a principled understanding of how to derive from an image of a heap of toy blocks (Fig. 10.18), a scene description that decomposes the mass of lines appearing in the image, into groups that reflect

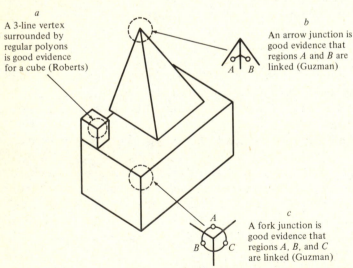

a
A 3-line vertex surrounded by regular polyons is good evidence for a cube (Roberts)

b
An arrow junction is good evidence that regions *A* and *B* are linked (Guzman)

c
A fork junction is good evidence that regions *A*, *B*, and *C* are linked (Guzman)

Figure 10.18   A blocks world scene analyzed with (*a*) the model-driven approach of the kind used by Roberts; (*b*) and (*c*) region linking of the kind used by Guzman. See text for details.

the blocks comprising the scene. The image to be analysed has somtimes been a photograph or TV picture of a real blocks world scene, sometimes a line drawing. This "toy problem" has the merit of being sufficiently simple to hold out the prospect of a reasonably early solution, while at the same time not being trivially easy. Various approaches have been explored, the progress of the research being marked by the successive elimination of representations by discovering their limitations.

The Model-Driven Approach

Study of the blocks world began in earnest with Roberts's (1965) classical paper which described a program that implemented the even more classical view (vide Helmholtz) that perception was a process cycling around the operations of detecting cues, selecting a hypothesis that is capable of making sense of them, drawing inferences from the hypothesis about further cues that *should* be present, checking these inferences with a search for further confirming/disconfirming cues, and so on. Roberts's program dealt with a blocks world constructed from variously sized cubes, wedges, and hexagonal 'cylinders.' It knew that the world contained only objects derived from these three kinds of blocks (which therefore served as prototypes), and its aim was to decompose the scene by using them as primitives.

The first stage of the program derived a line drawing of the scene from a photograph (cf. Marr's primal sketch, done with much less sophistication, utilising a single-edge detecting operator, as was customary at the time). Next, configurations of lines were detected as 'good cues' to a possible prototype. For example, a picture vertex surrounded by three regular polygons is a very good cue for a cube (Fig. 10.18*a*), a vertex of three lines in an arrowhead configuration is less good evidence (e.g., the tip of the pyramid in Fig. 10.18). The selected prototype became a hypothesis that was then tested for its fit to the image data by a process that explored whether the prototype could be suitably "stretched" by deformations preserving the geometrical integrity of the prototype. If the hypothesis survived the test, then it was accepted and the program went on to deal with another part of the image. If it did not, then another prototype was considered and/or other cues selected. All stages of the program were "model driven" (the models being the prototypes), except for the initial line-finding phase. And as far as the latter is concerned, some workers in the same tradition as Roberts (1965) even incorporated model testing into that phase as well (Falk, 1972; Shirai, 1973), in an attempt to overcome some of the (then surprising) difficulties that were experienced with extracting a good line description from a messy TV image.

The model-driven approach is characterised by the interpretation of input data, using specific knowledge about particular objects or object classes. It is important to distinguish the use of that kind of knowledge from the use of general knowledge about the world, such as that which underpins Marr's use of grouping principles for obtaining the full primal sketch. A visual system relying only on general knowledge of the world would be deemed "low level" or "bottom up," even if, as in the case of Marr's primal sketch, it is manifestly within the "constructivist," "interpretative," "representational" traditional of vision research (and therefore in contrast to the Gibsonian one of treating perception as an "immediate pickup of information" that requires no processing of any sort on the part of the perceiver; see Ullman [1981], for a critique of Gibson with which we heartily concur and for the replies of present-day Gibsonians).

Region Linking

The model-driven approach to the blocks world has endured, incorporating along the way insights derived from the next evolutionary strand that emerged, the bottom-up approach. The latter work originated in Guzman's (1968) program SEE which tried to segment line drawings of blocks world scenes by seeking links between the adjacent image regions. The underlying idea was to group together regions in the picture that derived from each body in the scene according to evidence offered by the different kinds of junction types that were present. For example, a fork is good evidence that its three bounding regions come from the same body and therefore that they are to be linked, whereas an arrow junction is evidence that only two of the regions that comprise it are related (Fig. 10.18). SEE utilised many such cues to establish in a first pass over the picture all links for which there was some evidence. In a second stage, SEE then interpreted that evidence to provide a coherent grouping of image regions, each group corresponding to a constituent body in the scene.

Problems abounded. To enable SEE to deal successfully with complicated scenes required the almost constant addition of new rules and modifications of old ones as counterexamples to its competence were discovered. The messy patchwork of rules that emerged (an example of Type 2 research discussed earlier) suggested a basic flaw in the approach and attention turned to a deeper bottom-up analysis of the task.

Line Labelling Using a Junction Dictionary

Guzman had sought to use coherence of evidence in the picture domain as a basis for segmentation in the scene domain. The next step was based on the insight that a search for coherence in the scene domain directly was really required, based upon a much more detailed use of what might be termed "the physics" of the situation, so that greater advantage could be taken of the geometrical constraints that are available. Attention thus turned to asking exactly what the lines in the picture could depict about the corresponding entities in the scene (Fig. 10.19).

Given the assumption that objects in the blocks world were arranged with no problematic accidental alignments, and avoiding for the moment problems to do with shadows, and so on, by continuing to work only with perfect line drawings, then each line in the image could be said to be the projection of an edge of a surface in the scene. Each edge (Fig. 10.19*a*) could either be of type:

- *concave connect* (produced by the junction of two touching surfaces, and with those surfaces forming a concave depth variation from the observer's viewpoint)
- *convex connect* (as concave connect, but with a convex depth variation from the observer's viewpoint)
- *occluding* (produced by one surface lying in front of another without touching it)

The aim then became deciding, for each line in the image, the kind of edge in the scene that produced it. In other words, the task was now construed as that of *line labelling*.

One way in which the physics of the situation provides powerful contraints is that although any line considered on its own has the three possible interpretations just described, not all the

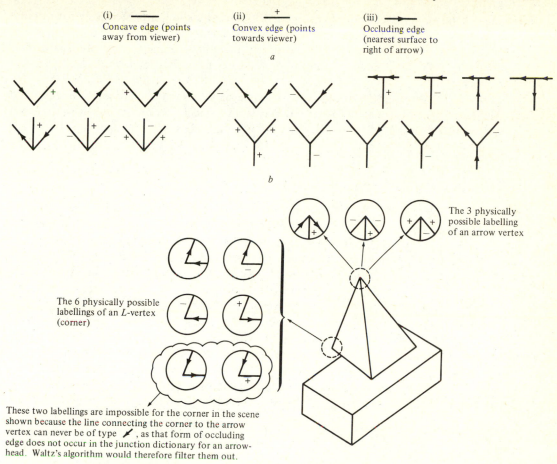

Figure 10.19   Waltz's line labelling algorithm. (*a*) Edge types and their associated line labels. (*b*) Dictionary of all possible interpretations of vertices of trihedral solids. (*c*) An example of Waltz-type filtering.

combinations at a vertex where lines meet can be interpreted as physically possible conjunctions of edges in the scene. For example, for 3-line vertices, only 8 of the 64 line-type combinations are physically realisable (Fig. 10.19*b*; 12 are allowable if T-junctions are regarded as a form of a 3-line vertex). It is therefore possible to use a "junction dictionary," specifing allowable types of vertex for each type of junction to limit possibilities. Furthermore, since a line has to represent the same kind of edge at both ends, it is easy to see in principle how an algorithm exploiting that "consistency constraint" can filter out impossible labellings (Fig. 10.19*c*). This scheme was independently proposed by Huffman (1971) and by Clowes (1971), and reached its zenith in Waltz's Ph.D. thesis. Thus Waltz (1975) relaxed almost all restrictions on lighting and shadow conditions, producing in his case a situation in which each line could have any one of 99 possible edge interpretations. He also lifted restrictions on the shapes of the blocks, so greatly increasing the allowable junctions and types of vertices that could arise. Much to everyone's surprise, he developed a filtering algorithm that could quite effectively cut through the horrendous combinatorial explosion of possibilities. The reason seems to be that some of the newly introduced junctions/vertices are relatively unambiguous, and they propagate their disambiguating influence through the entire network when consistency between neighbouring vertices is sought.

Waltz's (1975) filtering algorithm is an example of a "relaxation" process, as described earlier in the chapter. As such, it is clearly to be categorised as Level 2 in nature, with the Level 1 content of his analysis being the designation of edge types and the specification of the inconsistencies to be filtered out.

Filtering in Gradient Space

Unfortunately, despite Waltz's impressive results, deep problems remained. His program produced on occasion anomalous labellings of possible objects and "legal" labellings of impossible objects (Fig. 10.20). It became apparent that the junction dictionary approach was fundamentally flawed because, by confining itself only to edge types, it has in principle no way of exploiting certain crucially important constraints about the relationships of surfaces in blocks world scenes. Consider, for example, Figure 10.20b: because the junction dictionary does not capture the concept of surface planarity, it accepts the "impossible object," not noticing that the surfaces A and B cannot be planar and hence that the object is illegal (blocks with curved surfaces are not allowed in the world dealt with by Waltz's program). An important development in trying to overcome this problem was the use of the gradient-space representation of surfaces to provide constraints and consistency checks on surface relationships (Huffman 1971). The gradient-space representation can be used, as it is by Kanade (1980) in his theory of the Origami world, as a further stage of filtering, following a stage of Waltz-type

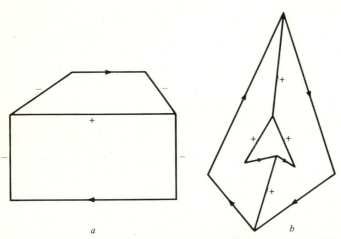

a   b

Figure 10.20 Labelling problems for Waltz's algorithm. (*a*) Anomalous (physically impossible) interpretation of a possible object. (*b*) False acceptance of an "impossible object." (*Source:* Adapted from Huffman, 1971.)

filtering of line labels; or as by Mackworth (1973), as a more direct way of deriving line labels without the use of a Huffman-Clowes junction dictionary at all.

Gradient space is a convenient representation for thinking about surfaces. It is a 2D coordinate system in which planes in 3D are represented as points, that is, each pair of 2D coordinates in the gradient-space graph (Fig. 21a) specifies the 3D orientation of surfaces or planes with respect to the observer's viewing position.

Gradient space can be thought of in the following way. Imagine a football covered with spines emanating from its center and sticking out from its surface. Each spine is normal to the

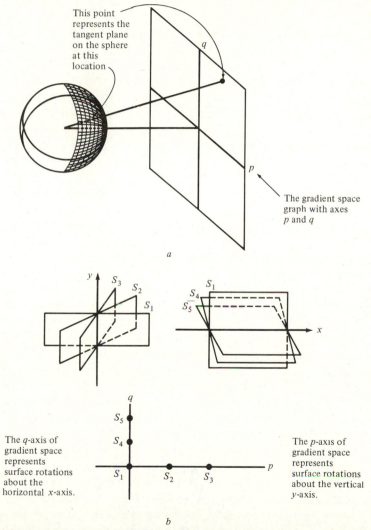

Figure 10.21   (a) Gradient space and the Gaussian sphere (see text). (b) Understanding gradient space in terms of surface rotations. (*Source:* Adapted from Marr, 1982.)

tangent plane touching the football's surface at the point where the spine is located. Now imagine all the spines extended outwards to intersect a plane. The gradient-space representation is a 2D graph lying in that plane. There is only one spine whose extension lies normal to the plane and the point where it intersects the plane is the origin of the gradient-space graph. (Obviously, the tangent plane at the point on the football's surface from which this spine arises will be parallel to the plane in which the gradient-space graph lies.)

Now consider the other spines extending from the football that intersect the gradient-space plane at some angle other than normal. The key feature of the gradient-space representation is that the coordinates of a point where a spine meets the plane are taken as a representation of the 3D orientation of the tangent plane at the point on the football's surface from which the spine projects. Each point in gradient space thus defines a surface with a particular 3D orientation.

What about the spines on the sides and back of the football pointing away from the plane? Exactly! Their absence from the gradient-space graph is a limitation of that representation. A mathematically more ideal representation is the Gaussian sphere. This is a 3D-coordinate system that may be regarded as the football with spines sticking out that was the starting metaphor, explaining the gradient-space concept (the sphere in Fig. 21a). In that representation the direction of each spine codes directly the orientation of the normal to the tangent plane of the surface. However, the relative simplicity of the gradient-space representation is only rarely outweighed by its disadvantages. Draper (1981) provides an appendix, giving a thorough technical introduction to gradient-space concepts and Ikeuchi and Horn (1981) give a clear mathematical description of its use in relation to the shape-from-shading problem.

Another way of thinking about the gradient space graph is shown in Figure 10.21b. The vertical axis in gradient space (labelled the q axis) represents the degree of surface rotation of a plane about the horizontal (x) axis in the image. Equally, the p axis in gradient space represents rotation of a plane about the vertical axis of its image. Combinations of p and q rotations will obviously be represented in the gradient-space graph by points lying off the p and q axes.

Note that in the gradient-space representation, the actual depth of the surface plane from the viewer is not made explicit, nor is the spatial extent of the plane. However, gradient space does capture the concave/convex relationship between adjoining surfaces, as illustrated in Figure 10.22. In considering that figure, begin by noting that a line in the image where two surfaces join or overlap (i.e., a line projecting from a connect edge or an occluding edge, respectively) appears in the gradient-space representation as a so-called "dual line" with an orientation at 90 degrees to the image line that gives rise to it. The importance of that fact, for which there are simple mathematical proofs (Mackworth, 1976), will become clear later. For the present, observe in Figure 10.22 that the position of points along the dual line is determined by the orientations of the surfaces they represent, so that the order of these points specifies whether the scene edge represented by the line is concave or convex.

As noted earlier, corners and edges of surfaces in the scene project into the image as junctions and lines, respectively. The Huffman–Clowes approach filters these by using a dictionary of junctions that exploits the fact that whatever description an edge has at one end provides a powerful constraint on what it can have at the other end. Attacking the same problem in the gradient-space representation, filtering proceeds by exploiting the more restrictive (but very similar) constraint that the regions on each side of an image line depict surfaces with the same slope along the entire length of the image line. This fact finds expression in the gradient-space graph in that a single dual line must necessarily represent the entire connecting

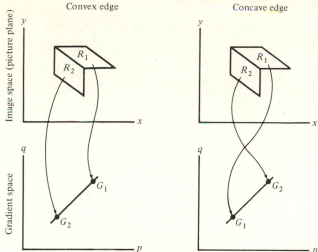

Figure 10.22 Mapping concave and convex edges into gradient space. (*Source:* After Kanade, 1982.)

edge between two planar surfaces. This consideration explains why Figure 10.20*b* is successfully rejected as an impossible object, using the gradient-space representation. Surface *A* must exist in the gradient-space graph as a single point, as must surface *B* (remember, they are planar surfaces and so all parts of them possess the same surface orientation with respect to the viewer). And yet, the connect edges between them on either side of the notch are not collinear, so that each edge would give rise to a different dual line (differently oriented because each dual line has to be at right angles to the junction between the surfaces that it represents—see previous discussion). Ergo, a contradiction exists, arising from the way the gradient-space representation captures information about surface orientations, and the "impossibility" of Figure 10.20*b* is recognised. The key point is that this has been achieved because working in gradient space allows the exploitation of constraints about surface properties, constraints that are missed by the line-labelling approach that confines itself simply to the properties of edges.

Another illustration of the way consistency between surface regions can be checked in gradient space is shown in Figure 10.23. The fork junction between regions R_A, R_B, and R_C, with gradients G_A, G_B, and G_C respectively, can be mapped into the gradient-space graph in only two ways, bearing in mind that each image line must give rise to a dual line that is perpendicular to itself. These two mappings can be translated or expanded in the gradient space without breaching this requirement (operations that would amount to changes in the gradients of the surfaces giving rise to the vertex in the image). However, the relative locations of the points in gradient space cannot be anything other than one of the two forms shown in Figure 10.23, and careful inspection of these will enable the reader to see that one of these depicts a vertex made up of three concave edges, the other a vertex made up of three convex edges. This is as it should be, as the junction dictionary work discovered that these were the only possible configurations for a vertex made up only of connect edges (what happens if one or more edge is occluding will be described later). The point of this illustration is, therefore, to show how gradient space can capture the constraints that are utilised by the junction dictionary approach, while at the same

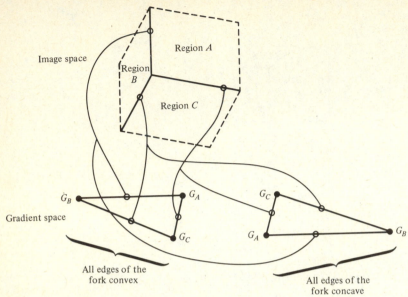

Figure 10.23   Gradient space representation of regions bounding a fork junction. The curved links show mappings between image lines and
their orthogonal dual lines in gradient space. Region A maps to
gradient space point G_A, region B to G_B, and region C to G_C.

time adding valuable extra information about surfaces that prevents at least some false
labellings and discovers some of the impossibilities that are missed by Waltz's algorithm.

So far so good: working in gradient space seems a clear advance on the junction dictionary
approach. However, Figure 10.24 shows an instance of an impossible object that is falsely
accepted, using gradient space. This is because its inconsistencies are not made explicit in that
space. Here again, as in Figure 10.20, surfaces A and B are separated by noncollinear edges on
either side of a notch, but now those edges are parallel. Unfortunately, the gradient-space
representation does not distinguish between the duals of parallel and collinear lines. This
limitation follows from the twin facts that gradient space does not represent the parts of plane
surfaces and dual lines represent only the orientation of edges. Hence, surfaces A and B in

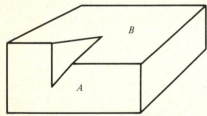

Figure 10.24   An impossible figure
"accepted" by gradient
space. (*Source:* After
Huffman, 1971.)

Figure 10.24 are "satisfactorily" represented as points on a single dual line, and the representation does not therefore label the picture as "impossible."

Junction Dictionary and Gradient Space Compared

Exploring these matters more deeply, the strategy of the junction dictionary approach can be described as follows: After a processing stage that locates lines and their intersections in the image, line junctions are classified on the basis of the number and configuration of their component lines. At each junction a list of physically possible labellings for each line corresponding to the particular junction type is created by consulting the junction dictionary, and then the whole network is checked for the consistency of the labels assigned to each end of lines in adjacent junctions. Apart from any other limitations the approach might have, it is important to realise that even if a consistent labelling is achieved, neither the qualitative shape of the objects in the scene nor even the relative orientation of any but connecting surfaces in the scene, is made explicit.

The strategy for obtaining a labelling using gradient space, as exploited by Mackworth (1973) in his program POLY, is essentially as follows: After a similar stage of early processing that locates lines and junctions but which also labels regions of the image, the task is to choose points in the gradient-space coordinate system that can represent those regions sensibly, that is, corresponding to possible surfaces in the scene in a mutually consistent fashion. This is done by choosing two adjacent regions and assuming that the line in the image that separates them derives from a connect rather than from an occluding edge. A dual line with orientation of 90 degrees to this line is drawn in gradient space in an arbitrary location and two points on it are arbitrarily assigned to represent the gradient of the two regions. This process selects a scale and an origin for the gradient-space graph (the latter is usually assigned to one of the chosen gradient points). Although this initial selection procedure is arbitrary, once these parameters are assigned it is possible to test for the consistency of putative connect edge assignments by solving simultaneous equations, relating the orientations of the dual lines and the coordinates of the surface gradient points lying on those lines for successive subsets of the image.

The labelling of occluding edges follows the connect labelling stage but operates outside the gradient-space representation. To understand how this is done in POLY, one must grasp the general principle that if the boundary lines separating two regions in the image are not collinear, then only one of them can be a connect edge, all the others must be occluding. Figure 10.25 illustrates this point: For region R, only one of its edges, a, can touch the plane P; the others must be occluding if the figure is not impossible (remember that all surfaces are assumed planar). This general principle follows from the simple geometric fact that two planes intersect

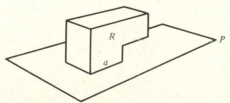

Figure 10.25   Only edge a of region R can
lie in the plane P.

in a straight line. The principle can be applied in consistency checks such as: "edge x could be a connect edge of type concave but if so then edge y which bounds the same region cannot be connect because it is not colinear with x; ergo, y must be occluding, unless of course x is the occluding edge, whereupon y must be connect. However, the second possibility is incompatible with . . . etc. etc." This informal sequence illustrates the kind of inconsistencies being filtered out. Moreover, with some thought it will be appreciated that for regions sharing a connect edge and an occluding edge, the sense of the connect edge (concave/convex) will enable a decision to be taken on the appropriate sense of a related occluding edge (i.e., which surface is in front of which). This is so because depending on the sense of a connect edge, the surface on one side of the edge must lie in a plane in front of the plane in which the other surface lies. (Fig. 10.26).

The gradient-space representation as utilised by Mackworth in his program POLY has serious limitations (even apart from the fact that the simple geometric relationships described here between the dual line in gradient space and the corresponding line in the image are true only if the viewing geometry is orthographic or a close approximation to it, i.e., if the depth in the scene is relatively small compared to the viewing distance). One of the major problems is that the information concerning the relative depths of surfaces from the viewer is not made explicit. The specification of a surface in 3D requires three parameters. Two of these correspond to the coordinates in gradient space (p, q), the third is to do with observer's distance (z) from the surface. This corresponds to the intersection of the plane in which the surface lies with the z-axis, that is, the axis normal to the coordinate system of gradient space and hence not represented in it. Mackworth (1973) found that the utilisation of depth information could greatly extend the power of POLY.

It is clear even from this brief overview that as understanding of the blocks world domain has progressed, the focus of the research has shifted substantially. Initially, in the model-driven paradigm, the task was to recover the 3D structure of the scene by mapping the projection of a stored model or prototype onto a representation of the image that made explicit the positions of

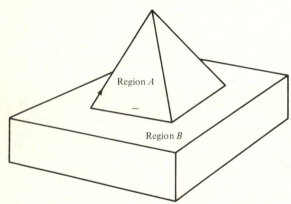

Figure 10.26   Connect edges can be used to determine the sense of occluding edges. Because the connect edge between regions A and B is concave ($-$), the occluding edge they share ($\rightarrow$) must be "occluding on the right."

the edges and surface junctions. Since then, the conception of the problem of low-level vision changed significantly (due largely to the insights of Horn and Marr), so that it is now seen in some sense as the discovery of the inverse transform of the imaging process. In the blocks world domain, this conception has moved research towards the development of a principled procedure that will recover all and only all the geometrically possible labellings of lines in the image. The progress of the research has been marked by the successive elimination of representations by discovering their limitations. Thus, the junction dictionary was recognised to be insufficient, however extended it was to handle shadows, complex objects, and so on, when it was realised that it could not in principle capture an important class of constraints that were derived from the 3D properties of planar surfaces and that it failed on certain types of pictures as a result. Similarly, counterexamples that point up fundamental limitations of the gradient-space representation were found (see Draper [1981] for a critical review), essentially for the same type of reason: If the task is to invert the imaging process to any realistic degree, then the representation must be capable of capturing the complexities of the 3D scene of which the image is a projection and gradient space fails to represent all the relevant information; or if it can be made to do so, by incorporating depth relationships relating to the z-axis (SUPER-POLY), it becomes very unwieldy (Draper, 1981).

Using the Sideness Constraint

One of the positive simplifying strengths of POLY was that it checked for consistency only over connect labels and used them to assign the sense of occlusion to nonconnecting edges. Connect labels are far more constraining than occlusion labels. This is because reasoning over connect labellings involves only the solution of numerically simple simultaneous equations, whereas the constraints provided by occlusion are relational and checking for consistency over a relational rather than a numerical data structure is very much more complex and much less intuitive. In particular, the concepts "in-front-of" and "behind" are not easily expressed in the 2D of gradient space, and perhaps are impossible to do so. Moreover, even if the relative depths of edges is utilised following further geometric analysis that extracts this information from the gradient-space representation (SUPERPOLY), it is still not easy to specify the relationships between bodies and the origin of the gradient space for different subsets of the image.

Recent work by Draper (1981) exploits and extends the ideas used by POLY during its assignment of occlusion labels to deal more generally with the line-labelling task. Utilising the insight that it is necessary to deal explicitly with surface depth relationships (in-front-of, behind), his program, Ellsid, uses an alternative method of surface-based reasoning which Draper calls "sideness reasoning," for example, if surface A is on this side of surface B, then.... This is much more geometrically intuitive than the gradient-space representation and sufficiently powerful to handle the problematic cases that POLY and the junction dictionary approach could not handle. Ellsid's strategy is essentially to check for consistency every conceivable labelling of a picture in terms of occluding and connecting edges, using the transitivity of the in-front-of and behind relationships which express the constraint of sideness. This is in contrast to the strategy employed in SUPERPOLY; first, solve for the gradient-space and depth relationships over connect edges, then use these constraints to assign occlusion relationships.

As Draper points out, a fundamental assumption underlying SUPERPOLY's strategy is that all the constraints derive from connect edges (obviously not so with mutually occluding but unconnected bodies) and if the system of equations for solving for the depth relationships of the connect edges are underdetermined, SUPERPOLY does not have the machinery to reason with the partial information. It is Draper's argument that to upgrade its competence would require the full algebraic panoply of the mathematical basis of gradient space, augmented with the machinery for reasoning in relational datastructures. On the other hand, by directly integrating both occlusion and connect edge information in a geometrically intuitive scheme that is inherently capable of reasoning over partial and weak constraints, the sideness-reasoning embodied in Ellsid seems to be the more natural representation. This is particularly so since Ellsid, exploiting the insights obtained from the critical evaluation of work both in the junction dictionary and gradient-space representations, has sufficient geometric power to produce all the consistent labellings of the lines in a blocks world drawing. It therefore achieves the major goal that blocks world research has struggled to attain.

But still the real problem remains unsolved! The development by Draper of powerful and general methods has revealed that in most cases even a simple line drawing has many geometrically consistent labellings, even without removing all the many domain restrictions that are usually employed. Many of these interpretations are extremely difficult to see for the human observer (people who work in this area say they improve with practice), although they could be made with pieces of paper and some dexterity. Thus, as Draper has pointed out, the attempt to improve on the Huffman–Clowes scheme as a *psychological* model by improving on its technical aims and abilities has met with resounding defeat.

Adding Geometrical Assumptions

This result brings to the fore a question that has often been raised but one that has exercised little directive influence on the field, namely; what are the important assumptions that the human brings to the perception of line drawings that enables him or her so readily to extract a single "natural" interpretation of the shape? Interestingly, recent work by Kanade and Kender (1980) shows that this does not force the adoption of a model-driven approach. The heuristics they have shown to be successful are derived from geometrical assumptions, and not from Roberts-like prototypes expressing object-domain knowledge. They make the following two assumptions:

1. If two lines are parallel in the picture, they are the projections of parallel edges in the scene.
2. Skewed symmetry in the image is the projection of a real symmetry in the scene. A skewed symmetry is one in which the two axes are not at right angles to each other (Fig. 10.27; in normal symmetry, of course, corresponding points lie on lines normal to the axis of symmetry).

The mathematical elaboration of these assumptions provides very powerful constraints on the location of the origin of the gradient-space coordinate system that effectively forces a unique orientation to the assigned to each surface. This in turn means that the natural quantitative shape of the object can be recovered. This is important because although Ellsid has sufficient geometric competence to complete the line-labelling task, its use of shape information

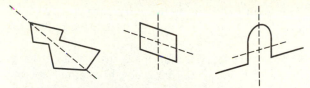

Figure 10.27   The skewed symmetry heuristic: "A skewed symmetry depicts a real symmetry viewed from some (unknown) view direction." (*Source:* After Kanade, 1981.)

is at best only qualitative: For example, "this may be joined to that, and if so this is in-front-of that . . . etc." Statements of the form: "this surface is at right angles to that one . . " are beyond its competence. Whether it can be extended to interpret its labellings in this way without dipping back into the gradient-space representation is a research question.

Meanwhile it is interesting to note the way in which studies from the areas of shape-from-shading, shape-from-texture, and shape-from-line-drawings are being unified by the sophisticated use of the gradient-space representation (in the case of the latter two areas, augmented by the same "psychological-geometrical" assumptions advanced by Kanade and Kender [1980]).

Blocks World Research and the Object Recognition Problem

It is clear that although research on the blocks world has contributed to the clarification of some important issues in image understanding and helped shape our present conceptions of low-level vision, the representations it has developed are limited in scope. They are related to what Marr has called the $2\frac{1}{2}$D sketch and Barrow and Tenebaum call "intrinsic images," viewer-centered representations making explicit the depths and orientations of visible surfaces (although a distinguishing feature of blocks world work has been to utilise a greatly restricted range of cues, compared with those considered for $2\frac{1}{2}$D sketch purposes, or for intrinsic images, for example, cues such as stereo, motion, and texture).

THE HOUGH TRANSFORM AND PARALLEL ARCHITECTURES

A frequent theme in earlier sections has been the need to build one representation by recognising structures in a lower one, for example, identifying the "signature tune" for an edge from channel primitives; discovering a 3D model that "fits" a 2D or $2\frac{1}{2}$D set of primitives. Throughout, our prime concern has been with issues at Level 1, that of computational theories underlying the creation of a given representation. We have given scant attention to Level 2, that is, to powerful algorithms that can serve Level 1 requirements, confining ourselves simply to relaxation processes. Of course, it may well turn out that special-purpose algorithms that are suitable only for a limited domain of Level 1 theories will be necessary in most instances, in which case Level 2 matters are probably best left to specialists who are the only ones who need to know about the details of algorithms that are applicable to their own narrow concerns.

However, in this section we introduce what presently appears to be an instance of a powerful general-purpose vision algorithm—the "generalised Hough transform," introduced by Ballard and Brown (1982).

The Hough transform is not a particularly novel idea but one of its major attractions is that it readily lends itself to implementation on the parallel hardware that is now becoming available more cheaply, with the wider use of VLSI techniques. This fact about the Hough is important to those who are interested in natural computation, because a highly distinctive characteristic of biological visual systems is that they exploit immense parallelism. Presumably one reason they do so is to overcome the handicap of having to use computing elements with 1 ms. cycle time. There are those, however, who would argue that there may be more to it than that. We doubt that the restriction until recently to von Neumann (serial) architectures has presented a crippling, or even a very serious, limitation to the development of computational theories of vision. In any event, the Hough transform seems to be leading a revival in the fortunes of highly connected "perceptronlike" neural network processes.

Perceptrons can be thought of as the neural embodiment of an evaluation function. Several processes input to a linear threshold device and if the sum of the inputs is greater than the threshold, then it fires. Perceptons can learn by arranging for the weights of the inputs to be adjusted according to whether or not the response of the device was appropriate. Essentially, if the response was a "false alarm," reduce the weighting of the inputs that contributed to the response; if the response was correct, increase the weights of the active inputs. Minsky and Papert (1962) dampened the excesses of early enthusiasm that perceptrons initially aroused, but now interest is being rekindled.

The Hough Transform Used for Template Pattern Recognition

Consider an image containing a target pattern of some kind that needs to be detected. One way of finding it is to apply a template of the pattern to every position of the image and measure its degree of agreement at each location. "Template correlation" is, of course, a classic problem area in the pattern-recognition and image-processing literature although not one of great interest in the field of image understanding. Template correlation is not, therefore, a topic we intend to review here in any depth, but a consideration of some of the problems that it encounters is a convenient way of introducing the Hough transform.

The major problem with using templates is, of course, that the target pattern is usually a considerably distorted version of the template in all but certain artifically constrained industrial environments (such as bank cheque number recognition). Thus, it is possible that the target pattern has been rotated and/or scaled in size (dilations or contractions) and/or translated in position and so on. To attempt to correlate a template with the input image in these circumstances with any hope of successful recognition means that some way has to be found to cope with the distortions. The Hough transform presents a way of doing this effectively and economically in many circumstances.

The first step is, of course, to define the template. This can take a variety of forms when using the principle on which the Hough is based, but we begin by introducing a definition that can take account of translations. In this case template definition starts with the selection of an arbitrary origin or a reference point on the pattern and then parts of the pattern are characterised with respect to that origin (Fig. 10.28). Usually it is not possible to describe an

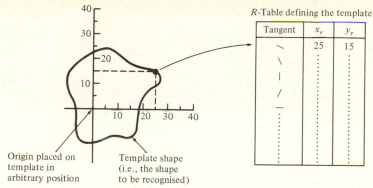

R-Table defining the template

Tangent	x_r	y_r
⟍	25	15
\	⋮	⋮
		⋮	⋮
/	⋮	⋮
—	⋮	⋮
⋮	⋮	⋮

Origin placed on template in arbitrary position

Template shape (i.e., the shape to be recognised)

Figure 10.28 The R-table of a Hough transform for dealing with translations.

analytic function for the pattern and so parts of the pattern have to be listed explicitly in what is known as an "R-table." A straightforward means of doing this is to code the x, y coordinates of locations on the contour of the pattern with respect to the arbitrary origin, together with the tangent of the contour at each location. It is important to realise, however, that the R-table can be drawn up by utilising any useful characteristics of the pattern for the task in hand. One way to think of it is as a definition of the spatial arrangement of features comprising a template.

The next step is to use the R-table to record the goodness-of-fit of the template to various parts of the image. This is done by finding a feature in the image of the type that is listed in the R-table (e.g., a point on a curve with a tangent value given in the R-table; Fig. 10.29). The feature is then accessed in the R-table and the "predicted" location of the origin of the template in the image is found, working on the assumption that the feature under consideration is indeed a part of the template in question (it will not be, of course, if the input image does not include the template pattern). The underlying idea here is that if the feature is part of the pattern, then it can be used to constrain the x, y position in image space where the origin of the template could lie. Accordingly, the predicted location is incremented in a suitable accumulator table that stores evidence as to the x, y translation of the pattern in the image. Another feature is then found and the same cycle of operations is repeated, namely, accessing the R-table to find the predicted image location for the origin of the template and incrementing the accumulator accordingly. When all the image features have been used to access (key into) the R-table, then the accumulator is inspected for maxima. As will readily be appreciated, if the features combine to form an example of the template, they will all increment the same cell in the accumulator, leading to an easily identifiable maximum showing the x, y translation of the template.

The great advantage of the Hough transform for effecting template correlation is the ease with which one can design an R-table to permit the consideration of pattern dimensions independently of one another. For example, it is an easy matter to examine the rotation and scale of a pattern independently of its position. This can be done with an R-table specifying a template by using feature dimensions of orientation and size, and with no entries for the x, y position. To illustrate this, suppose that recognition was required for 2D patterns whose primitives were straight-line segments described by length (L) and orientation (Θ). One could design an R-table listing L and Θ for each line segment appearing in the template pattern (Fig.

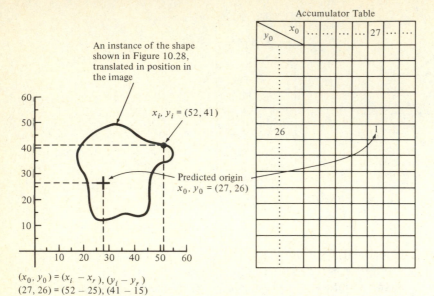

$(x_0, y_0) = (x_i - x_r), (y_i - y_r)$
$(27, 26) = (52 - 25), (41 - 15)$

Figure 10.29 Incrementing an accumulator table using information from the R-table. The tangent at the point x_i, y_i is used to access the R-table to discover x_r, y_r, thus enabling the position of the origin of the shape to be calculated. This predicted position is logged in the accumulator table. After many entries (one for each tangent occurring in the shape to be recognised), the accumulator will contain a more or less blurred maximum, according to whether the shape to be recognised is an example of the template shape.

10.30). Now imagine that a line of length L' and orientation Θ' is found in the image. It could be an instance of a line in the template where $L' = s.L$ and $\Theta' = r.\Theta$, and where s and r are size and rotational scaling parameters, respectively, that match the image line to an entry in the R-table. Accordingly, an accumulator table with axes of size and rotation is incremented such that the particular feature being considered is taken as evidence for the template pattern appearing in the image with a given size/rotation (s, r) pairing.

The clever aspect of this treatment is the way the Hough transform allows an easy projection of a multidimensional space (in our example, a pattern appearing in the image with dimensions of translation, size, and rotation), onto one of lower order (here size and rotation only). More will be said about this later, when the possible merit of using the Hough for modelling some low-level properties of human vision is considered.

The end result of this kind of Hough transform is usually a set of fairly blurred maxima in the accumulator table. However, having detected maxima corresponding to particular sizes and rotations, one can then eliminate from the image all line segments that did not contribute to them. This results in a greatly improved signal-to-noise ratio, with input features containing candidate exemplars of the target pattern at known sizes and rotations. It is then a simple matter to locate the target pattern by using an R-table, giving an x, y position that is "tuned" for the appropriate size and rotation.

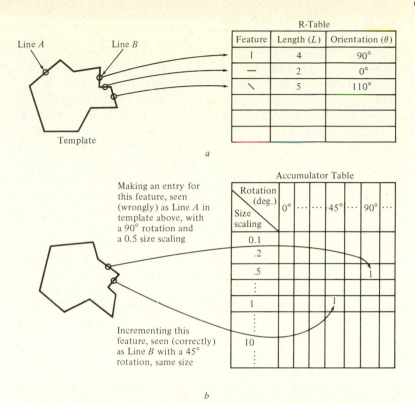

R-Table

Feature	Length (L)	Orientation (θ)
|	4	90°
—	2	0°
\	5	110°

a

Making an entry for this feature, seen (wrongly) as Line A in template above, with a 90° rotation and a 0.5 size scaling

Incrementing this feature, seen (correctly) as Line B with a 45° rotation, same size

Accumulator Table

Rotation (deg.) Size scaling	0°	···	···	45°	···	90°	···
0.1							
.2							
.5						1	
⋮							
1			1				
⋮							
10							
⋮							

b

Figure 10.30 A Hough transform for dealing with distortions of size and rotation (translations ignored in this example). (*a*) Defining the R-table (*b*) Above shape, rotated 45° but of same size, being used to increment an accumulator table. Only two entries are shown for simplicity, but each feature in the shape to be recognized will generate many entries, allowing for all possibilities of scaling features appearing in the R-table.

Note that it is an attribute of the Hough transform that the R-table implicitly embodies constraints that are derived from the relative positions of the primitives, which is why it permits patterns to be distinguished that have similar components but a different spatial arrangement of them. Given also that a wide range of pattern primitives can be used, it is clear that the Hough transform is an extendable and generalisable engine for multidimensional correlations that are readily tailored to exploit features and constraints of arbitrary complexity.

The scope of the Hough transform is so wide that it is worth emphasising that it is only within the context of a particular scheme or usage that it can be evaluated. For example, it would be possible to design the R-table to allow variations within limits of the relative positions of the primitives, or even subsets of them. Also, the process of incrementing the accumulator is, of course, amenable to all sorts of special-purpose weighting-of-evidence stratagems that seem sensible in a particular application. It is, therefore, quite clearly a Level 2 algorithmic tool that is capable of being tailored to suit the requirements of a potentially very wide range of Level 1 theories.

An Example of the Hough Being Used for 3D Object Recognition

One interesting application of the Hough is that of Ballard and Sabbah (1981) who propose a scheme for the recovery and recognition of 3D shapes. Their representation of the 3D shape is object centered, surface based, and unorganised, in that the surface primitives are local surface patches with no intrinsic organisation (it is essentially a Gaussian sphere representation). The R-table corresponding to a particular shape is a histogram of the surface normals that are described in an object-centered coordinate system (probably a representation that is appropriate only for relatively simple symmetrical and smooth objects: one could imagine acute difficulties for the surface equivalent of random noise—a crumpled newspaper). Although Ballard and Sabbah are not explicit about their full procedures (they confine themselves to reporting, by their own admission, a simple demonstration), it seems that the scene they deal with is either relatively sparse and/or that it has been processed to at least the stage of the recovery of a quantitative 3D structure and connectivity (and possibly even segmented into objects). Their strategy is to find first the 3D rotation of the template objective that best fits the surface description of the image. This in done in an exactly analogous way to the simple 2D pattern case previously described, with the orientation of the surface normals of regions in the image accessing the R-table. Then, after thinning the image by using the kind of filtering heuristic described for 2D patterns, but now excluding from further consideration regions that do not contribute to a maximum, the input data are reexamined. This is done by exploiting the constraints of adjacency/connectivity of surfaces and/or the shape of surfaces, using a Hough transform that allows rotations in 3D (the accumulator is three-dimensional to allow capturing rotations of the input object in 3D space). In this second stage, which exploits the shape of the object's surface (no details are given of how to deal with curved regions so we must assume they are planar), the entire 2D pattern-recognition scheme is extended to handle rotations of planar shapes in 3D. However, is obviously much reduced in scope because the previous stage has recovered the actual rotations, and so the task has essentially become one of recovering the 2D-positional translation of the projection of the surface shape. Ballard and Sabbah's work is clearly interesting for its use of a Hough transform in the context of 3D-shape representation, but its detailed evaluation must await the test of a large-scale implementation.

OVERVIEW

The Hough transform is a very exciting development, whose potential has yet to be fully explored. Feldman and Ballard (1981) and their colleagues have begun an extensive program of research into its application to problems in low-level vision, with encouraging results in implementations that recover and utilise what Barrow and Tenebaum (1978) have called "intrinsic images." As mentioned ealier, these are maps using a viewer-centered image coordinate system that make explicit aspects of visible surfaces (maps laid out in a spatial system that biologists would term "retinotopic").

One of the strengths of the generalised Hough transform is the ease with which it decouples interdependence between dimensions in multidimensional feature space. The sequential processing of subspaces or projection of multidimensional feature spaces onto spaces of lower dimensionality enables the conjunction of features to be processed with considerable economy and flexibility. Indeed, it could be said that the Hough provides a plausible deflection of, if not a complete answer to, what has become known in the psychological and neurophysiological literature as the problem of "the grandmother cell" (or for some the "yellow Volkswagen" or the "rusty Fiat" problem). That problem is: How do we recognise and/or represent objects with arbitary and novel conjections of features? Do we have a cell/unit/template for every conceiveable instance of every object we can recognise? This question has its origin as a *reductio ad absurdum* challenge to the optimistic excesses of psychologists who are overimpressed by the physiological discovery of "feature-detectors" in the visual cortex of the cat and monkey, without regard to the sobering considerations of combinatorial explosions. Of interest in this context is the way in which the Hough transform can be implemented in networks of simple neuronlike processes. And therefore it becomes of considerable interest to note the neurophysiological evidence for the existence of several retinotopic maps in monkey visual dimension, such as colour, orientation, motion, and so on (but whether an area that is specific for surface orientation exists is not known). Thus, it is tempting to speculate that the visual cortex implements something rather like the Hough in dealing with the problem of decomposing multidimensional feature spaces.

The idea that it is possible to compute complex functions by using networks of simple perceptronlike processes is currently having a revival in computer vision. Advocates of this "connectionist" approach emphasise the contrast with the classical AI approach based on symbolic computations, arguing that their parallel-processing methods are certainly more akin to the style of computation that the brain uses (a point that few workers would challenge). They argue with justification that the sort of data structures and memory access and update supported by current computer architectures are potentially misleading analogies for the sort of procedures that are used by the brain, and furthermore, there is no way that they could be run in real time on biological hardware.

But however true that may be, the distinction between the theory and the engine running it is blurred only at one's peril. The science of computations in networks of simple but richly connected units is undoubtedly more likely to be relevant to the understanding of brain than computer science based on von Neumann architectures. But for the scientist in AI, at least for those working in vision, an understanding of the structure of the information-processing problem is logically of prior concern (Level 1), and that concern is not to be confused with questions about implementations either at the algorithm or the hardware levels (Levels 2 and 3).

The danger here is that the appeal to parallelism can be a good way of hiding the problem, which is to devise a theoretically adequate representational scheme independently of what machine it will run on. Of course, it is possible that once we understand parallel architectures insights will occur into the problem of shape representation that were not possible beforehand. However, it is extremely debatable whether, for example, Waltz's filtering algorithm was in any way delayed in its conception by familiarity with only von Neumann machines, despite the fact that Waltz's algorithm is intrinsically well suited to parallel implementation.

Indeed, it must be remembered, and this is the really important point here, that Waltz's algorithm is just that—an algorithm. It is not in itself the solution to an interesting vision problem. Rather, it is an interesting solution to the problem of constraining a combinatorial explosion of possible interpretations by eliminating inconsistencies. Once again, the danger here is that of confusing the different levels at which an information-processing task must be understood. Thus, those who debate whether property lists (LISP structures), frames, production systems, Hough transforms, and so on are good representations are confusing the level of the machine with the topmost level, the solution of the computational problem that is going to run on it. In our laboratory we are using a version of the Hough transform as the algorithmic engine on which to run a particular theory of stereopsis. Previously the same theory had been implemented by using a Waltz-like filtering algorithm. Both the algorithm and the theory are equally important, only the theory is more so!

The general point here is that the discovery of a representation for the description of shape, by which we mean a formal scheme and the proof of its adequacy, is at a completely different level from that at which questions about the kind of machine it will run on are appropriate. The design of a representation for shape requires answers to questions such as those provided by Marr and Nishihara in their analysis of the problem: What are the features that are suitable as primitives for what class of objects? Should they be surface based, volumetric, or both? What sort of organisation should they have? How can we square the stability/sensitivity equation? Is there any formal test of adequacy or completeness? and so on.

This is not to deny that collaboration across the different levels is the optimal research strategy; it is only to repeat the truism, so clearly demonstrated by Chomsky (1965) in the context of language, that it is difficult if not misguided to study the learning of a task without first acquiring an understanding of what is actually being learned. Similarly, in vision, an understanding of the architecture of the visual cortex by itself has added little if anything to our understanding of information-processing tasks that in their complex interrelationships collectively form the competence called *visual perception*. If there is any particular role that is specific to the artificial intelligence or computational approach to the study of vision, it is to make explicit the structure of the task (cf. Chomsky's competence) that underlies the remarkable benchmark performance of biological vision machines. Implementation details falling within the domain of the neurophysiologist and the psychophysicist may or may not illuminate the advance to understanding that competence, and may or may not be interesting depending upon personal tastes. What is clear is that understanding visual competence at the computational level is in a logical category prior to that of understanding implementation.

REFERENCES

Ballard, D.H., and Sabbah, D. 1981. On shapes. *Proc. IJCAI7*, 607–612.

Barrow, H. G., and Tenenbaum, J. M. 1978. Recovering intrinsic scene characteristics from images. In Hanson, A. R., and Riseman E. M., (Eds.), *Computer Vision Systems*. New York: Academic Press.

Barrow, H. G., and Tenenbaum, J. M. 1981. Computational vision. *Proc. IEEE* 6: 572–595.

Binford, T. O. 1981. Inferring surfaces from images. Special Issue on Vision. *Artificial Intelligence* 17: 205–244.

Campbell, F. W. C., and Robson, J. G. 1968. Application of Fourier analysis to the visibility of gratings. *J. Physiol. Lond.* 197: 551–556.

Chomsky, N. 1965. *Aspects of the theory of syntax*. Cambridge, Mass.: MIT Press.

Clowes, M. B. 1971. On seeing things. *Artificial Intelligence* 2:79

Draper, S. 1980. Reasoning about line-drawing interpretation. Ph.D. thesis. University of Sussex.

Draper, S. 1981. The use of gradient and dual space in line-drawing interpretation. Special Issue on Vision. *Artificial Intelligence* 17: 461–493.

Falk, G. 1972. Interpretation of imperfect line data as a three-dimensional scene. *Artificial Intelligence* 3: 101–144.

Feldman, J. A., and Ballard D. 1981. Computing with connections. Technical Report No. 72, Rochester: Department of Computer Science, University of Rochester.

Guzman, A. 1968. Decomposition of a visual scene into three-dimensional bodies. *AFIPS Fall Joint Conferences* 33: 291–304.

Haralick, R. M. 1980. Edge and regional analysis for digital image data. *Compute. Graph. Image Process.* 12: 60–73.

Hubel, D. H., and Wiesel, T. N. 1959. Receptive fields of single neurones in the cat's striate cortex. *Journal of Physiology.* 148: 579–591.

Huffman, D. A. 1971. Impossible objects as nonsense sentences. In R. Meltzer and D. Michie (Eds.), *Machine intelligence 6.* New York: Elsevier, 295–323.

Ikeuchi, D., and Horn, B. K. P. 1981. Numerical shape from shading and occluding boundaries. Special Issue on Vision. *Artificial Intelligence* 17: 141–184.

Julesz, B. 1981. Textons, the elements of texture perception, and their interactions. *Nature* 290: 91–97.

Kanade, T. 1980. A theory of origami world. *Artificial Intelligence* 13: 279–311.

Kanade, T., and Kender, J. 1980. Skewed symmetry: Mapping image regularities into shape. CMU–CS–80–133, Computer Science Dept., Carnegie-Mellon University.

Kender, J. 1980. *Shape from Texture.* Technical Report CMU-C5-81-102. Pittsburgh: Department of Computer Science, Carnegie-Mellon University.

Mackworth, A. K. 1973. Interpreting pictures of polyhedral scenes. *Artificial Intelligence* 4:121–137.

Mackworth, A. 1976. Model driven interpretation in intelligent visual systems. *Perception* 5: 349–370.

Marr, D. 1976. Early processing of visual information. *Phil. Trans. Roy. Soc. Lond. B.* 275: 483–524.

Marr, D. 1977a. Artificial intelligence—A personal view. *Artificial Intelligence* 9:37–48.

Marr, D. 1977b. Analysis of occluding contour. *Proc. Roy. Soc. Lond. B* : 441–475.

Marr, D. 1982. *Vision.* San Francisco: Freeman.

Marr, D., and Hildreth, E. 1980. Theory of edge detection. *Proc. Roy. Soc. Lond. B.* 207: 187–217.

Marr, D. and Nishihara, H. K. 1978. Representation and recognition of the spatial organisation of three-dimensional shapes. *Proc. Roy. Soc. Lond. B* 200: 269–294.

Marr, D., Poggio, T., and Ullman, S. 1979. Bandpass channels, zero-crossings, and early visual processing. *J Opt Soc. Am.* 69: 914–916.

Marr, D., and Ullman, S. 1981. Directional selectivity and its use in early visual processing. *Proc. Roy. Soc. Lond. B.* 211: 151–180.

Mayhew, J., and Frisby, J. 1981. Psychophysical and computational studies towards a theory of human stereopsis. Special Issue on Vision. *Artificial Intelligence* 17:349–386.

Poggio, Nielson, K., and Nishihara, K. 1982. Zero crossings and spatiotemporal interpretation in vision. AI Memo No. 674. Cambridge, Mass.: MIT AI Lab.

Roberts, L. 1965. Machine perception of three-dimensional solids. In J. Tippett (Ed.), *Optical and electro-optical information processing.* Cambridge, Mass.: MIT Press, 159–197.

Shirai, Y. 1973. A context-sensitive line finder for recognition of polyhedra. *Artificial Intelligence* 4: 95–119.

Ullman, S. 1979. *The Interpretation of Visual Motion.* Cambridge, Mass. MIT Press.

Ullman, S. 1981. Against direct perception. *Brain and Behavioural Sciences.*

Waltz, D. 1975. Generating semantic descriptions from drawings of scenes with shadows. In P. Winston (Ed.). *The psychology of computer vision.* New York: McGraw-Hill.

Wilson, H. R. 1983. Psychophysical evidence for spatial channels. In Braddick, O. L., and Sleigh, A. (Eds.), *Physical and Biological Processing of Images.*

Wilson, H. R. and Bergen, J. R. 1979. A four mechanism model for spatial vision. *Vision Research* 19: 19–32.

Wilson, H. R., and Giese, S. C. 1977. Threshold visibility of frequency gradient patterns. *Vision Research* 17: 1177–1190.

Zucker, S. W. 1982. Early orientation selection and grouping processes: Type I and Type II processes. Technical Report 82-6. Computer Vision and Graphics Laboratory. Montreal: Department of Electrical Engineering, McGill University, Canada.

Annotated Bibliography

If you want to plunge in at the deep end, the Special Issue on Vision of *Artificial Intelligence* (17: 1–508, 1981) is a good place from which to jump for those who can stand heights, but a better introduction to the subject might be to start with two really excellent tutorial reviews of recent developments in the area:

Barrow, H. G. and Tenenbaum, J. M. "Computational Vision." *Proc. IEEE* 6: 572–595, 1981.

Brady, M. "Computational Approaches to Image Understanding," *Computing Surveys* 14:1: 2–78, 1982.

If expense is no object and you would like a thorough textbook treatment of a wide range of computer vision techniques and algorithms:

Ballard, D. H., and Brown, C. M. *Computer Vision.* Englewood Cliffs, N.J: Prentice-Hall, 1982.

Marr's work has been published in the *Proceedings* and *Transactions of the Royal Society of London B* as a series of major papers, 1976–1980. But the best summary and introduction to his work, and also of his colleagues in the vision group he founded at MIT, is his book:

Marr, D. *Vision.* San Francisco: Freeman, 1982.

A good summary statement of his work is:

Marr, D. "Representing Visual Information—A Computational Approach." In Hanson, A. R., and Riseman, E. M. (Eds.), *Computer Vision Systems.* New York: Academic Press, 1978.
This book also contains other articles that are worth reading for the state of the art, circa mid-1970's.

Other Marr papers cited here are:

Marr, D. "Artificial Intelligence—A Personal View." *Artificial Intelligence* 9: 37–48, 1977.

Marr, D. "Analysis of Occluding Contour." *Proc. Roy. Soc. Lond. B* : 441–475, 1977b.

Marr, D., and Nishihara, H. K. "Representation and Recognition of the Spatial Organisation of Three-Dimensional Shapes. *Proc. Roy. Soc. Lond. B.*200: 269–294, 1978.

For the primal sketch and related references cited here:

Binford, T. O. "Inferring Surfaces from Images." Special Issue on Vision. *Artificial Intelligence* 17: , 1981.

Davis, L. S., and Rosenfeld, A. "Cooperating Processes for Low Level Vision: A Survey." Special Issue on Vision. *Artificial Intelligence* 17: 245–264, 1981.

Haralick, R. M. "Edge and Regional Analysis for Digital Image Data." *Comput. Graph. Image Process.* 12: 60–73, 1980.

Hubel, D. H. "Exploration of the Primary Visual Coetex, 1955–78. *Nature* 299: 515–524, 1982.

Marr, D. "Early Processing of Visual Information" *Proc. Roy. Soc. Lond. B* 275: 483–524, 1976.

Marr, D., and Hildreth, E. "Theory of Edge Detection" *Proc. Roy. Soc. Lond. B* 207: 187–217, 1980. (Also, Hildreth's Masters thesis. AI Memo No 579. Cambridge, Mass.: MIT AI Lab., 1980.)

Marr, D., Poggio, T., and Ullman, S. "Bandpass Channels, Zero-Crossings, and Early Visual Processing." *J. Opt. Soc. Am.* 69: 914–916, 1979.

Poggio, T., Nielsen, K., and Nishihara, K. "Zero Crossings and Spatiotemporal Interpretation in Vision." AI Memo No 674. Cambridge, Mass.: MIT AI Lab, 1982.

Shirai, Y. A Context-Sensitive Line Finder for Recognition of Polyhedra." *Artificial Intelligence* 4: 95–119, 1973.

Zucker, S. W. "Early Orientation Selection and Grouping Processes: Type I and Type II Processes." Technical Report 82–6. Computer Vision and Graphics Laboratory, Department of Electrical Engineering, McGill University, Montreal, Canada, 1982.

For general psychology of low-level vision:

Frisby, J. *Seeing: Illusion Brain and Mind.* Oxford: Oxford University Press, 1980. (This is the best introduction to vision that is available, with lots of figures, and a layman's guide to visual neurophysiology—cheap too!)

Julesz, R., and Schumer, R. "Early Visual Perception." *Ann. Rev. Psy.* 32: 575–627, 1981.

Ullman, S. "Against Direct Perception." *Brain and Behavioural Sciences* 1981. (This discusses the Gibsonian approach to perception).

For the spatial frequency channels story:

Campbell, F. W. C., and Robson, J. G. "Application of Fourier Analysis to the Visibility of Gratings." *J. Physiol. Lond.* 197: 551–556, 1968.

Wilson, H. R. "Psychophysical Evidence for Spatial Channels." In Braddick, D. L., and Sleigh, A. (Eds), *Physical and Biological Processing of Images: Proceedings of the Rank Prize Fund Symposium.* 1983.

Wilson, H. R. and Bergen, J. R. "A Four Mechanism Model for Spatial Vision" *Vision Research* 19: 19–32, 1979.

Wilson, H. R., and Giese, S. C. "Threshold Visibility of Frequency Gradient Patterns." *Vision Research* 17: 1177–1190, 1977.

For texture perception:

Julesz, B. "Textons, the Elements of Texture Perception, and Their Interactions." *Nature* 290: 91–97, 1961.

Kender, J. "Shape from Texture. Ph.D. thesis. Technical Report No. CMU-CS-81-102. Pittsburgh: Department of Computer Science, Carnegie-Mellon University, 1980.

Stevens, K. "The Visual Interpretation of Surface Contours." Special Issue on Vision. *Artificial Intelligence,* 17: 47–74, 1981.

For intrinsic images:

Barrow, H. G., and Tenenbaum, J. M. "Recovering Intrinsic Scene Characteristics from Images." In Hanson, A. R. and Riseman, E. M. (Eds.), *Computer Vision Systems.* New York: Academic Press, 1978.

Barrow, H. G., and Tennenbaum, J. M. "Computational Vision." *Proc. IEEE* 6:572–595, 1981.

For shape from shading:

Ikeuchi, K., and Horn, B. K. P. "Numerical Shape from Shading and Occluding Boundaries." Special Issue on Vision. *Artificial Intelligence* 17: 141–184, 1981.

For 3D object recognition:

Brooks, R. A. "Symbolic Reasoning Amongst 3D Models and 2D Images." Special Issue on Vision. *Artificial Intelligence,* 17: 285–348, 1981.
Marr, D., and Nishihara, H. K. "Representation and Recognition of the Spatial Organisation of Three-Dimensional Shapes." *Proceedings Royal Society London B* 200: 269–294, 1978.
Ullman, J. R. "Aspects of Visual Automation." In Braddick, O. L., and Sleigh, A. (Eds.), *Physical and Biological Processing of Images: Proceedings of Rank Prize Fund Symposium.* London: Springer-Verlag, 1983.

A good nontechnical introduction to the blocks world AI vision domain can be found in:

Boden, M. *Artificial Intelligence and Natural Man.* Hassocks, England: Harvester Press, 1977.
    This is an Open University set book and is recommended highly as a general introduction to AI. It contains references to all the classic papers (Roberts, Guzman, Huffman, Clowes, Waltz).

For those really wanting to get into current blocks world research:

Draper, S. "Reasoning About Line-Drawing Interpretation." Ph.D. thesis. University of Sussex. (See also:
    Draper, S. "The Use of Gradient and Dual Space in Line-Drawing Interpretation." Special Issue on Vision. *Artificial Intelligence,* 17: 461–493, 1981. Draper gives references for the Mackworth papers, too).
Elcock, E., and Michie, D. (Eds.). *Machine Intelligence (9).* London: Ellis Horwood, 1977. (This contains articles by Huffman and Mackworth. The article by Mackworth is an important criticism of "classic" programs in the block world domain.)
Kanade, T. "A Theory of Origami World." *Artificial Intelligence* 13: 279–311, 1980. See also:
    Kanade, T. Memo CMU-CS-79-153. Pittsburgh: Department of Computer Science, Carnegie-Mellon University, 1979.
    Kanade, T. "Recovery of the Three-Dimensional Shape of an Object from a Single View." Special Issue on Vision. *Artificial Intelligence* 17: 409–460, 1981.
Kender, J. "Shape from Texture." Technical Report No. CMU-C5-81-102. Pittsburgh: Department of Computer Science Carnegie-Mellon University, 1980.
Mackworth, "Model Driven Interpretation in Intelligent Visual Systems." *Perception* 5: 349–370, 1976.
Winston, P. *The Psychology of Computer Vision* New York: McGraw-Hill, 1975. (This contains articles by Horn and Waltz among others.)

For motion perception:

Longuet-Higgins, H., and Prazdny, K. "The Interpretation of a Moving Image." *Proc. Roy. Soc. Lond. B* 208: 385–397, 1980.
Marr, D., and Ullman, S. "Directional Selectivity and Its Use in Early Visual Processing." *Proc. Roy. Soc. Lond. B* 211: 151–180, 1982.
Ullman, S. *The Interpretation of Visual Motion.* Cambridge, Mass. MIT Press, 1979.

For stereopsis:

Grimson, W. "A Computer Implementation of a Theory of Human Stereo Vision." *Proc. Roy. Soc. Lond. B* 292: 217–253, 1981.

Marr, D., and Poggio, T. "A Theory of Human Stereopsis." *Proc. Roy. Soc. Lond. B.* 204: 301–328, 1979.

Mayhew, J., and Frisby, J. "Psychophysical and Computational Studies Towards a Theory of Human Stereopsis." Special Issue on Vision. *Artificial Intelligence* 17: 349–386, 1981.

Mayhew, J. and Longuet-Higgins, C. "A Computational Model of Binocular Depth Perception." *Nature* 297: 376–379, 1982.

For the Hough transform and parallel-connectionist schemes, see the following. 'TR' refers to technical reports, which may be obtained from the Computer Science Department, University of Rochester, Rochester, NY 14627.

Ballard, D. H. "Parameter Networks: Towards a Theory of Low Level Vision." TR 75, 1981.

Ballard, D. H. and Sabbah, D. "On Shapes." *Proc. IJCAI7.:* 607–612, 1981.

Feldman, J. A. "Memory and Change in Connection Networks." TR 96.

Feldman, J. A. "Four Frames Suffice: A Provisionary Model of Vision and Space." *TR* 99.

Feldman, J. A., and Ballard, D. "Computing with Connections." *TR* 72.

Hinton, G. E. "Shape Representations in Parallel Systems." *Proc. IJCAI7.:* 1088–1096, 1981.

Hinton, G., and Anderson, J. (Eds.). *Parallel Models of Associative Memory.* Hillsdale, N.J.: Erlbaum, 1981.

Marr, D. "A Theory for Cerebral Cortex." *Proceedings Royal Society London B* 176: 161–234, 1970.
    Question: Why did Marr, arguably one of the best visual scientsts for years, stop work on modelling neural networks (i.e., parallel-connectionist schemes) and start working on low-level visual representations?? Did he change levels?

Minsky, M., and Papert, S *Perceptrons.* Cambridge, Mass: MIT Press, 1968.

Journals

The major publication outlet seems to be the AI Lab Memos of the major U.S. AI/computer science departments. *AISB Quarterly* and the *SIGART Newsletter* are sources for notifications of recent work. See the notes at the end of Chapter 5 for information about how to obtain these.

As far as regular journals are concerned, the MIT group seems to have adopted the *Proceedings* and *Transactions of the Royal Society of London* as the outlet for the final polished version of their lab memos. With the notable exception of the Special Issue on Vision. *Artificial Intelligence* provides only a trickle, compared with *Computer Graphics and Digital Image Processing,* which contains both theoretical papers, as well as articles about programs for finding lungs in chests and solutions to other applied problems. Every year it contains a bibliography by Rosenfeld of the previous year's image-processing publications. In 1981–1982 there were more than 900! Many of these are by engineers for engineers and address problems of bandwidth compression, transmission, and restoration techniques, computer-aided tomography, and medical imaging, and so on. Not for the unsophisticated.

CHAPTER 11

NATURAL LANGUAGE PROCESSING

GRAEME RITCHIE
and
HENRY THOMPSON

HISTORICAL SURVEY

There are a variety of possible reasons for studying natural language processing (NLP). The two most common aims are the theoretical investigation of human language and more natural man-machine communication. The emphasis in this chapter will be more on the former, but many of the same issues arise regardless of the overall aim.

Although some NLP research claims to be purely theoretical, and does not involve actual implementation, this is highly untypical. NLP is generally investigated by writing computer programs, and the kinds of programs that are constructed are quite varied—question-answering (e.g., Woods et al. [1972]; Hendrix et al. [1978]; see Simmons [1965] for a review of early work), general "front-ends" (e.g., Bobrow et al. [1977]), dialogue (e.g., Perrault et al. [1978]), machine translation (see Bar-Hillel [1960]; Wilks [1973]), paraphrasing (e.g., Schank et. al. [1975]; Boguraev [1980]).

In the very early days of computing, the U.S. military provided large sums of money for research into machine translation (MT), without much success. The main outcome was a realisation that human language is extraordinarily complicated and that considerably more research into grammar and meaning was needed before we could think about automating these processes (see Bar-Hillel [1960], ALPAC [1966]). It is interesting to notice that MT is having something of a revival in the early 1980s, as commercial and political pressures are demanding the development of MT programs, however limited (Toma, 1977; Rolling, 1978).

In the 1960s, a few isolated NLP programs were written (see Feigenbaum and Feldman [1964]; Minsky [1968] for the main examples) but there was little coherence or theoretical basis to the field.

Keyword Matching

Most of the NLP programs that claimed to carry out some task other than just parsing (e.g., problem-solving, question-answering) were based on crude searches for keywords or patterns in the input string. One program from this period that is worth mentioning is the ELIZA system of Weizenbaum (1966, 1967), since it carried the keyword approach to an absurd (but impressive) extreme. It carried on a "conversation" with a user, via a terminal, about any topic that the human chose, and never seemed lost for a response. For example:

> USER: Men are all alike.
> ELIZA: **In what way?**
> USER: They're always bugging us about something or other.
> ELIZA: **Can you think of a specific example?**
> USER: Well, my boyfriend made me come here.
> ELIZA: **Your boyfriend made you come here.**
> USER: He says I'm depressed much of the time.
> ELIZA: **I am sorry to hear that you are depressed.**
> USER: It's true. I am unhappy.
> ELIZA: **Do you think coming here will help you not to be unhappy?**
> USER: I need some help, that much seems certain.
> ELIZA: **What would it mean to you if you got some help?**

The program was based on very simple tricks, and its response were of two kinds:

1. stock phrases (e.g., "In what way?")
2. standard patterns with fragments of a previous input sentence inserted into them (e.g., "I am sorry to hear that . . . ?" "Tell me more about . . ."), with various adjustments (e.g., changing "my" to "your")

These techniques (with a few enhancements) produced an amazing level of fluency, but it would be difficult to argue that the program was "understanding" to any degree. This illustrates the difficulty of judging a program by its output, or of defining understanding in terms of behaviour, since programs written in this crude way could often deceive people into believing that the output was coming from an actual person; that is, they could pass what is sometimes called the "Turing test" for intelligence. (See Boden [1977, Chapter 5] for a good discussion.)

Transformational Grammar

Until about 1965, there was very little overlap between computational work on NLP and research in theoretical linguistics. In the latter area, transformational grammar, or "TG"

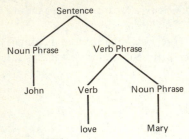

Figure 11.1

(Chomsky, 1957, 1965) had become dominant. Chomsky's main idea was that the most appropriate syntactic structure for a sentence was not a tree that was directly built on the original words but was a "deep structure" in which the original "surface structure" might be considerably rearranged. The relationship between deep structures and ordinary surface structures was then specified by rules called *transformations* which were tree-manipulating operations. For example, the deep structure for "John loves Mary" might be as in Figure 11.1, whereas the structure for "Mary is loved by John" would be as in Figure 11.2. In this way, superficial differences between sentences were removed, and the deep structure showed all the significant information in a standardised format.

It must be stressed that this was not intended as a computational theory (i.e., transformations were statements of relations between possible trees, not processing rules). TG was not widely adopted as a computational model, although there were one or two attempts at "reverse transformational parsing" (e.g., Zwicky et al. [1965], Petrick [1973], Plath [1973]; see King [1983a] for a review). The most successful TG-inspired programs accepted the idea of deep structure (i.e., a standardised structure) but performed the surface-to-deep conversion by any computational technique that seemed to work (rather than sticking strictly to Chomskian transformations).

There were various purely syntactic parsers that were written throughout the 1960s, (e.g., Kuno [1965]), using a variety of techniques, but these had little pretence to performing any semantic processing. Some of the later programs (e.g., Thorne et al. [1968], Bobrow and Fraser [1969]) built a deep structure in the sense of Chomsky (1965), but instead of using transformational rules to process the string, the programs used "augmented transition network grammars" (discussed later).

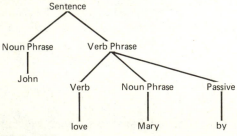

Figure 11.2

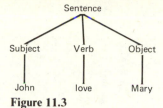

Figure 11.3

Case Frames

Once the step had been taken to postulate a structure for a sentence other than the superficial one, various ideas were put forward for modifications of deep structure. One of the most popular of these was known as "case grammar," which can be viewed in the following way. The point of having deep structures like those previously given is to show the main relationships among the constituents, such as subject, object, and so on. That is, the diagram in Figure 11.2 for "**Mary is loved by John**" is really expressing something like the configuration in Figure 11.3. Then if we are going to represent the relations among items in this way, why bother clinging to notions like "subject," which is essentially concerned with surface structure, rather than with meaning? Let us introduce a set of semantically useful roles that can be used (for our new style of deep structure), and mark each verb with a list of the roles that are relevant to it (its "case frame"). For example, "**John hit Mary with a hammer**" would be sketched as in Figure 11.4.

The dictionary entry for "hit" would then include a case frame, noting that it required an *agent,* an *object* and (optionally) an *instrument*. The idea of *deep cases* was popularised within TG by Fillmore (1968), but it has been adopted and modified widely in artificial intelligence (AI) (see Bruce [1975] for a review). Fillmore originally intended that cases should not be just arbitrarily labelled slots around a verb, but that there should be some universal, semantically significant set of cases that could be used to define possible case frames. (See Charniak [1975], Wilks [1976], Ritchie [1980, Sec. 6.4] for discussions of what might count as a "case-based" system.)

The introduction of case frames is a step away from the concept of a purely syntactic deep structure, towards the use of a more semantic structure.

Augmented Transition Network Grammars

In the late 1960s, a technique (and notation) for writing syntactic recognition grammars was developed by Woods (1970) and (independently) by Dewar et al. (1969). This was the "augmented transition network grammar" (ATN grammar), an idea that has subsequently

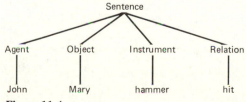

Figure 11.4

Noun Phrase:

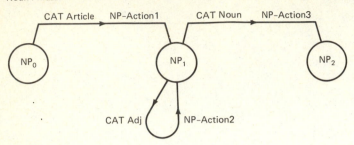

Figure 11.5

been much used (and abused). (See Bates [1978] or Johnson [1983] for a full introduction to ATNs.)

A parsing grammar is represented as a set of diagrams or networks that display the possible orderings of constituents in a sentence and the various options the parser will have at any stage in the processing. The parsing program scans the networks as it works through the sentence, making choices and carrying out actions as specified by the networks. The network grammar can be thought of as a highly specialised flow diagram.

For example, a simple noun phrase could be described by the network in Figure 11.5. The circled points in the network are called *states* and the connecting lines are known as *arcs*.

The interpretation of this network is roughly thus:

> When at state NP0: if the next word is in category **Article**, perform **NP-Action1** and move on to state **NP1**.
> When at state NP1: if the next word is in category **Adj**, perform **NP-Action2** and return to state **NP1**; if the next word is in category **Noun**, perform **NP-Action3** and move to state **NP2**.

The actions on the arcs can be operations to build syntax trees like those shown earlier (e.g., **attach X as NP node**), or any other actions that the parser designer thinks suitable. The ATN interpreter has several storage locations (usually referred to as "registers"), which can be used to hold half-built structures, or other working data. This allows the parser the freedom to do any computation at all (not just building a simple tree left to right). The tests on the arcs (e.g., **CAT**) can also be for a specific word (e.g., [**WRD** "to"]), or can refer to a phrase or clause category. This latter facility (known as the **PUSH** arc) is the way that constituents within constituents can be processed, as follows. As the parser works through the sentence, it is likely to encounter constituents (i.e., phrases or clauses) inside each other. For example:

> The man [who you met] gave the daughter [of the host] a present.

This nesting may occur to some depth:

> I told Alf that [you thought that [Bill knew. . .]].

Sentence:

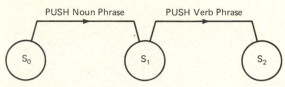

Figure 11.6

Hence, the parser has to have some way of suspending the constituent it is working on, parsing the inner phrase, and resuming where it left off with the outer phrase. This is achieved in the following way. The parser contains different procedures for parsing different types of constituents, and these are called by each other (recursively if necessary). Thus, the "noun phrase procedure" can call the "relative clause procedure," thereby causing a relative clause to be processed within a noun phrase.

In a simple parser, the tree building can be directly linked to the flow of control between the different parsing procedures. That is, each procedure can attach its own result (a subtree) to the main tree as it finishes. In this way, the tree will automatically build up, reflecting the way that the parsing procedures were called.

In an ATN grammar, each network can be thought of as a parsing procedure, and the PUSH arc is taken as an invocation of another network. For example, the network in Figure 11.6 specifies that a **Noun Phrase** should be sought first, then a **Verb Phrase**.

The ATN grammar should then contain other networks, labelled **Noun Phrase** and **Verb Phrase**, which can be scanned by the parser while it is carrying out the PUSH arcs. The temporary use of these other (sub)networks before returning to the S0-S1-S2 network constitutes the calling of parsing procedures previously described. (Those familiar with the details of procedure calls in programming languages may notice that the notation PUSH <sub-network> is slightly misleading; what the ATN interpreter actually does is push (onto a control stack) information about the current network (next state is S1, etc.) and then start at the initial state of the subnetwork).

LUNAR

One of the largest and most successful question-answering systems using AI ideas of around 1970 was the lunar sciences natural language information system, commonly known as the LUNAR system (see Woods [1977]).

This system had a separate syntax analyser and semantic interpreter. The parser, written in ATN form, built a Chomskian deep structure for an input sentence, using the storage facilities of the ATN (registers) to reorder constituents as necessary. The semantic rules were designed to operate on this tree structure, building data-base queries that reflected the meaning of the question or command that had been parsed. These queries were executable commands in a special procedural data-base language (Woods, 1968). Woods (1977) gives a syntactic structure like that in Figure 11.7 for the input sentence:

HOW MANY SAMPLES ARE THERE?

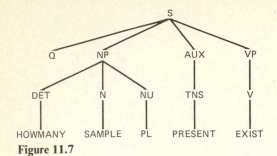

Figure 11.7

The semantic structure is then the following query program:

```
(FOR THE X15/
    (SEQL (NUMBER X15/
        (SEQ SAMPLES: T)):
            T;
    (PRINTOUT X15)))
```

The system was used in various tests and responded successfully to queries such as:

- What is the average concentration of iron in ilmenite?
- Give me the modal analyses of those samples for all phases.
- How many rocks have greater than 50 ppm nickel?
- Of the type A rocks, which is the oldest?

Although it mainly had to deal with queries about its stored information concerning moon-rock samples, and was not a general-purpose natural-language front end, the system was quite impressive in its performance.

SHRDLU

In 1970, the SHRDLU program (Winograd, 1972) had an overwhelming effect on research into NLP. This was a dialogue system that could converse with a human user about a simple table-top world containing building blocks. The program had a (very crude) simulation of a "hand" and "eye" which it could use within the simulated "BLOCKS world."

The program contained a syntactic parser, written by using a special-purpose high-level language called PROGRAMMAR which provided much of the same facilities as an ATN interpreter. The syntax tree thus built was acted on by various "semantic specialists" (LISP procedures) which constructed semantic structures, represented as expressions or commands in another special-purpose programming language, Micro-Planner. The system evaluated the pieces of Micro-Planner program in the computational environment of the BLOCKS data base, and this constituted the response to the original input sentence—for example, examining the world model to find something, or carrying out a command in that world. (See Boden [1977,

Chap. 6] for a brief description.) This arrangement allowed such conversational exchanges as the following:

USER: pick up a big red block.
SHRDLU: **OK**
USER: grasp the pyramid
SHRDLU: **I dont understand which pyramid you mean.**
USER: what does the box contain?
SHRDLU: **The blue pyramid and the blue block.**
USER: what is the pyramid supported by?
SHRDLU: **The box.**
USER: how many blocks are in the box?
SHRDLU: **Four of them.**

This excerpt of dialogue has been chosen here to reflect what was generally possible in such systems at the time. The full published version contained a long conversation that Winograd (1972) had carried on with the program, annotated with his explanations of what the program was doing as it conversed and containing such passages as:

USER: How many things are on top of green cubes?
SHRDLU: **I'm not sure what you mean by "on top of" in the phrase "on top of green cubes." Do you mean:**
1. Directly on the surface.
2. Anywhere on top of?
USER: 2
SHRDLU: Three of them.
. . . . .
. . . . .
USER: Will you please stack up both of the red blocks and either a green cube or a pyramid?
SHRDLU: **OK.**
. . . . .
. . . . .
USER: There were five blocks to the left of the box then.
SHRDLU: **No, only four of them: the red cube, two large green cubes and a large red block.**

The dialogue looked very impressive, and it was largely this that led to the system being hailed as a great breakthrough (despite the lesson of the ELIZA program). This work persuaded many sceptics that computers could be made to *understand* language in some real way and reassured those in artificial intelligence who were doubtful. This renewed faith escalated, and by the mid-1970s NLP was again a flourishing research area. Although people wrote bigger and more complex programs, the theoretical advances were not startling. In a way, this apparent lack of success could be attributed to the attitudes instilled by the Winograd tour de force. The SHRDLU "sample dialogue" was a one-off event, but the AI community adopted it as representing the current state of knowledge in NLP. This generated the false assumption that most of the substantive problems had been solved and that fast progress was possible.

SHRDLU's main features were:

1. a syntactic parser with a fairly wide coverage that built surface structures that were not simply trivial category labellings
2. an attempt to explore the idea of "procedural semantics" (see subsequent discussion) in an implementation
3. the integration of many components, all exemplifying the contemporary level of performance, into a whole system.

Of course, one program does not constitute a complete theoretical solution to the major problems, and so the euphoria stimulated by SHRDLU was slightly ill-founded. Hence, the AI community was struggling with a distorted view of what was possible and overlooked the fact that we still did not have an adequate theory of language.

The Swing to Semantics

Although both LUNAR and SHRDLU had nontrivial semantic components, they both contained a syntactic analyser that performed the first essential processing of the sentence. Such systems could, in retrospect, be viewed as transitions between the purely syntactic parsers of the early and mid-1960s and some of the systems of the early 1970s. The emphasis until then had been on syntax, with surprisingly little discussion of semantics; the early 1970s saw a reversal of that trend, to the extent that AI workers studying syntax were looked upon as little better than members of the Flat Earth Society. There were even claims that sentence understanding did not require syntactic analysis, since syntax seemed (to some AI workers) to have no obvious bearing on meaning. This was a symptom of the extent to which "autonomous syntax" had been studied without reference to semantic issues during the 1960s, causing people to feel that there was no intimate relationship between syntax and semantics (despite the systematic syntax-semantics relationship incorporated into LUNAR and into SHRDLU).

Perhaps the most vociferous advocate of nonsyntactic approaches to NLP was Schank (1972, 1975a,b), who put forward a general form of "meaning representation" for natural language (discussed in later section), and proposed that such meaning structures made syntactic parsing unnecessary.

Riesbeck (1974, 1975a,b) wrote a "conceptual analyser" within this framework, which analysed sentences by building the input directly into a conceptual structure. The control structure in the analyser was essentially as follows. The processing rules were in the form of "requests," which were pairs of a *test* and an *action* and each word had a set of requests stored in its lexical entry. The analyser, in scanning a sentence, maintained a list of *active requests,* and the requests of each input word were added to this list as the words were encountered. Whenever the test of an active request was found to be true, the resulting action was executed. One advantage was supposed to be that this would cause the correct meaning to be selected automatically for ambiguous words, since the only sense of a word that would be detected by the analyser would be one that some currently active request (activated by the previous context) was seeking. Hence, if only one particular meaning is "predicted" on conceptual grounds, it alone will cause active requests to fire.

The other main claim made by Riesbeck (1975b) was that his analyser avoided the need for syntactic information, but this has been strongly disputed. Inspection of his example "requests" reveals the presence of much traditional syntax—for example, tests such as Is input an NP?, syntactic nesting devices for analysing noun phrases, and registers labelled SUBJ and OBJ for holding surface subject and object. (See Ritchie [1983], Charniak and Wilks [1975, Chap. 9] for criticisms of this approach).

Wilks (1973, 1976a,b) outlined an approach in which semantics was claimed to be a central mechanism, based on matching simple semantic patterns against the input sentence, and depending on the notion of *preference* between different possible matches (rather than simple outright rejection). This was part of a machine-translation system at Stanford University in the early 1970s and used a large number (several hundred) of "primitives," which were atomic symbols such as MAN, FOLK, PART. These items, when grouped into trees, made "formulae," and each word sense had a formula to represent its meaning. Thus, a word with several senses would have several different formulae stored in the dictionary. For example, Wilks (1978) shows two senses of the verb grasp (namely, understanding an idea, and taking hold of a physical object). Each formula has a particular primitive that is its "head" (usually at the top-right corner of the tree of primitives) and which gives the broad category that the sense falls into (e.g., for the two senses of grasp the heads are THINK and SENSE).

The processing rules include "templates," which are patterns, usually of three primitives. For example, the template [MAN CAUSE MAN] would underlie the two sentences John hit Bill and Fred hated Joe. The input sentence is passed through an initial "fragmenter" which clusters the words into small phrases or groups. A template matcher then tries to find, for each fragment, a template (or several) that will match it, in the sense that three words in the fragment have formulae whose heads match those in the bare template. The resulting structure (i.e., template plus matching formulae) is a "filled template," and the semantic representation of the string is given, at this stage, by the sequence of filled templates thus constructed. Further routines then try to find links between these filled templates in various ways, using (among other things) rules called "paraplates" which specify how adjuncts may be fitted into case slots (to use conventional terminology for a moment).

The essential characteristic of this system (other than its lack of emphasis on syntax) is the use of semantic preference. Whereas many systems (e.g., Winograd [1972]) use the linguistic notion of "selectional restrictions" (Katz & Fodor, 1963) to reject semantically anomalous constructions, Wilks' analyser merely *prefers* some combinations to others. In this way, slightly nonstandard subjects and objects may be allowed (e.g., My car drinks gasoline), but ambiguity is resolved by selecting the *most preferred* reading. This assessment is done after the filled templates have been constructed, by checking how many of the preferences that are specified in the formulae have been satisfied by the neighbouring items.

As in the case of Riesbeck's system, the system is not really nonsyntactic, since both the fragmenting and the later "tying together" routines use a large amount of syntactic information. In particular, the fragmenting (which is wholly syntactic) occurs before the semantic template matching, and there is no facility for "feedback" (i.e., revoking fragmentation decisions). (See Boguraev [1980] for a detailed discussion of this approach.)

Scripts

In the mid-1970s, the Minsky (1975) notion of a "frame" had a strong influence throughout AI. Within NLP, the main frame approach was the "script" (Schank & Abelson, 1975). This was a frame with some kind of time sequence added, so that a script could describe a stereotyped sequence of actions or events. Schank and his colleagues spent some time writing programs that could understand simple stories on the basis of having scripts for the activities being described (Lehnert, 1977). For example, the SAM program is supposed to understand and answer questions about short stories concerning everyday activities (e.g., eating in a restaurant). The essential point is that a typical verbal account of an activity does not furnish all the details—a storyteller assumes that the listener can fill in the gaps, using assumptions about the "normal" course of events. Scripts are supposed to be complex patterns that describe these normal examples of the activity.

This approach has also been applied to the comprehension of news items (see Schank et al. [1980]). Since the style of news reporting is itself stereotyped in its presentation of information, the question arises of whether a script should represent the prototypical *event* or the typical way that such an event is *reported*. If the latter course is followed, scripts then become relations of "text grammars" (cf. Petofi and Rieser [1974]).

It should be emphasised that this line of work is concerned with the higher-level inferences that happen during language understanding, not with the lower-level grammatical processing of sentences. The latter (news report) work, for example, depends very strongly on the use of keywords in the text (see Wilks [1983] for comments on this).

Deterministic Parsing

Marcus (1978, 1980) has written a parser that produces linguistically approved structures (compatible with Chomsky's extended standard theory—see Radford [1981]), and which will analyse sentences without having to consider multiple possibilities during the analysis process. His claim is that humans normally parse sentences "deterministically" (i.e., following only the correct path through the grammar) and that parsers written to perform in a similar manner will reveal interesting aspects of human language (see Chap. 9 for a fuller description of the proposed mechanism, and Sampson [1983] for a theoretical discussion). Unfortunately, the idea has not been tested on a wide enough range of sentences to substantiate this hypothesis.

Practical Parsers

In the past few years, there has been a marked trend (at least within the United States) towards the construction of large, efficient parsers for use as front ends to data bases or intelligent systems. In many cases, the mechanisms used are quite interesting theoretically, but the emphasis is more on having a stable, usable parser that covers a reasonably wide range of English and responds in an acceptably short time. For example, the work at BBN (Bobrow & Webber, 1980a,b; Brachman et al., 1979), and at SRI (Hendrix et al., 1978) is very much within practical guidelines. This is in contrast to experimental NLP systems (typically, Ph.D. projects that are fragile, unstable, and have narrow coverage and hopeless response time).

The LADDER system (Hendrix et al., 1978) is a data-base query system that includes an English language component called INLAND, allowing queries such as:

- What is the length of the Constellation?
- To what country does each merchant ship in the North Atlantic belong?
- What is the current position of the Kennedy?

The INLAND interface was constructed using LIFER, which is a general facility for writing parsing grammars (Hendrix, 1977). LIFER allows the programmer-linguist to define rules that are like context-free grammar rules with arbitrary actions attached (somewhat similar to the "definite clause grammars" of Pereira and Warren [1980]).

Conversational Structure

One area that was relatively neglected in the 1960s and early 1970s, but which seems likely to be an extremely important research field in the near future, is the study of dialogue. Some linguists and philosophers had discussed conversation from a theoretical point of view (e.g., Austin [1962]) but implemented NL systems had fairly rudimentary user interfaces that usually handled each sentence in isolation.

More recently, it has been realised that it is essential (for both practical and theoretical purposes) to build up a richer description of what occurs during a natural language dialogue, in terms of the goals and plans of the participants and the view that each person has of the other (and of his views). This kind of factor is relevant not only to why a person says something, but also to the way that the utterance is phrased. (See Grosz [1977], Perrault et al. [1978], Perrault and Allen [1980], Brady [1983].)

Further Reading

This has been a brief summary of some of the background ideas to current work in natural language processing. There are a few major areas that were not covered, such as sentence generation (Davey, 1974; Goldman, 1975; Boguraev, 1980; McDonald, 1980) and speech understanding (Woods et al., 1976; Lowerre, 1976; McCracken, 1978). Further background material can be found in Charniak and Wilks (1975), Boden (1977), Winograd (1983), and King (1983). However, the best way to grasp the issues involved is to write programs that handle actual language; in the next section, we will consider some of the issues that arise when attempting to do this.

BASIC ISSUES AND PROBLEMS

Language is a means of communication, and as such it is of interest in the computational context. If computers are to communicate by means of natural language, then two fundamental problems must be addressed: What is communicated? and How does an utterance accomplish this communication? Within the context of building computer systems, this amounts to asking: What representation should be used to capture the meaning of an utterance? and What process should be used to capture the relationship between this representation and the sounds/characters that are present within an utterance? Needless to say, many different approaches to these questions are being pursued within the field at the moment—there is no one accepted answer. The remaining sections of this chapter provide an overview of the issues and terminology that are involved in each case and try to delineate the various positions of significance.

Constructing a Semantic Theory

Perhaps the greatest problem that arises in any attempt to build a computer system that is capable of understanding natural language is that of meaning. There is still no well-defined, properly understood, adequate theory of meaning, despite centuries of philosophy (and a few decades of so-called "machine representation of knowledge"). In comparison to the field of syntax, where various techniques are available, some of which achieve a high level of adequacy, semantics is making slow progress. This section will briefly summarise some of the elementary issues that arise in trying to represent "meaning," and mention some of the more common representational techniques within AI.

There are two main ways of building a theory of meaning for a natural language like English:

1. One could adopt an existing, well-defined, clearly understood mathematical formalism (e.g., predicate logic, discussed later) and use this to describe the meanings of sentences and texts. The advantage here is that the notation and procedures that are involved are well defined, and precise statements can be proved about the theory (see Hayes [1977]). The disadvantage is that the characteristics of the mathematical system chosen may not be a very close match to those of English, and one then has to force the language into the mould provided by the mathematics. One could also start modifying the mathematical definitions to bring the system closer to English, but this must be done very carefully if the purity and precision of the original system are not to be destroyed; the most notable attempt in this direction is the logic of Montague (see Thomason [1974]).

2. One could try to build a special-purpose notation for representing natural language meanings. The advantage of this is that there is no committment to spurious constructs—the only items put into the theory are those that seem to be necessary to describe English. Unfortunately, devising new notations is a confusing path, full of conceptual pitfalls. The new "semantic notation" is likely to be ill-defined, and its properties will not be amenable to precise analysis (see Hayes, 1974, 1977, 1979).

Both these routes are used widely in AI, and heated arguments are sometimes heard between dedicated practitioners of the different styles. In the remainder of this chapter, we will look mainly at some of the ideas that have come out of approach (2), but we will start with a brief (and rather inadequate) summary of predicate logic (the main mathematical contender).

Predicate Logic

The mathematical formalism that is most often discussed as a simple, well-understood representation of meaning is first-order predicate logic. It is impossible to give a full explanation of the ideas involved, but some of the salient features can be mentioned. (See Stoll [1979] for an elementary treatment, or Mendelson [1964] and Schoenfield [1967], for more mathematical expositions.)

There is a set of symbols, and rules for combining these into *terms* and *sentences*. There are also rules of *inference*, which state how a given set of sentences may be extended to contain other sentences. A logical system will have an initial set of sentences ("axioms"), and any sentence that can be derived from these axioms, using the inference rules, is called a "theorem" of the system. All these are purely formal manipulations of the symbols—there is no meaning or interpretation assigned to the symbols in this.

The standard way of giving meaning to these symbols is to regard the "terms" as referring to objects in some set (the "model"), and the sentences as being statements about these objects and relations among them. This depends on pairing up symbols in the logic with objects (and relations) in the model, and using interpretation rules (*truth-conditions*) to state how the meaning (*truth-value*) of a complex sentence depends on the truth or falsity of its component parts. For example, suppose we have two terms BOOK1 and TABLE2, and a sentence ON(BOOK1, TABLE2). This might be given an interpretation in which BOOK1 and TABLE2 refer to a particular book and a particular table, and the symbol ON is interpreted as meaning is on top of. Then ON(BOOK1, TABLE2) would be true in this model if (and only if) the object referred to as BOOK1 were on top of the object referred to as TABLE2. Symbols like ON in this example that are used to make statements and which can refer to relations that may or may not hold, are called *predicates*.

The inference rules are designed so that, starting from axioms that are "true" of a model, only true theorems will be produced. That is, the whole mechanism is carefully constructed so that the two notions of "being a theorem" (which is determined solely by manipulating the sentences symbolically) and "being true in a model" correspond. In this way, the logic is a well-defined notation in which exact descriptive statements can be formulated about any model (i.e., set of objects with relations between them). Moreover, purely formal manipulations of these symbolic statements (i.e., inference) can be used to produce further valid descriptions of that same model, without direct reference to the model itself.

The logic outlined here is referred to as "first-order," because the only allowable statements are about the truth or falsity of the relationships among objects in the model, not about the definitions or properties of the relations themselves. In higher-order logics, it is permissible to form statements that describe the nature of the relations.

What is the relevance of this to natural language? One rather simplified approach to providing a "semantic structure" for English is to associate a logical "sentence" with each English sentence. For example,

"John loves Mary": $L(J, M)$
"x hates y": $H(x, y)$
"x is a mouse": $M(x)$
"x is a cat": $C(x)$
"All mice hate all cats": $(\forall x)(\forall y)((M(x) \land C(y)) \Rightarrow H(x, y))$

(where $\forall x$ means that the following statement is true for all choices of x, $\land$ means that the statements it connects are both true, and $\Rightarrow$ means that if the preceding statement is true, then that which follows is also true).

This may work as long as we consider only examples that make simple assertions about relations among objects in a very straightforward way. But this becomes difficult for less trivial examples, such as:

Many people believe that large corporations have always tried to undermine organisations whose activities they regarded as likely to harm the interests of international trade.

This difficulty does not mean that logic is inappropriate as a representational tool for natural language semantics, but it casts doubt on any naive attempt to tie up the objects and relations of a logic model with real-world objects and relations in a very simple way, and to associate logical formulae with English sentences directly. The powerful techniques of logic (even first-order predicate logic, as already discussed) could be used in some other way as a descriptive apparatus within a semantic theory, perhaps by introducing a more subtle notion of what the objects and relations are that underlie natural language (e.g., introducing various abstract objects). Alternatively, it may be necessary to introduce more complex logics. For example, "modal" logics (in which notions of "possibility" and "necessity" can be expressed—Hughes and Cresswell [1973]), "tense" logics (in which time sequences can be described—Prior [1967]), or higher-order logics (in which statements can be expressed not only about the basic objects but also about the relations and functions that are defined in the model).

Problems in Designing a Meaning-Representation

Let us start by sketching some of the requirements of a semantic system and mentioning some of the common pitfalls. The semantic representation should not be just a rearrangement of the English words with some (meaningless) notation thrown in. Such a representation in itself does not explain or describe anything. For example, we might be tempted to write the meaning of

"John loves Mary"

as

LOVE(JOHN, MARY)

This could perhaps be justified by saying that this indicates a relation (LOVE) that holds between two entities (JOHN and MARY) (as in predicate logic). However, this simplistic approach fails in more complex examples. For example:

"Mary left the house before she could achieve anything."

BEFORE(LEAVE(MARY, THE(HOUSE)), POSSIBLE(ACHIEVE(MARY, ANYTHING)))

It becomes difficult to claim that this represents relations among entities here—not only would BEFORE, ACHIEVE and POSSIBLE have to be very complex (i.e., this formula does not really show their meaning in any way—see additional comments in the next section), but what kind of *entity* is ANYTHING? Moreover, what kind of *relation* is THE?

Allied to this problem is the need for a semantic notation to have some clear interpretation. In the same way that a syntax tree can be justified by its suitability for conversion into semantic form, the semantic representation must be useful for further manipulation (e.g., inference, retrieval of information). It is no use writing down superficially attractive formulae or elegant diagrams, if there is no indication of how these notations actually *mean* something or how they can be used (see Woods [1975a]).

Semantic Primitives

One popular approach in work on semantics is "decomposition into primitives." The idea is that meaning can be expressed in terms of some standard set of features or relations and that all meanings can be represented by reducing them to a configuration of these basic elements [e.g., Katz and Fodor [1963]; see Bolinger [1965] for a criticism). Binary semantic features have traditionally been used for classifying simple objects, but this is not subtle enough for much else. For example, we could perhaps persuade ourselves that the meaning of **dog** is

(+ANIMATE, −HUMAN, +QUADRUPED, +CANINE)

and that the meaning of **bone** is

(−ANIMATE, +PHYSICAL, +ANIMAL, +OSSEOUS)

but what would we do to represent the meaning of **The dog ate the bone**? Simply heaping binary features together does not retain the relevant structural information (e.g., who is eating what). Katz and Fodor (1963) tried to get around this by including some structuring in their sets of "semantic markers" (their version of "features"), but their theory was never fully formalised. A slightly more sophisticated approach has been proposed by various linguists and AI workers. This involves using a set of primitive relations to describe all meanings. The actual details vary from one theory to the next. For example, it has been suggested that the meaning of **John killed Mary** could be represented as

CAUSE(JOHN, BECOME(NOT(ALIVE(MARY))))

(See McCawley [1971], Fodor [1970].) The warnings given earlier about thinking that you have captured the meaning because you have scribbled a plausible definition are still relevant—calling your relations primitive does not make them magically meaningful. Another version of the primitives approach was proposed, within AI, by Schank (1975a,b) and Schank et al. (1975). He suggested that a certain small set of relations would serve to depict all natural language meanings (in any language). His suggested set of linking relations included:

INGEST: person transfers something to his inside
$<\equiv$: one concept or event causes another
INC(n): change in a scale of size n
PART: one thing is a part of another
$<=>$: this configuration of elements represents an event
CHANGE: change in state

There were also various other labels (e.g., cases), and in fact, only *actions* were decomposed into primitives—other items (e.g., descriptions of things) used other categories. A sentence such as **John liked the food** might be represented roughly as in Figure 11.8 (modifying Schank's own peculiar graphical notation):

The advantage of this kind of approach is supposed to be that similarities in meaning can be captured by structures having similar or identical subparts and that more subtle inferences are possible (e.g., that after **John liked the food**, the food is in John's stomach). Once detailed general rules are provided to make the requisite matches and inferences (see Rieger [1975] for an early version), these diagrams are an improvement on the simplistic formulae cited earlier. It

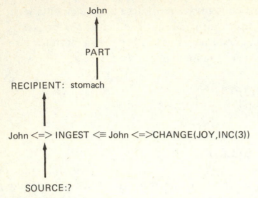

SOURCE:?

Figure 11.8

is important to bear in mind, in cases like this, that it is the whole system (symbolic structures *and* inference rules) that should be assessed—the validity or otherwise of the representation cannot be determined merely from an inspection of the graphical form.

The disadvantage of an approach *wholly* based on primitives is that it does not admit the relevance of larger chunks than the actual primitives. For example, the fact that English has words for certain terms suggests that these constitute, for the English speaker, integral units of meaning and that a NLP system should perhaps treat them as units. This could be achieved by describing meaning at several levels—for example, in larger units, corresponding to words, and in "expanded" form, giving the underlying meaning in primitive terms (cf. Norman and Rumelhart [1975]). If we do not use larger items (than the primitives) for meaning-manipulations, then operations such as inferences and retrieval become horrendously complicated. (If you have ever written a large program in assembly code without the benefit of macros or subroutines, you may have some idea of the difficulties involved). On the other hand, if we do allow "unexpanded" blobs of meaning to be used, the NLP system will be continually having to make choices about the need to decompose these units. For example, suppose the system wants to compare two statements to see if they mean the same; should it decompose both of them? one of them? decompose all of both of them, or only parts of both of them? The extra processing could become considerable.

Semantic Networks

The convention of representing relations by labelled graphs (as in the preceding example) is very common in AI. It provides a handy way of depicting a complex set of interrelations, and this has led many workers (perhaps misguidedly) to think of these graphical notations as constituting a theory of meaning. These labelled diagrams are usually referred to as "semantic nets" or "semantic networks," but whether they form a new way of representing meaning depends very much on what is put in the networks. (See Findler [1979] for a wide sample of the field and Ritchie and Hanna [1983] for a review). Usually, the network represents relations between entities, where an entity can be either a specific object (e.g., John) or a general concept (e.g., dog). These meaning-relations can be regarded as being either "real-world" relations (like loves, supports, ingests) or organisational links (like inc in the preceding diagram, or the

object link between a verb-meaning and its object-meaning). To propose a theory of meaning based on semantic nets, one should specify (among other things):

- What organisational links are available
- How the various types of links and nodes can be connected
- What operations can be performed on these combinations of links and nodes

In the past, most proposals for semantic net systems have not made such details clear (relying on a few sample diagrams and the reader's intuitions), and many confusions have crept in concerning the use of network notation (see Woods [1975a] for a good critique). Some of the deficiencies that have occurred are:

- not distinguishing the extension of a set (e.g., the set of **all dogs**) from the concept defining that set (e.g., the definition of a **dog**)
- confusing set-inclusion (**a dog is a mammal**) with set-membership (**Fido is a dog**); usually this is embodied in the use of a single type of ISA link between nodes
- not specifying what the import of an arc in a network is; that is, Can an arc (link) be scanned equally easily in both directions? Are there connections between nodes other than by the arcs shown?
- losing much of the expressive power of traditional logic (e.g., the ability to include quantified statements like **for all x . . .** and **there exists an x . . .**) without substituting any useful facilities to compensate.

In general, most semantic net notations suffer from the aforementioned problem—they are notations without any properly defined meaning. Hayes (1977) has argued that most "knowledge representation formalisms" are in fact reinventions of traditional logics. It is certainly rare to see a semantic network facility that could not be achieved equally well in some conventional logical formalism, but it is perhaps an overstatement to say that semantic nets are simply notational variants of existing logics—until the meaning of a network notation is defined fully, this is an open question.

One idea that has become commonly associated with semantic networks is "inheritance." Nodes in the network are arranged into a hierarchy, in which more general concepts have more general properties, and the more specific concepts or individuals are treated as having all the properties of the nodes to which they are connected by inheritance links. This gives a very economical representation, since properties associated with many items need only be inserted at one place in the net. For example, if the network contains the information that Albert is an elephant, and the **elephant** node has data giving the typical colour as **grey**, then the system should be able to respond to the question **what colour is Albert?** by letting the Albert node inherit properties from the **elephant** node. In a system of a realistic size, this leads to important questions of processing for any inference mechanism. The main issue is: When should the inheritance occur during processing (cf. the preceding comments on decomposition into primitives)? That is, each node is normally linked to a vast amount of inheritable properties, any of which might be pertinent to the current task, and it is very difficult for the inference process to know whether to start considering all possible inheritable properties for every node it is handling (see Fahlman [1979], McDermott [1975a,b], Bundy and Stone [1975]).

Procedural Semantics

Another idea that is often proposed for semantic representation is that of "procedural semantics." This is based on the intuition that certain kinds of knowledge are better thought of not as static data structures but as procedures that can be executed (Winograd, 1972). This attitude has never become clearly formulated as a theory, but it manifests itself in various forms throughout AI. Some versions of this are rather bizarre; for example, it has been argued that "knowing" the meaning of grasp is roughly equivalent to having a procedure that will, when carried out, grasp an object. This seems incoherent—does that mean that you cannot understand the word *swim* unless you can swim? A slightly more subtle and abstract form of procedural semantics suggests that many meanings can best be described as procedures that operate on other meanings. For example, the meaning of the word *the* is a procedure that searches the context for an example of the item in question (Rumelhart & Norman, 1973); thus the meaning of *the pyramid* is a procedure that looks about for a recently mentioned pyramid (Winograd, 1972). This is a useful way of looking at certain words, but it needs some refinement before it will work as a full theory (see Ritchie [1980, Chap. 6]).

In particular, where do these procedures operate? In the outside world (enabling the language user to pick up pyramids, etc.) or in some internal "memory" (enabling the language user to talk about items that are not currently accessible in the outside world)? Also, it has been suggested that the procedural meaning of a question is a program that, when executed, will answer the question. It is not clear exactly whether the analogy is between understanding a question/command and constructing this procedure, or between answering/obeying the utterance and executing the procedure. It is possible to understand a question without working out the answer, and possible to decide the answer without replying, so presumably these stages must be reflected in the procedural model. The hard-line version of procedural semantics, in which all semantic structures are procedures (i.e., a direct adoption of the programming techniques used by Woods [1968] and Winograd [1972]) is probably not held by anyone (except perhaps Johnson-Laird [1977]). There is, nevertheless, a widespread sympathy for a more general form of procedural semantics, in which language understanding is looked on as a form of processing, not only in the conversion from words to meaning, but also in the definition of what a meaning is (see Winograd [1976]). Sentences, in this view, are regarded as attempts by a speaker to create an effect in the hearer (e.g., identifying something being referred to, remembering a fact, carrying out some task), and it is unrealistic to talk of *the meaning* simply as a data structure; we must also ask what the speaker or hearer would do with this meaning under particular circumstances (cf. Davies and Isard [1972]).

Frames

For many years, AI approaches to knowledge representation paid little attention to grouping or organising; the knowledge was seen as a large, multiply-connected network. Since about 1970, attempts have been made to impose more order on this mass.

One organisational technique that became enormously fashionable in the mid-1970s was the "frame" (Minsky, 1975). A *frame* was a cluster of procedures and data, all of which referred to some topic or subject matter, so that whole clumps of knowledge could be moved around memory together. The underlying intuition was that humans do not always work things out from first principles; instead, they have vast chunks of standard knowledge about previously encountered situations, which allow them to make assumptions about normal patterns of things. A frame was intended to be a block of stereotyped knowledge that could be deployed under appropriate circumstances to avoid the need for perceiving or working out all the details every time. Each frame would have a number of "slots," each with a cluster of attached information. The slots indicated parts of the whole frame, and the contents of the slots would vary with different uses of the same frame (in the same way that parameters of a procedure can vary). The information attached to a slot could include a "restriction" (i.e., a type-check on the possible fillers), a "default" (i.e., a value to be used if none had been explicitly inserted) and various procedures (e.g., "demons" to be executed when something is put in the slot). One attempt to construct a complete natural language system based on frames was the computerised travel agent facility of the GUS project (Bobrow et al., 1977). This contained frames for typical items such as trips, customers, dates, and so on. The frame for a dialog had slots for a client, a time of occurrence, and a topic; the latter could be filled with an instance of the Trip-Specification frame, which in turn had slots for a HomePort, a ForeignPort, an OutwardLeg, an AwayStay, and an InwardLeg.

Like many AI approaches to meaning, the frame has remained a rough intuitive notion, without ever becoming a precise theory, although there have been one or two attempts at "frame languages" (e.g., Roberts and Goldstein [1977], Bobrow and Winograd [1977a,b], Brachman [1979]) and many papers (and programs) have been inspired by these ideas (e.g., Metzing [1979]).

The problem of representing meaning is vast and relatively unsolved. It would not be misleading to say that the whole question of meaning is an open problem. Although some of the approaches that have evolved within AI may lead to useful insights concerning the use of knowledge in natural language communication, there is a great deal of work to be done.

INTERPRETATION AND PRODUCTION: FROM FORM TO CONTENT AND BACK AGAIN

Even supposing a solution to the problem of choosing a representation addressed in the previous sections (and some such solution must be adopted in any language processing system), we are still only halfway there. There remains the separate question of, How, given an utterance, do we arrive at a representation of its meaning (*interpretation*)? and/or, given a chunk of meaning representation, How do we arrive at an utterance that expresses it (*production*)? (Just how separable they are is one of the issues that divides people—we will come to that later).

For the purpose of exposition, we will simplify the problem along three dimensions: We will take "form" to refer to character strings, not sound waves, thus avoiding issues of speech recognition and production; We will focus on English, with only occasional references to the dangers of such linguistic myopia; We will focus on interpretation at the expense of production, as this is where most of the work has been done. We have thus reduced the problem to that of specifying a function from English utterances in the form of character strings to meaning in the form of some representational calculus.

Decomposing the Problem into Stages

In attempting to formulate a computational solution to this problem, we will follow standard practice and seek a decomposition into stages. Linguistics provides us with such a decomposition, using the name *morphology* for the first stage.

Virtually all computational systems extant respect this first division, distinguishing between a state that identifies words and affixes in the input character string and looks them up in various dictionaries, and all subsequent processing. The location of the boundaries between the subsequent stages, as well as their number, are much more contentious.

Beyond presenting a very simple partial solution in this chapter we will have nothing further to say about the morphological stage. This is not to suggest that there are no outstanding problems here—even English, which is relatively speaking well behaved in this respect, presents difficulties when one wishes to deal with the whole of the 200,000+ vocabulary, and once one looks at other languages, things get worse. The interested reader is referred to Kay (1977) and Kaplan and Kay (1982) for further discussion.

Syntax: Pro and Con

The traditional linguistic analysis consisted of three further stages: *syntax, semantics,* and *pragmatics*. This division goes back at least as far as Morris (1938) and has received a number of different interpretations. Loosely speaking, the syntactic stage is concerned with grammatical, structural analysis without regard to meaning, the semantic stage is concerned with local, literal meaning without regard to context, and the pragmatic stage is concerned with full-blooded communicative content. It is fair to say that the major division of opinion within AI as regards natural language interpretation is whether or not this division is approximately correct, that is, whether a division of the interpretation process into three such stages is the right first step. In practice it is the independent existence of a syntactic stage that is the issue.

It would not be appropriate to attempt to recapitulate the arguments on both sides of this issue here. But we do want to make clear what the disagreement is truly about, because the fundamental point is often clouded by a separate, related issue. Given a complex process whose computational realisation is decomposed into stages, there are two architectural issues that must be settled: How many stages are there? and What is their relationship with each other? If we carry the computational analysis one step further, and suppose that each stage is realised as a specialised process that interprets some specialised knowledge base, then the first issue is one of how many distinguishable sorts of process/knowledge pairs are appropriate, and the second is one of control flow between the processes. We take it that the first of these is the major theoretical question and the second is subsidiary to it.

The mistake that is often made here is to assume that support for a syntactic stage in the interpretation process involves a claim of hermetically sealed autonomy as far as control flow is concerned, but this is neither necessarily the case in the abstract nor often the case in practice. A survey of various systems with respect to this issue can be found in Ritchie (1983). The real issue is whether or not it is useful or necessary to distinguish information about syntactic structure from other (e.g., semantic or contextual) information. Such a distinction *does* imply a concomitant distinction between processes that are suitable to the different sorts of information—it does *not* imply that those processes are completely independent.

Most of those who assert that such a distinction is not useful or necessary (sometimes one, sometimes the other, sometimes both) are associated more or less directly with Roger Schank (1975b). It is in their attitude towards ambiguity that the difference between the two positions can most easily be seen. Consider the utterance Robin banks with Barclays. As a first step in interpreting it, morphological and lexical analysis will reveal an ambiguity—the characters b a n k s are not univocal in English. A caricature of the asyntactic position proceeds as follows:

> My dictionary tells me that this string of characters either refers to the edges of bodies of water, to financial institutions, or to the process of using a financial institution. Similarly, it tells me that Robin refers to a human, and Barclays to a particular financial institution. There is only one sensible way of combining these meanings into a single coherent meaning—The human named Robin uses the financial institution named Barclays.

whereas a caricature of the syntactic position would be

> My dictionary tells me that Robin is a proper noun, banks either a plural noun or the third person singular of a verb, with a preposition and Barclays another proper noun. My grammar tells me that well-formed utterances in English can consist of the sequence proper noun, verb, preposition, proper noun, but that the sequence proper noun, noun, preposition, proper noun is not a well-formed English utterance. Therefore banks is in this case a verb.

Two things should be clear about the differences between the two approaches: The first carries us further than the second, which as described has not extracted any meaning from the utterance as yet, and the second has reference to a knowledge base of grammatical and structural information that is not used by the first, which performs its operations entirely in terms of meaning. It should also be noted that the first makes crucial use of the notion "sensible way of combining . . . into a single coherent meaning." Its dependence on this notion makes this approach suspect from a practical point of view, as effectively discharging this notion in a working system is an open-ended and extremely daunting problem. It is also theoretically suspect, as it denies the relevance and utility of grammatical and structural information. For this reason, among others, in what follows we will assume that some form of the second approach is what is wanted. This will also allow us to take advantage of noncomputational linguistic theory.

Syntax: Grammar and Parsing

The goal of the syntactic stage, then, is to take morphologically and lexically analysed utterances and produce from them some form of syntactic structures. We assume the standard computational division of labour mentioned at the very beginning of this chapter between process and knowledge base. The knowledge base for the syntactic stage is called a *grammar*. It is an expression of the structural regularities of a given language. The process that operates over the grammar to produce structures from utterances is called a *parser*. The choice of parsing mechanism is to some extent independent of the way in which the grammar is expressed (the *grammatical formalism*), and it is very important to keep the two distinct.

The output of the parser may be of various sorts—surface structure trees, deep structure trees, functional or relational structures—depending on the linguistic theoretical basis for the interpretation system and its overall structure. Thus, for example, Marcus (1980) produces extended standard theory surface structures (Chomsky, 1975), Woods (1970) produces standard theory deep structures (Chomsky, 1965), Thompson (1981) produces generalized phrase (surface) structures (Gazdar, 1981), and Kaplan produces functional structures (Kaplan & Bresnan, 1982). But all these systems are constrained by the nature of language to confront a number of basic issues, which we will now discuss.

Ambiguity

The aspect of natural language that underlies many of the variations in approach to interpretation and parsing is *ambiguity*. Three kinds of ambiguity will concern us: structural, form class, and word sense. Structural ambiguity comes about when an utterance can be analysed as having more than one syntactic structure. For example, the utterance You can have peas and beans or carrots can be analysed in one of two ways, as indicated by the bracketings [peas and beans] or carrots versus peas and [beans or carrots]. Form class ambiguity comes about when a given word may be analysed as more than one part of speech. For instance, saw may be either a noun or a verb, plastic either an adjective or a noun, and so on. Form class ambiguity necessarily gives rise to structural ambiguity as well, as in the famous example He saw her duck. The words her and duck are both form class ambiguous. Taking her as a possessive pronoun and duck as a noun, we get a structure for the utterance of ⟨noun phrase, verb, noun phrase⟩—a duck was seen. Taking her as a personal pronoun and duck as a verb, we get a structure of ⟨noun phrase, verb, [noun phrase, verb]⟩—an act of ducking was seen. Finally, word sense ambiguity comes about when a given word of a given form class may still have more than one meaning. For example, in the utterance When I came in they were talking about planes the word plane, taken as a noun, may refer to (at least) a flying machine, a geometrical surface or a woodworking tool. Word sense ambiguity can be taken to be of no syntactic significance, but clearly form class and structural ambiguity are of crucial concern in parsing. In this connection, a further distinction must be made, between *global* and *local* ambiguity. The examples given so far have all been of global, that is, cases where entire utterances are ambiguous. Local ambiguity refers to situations where portions of utterances are ambiguous, even though the utterance as a whole is univocal. For example, if we compare two utterances, The plastic covers the table and The plastic covers protect the table, we can see that the partial utterance the plastic covers is locally ambiguous. Local ambiguity seems to be characteristic of natural languages, although one is typically not aware of this in everyday language use. Once one attempts to approach language mechanically, however, it becomes overwhelmingly apparent and exerts a considerable influence on system design. We will return to this issue later.

Parsing: Terminology and Issues

In order to illustrate a number of points regarding parsing, we will use the following very simple context-free phrase-structure grammar for a small fragment of English:

S –> NP VP	Art –> the	Adj –> plastic
NP –> Art N	N –> plastic	N –> cloths
NP –> Art Adj N	N –> covers	N –> table
VP –> V NP	V –> covers	V –> protect

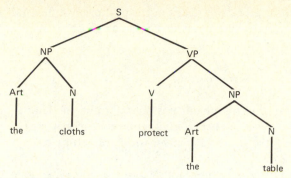

Figure 11.9

Although this is not the place for a detailed discussion of phrase structure grammars, a few terms can usefully be defined here: S is the *initial* or start symbol; S, NP, and VP are the *nonterminal* symbols; Art, Adj, V, and N (the lexical categories) are the *preterminal* symbols, and the English words are the *terminal* symbols.

This grammar is a repository for information about well-formed English utterances. A number of issues arise as we try to put the grammar to work in parsing a particular utterance, say the cloths protect the table, which has the structure given in Figure 11.9.

Top-Down Versus Bottom-Up

First, we must choose where to start—with the grammar or with the utterance. On the one hand, we can ask "I want to find an S—what do I need? Ah, an NP. Well, how do I find an NP? One way requires an Art first, and I have one. Ok, what do I need next, etc." This way of proceeding is called *top-down,* or *hypothesis driven,* for obvious reasons. We start from the top of the tree, and work down through the grammar, trying to get to the words of the utterance. We start from the hypothesis that what we have is an S, and try to find out how, by breaking the hypothesis down into subsidiary, smaller hypotheses. Many computer language parsers operate in roughly this fashion, using what is called the *recursive descent method.* A recursive descent parser consists of a collection of functions, one per constituent type, which reflect in explicit calls to one another the scenario at the beginning of this paragraph.

Alternatively, we could have said "Well, the first thing I see is the, which is an Art—What can I do with it?—nothing by itself. What else do I have?—the word cloths, which is an N. Ah, an Art followed by an N make an NP—What can I do with that?—nothing by itself. What else do I have? etc." This way of proceeding is called *bottom-up* or *data driven,* again for obvious reasons. We start from the words at the bottom of the tree and try to work up to S, using the grammar as a guide. We start from the data and try to piece it together into bigger and bigger chunks until we have only one. So-called shift-reduce parsers for computer languages operate in more or less this fashion, working with a buffer of symbols to be analysed, and either *shifting* a new symbol in at the end, or *reducing* an initial substring to a single symbol, as per some rule in the grammar.

Another choice we have, already made implicitly, is whether to run *left to right* or alternatively *right to left,* saying, for example, "here we have an N, preceded by an Art, that's an NP. Preceding the NP is a V—that makes a VP, etc." A desire for psychological plausibility may lead most parser designers to prefer left-to-right processing, but there is no a priori difference from a technical standpoint, and some grammars may actually be parsed more efficiently "backwards."

Nondeterminism

The processing correlate of form class and structural ambiguity is nondeterminism. That is, during the parsing of locally or globally ambiguous utterances, the situation may arise when the state of the analysis so far, the grammar, and the focus of the parser within the utterance, are insufficient to determine uniquely the next step.

For example, suppose we were parsing the utterance **the plastic covers protect the table** proceeding left to right, bottom-up. After noting **the** as an **Art**, we have a choice when we get to **plastic**. Either it is an **Adj**, and we proceed with the rule (**NP** $\rightarrow$ **Art Adj N**), or it is an **N**, in which case by the rule (**NP** $\rightarrow$ **Art N**) we have a complete **NP**. The latter choice would be wrong, but in another utterance, such as **the plastic covers the table**, it would be correct.

There are three available responses to the problem of nondeterminism. One is to say that by extending the focus of the parser sufficiently, the problem can be made to disappear effectively. One can extend the focus of the parser by either introducing interaction with other stages of the interpretation process or considering more than one word in the utterance. Either semantic and contextual information about the alternatives under consideration will be sufficient to reject all but one possibility, or looking ahead in the utterance will do so. Note that in the preceding example we would have to look ahead not just to **covers**, but beyond to **protect** before knowing the answer, as **covers** is form class ambiguous as well. Some combination of these approaches has been advocated in one way or another by Marcus (1980), Church (1980), Milne (1982), and Berwick (1982). It remains to be seen how much and just what sort of lookahead is necessary for English, and whether this approach will work for languages such as Japanese which are basically postfixing (verb final with postpositions and prenominal relative clauses), rather than prefixing (verb medial with prepositions and postnominal relative clauses), as English is. The following Japanese sentence, which means **This is a book that I have written**, suggests where some of the problems lie:

> Kore wa watakusi ga kaita hon desu
> this   I   wrote book is

The other two approaches both accept nondeterminism and implement it on our deterministic machines. The first is called *backtracking*. At each point where more than one alternative exists, the parser notes this, pursues one to its conclusion, and then "backs up" to a choice point and pursues a different alternative. This can be seen as a *depth-first* search through the tree of alternative analyses. If only one analysis is required the process can be terminated immediately when one is found—otherwise, all analyses will eventually be found.

The second approach is called *parallelism*. It can be seen as a breadth-first search through the tree of alternative analyses. At each point where more than one alternative exists, all paths are pursued simultaneously. True parallelism requires multiple processors. *Pseudo*parallelism, where a single processor "timeshares" among the different paths, pushing each forward a bit at a time, is thus more common (for the time being at least). In this approach all analyses are found more or less simultaneously.

It should be clear that attempting to avoid nondeterminism binds the grammar more tightly to the parser. A nondeterministic parser can support a wide range of grammatical formalisms, with little constraint on the form or content of particular grammars. A deterministic parser, on the other hand, obliges those who write grammars for it to produce unambiguous grammars, in the extended sense previously described. The way in which this is done will depend on exactly what mechanisms the deterministic parser provides for coping with local ambiguity.

To end where we began: It is the ambiguity of natural language that makes parsing an issue at all. The amazing fact is that although local ambiguity pervades our speech to an incredible extent, we are rarely aware of or troubled by it. Any natural language interpretation system must confront this issue in some way, regardless of the particular language-processing task for which it is functioning as an aid.

Bibliography

Abbreviations used—IJCAI: International Joint Conference on Artificial Intelligence; AISB: Society for the Study of Artificial Intelligence and Simulation of Behavior Conference on Artificial Intelligence; TINLAP: Workshop on Theoretical Issues in Natural Language Processing (Vol. 1 edited by Schank and Nash-Webber, Vol. 2 edited by Waltz—see details below); CACM: Communications of the Association for Computing Machinery; JACM: Journal of the Association for Computing Machinery.
*Indicates general or background material.

ALPAC. "Languages and Machines: Computers in Translation and Linguistics." Report by the Automatic Language Processing Advisory Committee, National Research Council, Pub. No. 1416, Washington, D.C., 1966.

Austin, J. L. *How to Do Things with Words*. Oxford: Oxford University Press, 1962.

Bar-Hillel, Y. "The Present Status of Automatic Translation of Languages." In Alt, F. L. (Ed.), *Advances in Computers,* Vol. I. New York: Academic Press, 1960.

Bates, M. "The Theory and Practice of Augmented Transition Network Grammars." In Bolc, L. (Ed.), *Natural Language Communication with Computers*. Berlin: Springer Lecture Notes in Computer Science 63, 1978.

Berwick, R. "Locality Principles and the Acquisition of Syntactic Knowledge." Ph.D. Thesis. Cambridge, Mass.: MIT AI Lab, 1982.

*Bobrow, D. G., and Collins, A. (Eds.). *Representation and Understanding: Studies in Cognitive Science*. New York: Academic Press, 1975.

Bobrow, D. G., and Fraser, J. B. "An Augmented State Transition Network Analysis Procedure." *IJCAI* 1: 557–567, 1969.

Bobrow, D. G., Kaplan, R. M., Kay, M., Norman, D. A., Thompson, H., and Winograd, T. "GUS: A Frame-Driven Dialog System." *Artificial Intelligence* 8: 155–173, 1977.

Bobrow, R. J., and Webber, B. L. "PSI-KLONE—Parsing and Semantic Interpretation in the BBN Natural Language Understanding System." In *Proceedings of the CSCSI/SCEIO Conference,* May, 1980a.

Bobrow, R. J., and Webber, B. L. "Knowledge Representation for Syntactic/Semantic Processing." *Proceedings of the First Annual National Conference on Artificial Intelligence,* 316–323. Stanford, Calif., August, 1980b.

Bobrow, D. G., and Winograd, T. "An Overview of KRL, a Knowledge Representation Language." *Cognitive Science* 1(1): 3–46, 1977a.

Bobrow, D. G., and Winograd, T. "Experience with KRL-0: One cycle of a knowledge representation language." *IJCAI* 5:213–222, 1977b.

*Boden, M. A. *Artificial intelligence and natural man.* Hassocks, Sussex: Harvester Press, 1977.

Boguraev, B. K. "Automatic Resolution of Linguistic Ambiguities." Technical Report No. 11. Cambridge, England: Computer Laboratory, Cambridge University, 1980.

Bolinger, D. "The Atomisation of Meaning." *Language* 41(4): 555–573, 1965.

Brachman, R. J. "On the Epistemological Status of Semantic Networks." In Findler, N. V. (Ed.), *Associative Networks.* New York: Academic Press, 1979.

Brachman, R. J. et al. "Research in Natural Language Understanding." BBN Report 4274. Cambridge, Mass.: Bolt, Beranek and Newman, 1979.

Brady, M. (Ed.). *Computational Models of Discourse.* Cambridge, Mass: MIT Press, 1983.

Bruce, B. C. "Case Systems for Natural Language." *Artificial Intelligence* 6: 327–360, 1975.

Bruce, B., and Newman, D. "Interacting Plans." *Cognitivie Science* 2: 195–233.

Bundy, A., and Stone, M. "A Note on McDermott's Symbol-Mapping Problem." *ACM SIGART Newsletter* 53: 9–10, 1975.

Charniak, E. "A Brief for Case." Working Paper 22. Geneva: Institute for Semantic and Cognitive Studies, 1975.

Charniak, E. "A Parser with Something for Everyone." Technical Report No. CS-70, Department of Computer Science, Brown University. Also in King, M. (Ed.), *Parsing Natural Language.* New York, Academic Press, 1983.

*Charniak, E., Riesbeck, C., and McDermott, D. *Artificial Intelligence Programming.* Hillsdale, N.J.: Erlbaum, 1980.

*Charniak, E., and Wilks, Y. (Eds). *Computational Semantics.* Amsterdam: North-Holland, 1975.

Chomsky, N. *Syntactic Structures.* The Hague: Mouton, 1957.

Chomsky, N. *Aspects of the Theory of Syntax.* Cambridge, Mass: MIT Press, 1965.

Chomsky, N. *Reflections on Language.* London: Fontana, 1975.

Church, K. M. On Memory Limitations in Natural Language Processing. Master's thesis. Cambridge, Mass.: MIT Laboratory for Computer Science, 1980.

Colmerauer, A. "Les Systèmes-Q ou un Formalisme pour Analyser et Synthetiser des Phrases sur Ordinateur." Internal Publication 43, Department d'Informatique, Université de Montreal, Canada, 1970.

Conway, M. E. "Design of a Separable Transition-Diagram Compiler." *CACM* 6: 396–408, 1963.

Davey, A. C. "Formalisation of Discourse Production." Ph.D. thesis. Edinburgh: University of Edinburgh, 1974. (Available from Edinburgh University Press as "Discourse production," 1978).

Davies, D. J. M., and Isard, S. D. "Utterances as Programs." In Meltzer, B., and Michie, D. (Eds.), *Machine Intelligence 7.* Edinburgh: Edinburgh University Press, 1972.

Dewar, H., Bratley, P., and Thorne, J. P. "A Program for the Syntactic Analysis of English Sentences." *CACM* 12: 476–479, 1969.

Earley, J. "An Efficient Context-Free Parsing Algorithm." *CACM* 13(2): 94–102, 1970.

Fahlman, S. E. *NETL: A System for Representing and Using Real-World Knowledge.* Cambridge, Mass.: MIT Press, 1979.

*Feigenbaum, E. A., and Feldman, J. (Eds). *Computers and Thought.* New York: McGraw-Hill, 1964.

Fillmore, C. J. "The Case for Case." In Bach, E. and Harms, R. T. (Eds.), *Universals in Linguistic Theory.* New York: Holt, Rinehart and Winston, 1968.

Findler, N. V. (Ed.) *Associative Networks.* New York: Academic Press, 1979.

Fodor, J. A. "Three Reasons for Not Deriving 'Kill' from 'Cause to Die.' " *Linguistic Inquiry* 1: 429–438, 1970.

Gazdar, G. "Phrase Structure Grammar." In Jacobson, P., and Pullum, G. (Eds.) *The Nature of Syntactic Representation.* Dordrecht: Reidel, 1981.

Goldman, N. M. "Conceptual generation." In Schank, R. C. (Ed.), *Conceptual Information Processing.* Amsterdam: North-Holland, 1975.

Grosz, B. "The representation and use of focus in a system for understanding dialog." *IJCAI* 5, 1977.

Hayes, P. J. "Some problems and non-problems in representation theory." *AISB-74:* 63–79, 1974.

Hayes, P. J. "In defence of logic." *IJCAI* 5:559–565, 1977.

Hayes, P. J. "The logic of frames." In Metzing, D. (Ed.), *Frames Conceptions and Text Understanding.* Berlin: de Gruyter, 1979.

Hendrix, G. G. "The LIFER Manual: A guide to building practical natural language interfaces." Technical Note 138, SRI Artificial Intelligence Center, Menlo Park, Calif., 1977.

Hendrix, G. G., Sacerdoti, E. D., Sagalowicz, D., and Slocum, J. "Developing a natural language interface to complex data." *ACM Transactions on Databases* 3 (2): 105–147, 1978.

Hughes, G., and Cresswell, M. *Introduction to Modal Logic.* London: Methuen, 1973.

Johnson R. "Parsing with transition networks." In King, M. (Ed.), *Parsing Natural Language.* New York: Academic Press, 1983.

Johnson-Laird, P. N. "Procedural Semantics." *Cognition* 5 (3): 189–214, 1977.

Kaplan, R. M. "Augmented Transition Networks as Psychological Models of Sentence Comprehension." *Artificial Intelligence* 3: 77–100, 1972.

Kaplan, R. M. "On Process Models for Sentence Analysis." In Norman, D. A., Rumelhart, D. E. and the LNR Research Group, *Explorations in Cognition.* San Francisco: Freeman, 1975.

Kaplan, R. M., and Bresnan, J. "Lexical-Functional Grammar: A Formal System of Grammatical Representation." In Bresnan (Ed.), *The Mental Representation of Grammatical Relations.* Cambridge, Mass.: MIT Press, 1982.

Kaplan, R. M., and Kay, M. "Word Recognition." Technical Report, Palo Alto, Calif.: Xerox Palo Alto Research Centre, 1982.

Katz, J. J., and Fodor, J. A. "The Structure of a Semantic Theory." *Language,* 39,(2): 170–210, 1963. (Also in *The Structure of Language.* Fodor, J. A. and Katz, J. J. (Eds.), Englewood Cliffs, N.J.: Prentice-Hall, 1964.)

Kay, M. "The MIND System." In Rustin, R. (Ed.), *Natural Language Processing.* Englewood Cliffs, N.J.: Prentice-Hall, 1973.

Kay, M. "Morphological and Syntactic Analysis." In Zampolli, A. (Ed.), *Linguistic Structures Processing.* Amsterdam: North-Holland, 1977.

Kay, M. "Algorithm Schemata and Data Structures in Syntactic Processing." In *Proceedings of the Symposium on Text Processing.* Nobel Academy, (to appear). (Also, CSL-80-12, Xerox PARC, Palo Alto, Calif., 1980.)

King, M. "Transformational Parsing." In King, M. (Ed.), *Parsing Natural Language.* New York, Academic Press, 1983a.

*King, M. (Ed.). *Parsing Natural Language.* New York: Academic Press, 1983b.

Kuno, S. "Predictive Analysis and a Path Elimination Technique." *CACM* 8, 687–698, 1965.

Lehnert, W. "Human and Computational Question Answering." *Cognitive Science* 1(1): 47–73, 1977.

Lowerre, B. T. "The HARPY Speech Recognition System." Ph.D. thesis. Pittsburgh: Department of Computer Science, Carnegie-Mellon University, 1976.

Marcus, M. P. "Diagnosis as a Notion of Grammar." *TINLAP* 1: 6–10, 1975.

Marcus, M. P. "A Computational Account of Some Constraints on Language." *TINLAP* 2: 236–246, 1978.

Marcus, M. P. *A Theory of Syntactic Recognition for Natural Language.* Cambridge, Mass.: MIT Press, 1980.

McCawley, J. D. "Pre-lexical Syntax." *Report of the 22nd Annual Round Table Meeting on Linguistics and Language Studies.* (Georgetown Monographs 22), 1971.

McCracken, D. "A Production System Version of the Hearsay-II Speech Understanding System." Technical Report No. CMU-CS-78-114. Pittsburgh, PA: Department of Computer Science, Carnegie-Mellon University, 1978.

McDermott, D. V. "Symbol-Mapping: A Technical Problem in PLANNER-like Systems." *ACM SIGART Newsletter* 51: 4, 1975a.

McDermott, D. V. "A Packet-Based Approach to the Symbol-Mapping Problem." *ACM SIGART Newsletter* 53: 6–7, 1975b.

McDermott, D. V. "Artificial Intelligence Meets Natural Stupidity." *ACM SIGART Newsletter* 57: 6–9, 1976.

McDonald, D. D. "Natural Language Production as a Process of Decision-Making Under Constraints." Ph.D. thesis. Cambridge, Mass. MIT, 1980.

Medress, M. et al. "Speech Understanding Systems: Report of a Steering Committee." *ACM SIGART Newsletter* 62: , 1977.

Mendelson, E. *Introduction to Mathematical Logic*. New York: Van Nostrand Reinhold, 1964.

Metzing, D. (Ed.) *Frame Conceptions and Text Understanding*. Berlin: de Gruyter, 1979.

Milne, R. W. "Predicting Garden Path Sentences." *Cognitive Science* 6(3): 349–373, 1982.

Minsky, M. *Computation—Finite and Infinite Machines*. (Introd. and Chap. 1). Englewood Cliffs, N.J.: Prentice-Hall, 1967.

*Minsky, M. (Ed.) *Semantic Information Processing*. Cambridge, Mass.: MIT Press, 1968.

Minsky, M. "A Framework for Representing Knowledge." In Winston (Ed.), *The Psychology of Computer Vision*. New York: McGraw-Hill, 1979.

Montague, R. "Universal Grammar." *Theoria* 36: 373–398, 1970a.

Montague, R. "English as a Formal Language I." In Visentini et al. (Eds.), *Linguaggi Nella Societa e Nella Tecnica*. Milan: , 1970b.

Montague, R. "Pragmatics and Intensional Logic." In Harman, G. and Davidson, D. (Eds.), *Semantics of Natural Language,* Dordrecht: Reidel, 1972.

Morris, C. "Foundations of the Theory of Signs." *International Encyclopedia of Unified Science* Vol. 1(2). Chicago: University of Chicago Press, 1938.

*Norman, D. A., Rumelhart, D. E., and the LNR Research Group. *Explorations in Cognition*. San Francisco: Freeman, 1975.

Pereira, F. C. N., and Warren, D. H. D. "Definite Clause Grammars for Language Analysis—A Survey of the Formalism and a Comparison with Augmented Transition Networks." *Artificial Intelligence* 13(3): 231–278, 1980.

Perrault, C. R., and Allen, J. F. "A Plan-Based Analysis of Indirect Speech Acts." *American Journal of Computational Linguistics* 6(3–4): 167–182, 1980.

Perrault, C. R., Allen, J. F., and Cohen, P. R. "Speech acts as a basis for understanding dialogue coherence." *TINLAP* 2: 125–132, 1978.

Petofi, J. S., and Rieser, H. (Eds.), *Studies in Text Grammar*. Dordrecht: Reidel, 1974.

Petrick, S. P. "Transformational Analysis." In Rustin, R. (Ed.), *Natural Language Processing*. Englewood Cliffs, N.J.: Prentice-Hall, 1973.

Plath, W. J. "Transformational Grammar and Transformational Parsing in the REQUEST System." In *Proceedings of International Conference on Computer Linguistics,* Pisa, 1973.

Prior, A. *Past, Present and Future*. Oxford: Oxford University Press, 1973.

Radford, A. *Transformational Syntax*. Cambridge, England: Cambridge University Press, 1981.

Rieger, C. "Conceptual Memory and Inference." In Schank, R. C. (Ed.), *Conceptual Information Processing*. Amsterdam: North-Holland, 1975b.

Riesbeck, C. K. "Computational Understanding: Analysis of Sentences and Context." Ph.D. thesis. Stanford, Calif.: Department of Computer Science, Stanford University, 1974.

Riesbeck, C. K. "Computational Understanding." *TINLAP* 1: 11–15, 1975a.

Riesbeck, C. K. "Conceptual Analysis." In Schank, R. C. (Ed.) *Conceptual Information Processing*. Amsterdam: North-Holland, 1975b.

Ritchie, G. D. "Augmented Transition Network Grammars and Semantic Processing." Technical Report CSR-20-78, Edinburgh: Department of Computer Science, University of Edinburgh, 1978.

Ritchie, G. D. *Computational Grammar—An Artificial Intelligence Approach to Linguistic Description.* Hassocks, Sussex: Harvester Press, 1980.

Ritchie, G. D. "Semantics in Parsing." In King, M. (Ed.), *Parsing Natural Language.* New York: Academic Press, 1983.

Ritchie, G. D., and Hanna F. K. "Semantic Networks: A General Definition and a Survey." *Information Technology: Research and Development* 2(3), 1983.

Roberts, R. B., and Goldstein, I. P. "The FRL Manual." Memo 409. Cambridge, Mass.: MIT AI Lab, 1977.

Rolling, L. "The Facts About Automatic Translation." In *Proceedings of the FID Symposium.* Edinburgh: University of Edinburgh, 1978.

Rumelhart, D. E., and Norman, D. A. "Active Semantic Networks as a Model of Human Memory." *IJCAI* 3: 450–457, 1973.

Rumelhart, D. E., and Norman, D. A. "The Active Structural Network." In Norman, D. A. and Rumelhart, D. E. (Eds.), *Explorations in Cognition.* San Francisco: Freeman, 1975.

*Rustin, R. (Ed.). *Natural Language Processing.* Englewood Cliffs, N.J.: Prentice-Hall, 1973.

Samlowski, W. "Case Grammar." In Charniak, E. and Wilks, Y. (Eds.), *Computational Semantics.* Amsterdam: North-Holland, 1975.

Sampson, G. "Deterministic Parsing." In King, M. (Ed.), *Parsing Natural Language.* New York: Academic Press, 1983.

Schank, R. C. "Conceptual Dependency: A Theory of Natural Language Understanding." *Cognitive Pscyhology* 3(4): 552–630, 1972.

Schank, R. C. "The Primitive ACTs of Conceptual Dependency." *TINLAP* 1: 34–37, 1975a.

Schank, R. C. (Ed.) *Conceptual Information Processing.* Amsterdam: North-Holland, 1975b.

Schank, R. C. "Using Knowledge to Understand." *TINLAP* 1: 117–121, 1975c.

Schank, R. C., and Abelson, R. P. "Scripts, Plans and Knowledge." *IJCAI* 4, 1975.

*Schank, R. C., and Colby, K. M. (Eds.) *Computer Models of Thought and Language.* San Francisco: Freeman, 1973.

Schank, R. C., Goldman, N. M., Rieger, C. J., and Riesbeck, C. K. "Inference and Paraphrase by Computer." *JACM* 22(3): 309–328, 1975.

Schank, R. C., Lebowitz, M., and Birnbaum, L. "An Integrated Understander." *American Journal of Computational Linguistics* 6(1): 1980.

*Schank, R. C., and Nash-Webber, B. L. (Eds.). *Proceedings of the Workshop on Theoretical Issues in Natural Language Processing (TINLAP 1).* Cambridge, Mass.: MIT, June 1975. (Available from ACM: may still be available from Association for Computational Linguistics.)

Schoenfield, J. *Mathematical Logic.* Reading, Mass.: Addison-Wesley, 1967.

Simmons, R. F. "Answering English Questions by Computer: A Survey." *CACM* 8: 53–70, 1965.

Stoll, R. R. *Set Theory and Logic.* New York: Dover, 1979.

Thomason, R. (Ed.) *Formal Philosophy: Selected papers of Richard Montague.* New Haven: Yale University Press, 1974.

Thompson, H. S. "Strategy and Tactics: A Model for Language Production." In *Papers from the 13th Meeting of Chicago Linguistic Society,* 1977.

Thompson, H. S. "Chart Parsing and Rule Schemata in GPSG." In *Proceedings of the 19th Annual Meeting of the Association for Computational Linguistics.* Alexandria, VA: Association for Computational Linguistics, 1981. (Also DAI Research Paper 165, Edinburgh: Department of Artificial Intelligence, University of Edinburgh).

Thompson, H. S. "Handling Metarules in a Parser for GPSG." In Barlow, M., Flickinger, D., and Sag, I. (Eds.), *Developments in Generalized Phrase Structure Grammars: Stanford Working Papers in Grammatical Theory,* Vol. 2, Bloomington, Ind.: Indiana University Linguistics Club, 1982.

Thorne, J. P., Bratley, P., and Dewar, H. "The Syntactic Analysis of English by Machine." In Michie (Ed.), *Machine Intelligence 3.* Edinburgh: Edinburgh University Press, 1968.

Toma, P. "Systran as a Multilingual Machine Translation System." In *Overcoming the Language Barrier. Third European Congress on Information Systems and Networks, Luxembourg.* Munchen: Verlag Dokumentation, 1977.

*Waltz, D. L. (Ed.) *Proceedings of the Second Workshop on Theoretical Issues in Natural Language Processing (TINLAP 2).* Champagne-Urbana, Illinois, July 1978. (Available from the Association for Computing Machinery.)

Weizenbaum, J. "ELIZA—A Computer Program for the Study of Natural Language Communication Between Man and Machine." *CACM* 9: 36–45, 1966.

Weizenbaum, J. "Contextual understanding by computers." *CACM* 10: 474–480, 1967.

Wilks, Y. "The Stanford Machine Intelligence Project." In Rustin, R. (Ed.), *Natural Language Processing.* Englewood Cliffs, N.J.: Prentice-Hall, 1973.

Wilks, Y. "An Intelligent Analyzer and Understander of English." *CACM* 18: 264–274, 1975a.

Wilks, Y. "Preference Semantics." In Keenan, E. L. (Ed.), *Formal Semantics of Natural Language.* Cambridge, England: Cambridge University Press, 1975b.

Wilks, Y. "Processing Case." *Amer. J. Comp. Ling.* 56: 1976.

Wilks, Y. "Making Preferences More Active." *Artificial Intelligence* 11(3): 197–223, 1978.

Wilks, Y. "Deep and Superficial Parsing." In King, M. (Ed.), *Parsing Natural Language.* New York: Academic Press, 1983.

Winograd, T. "*Understanding Natural Language.*" New York: Academic Press, 1972.

Winograd, T. "Towards a Procedural Understanding of Semantics." *Revue Internationale de Philosophie,* 3–4(117–118): 260–303, 1976.

Winograd, T. "On Some Contested Suppositions of Generative Linguistics About the Scientific Study of Language." Memo AIM-300. Stanford, Calif.: AI Laboratory, Stanford University, 1977. (Also *Cognition* 5(2): 151–179.)

*Winograd, T. *Language as a Cognitive Process, Vol. I: Syntax.* Reading, Mass.: Addison-Wesley, 1983.

Woods, W. A. "Procedural Semantics for a Question-Answering Machine." *Proceedings of Fall Joint Computer Conference,* 457–471, New York, 1968.

Woods, W. A. "Transition Network Grammars for Natural Language Analysis." *CACM* 13, 591–606, 1970.

Woods, W. A. "An Experimental Parsing System for Transition Network Grammars." In Rustin R. (Ed.), *Natural Language Processing.* Englewood Cliffs, N.J.: Prentice-Hall, 1973.

Woods, W. A. "What's in a Link?—Foundations for Semantic Networks." In Bobrow, D. G., and Collins, A. (Eds.), *Representation and Understanding: Studies in Cognitive Science.* New York: Academic Press, 1975a.

Woods, W. A. "Some Methodological Issues in Natural Language Understanding Research." *TINLAP* 1: 134–139, 1975b.

Woods, W. A. "Lunar Rocks in Natural English: Explorations in Natural Language Question Answering." In Zampolli, A. (Ed.), *Linguistic Structures Processing.* Amsterdam: North-Holland, 1977.

Woods, W. A. et al. "Speech Understanding Systems—Final report." BBN Report 3438. Cambridge, Mass.: Bolt, Beranek and Newman, 1976.

Woods, W. A., Nash-Webber, B. L., and Kaplan, R. M. "The Lunar Sciences Natural Language System: Final Report." BBN Report 2265. Cambridge, Mass.: Bolt, Beranek and Newman, 1972.

Woods, W. A., and Makhoul, J. "Mechanical Inference Problems in Continuous Speech Understanding." *Artificial Intelligence* 5: 73–91, 1974.

*Zampolli, A. (Ed.) *Linguistic Structures Processing.* Amsterdam: North Holland, 1977.

Zwicky, A. et al. "The MITRE Syntactic Analysis Procedure for Transformational Grammar." *Proceedings of Fall Joint Computer Conference.* New York, 1965.

CHAPTER 12

INDUSTRIAL ROBOTICS

WILLIAM F. CLOCKSIN
and
PETER G. DAVEY

INTRODUCTION

Since the 1950s, industrial automation has been the province of the production engineer and control engineer. To the production engineer, industrial robotics simply concerns the development of advanced machine tools in which the possibilities offered by modern control and computing systems are used to provide greater flexibility and adaptability. The basic machinery is not really new. For example, a considerable amount of logic circuitry is contained in controllers of machine tools (milling machines, lathes, and machining centres) and special-purpose assembly equipment such as that used for producing small consumer items such as light bulbs and "disposable" ball-point pens. What is new is that recent advances in microelectronics and software technology provide the potential to increase the complexity and hence the apparent "intelligence" of robotic tools.

Advanced robotic manufacturing equipment offers the possibility that the form of the final product needs only to be roughly known when the initial investment in the production machinery is made. Such a production line would be "programmable" so that changes in the design of the product could be accommodated by reprogramming existing equipment instead of dismantling and rebuilding special-purpose machinery. The purpose of this chapter is to describe what today's industrial robots actually are, what jobs they are doing, how their use is justified, and the kind of improvements that industry would like to see tomorrow.

A LOOK AT MANUFACTURING

Figure 12.1 shows a general model of what abstract tasks are involved in a typical manufacturing plant. This model usually applies whether the plant is a multimillion pound industrial complex for building motorcars, or a cottage business making leather handbags. Fed into the plant are raw materials, component parts, and tools. These items must be unloaded from conveyances such as trucks and trains, unpacked from their containers, and stored in the factory stores. The operations usually performed on the materials are machining (milling or carving into shape); fabrication (stamping, pressing, punching, bending); assembly (bolting, welding, sewing, inserting); preparation and finish (painting, polishing); and finally, testing and inspecting the product. At each stage of the process, parts and tools are loaded and unloaded, materials are added or removed, and parts are mated and measured. While work is in progress, there are subassemblies, and jigs and fixtures to help hold parts and subassemblies. These must all be stored and unstored as the occasion demands. The finished product must be unstored, packed into a container, loaded on a conveyance, and taken away.

When considering these tasks, it is helpful to examine the time interval between when a decision is made to do the task and when the task is actually carried out. Such intervals constitute a decision timing spectrum. For example, it is possible that the time interval for a decision to do an assembly can be very long. From the time we decide to assemble a motorcar to the time we begin the work can vary from days to months. In other applications, the time interval is short: when welding, the decision how to move the torch to follow the seam must be made immediately. In yet other applications, the time interval is actually negative. For example, if an error occurs, we can only decide how to recover from the error after it occurs, but this time interval should be short. A longer negative interval is acceptable for production

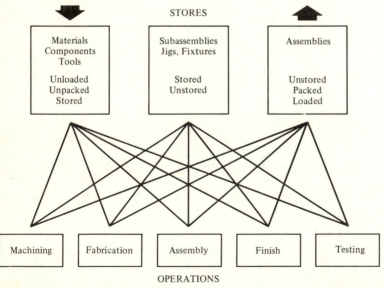

Figure 12.1

analysis (or "learning"), where it may be necessary to perform the task many times in order to establish what the trend is.

Such a spectrum can help us to decide what form of automation is appropriate, and thus how to distribute computational resources when designing robots and writing the programs to control them. For example, it is worth spending a lot of time planning an assembly task. It is expensive to debug entire production lines if there is a bug in the generated assembly plan. On the other hand, sensor-controlled robots must be able to react to external changes in fractions of seconds. Error recovery should commence a short time after the error is detected so that the undesirable effects do not propagate along the production line to other machinery.

The factory environment is not inherently orderly. Some sources of disorder cannot be controlled, such as variability of batch requirements due to unpredictable demands for products made in batches. Other uncontrollable factors are characteristics of the human work force: variations in the quality of work; variations in the rate of production; and errors of interpretation, implementation, and documentation. On the other hand, some disorders are potentially controllable or predictable, such as consistency of raw materials and processes; control of production flow; and control of machine output in terms of quality and rate. Of course, controlling such disorders may be very expensive and not worthwhile.

The factory environment is likely to be very different from the relatively comfortable office or laboratory in which robot software is written. To take automotive assembly, for example, there is electrical interference from welding; there is loud noise; and the lighting is of unpredictable brightness, flicker, and spectral content. These can interfere with electrical circuits, ultrasonic sensors, and visual/infrared sensors. Buttons are pressed with greasy fingers and gloved hands. Smoke, sparks, and molten metal that spatter from the welding process can also interfere with sensing. In a chemical plant, powders, aerosols, and corrosive vapours are present. These work their way into the mechanics and sensors of a robot. Furthermore, in many industrialised countries, the government specifies strict regulations about the health and safety of workers who interact with machinery. The purpose of this catalogue of horrors is not to discourage the would-be robot designer but to describe real and challenging problems that can stimulate good academic research and profoundly influence the design of "intelligent" robot software and hardware.

ROBOTS

One way to describe what is required of robots is to explain what nonflexible machinery is like. In manufacturing plants that do not have robots, all the tools that construct the product need to be specially designed and built. Jigs and fixtures hold specific parts at a specific location in space. These are purpose-built mechanisms that cost a lot of money. Much of the expense in building motorcars, for example, is actually in building the tools that build the motorcars. A jig for holding, turning over, and welding a motorcar chassis may cost a million pounds to design and build. Once it is built, it does only one job. If even minor modifications to the motorcar design are required, it may be necessary to dismantle and rebuild at least part of the jig.

Flexible devices, in the form of robots, can provide three improvements to this situation. First, the robot (or a team of robots) could act as a jig, holding subassemblies in specified ways.

If modifications are required in how the part is held, then it is much cheaper to reprogram the robots than it is to dismantle and rebuild the special-purpose equipment. Second, much of the expense of jigs is a result of the fact that they are precision machines that will hold the parts to within fractions of a millimetre of a known position. It is much less expensive to design and build jigs that are not so precise (and also, robots are not that precise). So if a robot can use sensors to locate accurately a feature of a part, given a rough estimate of its position, then we can compare the cost of providing precision machinery with the cost of using sensor-equipped robots. A compelling analogy here is with the human hand, which although not a precision device on its own, is normally used together with tactile and visual feedback to enhance its dexterity and repeatability. Third, robots can be used in jobs that are too dangerous for people, such as welding and paint spraying. In certain factories, these are jobs that are so dangerous that people are (quite rightly) unwilling to do them for fear of injury or chronic illness. For example, welding produces toxic and carcinogenic fumes, splatters of molten metal, and intense radiation that may cause eye injury and skin cancer. The welder must take up awkward positions in hot, confined spaces while weighted down with equipment and protective clothing. These advantages of robots are among those considered when justifying the use of robots in industry. We will return to this topic later.

The current robots on the market consist of a mechanical arm, actuators, encoders, a controller, and a power source. The arm can be articulated (Fig. 12.2), rather like a human

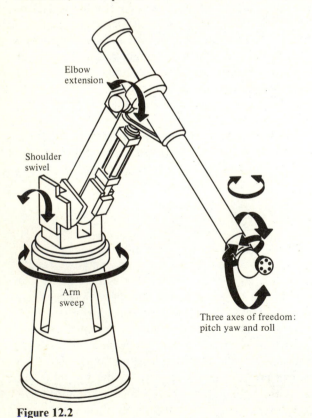

Elbow
extension

Shoulder
swivel

Arm
sweep

Three axes of freedom:
pitch yaw and roll

Figure 12.2

arm, or it could have a cartesian configuration rather like a gantry crane. Even more common are "polar" and "cylindrical" configurations. There are normally anywhere from three to six joints, each of which is said to provide one "degree of freedom." Six degrees of freedom are the minimum required for the robot to place the tool at any (X, Y, Z) point and (pitch, roll, yaw) angle in space. Each joint can be prismatic (sliding in and out) or revolute (rotational). The actuators are what move the joints: These can be electric motors, hydraulic actuators, or pneumatic actuators. Hydraulic actuators are preferred only where the highest power-to-weight ratio is required. Electric actuators are precise and easily controlled, so these meet most of the requirements. Pneumatic actuators have few advantages other than very low cost. The robot uses encoders to sense the amount by which each joint is actuated. This enables servomechanism control of each joint by comparing the desired joint position with the actual one, and feeding the error signal to the actuator for that joint. As with other sensors, faster operation can be obtained by feeding back proportional, differentiated, and integrated error signals; the study of these issues is the province of the control engineer. Encoders are usually implemented by using synchro-resolvers, optical shaft encoders, or potentiometers, either singly or in combination.

The controller provides the interface between the electromechanics of the robot and the commands from the user. The controller is usually based on one or more microprocessors. The controller handles servomechanism control of the motors, detects joint limits and error conditions, maintains operating modes (teach, single step, auto), and stores the user's program. More sophisticated controllers provide facilities for off-line programming, transformation of coordinate systems, and links to other machines and sensors. The power source of the robot is normally supplied through the normal electricity distribution network, but additional supplies of compressed air or hydraulic pumps are required for those joints that are actuated by pneumatics or hydraulics.

Among the dimensions on which such robots vary are the load capacity (at rest) of the robot, the precision at which the robot can repeatedly move to a specified point in space, the type of actuators used, and how many axes of movement are normally supplied. Many industrial robots have a geometry resembling Figure 12.2, with revolute joints. Other geometries include prismatic "forearms," based on rack and pinion and five degrees-of-freedom arms, with pitch and roll being the only angular motions at the wrist.

"TEACHING" ROBOTS WHAT TO DO

When specifying how the robot is to move, the programmer must provide information in the form of a program, rather as in a computer program. The process of programming the robot's movements is known in the industrial robotics trade as "teaching." The notion of programming for which robot controllers cater is rather more impoverished than what a typical computer programming language might offer. The basic function is to move each of the robot's joints to a specified position. This has the effect of moving the tool in the robot's "hand" to a desired position and orientation in space. Three kinds of information must be specified: geometric, motion, and action.

1. *Geometric*. It must be possible to specify the position and orientation of the tool in the hand of the robot's arm. Different robot controllers provide different means of specifying this,

and various coordinate systems can be used. Some robots permit the programmer to manually drive each joint of the robot into a particular configuration and then to store the resulting coordinates in the program. This is "teaching by showing." More sophisticated controllers allow the programmer to specify positions and orientations in terms of cartesian "world" and "tool" coordinate systems, so that movements can be specified relative to the tool tip, or relative to the jig, for example. This feature depends on the controller having a kinematic model of the robot arm. The model usually takes the form of about a dozen equations having trigonometric and other nonlinear terms. The computational power needed to use the model to transform between tool coordinates and joint positions in real-time (say 50 to 100 transformations per second) is just within the reach of today's fast 16-bit microprocessors.

2. *Motion.* When moving from one programmed point to another, the robot requires information about when to accelerate and decelerate and whether a straight line or a curve must connect the points. The least sophisticated controllers, at least from the programmer's point of view, offer only a "continuous path" mode. In this case, the programmer leads the robot arm through arbitrary movements, and the controller stores these movements and plays them back when required. No internal geometric coordinates are made available to the programmer. Continuous path control is used mainly for paint spraying, where a smooth trajectory is required, but where the programmer does not find it necessary to manipulate an internal representation of the taught path. Most robot controllers work in a "point-to-point" mode, in which an internal representation of programmed points is available, but the actual trajectory between the two points is not under the control of the programmer. The robot will not necessarily connect the points by a straight line, but may do so by a curve that depends on the rate at which the individual joint angles are incremented by the controller. More sophisticated controllers, working in a "world" coordinate system, can interpolate world coordinate points on the line connecting the two programmed points and transform between world coordinates and joint angles in real time along the line. Also, the velocity of a movement is important. In arc welding, for example, a specified constant velocity is needed. In other applications, the velocity may not be what is specified, as long as the motion is completed before a specified point in time.

3. *Action.* The robot's end effector can be equipped with tools that are specific to the job, such as grippers, grinders, routers, drills, spray nozzles, welding torches, cutting torches, jigs, saws, polishers, and so forth. These tools need to be switched on and off at times that are specified in the program. Also, the robot may need to examine the state of a number of switches, such as limit switches and interlock switches. For this reason, most controllers offer some uncommitted input/output ports for the use of the customer.

Successive movements of the robot arm must be ordered in a specified sequence. Normally, the controller executes one "taught" instruction after another in the order that is specified in the program. However, as with computer programming languages, it is often necessary to alter the order of execution at runtime. The decision can be based on variables that are internal to the program, as with conditionals in computer programming languages. Or, the decision must be based on combinations of conditions in the work environment. This is what sensing is all about, and rudimentary sensors are being fitted to some robots in today's factories. These sensors include limit switches, torque sensors to detect if a motor is being stressed (useful in grinding and sawing), and photocells to detect the absence or presence of a part in a specified place.

JUSTIFICATION FOR USING ROBOTS

Now that we have seen what today's robots offer the production manager, we turn to how the use of such flexible devices on the factory floor can be justified. We have already touched on two advantages of using robots: to automate tasks that are too dangerous for people to do and to reduce the cost in adapting a factory to produce a modified product. This reduces the lead time to develop new models and new products. Here are a few more advantages:

1. *Reduce Wasted Investment in Work-in-Progress.* An important cost of running a factory is in storing subassemblies that are not being used and in transporting subassemblies between work stations and stores. Faster and more uniform work-cycle times that are offered by robots can reduce costly bulges in the production pipeline. Automated conveyances that are controlled by a supervisory communications network can also help.
2. *Better Use of Major Capital Plant.* A robot used for paint spraying is likely to yield savings of materials (paint) of up to 50 percent. Furthermore, exhaust air volumes can be halved. In welding, for example, robots can move from one part to another more quickly than can be done with manual welding. This means that the time spent actually welding is a larger proportion of the total working time.
3. *Low Cost for Custom Designed Products.* Flexible automation provides the potential to manufacture custom designed products in small batches, with the low cost associated with mass production.
4. *Higher Quality Products.* Increased automation brings about more consistent production, and as a result of this and quick reprogrammability, a product of higher quality.

All of these advantages can work directly toward increasing productivity (the amount of product manufactured per unit of time) and toward retaining or increasing market share.

It is clear that increased automation results in social consequences. These are important issues that bear careful consideration. The most immediate consequence is that jobs are less likely to be lost in the firm or country that is able to automate widely, since its market share is likely to increase. Certain other advantageous side effects accrue if robotics is carefully introduced by enlightened management. For example, flexible automation narrows the gulf between the production engineer and the design engineer, so that closer interaction is possible. Furthermore, with dangerous and soporific tasks being carried out by robots, manual labour would bring to bear a mix of tasks in a given job, which is more satisfying than doing a single repetitive task day in and day out.

With regard to automation in the motorcar industry, one so-called advantage that journalists are fond of relating is that robots do not take coffee breaks. Perhaps in reply it should be pointed out to them that robots do not buy motorcars, either!

ADVANTAGES OF INTELLIGENT ROBOTS

So far we have dealt with robots as they exist in factories today. Many of the tasks that robots now carry out in industry require no sensors at all, but the robots that appear in this decade are going to have much in the way of sensory equipment, that is, vision, hearing, touch, and so forth. It is the robot's use of such sensors that will allow them to carry out jobs that they could not possibly tackle today.

The tasks that robots cannot do now are characterised by the fact that the world in which the robot is operating is imperfect or variable. Take, for example, the arc welding of pressed steel sheets about 1 or 2 millimetres thick. It is impossible to teach the robot in advance the precise location of where the seams are to be welded, because of tolerances in the pressing process and the movement of the metal during heating, and because sheet steel varies in flexibility. Another example is in cleaning the burrs from castings. If the casting process were so precise that the positions of burrs were known in advance, then they could be eliminated during casting. The whole point is that the burrs are essentially random in size and position, and a robot whose job it is to remove them can best work by feeling or seeing where they are.

Robots need to be able to cope with the inevitable errors that occur during the manufacturing process. Consider a spectrum of error severity that classifies errors and possible ways to recover from them. Suppose the robot is attempting to insert a peg into a hole. The least severe error is when the robot is given a situation that can be corrected by altering some variables at runtime. In this case, the hole may be displaced from its expected position. This can happen because of cumulative errors in parts tolerances, imperfect fit of parts, or perhaps wear in the driving system of the robot. A robot should be able to sense the actual position of the hole and to insert the pin in the sensed hole.

The next most severe error occurs when the robot must change its strategy at runtime. For example, the hole may be plugged with a plastic bung. Or, the view of the hole may be obscured by shavings and burrs left over from when the hole was drilled. Such conditions can be specified by a "messy looking" hole. A typical action to take in this case might be to ream out the hole.

The most severe error occurs when it is necessary as a result of the preceding conditions to abandon the task. This might be necessary if the robot cannot reach the hole or if a hole cannot be detected or if the pin becomes stuck or if the pin falls out of the robot's gripper. Also included in this category of errors is power failure, tool breakage, manual intervention by pressing an emergency stop button, and so forth. If the robot is engaged on a task when such errors occur, it is desirable to retain the entire computational state of the task so that the robot can either resume the task or withdraw from it safely after the problem has been rectified.

When looking at the tasks that robots carry out, one would find it helpful to classify them on a rough scale of increasing disorder in their environment, like this:

1. *Spraying and Coating of Powders, Paints, and Adhesives.* Some sensory feedback is an advantage if we wish the robot not to paint thin air when a part is unexpectedly removed.
2. *Arc Welding.* Sensory feedback becomes more desirable as tolerances worsen due to the unpredictable flexibility of thin sheet steel.
3. *Foundry and Deburring.* Sensory (force) feedback is essential to prevent tool breakage.
4. *Mechanical and Electronic Assembly.* It is seldom economic to position parts accurately enough so that they could be assembled completely by dead reckoning.
5. *Clothing and Rubber Industries.* Robotic manufacture with intrinsically floppy materials is particularly demanding on sensory feedback.
6. *Maintenance.* Pipes and pressure vessels in chemical plants are often in dangerous locations,

and they must be inspected and repaired occasionally. Such applications are dependent on sensory feedback, especially in difficult and dangerous environments.

Apart from overcoming problems of disorder in the environment, results of research into artificial intelligence and adaptive control should be able to bring other advantages to robotic devices. Although technically difficult, there may be possibilities for using linkages that are less stiff and include more play than at present, where these deficiencies are compensated for by sensory control systems. Again, the human arm that is controlled by senses of touch and vision is a tempting precedent. Research on compliance is a step in this direction. Since mechanical components seem certain to increase in cost while sensory and computing components will become cheaper, there is a potential here for achieving less expensive robots. Better control by overall sensory feedback will also result in the position accuracy of a robot relative to its workpiece being greater than the absolute accuracy of either. This is particularly important for delicate assembly work and in achieving fast cycle times.

RESEARCH AND DEVELOPMENT TOWARD THE INTELLIGENT ROBOT

There is a demand for robots that are faster, cheaper, and more accurate. Additionally, users are hoping for robotic systems that provide for better communication between components of the system. For example, coordinating the activity of two or three dozen robots on an assembly line is practically impossible without the use of at least one supervisory processor. Yet, many such systems that are installed in industry today consist of individually programmed robots that use perhaps one or two semaphores to communicate with a single neighbour down the assembly line. Users are also demanding robots that are more tolerant of disorder and imperfection in tools and parts, while maintaining high reliability. The cost of maintaining perfect order in a factory and its suppliers may be prohibitively high.

To meet these needs robot research includes the following aims:

- better dynamic control of robots to produce cheaper machines that are able to operate faster under heavy loads
- better visualisation of robot workplaces at the planning stage
- unmanned industrial trucks that are able to navigate without guidance wires
- robot arc welding systems that are able to cope with poorer fitup and to move within confined spaces
- improved gripper concepts, especially for flexible material
- integral use of robots with computer-aided design systems for complex tasks including assembly
- sensors with cheap, integral processor power
- inspection by robot, especially supervisory software to allow the process to adapt according to results of inspection and calibration

For those interested in pursuing robotics research, some less explored areas of research include:

· independent metrology of the end effector
· radical improvement in arm construction
· design of supervisory software
· process technology of assembly tasks

We feel it is sensible to channel the main research and development effort toward intelligence in robots over the next few years into industrial robotics, instead of, say, robots for undersea, agriculture, or mining work. The reasons for this are threefold. First, the level of variability can be kept relatively low, with small increments of sophistication in the problems tackled; this can help to ensure technical success. Second, as there are many jobs in industry that now appear dangerous for humans to do, developments are likely to be socially acceptable. Third, the survival of industrialised societies depends partly on raising productivity, in order to help to ensure that research funding will be available.

Several paths for research and development in industrial robotics look as though they will eventually merge. The first is the further application and development of the familiar "universal" robot such as that depicted in Figure 12.2. This type of robot is already becoming somewhat specialised: paint-spraying robots no longer resemble spot-welding robots. These are regarded as devices that are taught relatively seldom and which then operate autonomously for periods from a few weeks to a few years.

The second path is the progressive improvement of dedicated automation machines by the addition of intelligent subsystems such as sensors, thus increasing their flexibility and adaptability to minor variations in the components being produced.

The third path is the addition of computing "intelligence" to take over the simpler and more repetitive tasks from the human operator in remote-manipulator devices. Much of the technology of the remote manipulator is identical to the universal robot, but since there is an operator in charge instead of a computer, more emphasis is placed on trying to achieve an optimal man-machine interface.

Fourth, there is continuous improvement in automatic inspection machinery. The development of fast noncontacting measuring devices will be of the greatest importance in providing the high-grade sensors that are needed to locate a workpiece accurately enough for assembly tasks.

Clearly, it is most important to choose correctly and to time research tasks in applying artificial intelligence techniques to robotics. If research is too early or too sophisticated in technique, then such projects may never really relate to real products or applications. Too late or too naive, and they may actually be behind industrial practice by the time they are complete. Correctly timed, their results will cause a dramatic increase in the rate that robots are applied to new tasks.

Bibliography

The following sources will be helpful in finding out more about robotics as practised in industry today.

Engleberger, J. F. *Robots and People.* Bedford, England: IFS Publications, 1980. Joe Engleberger is the president of Unimation, Inc., the largest of the early robot manufacturers in the United States and somewhat of a legend as the "father" of the first successful industrial robot.

Groover, M. P. *Automation, Production Systems, and Computer-Aided Manufacturing,* Englewood Cliffs, N.J.: Prentice-Hall, 1980. Provides a comprehensive and detailed survey of various topics in production automation, industrial robots, computer-aided design and manufacturing, machine tool programming, flexible manufacturing systems, and materials requirements planning. Almost everything is here in one book.

Simons, G. L. *Robots in Industry.* Birmingham, England: National Computing Centre, 1980. This 200-page book covers in detail all the aspects mentioned in this chapter. The book concentrates more on specification and performance of existing industrial robots and cost-benefit analysis.

British Robot Association. A professional body that promotes the use of robots in industry, and sponsors a series of yearly conferences that publishes proceedings and accepts AI-related papers. Relevant conferences are the *International Conference on Assembly Automation,* and the *International Conference on Robot Vision and Sensory Controls.*

IFS Publications, in association with the British Robot Association, publishes and distributes a variety of books and magazines (such as those previously listed), dealing with all aspects of industrial robots, with emphasis on management, marketing, and engineering. Their principal quarterly magazine is *The Industrial Robot.* The address of both bodies is: 35–39 High Street, Kemston, Bedford MK42 7BT, England.

International Journal of Robotics Research. A new quarterly journal that promises to be a reputable forum for research in robotics. Published by MIT Press, Cambridge, Mass.

International Symposium on Industrial Robotics. A yearly conference, now in its 13th year, publishes a lengthy proceedings. Papers on AI-related topics are accepted.

CHAPTER 13

TEXT PROCESSING

PAUL LEFRERE

INTRODUCTION

> As a rule of thumb, anything as easy to learn as a typewriter is as useful as a typewriter. (Finseth, 1982, p. 302)

Text editing is sometimes described as an example of "information technology," since it involves manipulation of information. Yet real information technology systems help with three more general needs: acceleration, augmentation, and delegation. *Acceleration* means speeding up the acquisition of a given piece of information (e.g., by linking a text editor to a data base). *Augmentation* refers to ways of assisting a user in the substance of the task, rather than the pace of the task. Augmentation can occur in two ways: saving so much time that a user decides to attempt a task or reducing the need for alertness or perseverance. *Delegation* refers to occasions when the system itself can use programmed criteria to make decisions that a user would otherwise make. A simple example would be "humanised" data input: letting a user fill in a form on a terminal in any order; here, the program will have to guess from earlier entries where an input such as DEC 20 should appear (in the field for the date or the field for computers?).

If only experienced users are to use a system, it may be possible to predict their needs and the roles they will have for the system. For example, consider the augmentation needs of programmers. Slips of various kinds are common when writing a program, but their effect can be reduced by using a language-directed editor. For those unfamiliar with them, these editors *know* the major structural characteristics of a programming language (i.e., its lexical, syntactic, and semantic aspects, as explained briefly later). So they can manipulate program structures rather than manipulate program text. This means that they can combine the text-manipulation functions of an on-line editor with the syntax-checking functions of a compiler—including checks for syntactic correctness *as text is entered*. Their advocates say that they allow speedier creation and modification of a program in terms of its syntactic structure (Morris & Schwartz, 1981; but see also Waters [1981] for a comparison of these syntax editors and the "Programmer's Apprentice": an editor that allows a user to build up a program from prototypical fragments or to modify it in terms of its logical structure).

Language-directed editors are interesting because they indicate what can be achieved with a system that is tailored to a particular and reasonably well-specified task. If the language-directed approach does save time, even a partial implementation of it might improve natural language or text editors. The problem here is the complexity of ordinary or natural language. We take for granted our ability to see that sequences of characters are combined into words, those words form sentences and those sentences convey the meaning of the text. We recognize as difficult the task of getting a program to "understand" the same text. One approach is to analyse the text as if it can be processed first *lexically,* then *syntactically,* and finally *semantically.* (Briefly, a lexical analyser takes a string of characters and identifies the individual words in the input; a syntactic analyser identifies sentences and implicit grammatical relationships; whereas a semantic analyser takes sentences and uses them to assign some meaning to the text.)

It is possible to reduce the complexity of ordinary language in specific domains—for example, special-purpose texts such as letters, memoranda, and technical documents. But even there it is difficult to build up an explicit syntactic/semantic description of what constitutes a valid document, let alone model how people produce such documents. It is not surprising that even the best of current "ordinary language" text editors have no intelligence—no sensitivity to and no understanding of what is being edited. This is a consequence of the ways in which the text is represented: all too often, this is in terms of characters of text and lines of text, rather than paragraphs and chapters. Accordingly, these editors are not oriented in a principled way to writing, reading, or even copy typing or editing, which may be one reason that both experienced users and computer-naive users take a significant time to master each editor they encounter (Embley & Nagy, 1981).

Earlier in this section we noted that it may be possible to predict most of the needs of experienced users. It may even be possible to get a good idea of their needs by asking them what they would like. But at the moment, there are more inexperienced computer users than experienced ones. If users are inexperienced, the needs they perceive and express may differ from their revealed or actual needs. One way to reveal probable needs is through the collection of detailed records (protocols) of users' interactions with computer systems, recording both their keystrokes and their verbal comments. Alternatively (or additionally), those protocols may include videotapes of users. Such protocols often reveal idiosyncratic difficulties. For example, ". . . one learner . . . did not know what the cursor was, a second . . . thought the printer was a person and yet a third . . . thought she herself was the printer" (Lewis & Mack, 1982, p. 389). Protocols also reveal more disturbing general problems, such as learners' tendencies to misapply their previous experience or to go beyond what they are told. Although some of the problems revealed in protocols may lie in the individual user, others may stem from a mismatch between designers' and users' conceptions of tasks. The next section considers this point in more detail.

Bush's "MEMEX"

Most of us find it easier to modify an existing document than to create a document on a blank sheet of paper. In accordance with this, the design of the 1980s Xerox "Star" work station assumes that users will create material by copying existing objects (paragraphs, icons, etc.) and then modifying them. A precomputing perspective on this is provided by one of the first information scientists, Vannevar Bush. In his view, although it was desirable to offer an information system that could be tailored to suit individual users, this could not be done without some model of information acquisition and creation.

Consider information creation: The order in which ideas come to you when you are drafting something may not be the order you decide upon for the final version. Bush restated this need to reorganize material as a need for an infinitely deep structure for document outlines. Another need Bush identified was being able to draw upon existing material. He observed that no piece of information stood alone: It had a context, such as interconnections or links with a literature on that subject. Further, he felt that authors would either follow those links or create new ones. His proposal was to use the technology of his time—microfilm—to store as separate images, each idea or section of a document (Bush, 1945). Each such image was to be made available via a random-access console which he called the MEMEX. This would hold all the documents a person ever read or wrote and would allow the user to peruse "trails" of documents, creating "new" documents not just by adding or substituting further images but by putting in new trails—new structures. Simplifying Bush's argument considerably, this would make more evident the difference between a typical minor contribution and something entirely new. In the former case, it might be for the most part a recompilation and annotation of documents already in the MEMEX, a merging of a diagram from document A and a paragraph from document B. Its "publication" would require no more than giving details of the *trail* taken through the common stored material ("read this paragraph, then look at that diagram"), together with details of any *annotations* (Fig. 13.1).

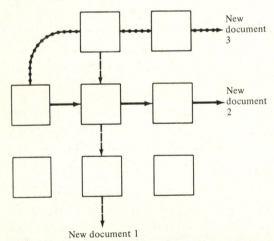

Figure 13.1 In a MEMEX, trails through existing pages are equivalent to new documents.

Like many grand ideas, Bush's speculations were unimplementable at the time but were resurrected when a new technology developed. In this case, it was computing, and the idea reemerged in 1965 in the form of Theodor Nelson's HYPERTEXT, which Nelson still hopes will one day "... store a body of writings as an interconnected whole, with linkages, and ... provide instantaneous access to any writings within that body" (Nelson, 1980, p. 1016). Subsequent workers concentrated on how to implement such ideas, rather than ask whether they really were appropriate to people's needs. For example, would a MEMEX help authors to overcome writing hazards such as not knowing where and how to begin writing or help writers to express ideas as text? Similarly, would readers find a random-access system as easy to browse through as a book? Current research with computer systems not too far removed from the MEMEX in capability indicates that readers might lose their way, forget where they had been and where they were going, and perhaps be distracted by the "joints" between one screen's worth of information and the next (e.g., Robertson et al. [1981], Fox and Palay [1982]).

Augment

One early attempt to produce a writer-oriented, computer-based system with some resemblance to HYPERTEXT took place in the NLS (on-line system) project. This is now generally referred to by its commercial name, AUGMENT (Engelbart & English, 1968). The AUGMENT system is essentially a community of shared files, with facilities for rapid search and linkage. Text documents can be represented as a collection of logical blocks of text, or "statements." Those logical elements are the ideas, be they sentences, paragraphs, diagrams or a row in a table. Superimposed on this basic data structure is a tree structure (analogous to a table of contents), so that users can define hierarchical relationships among the basic building blocks of a document, such as chapter headings, opening and closing paragraphs, and so forth. This allows each document to be accessed and displayed in many ways. For example, an initial browse can be at the top two levels, dropping to a detailed level for a particular topic, then returning to the top levels. Cross references to other levels or to other documents can also be inserted and followed up. In many ways, this is analogous to searching through a conventional data base—but here the data-base management system allows you to carry out interactive searches on free-form narrative information. A similar flexibility applies to editing.

The MEMEX/AUGMENT ideas are worth remembering for one important reason: They illustrate the possibility of distinguishing between people's conceptions of documents, how a document is presented to a particular user, and how that same document is represented inside a machine. To do this, we need an appropriate structural representation of a document. Imagine two different users, one who thinks of writing in terms of adding more words to a document, while the other sees a document as containing logical objects to be manipulated in an iterative process. One possible way of satisfying both their needs is to parse their text file into a canonical representation, a data structure that is an inside-the-machine form of the original document. That internal form could, of course, be unparsed back into a text file after editing. For example, if you use BASE (the AUGMENT editor), you can edit a document in two ways: First as if the internal representation were text; that is, you can use text editing commands at the level of characters, lines, and paragraphs, and so on, knowing that the effect of those commands will be mapped back into the structure on execution. Second, you can rearrange or process any of the logical blocks of text you identified, such as chapter headings or rows and columns in a table.

This is done by means of **structure** editing commands, directed at those structural elements and operating directly on their internal representation. Logically, it is unnecessary to know the details of this internal representation, whichever way you choose to edit your document. (This leaves unanswered the empirical question of whether users *will* want to know how the machine works.)

Although structural representations are useful in theory, it is rare for users to take full advantage of them. This may indicate that when working on them, people do not think of documents in this way. Perhaps a "perception of structure" model only applies to skilled writers and readers. Alternatively, it may be a valid model that has been poorly implemented. For example, one problem with many terminals is that what you see on the screen is not what you get as hard copy (the printed version of the text). Another related problem is that, at least with traditional data/procedure-oriented software, structural information has to be added to the document by the user.

COMMAND-BASED EDITORS

Fifteen years ago it seemed that every computer scientist was designing and implementing his own programming language. Nowadays he seems to build an editor instead (Scowen, 1981, p. 886).

Many of the editing programs that have appeared over the past 3 to 4 years are deficient in three ways: (1) They appear to be written to cope with the fast-disappearing constraint of limited access to cpu time and system memory, (2) They are written for slow and unsophisticated "glass teletypes," rather than high-resolution bit-map displays, (3) They are based on designers' intuitions rather than on empirically derived principles.

The solution is not so simple as letting users extend or modify the editor, as is possible in EMACS (Stallman, 1979). One reason for this is the problem of implementation: An extensible editor can grow to great size (and so be slow to run), there may be no source code to modify it (particularly likely with commercial editors), and it may be difficult to transfer the editor from one machine or operating system to another. These practical concerns are important in the short term but may distract us from considering user-related factors.

Consider first one of the most difficult kinds of text editors to learn to use—the line-oriented editor. This has "command modes" in which requested commands typically take the form r5i/new text/, that is, a cursor or internal marker will move right five spaces and then the words new text will be inserted. Such commands are parsed into (say) an editing operation (e.g., INSERT, as here) and associated data. The latter might be a combination of literal character string data (the text to be inserted) and positioning data (e.g., the precise place in the file for the start of the editing operation). With such an editor it is easy to forget which mode you are in and so type in a command that is inappropriate in that mode. Even when you don't make this mistake, a mode-based editor can make simple jobs difficult if it is insensitive to context. An apocryphal illustration of this is provided by Larry Tessler (1981, p. 90), who imagines an editing session in which you try to copy text from a file whose name you find you can't remember:

[type] the COPY-FROM command . . . [When it asks] "from what file?" . . . leave FROM-WHAT-FILE mode, leave COPY-FROM mode, SAVE the edited text, EXIT from the editor to

the executive, issue the **LIST-FILES** command, look for the name you want ([quickly—because] you can't scroll backwards in that mode), **TERMINATE** the list command, **EXIT** from file management to the executive, re-enter the **EDITOR**, issue the **COPY-FROM** command, and . . . simply type the name.

A context-sensitive editor, on the other hand, might *know* as soon as you issue the **COPY-FROM** command that if you do not type in a file name immediately, it should display the names of files that are available for copying.

Although line-oriented systems are still used, screen-oriented programs are now more common. Many of these are menu-based; if the prevailing menu is permanently on view, there is less chance of forgetting which mode one is in. Even so, such programs probably take longer than necessary to master, partly because of the lack of consensus among designers over the names to give to particular functions (e.g., Does **Delete** mean the same as **Erase**?).

Users can be confused further by the variety of methods that are used to designate commands: Although most documents contain alphanumeric characters rather than control characters, some editors use "ordinary" letters for commands; others use control characters or escape sequences; a few programs use all three! Again, there are levels of agreement and disagreement within groups: Those who believe that commands should have single-letter abbreviations fall into two camps—mnemonically bound and positionally bound (Finseth, 1982). An example of a set of mnemonics is **F** for Forward, **B** for Back one character, **N** for Next line and **P** for Previous line; and an example of a set of positional abbreviations is using the relative positions of **E**, **X**, **S**, and **D** (in a diamond on a QWERTY keyboard) to signify movement up, down, left and right.

Examples such as these indicate the shortcomings of intuition and subjective experience when considering users, but until relatively recently, there were few analytical tools for assessing the relative merits of interface designs. In the next section we look at some approaches to characterizing interactions among users, tasks, and keyboard-based systems.

"WYSIWYG" and Formatting

The current paradigm in designing text editors is WYSIWYG: What You See Is What You Get. With most text-handling systems, this does not happen: document composition typically involves a formatting stage. Formatting can involve postprocessing of a complete text file or immediate interaction. In the former, batch-oriented case, an input file must contain the structural information as markup commands (Fig. 13.2); even if only a local change in layout is

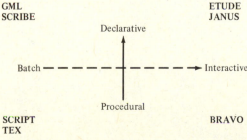

Figure 13.2   How different systems handle document markup.

required, the whole file must be compiled to produce a formatted output file. In the latter, interactive case, the traditionally separate functions of "text editor" and "text formatter" are combined so that any part of the formatted document can be viewed and edited immediately.

An important distinction here is that between *declarative* and *procedural* approaches. These terms are commonplace in programming but have an extended application in AI. In programming, an example of a procedure is a subroutine, which can be defined at one stage and called at a later stage in a program: It separates the internal details of the implementation of an operation from its external behaviour—the parameters it receives, the values it returns, and any side effects it has. A declaration, by contrast, allows postspecification of the type, scope, initial value, and so on of the variable to which it refers. I will give subsequently a text-handling example of the difference between declarative and procedural approaches; for a discussion of their significance for modelling human skills in general, see Ellis (1974).

The procedural approach to formatting is a traditional one. Here, you must specify in advance what the actions are to be (Fig. 13.3). Each part of the document has to be tagged by inserting a control word, such as .spacing 2 to indicate that the final document will be double spaced at this point. Each control word can have an abbreviation, such as .S 2, but even so its insertion can be both time consuming and a relatively unnatural part of document preparation. Also, any system able to cope with sophisticated layouts such as mathematics setting will have a large number of primitive controls to direct actions, such as skipping lines, indenting, and changing founts.

In a declarative system, on the other hand, you need not prespecify the actions of the formatter. Each part of the document still has to be tagged (Fig. 13.4), but the tags identify elements rather than actions associated with elements. Typical elements in a latter would include the opening and closing salutations. Each is recognized by its explicit markup and is mapped to a control procedure associated with it for the particular processing run. The advantage over a procedural system is obvious when you think of tasks like adding a new item to the top of a list. With a procedural system, *you* would have to renumber the list items—and any footnotes associated with the list. Worse, the new item might push the footnote away from the table, because most procedural systems cannot keep references together.

Much of the "housekeeping" that is necessary in procedural systems is taken care of in

```
.sk1
'Markup' information serves two purposes:
.sk1
.tb4
.of4
1.TABit separates logical elements; and
.sk1
2.TABit specifies the processing functions to be
performed on those elements.
.of0
```

Figure 13.3 Procedural commands in 'SCRIPT'. .sk means skip, .tb means tab, .of means offset.

:paragraph.
To change a light bulb:
:numbered-list.
:item
Remove chandelier.
:footnote.
Omit steps 1 and 4 if
there is no chandelier.
:end-footnote.
:item.
Remove old light bulb.
:item.
Insert new light bulb.
:item.
Replace chandelier.
:end-list.
:paragraph.
Ensure that the power is
off before you start.

To change a light bulb:
1. Remove chandelier.[1]
2. Remove old light bulb.
3. Insert new light bulb.
4. Replace chandelier.
Ensure that the power is off
before you start.

---

[1] Omit steps 1 and 4
if there is no chandelier.

Figure 13.4   Declarative commands in 'GML' (left: original markup; right: formatted document).

declarative systems such as TEX (Knuth, 1979), GML (Goldfarb, 1981), and JANUS (Chamberlin et al., 1981). But the user must still specify how each tag or combination of tags should be formatted. The ease with which a user can do this depends on whether the system is interactive and can show the effects of a given set of formatting instructions; if the system is not interactive, this will impose a considerable mental load on most users (who may not be able easily to visualise how a document will look after formatting).

The designer of an interactive declarative system must consider how to display both the text of the document and the high-level markup tags that define its structure. In JANUS, for example, users have a two-screen work station, with simultaneous, side-by-side display of each page from the final formatted version and the corresponding page in the "marked-up" document. By contrast, with ETUDE (Good, 1981) users have a single screen that is split into windows (Fig. 13.5). This places constraints on the space that is available for tags but may make the system easier to use, because what you see in the main window *is* what you get.

STUDYING USER-COMPUTER INTERACTION

Psychology is often criticized for its impracticality and its concern with minutiae while at the same time the crucial problems impeding many engineering developments are problems of psychological performance. (Card & Newell, 1981, p. 240).

<table>
<tr><td colspan="2" align="center">INTERACTION WINDOW</td></tr>
</table>

INTERACTION WINDOW

March 30, 1981   1:20 pm   Document: letter.BodyText
There are no chapters in a letter. Press **menu** for alternatives.

FORMAT WINDOW	TEXT WINDOW
returnaddress	MIT Laboratory for Computer Science March 30, 1981
address	John Jones Smithburg
salutation	Dear Mr. Jones,
body,paragraph	We are pleased to hear of your interest in the ETUDE text for- matting system. It satisfies two of our main design aims:
number,item	1. ETUDE should be easy to use. In particular, a user should not be reluctant to try a command for fear of losing the cur- rent document.
item	2. A user of ETUDE should not be concerned with the details of a document's formatting (margins, type faces, etc.)
paragraph	If you have any further questions, do not hesitate to contact me.
closing	Sincerely, A Designer

Figure 13.5   Using windows for interactions, formatting, and text (based on Good, 1981).

There is no single, uniform approach that designers can adopt for studying user–computer interactions. The reasons for this include: the large number of variables involved (e.g., user background, the nature of the tasks) and the problem of characterizing the overall performance of the combination of user and system. There are many criteria for measuring performance. For example, Card et al. (1980) list:

- acceptability (users' subjective evaluation)
- concentration (the number of things for users to bear in mind)
- errors (their number and significance)
- fatigue (over an extended period of use)
- functionality (the range of tasks that users can reasonably undertake)
- learning (the time it takes a novice to learn how to carry out a given set of tasks)
- time (how long it takes to carry out a given set of tasks).

These have long been studied (mostly for tasks outside computing) by applied psychologists. Much of this research could help designers, by giving them a better understanding of the psychological determinants of the overall performance of the combination of user, task, and computer. Because of this, some psychologists are trying to establish the discipline of "cognitive engineering." They hope to refine a number of possible design tools, including:

- analysing tasks (identifying rational means to accomplish particular tasks or goals)
- using knowledge of psychological processing mechanisms, combined with task analysis, to predict human performance on specific tasks (discussed later)
- studying people's spontaneous interpretations of systems; some of those "mental models" (Gentner & Stevens, 1983) will be more helpful to users than others, so predicting fruitful ways of describing a system might be possible
- analysing human errors; this can help to optimize performance and to minimize either the incidence of errors or the effect of errors; an application of this topic is described in the next section

The most useful of these particular tools, I believe, will turn out to be the analysis of error. Errors have been studied in some detail by Norman (1982), who carefully distinguishes between "mistakes" (errors in one's intention) and "slips" (errors in carrying out the intention). He has classified three types of slip in psychological terms: (1) slips in the formation of intention, (2) slips resulting from faulty activation of schemas, and (3) slips resulting from faulty triggering of schemas. Examples of (1) include "mode errors" and "description errors": respectively, typing text while in command mode in a mode-driven editor and typing a command sequence that is similar to the intended one (e.g., when trying to move to the end of a marked block of text in WordStar, for which the command is controlQK, typing controlKQ instead may delete all one's editing). Examples of (2) and (3)—the schema slips—include typing a similar but more frequently used sequence instead of the desired but uncommon sequence and failure to carry out a necessary action at the right time or at all. The power of this approach is demonstrated later.

Simulating Skilled Typing

By way of illustration of what can be achieved by looking at errors, consider the task of becoming a skilled typist. Here, becoming expert involves a change from doing only a single action at a time ("see-and-peck" typing) to touch-typing, using both hands at once. This task is of interest because it involves overlapping, cooperative performance of several simultaneous acts.

According to Rumelhart and Norman (1981), skilled typists move their hands towards the keys in parallel, tend to type in units at the word level or smaller and find cross-hand strokes take longer to master and type than sequences involving only within-hand strokes. The most familiar errors that are made by skilled typists, they found, are doubling errors, misstrokes, and transpositions.

Rumelhart and Norman's error data were used by them to construct a model of typing whose output display ("hands" and "fingers" moving over a keyboard) can itself be monitored for errors as it types. Its actions are controlled by means of schemata: The schema for a word such as **very** would be activated by the model's perceptual system and parser, which would activate

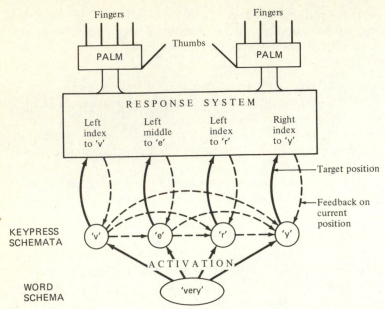

Figure 13.6   How activations interact when typing the word **very**. The dotted lines depict inhibition of other schemata. (*Source:* After Rumelhart and Norman, 1981.)

subsidiary schemata for keypresses (Fig. 13.6). Each of those keypress schemata specifies a target position relative to the centre of the keyboard. That information is then sent to the response system. This must transform the current position of each finger into its target position by correctly reconfiguring the positions of the palms and fingers.

Each keypress schema inhibits the subsequent schemata, to ensure that keys are depressed in the intended sequence. Errors occur because the activation values are noisy. Their computer simulation of typing emulates many of the major phenomena, such as typing **bokk** rather than **book**, as well as providing a reasonably good account of the timing patterns observed among skilled typists.

The Keystroke-Level Model

In addition to studies of error, a knowledge of psychological processing mechanisms can be combined with task analysis to predict human performance on specific tasks. The most convincing research on this takes a narrow focus, as with studies of copyediting by experts: This represents a combination of a relatively well-specified task, tackled by users for whom it is routine. In any such study, there is a need for appropriate ways of measuring performance. Since many text-handling devices are keyboard instruments, a natural metric for keyboard-based tasks such as copyediting is a timed record of users' key depressions. One purpose in recording key depressions is to use that data to build a model of the time that is taken to perform a given task. An example of such a model is the "keystroke-level model," developed by Card et al. (1980). The problem that Card and his co-workers addressed is how to predict the minimum time an expert user will take to execute a task on a system, if the user makes no errors. Their model requires a detailed specification of the task (including details of any subtasks), the method used for the task, the system's command language, the system's response time, and the motor-skill parameters of the user. Given this information, it is possible to calculate the "execution time" on each component of the task (i.e., the time that is taken by the user to carry out that subtask, once he or she has decided upon the method). That calculated time can be compared with actual times, obtained by collecting detailed records, or "protocols," of interactions between the user and the system.

The execution time is the sum of the following times: the system response time for each action within a subtask, the time that is spent mentally preparing for executing each physical action, and the times that are taken on individual physical actions.

We can get an idea of what is involved in calculating the execution time on a task if we examine the task of moving down a line, then replacing one five-letter word by another one. Card et al. (1980) list two methods: one is for a particular screen-based editor, the other is for a line-oriented editor. Each method has seven steps. In their screen-based system, these are: reach for pointing device; point to word; select word; home on keyboard; call replace command; type new word; terminate type-in. In the line-oriented system, these are: jump to next line, call substitute command, specify new word, terminate argument, specify old word, terminate argument, terminate command. Each of those steps had an associated performance time or combination of times (e.g., the time to type in the new five-letter word was assumed to be five times the average time to press a key—approximately 0.2 seconds for an average skilled typist). The predicted overall execution times were fairly accurate: 6.2 seconds for the screen-based system versus 8.4 seconds for the line-oriented one.

Card et al. (1980) raise the interesting question of whether their model can be simplified, yet still produce reasonable predictions of execution times. For example, one could (1) use a single constant time for all operations, (2) count users' motor-movements only and multiply the total time for these physical operations by a "mental overhead" constant, or (3) count the number of keystrokes only. Each of these substantially degrades accuracy but can lead to useful approximations.

No specialized psychological knowledge is required to use the keystroke-level model. All that is required from designers is that they specify in detail the significant operations that are required to accomplish a given task. Given this, they can *predict* and *quantify* the error-free performance of skilled users to a useful degree of accuracy. The tasks to which we can apply this model range in complexity from the correction of a marked-up manuscript (with its subtasks of word insertions, substitutions, and moving sentences within paragraphs) to tasks such as adding a box to a diagram or removing overlapping graphic elements using a graphic editor with or without visual equivalents—"iconic representations"—of the commands.

Card and his co-workers (1980) emphasize that their keystroke-level model was built to predict only the time that is taken by an expert to perform a routine task. They point out that the system designer must consider other users, other tasks, and other aspects of performance. In my view, another way in which designers may be able to improve the lot of users is to design systems or programs to which users can delegate more aspects of their tasks. As seen in the next section, before designers can do this they must learn more about the details of those tasks and consider ways of providing their systems with an internal representation of aspects of the task.

ADVANCING THE STATE OF THE ART

> ... if we program ... to imitate paper, as is the case for the current generation of text editing systems, we will never know if qualitative improvements in the handling of words can be obtained. (Goldstein, 1981, p. 147)

A good example of a personal office computer is the Xerox "8010 Star Information System." This is a high-performance machine: it has a $10\frac{1}{2}$ inch by $13\frac{1}{2}$ inch bit-mapped display screen with a resolution of 72 dots per inch; a minimum of 10 megabytes of disc memory and 512K of main memory (compared with the 600K-disc and 64K-RAM memory of typical 8-bit microcomputers); its cursor movement is via a high-speed "mouse" pointing device; and the system has a 10-megabits-per-second link to other users and to laser printers.

The Star's user-interface was designed according to the maxim "simple things should be simple; complex things should be possible" (Smith et al., 1982, p. 274). It is worth looking briefly at some details of that interface to see how the designers avoided the worst aspects of "programming to imitate paper." Their design has seven major features:

- appropriate conceptual model
- consistency of mechanisms and commands
- modeless interactions
- seeing and pointing rather than remembering and typing
- simplicity
- user tailorability
- what you see is what you get

The conceptual model is an electronic desktop. The screen can show simultaneously both a facsimile of a printed page and up to 154 "icons"—pictures of familiar objects such as files—scattered anywhere on it. Users can tailor the screen to their way of working by choosing the size, shape, position, and number of icons they want on their "desk." Each icon is a concrete object, in the sense that it can be manipulated. For example, a document can be filed by moving its icon to a picture of a file drawer: it is first selected by pointing to it with the mouse (and pressing a button on the mouse); it can then be moved—or a user can decide instead at that stage to copy or delete it—by pressing an appropriate key. By its similarity to a physical office, the Star's user model preserves people's familiar ways of working and the value of their existing knowledge; as one consequence, it reduces users' need for training.

The icon idea is applied consistently to all user interactions. For example, consider the way that keys are labelled on the Star, which can have a user-defined textual and/or graphical character set of size 2^{16}. Icons provide a neat solution to labelling each key: A set of icons can be displayed or modified in a "keyboard-interpretation window" to show how the keyboard is to be interpreted at a particular time; the user can choose whether to type at the "real" keyboard or to copy icons from that window.

Consistency extends to mechanisms and to commands; for example, the same mechanism (a particular button) is used to select a character, an icon, or a graphic line. Similarly, the commands perform the same way, regardless of the object being worked on. So the same set of actions is involved whether one is moving either text within a document, a document to a folder, or a line in an illustration. "Mode" problems are reduced by devoting certain keys to invoking functions and by changing the shape of the cursor according to the state of the system.

Ease of use is ensured further in three ways:

- using the screen as a "visual aid to memory," to show everything relevant to a task (e.g., having menus that users can see and point to, rather than having to remember and type commands)
- empirically based simplicity (e.g., people found it easier to learn to use a mouse with two keys, each with a tiny range of functions, than to use a mouse with one key combining those functions)
- having a little redundancy (e.g., frequently used commands such as underlining are available both in a consistent fashion (via the mouse, selecting from an appropriate menu) and via dedicated keys

Areas of Future Work

Although the Star's designers have addressed many of the issues that were raised previously, they emphasize the continued need for a more rigorous approach to interface design. AI is a necessary component of that more rigorous approach. This is because interfaces should be well matched to task and to user, yet we currently lack sufficiently detailed models of any but the simplest text-handling tasks—and then only for expert users. We should be working towards the development of such models, which will have some combination of the following attributes: computationally realizable, empirically based, psychologically plausible, and task-sensitive. Examples of attractive ideas are programs that claim to assess the "readability" of text or to improve its readability by varying its layout (Macdonald, 1980; see Fig. 13.7). These particular programs may well do what they say, yet McDermott (1976) has demonstrated in an AI context

---

a Original text:

"A useful theory of design would combine general principles with specific task requirements. It would also be explicit about the means of doing this, that is, describe precisely how a particular design problem might be solved."

b Final output:

"A useful theory of design
would combine general principles
with specific task requirements.
It would also be explicit about the means of doing this,
that is, describe precisely
how a particular design problem might be solved."

Figure 13.7   An example of a Writer's Workbench program (This 'Chunks' text into theoretically meaningful segments.)

that the name given to a program or to a program fragment may not match its actual function.

Our understanding has even more gaps when we look at the complexities of information retrieval. For example, we do not know the effect on readers' search strategies of new information, such as "citing statements"—qualifying statements in one document (or part of a document) about other documents (or sections of that document) which it cites; nor do we know how users' search strategies alter as they become more familiar with a data base (but see Holland's 1980 work on designing a system that learns by making inferences about the success of past searches and adapts accordingly).

One recent exploratory study of information retrieval (Weyer, 1982) shows what can be done. This study of an "electronic book" starts with the assumption that users may require help: help not only with augmenting and suggesting search methods but also with managing the found information (i.e., where has the user looked and what should be looked at next). As Weyer remarks, earlier work provided few clues for him "about how to improve . . . electronic information systems . . . actual systems often [just imitate] . . . traditional media, functioning merely as automated page turners." He kept both a transcript of users' comments and data files of each user's interactions; where the transcript was unclear, those data files could be replayed in sequence to show what a user saw on the screen at a given moment. The results indicated the potential value of "an explicit model of tactics and their realization through the browser [which] could aid in evaluating the strengths and weaknesses of interface designs" (Weyer, 1982).

Information generation is even more complex than information retrieval. The prototypical example is the act of writing. Research on this topic falls under the general rubric of research into the intellectual *processes* (e.g., planning, problem solving and inference) which underlie many text-handling tasks. Writing is a task that is undertaken under multiple constraints, including "the requirement for correct grammar, appropriate tone, accuracy of meaning and smooth transition" (Hayes & Flower, 1980, p. 390). If some of those constraints can be removed with computer help, writing itself may become less difficult. This is the rationale for the work by Larry Frase and his Bell Laboratories co-workers (MacDonald, 1980) on the UNIX-based suite of programs called "The Writer's Workbench." Those programs can be used in batch mode to evaluate surface features of text such as certain measures of readability, sentence and word length, sentence openers, sentence types, and word usage.

Help with the process of text-*assessment* is more common than help with text-*generation*. This may be because the latter is still relatively unknown territory. Even if we had a clear idea of the processes involved in writing, it would not be a simple matter to determine the actual usefulness of computer-based aids to writing. For example, one needs to consider how to assess the style and the content of the writing itself (Hirsch & Harrington, in Frederiksen & Dominic, 1981). The quality of the writing produced with computer assistance will also depend on people's familiarity with a word processor as a writing medium (see Gould, 1981), as well as on the complexity of the writing task, relative to their experience. One currently uninvestigated factor here is the effect of providing word processors that have readily extensible facilities; using those facilities may alter people's "locus of control" and "perception of task."

Two approaches to help people to write that are of particular interest are those of Sharples (1981) and Goldstein (1981). Sharples has provided children with a word processor/text transformer, an automated thesaurus and dictionary, a spelling corrector, a story planner, and a sentence generator. Goldstein has experimented with more sophisticated planning aids, which allowed him to delegate to the program the need to remind him of constraints (e.g., on the length of an article) and to prepare and compare multiple drafts. Goldstein (1981, p. 147) has suggested that writers could benefit from programs that "articulate a formal theory of argument structure," providing "planning schemata to represent different arguments such as argument-by-induction, argument-by-authority, and argument-by-deductive proof ... with slots for the various positions that an argument requires."

Although there is value in looking at aids to writing as a creative act, specialised subtopics may also be worth studying, especially if their study may help to solve a common problem. One such problem is how to impose structure on parts of a document. We can see this with two examples. Consider first the task of creating effective tables. This can be split into two subtasks: creating a table and modifying the content and/or layout of the table to make it effective. Programs to help with the latter subtask can be aids to decision making (see discussion on augmentation) or can be quasi-intelligent (delegation). The task of manipulating the table requires the following interactive facilities:

- changing axes (rows to columns)
- changing the sequence of items in vertical or horizontal rows (e.g., from alphabetical to numerical order)
- alternating among full, rounded, and summary data
- positioning footnotes to fall directly below their headings

Implementating such facilities will be difficult if the components of the table are not already tagged (as in document markup). This difficulty underlies a second example: the seemingly unrelated problem of how to recognize and check citations in documents.

Citations and references have stereotyped components (e.g., type of source, date, edition, author, and editor). When one or two of those components are missing, we can readily recognise this, even though authors rarely explicitly tag each component (as in a data base where entries are in "fields"). The task of checking references is made difficult by incomplete citations, or citations whose parts are in arbitrary order. It is an example of practical pattern matching and inferences, which could have commercial value (as in automated reference checking in data-bases), particularly if combined with a query-formulation program (Williams, 1980).

It is not obvious how to recognise structural elements such as rows or columns in a table or dates and authors in a reference. The problem is much reduced if we can arrange for some or all the elements to be tagged automatically. This is much more difficult to arrange with traditional data/procedure-oriented systems than with object-oriented systems such as SMALLTALK-80, so a brief discussion of the latter is in order. That language is structured around a single metaphor of communicating objects. Many objects may be similar, representing the same kind of thing and differing only in some specific property. A group of similar objects form a class; the objects themselves form instances of that class. A new class can be created to *inherit* the internal and external description of an already existing class; it is then a subclass of the original class and can modify its inherited description by adding new messages to which its instances respond, or by modifying the way in which the response to a message is carried out.

The difference between an object-oriented and a traditional system can be seen by

> This is a paragraph whose height may be varied by changing the paragraph width and/or the number of words. The box surrounding this paragraph must fit around it precisely in either case.

> This is a paragraph whose height may be varied by changing the paragraph width and/or the number of words. The box surrounding this paragraph must fit around it precisely in either case.

Figure 13.8   A document with the constraint that text must just fill a box

considering how screen windows are dealt with in each case. In both, we would want the windows to contain text, have titles, and be movable—overlapping, if necessary. Conventionally, we would have data and procedures; the data would represent things like the location, size, and contents of a window, whereas the procedures would be treated as independent of the data. To manipulate a window, you would need procedures describing the details of the manipulation. So to *move* a window, you would call the procedure that moves windows and then pass to it the data representing the window and its new location—making sure it was the appropriate data for that procedure, of course. By contrast, windows can be treated as containing their own built-in methods for being manipulated—they can be treated as objects, which represent both information and its manipulation. Objects determine how to manipulate themselves on the basis of messages they receive. In other words, the messages do *not* call a procedure, they invoke a manipulation—like telling someone *what* you want to happen, not *how* to do it. For example, consider the problem of layout. Although this can be dealt with manually, a more powerful approach uses the idea of *objects subject to constraints*. Figure 13.8 shows an example from THINGLAB (Borning, 1981), a SMALLTALK extension.

In SMALLTALK as implemented in the Xerox Star, the objects that the user sees are icons—icons that represent system files, devices and functions. Each document has a "property sheet," normally unseen, which contains the graphic parameters in effect at any point. This makes for a system that is rich in function yet simple and consistent to operate. Another benefit of that approach is that it helps to solve the problem of how to achieve *built-in* recognition and processing of structural elements. Instead of having to remember explicitly to add declarative tags, an author can do this inadvertently and with a lower mental overhead—because the range of icons that are available in such systems could be extended to include headings, tables, and other common and obvious structural elements. So this might be the easiest way of providing a partial solution to the tagging problem. To go further will require studies of the mistakes made by naive computer users (Stevens, 1980).

CONCLUSIONS

Many of the problems of text editing are *representation* problems. When structural elements are appropriately represented, the result can be a system that is rich in function yet simple and consistent to use. This can facilitate the provision of facilities of commercial significance, for formatting or for information retrieval and manipulation. There are good prospects for extending user interfaces to provide increased support for common yet complex tasks such as writing.

References

Bush, V. 1945. As we may think. *Atlantic Monthly* 176(7): 101–108.

Card, S. K., Moran, T. P., and Newell, A. 1980. The keystroke-level model for user performance time with interactive systems. *Communications of the ACM* 23: 396–410.

Card, S. K., and Newell, A. 1981. Are we ready for a cognitive engineering? In *Proceedings of the Seventh International Joint Conference on Artificial Intelligence,* August 24–28, Vancouver, B.C., pp. 240–242.

Chamberlin, D. D., King, J. C., Slutz, D. R., Todd, S. J. P., and Wade, B.'W. 1981. JANUS: An interactive system for document composition. *ACM SIGPLAN Notices* 16(6): 82–91.

Embley, D. W., and Nagy, G. 1981. Behavioral aspects of text editors. *Computing Surveys* 13(1): 33–70.

Engelbart, D. C., and English, W. K. 1968. A Research Center for Augmenting Human Intellect. *AFIPS Conference Proceedings,* 33, San Francisco, Calif., pp. 395–410.

Finseth, C. A. 1982. Managing words: What capabilities should you have with a text editor? *Byte* 7(4): 302–310.

Fox, M. S., and Palay, A. J. 1982. Machine-assisted browsing for the naive user. In Divilbiss, J. L. (Ed.), *Public Access to Library Automation.* Champaign, Ill.: University of Illinois.

Goldfarb, C. F. 1981. A generalized approach to document markup. *ACM SIGPLAN Notices* 16(6): 68–73.

Goldstein, I. 1981. Writing with a computer. In *Proceedings of the Third Annual Conference of the Cognitive Science Society,* August 19–21, Berkeley, Calif., pp., 145–147.

Good, M. 1981. Etude and the folklore of user interface design. In *Proceedings of the ACM Special Interest Group on Programming Languages/SIGOA Symposium on Text Manipulation,* June 8–10, Portland, Ore., pp. 34–43.

Gould, J. D. 1981. Composing letters with computer-based text editors. *Human Factors* 23(5): 593–606.

Hayes, J. R., and Flower, L. S. 1980. Writing as problem solving. *Visible Language* 14: 388–399.

Holland, J. H. 1980. Adaptive algorithms for discovering and using general patterns in growing knowledge bases. *International Journal of Policy Analysis and Information Systems* 4: 245–268.

Lewis, C., and Mack, R. 1982. Learning to use a text processing system: Evidence from "thinking aloud" protocols. In *Proceedings of Conference on Human Factors in Computer Systems.* ACM Washington Chapter, Washington, D.C., pp. 387–392.

Macdonald, A. H. 1980. Pattern matching and language analysis as editing supports. In Frase, L. T. (Ed.), *Symposium on Computer Aids for Writing and Text Design.* AERA Conference, Boston.

Morris, J. M., and Schwartz, M. D. 1981. *The design of a language-directed editor for block-structured languages.* In *Proceedings of the ACM Special Interest Group on Programming Languages/SIGOA Symposium on Text Manipulation,* June 8–10, Portland, Ore., pp. 28–33.

Nelson, T. H. 1980. Replacing the printed word: A complete literary system. In *Information Processing 80 (IFIP).* Amsterdam: North-Holland, pp. 1013–1023.

Robertson, G., McCracken, D., and Newell, A. 1981. The ZOG approach to man-machine communication. *International Journal of Man-machine Studies* 14: 461–488.

Rumelhart, D. E., and Norman, D. A. 1981. An activation-trigger-schema model for the simulation of skilled typing. In *Proceedings of the Third Annual Conference of the Cognitive Science Society,* August 19–21, Berkeley, Calif., pp. 281–282.

Scowen, R. S. 1981. A survey of some text editors. *Software-Practice and Experience* 11: 883–906.

Sharples, M. 1981. Microcomputers and creative writing. In Howe, J. A. M., and Ross, P. M. (Eds.), *Microcomputers in Secondary Education: Issues and Techniques.* London: Kogan Page.

Smith, D. C., Irby, C., Kimball, R., Verplank, B., and Harslem, E. 1982. Designing the Star user interface. *Byte* 7(4): 242–282.

Stallman, R. M. 1979. EMACS: An extensible, customizable, self-documenting display editor. AI Memo. 519, MIT. Also, in *Proceedings of the ACM Special Interest Group on Programming Languages/ SIGOA Symposium on Text Manipulation,* June 8–10, Portland, Ore.

Stevens, D. F. 1980. Some cautionary aphorisms for user-oriented computer management. In *Information Processing 80 (IFIP).* Amsterdam: North-Holland, pp. 791–796.

Tessler, L. 1981. The Smalltalk environment. *Byte* 6(8): 90–147.

Waters, R. C. 1981. A knowledge-based program editor. In *Proceedings of the Seventh International Joint Conference on Artificial Intelligence,* August 24–28, Vancouver, B.C., pp. 920–926.

Annotated Bibliography

Borning, A. "The Programming Language Aspects of Thinglab, a Constraint-Oriented Simulation Laboratory." *ACM Transactions on Programming Languages and Systems* 3: 353–387, 1981.

A very readable account on how constraints can be satisfied in a Smalltalk-based system. Example range from physics and geometry to document-related topics such as that the height of a bar in a bar chart must correspond to and vary with an entry in a table.

Bush, V. "As We May Think." *Atlantic Monthly* 176(7): 101–108, 1945.

An influential article, now mainly of historical interest.

Card, S. K., Moran, T. P. and Newell, A. "The Keystroke-level Model for User Performance Time with Interactive Systems." *Communications of the ACM* 23: 396–410, 1980.

Without using a particularly complex model, the article explains how to predict the time an expert takes to carry out a keyboard task.

Card, S. K., and Newell, A. "Are we ready for a Cognitive Engineering?" In *Proceedings of the Seventh International Joint Conference on Artificial Intelligence.* August 24–28, Vancouver, B.C., 1981, pp. 240–242.

Describes their "model human processor." This model of the mind has three partially coupled processors, a perceptual processor, a cognitive processor, and a motor processor. The model allows quantitative and fairly realistic estimates to be made of best possible performance, as shown for Morse Code listening rate; reaching to a button; and reaction time.

Chamberlin, D. D., King, J. C., Slutz, D. R., Todd, S. J. P. and Wade, B. W. "JANUS: An Interactive System for Document Composition." *ACM SIGPLAN Notices* 16(6): 82–91, 1981.

Starts with a useful classification of present systems (batch vs. interactive; text only vs. images and text; procedural vs. declarative). Then gives a readable discussion of the constraints to be satisfied by page-formatting programs.

Ellis, A. B. *The Use and Misuse of Computers in Education.* New York: McGraw-Hill, 1974.

An introductory and largely nontechnical text on how people think about computers and how those perceptions are related to our ability to think procedurally. Some parts remain fresh.

Embley, D. W. and Nagy, G. "Behavioral Aspects of Text Editors." *Computing Surveys* 13(1): 33–70, 1981.

A comprehensive account of methods that are used to study how people utilize text editors, which delineates promising research areas. See also their paper "Can We Expect to Improve Text Editing Performance?" In *Proceedings of Conference on Human Factors in Computer Systems,* March 15–17, Gaithersburg, Ma., 1982.

Engelbart, D. C. and English, W. K. "A Research Center for Augmenting Human Intellect." In *AFIPS Conference Proceedings, 33,* San Francisco, 1968, pp. 395–410.

Describes a system that is still available under TWENEX, with some powerful facilities even now absent from many systems but designed at a time when not that much was known about how people write. Other "augmentation" ideas that might be implementable with current technology are contained in Sass, M. A., and Wilkinson, W. D. (Eds.), *Symposium on Computer Augmentation of Human Reasoning* Washington, D.C.: Spartan Books, 1965.

Ericsson, K. A. and Simon, H. A. "Verbal Reports as Data." *Psychological Review* 47(3): 215–251, 1980.

The paper to look at before you undertake protocol studies.

Finseth, C. A. "Managing Words: What capabilities Should You Have with a Text Editor? *Byte* 7(4): 302–310, 1982.

Singles out really useful features in a text editor.

Fox, M. S., and Palay, A. J. "Machine-Assisted Browsing for the Naive User." In Divilbiss, J. L. (Ed.), *Public Access to Library Automation.* Champaign, Ill.: University of Illinois, 1982.

Some good ideas for new tools for document handling. But see Weyer.

Frederiksen, C. H. and Dominic, J. F. *Writing: Process, Development and Communication.* Hillsdale, N.J.: Erlbaum, 1981.

The second of two edited collections whose themes are: How can we learn more about writing? and, How can we learn more about the interaction between teaching to write and learning to write? The views presented come from AI-related disciplines and other such as anthropology, sociolinguistics, and rhetoric.

Gentner, D. and Stevens, A. (Eds.). *Mental Models.* Hillsdale, N. J.: Erlbaum, 1983.

Contains a variety of papers exploring the use of analogy and metaphor in understanding or explaining physical and computer systems.

Goldfarb, C. F. "A Generalized Approach to Document Markup." *ACM SIGPLAN Notices,* 16(6): 68–73, 1981.

Describes a "generalized markup language" (GML), which is rigorous and allows us to process documents by using existing programming and database techniques.

Goldstein, I. "Writing with a Computer." In *Proceedings of the Third Annual Conference of the Cognitive Science Society,* August 19–21, Berkeley, Calif., 1981, pp. 145–147.

Argues that current text-editing systems are programmed to imitate several undesirable features of paper and suggests new designs that may lead to qualitative improvements in our writing ability.

Good, M. "Etude and the Folklore of User Interface Design." In *Proceedings of the ACM Special Interest Group on Programming Languages/SIGOA Symposium on Text Manipulation,* June 8–10, Portland, Ore, 1981, pp. 34–43.

Describes a well-thought-out text editor. But see the papers by Chamberlin and by Goldfarb for details of programs such as BRAVO, GML, JANUS, and EMACS (plus the last paper in those Proceedings—itself a short annotated bibliography of background material).

Gould, J. D. "Composing Letters with Computer-Based Text Editors." *Human Factors* 23(5): 593–606, 1981.

Compares planning, formatting, editing, and other activities for authors using longhand (and also dictating and speaking) as against using text editors.

Hayes, J. R. and Flower, L. S. "Writing as Problem Solving." *Visible Language* 14: 388–399, 1980.

Similar to their paper in Frederiksen but lists further interesting papers on writing and information design.

Holland, J. H. "Adaptive Algorithms for Discovering and Using General Patterns in Growing Knowledge Bases." *International Journal of Policy Analysis and Information Systems* 4: 245–268, 1980.

Examples from information science involve familiar AI problems: inferring patterns, associations, and predictions. Covers learning of new production rules, generalization, focus of attention, and conflict resolution between competing productions.

Knuth, D. E. *TEX and Metafont: New Directions in Typesetting.* Bedford, Mass: Digital Press, 1979.

A definitive book on the principles of sophisticated text formatting. Knuth outlines some of the mathematical principles involved in text layout and novel typeface design and describes a practical computer system that allows book authors to communicate complex formatting specifications in a form that is suitable for use by commercial phototypesetting machines.

Lewis, C., and Mack, R. Learning to Use a Text Processing System: Evidence from "Thinking Aloud" Protocols. In *Proceedings of Conference on Human Factors in Computer Systems.* ACM Washington Chapter, Washington, D.C., 1982, pp. 387–392.

Describes techniques for studying the characters of naive users; for monitoring their use of training manuals and for relating their difficulties to interface design.

Macdonald, A. H. "Pattern Matching and Language Analysis as Editing Supports." In Frase, L. T. (ed.), *Symposium on Computer Aids for Writing and Text Design. AERA Conference, Boston, 1980.*

Describes the Bell Laboratories' "Writers Workbench"—A suite of programs that are available under UNIX. These programs assess writers' styles in various ways (e.g., "readability" indices) and suggest different phrasings and layouts.

McDermott, D. "Artificial Intelligence Meets Natural Stupidity." *ACM SIGART Newsletter* 57: 4–9, 1976.

Why does it matter what you call a program? Read this series of cautionary examples and see.

Morris, J. M., and Schwartz, M. D. "The Design of a Language-Directed Editor for Block-Structured Languages." In *Proceedings of the ACM Special Interest Group on Programming Languages/ SIGOA Symposium on Text Manipulation,* June 8–10, Portland, Ore., 1981, pp. 28–33.

Briefly reviews the features of language-directed editors in different languages (e.g., LISP) and describes another for PASCAL. See also the paper by Waters.

Nelson, T. H. Replacing the Printed Word: A Complete literary system." In *Information Processing 80 (IFIP)* Amsterdam: North-Holland, 1980.

From the man who brought us visions of HYPERTEXT, details of an interesting MEMEX-like proposal, "Project Xanadu." His ideas are nothing if not ambitious (e.g., his 1974 "A conceptual framework for man-machine everything" and other gems he cites here).

Norman, D. A. "Steps Toward a Cognitive Engineering: Design Rules Based on Analyses of Human Error." In *Proceedings of Conference on Human Factors in Computer Systems.* ACM Washington Chapter, Washington, D.C., 1982, pp. 378–382.

Shows how system design details could be derived from a classification of human errors.

Robertson, G., McCracken, D. and Newell, A. "The ZOG Approach to Man-machine Communication." *International Journal of Man-machine Studies* 14: 461–488, 1981.

Describes a rapid-response, large network, menu-selection system that has been used (among other things) as a computerised reference library.

Rumelhart, D. E. and Norman, D. A. "An Activation-Trigger-Schema Model for the Simulation of Skilled Typing." In *Proceedings of the Third Annual Conference of the Cognitive Science Society,* August 19–21, Berkeley, Calif., 1981, pp. 281–282.

A neat simulation of a complex motor task. (More details are given in their "Simulating a Skilled Typist: A Study of Skilled Cognitive-Motor Performance." Technical Report No. 102. San Diego: Center for Human Information Processing, University of California, 1982.)

Scowen, R. S. "A Survey of Some Text Editors." *Software Practice and Experience* 11: 883–906, 1981.

Considers the tasks, constraints, and user interfaces for several editors, giving examples of the necessary interactions.

Sharples, M. "Microcomputers and Creative Writing." In Howe, J. A. M., and Ross, P. M. (Eds.), Longon: *Microcomputers in Secondary Education: Issues and Techniques,* London: Kogan Page, 1981.

A clear description of aids to creative writing.

Smith, D. C., Irby, C., Kimball, R., Verplank, B. and Harslem, E. "Designing the Star User Interface." *Byte* 7(4): 242–282, 1982.

A most readable explanation of the merits of adhering to a small set of cogent design principles.

Stallman, R. M. EMACS: "An Extensible, Customizable, Self-documenting Display Editor." AI Memo. 519, Cambridge, Mass.: MIT, 1979. Also, in *Proceedings of the ACM Special Interest Group on Programming Languages/SIGOA Symposium on Text Manipulation,* June 8–10, Portland, Ore.—see Good.

As self-explanatory as its title. EMACS is a general-purpose editor, particularly suitable for LISP.

Stevens, D. F. "Some Cautionary Aphorisms for User-Oriented Computer Management." In *Information Processing 80 (IFIP)*. Amsterdam: North-Holland, 1980, pp. 791–796.

A concise and entertaining set of illustrations of, among other things, our capacity for random behaviour when using computers.

Tessler, L. "The Smalltalk Environment." *Byte* 6(8): 90–147, 1981.

One of over a dozen articles on Smalltalk-80 in a special issue of *Byte*. (Volume 7(8) gives a similar overview of Logo.) Tessler's article has some excellent general illustrations of the hardware and the high-resolution graphics but is worth reading mostly for its discussion of how object-oriented "windows" can be used in editing.

Waters, R. C. "A Knowledge-Based Program Editor." In *Proceedings of the Seventh International Joint Conference on Artificial Intelligence,* August 24–28, Vancouver, B.C., 1981, pp. 920–926.

Describes an interactive programming assistant system with four parts: an analyser (to build an abstract representation or "plan" for a program); a coder (to create appropriate program text); a library of plans; and a plan editor. Compares this system with programming language syntax editors such as Mentor and Gandalf.

Weyer, S. A. "The Design of a Dynamic Book for Information Search." *International Journal of Man-machine Studies* 17: 87–107, 1982.

Explores how people look for information and how the design of the search tool—here, a dynamic book implemented in Smalltalk—can affect the process.

Williams, P. W. "Intelligent Access to Online Systems." In *Proceedings of the Fourth International Online Information Meeting,* Oxford: Learned Information; 1980.

Describes a non-AI solution to such problems as having to remember how to access and interrogate particular data bases and having to key in such directions manually.

CHAPTER 14

PLANNING AND OPERATIONS RESEARCH

LESLEY DANIEL

INTRODUCTION

A particular aspect of the artificial intelligence study of problem solving is that of automatic plan generation—that is, using a computer program to produce a plan, a sequence of actions that will transform the world from some given initial state to a desired goal state. Typical planning problems in human problem solving might be to find plans to cook a meal, to decorate a room, or to make a journey from London to Paris. A striking characteristic of human problem solving is its flexibility—a person of average intelligence would cope quite efficiently with each of the three preceding situations.

People are good at extracting from the myriad of facts that are true in any state of the world exactly those that are relevant to the problem in hand. They are also good at considering only the most suitable actions to solve the problem.

Computer problem solvers cannot handle such complexity and the task of automatic plan generation was formulated as a problem in a very restricted world. A typical world that could be handled by most of the programs we will be considering would contain only a few objects (e.g., three boxes and a robot) and a small repertoire of actions that could be considered in forming a plan (e.g., pushing a box from one location to another and moving to a particular place). The states of the world will be distinguished by only a few facts (e.g., the location of the objects) and many more will be ignored (e.g., the weight of an object, the age of the robot, the size of the room, whether the sun is shining, the day of the week, etc.) Thus, a typical planning problem might be presented in the following way:

The World

The world in which the planning program must generate plans has:

- a Robot—R
- three boxes—B1, B2, B3
- four locations—a, b, c, d
- two actions—PUSH and GOTO

States of the World

The states of the world are fully specified by a set of predicates stating the location of every object. For example:

$$S1 - at(B1, b) \wedge at(B2, c) \wedge at(B3, d) \wedge at(R, a).$$

The predicate at(B1, b) means that the box labelled B1 is located at position b. In the state S1 defined here, B1 is at b, B2 at c, B3 at d, and the robot at a, as shown in Figure 14.1.

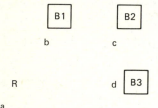

Figure 14.1

Actions

Actions are fully specified by stating what conditions must be true before an action can be applied and the facts that are made true and untrue by the action.

We may, for example, define an action of pushing an object from one place to another as follows:

PUSH(obj, x, y)

—push any object from any x to any y for all values of obj, x, y.

The preconditions define which facts must be true before the action can take place—that is, the robot and the object must both be at the same place:

preconditions: at(obj, x) $\wedge$ at(R, x)

The effects of the action are defined by an **add-list** (all the facts made true by the action) and a **delete-list** (all the facts that will no longer be true after the action).

add-list: at(R, y); at(obj, y)
delete-list: at(R, x); at (obj, x)

With such a formulation, we might present the planning system with the following initial state:

$$S_o - at(B1, b) \wedge at(B2, c) \wedge at(B3, d) \wedge at(R, a)$$

as shown in Figure 14.1, and a goal state:

$$S_g - at(B1, x) \wedge at(B2, x) \wedge at(B3, x)$$

That is, we want all the boxes collected together in one place. Figure 14.2 shows one possible solution.

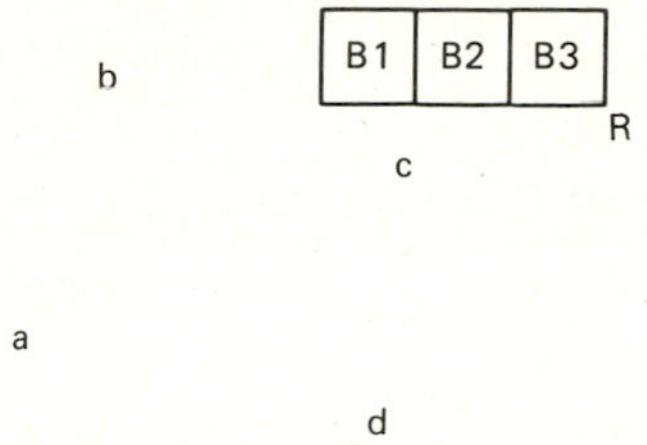

b

| B1 | B2 | B3 |

R

c

a

d

Figure 14.2

The problem is to find a plan, i.e. a composition of actions that will achieve the goal from the initial state. For this particular problem, an acceptable plan would be GOTO(b); PUSH(B1, b, c); GOTO(d); PUSH(B3, d, c), which would result in the state $S' - at(B1, c) \wedge at(B3, c) \wedge at(B2, c) \wedge at(R, c)$, in which the goal is satisfied. If a plan is linear (a sequence of actions as previously described), the problem can be represented as a path-finding problem in a "search tree" by considering each state as a "node" and each action as a "branch." In a given state, several actions may be applicable—that is, those whose preconditions are true in the state. From a particular initial state we may choose to apply each candidate action and obtain several successor states. In turn we can consider each of these new states and apply applicable actions to generate new successor states. A search tree for the previously discussed problem is shown in Figure 14.3. Only part of the tree is included and goal states are marked by asterisks.

We can see that a plan is a path through the search tree from the initial state to one in which the goal is satisfied. For the preceding example, the solution path is highlighted in bold. We may also note that since at every node many choices can be made (even though some are less sensible than others), the tree soon grows very large and there may be many feasible plans, some more efficient than others.

We can summarize the planning approach as follows:

· The world is described by a set of facts that define distinct states.
· The planning system has a repertoire of primitive actions (operators) that can be combined to achieve a given goal.

· The actions are defined by the conditions that must be true before they can be applied and the effects they have on the world—the facts that are made true and those that are made untrue.

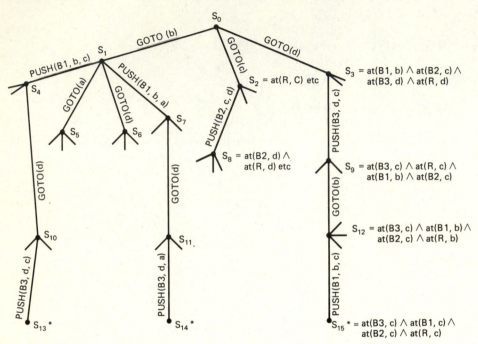

Figure 14.3   Part of search tree for achieving at (B1, x) $\wedge$ at (B2, x) $\wedge$ at (B3, x)

SEARCH STRATEGIES

If we consider the problem of plan generation as one of exploring a tree of states, we can immediately distinguish among three strategies for searching the tree.

Forward Search

Starting from the initial state, applicable operators are identified to produce successor states. A state is chosen for expansion, possibly using a "heuristic evaluation" function as a measure of the value/promise of each state (see, e.g., Nilsson [1971]), and the search tree grows until a state is found in which the goal is satisfied.

A typical evaluation function might be the number of facts that are to be made true in the goal state that have already been achieved in the current state.

In the planning problem, the number of applicable operators in any state is large and, unless there is some measure of proximity to the goal and the relevance of candidate operators, the tree will grow exponentially.

Backward Search

The backward search strategy is to work backwards from the goal state to the initial state, considering how to satisfy the preconditions of actions that will achieve the desired goal. Even if only relevant actions (i.e., those that will achieve one or more goals) are considered, some of those that are introduced may be impossible to apply and such a strategy can only work if it incorporates some measure of proximity to the initial state. With backward search, the problem solver is always trying to achieve the preconditions of the actions to be applied and the nodes in the search tree correspond to lists of these subgoals rather than to actual states of the world.

Means–Ends Analysis

The notion of means–ends analysis (introduced by Newell, Shaw, and Simon [1959] in the general problem solver program—[GPS]) is an attempt to avoid the pitfalls of the previous strategies. The idea is to start from the goal state and apply just those actions (means) that can contribute to the goals (ends). As soon as an action's preconditions are true, it is applied and a new state is generated. If no relevant action can be applied, a new subgoal (i.e., the preconditions of a relevant action) is added to the list of goals to be achieved. In means–ends analysis, preference is given to those actions whose preconditions are most nearly true in the current state.

STRIPS

In this section we describe an early planning system called *STRIPS*, the Stanford Research Institute problem solver (Fikes & Nilsson, 1971), which used means–ends analysis. STRIPS was designed as the problem-solving component of a mobile robot called SHAKEY. SHAKEY lives in a world of seven rooms connected by doors and containing several large boxes that it can push around. A typical task for SHAKEY might be to push a box from one room to another. First it uses its planning system to form a plan from its *primitive operators* (e.g., go to a location, push box, open door) and then executes the plan by using an action routine for each operator.

The problem-solving strategy that is used by STRIPS can be summarized as follows:

- Try to prove the goal G is true in the initial state S_o: STRIPS uses a theorem prover to try to prove that the assertions in the goal are satisfied. The theorem prover will either return successfully or return the facts that cannot be made true. For example, if the goal and initial state were

    G – at(B1, x) $\wedge$ at(B2, x)
    S_o – at(B1, a) $\wedge$ at(B2, b)

the theorem prover might set x to a, satisfying the assertion at(B1, a) but returning at(B2, a) as the difference between the initial state and the goal state.

- A failed proof will yield the difference between the current state and the goal that must be reduced.
- Look for the actions to reduce this difference—suitable actions can be found by consulting their **add-lists**—that is, the facts that are made true. The action PUSH(obj, x, y) is a suitable action for achieving at(B2, a) since its **add-list** contains the fact at(obj, y).
- Try to apply the action—satisfying the precondition of the chosen action becomes a new subgoal that must be achieved in order to achieve the main goal. As soon as an action's preconditions are achieved, apply the action and produce a new state.
- Every time a new state is produced, try to prove that the goals (and their subgoals) are true.

We can see how STRIPS would generate plans in a world containing three blocks A, B, C, standing on a table, and a single action of moving a block from one location to another.

STACK(x, y, z) moves a block x from y to z, where x can be A, B, or C and y and z can be A, B, C, or a table. This is expressed as follows:

> *preconditions:*   on(x, y) $\land$ clear(x) $\land$ clear(z)
> *add-list:*   on(x, z); clear(y)
> *delete-list:*   on(x, y); clear(z)

STRIPS also has a class of facts that are always true, for example,

> clear(table).

We can propose an initial state:

> S_o — on(C, A) $\land$ on(B, table) $\land$ on(A, table) $\land$ clear(C) $\land$ clear(B)

and a goal state

> S_g — on(A, B) $\land$ on(B, C)

which are shown in Figure 14.4. Note that the goal does not completely specify a state but simply is a subset of facts that must be true.

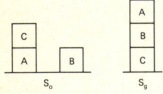

Figure 14.4

In trying to prove the goal true in the initial state, STRIPS comes up with the difference on(A, B) $\land$ on(B, C).

Consulting the **add-list** of the operator STACK(x, y, z), we see that the assertion on(A, B) can be made true by the action

> STACK(A, y, B) (i.e., set x = A, z = B)

and the assertion on(B, C) can be made true by the action

STACK(B, y, C) (i.e., set x = B, z = C)

In order to apply the first action, STRIPS must achieve the subgoals

on(A, y) ∧ clear(B) ∧ clear(A)

which yields a difference

clear(A)

if y = table.

At this stage the world is still in the initial state and STRIPS is working on the stack of goals:

clear(A) ∧ on(A, B) ∧ on(B, C)

The action that is relevant to achieving clear(A) is STACK(x, A, y) whose preconditions on(x, A) ∧ clear(x) ∧ clear(y) are true in S_o if x = C and y = table. The action is applied and STRIPS tries to achieve its stack of goals in the new state.

S_1 — on(A, table) ∧ on(B, table) ∧ on(C, table) ∧ clear(A) ∧ clear(B) ∧ clear(C).

The search tree that is generated for this problem is shown in Figure 14.5. In order to keep the diagram simple, we show only some of the possible states.

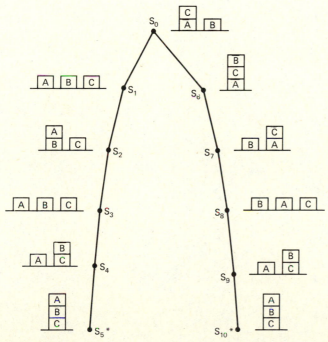

Figure 14.5

The goals and associated actions for each branch are as follows:

$S_o - S_1$: The planner is trying to achieve the goals in the order

on(A, B) $\wedge$ on(B, C).

An appropriate action for the first goal is

STACK(A, y, B)

which introduces the new subgoal

clear(A).

An appropriate action is

STACK(C, A, table)

which can be applied in S_o.

$S_1 - S_2$: The planner tries to achieve

on(A, B)

by applying the action

STACK(A, table, B).

$S_2 - S_3$: The planner tries to achieve

on(B, C).

An appropriate action is

STACK(B, y', C)

which introduces the subgoal

clear(B).

An appropriate action is

STACK(A, B, table)

which can be applied in S_2.

$S_3 - S_4$: The planner tries to achieve

on(B, C)

by applying the action

STACK(B, table, C).

$S_4 - S_5$: The planner tries to achieve

on(A, B)

by applying

    STACK(A, table, B).

By attacking the goals in a different order, the planner finds a different solution path:

$S_0 - S_6$: The planner has ordered the goals

    on(B, C) $\wedge$ on(A, B).

An appropriate action is

    STACK(B, table, C).

$S_6 - S_7$: The planner tries to achieve

    on(A, B).

An appropriate action is

    STACK(A, y'', B)

which introduces the new subgoal

    clear(A).

An appropriate action is

    STACK(C, y'', z')

which yields the new subgoal

    clear(C).

An appropriate action is

    STACK(B, C, table).

$S_7 - S_8$: An appropriate action for

    clear(A)

is

    STACK(C, A, table).

$S_8 - S_9$: An appropriate action for

    on(B, C)

is

    STACK(B, table, C).

$S_9 - S_{10}$: An appropriate action for

    on(A, B)

is

STACK(A, table, B).

We can see that even for such a simple problem the search tree is quite large. The choices arise for two reasons:

1. Even with a single operator, there are several actions that are relevant to any situation—for example, in state S_2 STACK(A, B, table) and STACK(A, B, C) are both relevant to achieving clear(A).
2. Even though in any state, STRIPS is always working on the goal at the top of its stack of goals, when a new state yields a new difference, there is a choice of how to order the goals with respect to the new difference.

Because the goals are held as a stack and STRIPS is only considering the top one at any one time, inefficient plans are generated with goals being achieved, then undone, then reachieved. In fact, the example we have considered is a particularly difficult one, for which STRIPS will not find the simplest solution. In state S_1 it will never try to stack B on C because it has previously committed itself to achieving on(A, B). On the other branch of the tree on(B, C) can be achieved immediately by applying an action to the initial state and must then be undone in order to achieve clear(A).

To summarize, STRIPS has several shortcomings that are addressed by subsequent planning systems:

1. The search tree is still large with many alternatives at each node.
   (a) There may be more than one failed proof that the goal is true in a given state with a difference corresponding to each proof.

   For example, an attempt to prove
   G_0—at(B1, x) $\wedge$ at(B2, x) $\wedge$ at(B3, x)
   in S_0—at(B1, a) $\wedge$ at(B2, b) $\wedge$ at(B3, c)
   will yield three differences:
   D_1—setting x = a gives   at(B2, a) $\wedge$ at(B3, a)
   D_2—setting x = b gives   at(B1, b) $\wedge$ at(B3, b)
   D_3—setting x = c gives   at(B1, c) $\wedge$ at(B2, c)
   (b) For a given difference there is a choice of order in which the goals should be achieved.
   (c) There may be a choice of actions to reduce the difference.
2. STRIPS keeps a stack of goals but at any time is considering only how to achieve the goal at the top of the stack. Consequently:
   (a) Because STRIPS doesn't keep track of the goals that are already achieved they may be undone by subsequent actions and have to be reachieved later—we need to *protect* the goals that are achieved—that is, not allow any actions to be applied that will delete them.
   (b) The goals are achieved in the order in which they are placed on the stack and this may lead to inefficient plans. In general, if we have a collection of subgoals that must all be achieved, it is best to tackle the most difficult first—we need a difficulty ordering on the goals.

HACKER, a planning program that was developed by Sussman (1973) at MIT, introduced the notion of protecting subgoals. However, the problem we have just considered is difficult for HACKER since once having achieved a goal, it can not be undone.

ABSTRIPS, a variant of STRIPS that was developed by Sacerdoti (1975a) at SRI, attached a difficulty ordering (called *criticality*) to the preconditions of each operation. Plans are found in several stages—in the early stages preconditions with low criticality are ignored, but these are taken into account in the later stages. Thus, a more detailed plan is obtained by filling in the gaps in the plan that become apparent when preconditions with low criticality are considered.

NOAH

In a later planning system called NOAH, Sacerdoti (1975b) extended this notion of planning at different levels of detail. NOAH (Nets Of Action Hierarchies) was the planning component of the computer-based consultant project at SRI. The aim of the project was to develop a computer system that could play the role of an expert advising an inexperienced human apprentice in the diagnosis of faulty electrical equipment. NOAH was the problem-solving and execution monitoring system that formulated plans for the assembly, dismantling, and repair of equipment such as water pumps.

The aim of the system was to generate plans at different levels of detail in order to interact with the apprentice at a level that matched his or her expertise—an experienced apprentice could cope with advice couched in terms of high-level actions while somebody with less expertise might need more detailed advice. Upon the request of the apprentice, the system provided instructions in progressively more detail for any step in the process.

The system was also able to monitor the apprentice's work and to generate plans dynamically so that when it became aware of an unexpected event, it could alter the instructions to the apprentice to deal effectively with the new situation.

Plans in NOAH are represented as partially ordered networks of actions—termed procedural nets—instead of linear sequences. Orderings between actions are only introduced as necessary: either because one action achieves a precondition of a successor action or because two actions interfere with each other. In a partially ordered plan, only some actions are ordered, whereas others are left to be done in any order (see Fig. 14.10).

The system develops a hierarchy of plans at different levels of detail. High-level plans are refined into more detailed versions by expanding high-level actions into partially ordered groups of subactions. Thus, the repertoire of primitive operators used by STRIPS and ABSTRIPS is replaced by a hierarchy where each high-level action can be decomposed into more detailed subactions.

The NOAH planning cycle can be summarized in three steps, as follows:

1. Expand the most detailed plan in the procedural net, providing a new, more detailed plan.
2. Criticise the new plan, performing any necessary reordering or elimination of redundant actions.
3. If more detail is required, then go to step 1.

The system uses three critics in its analysis of each planning stage:

1. *Resolve Conflicts Critic*. If action A deletes an expression that is a precondition of another action B, a conflict occurs that can be resolved by ensuring that A is not executed until after B.
2. *Use Existing Objects Critic*. This critic helps bind free variables in such a way as to make the plans efficient. For example, in trying to clear a box B, the action STACK(C, B, x) may

appear in the plan (where at this stage x is still a free variable). In examining the plan, the *use existing objects critic* might find that setting x equal to D would achieve the goal on(C, D) which exists elsewhere in the plan.

3. *Eliminate Redundant Preconditions Critic.* Merges goal nodes whenever possible. If a goal appears at several places in the plan, NOAH tries to use a single action to achieve the goal and keep it true for as long as it is required (i.e., until all actions that require the goal as a precondition are complete).

The Table of Multiple Effects

NOAH builds a table of multiple effects by making an entry for each expression that is asserted or denied by more than one node in the current net. Those expressions that are deleted by the node for which they are a precondition are eliminated. For example, clear(B) is a precondition for the action PUTON(A, B) which also deletes it—since no interaction can be involved in such a deletion, it can be eliminated. The *resolve conflicts critic* uses the table of multiple effects to find cases where an action deletes the precondition of another action.

NOAH on a 4-Block Problem

We will now follow NOAH through a 4-block problem which is an extension of the earlier 3-block problem.

The problem posed to NOAH is, given an initial state, as illustrated in Figure 14.6, to stack the blocks in a tower:

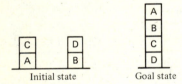

Initial state   Goal state

Figure 14.6

Figure 14.7 illustrates the notation to be used in the following diagrams:

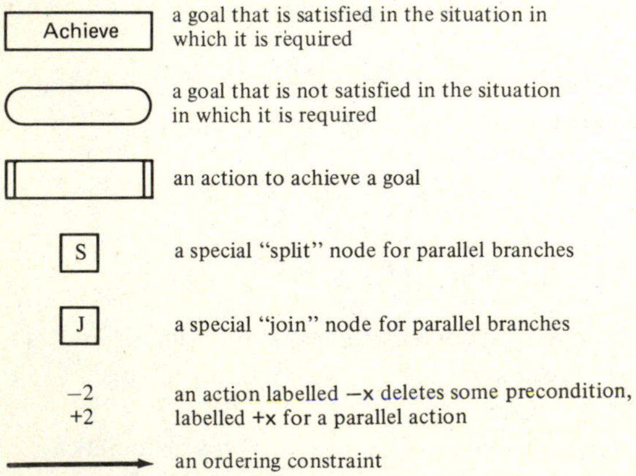

Achieve	a goal that is satisfied in the situation in which it is required
	a goal that is not satisfied in the situation in which it is required
	an action to achieve a goal
S	a special "split" node for parallel branches
J	a special "join" node for parallel branches
−2 +2	an action labelled −x deletes some precondition, labelled +x for a parallel action
→	an ordering constraint

Figure 14.7

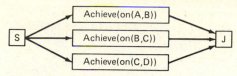

Figure 14.8

NOAH first sets up a network containing three goal nodes (one for each goal in the original problem) as shown in Figure 14.8.

The net is expanded by replacing the goal nodes by actions to achieve the goals and any preconditions of those actions. For example, the goal Achieve(on(x, y)) can be achieved by the operator **PUTON**(x, y) with preconditions **clear**(x) and **clear**(y) (Fig. 14.9).

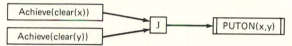

Figure 14.9   Expansion of Achieve (on (x, y)

If there is more than one relevant operator, the system has to choose between alternative expansions of the procedural net.

Expanding Figure 14.8, and allowing for the fact that **clear**(C) and **clear**(D) are already achieved in the initial state, the new network looks like that shown in Figure 14.10.

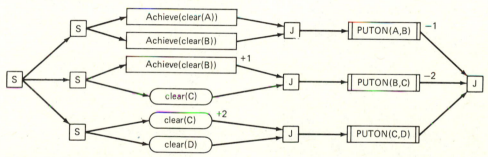

Figure 14.10

The *remove conflicts critic* finds that in two cases a precondition ($+$x) is deleted by a parallel operation ($-$x). These conflicts are found from the table of multiple effects. Each conflict is removed by introducing a new precedence relation to put the goal that has a deleted precondition before the negating action. For example, **PUTON**(B, C) must be done before **PUTON**(A, B).

Redundant preconditions in parallel branches are eliminated. For example, **clear**(C) is a precondition of **PUTON**(C, D) and remains true for **PUTON**(B, C) (Fig. 14.11):

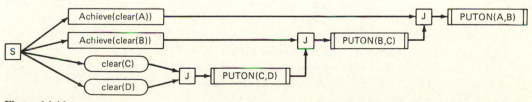

Figure 14.11

By consulting available expansions, NOAH discovers that the goal clear(A) can be achieved by moving the block on A, so the goal node is replaced by an action and new preconditions. Similarly, clear(B) is replaced by an action to put D elsewhere (Fig. 14.12):

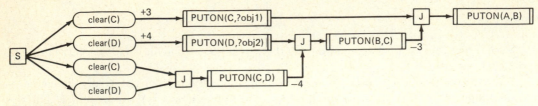

Figure 14.12

Two new conflicts are found from the table of multiple effects and removed by *linearization.* NOAH uses the table of multiple effects to find assertions that are denied by one node (e.g., PUTON(C, D) denies clear(D)) and asserted by another (e.g., the goal node clear(D) asserts clear(D)). The linearization is the introduction of a precedence relationship to ensure that PUTON(D, ?obj2) occurs before PUTON(C, D). Analogously, linearization ensures that PUTON(C, ?obj1) occurs before PUTON(B, C) (Fig. 14.13):

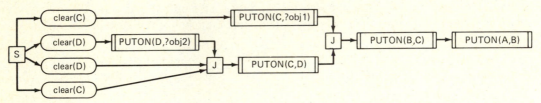

Figure 14.13

The system tries to remove redundant preconditions and actions by trying to match unspecified arguments with objects in parallel actions. For example, ?obj1 in action PUTON(C, ?obj1) can be matched with D in PUTON(C, D) and the two parallel actions merge.

The final net is as follows with clear(D) and clear(C) achieved in the initial state (Fig. 14.14):

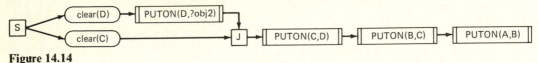

Figure 14.14

Some Restrictions of NOAH

1. *Choice of Operator.* Actions are only introduced into the procedural net if they are relevant to a goal that is being considered. If more than one operator is relevant, a choice is made and alternatives are kept as backtrack possibilities. However, when a particular plan fails to find a solution, no information is kept about the reason for the failure and the system simply backs up to a higher level network and chooses an alternative action.
2. *Restrictions on Linearization.* In removing conflicts from the network, NOAH only considers one possible linearization.

However, if we look at interactions in more detail we can see that, in general, two ways of removing the interaction are possible.

Consider two parallel actions where one deletes the precondition of the other (Fig. 14.15):

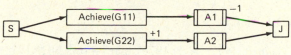

Figure 14.15

NOAH would remove this interaction by putting action **A2** before **A1**, thus (Fig. 14.16):

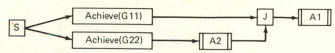

Figure 14.16

In fact, the interaction could also be removed by putting **A1** before the goal to **Achieve(G22)**, thus (Fig. 14.17):

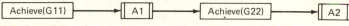

Figure 14.17

Because not all possibilities are considered, NOAH might fail to find solutions to problems for which solutions could be found by considering alternative linearizations.

In fact, a special case of problems that are impossible for NOAH are those involving double interactions. For example, suppose we wanted a robot to move two adjacent boxes, one at a time, from **LOC1** to **LOC2** (Fig. 14.18):

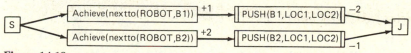

Figure 14.18

NOAH would remove the first interaction by placing **PUSH(B1, LOC1, LOC2)** before **PUSH(B2, LOC1, LOC2)** and then be unable to resolve the second conflict (NOAH's only means to resolve the second conflict is by placing **PUSH(B2, LOC1, LOC2)** before **PUSH(B1, LOC1, LOC2)**).

In fact considering the alternative way of resolving conflicts means that two possible linearizations become apparent (Fig. 14.19):

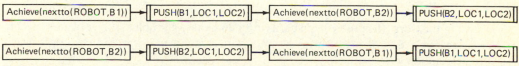

Figure 14.19

A further problem with NOAH arises because the table of multiple effects contains any expression that was added and deleted by more than one node (not necessarily goals). Thus, spurious interactions might be detected.

PLANNING AND OPERATIONS RESEARCH

The rest of this chapter describes a project (Daniel, 1977; Tate, 1976) that follows NOAH in the use of partially ordered networks of actions to represent a plan at any stage of development. Such networks are in a suitable form for the use of critical path analysis techniques having only those ordering constraints that are imposed by the fact that either

- an action achieves a condition for a subsequent action, or
- an action interferes with an important effect of another action and must be removed outside its range.

We adopted Sacerdoti's (1975a) philosophy of hierarchical planning, where planning proceeds in stages at progressively greater levels of detail, and at each stage, the current plan is represented as a graph where the nodes represent actions (or goals to be achieved) and the edges represent ordering relations (links) among them. The graph is refined by expanding each node into a more detailed subnetwork of nodes and adjusting the orderings accordingly.

In the first phase of the project, we were concerned with the development of a general hierarchical planning system; our intention has been not only to write programs that perform well in a particular problem domain but to structure the programs so that the various aspects of the planning process can easily be identified. Accordingly, the problem was attacked under several headings:

- *Task Formalism*. This is a formalism for defining a hierarchy of actions and goals.
- *Planner*. This is a program that uses the task formalism to generate plans in the hierarchic manner previously described.
- *Optimization Procedures*. Considerations of efficiency are important and the planner must produce cost-effective plans, since we are interested in practical problems. Accordingly, we have developed criteria for choosing efficient alternatives.
- *Modifying Plans*. A decision graph has been implemented to record the relationships among decisions that were made in generating a plan and allow appropriate modification of the plan to recover from failure.

In the second phase of the project, the general planning system was adapted to cope with a practical application to the problem of repeatedly generating plans for the annual overhaul of power stations.

Task Formalism

At the outset of the work, the problem of specifying a domain to a problem solver in a hierarchic fashion was recognized as being of primary importance, and a uniform and straightforward method of description was sought.

The formalism allows high-level definitions of a task to be given; each part of which can be expanded into lower-level descriptions and so on down to some arbitrary level that the user of the program requires as output. Each lower-level component can be specified in a modular way—not requiring knowledge of the exact form of the other components.

The specification of an action must specify how it may be expanded into more detailed subactions (there may be alternative expansions for an action, e.g., different methods for installing electrical wiring), and how the constituent actions relate to each other. Rather than explicitly expressing ordering constraints in terms of precedence relations between actions, the task formalism allows specification of the conditions that must hold before an action can start (e.g., the walls of a house must be finished before the roof can be built) and the changes an action makes to the world (i.e., making some conditions true and some false), leaving the planning system to deduce feasible ordering relations. Thus, the task formalism allows individual actions to be specified independently of other actions in the plan.

The task formalism allows the specification of a hierarchy of actions in terms of schemas (called *opschemas*) for an expansion that specifies:

- *Pattern*. The pattern of an opschema determines for which actions the expansion is suitable.
- *Expansion*. The constituent actions (or goals) are specified as a partial order.
- *Conditions*. The conditions that are required by the constituent actions.
- *Effects*. The changes that are made to the world model.

Planner

The planning system uses a hierarchic specification of the problem domain, expressed in the task formalism, to plan at progressively more refined levels of detail. At each level the plan is represented as a graph, where the nodes represent actions (or goals) and the edges represent ordering relations between them. Each node has associated with it:

- *Node Type:* action, goal, phantom (a goal that has been achieved in another part of the plan)
- *Pattern:* the expansions for a node are found by matching its pattern against the patterns of opschemas
- *node context:* contains the effects of the node
- *parentnode:* the node was inserted as a result of the expansion of its parentnode
- *prenodes:* a list of nodes linked immediately before this one
- *succnodes:* a list of nodes linked immediately after this one

Two other data structures are build by the planner:

- **TOME**: The Table Of Multiple Effects stores information about facts that are made true or false at different nodes.
- **GOST**: The GOal STructure records the conditions on nodes along with the contributors to a condition (those nodes that make the pattern true). The goal structure thus specifies a set of time "ranges" for which the truth of certain conditions must be maintained. The use of goal structure in problem solving was first described by Tate (1974, 1975).

The planning cycle consists of expanding nodes in the network—that is, replacing a high-level action by a subnetwork of more detailed actions—and then looking for interactions with other parts of the plan.

Goal nodes are expanded by first looking to see whether the goal is already achieved by some other action in the plan, and if necessary, adding links to make the goal true at the point that is required (e.g., in overhauling machinery, it is necessary to remove the cover to gain access to a component and worthwhile to look to see whether an action to remove the cover has already been included because of a repair to another component). If so, the node is then made a phantom node and a record of this fact is kept by adding a phantom condition to the GOST. If the goal node cannot be made a phantom, it is expanded, in the same way as an action node, by finding an expansion opschema whose pattern matches the pattern of the node.

The expansion of a node causes the introduction of new conditions (on the new nodes) and new effects, and the planner seeks to ensure that the conditions are satisfied and the effects do not interfere with conditions on other nodes in the network. It may be necessary to add new links to the network to remove an endangered condition out of the range of a node that denies the condition (e.g., in a house-building task, it is necessary to have access to brickwork before electrical wiring can be installed; plastering the brickwork denies this access and therefore cannot be done until after the wiring has been installed). The planner uses the GOST and TOME to find interactions only on goal nodes.

In general, an interaction involves three nodes (A, B, and C, as shown in Fig. 14.20). If action A achieves a condition that is required by action B and made untrue by action C, an interaction occurs unless C is already a predecessor of A or a successor of B. The interaction can be resolved by adding a link to ensure that C is outside the range of the condition in question. Three cases must be considered:

- The interaction is totally *unconstrained* because C is parallel to both A and B—in this case, the interaction can be resolved either by linking C as a predecessor of A or as a successor of B.
- The interaction is *constrained* because C is already linked as a successor of A—the interaction must be resolved by linking C as a successor of B.
- The interaction is *constrained* because C is already linked as a predecessor of B—the interaction must be resolved by linking C as a predecessor of A.

Figure 14.20

Optimization Procedures

Since we are interested in practical problems, considerations of efficiency are important and the planner must produce cost-effective plans. A preliminary step was to determine criteria for judging the efficiency of alternative plans. Such plans have a set of constituent actions, each with cost of execution and duration. A suitable measure of the efficiency of a plan must trade-off the total cost of the constituent actions against the overall duration of the project. In many cases it is easy to assign either an overhead cost to the duration of the project or a penalty cost to any delay beyond a fixed duration. If the project in question is the overhaul of a power station, the cost of having the station out of action can be measured as the additional cost of generating power by a less efficient alternative. For example, the overhead cost per day may be greater for a modern nuclear power station than for an old coal-fired station. It is very common for building contractors to insert penalty clauses in their contracts, whereby they undertake to make penalty payments for delays beyond an agreed completion date.

One possible formulation of the problem of generating an efficient plan is that of choosing a set of activities P which will perform the specified task at minimum cost, where the cost depends on the cost of performing individual actions and an overhead that depends on the length of time that is taken for the whole plan.

Thus, the total cost can be expressed as

$$C = \sum_{i \in p} C_i + kT.$$

where

c_i is the cost of the ith job
k is the overhead cost per day
T is the duration of the project in days

There have been several studies (e.g., Crowston and Thompson [1967]) that have assumed that the choices of alternative actions can be incorporated into a single graph that allows alternatives to have different predecessors, and in previous work (Daniel, 1974) we have considered ways of searching such a graph for a good solution.

We now consider such an approach to be inadequate for the following reasons:

· The complexity of carrying along alternatives is too great because of the combinatorial explosion of interactions among different actions.
· The representations proposed for networks with alternatives are inadequate for the complexity of the problem.

An alternative approach to the problem of choosing efficient plans suggests that plans can be generated at different levels of detail and that, at each level in the hierarchy, choices can be made between different actions and different ways of resolving interactions. Thus, no alternatives are kept in the network as it is expanded to the next most detailed level, but efficiency criteria are considered when choices are being made.

Here we are suggesting an extension of NOAH's planning strategy to provide efficient as well as feasible plans.

Modifying Plans

At various stages in the planning process, choices are made among alternatives. However well organized the planner, there is always the possibility that a wrong choice will be made, resulting in either an infeasible or a very inefficient solution. Recovery from such a failure involves identification of the decision that is responsible for the failure and appropriate modification of the current plan. In order to facilitate such modification procedures, one can use a separate structure, called a *decision graph,* to record the relationships among decisions that are made in generating a plan.

Hierarchical planning corresponds to choosing among alternative plans at each level in the hierarchy. Because, at each level, the planner is working on a complete plan, global information is available to direct the choice, and moreover, because high level plans have relatively few actions, it is possible to make a comprehensive investigation of the search space for that particular level. A planner that explored the whole search space at each level of detail and did not backtrack between levels would have a complete search space as shown in Figure 14.21.

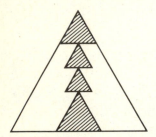

Figure 14.21

The expectations of such a system are:

· It is possible to explore all alternatives at each level of detail in order to yield the "best" plan according to some criterion.
· It is not necessary to back up to higher-level choice points—the "best" plan at a particular level will always generate a good plan when examined in more detail.

In fact, the search space at a particular level is often large, and since high-level plans must be inaccurate, the decisions made at these levels sometimes prove to be wrong and must be reversed. For example, in planning how to move an object from one room to another, a particular door may be chosen which, on closer investigation, proves to be locked. Consequently, in designing a search strategy, one must consider how to structure the search within a particular level in order to get a good solution without necessarily searching the whole space and how to recognize when one must back up to a decision that is made at a higher level of detail.

The decision graph, based on Hayes's (1975) work on a journey planner, allows the system to back up and undo decisions that were made at higher levels without throwing away all the work that was done following the original decision. Only the affected parts of the network are modified when a decision is undone.

The basic assumption behind the structure of the decision graph is that the decisions that are made in generating a plan are of two types:

· choice of expansion for a node
· choice of links to remove an interaction

Such choices are interrelated inasmuch as an interaction and consequent link may depend on a particular choice of expansion. The purpose of the decision graph is to record such relationships. Every node in the plan (net node) points to a node in the decision graph (*d*-node), corresponding to the expansion that introduced it. Every time an expansion (or phantom) is made, a node is set up in the *d*-graph with pointers to:

- the net node being expanded
- the parent *d*-node—that which introduced the net node being expanded
- the new net nodes, introduced by the expansion
- any subsequent expansions of these nodes
- any interaction *d*-nodes that are consequent on this expansion
- any phantom *d*-nodes corresponding to phantom links, using a pattern achieved by the expansion
- in the case of a phantom—any *d*-node corresponding to a phantom link that is required to establish the phantom goal

Every time a link is introduced to enable the creation of a phantom net node, a *d*-node is introduced with pointers to:

- the net node and corresponding *d*-node made into a phantom
- the net node and corresponding *d*-node achieving the pattern

Every time a link is introduced to remove an interaction, a *d*-node is introduced with pointers to:

- the link being introduced
- the net node and corresponding *d*-node that needs the condition involved in the interaction
- the net node and corresponding *d*-node that achieves the condition in question
- the net node and corresponding *d*-node that deletes the condition in question

Satisfying Conditions and Removing Interactions

The task formalism allows several types of conditions to be specified, but the two that proved most useful were:

- *Supervised Conditions*. Conditions that are achieved within the expansion containing the node for which they are needed—that is, actions that make them true are included in the opschema.
- *Unsupervised Conditions*—Conditions that are expected to be achieved by an action in another part of the plan—that is, their contributors are not specified and must be determined by the planner.

Ensuring that unsupervised conditions are satisfied often involves adding links to the network, thus constraining later attempts to remove interactions or satisfy conditions. Consequently, it is important that such conditions be satisfied as soon as possible. In our latest planning system, unsupervised conditions are satisfied at every level before proceeding to the next most detailed level.

For the same reason, constrained interactions are removed immediately, whereas those that can be resolved in two ways are only removed when all nodes at one level have been expanded.

An Example

Here we show different levels of parts of a plan to build a house (Figs. 14.22 and 14.23)

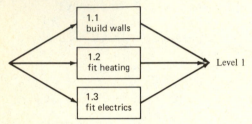

Figure 14.22

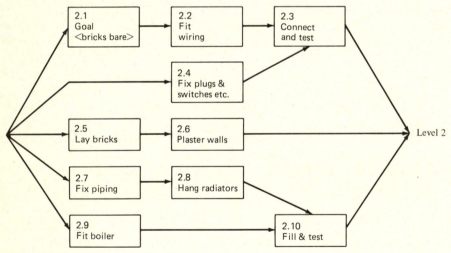

Figure 14.23

When the nodes in the level 1 plan are expanded to those at level 2, some new conditions and effects are introduced.

CONDITIONS: unsupervised ⟨bricks laid⟩ needed-by 2.2
unsupervised ⟨wall surface complete⟩ needed-by 2.4
unsupervised ⟨wall surface complete⟩ needed-by 2.8
supervised ⟨bricks bare⟩ needed-by 2.2 added-by 2.1

EFFECTS: *add*   ⟨bricks laid⟩ by 2.5
                              ⟨wall surface complete⟩ by 2.6
                              ⟨bricks bare⟩ by 2.5
           delete ⟨bricks bare⟩ by 2.6

Links must be added to make the unsupervised conditions true and an interaction is detected between the condition needed by 2.2 and deleted by 2.6. The interaction can be removed by linking 2.6 either before 2.1 or after 2.2 and the choice depends on trading-off a possible delay to successors of 2.6 against the cost of making the goal of 2.1 true (Note: It is already made true by 2.5, but this cannot be maintained if 2.6 precedes 2.1). The network resulting from one choice is shown in Figure 14.24:

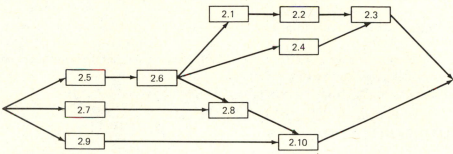

Figure 14.24

The choice of ways to remove the interaction could cause difficulty in a plan where the walls were not plastered but panelled with wood. In such a case it would not be possible to gain access to the brickwork to fit wiring, whereas if the walls were plastered, the plaster could be cut and then patched up.

The decision graph, shown in Figure 14.25, records the relationship among some of the decisions that were made in generating the plan. The only way in which a plan can be modified is to undo one of the two kinds of decisions involved in the plan—that is to remove an expansion or a link (either a phantom link or an interaction link).

Removing a phantom link is very straightforward, only requiring that the net-node in question be reinstated as a goal node and that the GOST and decision graph be modified

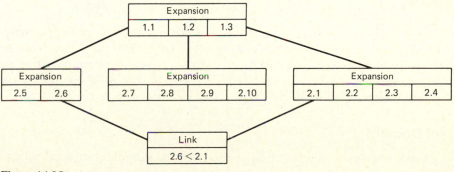

Figure 14.25

accordingly. Removing an interaction link involves choosing either an alternative way to remove the interaction or undoing an expansion that introduced one of the actions that is involved in the interaction.

The steps involved in undoing an expansion are:

1. Trace down the decision graph and the net nodes (and their expansions, if any) and links that are dependent on the expansion.
2. Remove these nodes and links and replace them by the single parent net node.
3. Find all remaining links that are connected to any removed net nodes and attach them to the parent net node.
4. Modify the TOME and GOST for every deleted net node as follows:
   (a) Remove all conditions and effects that are needed/achieved by the deleted node and not the replaced node.
   (b) Remove them as contributors to any condition that is not achieved by the replaced node.
5. For all conditions that now have no contributors, undo the expansion that was dependent on it (i.e., phantom nodes replaced by goal nodes).
6. Look for interactions arising from the removal of links from the graph.

A PRACTICAL APPLICATION

For a practical application involving the generation of networks of the size that is usually used for critical path analysis techniques (several hundred activities), it was important to avoid large search spaces. We looked for an application where a large class of networks was required, each member of the class having great similarities with all the others, but having important differences that required a new network to be generated for each individual project. The advantages of such a problem domain are:

- There are enough historical data of plans that have been previously generated to allow an action hierarchy to be set up.
- The choice of plans to be generated is sufficiently restricted to keep the search space under control.
- The difference among individual plans is sufficient to make it worthwhile to have a system that aids in their generation.

The chosen application was the annual overhauling of power stations where each annual overhaul is different from previous years but still has the same overall structure. Another possible application might be the construction of a set of houses of a particular type but where, in each individual case, there are choices to be made between restricted alternatives about things such as type of heating, type of flooring, type of bathroom fixtures, and so on.

The Problem Domain

Within the large task of power-station overhaul we selected the subproject of overhauling a turbine as being the size of problem with which the planning system should cope. The networks involved usually have more than five hundred activities but the problem is highly structured as follows:

- A turbine consists of four sections: high pressure, intermediate pressure, and two low pressure sections.
- Overhauls on each of the four sections can proceed independently, except for one alignment check along the whole length of the rotor.
- The overhaul of a section comprises the removal of layers of covers and the rotor, giving access to various components in the process, and replacement of parts as access is no longer required.
- An individual overhaul varies from previous ones inasmuch as different components may or may not be overhauled and there are different types of overhaul for each component. The choice of which type of overhaul is to be done on each component (or whether it is to be overhauled at all) is totally at the discretion of the user. The planner has merely to work out the consequences of each decision—for example, ensuring that access is gained.

It seemed natural to define the action hierarchy in terms of three levels giving networks of about 70 nodes, 300 nodes, and 750 nodes. Figures 14.26 to 14.28 show typical actions at each level. Only those conditions and effects that were involved in interactions were mentioned when using the task formalism to specify opschemas. These were relatively few at each level of detail, since in most cases the ordering within expansions, which was passed down to lower-level networks, took care of most potential interactions. In this particular application, there are no choices to be made among alternative expansions (such choices are decisions to be made by the user of the system), and in all cases, interactions can only be removed in one way. Consequently, the process of the planning problem is that of finding and removing the interactions among different parts of the plan.

Achieving Goals

The planning system now distinguishes among goal nodes, action nodes, and query nodes. *Query nodes* are a means of allowing the user to choose whether certain actions should be included in the plan—for example, whether to overhaul the high-pressure section of a turbine. When a query node is encountered, the user is asked whether the corresponding action should be included. If the user responds "no" the action will not be included, otherwise the action will be included and expanded.

In general, an expansion will include several goal nodes that are used to avoid redundancy in cases where several actions share preconditions. For example, two different components A and B may be located under the same cover. If A is to be overhauled, then it will not be necessary to remove the cover again for B. However, if A is not included, then an action must be introduced to remove the cover for B. Thus, the opschemas for B will have the following expansion:

```
1 goal ≪ Remove top cover ≫
2 action ≪ Overhaul component B ≫
3 goal ≪ Replace top cover ≫
orderings    1 → 2    2 → 3
```

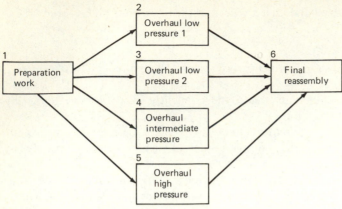

Figure 14.26 Planning network for turbine overhaul task.

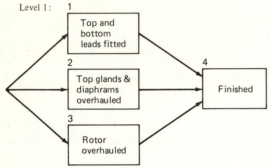

Figure 14.27 First level expansion of "overhaul high pressure" action.

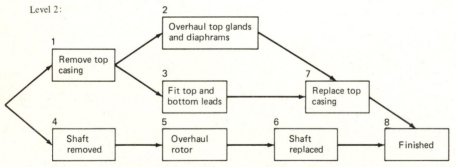

Figure 14.28 Second level expansion of "overhaul high pressure" action.

The actions to remove and replace the cover should naturally be included in the same network as the action to overhaul **B**. In the planning system the two goal patterns are marked as having the same level as that of the pattern that is currently being expanded. In this way they will both be expanded (i.e., the goal replaced by actions) before the action to overhaul **B** is expanded.

The Planning Cycle

The planner operates at distinct levels (in this case, three) and tries to tie up as many loose ends as possible before going on to the next level of detail. Each pattern is marked with a level and only those whose levels are equal to the current one will be expanded. For a particular level the steps for the cycle are as follows:

1. Increment net level to current level.
2. Expand a node whose level is equal to current level. If there is none, go to step (8).
3. If there are any query nodes in the expansion, interrogate user and act accordingly.
4. Introduce new nodes into network.
5. Try to satisfy unsupervised conditions—if any cannot be satisfied, keep a note.
6. Look for interactions involving nodes in the current expansion. All constrained interactions are removed immediately—unconstrained interactions are stored, to be removed when they become constrained or at the end of the cycle.
7. Go to step (2).
8. Remove any outstanding unconstrained interactions.
9. Go to step (1).

We can now follow through the representation in the task formalism of part of the action hierarchy for turbine overhaul—the overhaul of the high-pressure section.

The highest level network for the turbine overhaul is shown in Figure 14.26.

Such a network can be represented in the task formalism as an opschema:

```
opschema turbine
pattern «turbine overhaul»
expansion    1 action «preparation work»
            ·2 query  «low pressure 1 overhauled»
             3 query  «low pressure 2 overhauled»
             4 query  «intermediate pressure overhauled»
             5 query  «high pressure overhauled»
             6 action «final reassembly»
orderings 1 → 2   1 → 3   1 → 4   1 → 5
          2 → 6   3 → 6   4 → 6   5 → 6
end;
```

The action "overhaul high pressure" can be expanded to the networks in Figures 14.27 and 14.28.

At the second level the unsupervised condition

«top casing replaced» can be satisfied.

The new unsupervised conditions «top casing removed» that are required by nodes 4, 5, and 6 in Figure 14.28 are made true by node 1 and untrue by node 7. The planner will remove the interaction and satisfy the conditions by linking 1 before 4 and 6 before 7. The interactions will not be removed until they have become constrained by the satisfaction of the unsupervised conditions.

A call to the system

plan goal «turbine overhaul»

will cause the planning program to use the preceding opschema, to set up the initial high-level network, as shown in Figure 14.26. The presence of query nodes causes the system to interrogate the user as to whether he or she wishes the corresponding actions to be performed. That is, does he or she wish to overhaul the intermediate pressure section in this particular overhaul (note that the query nodes can occur at every level in the hierarchy, thus allowing refinement of the particular type of overhaul required). If the user answers "no," the node type will be changed to phantom and the goal will be set to true in the initial state—thus, no expansion of this high-level node will be made at any stage. If the user answers "yes," the node type will be set to goal, and at some stage, the planner will seek to achieve the goal either as a result of some other action already in the plan or by introducing new actions.

We have set up the action hierarchy for the overhaul of a turbine for a power station, and the planning system operates effectively to produce networks of the type in current use.

As already stated, there is no requirement in this particular application for the planning system to make any choices since:

- Choices among alternative expansions are made by the user—that is, in specifying the exact type of overhaul that he or she wishes to have performed.
- All interactions become constrained at each level of detail—by either the time they are identified or the introduction of links to satisfy unsupervised conditions before they are re- solved. (In the current implementation, unconstrained interactions are not resolved until the very end of each level of expansion.)

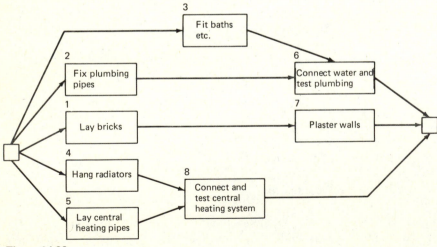

Figure 14.29

However, it is reasonable to expect that in very similar applications (e.g., different types of overhaul or construction tasks), the problem of choices will arise. Limited choices between alternative expansions might arise because there is more than one way to perform a task (one being fast and expensive, the other being slow and cheap), the "best" choice being dependent on the criticality of the task in question—that is, its relationship in other parts of the project.

Again, it is easy to envisage occasions where choices among alternative ways of resolving interactions need to be made by the planning system.

The considerations to be taken into account when making such choices can best be illustrated by a variant of the earlier example for house-building. When the network shown in Figure 14.29 is examined for interactions the following conditions and effects are discovered:

CONDITIONS: unsupervised <bricks laid> needed-by at 2
unsupervised <wall surface complete> needed-by 4
unsupervised <bricks bare> needed-by 2

EFFECTS *add* <bricks laid> by 1
<bricks bare> by 1
<wall surface complete> by 7
delete <bricks bare> by 7

A sensible planner would satisfy the supervised conditions (which involve no choices) before resolving the interaction between nodes 2 and 7. When the supervised conditions are satisfied, the network is as in Figure 14.30:

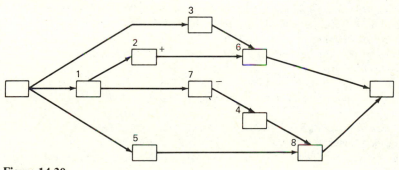

Figure 14.30

There is now an interaction because the unsupervised condition <bricks bare> that is needed by node 2 is deleted by node 7. The interaction can be resolved in two ways:

1. Add a link that means that 7 cannot start until node 2 has finished and 7's successors will be delayed; or
2. Link 7 before 2 and expect that the condition must now be established by the addition of a new action into the network.

Thus, we see that the problem of choosing how to resolve the interaction involves trading-off possible delays in the project against the cost of introducing additional actions. However, if no radiators were being fitted, the alternative resolution would be more satisfactory.

The planner in use, NONLIN (Tate, 1976), has the ability to cope with this, and the present turbine overhaul system needs only minor modification to cope with such choices. In Daniel (1977) we describe a search strategy for such applications.

This chapter represents one example of combining AI reasoning techniques with more conventional approaches to mathematical modelling. We expect in the future to see the emergence of powerful systems based upon a synthesis of techniques drawn from Operations Research, statistical inference, linear programming, and symbolic computation.

Bibliography

Crowston, W., and Thompson, G. L. "Decision CPM: A Method for Simultaneous Planning, Scheduling, and Control of Projects." *Operations Research* 15: 407–426, 1967.

Daniel, L. M. "And/or Graphs and Critical Paths." In *Proceedings of the International Conference on Information Processing,* 1974.

Daniel, L. M. "Planning: Modifying Non-linear Plans," DAI Working Paper 24. Edinburgh: Department of Artificial Intelligence, University of Edinburgh, 1977.

Fikes, R. E., and Nilsson, N. J. 1971. "STRIPS: A New Approach to the Application of Theorem Proving to Problem Solving," *Artificial Intelligence* 2: 189–208, 1971.

Hayes, P. J. "A Representation for Robot Plans." In *Proceedings of the Fourth International Joint Conference on Artificial Intelligence,* Tbilisi, U.S.S.R., 1975.

Newell, A., Shaw, J. C., and Simon, H. A. "Report on a General Problem-Solving Program." In *Proceedings of the International Conference on Information Processing,* UNESCO House, Paris, 1959, pp. 256–264.

Nilsson, N. J. *Problem Solving Methods in Artificial Intelligence.* New York: McGraw-Hill, 1971.

Sacerdoti, E. D. "The Non-linear Nature of Plans." In *Proceedings of the Fourth International Joint Conference on Artificial Intelligence,* Tibilisi, U.S.S.R., 1975a.

Sacerdoti, E. D. "A Structure for Plans and Behaviour." *SRI Technical Note 109.* Menlo Park, Calif.: AI Center, Stanford Research Institute, 1975b.

Siklossy, L., and Deussi, J. "An Efficient Robot Planner Which Generates Its Own Procedures." In *Proceedings of the Third International Joint Conference on Artificial Intelligence,* Stanford, Calif., 1973.

Sussman, G. J. *A Computational Model of Skill Acquisition.* Amsterdam: North-Holland, 1973.

Tate, A. "INTERPLAN: A Plan Generation System Which Can Deal with Interactions Between Goals." Memo MIP-R-109. Edinburgh: Machine Intelligence Research Unit, University of Edinburgh, 1974.

Tate, A. "The Use of Goal Structure to Direct Search in a Problem Solver." Ph.D. thesis. Edinburgh: University of Edinburgh, 1975.

Tate, A. "NONLIN: A Hierarchic Non-linear Planner." DAI Memo 25. Edinburgh: Department of Artificial Intelligence, University of Edinburgh, 1976.

CHAPTER 15

INSIDE AN EXPERT SYSTEM: A RATIONAL RECONSTRUCTION OF THE MYCIN CONSULTATION SYSTEM

JADZIA CENDROWSKA
and
MAX BRAMER

INTRODUCTION AND RATIONALE

Much attention has recently been focussed on the field of expert systems development, not least as a result of the Japanese Fifth Generation Computer project.

This chapter describes a "rational reconstruction" of part of MYCIN, arguably the best known and most significant expert system currently in existence.

There are two principal reasons why the authors consider that work of this kind is of value at the present time.

1. The technique of "rebuild and improve" is likely to be a very effective means of gaining considerable practical knowledge and experience in a relatively short time for those who

wish to develop working systems without going through a lengthy preliminary apprentice-ship of research and theoretical study. This is a technique that Japanese industry has frequently used to good effect in the past.

2. A sufficient number of working systems have now been developed to make the synthesis of a coherent body of underlying theory a practical possibility.

Although it would undoubtedly be of great value to develop such a body of theory in as much detail as possible, both to aid the effective production of further systems and to indicate areas in which further research is needed, there are a number of obstacles to doing so.

Expert systems work is derived from research in artificial intelligence, a field in which the complaint is often made that published accounts of research frequently do not directly correspond to actual working programs (if such programs exist at all) and often give a misleading impression of what has been achieved.

Without wishing to defend bad practices, there are difficulties involved in artificial intelligence research that make accurate appraisal particularly difficult. The field is generally concerned with domains (such as medical diagnosis or language understanding) where the "success" of a program is difficult to measure and can usually only be judged in terms of selected examples. It is clearly not possible to show every feasible example, and so the value of a program is inherently uncertain.

The programs themselves are often large and extremely complex and thus not usually suitable for publication. Inevitably, published accounts tend to be in simplified form and this effect is compounded as second- and third-hand versions appear in textbooks and survey articles. For example, MYCIN is usually described as using production rules and a backward-chaining control structure, which although true is a serious oversimplification. Unfortunately, it may well be that the detailed information lost in this way is of crucial importance for the researcher who desires to build on the work.

A particular feature of AI programs is that they are generally written to illustrate a particular theory, and if judged successful, it is this theory that will be featured in published accounts. However, it may be the case that the program's success derives less from the embodied theory than from the author's skill in writing and "fine tuning" the program. Authors are not well placed to be able to judge such matters objectively and an extremely detailed subsequent analysis may be needed to identify what has been learned, even from the most acclaimed of systems.

This chapter is concerned with the rational reconstruction of a major expert system.

It must be stressed that the aim of a rational reconstruction is not to rebuild an existing system in an exactly identical form (which is virtually impossible with any computer system of any appreciable size). Rather, it is to analyse the system in close detail, from a re-engineering viewpoint, piecing together the information given in a number of different accounts, if necessary—much as an archaeologist combines the evidence from different parts of an excavation to form a composite view of a site.

To demonstrate the accuracy of the analysis, one should build a replacement for the most important part (or parts) of the original system, perhaps in a different language, which corresponds as closely as possible to the published descriptions and examples of program performance. In this way, any discrepancies between description and performance can be highlighted and analyzed in detail.

The value of performing such a reconstruction lies substantially in what is learned from achieving it, but the finished product is also likely to be of value since it represents, in a sense, the "essence" of the original system—the principal routines and data structures, for example, rather than the input/output routines, debugging facilities and so on, which although crucial for practical use are of no particular interest and merely complicate the original system.

MYCIN is singled out for attention in this paper, not in any spirit of criticism, but because of its apparent considerable success and its status in the expert systems field.

It is the authors' view that a thorough understanding of the strengths and limitations of the techniques of knowledge representation and manipulation embodied in MYCIN is likely to be of considerable value to the serious researcher or system developer, as a basis for further work.

MYCIN is a rule-based expert system, developed by Edward Shortliffe and others at the Stanford Heuristic Programming Project, in collaboration with the Infectious Diseases Group at the Stanford Medical School, which was designed to assist physicians in the diagnosis and treatment of diseases caused by certain kinds of bacterial infection. MYCIN seeks to model the decision process by which the expert consultant performs a diagnosis and selects a suitable treatment.

This chapter presents a detailed analysis and a partial reconstruction of MYCIN's control structure and the data bases used for the diagnosis phase of the decision process. The main source employed is Edward Shortliffe's book *Computer-based Medical Consultations: MYCIN,* referred to as Shortliffe (1976), and a Ph.D. thesis by William van Melle on a closely related system, EMYCIN. This thesis is referred to as van Melle (1980). A brief account of the evolution of the MYCIN system and its relationship to EMYCIN is given in a later section. It is important to appreciate, however, that MYCIN is a complex system that has undergone numerous modifications over a lengthy period of time. The version described here is an amalgam of several of these versions, which includes some important features that are not described in Shortliffe (1976). Embellishments introduced in the most recent versions of MYCIN have not necessarily been included. Although this reconstruction generally follows the published descriptions closely, in some cases "interpolations" have been made where the descriptions that are available are imprecise, and some other implementation details have been changed in the interests of uniformity.

Minor details of no theoretical significance (such as the exact format in which a date should be entered) have occasionally been changed in this reconstruction. However, important details (e.g., of MYCIN's control structure) have been closely scrutinised. A listing of a reconstructed version of MYCIN, known as RMYCIN, which closely follows the description given in this chapter, is given in Cendrowska and Bramer (1982), from which this chapter is adapted. Specimen output from RMYCIN is given in the appendix.

Although MYCIN itself is written in LISP, the reconstruction (RMYCIN) employs the programming language POP-2. This design decision should not be taken as advancing the claims of that language for expert systems development, but as a means of identifying those features of a programming language that are particularly necessary or desirable in constructing such systems.

Attention is focussed, *inter alia,* on the production rules, the goal-directed backward chaining of rules that comprises the control structure and the parameters and context types that are employed, together with the data structures created during a consultation and the system's use of "certainty factors" to handle uncertain information.

A detailed account is given of how a typical consultation proceeds and some variants that can occur are considered. Developments to MYCIN since its original implementation in 1976 to improve performance and efficiency are also described, together with a brief account of its generalised version EMYCIN.

The chapter identifies a number of gaps in the original reporting of MYCIN and presents a critique of a number of its features and an appraisal of the value of a MYCIN-like approach as a starting point for further expert systems development.

SYSTEM OVERVIEW

Work on the MYCIN project started in 1972. The task was to design a system that could play a similar role to that of a human specialist in infectious diseases. Thus, it was to interact with a physician to collect all the relevant information that is available about a patient under consideration, and then to examine this information for evidence upon which to base a diagnosis and recommendation for therapy.

The human specialist tackles the problem of selecting an appropriate therapy in four stages, namely:

1. determining if the patient has a significant infection, and if so
2. determining the likely identity of the offending organism(s)
3. deciding which drugs are likely to be effective in general, and
4. choosing the most appropriate drug for the patient.

This decision process is a complex one, relying heavily on clinical judgment and experience. MYCIN tries to model the chain of reasoning that is used by the specialist by embodying his or her judgmental knowledge in the form of production rules.

The program collects relevant information about the patient (e.g., his or her clinical condition, symptoms, medical history, or details of any laboratory findings), by conducting an interactive dialogue with the physician. It asks the basic questions first. The information entered by the physician in response to these questions is used by the rules in an attempt to make a diagnosis. If, during this process, further information is required, the system will either try to infer the information from the data it has already acquired, or it will ask the physician. As soon as a reasonable diagnosis can be made, MYCIN will compile a list of possible therapies, and on the basis of further interaction with the physician, will choose the most appropriate one for the patient.

The rules are frequently of a tentative kind, indicating, for example, that certain symptoms imply a conclusion only to some level of certainty. The ability to "reason with uncertain information" is an important feature of MYCIN.

MYCIN has many features to heighten its acceptability to physicians. It is easy to use. The system is tolerant of spelling or typing mistakes and can recognize synonyms. It communicates with the user in a subset of English, so that no training is required to use the system. Because of the modularity of the rules, MYCIN is easy to update, and so can accommodate the changes to which the medical domain is prone. The system also provides an explanation facility, which allows the users to ask questions, so that they can understand for themselves how MYCIN makes its decisions.

The entire MYCIN system comprises three subprograms (see Fig. 15.1): the consultation program, the explanation program, and the rule acquisition program. It stores its information in two data bases: a *static data base* that contains all the rules used during a consultation, and a *dynamic data base* which is created afresh for each consultation and contains patient information and details of the questions that are asked in the consultation to date. When the physician feels that he needs advice about the management of a particular patient, he enters the system by starting the consultation program. The ensuing interaction is the core of the program during which the system asks the necessary questions, draws its inferences, and makes its recommendations as to the diagnosis and therapy. A typical consultation lasts about 20 minutes. The questions asked depend on the answers that were previously given and are only asked if the information cannot be inferred from data already acquired. They are asked in a logical sequence so that the physician can follow the course of the consultation. Redundancy is avoided. If the physician feels that some part of the consultation is obscure, for example, if he cannot see the reason for a particular question, he can temporarily adjourn from the consultation to ask for clarification. The system can then explain the reason for the question and give examples of the type of answer it expects. Afterwards, the physician can return to the basic consultation without having to retrace his steps from the beginning.

When the consultation is over, the system passes automatically to the second subprogram, the explanation program, which answers questions from the user and explains its line of reasoning. It does this by showing an English version of the rules that are used, to explain why it needed a particular piece of information, and how certain conclusions were reached. The main purpose of this is to allow physicians to decide if MYCIN's reasoning is sound and to reject its advice if they feel that it is not sound. Without this feature MYCIN would be totally unacceptable to the medical profession, as a physician would be reluctant to give medication unless he was certain that it was the appropriate therapy for his patient.

The third subprogram is the rule-acquisition program, for use by experts only. If an expert

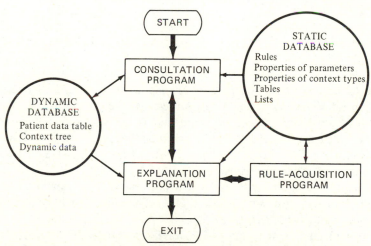

Figure 15.1   Flow of control and information within the MYCIN system. Flow of control is indicated by heavy arrows: Flow of information by light arrows. (*Source:* Adapted from Shortliffe, 1976, p. 46.)

feels that a rule is missing or incomplete, he or she can use this program to correct the error by entering a new rule or modifying the old one.

This chapter concentrates almost entirely on MYCIN's consultation program, although features of relevance to the other two constituent programs are also occasionally mentioned.

In particular, the description is focussed on the first two stages in the decision process as previously listed, namely, deciding whether the patient has a significant infection, and if so, determining the likely identity of the offending organism(s). The description is therefore limited to describing how the consultation program uses rules to interact with the user and build the data structures containing the clinical information that was gained during the consultation. Correspondingly, RMYCIN uses a subset of MYCIN's rules to infer the identity of the infecting organism(s) but does not proceed to propose a treatment. Adding this facility to the program would require detailed information about drug sensitivities and their interactions that at present is unavailable to the authors and of no particular value for the present purpose.

The third stage is, in fact, implemented in MYCIN in conventional procedural rather than rule-based form. (The final stage is once again rule based.)

OVERVIEW OF THE MYCIN CONSULTATION SYSTEM

As a consultation proceeds, MYCIN builds up information about a number of entities in its domain, such as an offending organism or the culture from which it was isolated. These entities are known as *contexts*. The information is either provided directly by the user or deduced by using rules.

There are a number of *context types* employed, of which the most important† are PERSON, CURCULS, and CURORGS, corresponding to the patient, 'current cultures', taken from the patient and 'current organisms', isolated from those cultures, respectively.

Contexts are arranged hierarchically in a tree structure, known as a *context tree,* which varies in detail from one consultation to another.

In every consultation, there is exactly one context of type PERSON (i.e., the patient himself or herself). This context has no "parent context" and serves as the root node of the context tree.

Contexts of every other type can occur as many times as necessary (including zero times). However, it turns out that at least one context of type CURCULS and one of type CURORGS must always exist in every consultation (and it would be pointless to take part in a MYCIN consultation in the absence of at least one current organism that is isolated from a current positive culture). Each context type except PERSON has a corresponding parent context type, thus a CURCULS context can only be a direct descendant of the PERSON, a CURORGS context can only be a direct descendant of a CURCULS context, and so on.

Figure 15.2 is an example of a typical context tree. Each node corresponds to a context and is labelled with a unique name (automatically assigned by MYCIN). The type of each context in the tree is shown in parentheses beside its name.

This figure represents a patient (the context named PATIENT-1 of type PERSON), from whom two current cultures (contexts CULTURE-1 and CULTURE-2 of type CURCULS) and one prior culture (context CULTURE-3 of type PRIORCULS) have been obtained. Two organisms

†1976 version.

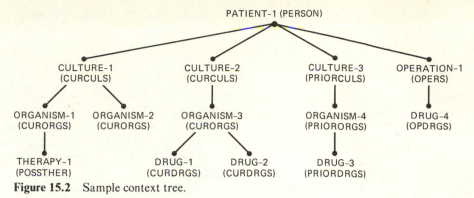

Figure 15.2   Sample context tree.

were isolated from the first current culture, and one each from the second current culture and the prior culture (contexts ORGANISM-1, ORGANISM-2, and ORGANISM-3 of type CURORGS and context ORGANISM-4 of type PRIORORGS, respectively). The patient is being treated for one of the current organisms, ORGANISM-3, with two different drugs (contexts DRUG-1 and DRUG-2 of type CURDRGS), and a possible therapy is being considered for recommendation for use against ORGANISM-1 (context THERAPY-1 of type POSSTHER). He or she has also been treated for the organism, ORGANISM-4, isolated from the prior culture (context DRUG-3 of type PRIORDRGS). The patient had a recent operation (context OPERATION-1 of type OPERS), during which a drug was administered (context DRUG-4 of type OPDRGS).

Although the context tree is of paramount importance, MYCIN is not initially provided with information about the contexts that are applicable to the current consultation.

Rather it creates, or *instantiates,* each context as the need for it is discovered. A consultation begins by instantiating a context of type PERSON. This action "drives" the entire consultation session as discussed in the following sections. Each instantiation of a context type, that is, each context, is automatically assigned a unique name, for example, CULTURE-1 or ORGANISM-3.

Each context type has an associated set of *clinical parameters* that applies to all contexts of that type but (in general) varies from one context type to another.

Thus, for example, the sets of parameters corresponding to context types PERSON, CURCULS, and CURORGS are named PROP-PT, PROP-CUL, and PROP-ORG, respectively.

PROP-PT includes parameters NAME, AGE, and SEX (the name, age, and sex of the patient), PROP-CUL includes parameter SITE (the site of the culture), and PROP-ORG includes parameter IDENT (the identity of the organism).

Finding the value of a clinical parameter is known as *tracing* the parameter. Ultimately, MYCIN is concerned with tracing the value of a single parameter, REGIMEN (in category PROP-PT) for context PATIENT-1.

REGIMEN is the "recommended treatment" for the patient under consideration.

Although the values of some clinical parameters (e.g., NAME, AGE, SEX) can be supplied directly by the user (the physician), the majority (including the value of REGIMEN) cannot be supplied and instead are *deduced* by MYCIN, using rules that link an unknown value of interest to the values of other parameters.

Thus, for example, in finding the value of REGIMEN, one must first find, *inter alia,* a possible value of IDENT for (i.e., the identity of) each current organism.

MYCIN uses production rules to embody its expert knowledge about infectious diseases, as inference rules of the general form:

IF *premise* THEN *action*

where **premise** generally involves testing the value of one or more parameters and **action** generally involves concluding the value of one or more further parameters.

Note that for many clinical parameters, MYCIN usually computes not one definitive value but a number of alternative possibilities, each with its own probability-like value called a *certainty factor*. This is a number between -1 and $+1$ and is used to indicate the degree of belief that the value of the clinical parameter is the true value.

A certainty factor of $+1$ indicates that the parameter is "known with certainty" to have that value. A certainty factor of -1 indicates that the parameter is known with certainty *not* to have that value. Certainty factors can be either computed or entered by the physician (as described further in later sections). Thus, the value of IDENT for ORGANISM-1 may be SALMONELLA (with certainty factor 0.4), PSEUDOMONAS (with certainty factor 0.3), and so on.

Each of MYCIN's rules is intended to correspond to an item of knowledge that is meaningful to the physician. Each rule has both an internal (stored) form and an external English translation. In the internal form, both the premise and the action part of a rule are held as a (LISP) list structure. Figure 15.3 shows an example of a rule in both forms.

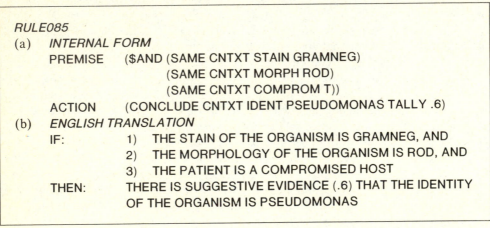

RULE085
(a)   *INTERNAL FORM*
       PREMISE   ($AND (SAME CNTXT STAIN GRAMNEG)
                        (SAME CNTXT MORPH ROD)
                        (SAME CNTXT COMPROM T))
       ACTION   (CONCLUDE CNTXT IDENT PSEUDOMONAS TALLY .6)
(b)   *ENGLISH TRANSLATION*
       IF: 1)   THE STAIN OF THE ORGANISM IS GRAMNEG, AND
                   2)   THE MORPHOLOGY OF THE ORGANISM IS ROD, AND
                   3)   THE PATIENT IS A COMPROMISED HOST
       THEN: THERE IS SUGGESTIVE EVIDENCE (.6) THAT THE IDENTITY
                   OF THE ORGANISM IS PSEUDOMONAS

Figure 15.3   One of MYCIN's rules. (*Source:* From Shortliffe, 1976, p. 75.)

MYCIN's control structure is (principally) a goal-directed *backward-chaining* of rules. At any point the program is working towards the goal of finding the value of some parameter of a context, that is, *tracing* the parameter, and it does this by invoking all the rules that make a conclusion about that parameter in their ACTION part.

For example, if the program were trying to deduce the identity of an organism (i.e., the value of its IDENT parameter), one of the rules invoked would be RULE085 (Fig. 15.3). In this case, the premise is the conjunction of three conditions.

If all the necessary parameters had already been traced, the premise could be determined to be either true or false and in the former case a conclusion could be made about the identity of the organism (with a suitable certainty factor). However, if the value of some parameter referenced in the premise had not been traced (e.g., the morphology of the organism), it would be traced immediately as part of the "evaluation" of the premise of RULE085. This might involve performing a similar process on rules that conclude a value for the MORPH parameter in their action parts.

Continuing in this way leads to a *depth-first search* of an implicit AND/OR tree that is formed by the constituent conditions of the rules. At the leaf nodes of this tree, the values of parameters are provided by the user in response to questions.

The aim of MYCIN's backward-chaining approach is to avoid asking questions unnecessarily. Instead, with a few exceptions, questions are asked only when needed to trace the value of a clinical parameter.

The consultation starts by instantiating the context PATIENT-1 as the root node of the context tree and then attempts to find the value of the REGIMEN parameter for that context (the reason for this is explained in the section on the control structure). There is a single relevant rule, called the *goal rule,* which leads to a deduction of the value of REGIMEN. Note that the physician cannot simply be asked the value of REGIMEN (and there would be little point in using MYCIN if REGIMEN were already known).

In order to find the value of REGIMEN, MYCIN traces the values of the parameters that are referenced in the PREMISE part of the goal rule. Again, the physician probably does not know these values, so the rules that infer these values have to be invoked, and the parameters in their PREMISE parts traced, and so on until the physician can supply some answers.

The preceding is a simplified description of how the consultation program of MYCIN operates. In the following sections this description is amplified and a "reconstruction" of the program's control structure and data structures is given.

CLASSIFYING CLINICAL PARAMETERS

Single, Binary and Multiple-Valued Parameters

There are three kinds of parameter: single-valued, binary, and multiple-valued. The majority of parameters are *single-valued,* for example, the value of IDENT for ORGANISM-1 (the identity of the organism) can logically have only one value. However, at any stage MYCIN can store a number of alternative values, each with a *certainty factor* from -1 to $+1$. Thus, the value of IDENT for ORGANISM-1 could be represented (in list form) as ((SALMONELLA 0.4) (PSEUDO-MONAS 0.3). . . .)

(The certainty factor of any value not included in the list is assumed to be zero.)

When a number of rules are used to deduce the value of a parameter, the certainty factors that are associated with each possible value will generally vary as further rules are invoked. If at any stage a value has a certainty factor of $+1$, all the others are deleted. A special case of the single-valued parameter is the *binary* or "yes/no" parameter, where the value is limited to one of two possibilities, yes or no. In this case, rather than storing certainty factors for both the value T ('true') and the value F ('false'), only the former is stored, for example:

((T 0.7))

Multiple-valued parameters are those that may reasonably have more than one value simultaneously, for example, a patient may be allergic to more than one drug. Assuming PATIENT-1 was known with certainty to be allergic to both penicillin and clindamycin, the value of the ALLERGIES property for PATIENT-1 would be the list ((PENICILLIN 1.0) (CLINDAMY-CIN 1.0)).

Note that for multiple-valued parameters, each possible value has its own independent certainty factor, from −1 to +1.

Labdata Parameters

A parameter is called labdata if it is one for which the user may be expected to know the value. This includes those parameters of which the user is very likely to know the value, such as NAME, AGE, and SEX for PERSON contexts, and those such as IDENT which may occasionally be known from laboratory reports but usually are not.

When MYCIN wants to trace the value of a labdata parameter, it first asks the user to supply its value.

If the value unknown is given, MYCIN attempts to use its rules to deduce the value of the parameter; otherwise the value that is entered by the user is accepted.

When tracing a non-labdata parameter, MYCIN begins by using its rules to deduce the value. If this produces an unreliable value†, and the value of the parameter can be asked for, MYCIN then asks the user to supply a value, otherwise the unreliable value is accepted.

Askable and Inferrable Parameters

Askable parameters are those for which it is permitted to ask the user for the value. All labdata parameters are necessarily askable.

Inferrable parameters are those whose values can be deduced by using the rules. A parameter may be both askable and inferrable, for example, IDENT (the identity of the organism).

In general, the existence of a non-labdata but askable parameter suggests that the value is not likely to be known to the user but may be calculated by him or her (possibly with some difficulty) if it cannot be reliably deduced. An example of such a parameter is ADEQUATE, that is, the dose of the drug is adequate.

An example of a non-askable (and hence non-labdata) parameter is REGIMEN, that is, the recommended treatment. In this case the value can only be deduced.

An example of a non-inferrable parameter is AGE, that is, the age of the patient.

Mainprops Parameters

For each context type, certain parameters are designated as Mainprops (i.e., "main properties"). These are parameters that are automatically traced as soon as a context is instantiated. The Mainprops parameters for a context of type PERSON are NAME, AGE, SEX, and REGIMEN. The automatic tracing of REGIMEN for the context PATIENT-1 *drives* a MYCIN consultation. All other parameters are only traced when needed.   When a new context is

---

†To be precise, its certainty factor, CF, satisfies $-0.2 < CF < +0.2$. A function KNOWN (described later) tests for this condition.

created, the tracing of any parameters that are currently being traced is suspended until the tracing of the **Mainprops** parameters for the new context is completed.

Apart from the special role of the **REGIMEN** property for a **PERSON** context, the use of **Mainprops** ensures that the most important parameters for each context (e.g. **IDENT** for a **CURORGS** context—the identity of an organism) are traced at an early stage. There is also the consideration that a user may expect and prefer to provide certain information when a context is instantiated, even if it turns out not to be needed until later (or not at all). This consideration may apply, for example, to the name, age, and sex of the patient and the site from which a culture was taken. (Note that parameter **NAME**—the patient's name—is not used by any of the rules but is obviously a useful piece of information to appear in the printed record of a consultation.)

CLASSIFYING RULES

Each of MYCIN's rules may reference parameters of one or more contexts in the context tree. Each rule is applied to a portion of the context tree containing these contexts and is classified according to which types of context are referenced. To be precise, the lowest context type in the tree that the rule may be applied to determines its category. As an example, RULE047 is given in Figure 15.4 in both internal form and English translation.

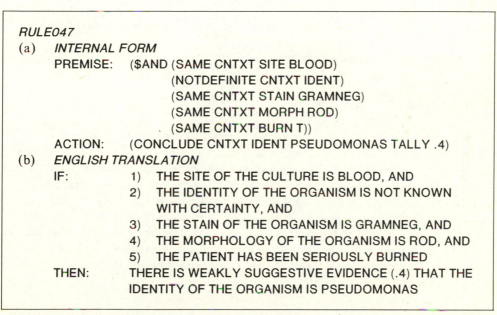

RULE047
(a) **INTERNAL FORM**
  PREMISE: ($AND (SAME CNTXT SITE BLOOD)
          (NOTDEFINITE CNTXT IDENT)
          (SAME CNTXT STAIN GRAMNEG)
          (SAME CNTXT MORPH ROD)
          (SAME CNTXT BURN T))
  ACTION: (CONCLUDE CNTXT IDENT PSEUDOMONAS TALLY .4)
(b) *ENGLISH TRANSLATION*
  IF: 1) THE SITE OF THE CULTURE IS BLOOD, AND
        2) THE IDENTITY OF THE ORGANISM IS NOT KNOWN
            WITH CERTAINTY, AND
        3) THE STAIN OF THE ORGANISM IS GRAMNEG, AND
        4) THE MORPHOLOGY OF THE ORGANISM IS ROD, AND
        5) THE PATIENT HAS BEEN SERIOUSLY BURNED
  THEN: THERE IS WEAKLY SUGGESTIVE EVIDENCE (.4) THAT THE
        IDENTITY OF THE ORGANISM IS PSEUDOMONAS

Figure 15.4   RULE047. (Source: Shortliffe (1976, p. 52))

This rule refers to parameters SITE, IDENT (twice), STAIN, MORPH, and BURN. Of these, BURN is a PROP-PT parameter (and therefore corresponds to a PERSON context), SITE is a PROP-CUL parameter, and IDENT, STAIN, and MORPH are all PROP-ORG parameters.

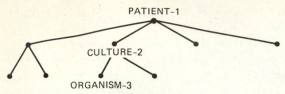

Figure 15.5   A context tree.

The rule is therefore applicable to a branch of a context tree containing three contexts, corresponding to a patient, a culture, and an organism, as shown in Figure 15.5. (If applied to the branch that is indicated, the rule would be concerned with parameters BURN of PATIENT-1, SITE of CULTURE-2, and IDENT, STAIN, and MORPH of ORGANISM-3.)

RULE047 is a member of the category ORGRULES, indicating that it may be applied to CURORGS contexts such as ORGANISM-3 (and, unavoidably, contexts that are higher up the tree).

Rules in category CULRULES may reference cultures and contexts that are higher in the tree (the only higher one that is possible being the PERSON context at the root node).

Rules in category PATRULES may only be applied to a context of type PERSON, that is, the root node, and so must make no reference to any contexts of other types.

Apart from the classification into categories, a rule is described as *self-referencing* if the value of one (or more) of the parameters that are referenced in the premise part is concluded in the action part.

Thus, RULEO47 is self-referencing, since the value of IDENT is tested in the premise part and concluded in the action part.

Self-referencing rules are discussed further in a later section.

THE STATIC DATA BASE

MYCIN has a static data base that contains its production rules and all the other fixed information that is needed by the consultation program. Every context type and every clinical parameter that is used by MYCIN has a number of properties that fully describe it. These properties enable the program to make all the correct associations between parameters and contexts and among the contexts themselves, and provide information that tells it which rules to invoke and when, when to ask a question, which question to ask, and what answers to expect. They also enable MYCIN to find the right position in the context tree for a particular context and indicate which basic questions to ask when a context is first instantiated.

The static data base is set up only once; when the system is being built, but it can be modified by experts using the rule-acquisition progam.

Properties of Rules

The following properties are stored in the static data base for each rule:

1.	PREMISE	the premise part (in list form)
2.	ACTION	the action part (in list form)

3.   CATEGORY†   the category to which the rule belongs
4.   SELFREF‡   whether the rule is self-referencing (1 = true, 0 = false)

RULE047, given in the previous section, could be held in the static data base in the form of "object-attribute-value" triples as follows:

OBJECT	ATTRIBUTE	VALUE
RULE047	PREMISE	($AND (SAME CNTXT SITE BLOOD) (NOTDEFINITE CNTXT IDENT) (SAME CNTXT STAIN GRAMNEG) (SAME CNTXT MORPH ROD) (SAME CNTXT BURN T))
RULE047	ACTION	(CONCLUDE CNTXT IDENT PSEUDOMONAS TALLY .4)
RULE047	CATEGORY	ORGRULES
RULE047	SELFREF	1

Object-attribute-value triples are implemented by means of LISP "property lists" in MYCIN. However, a tabular representation is used throughout this chapter, as it is probably more meaningful to the general reader.

Properties of Clinical Parameters

Up to thirteen values are stored in the static data base for each clinical parameter, for use by both the consultation and the explanation programs.

1.   MEMBEROF†   The name of the corresponding category of clinical parameters (e.g., PROP-CUL).

2.   VALUTYPE†   The type of parameter (single-valued, yes-no or multiple-valued)

3.   EXPECT   Permissible values of an askable parameter. (When a value is entered by the user in reply to a question, it is checked against the value of this property.)

(YN)   denotes a yes-no answer is required.

(NUMB)   denotes that the value expected is a number

†An interpolation.
‡A simplification. MYCIN computes whether or not a rule is self-referencing, but it is straightforward for the system builder to supply the information instead.

(ONEOF ⟨list⟩) denotes that the value
must be a member of
⟨list⟩

(ANY) denotes that there is no restriction
on the value the parameter may
have.

4.   PROMPT   The question to be asked when MYCIN
needs to know the value of a single-valued or
a yes-no parameter, for example,
(Enter the identity (genus) of * :)
When the question is asked, the contents of
the list are printed out, with the asterisk replaced by the name of the relevant context
(e.g., ORGANISM-3).

5.   PROMPT1   The question to be asked when MYCIN
needs to know the value of a multiple-valued
parameter, for example, the value of
PROMPT1 for parameter ALLERGIES is:
(Is the patient allergic to (VALU)?)
If the value of ALLERGIES were needed to
test whether a clause in the premise of a rule
such as (SAME CNTXT ALLERGIES PENI-
CILLIN) were satisfied, the value of
PROMPT1 would be printed out with (VALU)
replaced by PENICILLIN.

6.   LABDATA   Whether the parameter is a labdata one.
7.   LOOKAHEAD   A list of all the rules that reference the parameter in their premise.

8.   UPDATED-BY   A list of all the rules that update the value of
the parameter. When the system needs to
infer this value, it invokes and attempts to
evaluate every rule in the UPDATED-BY list
in turn (amending the associated certainty
factors each time).

9.   CONTAINED-IN   A list of all the rules that reference the parameter in their ACTION clause but do not
update its value.

10.   TRANS   Every function, clinical parameter, context
type, list, and table that is stored in MY-
CIN's static data base has a TRANS property, which is used for translating the rules into
English for explanation purposes. For example, if the physician wishes to see RULE047,
it needs to be shown in an easily understandable form. A translation function uses the

		TRANS property of each term that is used in the internal form of a rule to produce an "English" form of the rule, which is likely to be more acceptable to the user than the "internal" form.
11.	DEFAULT	Only applies to those parameters where the expected value is a number. It indicates the units that are used (e.g., days or grams).
12.	CONDITION	A LISP expression that is executed before a question is asked of the user. If the condition is true, the question is *not* asked. For example, if the genus of an organism is not known, there is no point in asking for its subtype. So the CONDITION property for SUBTYPE is the LISP expression (NOTKNOWN CNTXT GENUS).
13.	ANTECEDENT-RULES-OF†	(See further discussion in later section.)

Properties (1), (2), and (10) must always be present for every clinical parameter.

Property (3) and either property (4) or property (5) must always be present for an **askable** parameter. Property (11) is frequently not needed. The other properties are all needed, but here and elsewhere MYCIN makes use of the feature of LISP that any property value that is not explicitly given has a default value of **NIL**. This value can be interpreted as either **false** (in the case of properties (6) and (12)) or "the empty list" (for properties (7), (8), (9) and (13)).

If there is no PROMPT (or PROMPT1) property for a parameter, MYCIN assumes that its value cannot be asked; if there is no UPDATED-BY property, it assumes that the value cannot be inferred; LABDATA, if absent, is assumed to be false, and so on. Figure 15.6 shows how these properties might be stored in the static data base.

Object (Parameter)	Attribute (Property)	Value
BURN	MEMBEROF	PROP-PT
BURN	VALUTYPE	BINARY
BURN	EXPECT	(YN)
BURN	PROMPT	(Is * a burn patient?)
BURN	LABDATA	1
BURN	LOOKAHEAD	(RULE047)
BURN	TRANS	(* HAS BEEN SERIOUSLY BURNED)

Figure 15.6. Properties of clinical parameters, stored as object-attribute-value triples.

†An interpolation.

Properties of Context Types

Up to ten values are stored in the static data base for each of the context types that are known to MYCIN. These are used every time a context is instantiated and also for checking that a rule is applied to the appropriate context.

1. ASSOCWITH The context type of the parent node. Each context type may be a direct descendant of only one other context type. For example, the ASSOCWITH property of CURORGS is CURCULS, indicating that a context of type CURORGS can only be instantiated as a descendant of a context of type CURCULS.

2. TYPE The name stem for contexts of this type. For example, the TYPE property of CURORGS is ORGANISM-. Every time a context of type CURORGS is created, a number is suffixed to ORGANISM- to give a unique name for the new context. (Numbers are suffixed in the order 1, 2, 3, and so on *separately* for each name stem. Note that more than one context type may have the same name stem.)

3. PROPTYPE The category of clinical parameters that corresponds to the context type (e.g., PROP-PT for type PERSON).

4. SUBJECT A list of the categories of rules that may be applied to a context of this type, for example, the list (PATRULES) for context type PERSON.

5. MAINPROPS A list of clinical parameters that are to be traced immediately whenever a context of this type is instantiated (see previous discussion on **Mainprops**).

6. TRANS Used by the explanation program for translation into English.

7. SYN Can be used for replacing the asterisk in the PROMPT property of the clinical parameters. For example, the PROMPT property of the parameter WHENCUL is **(Please give the number of days since ∗ was obtained).** The asterisk can be replaced by the name of the context (say, CULTURE-1, of type CURCULS), or it can be replaced by a string of characters that are derived from the SYN property of CURCULS, which is (SITE (the ∗ culture)). The asterisk in the SYN property is replaced by the value of the specified parameter, for example, if the SITE of CULTURE-1 is BLOOD, then (the ∗ culture) becomes (the blood culture), and thus the prompt for WHENCUL becomes **(Please give the number of days since the blood culture was obtained).**

8. PROMPT1 The question to be asked to find out whether any contexts of this type exist. A yes-no answer is expected; if it is **yes** the *first* such context is immediately instantiated.

9. PROMPT2 After the first context of this type has been created, PROMPT2 gives a question that is asked to discover whether there are further contexts of the same type (if the answer yes is given, a further context is instantiated and the question is asked again).

10. PROMPT3 Replaces PROMPT1 for those context types for which there must always be at least one corresponding context (such as CURCULS and CURORGS). PROMPT3 is a statement (not a question) that is printed out immediately before the first such context is instantiated. (MYCIN then continues by asking repeatedly about further contexts, using PROMPT2 as above.)

Of these properties, all will normally be required for each context type (with the possible exception of SYN), except that only one of PROMPT1 and PROMPT3 is appropriate for any particular context type. Any property value that is not explicitly given has a default value of NIL.

Other Static Data

Other static data is also stored by MYCIN (not in the "standard" object-attribute-value triple form). This includes lists and tables that can be referenced by the rules, such as a list of all the organisms known to MYCIN, and lists of sterile sites and nonsterile sites, which are used primarily to avoid redundancy. For example, MYCIN has many rules that contain the clause (SAME CNTXT SITE (LISTOF STERILESITES)). The function LISTOF retrieves the list STERILESITES from the static data base and this list of values is effectively used by function SAME as its third argument. This avoids having to give all the elements of the list explicitly each time it is used.

The tables include a table of the staining characteristics, morphology and aerobicity of each organism known to MYCIN, and a table of the normal flora that are associated with each site known to MYCIN. (See the section on special functions for a description of how these tables are used.)

THE DYNAMIC DATA BASE

MYCIN makes use of a dynamic data base, which is set up afresh for each consultation. This contains data of the kinds described below. In each case, the data can be thought of as taking the form of object-attribute-value triples.

1. *patient data,* that is, the values of clinical parameters (as supplied by the physician or inferred by the program)
2. so-called *dynamic data,* which records the details of acquisition of data mainly for explanation purposes
3. properties of context types† that are used when instantiating contexts
4. information about the context tree as it is built up†

Each of these kinds of data is described in turn in the following subsections. Note that the term *patient data base* is used to denote the patient data part of the dynamic data base.

Patient Data

The following figure (Fig. 15.7) gives an example of how patient data might appear in the patient data base, in tabular form. Each entry is referred to as a *patient data triple.* Notice that for patient data the value entry in the data base consists of three parts: a list followed by two integers.† Ignoring the two integers at present, each sublist of the list gives one possible value of the clinical parameter (for the specified context) and its associated certainty factor. This certainty factor may have been computed (see section on functions used in the action parts of rules), or it may have been supplied by the physician. If the physician is unsure of the answer to a question that is generated by MYCIN, he can enter the value that he is uncertain of, followed

---

†Interpolation.

Object (context)	Attribute (parameter)	Value
PATIENT-1	SEX	((MALE 1.0)) 1 0
ORGANISM-1	IDENT	((KLEBSIELLA 0.6) (HAFNIA 0.4)) 1 0
PATIENT-1	ALLERGIES	((PENICILLIN 1.0) (AMPICILLIN 1.0)) 1 0

Figure 15.7   Patient data triples (showing associated certainty factors).

by an integer between -10 and $+10$ to indicate the degree of belief that it is the true value. This integer is then converted directly to a certainty factor between -1 and $+1$.

Figure 15.7 shows that for the first entry, SEX of PATIENT-1, there is only one value, and it is known with certainty (certainty factor 1.0). For the second entry, IDENT of ORGANISM-1, there are two alternative values present, with certainty factors of 0.6 and 0.4. Both SEX and IDENT are single-valued parameters. The third entry shows a multiple-valued parameter ALLERGIES. In this case, there are two alternative values that are present, each with its own *independent* certainty factor (both are known with certainty).

The two integer values that are included in each value entry in the data base are (from left to right) an istraced flag and an isbeingtraced flag. Whenever MYCIN needs to know the value of a clinical parameter, it attempts to look it up in the patient data base if possible. The istraced flag is used to indicate that the parameter has been traced to ensure that it is not traced again. Note, however, that this flag is ignored for multiple-valued parameters. If the parameter has not already been traced (or is multiple-valued), it is asked for from the user and/or deduced by using MYCIN's collection of rules that are stored in the static data base. Once the value has been found, the istraced flag is set in the corresponding entry in the dynamic data base. The isbeingtraced flag is used to indicate that the parameter is in the process of being traced. As many rules can reference the same parameter in their premises, it is possible for an invoked rule to call for the tracing of a parameter that is already in the process of being traced. The use of the isbeingtraced flag allows such reasoning loops to be detected and the invoked rule is then rejected. An exception to this occurs with the use of self-referencing rules, which do not call for the parameter to be traced, but ignore the isbeingtraced flag.

Dynamic Data

MYCIN collects information about the acquisition of data during a consultation, for use principally by the explanation program, to enable it to answer questions that are asked by the user and explain its reasoning. When the value of a clinical parameter becomes known, a record of how it was acquired is kept in the dynamic data base. If the value was inferred, a list of the rules that were used for that purpose is also kept. MYCIN also keeps a record of the questions that are asked of the user, together with the replies obtained, and the order in which they were asked. This enables the valuable facility to be provided whereby the user can amend one (or more) of his or her previous answers without having to rerun the consultation from the beginning.†

†For further details of this facility, see Shortliffe (1976, pp. 148–150).

Properties of Context Types†

The use made of the PROMPT1 or PROMPT3 property and the PROMPT2 property during context instantiation was described in the section on properties of context types. For this process to work properly, a record is needed of whether or not the PROMPT1 question (or the PROMPT3 statement) has been used and whether or not the user has indicated that there are no further contexts of that type.

At the beginning of a consultation, MYCIN stores in its dynamic data base the value of two properties for each context type except PERSON.

For each context type, property ASKABLE has value 1 and property PASKED has value 0†.

Thus, part of the dynamic data base might look like this (Fig. 15.8):

Object (Context type)	Attribute (Property)	Value
CURCULS	ASKABLE	1
CURCULS	PASKED	0

Figure 15.8   "Dynamic" properties of context types.

When a context type is to be instantiated, the program uses these "flags" to find out which prompt to use. Initially, ASKABLE is 1 and PASKED is 0, indicating that no contexts of that type have yet been instantiated. Either PROMPT1 (a question) or PROMPT3 (a statement) is then used, as appropriate, and the value of PASKED is set to 1.

Assuming there are further contexts to instantiate, ASKABLE will still be 1 but PASKED will now also be 1, indicating that PROMPT2 should now be used to ask whether another context of this type is to be instantiated. If the answer is YES then the new context will be created and PROMPT2 will be used again. If the answer is NO (or if the answer to PROMPT1 is NO), ASKABLE is set to 0, and no more contexts of this type are created.

A fourth property of context types for which a value is stored in the dynamic data base is NEXTNUM†. This is an integer that is appended to a 'name stem' such as ORGANISM- (see the TYPE property of context types in the section on that subject) every time a context is created. Each context type has its own NEXTNUM value. All are automatically set to 1 whenever MYCIN is invoked.

Information About the Context Tree

Information is held in the dynamic data base that corresponds to the 'linkage' of the context tree as it is built up during the consultation.

For each context, the values of the following three properties are stored.†

†Interpolation.

1. CTTYPE the corresponding context type
2. PARENT the name of the parent node (NIL in the case of the root node)
3. DESCENDANTSOF a list of the names of the direct descendants.

Thus, the dynamic data base might include the following triples (Fig. 15.9):

Object (Context)	Attribute (Property)	Value
PATIENT-1	CTTYPE	PERSON
PATIENT-1	PARENT	NIL
PATIENT-1	DESCENDANTSOF	(CULTURE-1 CULTURE-2)
CULTURE-1	CTTYPE	CURCULS
CULTURE-1	PARENT	PATIENT-1
CULTURE-1	DESCENDANTSOF	(ORGANISM-1 ORGANISM-2)

Figure 15.9   Information about the context tree.

USING RULES TO INFER THE VALUES OF CLINICAL PARAMETERS

Each of MYCIN's rules is of the form

IF *premise* THEN *action*

where *action* usually involves concluding a value for a clinical parameter for a particular context (say, that IDENT for ORGANISM-2 is PSEUDOMONAS with some certainty factor).
The premise part of each rule is of the form

($AND clause1 clause2 clause3. . . .),

and the premise is true overall if and only if all its constituent clauses are true.
Each clause is a list such as

(SAME CNTXT SITE BLOOD).

The first entry in the list is a predicate function name and the other elements are the arguments to which the function should be applied. Evaluating such a clause generally involves making some form of equality test on the value of a parameter (which itself may or may not have been traced at that stage—in the latter case, the parameter is immediately traced).
To evaluate the premise of a rule, MYCIN works through the constituent clauses from left to right. If any is false, the rule is immediately rejected. If the entire premise is satisfied, MYCIN evaluates the action part of the rule. This normally has the effect of adding the values of one or more clinical parameters to the dynamic data base, or updating those values already there.
An entry that occurs frequently in both the premise clauses and the action parts of rules is the word 'CNTXT'.
CNTXT is a variable for which there is substituted the name of the relevant context whenever a rule is used and this can vary from one part of a rule to another.

EXAMPLE

As a concrete example, consider the problem of tracing the value of the IDENT parameter for the context ORGANISM-2 in the following context tree (Fig. 15.10):

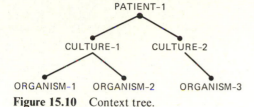

PATIENT-1

CULTURE-1   CULTURE-2

ORGANISM-1   ORGANISM-2   ORGANISM-3

Figure 15.10   Context tree.

Note: For this example it will be assumed for simplicity that this is the entire context tree that is needed for the consultation, that the existence of these six contexts is already known, and that the appropriate "linkage" information for the tree (three values for each context) is already stored in the dynamic data base (see previous section on context trees). In fact, however, MYCIN only instantiates contexts as the need for them is discovered. This point is discussed in detail later.

In order to infer the value of IDENT for context ORGANISM-2, the UPDATED-BY property for IDENT in the static data base is examined. This gives a list of the names of rules that update the value of the IDENT parameter, including RULE047. All these rules are invoked (used) in turn to find the required value of IDENT for ORGANISM-2. Note, however, that if at any stage a rule concludes the value of IDENT with certainty (certainty factor 1), the remaining rules are ignored. The internal form and English translation of RULE047 are reproduced here for convenience (Fig. 15.11):

RULE047

(a)   *INTERNAL FORM*
    PREMISE: ($AND (SAME CNTXT SITE BLOOD)
                        (NOTDEFINITE CNTXT IDENT)
                        (SAME CNTXT STAIN GRAMNEG)
                        (SAME CNTXT MORPH ROD)
                        (SAME CNTXT BURN T))
    ACTION: (CONCLUDE CNTXT IDENT PSEUDOMONAS TALLY .4)
(b)   *ENGLISH TRANSLATION*
    IF: 1)   THE SITE OF THE CULTURE IS BLOOD, AND
        2)   THE IDENTITY OF THE ORGANISM IS NOT KNOWN
            WITH CERTAINTY, AND
        3)   THE STAIN OF THE ORGANISM IS GRAMNEG, AND
        4)   THE MORPHOLOGY OF THE ORGANISM IS ROD, AND
        5)   THE PATIENT HAS BEEN SERIOUSLY BURNED
    THEN: THERE IS WEAKLY SUGGESTIVE EVIDENCE (.4) THAT THE
        IDENTITY OF THE ORGANISM IS PSEUDOMONAS.

Figure 15.11   RULE047. (The meaning of TALLY in the action part of the internal form is described later.)

This is the general form of RULE047 but to find the value of IDENT for ORGANISM-2 it is necessary to substitute appropriate values for each occurrence of CNTXT. This can be achieved in a number of ways. For example, the static and dynamic data bases may contain entries as shown below:

Static Data Base

OBJECT	ATTRIBUTE	VALUE
BURN	MEMBEROF	PROP-PT
SITE	MEMBEROF	PROP-CUL
IDENT	MEMBEROF	PROP-ORG
STAIN	MEMBEROF	PROP-ORG
MORPH	MEMBEROF	PROP-ORG
PERSON	PROPTYPE	PROP-PT
CURCULS	PROPTYPE	PROP-CUL
CURORGS	PROPTYPE	PROP-ORG

Dynamic Data Base

OBJECT	ATTRIBUTE	VALUE
ORGANISM-2	PARENT	CULTURE-1
CULTURE-1	PARENT	PATIENT-1
PATIENT-1	PARENT	NIL
PATIENT-1	CTTYPE	PERSON
CULTURE-1	CTTYPE	CURCULS
ORGANISM-2	CTTYPE	CURORGS

The first clause of RULE047 is (SAME CNTXT SITE BLOOD). To make the correct substitution for CNTXT, MYCIN needs to find a context on the "current branch" of the tree (i.e., the path from the root node to the context ORGANISM-2), of which the parameter SITE can be an attribute. The entries in the static data base show that SITE is a member of the category PROP-CUL. MYCIN examines each context on the current branch, starting with ORGANISM-2, as this is the context for which RULE047 was invoked. The CTTYPE property (in the dynamic data base) shows that ORGANISM-2 is of type CURORGS which is described by clinical parameters of the category PROP-ORG (the PROPTYPE property in the static data base). As SITE is of category PROP-CUL, it obviously cannot be an attribute of ORGANISM-2, so MYCIN uses the dynamic data base to find the PARENT of ORGANISM-2. This is CULTURE-1. CULTURE-1 is of type CURCULS, which is described by parameters of category PROP-CUL. This corresponds with the category of SITE so CULTURE-1 is substituted for CNTXT in the first clause of RULE047, and the clause is evaluated. The process is repeated for each clause in turn.

Had the rule referred to a context type below ORGANISM-2 in the tree, then it would have been applied to each descendant of ORGANISM-2 of this type in turn (these contexts having been instantiated as soon as the rule was invoked).

Each of the premise clauses is evaluated in turn until (1) one of them is found to be false or (2) all the clauses are found to be true.

In case (1), the rule is immediately abandoned and MYCIN goes on to the next relevant rule.

In case (2) the entire premise is satisfied and MYCIN evaluates the action part of RULE047, by applying the CONCLUDE function to its five arguments, to add an updated value of IDENT for ORGANISM-2 to the patient data base.

The functions that are used in the premise clauses and the action part of MYCIN's rules (including SAME, NOTDEFINITE, and CONCLUDE) are described in the next section.

FUNCTIONS USED IN APPLYING RULES

Simple Functions in Premise Clauses

MYCIN uses many different simple functions in the premise clauses of its rules. These act on the patient data triples in the dynamic data base, and (except for functions SAME and THOUGHTNOT described below) return a truth value. Each time a clause is to be evaluated, MYCIN first checks that the clinical parameter that is referenced in the clause has been traced and, if not, asks for or infers its value. It then applies the function to the appropriate patient data triple. The simple functions that are used in premise clauses of rules are described briefly below. More precise details are given in Shortliffe (1976, pp. 101–105) and van Melle (1980, pp. 155–159).

1. Functions KNOWN, NOTKNOWN, DEFINITE, and NOTDEFINITE are concerned not with the actual value of a parameter but with whether or not it is known. Thus, for example, (KNOWN ORGANISM-1 IDENT) is **true** if and only if the identity of the organism is known with a certainty factor greater than 0.2 (to be more precise, if any of the alternative values that are listed for the parameter in the dynamic data base has a certainty factor greater than 0.2). Function NOTKNOWN is **true** when function KNOWN is **false** and vice versa. (DEFINITE ORGANISM-2 IDENT) is **true** if and only if the identity of the organism is known with certainty. Function NOTDEFINITE is **true** when function DEFINITE is **false** and vice versa.

2. Functions SAME and THOUGHTNOT both return either **false** or a *numerical* value signifying **true**.

   For example, the clause

   (SAME ORGANISM-2 STAIN GRAMNEG)

tests whether the certainty factor that is associated with a value of GRAMNEG for the STAIN property of ORGANISM-2 is greater than 0.2. If so, the clause is considered **true** and the value of the certainty factor is returned. If not, the value **false** is returned.

The clause (THOUGHTNOT CULTURE-1 SITE BLOOD) is **true** if the certainty factor that is associated with a value of BLOOD for the SITE property of CULTURE-1 is less than −0.2, otherwise it is **false**. If the clause is **true**, the value returned is the *negative* of the certainty factor concerned.

3. Functions NOTSAME, MIGHTBE, VNOTKNOWN, DEFIS, NOTDEFIS, DEFNOT, and NOTDEFNOT are all concerned with the certainty factor with which the value of a parameter is known to be true and all return truth values. Thus, for example,

(DEFIS ORGANISM-2 STAIN GRAMNEG)

is **true** if it is known with certainty that the value of the parameter STAIN for ORGANISM-2 is GRAMNEG, otherwise it is **false**.

The functions of types (2) and (3) can all take a *list* of values, instead of just a single value, for their third argument.

For example, (SAME CULTURE-2 SITE (LISTOF STERILESITES)) retrieves all the alternative values of the SITE property for CULTURE-2 from the dynamic data base, disregarding all those whose values are not in the list STERILESITES. The largest certainty factor for those values remaining is then selected for use in evaluating the value of the SAME function.

4. Functions are available that can be applied to those clinical parameters that have a numerical value and which return a truth value.

Thus, (GREATERP PATIENT-1 AGE 13) is true if the patient's age is over 13, and false otherwise. Other arithmetic relations are evaluated by functions LESSP, GREATEQ, and LESSEQ.

Special Functions

MYCIN has special functions for referencing the knowledge tables in the static data base. These set up temporary data structures for use by other functions in premise or action clauses. (SAME CNTXT IDENT (LISTOF (GRID1 (VAL1 CNTXT PORTAL) PATHFLORA))) is an example of such a clause. GRID1 is one of the special functions†. It takes two arguments—a parameter and the name of a knowledge table. In this case, the parameter is computed. (VAL1 CNTXT PORTAL) retrieves the most highly confirmed value for the portal of entry of CNTXT (an organism) from the patient data base (tracing the value if necessary). This is then used to index the knowledge table PATHFLORA, which contains a list of likely pathogens to be found at each site known to MYCIN. The result is a list of organisms, which is then used by the function SAME as its third argument.

Mapping Functions‡

Some of MYCIN's rules reference more than one branch of the context tree. These rules are invoked when information is needed about contexts that are not on the current branch (e.g.,

---

†For a discussion of other special functions see van Melle (1980, pp. 162–163).

‡Mapping functions are not described by Shortliffe (1976), but are described in detail by van Melle (1980). The reader is referred to the latter source for further information.

PRIORORGS). In cases where no such contexts have yet been created, evaluation of the rule is suspended, the necessary contexts are instantiated, and the rule evaluation then continues. However, the basic control structure cannot be used to relate contexts in different branches of the tree. To overcome this problem, special functions, called *mapping functions,* are used.

THEREARE is one such function. It takes five arguments, MAPSET, PRED, FREEVAR, ANSET, and DUPLES. MAPSET is a function that, when evaluated, returns a list of contexts of a specified type. PRED is a clause, or conjunction of clauses, of the same form as a rule premise. Each element in the list returned by MAPSET is assigned to a local variable (specified by the third argument—FREEVAR), and PRED is evaluated using FREEVAR in place of CNTXT. The result may be a list of contexts that satisfy the conditions in PRED, or it may be a list of context-certainty factor pairs. The fourth argument—ANSET—is the name to be given to this list, and DUPLES is a flag that is set if certainty factors are required.

The MAPSET argument of THEREARE uses one of three functions for selecting contexts:

- (GETALL CTYPE) returns a list of all contexts of type CTYPE.
- (GETOFFSPRING CNTXT CTYPE) returns a list of descendant contexts of CNTXT of type CTYPE.
- (APPEND LIST1 LIST2 . . .) appends its list arguments into one long list.

Other functions that are used by mapping functions include SAMEANS and NOT-SAMEANS.

(SAMEANS CNTXT FREEVAR PARM) returns **true** if CNTXT and FREEVAR have the same value for the parameter PARM.

(NOTSAMEANS CNTXT FREEVAR PARM) returns **true** if CNTXT and FREEVAR have different values for PARM.

This is an example of a possible rule using mapping functions[†]:

IF: THERE IS A PRIOR ORGANISM WHICH MAY BE THE SAME AS THE CUR-RENT ORGANISM

THEN: IT IS DEFINITE (1.0) THAT THESE PROPERTIES—IDENTITY—SHOULD BE TRANSFERRED FROM A PRIOR ORGANISM WHICH MAY BE THE SAME AS THE ORGANISM TO THIS CURRENT ORGANISM.

This is a CURORGRULE, invoked to find out about the identity of a current organism, but PRIORORGS are referenced in the PREMISE. When MYCIN tries to evaluate the rule, it will first have to find all the descendants of PATIENT-1 of the context type PRIORORGS. If these have not yet been instantiated, they are now, together with the PRIORCULS context(s), in the normal fashion.

Functions Used in Action Parts

There are a number of functions that are used in the action part of a rule, of which the most commonly used is CONCLUDE.

[†]Rule 021 in Shortliffe (1976, p. 59). Note, however, that this version of MYCIN does not, in fact, use mapping functions.

CONCLUDE adds a patient data triple to the dynamic data base with a certainty factor that is calculated from the certainty factor of the premise and the certainty factor of the rule, as described below. If the triple already exists (by a previous conclusion), its old certainty factor is combined with the new one.

The certainty factor of the premise of a rule is the minimum of the certainty factors of its component premise clauses. (Functions **SAME** and **THOUGHTNOT** return a numerical value, other functions return a truth value and the value **true** is taken as equivalent to the number one for this purpose. So if functions **SAME** and **THOUGHTNOT** do not occur, **TALLY** is 1 by default.) Multiplying this value by the certainty factor of the rule gives the certainty factor to be associated with a new triple.

The **CONCLUDE** function takes five arguments, thus, for example, the action part of a rule might be

(CONCLUDE ORGANISM-2 IDENT SALMONELLA TALLY 0.4)

The fourth argument is always the variable **TALLY**, which is used to hold the certainty factor of the premise. The fifth argument is the certainty factor of the rule, which expresses the expert's degree of confidence in the conclusion. If in a particular case **TALLY** were 0.8, say, the certainty factor to be associated with the value **SALMONELLA** (as the identity of ORGANISM-2) in a new triple would be 0.32.

If there were already a triple in the dynamic data base with a certainty factor of C_1, say, and the newly calculated certainty factor were C_2, these values would be combined to give a new certainty factor, Cfcombine(C_1, C_2) and the dynamic data base would be updated accordingly. The formula† used for this purpose depends on the signs of C_1 and C_2 as follows:

$$\text{Cfcombine}(C_1, C_2) = C_1 + C_2 \times (1 - C_1) \text{ if } C_1 > 0 \text{ and } C_2 > 0$$

$$= -\text{Cfcombine}(-C_1, -C_2) \text{ if } C_1 < 0 \text{ and } C_2 < 0$$

$$= \frac{C_1 + C_2}{1 - \min(|C_1|, |C_2|)} \text{ if } C_1 \times C_2 < 0$$

With the combination of 1 and −1 defined to be 1.

A DETAILED ANALYSIS OF THE CONTROL STRUCTURE

A consultation session with **MYCIN** starts with the instantiation of the root node in the context tree, a context of type **PERSON**. Instantiating a context involves three steps:

1. The context is assigned a unique name.
2. It is added to the context tree.
3. The parameters in the context type's **MAINPROPS** list (stored in the static data base) are immediately traced.

---

†(*Source:* van Melle [1980, p. 41].) For a discussion of other conclusion functions, see van Melle (1980, pp. 159–162).

In the case of the root node, the name assigned for the first consultation in a MYCIN session is PATIENT-1.

The MAINPROPS property for context type PERSON is the list (NAME AGE SEX REGIMEN). Thus, MYCIN must immediately trace the value of each of these four parameters in turn. Once all four values have been traced, the consultation program terminates. (Note: Finding the value of REGIMEN—the recommended treatment for the patient—is the ultimate aim of all MYCIN consultations.)

1. NAME, AGE, and SEX are all LABDATA parameters and are automatically asked of the user. The values supplied by the user are stored as patient data triples in the dynamic data base, and the system goes on to trace the clinical parameter REGIMEN.
2. REGIMEN is a non-LABDATA parameter and the system thus proceeds to infer its value, by invoking the only rule that references REGIMEN in its action part, the goal rule, RULE092.

RULE092 is one of MYCIN's PATRULES and is therefore applicable to a context of type PERSON. The goal rule defines the four-stage decision process referred to in the first section, as follows:

RULE092

IF:	1)	THERE IS AN ORGANISM WHICH REQUIRES THERAPY, AND
	2)	CONSIDERATION HAS BEEN GIVEN TO THE POSSIBLE EXISTENCE OF ADDITIONAL ORGANISMS REQUIRING THERAPY, EVEN THOUGH THEY HAVE NOT ACTUALLY BEEN RECOVERED FROM ANY CURRENT CULTURES
THEN:		DO THE FOLLOWING:
	1)	COMPILE A LIST OF POSSIBLE THERAPIES WHICH, BASED UPON SENSITIVITY DATA, MAY BE EFFECTIVE AGAINST THE ORGANISMS REQUIRING TREATMENT, AND
	2)	DETERMINE THE BEST THERAPY RECOMMENDATIONS FROM THE COMPILED LIST
OTHERWISE:		INDICATE THAT THE PATIENT DOES NOT REQUIRE THERAPY

The premise of this rule references the two clinical parameters, TREATFOR and COVERFOR (in the first and second clauses, respectively) both of which are PROP-PT parameters (otherwise the rule would not be a PATRULE) and both of which are yes/no parameters. It is the evaluation of these clauses that causes the lengthy consultation.

TREATFOR (i.e., there is an organism that requires therapy) is a non-LABDATA parameter, so the system will try to infer its value by invoking all the rules listed by its UPDATED-BY property. The first of these might be RULE090†:

IF:	1)	THE IDENTITY OF THE ORGANISM IS KNOWN, AND
	2)	THERE IS SIGNIFICANT DISEASE ASSOCIATED WITH THIS OCCURRENCE OF THE ORGANISM
THEN:		IT IS DEFINITE (1.0) THAT THERE IS AN ORGANISM WHICH REQUIRES THERAPY

†Interpolation and simplification.

This is a CURORGRULE. Its CATEGORY is checked and found to be applicable only to the context type CURORGS. As the context currently under consideration (PATIENT-1) is not of the type CURORGS, MYCIN attempts to identify all the descendants of PATIENT-1 of type CURORGS (using the context tree that is stored in the dynamic data base). Here the main consultation has to stop temporarily because, of course, no contexts of type CURORGS have yet been instantiated, and MYCIN now attempts to create them.

The program first checks whether contexts of type CURORGS can be direct descendants of a context of type PERSON and finds that they cannot. The ASSOCWITH property of context type CURORGS is CURCULS, indicating that CURCULS is the necessary parent context type of CURORGS. Accordingly, MYCIN checks whether it is possible to instantiate contexts of type CURCULS.

Since the ASSOCWITH property of CURCULS is PERSON and a PERSON context already exists, it is possible to instantiate CURCULS contexts as direct descendants of PATIENT-1 and the system proceeds to do so. When contexts of a particular type are being instantiated, MYCIN makes use of the PROMPT1, PROMPT2, and PROMPT3 properties of that context type.

If there is a PROMPT1 property, this indicates that there may not necessarily be any contexts of the type in question for some consultations. If instead there is a PROMPT3 property, this indicates that there must always be at least one context of that type descending from the corresponding parent node. Both CURCULS and CURORGS are of this latter kind, since there must always be at least one current culture taken from the patient and at least one organism that is isolated from each current culture. In either case, the value of the 'PROMPT' property is printed out as a question to the user.

When attempting to create a second context of the same type, the PROMPT2 property is printed out to ask the user if there are any more contexts of that type. If the user replies that there are, one is instantiated, followed by the PROMPT2 question being asked again until a negative answer is received.

The question is then marked in the dynamic data base as 'not askable', by changing the value of the ASKABLE property for the context type to zero.

In the present case, the effect is that the first context of type CURCULS is instantiated and named CULTURE-1. The descendants (at least one) of CULTURE-1 are now instantiated in turn until the user indicates that there are no more. If there were two of these, they would be named ORGANISM-1 and ORGANISM-2. MYCIN then asks the user if there is a second current culture. If there is, it is instantiated as CULTURE-2 and its descendant current organism(s) are then instantiated. The procedure continues in this way, with CULTURE-3, CULTURE-4, and so on, as long as necessary.

At the end of this process, the context tree might look like that in Figure 15.12.

As each context is instantiated, its MAINPROPS parameters are traced.

For context type CURCULS, the elements of the MAINPROPS list are SITE and WHENCUL. Both of these are LABDATA parameters that cannot be inferred and hence must immediately be provided by the user when a CURCULS context is instantiated.

For context type CURORGS, the MAINPROPS list contains IDENT, STAIN, MORPH, and SENSITIVS. These are also LABDATA parameters. However, if IDENT (the identity of the organism) is known with certainty, the values of STAIN and MORPH are not requested from the user but are looked up in so-called "knowledge tables." To arrange this, MYCIN makes use of antecedent rules, which are described further in a subsequent section.

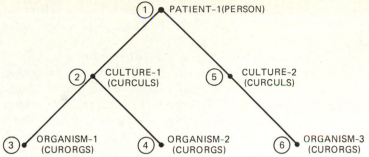

Figure 15.12   Construction of context tree. The circled numbers indicate the order in which the contexts are instantiated.

   The following sequence of events describes how the parameter IDENT for ORGANISM-1 is traced:

1. The triple (ORGANISM-1 IDENT ()) is added to the patient data base and its isbeingtraced flag is set.
2. MYCIN retrieves the PROMPT property of IDENT (in the static data base), namely, **(Enter the identity (genus) of *:)**. The asterisk is replaced by **ORGANISM-1** and the question is printed. Let us assume that the physician replies UNKNOWN.
3. The istraced flag that is associated with the triple is checked. At this stage it is still set to 0.
4. The list of rules that conclude about IDENT is retrieved from the UPDATED-BY property of IDENT in the static data base, and the first of these is invoked. This might be RULE156:

    RULE156
    PREMISE: ($AND (SAME CNTXT SITE BLOOD)
                        (SAME CNTXT STAIN GRAMNEG)
                        (SAME CNTXT MORPH ROD)
                        (SAME CNTXT PORTAL URINE)
                        (NOTSAME CNTXT GU T)
                        (NOTSAME CNTXT INFECT CYSTITIS))
    ACTION: (CONCLUDE CNTXT IDENT ECOLI TALLY .6)

5. MYCIN now checks to see if RULE156 is applicable to the current context. The system is trying to find out about the identity of ORGANISM-1, so this is the current context and is of type CURORGS. RULE156 is one of the CURORGRULES, and is therefore applicable.
6. The rule is applied.
7. The first clause is (SAME CNTXT SITE BLOOD). SITE is a PROPCUL parameter, so MYCIN uses the context tree to find the culture that is related to ORGANISM-1. This is CULTURE-1 and its SITE has already been traced (this will always be the case, since SITE is a MAINPROPS parameter of CURCULS). If the value of SITE is not BLOOD, then the rule is abandoned and the next one in the list is invoked.
8. Assuming that the rule has not been abandoned, the next clause is evaluated. This refers to the STAIN of the organism, and is therefore applicable to the current context. It has not yet

been traced but is a **LABDATA** parameter, so the information is initially requested from the user. The value entered by the user is added to the patient data base and checked by the function **SAME** to evaluate the clause.

 9. and 10. Step 8 is repeated for the parameters **MORPH** and **PORTAL**, in turn.

11. (NOTSAME CNTXT GU T) is the next clause to be evaluated. GU is a **PROP-PT** parameter, being concerned with whether or not the patient has had a genito-urinary manipulative procedure. The applicable context is therefore **PATIENT-1** and the system attempts to trace the value of GU for **PATIENT-1**. This is a **LABDATA** parameter, so its value is asked, but it also has an **UPDATED-BY** property, so it can be inferred. If the user does not know its value, that is, the parameter is not flagged to indicate that it has been traced (see section on patient data), its **UPDATED-BY** list of rules is retrieved and the rules are invoked one at a time. Once all the rules have been evaluated, the system updates the patient data base and applies the function **NOTSAME** to GU of **PATIENT-1**.

12. The last clause of the premise of RULE156 is slightly different. Whereas the clinical parameters traced so far have been single-valued or yes-no parameters, **INFECT** is multiple-valued, and as such, can procure many answers from the user. MYCIN is only concerned, at this stage, with whether or not the patient has cystitis. The **PROMPT1** property is therefore modified (see section on properties of clinical parameters), so that the system asks just this question, expecting a yes-no answer.

13. Assuming that all the clauses have been evaluated and have returned **true**, the function $AND returns **true** and the ACTION part of the rule is evaluated.

14. The certainty factor is calculated (see section on functions used in the action parts of rules), and the triple (ORGANISM-1 IDENT ()) in the patient data base is updated to (ORGANISM-1 IDENT (ECOLI 0.6)) (assuming TALLY = 1).

15. The evaluation of RULE156 is now completed, so the next rule in the UPDATED-BY list for **IDENT** is invoked. Each clause in its premise is evaluated in turn, and if all return **true**, then the ACTION part is evaluated. If this again concludes that the identity is ECOLI, then only the certainty factor that is associated with the existing triple is modified, otherwise a new value is added, with its own certainty factor.

16. Each rule is invoked in turn until the list is exhausted or a conclusion is made with certainty. The **istraced** flag that is associated with the triple is then set to 1, the **isbeingtraced** flag is set to 0, and the system continues instantiating the remaining **CURORGS** contexts (as described earlier).

17. Once all these **CURORGS** contexts have been instantiated, and the identities of the organisms determined, the parameters TREATFOR and COVERFOR can be concluded about, returning control to the ACTION part of the goal rule, RULE092.

A departure from this sequence takes place if an invoked rule is not applicable to the current context (as was the case before CURCULS or CURORGS had been instantiated, when RULE090 was invoked. In such a case, MYCIN determines to which context type(s) the rule is applicable, finds all the descendants of the current context of that type, instantiating them if necessary, and tries to apply the rule to each of those. So RULE090 is applied to each of the CURORGS context types once they have all been instantiated.

Also, the dynamic data base is referred to before evaluating each clause of a rule, and if the parameter to be traced is already being traced, the rule is abandoned.

To summarise, MYCIN invokes the goal rule to try to infer the REGIMEN for PATIENT-1. In order to do this, it needs to trace the clinical parameters that are referenced in the PREMISE of the rule—TREATFOR and COVERFOR—by invoking all the rules that conclude about these parameters. As each rule is invoked, MYCIN has to trace the parameters in its PREMISE by invoking further rules, and so on.

DEPARTURES FROM THE BASIC CONTROL STRUCTURE

In general, a rule is only triggered by the need to find out the values for clinical parameters that are concluded about in its ACTION part. At any one time, therefore, the system is working towards some subgoal that eventually will lead to the top goal. However, there are some departures from this basic "backward-chaining" mechanism.

MAINPROPS

The use of MAINPROPS as described in the previous section is a substantial departure from the normal backward-chaining inference mechanism of MYCIN, whereby values are only traced when needed.

MAINPROPS parameters are always traced, either by asking the user, by deduction—using rules—or both, whether or not they are eventually needed. The justification for this procedure lies in the view that there is certain information such as name, age, and sex of the patient and the identity of an organism (in cases where it is already known to the user), that the user would *prefer* to be asked for immediately when a context is created; even if it is not needed either at once or (in the case of name, for example) ever. In addition, there are some parameters such as REGIMEN that are certain or extremely likely to be needed and which are therefore traced straightaway. The use of MAINPROPS parameters may therefore be justified as a feature that adds *structure* to a consultation with MYCIN and thus may make it more acceptable to physicians.

Antecedent Rules

If a conclusion about a clinical parameter is made with certainty, the system retrieves a list of rules that reference this parameter in their PREMISE and considers each rule in turn. In each case, if no further parameters have to be traced (i.e., if the PREMISE is entirely known), the rule is applied to the current context.

Here is an example of an antecedent rule:

IF: THE IDENTITY OF THE ORGANISM IS KNOWN WITH CERTAINTY
THEN: IT IS DEFINITE (1.0) THAT THESE PARAMETERS—GRAMSTAIN MORPHOL-
       OGY AEROBICITY—SHOULD BE TRANSFERRED FROM THE IDENTITY OF
       THE ORGANISM TO THIS ORGANISM

This is one of the rules that reference the knowledge tables in the static data base. Invoking it causes the system to look up the identity of the organism in the table to find out the values for

STAIN, MORPH, and AIR of the organism. These values are then stored in the patient data base to be readily available when needed.

The use of antecedent rules is limited—there are only about forty such rules (van Melle [1980]) and they are used primarily to avoid asking redundant questions. Extensive use of antecedent rules would cause the system to "chain forwards" and lose its goal-directed approach.

Self-Referencing Rules

Self-referencing rules are a departure from the normally strict modularity of knowledge that is contained in rules. They are rules that reference the same clinical parameter in both their PREMISE and ACTION parts. RULE040 is an example:

```
RULE040
PREMISE:    ($AND (SAME CNTXT SITE BLOOD)
                  (MIGHTBE CNTXT IDENT PSEUDOMONAS)
                  (SAME CNTXT SKINLES T))
ACTION:     (CONCLUDE CNTXT IDENT PSEUDOMONAS TALLY .8)
```

which is translated as:

```
IF:      1)   THE SITE OF THE CULTURE IS BLOOD, AND
         2)   THE IDENTITY OF THE ORGANISM MAY BE PSEUDOMONAS, AND
         3)   THE PATIENT HAS ECTHYMA GANGRENOSUM SKIN LESIONS
THEN:    THERE IS STRONGLY SUGGESTIVE EVIDENCE (.8) THAT THE IDENTITY OF
         THE ORGANISM IS PSEUDOMONAS.
```

RULE040 would be invoked while the system was trying to find out about IDENT. However, the value of IDENT is needed to evaluate the PREMISE of the rule, and as it is already being traced, the rule would normally be abandoned. To overcome this problem, the UPDATED-BY list of rules for IDENT has to be scanned, and the self-referencing rules have to be separated from the ordinary rules. The ordinary rules are evaluated first, and only when some conclusion has been made about the value for IDENT are the self-referencing rules invoked. They ignore the "is-being-traced" flag and serve only to reinforce the certainty factor that is associated with the existing patient data triple. They are designed to prevent unreasonable or illogical questions being asked. For example, RULE040 asks about the typical skin lesions found with pseudomonas infections, but the only time an expert would ask this question would be if pseudomonas were already suspected, so MYCIN does not ask the question unless pseudomonas is known to be a possible identity.

Mapping Functions

MYCIN's mapping functions constitute a major departure from the basic control structure. See the earlier section on mapping functions for details.

THE EVOLUTION OF MYCIN

The original implementation of MYCIN, described by Shortliffe (1976), contained about 200 rules that were relevant to the domain of bacteremia. It could recognise about fifty organisms by collecting information about the patient which was organised into a context tree of up to ten context types, described by about sixty parameters. During this time various problems with data organisation were highlighted and the original idea of the backward-chaining mechanism had to be modified to cater for self-referencing rules, MAINPROPS parameters, and the need to reference more than one branch of the context tree.

After implementation, work on the project continued in three directions simultaneously. MYCIN's explanation facility was substantially extended and improved, by Carli Scott and others, with the purpose of introducing a domain-independent feature that enabled the physician to ask questions during the consultation. The domain was broadened to include the diagnosis and treatment of meningitis infections, which involved further discussions with medical specialists and resulted in a data base of 350 rules, a context tree of eleven context types (the context type INFECTION was introduced) and twenty extra parameters. This expansion caused new problems with the efficiency of the system. Three new features were introduced in an attempt to solve some of these problems, namely:

- *Metarules*. Used for pruning or reordering a long list of rules that were retrieved from the static data base for inferring the value of a parameter.
- *Unitypath*. Used for searching such a list of rules for one whose premise is known with certainty and which makes a definite conclusion, that is, has a certainty factor of 1.0. If this rule is evaluated successfully, no other rules need to be invoked.
- *Preview*. Used for searching the premise of an invoked rule for a clause already known to be false. If such a clause exists, then the rule is rejected immediately without tracing the parameters that are referenced in the preceding clauses, thus saving a lot of unnecessary computation.

At the same time, William van Melle began developing a domain-independent system based on MYCIN's control mechanism and data structures, which he called EMYCIN (Essential MYCIN). He recoded the MYCIN program to remove all its domain-specific knowledge, created a set of mapping functions to deal with some of this knowledge which was previously encoded in the program, added antecedent rules and some extra bookkeeping functions, and altered the certainty factor mechanism. He also added a rule compiler to increase efficiency and designed a subsystem to aid the construction and maintenance of a knowledge base.

MYCIN was then reimplemented in EMYCIN (1980), with a rule base of 450 rules and thirteen context types, described by about 200 parameters. Other knowledge bases (in different domains) were also constructed by using the EMYCIN framework (e.g., PUFF, HEADMED, SACON, CLOT), and the project was renamed the Knowledge-Based Consultation Systems Project.

ANALYSIS AND CRITICAL REVIEW

In this section, some of the features that make a programming language suitable for implementing an expert system such as MYCIN are considered and comments on a number of aspects of MYCIN are made.

Choice of Language

Although it has to be conceded that once a complex system has been constructed, it can possibly be rewritten (in principle) in virtually any high-level language, such as FORTRAN, there is no doubt that the so-called "artificial intelligence programming languages" have distinct advantages for developing an expert system such as MYCIN. MYCIN itself is implemented in LISP, which among many other facilities has three particularly helpful features.

1. Lists of arbitrary complexity containing elements of any kind can be processed in an extremely sophisticated way.
2. Each atom, such as ORGANISM-2, automatically has a *property list* by means of which values of any kind can be assigned to arbitrary properties of that atom. Thus, for example, the list ((SALMONELLA 0.4) (ECOLI 0.6)) can be made the value of the IDENT property of ORGANISM-2. It is additionally helpful in that it is not necessary to specify in advance which properties an atom may possess and that an unassigned value of any property automatically has a specific value (NIL) by default.
3. A list, such as (CONCLUDE CNTXT IDENT PSEUDOMONAS TALLY .6) can be treated as data (e.g., be input, modified, or output) by some parts of a program and evaluated as a function (the first element) applied to its arguments (the remaining elements) by others. Thus, for example, a specific value (such as CULTURE-1) can be substituted for an item in a list (such as CNTXT) before the list is evaluated as a function invocation.

Reimplementing MYCIN in any "conventional" language, such as PASCAL, would encounter severe difficulties because of the absence of these features.

In the case of RMYCIN, the system was implemented in POP-2, an AI programming language developed at the University of Edinburgh in Scotland. This choice of language was made principally as a means of comparing the two languages LISP and POP-2 as vehicles for developing systems of this kind, not as a means of advocating the use of POP-2. POP-2 would appear to be a most satisfactory choice for this purpose, although probably not so satisfactory as LISP in this case. In interpreting this comment, one should bear in mind that the data structures and many other features in RMYCIN are very closely related to those in MYCIN, and so it would be very surprising if LISP had not turned out to be a more suitable choice. Adjusting the internal representation to suit the features of POP-2 more closely might change the balance quite significantly. (A similar statement could *not* be made with any confidence in the case of conventional languages such as PASCAL, ALGOL-68, FORTRAN, COBOL, or BASIC.)

In terms of features (1) to (3) above, POP-2 is of similar power to LISP for list processing but is less powerful for items (2) and (3). The effect of having property lists was simulated by defining, for example, a record type ORGANISM with components DESCENDANTSOF, etc.

When a specific ORGANISM such as ORGANISM-2 is instantiated a "dummy record" with every element NIL is assigned to it, after which it is permitted to refer or assign to, for example, DESCENDANTSOF(ORGANISM-2). It is particularly valuable that POP-2, like LISP, allows elements of any kind, such as lists of lists, to be the value of a record component. Although POP-2 does not have property (3), previously listed, as a standard feature, it can be implemented by means of a function call in a straightforward manner. In RMYCIN, this function is called EVAL. If add is a function that takes two numerical arguments and returns their sum as its value, then [add 3 4] is a list of three elements, but eval([add 3 4]) is a function call that returns the value **7**, that is, the value of add(3,4).

To summarise, the experience gained from this reconstruction strongly suggests that for building systems such as MYCIN, a language with the flexibility and power of LISP, especially its list-processing features, is likely to be required in practice, but that POP-2 could be considered as a reasonable alternative to LISP as an implementation language.

Critical Analysis

MYCIN is often presented as an outstanding example of the value of the expert systems methodology, and its generalised version EMYCIN is often regarded as a general-purpose vehicle for constructing an expert system for any domain simply by adding further rules. Moreover, the popular impression of MYCIN is that of a system with a simple backward-chaining control structure acting on a body of rules. The control structure has been considered in detail earlier in this report and it is clear that there are many deviations from simple backward chaining, in particular, the use of antecedent rules, self-referencing rules, mapping functions, and the Mainprops property of context types. Although the facilities provided by EMYCIN are general in the sense of not being dependent on any one domain of discourse, it is far from certain that they would be useful or appropriate in general.

Although MYCIN's knowledge is largely rule based, there is an important component, namely, the creation of a list of potential therapies and the choice of the apparent first choice drug, which is algorithmic in nature. These are programmed explicitly in a series of relatively complex LISP functions. Shortliffe (1976) comments "if the goal-oriented control structure we have developed is truly general, one would hope that algorithmic approaches to the construction and ordering of lists could also be placed in decision-rule format. We therefore intend to experiment with ways of incorporating the remainder of MYCIN's knowledge into decision rules." However, this does not seem to have been accomplished.

In this section, a number of other aspects of MYCIN (or more accurately EMYCIN) are highlighted, some of which bear on its generality as a standard framework for constructing expert systems; others identify hidden restrictions in the use of the system and a number of questionable features, especially in connection with certainty factors.

How General is EMYCIN?

The most significant and obvious restriction on the use of EMYCIN is that it is designed to be used to build *consultation* systems. Van Melle (1980) states:

> EMYCIN was not designed to be a general-purpose representation language. It is thus wholly unsuited for some problems. Even those domains that have been successfully implemented have demonstrated some of the inadequacies of EMYCIN. . . .

EMYCIN is designed to handle tasks that can be posed in the form of providing consultative advice. The system takes as input a body of measurements or other information pertinent to a case, and produces as output some form of recommendation or analysis of the case. The framework seems well suited for some deductive problems, notably some classes of fault diagnosis, where a large body of input measurements (symptoms, laboratory tests) is available and the solution space of possible diagnoses can be enumerated. It is less well suited for "formation" problems, where the task is to piece together existing structures according to specified constraints to generate a solution. Among other classes of problems that EMYCIN does not attempt to handle are simulation tasks, and tasks involving planning with stepwise refinement.

These limitations derive largely from the fact that EMYCIN has chosen one basic, readily understood representation for the knowledge in a domain: production rules applied by a backward-chaining control structure, and operating on data in the form of associative triples. . . . The fact that rules are expected to be judgmental suggests that the knowledge of some domains may not be effectively represented in rules. Some of the simpler knowledge bases (PUFF, SACON) make little or no use of the inexact inference mechanism provided by CFs. More efficient representations may exist for the precise knowledge existing in such domains; e.g., much of the SACON rule set might be more concisely and lucidly represented as decision tables. However, even in such cases it is still practical to build a reasoning program from EMYCIN as a first test of the inference rules written by an expert. While many of the system's complicated features, such as certainty factors and the context tree, may go unused in the simpler systems, those features do not substantially burden a program that does not use their extra generality. The goal-directed, depth-first, backward-chaining control structure EMYCIN uses to apply the rules is perhaps the greatest limitation on the nature of the task an EMYCIN consultant can handle. Backward chaining works well for simple deductive tasks, but as soon as a problem poses additional constraints on the means by which reasoning can or should be performed, more sophisticated control mechanisms may be required. (pp. 138, 143–144)

One particular feature of an EMYCIN-based consultation system is that contexts are instantiated only when needed. This leads to considerable complexity of implementation (as shown previously) but is desirable in the case of MYCIN to avoid providing information about operations, prior cultures, and so on of no importance to the current consultation.

However, there may be other consultation domains where a set of contexts will always need to be instantiated eventually and it would be a considerable simplification to do so at the beginning of a consultation. (An example might be a system to calculate entitlement to Social Security benefits, where information about a claimant's dependents would virtually always be needed and might best be provided together early in a consultation.)

Most of MYCIN's rules reference only one branch of the context tree at a time, thus "focussing" the questions, which would otherwise appear to be asked at random. Some problems do arise, however, with rules that reference contexts on different branches of the tree and these are dealt with by the use of mapping functions. However, the need for such functions suggests that a context *tree* may not be the most appropriate data structure in general, and it would be interesting to consider the use of a context *network* as an alternative.

Apart from the preceding, there are a number of detailed restrictions on the use of a system that is constructed using EMYCIN.

Since instantiating the root node initiates the reasoning chain for a consultation, the parameter to be traced as the goal of the consultation (REGIMEN in the case of MYCIN) must be included in the Mainprops list of the root node.

All Mainprops parameters must be either single-valued or binary, because a multiple-valued parameter is only traced to establish if it has one particular possible value (not to establish all the values it possesses), and no such specific value is specifiable when the parameter is on the Mainprops list.

Multiple-valued parameters also cannot satisfactorily be used as arguments of the KNOWN function since, for example, testing whether KNOWN was satisfied for parameter ALLERGIES in MYCIN would return the answer **true** if even one value were known. However, this would not indicate that all the patient's allergies were known (which would be the point of applying the test).

Weaknesses of the EMYCIN Approach

A detailed analysis reveals a number of detailed faults in the EMYCIN framework, several of them involving the use of certainty factors. The MYCIN model of propagating certainty factors of both rules and facts through a network of relationships has been analysed by Adams (1976). He proves that a substantial part of the model can be derived from and is equivalent to standard probability theory, with assumptions of statistical independence, although there are also important differences. By this means a number of shortcomings in the MYCIN model are identified. In particular, there are interdependence restrictions that need to be applied to the estimation of certain parameters (measure of belief and measure of disbelief in a hypothesis, supplied by the physician) to maintain internal consistency, but which are not included in the MYCIN model. In addition, the use of certainty factors as a means of ranking hypotheses is also suspect, since examples can be given of cases where, of two hypotheses, the one with the lower probability would have the higher certainty factor. On the basis of Adams' analysis, it would seem that the MYCIN model has serious limitations. With the development of EMYCIN as a domain-independent expert system building tool, this matter is potentially of great importance.

It is interesting that such a flawed method should give results that are apparently acceptable in practice. Adams (1976) comments: "empirical success of MYCIN ... stands in spite of theoretical objections of the types discussed. ... It is probable that the model does not founder on the difficulties pointed out because in actual use the chains of reasoning are short and the hypotheses simple. However, there are many fields in which, because of its shortcomings, this model could not enjoy comparable success."

Van Melle (1980, p. 14 ftn.) states that there is no requirement for certainty factors in EMYCIN to sum to 1, since they are not probabilities. Thus, it is conceivable that more than one possible value of a parameter could have a certainty factor of $+1$, that is, be considered "known with certainty." This seems to be unsatisfactory, particularly since it would seem that EMYCIN follows the practice of MYCIN, whereby if the certainty factor of one possible value is calculated to be $+1$, all other values and their certainty factors are automatically deleted from the dynamic data base (including any with certainty factor $+1$ which may already be there).

A serious potential weakness of the EMYCIN method of manipulating rules is that premise clauses for which no reliable truth value can be established are regarded as false. For example, consider RULE 156 as previously discussed.

One clause of the premise is (SAME CNTXT MORPH ROD). Now suppose that for a particular consultation it was not possible to establish a value for the morphology of a specific organism with a certainty factor greater than 0.2. This clause would be considered false and hence the whole premise would be false. However, it might still be the case that the morphology really was rod, since it cannot be assumed that all the rules that are necessary to deduce morphology are included in the system.

The use of the value 0.2 as a "threshold" between known and not known is obviously arbitrary in any case.

Although the facility for the physician to enter a certainty factor with a data value is available, it is not used to great effect in MYCIN. In almost all cases, data entered is of a kind that will either be known with certainty or not at all (e.g., name of patient). Parameters that the physician might estimate are usually non-labdata, and thus should normally be deduced by using rules without giving the physician an opportunity to enter a value. A parameter that is labdata and for which it might occasionally be realistic to enter a definite value is IDENT. If instead an estimated value (with certainty factor, say, 0.4) is entered, the system will accept it and not attempt to deduce the value. If such an estimate is deliberately withheld by the physician (to force the system to deduce the value instead), then there is no way in which the physician's estimate can be made use of by the system in calculating the value of IDENT, even though it might be an extremely useful piece of evidence.

There is also a problem with EMYCIN's treatment of circular reasoning. For example, if there are rules of the form

1. *if* A *then* B
2. *if* B *then* C
3. *if* C *then* A

and the value of A needs to be traced, rule (3) would be invoked. This will cause rule (2) to be invoked in order to trace parameter C, and this will in turn cause rule (1) to be invoked to trace parameter B. Since the value of A is required in the premise of rule (1) and A is already being traced (rule (3)), a circularity is detected and rule (1) is abandoned. However, rule (1) is not in itself faulty and might be of great importance, particularly if it were to conclude with certainty.

Self-referencing rules, although a valuable feature in themselves, have the highly undesirable characteristic that the order in which they are executed can be significant if they conclude the value of some parameter and include either function SAME or function THOUGHTNOT in the premise part. For example, consider the two self-referencing rules (A) and (B) that follow:

Rule (A)

```
PREMISE:   ($AND (SAME CNTXT BURN T)
                 (SAME CNTXT IDENT PSEUDOMONAS))
ACTION:    (CONCLUDE CNTXT IDENT PSEUDOMONAS TALLY 1.0)
```

Rule (B)

PREMISE: ($AND (SAME CNTXT SKINLES T)
                         (SAME CNTXT IDENT PSEUDOMONAS))
ACTION: (CONCLUDE CNTXT IDENT PSEUDOMONAS TALLY 1.0)

If the dynamic data base contains the triples

ORGANISM-1	IDENT	(PSEUDOMONAS 0.3)
PATIENT-1	BURN	(T 1.0)
PATIENT-1	SKINLES	(T 0.3)

then the order in which the rules are applied to trace the value of IDENT for ORGANISM-1 is significant as shown by the following calculation.

CASE 1: RULE (A) IS APPLIED FIRST
When rule (A) is evaluated, TALLY becomes set to 0.3 (the SAME function returns **1.0** for the first clause and **0.3** for the second, using the certainty factor of PSEUDOMONAS from the dynamic data base, and the minimum is taken). Multiplying TALLY by 1.0, the certainty factor of rule A, gives **0.3**, and the new value calculated for the certainty factor of PSEUDOMONAS, using the formulae given in a previous section

$$(C_1 + C_2 - C_1 \times C_2), \text{is } 0.3 + 0.3 - 0.3 \times 0.3 = \underline{0.51}$$

The dynamic data base is then updated to contain

| ORGANISM-1 | IDENT | (PSEUDOMONAS 0.51) |

Applying rule (B) to this updated data base, TALLY for this rule becomes **0.3** (returned by the clause (SAME CNTXT SKINLES T)) and multiplying this by 1.0 (the certainty factor of rule (B)) again gives **0.3**. The formula $C_1 + C_2 - C_1 \times C_2$ now gives a new value for the certainty factor of PSEUDOMONAS of

$$0.51 + 0.3 - 0.51 \times 0.3 = \underline{0.657}$$

and this value is now inserted in the dynamic data base.

CASE 2: RULE (B) IS APPLIED FIRST.
When rule (B) is evaluated, for the "original" version of the dynamic data base, which contains the triple

| ORGANISM-1 | IDENT | (PSEUDOMONAS 0.3) |

TALLY becomes **0.3**. This is multiplied by 1.0 (the certainty factor of rule (B)) for use in the formula $C_1 + C_2 - C_1 \times C_2$ which now yields

$$0.3 + 0.3 - 0.3 \times 0.3 = \underline{0.51}$$

Thus, the dynamic data base is modified to contain

ORGANISM-1   IDENT   (PSEUDOMONAS 0.51)

Rule (A) is now evaluated, using this updated data base, and TALLY becomes **0.51**. Multiplying this by the certainty factor of rule A and applying the formula $C_1 + C_2 - C_1 \times C_2$ gives

$$\textbf{0.51} + \textbf{0.51} - \textbf{0.51} \times \textbf{0.51} = \underline{\textbf{0.7599}}$$

The reason for this discrepancy in the two results is that function SAME (and also function THOUGHTNOT) returns a numerical truth-value rather than simply **true**. The example that is given does not seem unreasonable and the difference in the calculated values could well be compounded if there were more than two self-referencing rules, concluding about the same parameter.

Conclusion

Despite the previous critical comments, the overall impression gained from performing this reconstruction has been one of an extremely sophisticated piece of software, carefully tuned to the needs of the infectious disease domain. The evolution of EMYCIN from MYCIN is itself worthy of considerable praise and the comments in this chapter should be viewed in that light.

Although it would be wrong to regard EMYCIN as an entirely general framework for building expert systems, even consultation systems, a careful study of the methods of knowledge representation and manipulation that are employed and the strengths and weaknesses of MYCIN and EMYCIN is likely to be of significant value to the developer of future systems. The preceding discussion is intended to point the way to future enhancements of the basic framework. There are many problems that need to be solved before a soundly based theory of expert systems can be presented, but the development of EMYCIN and MYCIN is a substantial step in that direction.

Bibliography

Adams, J. B. "A Probability Model of Medical Reasoning and the MYCIN Model." *Mathematical Biosciences* 32: 177–186, 1976.

Cendrowska, J., and Bramer, M. A. "A Rational Reconstruction of the MYCIN Consultation System." Open University Technical Report. November 1982.

Davis, R., Buchanan, B., and Shortliffe, E. "Production Rules as a Representation for a Knowledge-Based Consultation Program." *Artificial Intelligence* 8: 15–45, 1977.

Shortliffe, E. H. "MYCIN: A Rule-Based Computer Program for Advising Physicians Regarding Antimicrobial Therapy Selection." Ph.D. thesis. Stanford University, Stanford, Calif., 1974.

Shortliffe, E. H. *Computer-based Medical Consultations: MYCIN*. New York: American Elsevier, 1976.

Shortliffe, E. H., and Buchanan, B. G. "A Model of Inexact Reasoning in Medicine." *Mathematical Biosciences,* 23: 351–379, 1975.

Shortliffe, E. H., Davis, R., Axline, S. G., et al. "Computer-Based Consultations in Clinical Therapeutics: Explanation and Rule Acquisition Capabilities of the MYCIN System." *Comput. Biomed. Res.* 8: 303–320, 1975.

Van Melle, W. "MYCIN: A Knowledge-Based Consultation Program for Infectious Disease Diagnosis." *Int. J. Man-Machine Studies* 10: 313–322, 1978.

Van Melle, W. "A Domain-Independent Production Rule System for Consultation Programs." *Proceedings of the Sixth International Joint Conference on Artificial Intelligence,* Tokyo, Japan, 1979, 923–925.

Van Melle, W. "A Domain-Independent System That Aids in Constructing Knowledge-Based Consultation Programs." Stanford Heuristic Programming Project Memo HPP-80-22, Stanford, Calif., 1976.

APPENDIX: SPECIMEN OUTPUT FROM RMYCIN

The following is an example of the output that is produced by the reconstructed version of MYCIN, known as RMYCIN. A consultation with RMYCIN (unlike MYCIN itself) ends when the program forms a conclusion about the identity of each offending organism (possibly that it cannot deduce its value).

Rather than proceed to offer a recommended therapy (which would involve knowledge about drugs that the program does not possess), RMYCIN then prints out the contents of the patient data base in the form of triples, followed by the context tree in tabular form.

```
--------PATIENT1--------
```
1) Enter the patient's name
: SMITH
2) Age
: 23
3) Sex
: male
4) I will refer to the first positive culture obtained for SMITH (PATIENT1) as:

```
--------CULTURE1--------
```
5) From what site was the specimen for CULTURE1 taken?
: blood
6)   Please give the number of days since the BLOOD culture (CULTURE1) was obtained:
: 2
7) I will refer to the first offending organism from the BLOOD culture (CULTURE1) as:

```
--------ORGANISM1--------
```
8) Enter the identity (genus) of ORGANISM1
: unknown
9) The stain (Gram or Ziehl-Neelson Acidfast) of ORGANISM1:
: gramneg
10) Is ORGANISM1 a coccus or a rod (etc.)?
: rod
11) Did ORGANISM1 grow aerobically?
: y

12) Did ORGANISM1 grow anaerobically?

: y

13) What is the suspected portal of entry of ORGANISM1?

: unk

14) Is there evidence that SMITH (PATIENT1) has MENINGITIS?

: y

15) Were any organisms that were significant (but no longer require therapeutic attention) isolated within the last approximately 30 days?

: y

--------CULTURE2--------

16) From what site was the specimen for CULTURE2 taken?

: csf

17) Please give the number of days since the CSF culture (CULTURE2) was obtained:

: 7

18) I will refer to the first organism isolated from the CSF culture (CULTURE2) as:

--------ORGANISM2--------

19) Enter the identity (genus) of ORGANISM2

: ecoli

20) Were any other organisms isolated from the CSF culture (CULTURE2)?

: n

21) Any other significant earlier cultures from which pathogens were isolated?

: n

22) Is there evidence that SMITH (PATIENT1) has BACTEREMIA?

: n

23) Has SMITH (PATIENT1) had a genito—manipulative procedure?

: n

24) Is the patient's illness with the ORGANISM1 a hospital-acquired infection?

: y

25) Is SMITH (PATIENT1) a burn patient?

: n

26) Is SMITH (PATIENT1) a compromised host (e.g., alcoholic, sickle-cell disease, immunosuppressed)?

: n

27) Any other organisms isolated from the BLOOD culture (CULTURE 1) for which you would like a therapeutic recommendation?

: n

28) Are there any other current cultures for SMITH (PATIENT1) from which organisms were isolated?

: y

--------CULTURE3--------

29) From what site was the specimen for CULTURE3 taken?

: csf

30) Please give the number of days since the CSF culture (CULTURE3) was obtained:
: 3

31) I will refer to the first offending organism from the CSF culture (CULTURE3) as:

--------ORGANISM3--------

32) Enter the identity (genus) of ORGANISM3
: unk

33) The stain (Gram or Ziehl-Neelson Acidfast) of ORGANISM3:
: gramneg

34) Is ORGANISM3 a coccus or a rod (etc.)?
: rod

35) Did ORGANISM3 grow aerobically?
: y

36) Was an attempt made to grow ORGANISM3 anaerobically?
: y

37) Did ORGANISM3 grow anaerobically?
: y

38) Is the patient's illness with the ORGANISM3 a hospital-acquired infection?
: unk

39) What is the suspected portal of entry of ORGANISM3?
: unk

40) Any other organisms isolated from the CSF culture (CULTURE3) for which you would like a therapeutic recommendation?
: n

41) Are there any other current cultures for SMITH (PATIENT1) from which organisms were isolated?
: n

42) How many cultures were positive for ORGANISM1?
: 2

43) On a scale of 0–4, where higher numbers indicate increasing severity, how would you rate SMITH (PATIENT1)'s degree of sickness?
: 3

44) Is SMITH (PATIENT1) febrile?
: y

45) How many cultures are there in the series?
: 2

46) Is ORGANISM1 normally found at this site?
: n

47) How many cultures were positive for ORGANISM3?
: 2

48) How many cultures are there in the series?
: 2

49) Is ORGANISM3 normally found at this site?
: n

[Patient Data Base]

PATIENT1	NAME	[[SMITH 1]]	1	0
PATIENT1	AGE	[[23 1]]	1	0
PATIENT1	SEX	[[MALE 1]]	1	0
PATIENT1	REGIMEN	[[T 1.0]]	1	0
PATIENT1	TREATFOR	[[T 1.0]]	1	0
CULTURE1	SITE	[[BLOOD 1]]	1	0
CULTURE1	WHENCUL	[[2 1]]	1	0
ORGANISM1	IDENT	[[PSEUDOMONAS 0.16] [ECOLI 0.4]]	1	0
ORGANISM1	STAIN	[[GRAMNEG 1]]	1	0
ORGANISM1	MORPH	[[ROD 1]]	1	0
ORGANISM1	AIR	[[FACUL 0.8] [ANAEROBIC 0.2]]	1	0
ORGANISM1	AIRGROW	[[T 1]]	1	0
ORGANISM1	ANGROW	[[T 1]]	1	0
ORGANISM1	ANTRY	[[T 1.0]]	1	0
ORGANISM1	PORTAL	nil	1	0
PATIENT1	INFECT	[[MENINGITIS 1] [BACTEREMIA −1]]	1	0
CULTURE2	SITE	[[CSF 1]]	1	0
CULTURE2	WHENCUL	[[7 1]]	1	0
ORGANISM2	IDENT	[[ECOLI 1]]	1	0
ORGANISM2	STAIN	[[GRAMNEG 1.0]]	1	0
ORGANISM2	MORPH	[[ROD 1.0]]	1	0
ORGANISM2	AIR	[[AEROBIC 1.0]]	1	0
PATIENT1	GU	[[T −1]]	1	0
ORGANISM1	HOSPITAL	[[T 1]]	1	0
PATIENT1	BURN	[[T −1]]	1	0
PATIENT1	COMPROM	[[T −1]]	1	0
CULTURE3	SITE	[[CSF 1]]	1	0
CULTURE3	WHENCUL	[[3 1]]	1	0
ORGANISM3	IDENT	[[PSEUDOMONAS 0.1] [ECOLI 0.4]]	1	0
ORGANISM3	STAIN	[[GRAMNEG 1]]	1	0
ORGANISM3	MORPH	[[ROD 1]]	1	0
ORGANISM3	AIR	[[FACUL 1.0]]	1	0
ORGANISM3	AIRGROW	[[T 1]]	1	0
ORGANISM3	ANTRY	[[T 1.0]]	1	0
ORGANISM3	ANGROW	[[T 1]]	1	0
ORGANISM3	HOSPITAL	nil	1	0
ORGANISM3	PORTAL	nil	1	0
ORGANISM1	SIGNIFI-CANCE	[[T 0.99916]]	1	0
ORGANISM1	NUMPOS	[[2 1]]	1	0
PATIENT1	SEVERITY	[[3 1]]	1	0
PATIENT1	FEBRILE	[[T 1]]	1	0
CULTURE1	NUMCULS	[[2 1]]	1	0
ORGANISM1	CONTAMI-NANT	[[T −0.88]]	1	0

ORGANISM1	NORMAL	[[T −1]]	1	0
ORGANISM3	SIGNIFI-CANCE	[[T 0.99916]]	1	0
ORGANISM3	NUMPOS	[[2 1]]	1	0
CULTURE3	NUMCULS	[[2 1]]	1	0
ORGANISM3	CONTAMI-NANT	[[T −0.88]]	1	0
ORGANISM3	NORMAL	[[T −1]]	1	0

[Context Tree]

	CONTEXT-TYPE	PARENT	DESCENDANTS
PATIENT1	PERSON	nil	CULTURE1
			CULTURE2
			CULTURE3
CULTURE1	CURCULS	PATIENT1	ORGANISM1
ORGANISM1	CURORGS	CULTURE1	
CULTURE2	PRIORCULS	PATIENT1	ORGANISM2
ORGANISM2	PRIORORGS	CULTURE2	
CULTURE3	CURCULS	PATIENT1	ORGANISM3
ORGANISM3	CURORGS	CULTURE3	

85 86 87 9 8 7 6 5 4 3